SYNTHESIS OF OPTIMUM CONTROL SYSTEMS

McGraw-Hill Series in Control Systems Engineering

JOHN R. RAGAZZINI AND WILLIAM E. VANNAH, *Consulting Editors*

SYNTHESIS OF
Optimum Control Systems

SHELDON S. L. CHANG

PROFESSOR OF ELECTRICAL ENGINEERING
NEW YORK UNIVERSITY

McGRAW-HILL BOOK COMPANY, INC.

New York   Toronto   London

1961

SYNTHESIS OF OPTIMUM CONTROL SYSTEMS

10515   THE MAPLE PRESS COMPANY, YORK, PA.

67175

c

TO GERTRUDE

PREFACE

There are two major directions in the development of automatic control systems:

1. Improvements in components
2. Making the best use of the components

The second aspect, which is generally known as system design, is the main topic of this book.

Up until 10 years ago, most literature on control systems regarded components as no more than transfer functions.   Admittedly, one of the most essential aspects of a component is its transfer function.   Admittedly also, experienced system designers do not regard components as transfer functions alone.   They use them merely for studying a closed-loop system's stability and response to medium-sized signals, but in selecting components to be used, a fair amount of attention is also paid to the system's power capacity, stability of its characteristics, internal noise, linearity, etc.   While this double-pronged approach—linear stability theory plus common sense—has been highly successful and is still being used by most servo designers, it is not adequate to cope with a complex system in which ultimate response characteristics are desired.   To design such a system, experience is insufficient, and experiments are likely to be too slow.

In the past decade, systematic treatments of the optimum-design problem, which considers one or the other limiting features of the so-called fixed (or unalterable) component in addition to its transfer function, have appeared in the literature.   In the author's opinion, there are four basic methods in this category:

1. Wiener's least-square optimization with quadratic constraint and its manifestations in nonstationary and sampled-data systems
2. The maximum principle and its forerunner, the "bang-bang" servo principle
3. Self-optimizing systems of various types
4. Computer optimization and control of nonlinear systems

vii

The present volume consists of a treatment of the above four basic methods plus two auxiliary topics:

1. Estimation and measurement of power spectra and correlation functions
2. An analysis of the changes in a closed-loop system's response because of component inaccuracies

The material selected is based on the author's opinion of what additional knowledge is most useful to a servo designer in his work, assuming that he has mastered the basic tools of the trade such as Laplace transforms, Bode plot, Nyquist plot, Evans's root-locus method, etc. This additional knowledge is treated in the simplest possible way (known to the author), but the reader is assumed to be fairly well prepared at least in undergraduate mathematics. Knowledge of contour integration is essential and of probability theory and statistics desirable but not necessary, as the prerequisite knowledge on this subject is treated briefly in Appendixes A and C. Matrix algebra is used in some parts of the book, but a reader can understand most of the book without it.

The book may be used as a graduate text by itself or as an auxiliary text in a graduate course based on one of the standard texts. It will also be useful as a reference book for servo designers and research engineers.

It is the author's pleasure to acknowledge the encouragement and good suggestions from Dean John R. Ragazzini of New York University, Dr. J. G. Truxal of Brooklyn Polytechnic Institute, Professor T. J. Higgins of the University of Wisconsin, and Dr. J. H. Chadwick of the Sperry Gyroscope Company. Many thanks are due to Miss Maryann Regan for typing most of the manuscript and also to Mrs. Mary Rooney, Mrs. Eleanor Gilmore, Mrs. Marie Trotta, and Mrs. Beatrice Schwartz for helping to make various revisions and corrections on the manuscript.

Sheldon S. L. Chang

CONTENTS

CHAPTER 1

INTRODUCTION

1-1. Some Remarks on the Technological Development of Feedback Control Systems. The modern theoretical development of feedback control systems started in the 1920s or 1930s and is marked by Minorsky's paper on the steering of ships (1922), Nyquist's paper Regeneration Theory (1932), and Hazen's paper Theory of Servomechanisms (1934). Before that, the development of feedback controls was mainly in the hands of inventors. While there were isolated instances of successful applications of the concept of feedback control, such as Watt's applications of the flyball governor to the steam engine (1788), Whitehead's torpedo control (1866), and Sperry's gyro stabilizer (1915), there were many, many more attempts that were left unrecorded because they failed. The lack of theory prevented consistent success and economical design toward a prespecified objective.

The theoretical developments made it possible for engineers to design satisfactory feedback control systems as daily routine, using such now classical methods as the Nyquist plot, Bode diagram, Nichols chart, and Evans's root-locus method. However, one common denominator of these design techniques is that they have been developed without critical consideration. Each method leads to one way or another of compensating a system so that it is stable and satisfies a set of more or less arbitrary performance requirements, e.g., rise time, bandwidth, error coefficients, peak overshoot, etc. As these requirements can be satisfied in many ways, the selection of system configuration as well as time constants of the compensating networks is left largely to the discretion or experience of the designer. There is no place in the above-mentioned techniques for many factors which are known by experience to be significant, e.g., the torque-to-inertia ratio of a servomotor, the noise in the sensing elements, etc. Consequently, the question of what makes the best system under actual operating environment and component limitations cannot be answered by these techniques alone.

In the past one or two decades, while the classical design techniques have been reaching their fruition, the trend of research work has veered toward optimization. This has been for good reason: The problem is no longer how to design one of many systems that work but to design the system that works best.   In many applications, notably fire-control and inertial-guidance systems, no degree of accuracy is too good; in missile-steering systems, no response is too fast.   When we try to improve the accuracy and speed of response of a system, the ultimate limits, which are reached sooner or later, are noise and saturation.   Any design technique, if it is to be realistic, must take due account of these factors.   The outstanding work in this direction is represented by Wiener's theory of optimum filtering and prediction.   However, as Wiener's theory was not intended originally for control systems, it did not give due consideration to the power limitations of the components.   This significant addition to the theory was due to Newton.   Other developments of wide engineering implications include the phase-plane technique or predictor control of

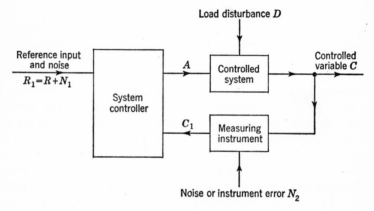

FIG. 1-1. Basic components in a feedback control system.

systems with simple saturation, the development of sampled-data systems, and the recent developments in self-optimizing systems.   The last is perhaps the culminating point of the trend toward optimization.   An ideal self-optimizing system learns about its environment and adjusts itself to optimum expected performance in a continual process of measuring and adjusting.   While developments in this area are still in their infancy, the importance of the self-optimizing concept cannot be over-emphasized.

1-2. The Given Conditions in a Servo-design Problem.   Perhaps the compelling need or reason for the recent developments and trends in servo theory can be understood by an examination of the problems facing a servo designer today.   In doing so, we shall also define a number of terms that will be useful later.

A general representation of a control system is shown in Fig. 1-1.   The controlled system may be a stabilized platform including a torque motor, a steering system including the control surface and its hydraulic drive, or a combination of a servomotor, gears, and marking pen. We assume that we may install instruments to measure whichever system variable we like. However, there is always the error or noise in measurement. The reference input may be transmitted from remote places, with unavoidable noise in the transmission link. Finally there are disturbing forces and moments applied to the load system. The elements possess varying degrees of inalterability. While a bigger and faster hydraulic drive, a better torque-to-inertia ratio in a motor-driven system, or a better signal-to-noise ratio in a measuring instrument is sometimes possible by using more expensive hardware, there is a limit on what one can do beyond any cost consideration. Furthermore, in order not to use expensive hardware unnecessarily, there is a point in investigating what is the best one can do with the given hardware.

By contrast, the system controller with its amplifiers and compensating networks, linear or nonlinear, is almost entirely up to the designer. While an increase in gain that requires an additional stage amplifier incurs some added expense, it is nowhere nearly comparable to the cost of a bigger hydraulic system. The noise in well-designed electronics is usually an order of magnitude lower than that of the measuring instruments and does not constitute a valid limitation on system gain. The saturation of amplifiers, if it is by noise of various types, can usually be alleviated by proper prefiltering. If an amplifier is saturated by an actuating error signal before the controlled system is saturated, economic considerations usually dictate a change of the setup. We can safely say that, at least in systems where high performance is at a premium, no limitation of any kind should be imposed on the controller itself.

Thus we may classify the elements in a control system into three categories:

1. The controlled system, which is also called the plant, the fixed component, or the unalterable component, meaning that its choice is usually not up to the servo designer
2. The measuring or sensing elements
3. The system controller

The first two items are more or less given, and a servo designer's job is essentially to design the system controller itself. However, that is only the first step. If we find it possible to design a controller to meet some given performance specification, the problem does not stop there. We are usually asked what is the best one can do with the given hardware (items 1 and 2). Sometimes we find it very difficult to meet the specified performance; then we must be prepared to answer the question: Is it at all possible to meet the specified performance with the hardware on hand?

Or, what improvement in the hardware is necessary in order to obtain the specified performance?

1-3. Some Classical Fallacies. These questions are difficult or impossible to answer if one knows only the classical techniques or theory. Compounding this, we shall see that some classical notions of performance and of what one can do with a system no longer represent the absolute truth. We shall confine our discussion to three areas:

1. System response to input
2. System response to load disturbance
3. Effect of variations in plant transfer function

Perhaps the best-known notion is the following: *The most desirable system response is the one with the shortest rise time and adequate damping.*

The above is no longer true when noise is considered. A shorter rise time also implies a larger passband for noise, which increases the over-all error. Another point is that what one can obtain on paper is different from what one would obtain in an actual system, because of plant saturation and a number of other factors. A shorter rise time usually means larger transient as well as noise input to the plant for the same reference input. Once the plant is saturated, the system is likely to be more sluggish than one which has a longer rise time on paper but operates in the linear range. A third point is that two systems with widely different pole-zero locations can have the same rise time and peak overshoot but a different order of magnitude of peak value of transient plant input. Considering the small-signal transient response alone is not enough, since a system with a lower peak value of plant input performs better when the reference input signal is large.

The best response to load disturbance is the stiffest one. In other words, the most undisturbable system is the best. This is not always true, depending on the available torque, rate, or power of the controlled system. For instance, in a platform-stabilization system we nearly always provide sufficient torque in the torque motor to balance out the disturbing moments. This is not so in the roll stabilization of an airplane or a ship and is even less so in a steering or attitude-control system. Consequently we try to balance out the disturbances as much as possible in a platform-stabilization system, the only limit to system bandwidth being instrument noise. In the roll stabilization of a ship we try to balance out nearly all the disturbing roll moment due to ocean waves when the sea state is not very heavy, so that the passengers can enjoy their voyage. However, in a really stormy sea, the roll moment is many times larger than the available stabilizing moment of the fins (or activated tanks, etc.), and all one can do is to use the fins to damp out the predominant resonant mode of the ship response to lessen the danger of capsizing. If the servo is designed with unduly large bandwidth, it would simply be jammed and would not serve any useful purpose at all. In steering and attitude-control systems, the rudder or control surface is used to keep a mean course or attitude, as its moment and speed of movement are not adequate to keep up with the instantaneous disturbances due to ocean waves or atmospheric turbulence.

From the frequency-response point of view, because of load inertia and other integration or resonant effects, some Fourier components of the load disturbance cause far more change in the controlled variable than others. When the stabilizing forces or moments at our disposal are limited, our problem is to design not the stiffest system but one which is properly selective, so that these forces or moments can be most effectively utilized.

The closed-loop response of a control system can be made as independent of plant transfer characteristics as one likes by using shunt compensation and increasing the gain of the inner loop. The problem of the sensitivity of closed-loop response to plant variations is one of the greatest current interest. An example of its practical application is the control of a ballistic missile. Within a relatively short time of less than a minute the Mach number changes from zero to 10 or higher and then to something undefined as the air pressure changes from 1 atm to practically zero. During the same period the mass changes as much as 10:1, with a corresponding shift of the center of mass. Obviously there is a drastic change in plant transfer characteristics; however, the closed-loop system response is required not only to be well damped but also to stay close to some specified performance at all times.

At first glance, one would think that the problem could be readily solved by using shunt compensaton with a large inner-loop gain. The inner loop, can be stabilized by introducing a sufficient number of zeros in the vicinity of the plant poles and keeping the poles of the compensating network far enough to the left. A close examination reveals that there is a definite relationship between the sensitivity function and the system's responses to load disturbance and instrument noise. This, together with the possible existence of transportation lag or nonminimum-phase effect in the plant, imposes a limit on how far we can go with inner-loop feedback.

Various ingenious schemes such as conditional feedback or the use of a model have been suggested, tried out, and published in the literature; however, from the analytical point of view, they are not different from the simple series-shunt compensation system. These points will become obvious from a discussion in the next section.

1-4. Basic Relations of Linearly Compensated Systems. With reference to Fig. 1-1, a control system is called linearly compensated if the controller is linear. It does not matter whether the controlled system and measuring instrument are linear or not. In other words, we can write an equation between R_1, C_1, and A:

$$A(s) = H_1(s)R_1(s) - H_2(s)C_1(s) \qquad (1\text{-}1)$$

where s is the Laplace-transform variable.

The above definition of a linearly compensated system can be generalized to include systems that have nonlinear elements in cascade with the controlled system, since these cascade elements can be viewed as part of the controlled system.

Our first basic relationship is that of equivalence: A linear system controller is completely specified by the transfer functions $H_1(s)$ and $H_2(s)$. Two system controllers with different configurations but the same $H_1(s)$

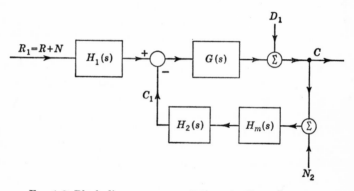

Fig. 1-2. Block-diagram representation of a linear system.

and $H_2(s)$ are completely equivalent as far as every aspect of the system response is concerned (such as stability and responses to input, to noise, to load disturbance, etc.).

When the problem is formulated in the form of Fig. 1-1, the equivalence relation is almost self-evident. The controlled system and measuring instrument are described by an equation relating $c_1(t)$ to all previous values of $d(t)$, $n_2(t)$, and $a(t)$:

$$c_1(t) = f[d(t'),n_2(t''),a(t'''),t] \qquad (1\text{-}2)$$

There is no need to discuss Eq. (1-2) except to note that it is completely independent of the system controller. Because Eqs. (1-1) and (1-2) determine $a(t)$, and consequently $c(t)$, the dependence of the controlled variable $c(t)$ on the system controller is only through the network functions $H_1(s)$ and $H_2(s)$. This proves the equivalence relation.

In case the controlled system and measuring instruments are linear, a basic relationship exists between the sensitivity function, system response to load disturbance, and system response to instrument noise. It can be derived as follows:

In Fig. 1-2, $G(s)$ and $H_m(s)$ are transfer functions of the controlled system and measuring instrument, respectively. The load disturbance is represented by its equivalent value $d_1(t)$ at the output end. Physically, $d_1(t)$ is the output variable if the control is completely cut off. The noise in the measuring instrument is represented by its equivalent value $n_2(t)$ of the measured variable. The closed-loop transfer functions C/R, C/D_1, and C/N_2 are defined as the response in C due to R, D_1, and N_2 alone. From an inspection of Fig. 1-2, we have

$$\frac{C}{R}(s) = \frac{H_1(s)G(s)}{1 + H_2(s)H_m(s)G(s)} \tag{1-3}$$

$$\frac{C}{D_1}(s) = \frac{1}{1 + H_2(s)H_m(s)G(s)} \tag{1-4}$$

$$\frac{C}{N_2}(s) = \frac{-H_2(s)H_m(s)G(s)}{1 + H_2(s)H_m(s)G(s)} \tag{1-5}$$

For an infinitesimal variation in $G(s)$ or $\Delta G(s)$, Eq. (1-3) gives

$$\frac{\Delta \frac{C}{R}(s)}{\frac{C}{R}(s)} = \frac{\Delta G(s)}{G(s)} \frac{1}{1 + H_2(s)H_m(s)G(s)} \tag{1-6}$$

The sensitivity function S is defined as

$$S = \frac{\Delta \frac{C}{R}(s) \Big/ \frac{C}{R}(s)}{\Delta G(s)/G(s)} \tag{1-7}$$

It represents the ratio of per-unit change in C/R to per-unit change in G and gives a quantitative measure of the dependence of the system transfer function to the plant transfer function. Equations (1-4) to (1-7) give

$$S = \frac{C}{D_1}(s) = 1 + \frac{C}{N_2}(s) \tag{1-8}$$

Because of the equivalence relation, Eq. (1-8) is completely independent of the system configuration. It holds as long as the system is linear.

Equations (1-3) and (1-4) imply that the transfer function C/R and C/D_1 can be independently selected. For any given $G(s)$, we can find H_1 and H_2 to give the desired C/R and C/D. However, Eq. (1-8) shows that the sensitivity of C/R to variations in G is closely tied to C/D_1 and C/N_2. In order to make C/R insensitive to variations in G, the loop gain

H_2H_mG must be maintained at some fairly high value for all possible values of G.   A sketch of the various gain functions is given in Fig. 1-3. The C/R function is approximately H_1/H_2H_m.   The loop gain (H_2H_mG) varies as G varies and must be allowed to decrease gradually beyond C/R on account of system stability.   Consequently, the system bandwidth to instrument noise is considerably higher than that of C/R, and the system's stiffness to load disturbance is also necessarily high over a wide band.   It is obvious that how far the noise bandwidth extends depends on how insensitive to plant variations the C/R function is made to be.

Thus we see that instrument noise and load disturbance are limiting factors to the degree of insensitivity that one can achieve in the system response function to plant variations.   Of course there are other limiting

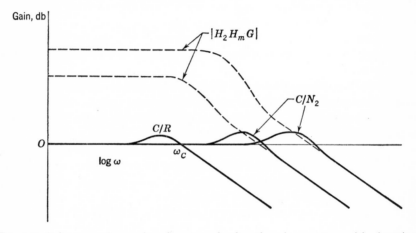

Fɪɢ. 1-3. Gain versus log ω of various transfer functions in a system with changing plant.

factors, e.g., transportation lag and high-frequency resonant modes of the plant.   While these high-frequency effects are not very significant in the passband of C/R itself, they nevertheless limit the extended gain bandwidth of H_mH_2G.

1-5. Scope of This Book.   The above is an illustration of the various factors entering into a control problem and how they are interrelated. Present control theory does not give a cookbook solution of every problem that may arise, but it does provide a number of basic tools for solving these problems.   To be more explicit, we have a number of idealized situations for which exact mathematical solutions are feasible.   Sometimes a control problem falls within one of these, and we have an immediate solution.   However, many problems do not fall into one idealized situation alone, and a direct mathematical solution is either too cumbersome or impossible with our present knowledge of mathematics.   The analytical methods that we use in solving idealized problems still can be used for an analysis of the effects of each individual factor involved and for providing some insight into what a good over-all solution should be. While it may be said that our present control theory is not complete, we must be thankful for this incompleteness, since without it the control field would no longer be an interesting and challenging one.

As mentioned in Sec. 1-2, the optimum performance, in whatever sense, that a system may achieve is limited only by factors in the controlled system or plant and in the environment of control, such as the presence of load disturbance and noise, etc., and by the unpredictable changes and variations of these factors. In the subsequent chapters we shall study the basic methods of analysis and synthesis which determine the optimum performance and optimum controller directly from these limitations. There are four such methods:

1. Wiener's least-square optimization with quadratic constraint, which is the simplest and most useful for linear systems with or without random disturbances.

2. Pontryagin's maximum principle for optimal control of a nonlinear system in the sense of minimal time or maximum range. A well-known forerunner and special case of the maximum principle is the "bang-bang" servo principle.

3. Self-optimizing systems or adaptive systems. A system of this kind measures, evaluates, and adapts itself to changing plant and environment.

4. Optimization and control by the use of a digital computer, which is more or less a catchall when everything else fails.

There are two essential phases of operation of a digital computer in control: (1) computations of the optimum performance and the optimum trajectory and (2) actual control of a system, utilizing the computed data. Dynamic programming and a digitized version of the maximum principle represent the basic mathematics upon which different computation procedures are based.

Besides the four basic methods of optimization, two closely related subjects are also treated:

1. Analysis and measurement of random processes. The concept of correlation, correlation functions, and spectral densities and the calculation and measurement of these functions are an essential part of control work.

2. Error analysis. An analysis of the errors or discrepancies caused by component inaccuracies on the closed-loop system response is as important a factor in control engineering as specification of tolerances is in a toolroom.

The above methods are useful not only for the design of complex systems but also for routine design of relatively simple systems. For instance, a graphical method realizing Wiener's optimization with quadratic constraint is the root-square-locus method. Its complexity is not much greater than that of the root-locus method, and it can be used in lieu of the latter. However, it gives directly from the plant transfer function and specified rise time or servo bandwidth the compensating network that has the least tendency to saturate the plant, among many that can be used to meet the performance specifications. Thus the method is an improvement over conventional linear design techniques. Similarly, the concept of "bang-bang" servo can be used to help select nonlinear compensating elements for systems which are easily saturable, although a complete realization of the bang-bang principle is difficult for high-order systems.

1-6. Nomenclature. There are some symbols and conventions which are used throughout this volume. The lower-case letters represent time functions. For instance, $r(t)$ represents the reference input, $c(t)$ the controlled variable, $i(t)$ an unspecified input function, $a(t)$ an unspecified system variable, and $\phi(t)$ the correlation function. Corresponding capital letters represent Laplace transforms of the time functions, for example, $R(s)$, $I(s)$, $C(s)$, etc. $G(s)$ and $H(s)$ represent open-loop system functions and transfer functions of components, with $g(t)$ and $h(t)$ as the respective impulse-response functions. Pertaining to sampled-data systems, an asterisk indicates sampling, for instance, $r^*(t)$ is the sampled $r(t)$, and $R^*(s)$ is the sampled transform, or transform of $r^*(t)$. $R(z)$ means the z transform of $r^*(t)$. An asterisk over a complex number indicates conjugation.

A bar over a time function represents averaging. A bar over a capital letter represents changing s to $-s$ or z to z^{-1}.

There are some symbols which are used consistently in the optimization procedure: $Y(s)$ and $Z(s)$ are defined in Sec. 2-4. The symbols $[\ \ ]_+$ and $\{\ \ \}^+$ are defined in Sec. 2-4.

The other symbols are defined as the occasion for their use arises.

CHAPTER 2

OPTIMUM SYSTEM WITH DETERMINISTIC INPUTS

2-1. Introduction. In this chapter we shall start with an exact solution of the problem of synthesizing a system with least-integral-square error subject to the power limitations of the controlled plant. While the problem as it stands does not have wide application, its usefulness is extended in the subsequent sections to the design of systems which meet the conventional requirements for response time, peak overshoot, etc., with least likelihood of saturation. The application of the method is then made easy by introducing the graphical root-square-locus method.

Simple application examples are given in the chapter to illustrate the method rather than its scope of application. It is obvious that the root-square-locus method can be applied to all design problems where the root-locus method is applicable.

2-2. Statement of the Least-square Optimization Problem. For the system of Fig. 2-1, the controlled plant with transfer function $G(s)$ is given, and a linear controller with unspecified configuration and control

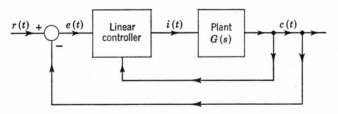

FIG. 2-1. A linear system with unspecified controller.

elements is to be designed. The design criterion is based on two figures of dismerit:

1. The integral-square error [subsequent to an input $r(t)$ applied at $t = 0$]:

$$J_1 = \int_0^\infty [e(t)]^2 \, dt = \int_0^\infty [r(t) - c(t)]^2 \, dt \tag{2-1}$$

2. The integral-square value of the control effort:

$$J_2 = \int_0^\infty [i(t)]^2 \, dt \tag{2-2}$$

The significance of J_1 is as follows:

1. Any error, positive or negative, contributes to the integral-square error a positive amount which increases with the magnitude and duration of the error.

2. Either a slow-rising characteristic or a large overshoot would increase the value of the integral-square error very significantly.

By limiting or requiring J_1 to be a minimum, we are, in effect, putting somewhat elastic restrictions on all three factors: response time, settling time, and peak overshoot. J_2 has similar significance relating to the control effort.

The design criterion may be either of the following:

a. Minimizing the system error within the limit of available control effort:

$$J_1 = \min \qquad (2\text{-}3)$$
$$J_2 \leq K_2 \qquad (2\text{-}4)$$

b. Minimizing the control effort with the tolerable system error specified:

$$J_2 = \min \qquad (2\text{-}3a)$$
$$J_1 \leq K_1 \qquad (2\text{-}4a)$$

There are two steps in the solution:

1. Determination of the optimum control ratio (or closed-loop transfer function) $(C/R)(s)$ from the design criterion, $G(s)$, and $r(t)$

2. Selection of a system configuration and compensating elements to give the optimum control ratio C/R

The second step is more or less routine and usually can be done in many ways.

2-3. Transformation into Frequency Domain, Parseval's Theorem. To facilitate mathematical manipulations we shall convert Eqs. (2-1) and (2-2) into the s domain. Let $a(t)$ be an arbitrary function which is zero for all negative values of t, is bounded for all values of t, and approaches zero at least as fast as $e^{-\epsilon t}$, as t approaches infinity, where ϵ is a small positive constant. We shall prove that

$$\int_0^\infty [a(t)]^2 \, dt = \frac{1}{2\pi j} \int_{-j\infty}^{j\infty} A(s)A(-s) \, ds \qquad (2\text{-}5)$$

where $A(s)$ is the Laplace transform of $a(t)$.

The above relation can be proved as follows: One of the $a(t)$'s on the left-hand side of Eq. (2-5) is written in terms of its inverse transform:

$$\int_0^\infty [a(t)]^2 \, dt = \frac{1}{2\pi j} \int_0^\infty a(t) \int_{-j\infty}^{j\infty} A(s)e^{st} \, ds \, dt \qquad (2\text{-}6)$$

Under the stated conditions for $a(t)$, Eq. (2-6) can be integrated first with respect to t.   The result is Eq. (2-5).   The conditions on $a(t)$ define a common region of convergence for the Laplace transforms $A(s)$ and $A(-s)$, as shown in Fig. 2-2.   We note that integration of s along the imaginary axis is within this region.

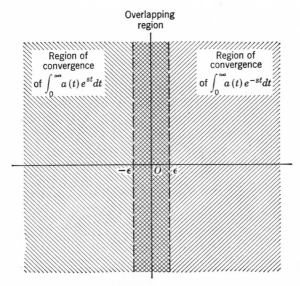

FIG. 2-2. Overlapping regions of convergence on the s plane.

Let $F(s)$ denote the control ratio $(C/R)(s)$.   The Laplace transforms of $c(t) - r(t)$ and $i(t)$ can be written as

$$C(s) - R(s) = [F(s) - 1]R(s) \tag{2-7}$$

$$I(s) = \frac{C(s)}{G(s)} = \frac{F(s)R(s)}{G(s)} \tag{2-8}$$

From Eqs. (2-5), (2-7), and (2-8), Eqs. (2-1) and (2-2) can be written as

$$J_1 = \frac{1}{2\pi j} \int_{-j\infty}^{j\infty} [F(s) - 1][F(-s) - 1]R(s)R(-s)\,ds \tag{2-9}$$

and

$$J_2 = \frac{1}{2\pi j} \int_{-j\infty}^{j\infty} \frac{F(s)F(-s)R(s)R(-s)}{G(s)G(-s)}\,ds \tag{2-10}$$

2-4. Solution of the Least-square Optimization Problem.   Following Lagrange's method of undetermined multipliers, Eqs. (2-3) and (2-4) can be written in one as

$$J_1 + k^2 J_2 = \min \tag{2-11}$$

Equation (2-11) can also be justified by simple reasoning.   For each value of k^2, there is a control ratio that satisfies Eq. (2-11), say $F_{0k}(s)$. When substituted into Eq. (2-10), each $F_{0k}(s)$ will give a value of J_2. Among all possible closed-loop transfer functions that yield the same value of J_2, $F_{0k}(s)$ gives the smallest value of J_1 because $F_{0k}(s)$ satisfies Eq. (2-11). To determine $F_0(s)$, we simply choose the one that gives the lowest J_1, among the $F_{0k}(s)$'s satisfying $J_2 \leq K_2$.

Obviously we are interested only in stable systems, and a condition on $F(s)$ is that all its poles be inside the LHP (left half plane). An arbitrary $F(s)$ can be written as

$$F(s) = F_{0k}(s) + \lambda F_1(s) \qquad (2\text{-}12)$$

where λ is a constant and $F_1(s)$ is a function of s. Since all the poles of $F(s)$ and $F_{0k}(s)$ are in the LHP interior, all the poles of $F_1(s)$ are in the LHP interior. On the other hand, given any $F_1(s)$ with all its poles in the LHP interior, and arbitrary constant λ, $F(s)$ of Eq. (2-12) represents a stable system function and is a candidate for the optimum system function $F_{0k}(s)$. Changing the sign of s in Eq. (2-12) gives

$$F(-s) = F_{0k}(-s) + \lambda F_1(-s) \qquad (2\text{-}13)$$

In the following mathematical manipulations, we shall use the shorthand notations F_{0k}, F_1, R, and G to represent $F_{0k}(s)$, $F_1(s)$, $R(s)$, and $G(s)$, respectively, and the shorthand notations $\bar{F}_{0k}$, $\bar{F}_1$, $\bar{R}$, and $\bar{G}$ to represent $F_{0k}(-s)$, $F_1(-s)$, $R(-s)$, and $G(-s)$, respectively. Evaluating Eqs. (2-9) and (2-10) for $F(s)$, we have

$$(J_1 + k^2 J_2)_{F(s)} = \frac{1}{2\pi j} \int_{-j\infty}^{j\infty} \left[(F_{0k} + \lambda F_1 - 1)(\bar{F}_{0k} + \lambda \bar{F}_1 - 1)R\bar{R} \right.$$
$$\left. + \frac{k^2(F_{0k} + \lambda F_1)(\bar{F}_{0k} + \lambda \bar{F}_1)R\bar{R}}{G\bar{G}} \right] ds = J_a + \lambda(J_b + J_c) + \lambda^2 J_d \qquad (2\text{-}14)$$

where
$$J_a = \frac{1}{2\pi j} \int_{-j\infty}^{j\infty} \left[(F_{0k} - 1)(\bar{F}_{0k} - 1) + \frac{k^2 F_{0k}\bar{F}_{0k}}{G\bar{G}} \right] R\bar{R} \, ds$$

$$J_b = \frac{1}{2\pi j} \int_{-j\infty}^{j\infty} \left[(\bar{F}_{0k} - 1) + \frac{k^2 \bar{F}_{0k}}{G\bar{G}} \right] R\bar{R}F_1 \, ds \quad = 0$$

$$J_c = \frac{1}{2\pi j} \int_{-j\infty}^{j\infty} \left[(F_{0k} - 1) + \frac{k^2 F_{0k}}{G\bar{G}} \right] R\bar{R}\bar{F}_1 \, ds \quad = 0$$

$$J_d = \frac{1}{2\pi j} \int_{-j\infty}^{j\infty} \left(1 + \frac{k^2}{G\bar{G}} \right) F_1\bar{F}_1 R\bar{R} \, ds$$

In Eq. (2-11) J_a is the value of $J_1 + k^2 J_2$ with F_{0k} as the system function, and J_d is always positive. By substituting $-s$ for s in J_b, it becomes J_c. It is therefore equal to the latter. Hence, the sufficient condition for F_{0k} to give the lowest value of $J_1 + k^2 J_2$ is simply that, for arbitrary $\bar{F}_1$, $J_c = 0$.

In the following we shall show that this is also a necessary condition. If $J_c \neq 0$ we can always choose a different λ satisfying the following conditions:

1. The magnitude of λ is small enough so that $\lambda^2 J_d < 2|\lambda J_c|$.
2. The sign of λ is such that $\lambda J_c < 0$.

Then for the $F(s)$ defined by Eq. (2-12), with the new value of λ, $J_1 + k^2 J_2$ is less than that for $F_{0k}(s)$, a result which contradicts the definition of $F_{0k}(s)$.

Now let us consider the equation

from $J_c, J_b = 0$

$$\int_{-j\infty}^{j\infty} \left[(\bar{F}_{0k} - 1) + \frac{k^2 F_{0k}}{G\bar{G}} \right] R\bar{R}\bar{F}_1 \, ds = 0 \qquad (2\text{-}15)$$

Since all the poles of $F_1(s)$ are inside the LHP, all the poles of $\bar{F}_1$ are inside the RHP (right half plane). It suggests a solution that all the poles of $[(\bar{F}_{0k} - 1) + k^2 F_{0k}/G\bar{G}]R\bar{R}$ be inside the RHP. We shall complete the path of integration of Eq. (2-15) by a large semicircle to the left, enclosing the entire LHP, as shown in Fig. 2-3. Since all the poles of the integrand are inside the RHP, the contour integral vanishes. The behavior of the integral at infinity remains to be examined. From the initial-value theorem of Laplace transforms we may evaluate the limiting values of the reference input r, controlled variable c_1, and control effort i, at an infinitesimal interval $0+$ subsequent to the step input:

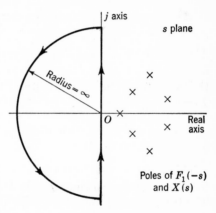

FIG. 2-3. Path of integration and locations of poles of $F_1(-s)$ and $X(s)$.

$$r(0+) = \lim_{s \to \infty} sR(s)$$

$$c(0+) = \lim_{s \to \infty} sF(s)R(s)$$

$$i(0+) = \lim_{s \to \infty} s\frac{F(s)R(s)}{G(s)}$$

The above equations are valid for the optimum system function $F_{0k}(s)$ as well as for any competing system function $F(s)$. Since $r(0+)$, $c(0+)$, $i(0+)$ are either finite or zero, the transform functions $R, FR, FR/G$, and their barred functions are all of the order of $1/s$. The integrand of Eq. (2-15) is made up of products of these factors and is therefore of the order of $1/s^2$. The semicircular part of the contour integral converges to zero as the radius approaches infinity. It follows that

$$\left[(F_{0k} - 1) + \frac{k^2 F_{0k}}{G\tilde{G}}\right] R\tilde{R} = X(s) \tag{2-16}$$

is a sufficient condition for Eq. (2-15). Here $X(s)$ is used to denote an arbitrary function of s with all its poles in the RHP interior.

Equation (2-16) is also the necessary condition for Eq. (2-15), because of the arbitrariness of $\tilde{F}_1$. If the expression $[(F_{0k} - 1) + k^2 F_{0k}/G\tilde{G}]R\tilde{R}$ has any poles in the LHP, a function $\tilde{F}_1$ could be selected so that the sum of residues would not vanish; Eq. (2-15) would then be violated. Thus Eq. (2-16) is the necessary and sufficient condition for $F_{0k}(s)$ to yield the minimum value of $J_1 + k^2 J_2$.

Equation (2-16) can be rewritten as

$$\left(1 + \frac{k^2}{G\tilde{G}}\right) R\tilde{R}F_{0k} - R\tilde{R} = X(s) \tag{2-17}$$

The function $1 + k^2/G\tilde{G}$ is not changed by replacing s with $-s$. Hence if α is a pole (or zero) $-\alpha$ must also be a pole (or zero). Consequently, the function can be factored into a function $Y(s)$ and an identical function $Y(-s)$ such that all the poles and zeros of $Y(s)$ are in the LHP:

$$1 + \frac{k^2}{G\tilde{G}} \equiv Y(s)Y(-s) \tag{2-18}$$

This process of factoring into two functions according to the pole-zero locations relative to the j axis in the s plane is called spectral factoring. The function that contains all the poles and zeros in the LHP (RHP) is denoted by braces { } around the original function and a plus (minus) sign at its upper right corner. We can write instead of Eq. (2-18)

$$Y(s) \equiv \left\{1 + \frac{k^2}{G\tilde{G}}\right\}^+ \tag{2-19}$$

Similarly, we can define a function $Z(s)$ by

$$Z(s) \equiv \{R(s)R(-s)\}^+ \tag{2-20}$$

In order not to break the continuity of the treatment, it is assumed at this point that the functions inside the braces do not have any poles or zeros on the imaginary axis. This restriction will be removed at the end of this section.

Substituting Eqs. (2-19) and (2-20) in (2-17) gives

$$Y\tilde{Y}Z\tilde{Z}F_{0k} - Z\tilde{Z} = X(s) \tag{2-21}$$

Dividing Eq. (2-21) by $\bar{Y}\bar{Z}$ gives

$$YZF_{0k} - \frac{Z}{\bar{Y}} = \frac{X}{\bar{Y}\bar{Z}} \tag{2-22}$$

The function $Z/\bar{Y}$ can be expressed as a partial-fraction expansion:

$$\frac{Z}{\bar{Y}} = \sum_i \frac{A_i}{s - \alpha_i} + \sum_j \frac{B_j}{s - \beta_j} \tag{2-23}$$

In Eq. (2-23) the α_i's are poles in the LHP, and the β_j's are poles in the RHP. Let [ ]$_+$ (and[ ]$_-$) be defined to represent the process of partial fractioning, retaining only the terms with poles in the LHP and RHP, respectively. Then, by definition,

$$\left[\frac{Z}{\bar{Y}}\right]_+ = \sum_i \frac{A_i}{s - \alpha_i} \tag{2-24}$$

$$\left[\frac{Z}{\bar{Y}}\right]_- = \sum_j \frac{B_j}{s - \beta_j} \tag{2-25}$$

Equation (2-22) can be written as

$$YZF_{0k} - \left[\frac{Z}{\bar{Y}}\right]_+ = \frac{X}{\bar{Y}\bar{Z}} + \left[\frac{Z}{\bar{Y}}\right]_- \tag{2-26}$$

Since all the poles of the expression on the left-hand side of Eq. (2-26) are in the LHP and all the poles of the expression on the right-hand side are in the RHP, we obtain as its solution†

$$YZF_{0k} = \left[\frac{Z}{\bar{Y}}\right]_+ \tag{2-27}$$

$$F_{0k} = \frac{1}{YZ}\left[\frac{Z}{\bar{Y}}\right]_+ \tag{2-28}$$

Once F_{0k} is determined, J_1 and J_2 can be evaluated as functions of k. As a rule, J_1 is an increasing function of k and J_2 is a decreasing function

---

† The two sides of Eq. (2-26) are equal to an unknown function of s which is analytic in the entire s plane. Therefore it must be a constant. To show that the constant vanishes, we shall examine the limit of the function YZF_{0k} as s approaches infinity:

$$Y \to \frac{k}{G} \qquad Z \to R$$

Therefore $\qquad\qquad YZF_{0k} \to k\,\dfrac{RF_{0k}}{G} = kI = \dfrac{ki(0+)}{s}$

Since both YZF_{0k} and $[Z/Y]_+$ are of the order of $1/s$ as s approaches infinity, the constant must be zero.

of k. The value of k is therefore given by

$$J_2(k) = K_2 \tag{2-29}$$

The above gives $F_0(s)$ for the optimizing problem defined by Eqs. (2-3) and (2-4). The problem defined by Eqs. (2-3a) and (2-4a) can be solved in exactly the same way. Equations (2-11) to (2-28) are equally applicable to the latter case, while Eq. (2-29) is replaced by

$$J_1(k) = K_1 \tag{2-30}$$

Example 2-1. An inertial load is to be driven by a servomotor through a gear train. The transfer function of the motor and load system can be represented as

$$G(s) \equiv \frac{C(s)}{I(s)} = \frac{K_T}{Ms^2} \tag{2-31}$$

where $c(t)$ is the load-shaft position in radians and $i(t)$ is the control winding current. The value of the constants are (referring to the load shaft)

$$K_T = 2 \text{ newton-m/amp}$$
$$M = 0.2 \text{ kg-m}^2$$
$$R = \text{control winding resistance} = 8 \text{ ohms}$$

Under the heaviest-duty condition there is, on an average, one step input every 2 sec with an rms amplitude of 0.5 radian. The amplitudes of the successive step inputs are independent. In order to keep the motor-temperature rise within allowable limits, the average copper loss of the control winding should not exceed 10 watts. Design a system controller which gives the least-integral-square error.

Solution. Since the successive step inputs are independent, their cross terms in the integral-square values of $e(t)$ and $i(t)$ average out, and these integral-square values can be calculated individually for each step input. In order not to exceed 10 watts in control-winding copper loss, we must have

$$\int_0^\infty R[i(t)]^2 \, dt \leq 10 \text{ watts} \times 2 \text{ sec}$$

or

$$\int_0^\infty [i(t)]^2 \, dt \leq {}^{20}\!/_8 = 2.5 \tag{2-32}$$

Equation (2-19) gives

$$Y(s) = \left\{ 1 + \frac{k^2 s^4}{100} \right\}^+ = (1 + as)(1 + bs) \tag{2-33}$$

where $a = \sqrt{(k/10)} \; \underline{/45^\circ}$ and b is its conjugate.

Now $R(s) = 0.5/s$ and has a pole at the origin. However, for all practical purposes we may write $R(s)$ as $0.5/(s + \epsilon)$, where ϵ may be the reciprocal of a billion years. While an exponentially decaying function with so long a half period is practically the same as a step function, it nevertheless satisfies the mathematical requirement of not having any poles or zeros on the imaginary axis. Equation (2-20) gives

$$Z(s) = \left\{ \frac{0.5}{s + \epsilon} \frac{0.5}{\epsilon - s} \right\}^+ = \frac{0.5}{s + \epsilon} \tag{2-34}$$

$$\left[\frac{Z}{\bar{Y}} \right]_+ = \left[\frac{0.5}{(s + \epsilon)(1 - as)(1 - bs)} \right]_+ = \frac{0.5}{(1 + a\epsilon)(1 + b\epsilon)(s + \epsilon)} \tag{2-35}$$

Substituting Eqs. (2-33) to (2-35) in (2-28) gives

$$F_{0k} = \frac{1}{(1 + as)(1 + bs)(1 + a\epsilon)(1 + b\epsilon)}$$

As ϵ approaches zero, it becomes

$$F_{0k} = \frac{1}{(1 + as)(1 + bs)} = \frac{1}{1 + \sqrt{0.2k}\, s + 0.1ks^2} \tag{2-36}$$

Substituting Eq. (2-36) in (2-10), we have

$$J_2(k) = \frac{1}{2\pi j} \int_{-j\infty}^{j\infty} \frac{-0.0025s^2\, ds}{(1 + \sqrt{0.2k}\, s + 0.1ks^2)(1 - \sqrt{0.2k}\, s + 0.1ks^2)} \tag{2-37}$$

An integral of this form can readily be evaluated by contour integration. However, as the work becomes rather tedious when the order of the system is high, it is advisable to use the Table of Integrals given in Appendix D. For the above integral we have

$$\begin{aligned} n &= 2 & a_2 &= 1 \\ a_0 &= 0.1k & b_0 &= -0.0025 \\ a_1 &= \sqrt{0.2k} & b_1 &= 0 \end{aligned}$$

$$J_2(k) = \frac{0.0025}{2 \times 0.1k \times \sqrt{0.2k}} = \frac{0.25}{\sqrt{80k^3}} = 2.5$$

Therefore $k = 0.05$. Substituting this value of k in Eq. (2-36) gives

$$F_0(s) = \frac{1}{1 + 0.1s + 0.005s^2} = \frac{C}{R}(s) \tag{2-38}$$

The control ratio of Eq. (2-38) can be readily realized by a system employing tachometer feedback, as shown in Fig. 2-4. The integral-square error is evaluated from Eq. (2-9):

$$\begin{aligned} J_1 &= \frac{1}{2\pi j} \int_{-j\infty}^{j\infty} \frac{(0.1s + 0.005s^2)(-0.1s + 0.005s^2)}{(1 + 0.1s + 0.005s^2)(1 - 0.1s + 0.005s^2)} \frac{0.5}{s}\left(-\frac{0.5}{s}\right) ds \\ &= \frac{1}{2\pi j} \int_{-j\infty}^{j\infty} \frac{0.0025(1 - 0.0025s^2)}{(1 + 0.1s + 0.005s^2)(1 - 0.1s + 0.005s^2)} ds \\ &= \frac{0.0025(0.0025 + 0.005)}{2 \times 0.005 \times 0.1} = 0.01875 \end{aligned} \tag{2-39}$$

In the above example, we have considered poles at the origin as poles at $\pm\epsilon$ in the calculations and let ϵ approach zero in the final result. Exactly the same results are obtained if, without using ϵ, we split these poles

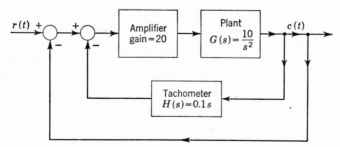

FIG. 2-4. Block diagram of an optimum system.

equally between Z and $\bar{Z}$ and treat the ones belonging to Z as if they were in the LHP and the ones belonging to $\bar{Z}$ as if they were in the RHP.   The latter method has the advantage of simplicity in algebraic manipulations. In case there are poles and/or zeros at other points on the imaginary axis, they can be treated in the same way.

Quite often the input to a system can be described as a random combination of step and ramp inputs or some other deterministic functions, and it is desirable to have the averaged values of J_1 and J_2 satisfying

$$\bar{J}_1 = \min$$
$$\bar{J}_2 \leq K_2$$

or vice versa.   The averaging process is weighted according to the frequencies of occurrence of the various types of inputs.   The solution is the same as above except that Eq. (2-20) is replaced by

$$\bar{Z}Z = \sum_i w_i \bar{R}_i R_i \tag{2-40}$$

In Eq. (2-40) w_i is proportional to the frequency of occurrence of the ith type of input R_i.

Another point worth mentioning is that the transfer function $G(s)$ is that between the output variable and the system variable the integral-square value of which we wish to limit.   The latter is not necessarily the conventional input variable.

2-5. Some General Results.   Let us examine the expression on the right-hand side of Eq. (2-28).   As $\bar{Y}$ does not have any poles in the LHP, the poles of the function $[Z/\bar{Y}]_+$ are the poles of Z only.   In the complete expression these poles are canceled out by Z in the denominator.   *Therefore the poles of the optimum control ratio are the zeros of Y and Z only.*

For the two commonly used deterministic inputs, Eq. (2-28) can be put into even simpler form:

1. *Step Input*

$$R(s) = \frac{1}{s}$$

$$F_{0k}(s) = \frac{s}{Y(s)} \left[\frac{1}{s\bar{Y}(s)} \right]_+ = \frac{s}{Y(s)} \frac{1}{Y(0)s} = \frac{1}{Y(0)Y(s)} \tag{2-41}$$

2. *Ramp Input*

$$R(s) = \frac{1}{s^2}$$

$$F_{0k}(s) = \frac{s^2}{Y(s)} \left[\frac{1}{s^2 \bar{Y}(s)} \right]_+ = \frac{s^2}{Y(s)} \left[\frac{1}{s^2 Y(0)} + \frac{Y'(0)}{s Y(0)^2} \right]$$
$$= \frac{1 + Ts}{Y(0)Y(s)} \tag{2-42}$$

where $T = Y'(0)/Y(0)$.

The constant $Y(0)$ can be determined by letting $s = 0$ in Eq. (2-18):

$$[Y(0)]^2 = 1 + \frac{k^2}{[G(0)]^2} \tag{2-43}$$

If the transfer function $G(s)$ has a factor s^n (where $n \neq 0$) in its denominator, $1/G(0)$ vanishes and $Y(0) = 1$.   Equations (2-41) and (2-42) give, respectively,

$$F_{0k}(s) = \frac{1}{Y(s)} \qquad \text{for step input} \tag{2-44}$$

$$F_{0k}(s) = \frac{1 + Y'(0)s}{Y(s)} \qquad \text{for ramp input} \tag{2-45}$$

Equations (2-44) and (2-45) will be given a physical interpretation.   An over-all open-loop transfer function $G_0(s)$ is defined by

$$\frac{C}{R}(s) = \frac{G_0(s)}{1 + G_0(s)} \tag{2-46}$$

For an optimum system,

$$\frac{1}{G_0(s)} = \frac{1}{F_{0k}(s)} - 1 \tag{2-47}$$

We shall examine the behavior of $G_0(s)$ for small values of s.   The function $Y(s)$ is expanded into a power series in s:

$$Y(s) = 1 + Y'(0)s + \tfrac{1}{2}Y''(0)s^2 + \cdots \tag{2-48}$$

For the step input, Eqs. (2-47) and (2-48) give

$$\frac{1}{G_0(s)} = Y'(0)s + \tfrac{1}{2}Y''(0)s^2 + \cdots \tag{2-49}$$

For the ramp input, Eqs. (2-47) and (2-48) give

$$\frac{1}{G_0(s)} = \frac{Y(s)}{1 + Y'(0)s} - 1 = \frac{\tfrac{1}{2}Y''(0)s^2 + \cdots}{1 + Y'(0)s} \tag{2-50}$$

The leading powers in Eqs. (2-49) and (2-50) are s and s^2, respectively. Therefore, *assuming $G(0) = \infty$, the optimum compensated system is a type 1 system for step inputs and a type 2 system for ramp inputs.   The optimum C/R is $1/Y(s)$ for the former case and $(1 + Ts)/Y(s)$ for the latter case, and T is selected to make the compensated system a type 2 system.*

If $G(0)$ is a constant, the control system is a regulator system and is inherently incapable of following a ramp input indefinitely.   The only meaningful problem then is the one with a step input.   Equation (2-41) shows that $F_{0k}(s)$ has the same poles and zeros as $1/Y(s)$, and Eqs. (2-41) and (2-43) give the d-c closed-loop gain as

$$F_{0k}(0) = \frac{1}{1 + k^2/[G(0)]^2} \tag{2-51}$$

With $F_{0k}(0)$ as given in Eq. (2-51), the steady-state value of $e^2 + k^2i^2$

is easily shown to be a minimum.   We shall leave the proof of this point to the reader.

2-6. Systems Meeting Conventional Specifications with Least Likelihood of Saturation.   The preceding sections give an exact solution of the optimization problem as formulated in Sec. 2-2.   However, very few control problems are so formulated.   The error criterion is usually not the integral-square error but a few somewhat arbitrarily defined descriptive parameters such as response time, settling time, peak overshoot, error coefficients, etc.   The input functon is known only in some approximate sense, and the limit on the control effort is usually not the i^2R loss but a nonlinearity in response such as is caused by saturation, range limitation, etc.

As we know, classical design methods do not consider the saturation problem.   While it is possible to make new assumptions and rewrite the saturation effect and other design conditions into exact form so that an exact solution can be made, the solution is usually quite tedious and one wonders if it is worth all that effort.   Presently we shall describe a method which does not give an exact solution of the saturation problem but is simple and is an improvement over the classical methods in that the saturation effect is at least considered in an approximate sort of way.

The method is essentially a reinterpretation of Eqs. (2-3a) and (2-4a). The specified response time determines approximately a value of J_1. If the saturable system variable is taken as $i(t)$ in Eq. (2-2), the likelihood of saturation is reduced by minimizing J_2.   We see that the design problem is then the same as the one defined by Eqs. (2-3a) and (2-4a).   However, instead of determining K_1 from the response time and k from K_1, k is determined directly from the response time, as follows: In an approximate sense, the response time is inversely proportional to the distance of the nearest pole to the origin.   Of course, it also depends on the number of poles at the nearest distance and on the locations of the other poles, etc., but as a first approximation these effects can be neglected.   Suppose that we define the response time t_p as the time it takes the system output variable to rise to 95 per cent of its equilibrium value after the application of a step input.   We find the following approximate relation quite useful:

$$t_p = \frac{\pi}{\omega} \tag{2-52}$$

The requirement on response time can be satisfied by selecting a k value such that the nearest isolated pole (not considering the poles in dipole pairs) is about π/t_p radians/sec from the origin.

To keep within the limit of specified peak overshoot is not a problem. We shall show in Sec. 2-8 that the peak overshoot of a system designed by the present method generally has a relatively low value and is well below the conventionally allowed 10 to 20 per cent. This is an expected result arising from minimizing the mean-square value of $i(t)$. As the natural frequency of the closed-loop system is usually not that of the plant $G(s)$, it takes an excessively large control effort to force the plant into an oscillatory motion.

If exceptionally low overshoot is required, it can be achieved by modifying the pole-zero locations of the optimum system, as will be discussed in the next section.

2-7. The Root-square-locus Method. Presently we shall derive a graphical method for determining the control ratio of an optimum system. In Sec. 2-5 we have shown that, with step and ramp inputs, the optimum control ratio can be readily calculated from the poles and zeros of $Y(s)$. Thus, once $Y(s)$ is determined, the problem is solved.

In the present chapter, we shall deal only with rational transfer functions which do not have any zeros in the RHP and leave the problems of transportation lag and nonminimum phase to be treated in Chap. 4. Presently we can write $G(s)$ as

$$G(s) = \frac{K \prod_{j=1}^{j=m} (s - z_j)}{\prod_{i=1}^{i=n} (s - p_i)} \qquad n > m \qquad (2\text{-}53)$$

Let q_i represent zeros of Y. Let Ω, P_i, Q_i, and Z_j represent $-s^2$, $-p_i^2$, $-q_i^2$, and $-z_j^2$, respectively. Equation (2-18) gives

$$Y\bar{Y} = 1 + \frac{k^2}{K^2} \frac{\prod_{i=1}^{n} (s - p_i)(-s - p_i)}{\prod_{j=1}^{m} (s - z_j)(-s - z_j)}$$

$$= 1 + \frac{k^2}{K^2} \frac{\prod_{i=1}^{n} (p_i^2 - s^2)}{\prod_{j=1}^{m} (z_j^2 - s^2)} = 1 + \frac{k^2}{K^2} \frac{\prod_{i=1}^{n} (\Omega - P_i)}{\prod_{j=1}^{m} (\Omega - Z_j)}$$

$$= \frac{(k^2/K^2) \prod_{i=1}^{n} (\Omega - P_i) + \prod_{j=1}^{m} (\Omega - Z_j)}{\prod_{j=1}^{m} (\Omega - Z_j)} \qquad (2\text{-}54)$$

The roots of Ω of the numerator polynomial on the right-hand side of Eq. (2-54) can be determined by the root-locus method, in which we take

$\left[\prod\limits_{j=1}^{m} (\Omega - Z_j) \right] \Big/ \left[\prod\limits_{i=1}^{n} (\Omega - P_i) \right]$ as the open-loop transfer function, and K^2/k^2 as the variable gain. The closed-loop poles so obtained are the Q_i's. Since the highest power of Ω in the polynomial is n, there are n Q_i's. It is also clear from Eq. (2-54) that z_j's are poles of $Y(s)$. Once the q_i's are calculated from the Q_i's, $Y(s)$ can be readily written as

$$Y(s) = \frac{Y(0) \prod\limits_{i=1}^{i=n} (1 - s/q_i)}{\prod\limits_{j=1}^{j=m} (1 - s/z_j)} \qquad (2\text{-}55)$$

By substituting Eqs. (2-43) and (2-55) in Eqs. (2-41) and (2-42), respectively, the optimum C/R for step and ramp inputs is readily determined.

We note that in the above method the only step which requires some effort is the determination of the Q_i's by the root-locus plot. Since the plot is made in the Ω plane, it will be referred to as the root-square-locus plot. Its advantage over the conventional root-locus method is that it starts with the pole-zero configuration of the fixed elements without specifying compensating networks and gives the closed-loop pole-zero configuration of the optimum system *including* the compensating networks for all values of gain. A design can be carried out in the following steps:

Step 1. Given the transfer function $G(s)$ with zeros z_1, z_2, . . . , z_i, . . . , z_m and poles p_1, p_2, . . . , p_n, where $n > m$, calculate z_1, z_2, . . . , z_m and p_1, p_2, . . . , p_n:

$$Z_i = -z_i{}^2$$
$$P_i = -p_i{}^2$$

Step 2. Plot the root locus of the new function with Z_i's as zeros and P_i's as poles. All such available means as the potential analog, a Spirule, etc., can be used. Corresponding to the same "gain," the set of points on the various loci constitute a set of root squares and will be denoted as Q_i's.

Step 3. Select the Q_i's according to system gain or the desired high-frequency performance. There are two typical ways of specifying the latter: system bandwidth, ω_1, or response time, t_p. If the bandwidth is specified, we shall choose the Q_i's so that the ones nearest the origin are at a distance somewhat less than $\omega_1{}^2$. If the response time is specified, the nearest Q_i's should be at a distance of approximately $(\pi/t_p)^2$. An exact determination of this distance is unnecessary in most cases to begin with, since the system bandwidth and response time are not precisely defined. If a more precise specification is to be met, a second or third trial may be indicated.

Step 4. Determine the closed-loop transfer function. After the selection of the Q_i's, the closed-loop poles are calculated as

$$q_i = \pm \sqrt{-Q_i}$$

The sign of the radical is so selected that the real component of q_i is always negative.

The control ratio which gives optimum step-input response is simply

$$\frac{C}{R}(s) = \frac{\displaystyle\prod_{j=1}^{m} (1 - s/z_j)}{A \displaystyle\prod_{i=1}^{n} (1 - s/q_i)} \tag{2-56}$$

where $A = 1 + k^2/[G(0)]^2$.

Step 4a. If optimum performance of the ramp inputs is desired, a new zero should be added to Eq. (2-56):

$$\frac{C}{R}(s) = \frac{(1 + Ts) \displaystyle\prod_{j=1}^{m} (1 - s/z_j)}{\displaystyle\prod_{i=1}^{n} (1 - s/q_i)} \tag{2-57}$$

where

$$T = \sum_{i=1}^{n} \left(-\frac{1}{q_i}\right) - \sum_{j=1}^{m} \left(-\frac{1}{z_j}\right) \tag{2-58}$$

Step 4b. Alternatively, if a larger velocity-error coefficient is required, a dipole pair near the origin can be added. The presence of the dipole pair, as long as it is close enough to the origin, does not affect appreciably the step-input response. The physical justification for such a procedure is that it gives optimum over-all response if there are also present other reference inputs which have a heavier concentration of power in the low-frequency region.

Let q_d and z_d represent the pole and zero of the additional dipole, and K_v represent the desired velocity-error coefficient. Then

$$\left(-\frac{1}{z_d}\right) - \left(-\frac{1}{q_d}\right) = \sum_{i=1}^{n} \left(-\frac{1}{q_i}\right) - \sum_{j=1}^{m} \left(-\frac{1}{z_i}\right) - \frac{1}{K_v} \tag{2-59}$$

The above equation gives one relation between z_d and q_d and leaves their exact location to be determined by other considerations, such as the power and frequency range of the low-frequency input. The exact location of z_d and q_d can be obtained by specifying the spectral density, as will be shown later.

Step 4c. While the peak overshoot of a system designed by the present method is low, in some exceptional cases the allowed peak overshoot may be even lower. One way to "doctor" the optimum system is to keep the magnitude of the characteristic frequencies unchanged, while the angles of the characteristic frequencies from the negative real axis are multiplied by a constant factor $h < 1$. If h is close to 1, $J_1 + k^2 J_2$ is not much different from its minimum value. A method for estimating the increment of $J_1 + k^2 J_2$ due to small deviations in $F_0(s)$ is given in Chap. 8.

Step 5. Determine the open-loop transfer function. The open-loop transfer function $G_0(s)$ can be determined from $F(s)$ as follows:

$$\frac{1}{G_0(s)} = \frac{1}{(C/R)(s)} - 1 \tag{2-60}$$

Once $G_0(s)$ is determined, the compensating network and amplifier can be obtained as the ratio $G_0(s)/G(s)$, where $G(s)$ is the transfer function of the fixed elements.

Example 2-2.† A hydraulic system for position control is to be designed. In response to a step input, it should have a response time of approximately 0.01 sec

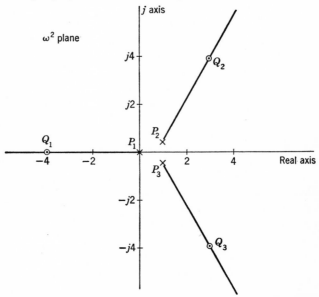

Fig. 2-5. Root-square-loci plot of an optimum system. P_1, P_2, P_3 are uncompensated open-loop poles and Q_1, Q_2, Q_3 are compensated closed-loop poles in the Ω plane.

with a peak overshoot of 15 per cent or less. The transfer function of the hydraulic valve and servomotor system is

$$G = \frac{K}{s[1 + 0.4(s/\omega_1) + (s/\omega_1)^2]}$$

† This example is taken from a paper by the author, Root Square Locus Plot—A Geometrical Method for Synthesis of Optimum Servo Systems, *IRE Conv. Record*, 1958.

where $K = 200$ radians/(sec)(in.) and $\omega_1 = 157$ radians/sec. Since the saturation is likely to occur at the hydraulic valve, its input is to be made as low as possible. The time constants of the solenoid and torque motor for actuating the hydraulic valve can be neglected.

Solution. There are three poles at 0 and at $(-0.2 \pm j0.98)\omega_1$, respectively. In plotting the root-square locus, it is expedient to use ω_1^2 as the base dimension. From step 1,

$$P_1 = 0$$
$$P_{2,3} = -(-0.2 \pm j0.98)^2\omega_1^2$$
$$= (0.919 \pm j0.392)\omega_1^2$$

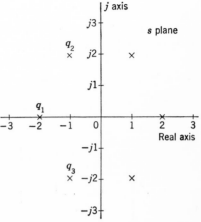

The positions of P_1, P_2, and P_3 are shown in Fig. 2-5. Taking P_1, P_2, and P_3 as open-loop poles and plotting the root loci as is done conventionally, we obtain the three root-square loci P_1Q_1, P_2Q_2, and P_3Q_3. In order to obtain a rise time of approximately 0.01 sec, the minimum distance is found to be $(\pi/0.01)^2 = 4\omega_1^2$. The nearest root is on the branch OA. Therefore $Q_1 = -4\omega_1^2$ and, correspondingly, $Q_2 = 4.84\omega_1^2 e^{j54.2°}$, $Q_3 = 4.84\omega_1^2 e^{-j54.2°}$. Taking the square roots of Q_1, Q_2, and Q_3 gives the six pole locations shown in Fig. 2-6. The ones in the LHP are the

FIG. 2-6. Diagram showing selection of closed-loop poles of the optimum system.

poles of the optimum control ratio: $-2\omega_1$, $2.2\omega_1 e^{\pm j117.1°}$. There are no zeros, and we obtain from Eq. (2-56)

$$\frac{C}{R}(s) = \frac{1}{(1 - s/q_1)(1 - s/q_2)(1 - s/q_3)}$$
$$= \frac{1}{[1 + 0.5(s/\omega_1)][1 + 0.414(s/\omega_1) + 0.207(s/\omega_1)^2]}$$

The open-loop transfer function is obtained from Eq. (2-60):

$$\frac{1}{G_0(s)} = \left(1 + 0.5\frac{s}{\omega_1}\right)\left[1 + 0.414\frac{s}{\omega_1} + 0.207\left(\frac{s}{\omega_1}\right)^2\right] - 1$$
$$= 0.914\frac{s}{\omega_1} + 0.414\left(\frac{s}{\omega_1}\right)^2 + 0.1035\left(\frac{s}{\omega_1}\right)^3$$
$$G_0(s) = \frac{1.095\omega_1}{s[1 + 0.453(s/\omega_1) + 0.11(s/\omega_1)^2]}$$

The required compensating network is obtained as the ratio $G_0(s)/G(s)$:

$$G_c(s) = \frac{K_a[1 + 0.4(s/\omega_1) + (s/\omega_1)^2]}{1 + 0.453(s/\omega_1) + 0.11(s/\omega_1)^2}$$
$$K_a = \frac{1.095\omega_1}{K} = 0.859 \text{ in./radian}$$

The above represents a resonant lead network, and K_a is the cascaded d-c gain of the error-sensing element, the amplifier, the resonant lead network, and the torque motor.

To compare the relative merits of the optimum system and a conventionally designed system, both systems were set up on an analog computer and tested with step inputs. The latter is designed on the basis of a pair of control poles at $1.46\omega_1 / \pm 60°$ and a third pole at $14.6\omega_1$. These closed-loop poles are so selected that the integral-square error of the system is the same as that of the optimum system. G_c of the conventionally designed system is

$$G_c(s) = \frac{1.04[1 + 0.4(s/\omega_1) + (s/\omega_1)^2]}{[1 + 0.615(s/\omega_1)][1 + 0.069(s/\omega_1)]}$$

Figure 2-7 shows the location of nonlinearity in the two systems. Figure 2-8 gives computer graphs corresponding to low inputs. The system input function is at the top, the system output is located in the middle, and the valve stroke is shown at the bottom. We see that, although the step-input responses of the two systems are comparable, the stroke is much lower for the optimum system. However, this is

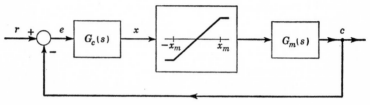

FIG. 2-7. Block diagrams of the two systems showing locations of nonlinearity. (*S. S. L. Chang, Root Square Locus Plot—A Geometrical Method for Synthesis of Optimum Servo Systems, IRE Conv. Record*, 1958.)

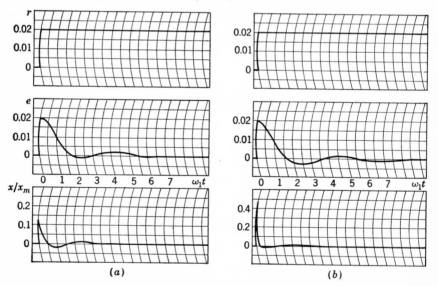

FIG. 2-8. Step-input response for small inputs. (*a*) Optimum system; (*b*) conventional system. (*S. S. L. Chang, Root Square Locus Plot—A Geometrical Method for Synthesis of Optimum Servo Systems, IRE Conv. Record*, 1958.)

not reflected in the system performance, as neither system is saturated. Figure 2-9 illustrates the situation with large inputs. Although the inputs to both systems are identical, they exhibit different degrees of saturation because of the difference in design. These tests clearly indicate the advantage of an optimized system.

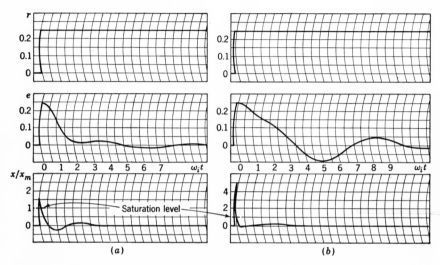

Fig. 2-9. Step-input response for large inputs. (a) Optimum system; (b) conventional system. (*S. S. L. Chang, Root Square Locus Plot—A Geometrical Method for Synthesis of Optimum Servo Systems, IRE Conv. Record, 1958.*)

2-8. Asymptotic Limit at Large Gain.

At this point, we are in a better position to investigate the general transient behavior of an optimum system that is designed on the basis of minimizing the integral- (or mean-) square error with constraint. Obviously, for very low system gains the response is more a reflection of the controlled system than of the design procedure. We shall study the transient response of an optimum system at its high-gain limit.

Assuming Eq. (2-53) to be the transfer function of the plant, we determine the poles of the optimum system by the root-square-locus plot. With reference to Fig. 2-10, in the asymptotic limit, m of the poles Q_1, Q_2, . . . , Q_m approach the m zeros Z_1, Z_2, . . . , Z_m. The remaining $n - m$ poles Q_{m+1}, Q_{m+2}, . . . , Q_n branch out along asymptotic lines which are at angles $[(2l - 1)/(n - m)]\pi$ with the real axis, $l = 1, 2, . . . ,$ $n - m$. In the limit, these $n - m$ poles are equidistant from the origin. From Eq. (2-56) we have

$$\frac{C}{R}(s) = \left[\prod_{j=1}^{m} \frac{1 - (s/z_j)}{1 - (s/q_j)}\right] \prod_{l=1}^{n-m} \frac{1}{1 - (s/q_{l+m})} \qquad (2\text{-}61)$$

As Q_j approaches Z_j, q_j approaches z_j, if all the zeros are in the LHP (i.e., the fixed component is of the minimum-phase type). The factors in the first brackets become dipoles at the various zeros and do not have much effect on the transient performance. The balance of the poles are equally spaced along a semicircle of radius q in the LHP, as shown in Fig.

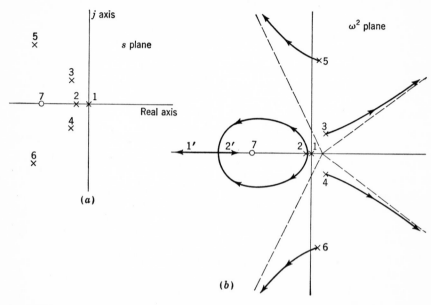

FIG. 2-10. Root-square loci of a typical system. (a) Pole-zero configuration of an uncompensated system; (b) root-square-loci plot of the optimum system.

2-11. These poles determine the response of the system. They are listed below:

$n - m = 1$:	$-q$
$n - m = 2$:	$-qe^{\pm j\pi/4}$
$n - m = 3$:	$-q, -qe^{\pm j\pi/3}$
$n - m = 4$:	$-qe^{\pm j\pi/8}, -qe^{\pm j3/8\pi}$

Correspondingly, the system response following a unit step input is

$n - m = 1$: $c(t) = 1 - e^{-qt}$

$n - m = 2$: $c(t) = 1 - 1.414e^{-0.707qt} \sin\left(0.707qt + \dfrac{\pi}{4}\right)$

$n - m = 3$: $c(t) = 1 - e^{-qt} - 1.155e^{-0.5qt} \sin 0.866qt$

$n - m = 4$: $c(t) = 1 - 2.414e^{-0.924qt} \sin (0.383qt + 45°)$
$$+ e^{-0.383qt} \sin (0.924qt + 135°)$$

The above functions are plotted in Fig. 2-12. We see that in all cases the overshoots are low and the oscillations are heavily damped.

In circuit theory, a network function of this type is called a Butterworth function. Its steady-state response decreases monotonously with frequency. To see this, one can readily derive from Eq. (2-61) that in the high-gain limit $(n' = n - m)$

$$F(s)F(-s) = \frac{1}{1 + (-s^2/q^2)^{n'}}$$

Therefore

$$|F(j\omega)| = \frac{1}{[1 + (\omega/q)^{2n'}]^{1/2}}$$

While the relation between peak overshoot and maximum modulus is inexact, it is still quite safe to say that a system with a steadily decreasing frequency-response characteristic does not have much of an overshoot.

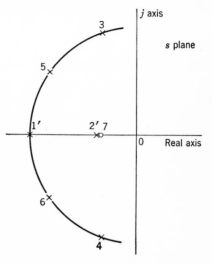

FIG. 2-11. Pole-zero configuration of an optimum system with very high gain.

Figure 2-12 also gives an indication of the degree of approximation of Eq. (2-52). The product qt_p is a function of $n - m$ or the number of

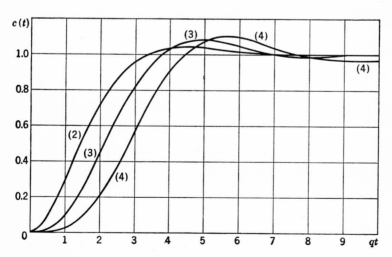

FIG. 2-12. Step-input response of optimum system in the high-gain limit.

isolated poles at the nearest distance:

$$n - m = 1: \qquad\qquad\qquad qt_p = 3.00$$
$$n - m = 2: \qquad\qquad\qquad qt_p = 2.96$$
$$n - m = 3: \qquad\qquad\qquad qt_p = 3.51$$
$$n - m = 4: \qquad\qquad\qquad qt_p = 4.16$$

We note that if the number of isolated poles at approximately the nearest distance is 1, 2, or 3 the approximation is quite good.

2-9. Total Design. Sometimes it is worthwhile to determine the functional relationship between the performance parameters and the parameters of the plant, including the saturation limits, etc. For instance, we may wish to investigate the functional relationship between the response time of a controlled vessel and the size of the control surface or to determine the relative merits of two interchangeable means of control, e.g., a jet versus a fin, or a hydraulic motor versus an electrical motor, etc. Obviously, the system response depends not only on the power element but also on the controller. To make the investigation meaningful, a reasonably good controller has to be designed or tailored to fit each size and type of power element. This is usually a time-consuming process. However, by using the method developed in the present chapter we can save time in making a large number of good designs. In cases where the criteria of performance and available control effort are exactly in the form of integral-square values, the functional relationships so derived are for controllers of the best possible design. Even in cases where these criteria are only approximate, as discussed in Sec. 2-6, the functional relationships are for controllers of uniformly good design, inasmuch as the uniformity in goodness can be gauged.

In a relatively simple case the problem can be solved analytically, as will be illustrated presently in an example. In a more involved case, we should need a large number of root-square-locus plots. However, the effort is still far less than that of making a large number of designs by conventional techniques and trying them out on an analog computer.

To illustrate the method, we shall use the motor-heating problem of Example 2-1 but assume a more general form of motor transfer function:

$$G(s) = \frac{C(s)}{I(s)} = \frac{K_T}{\eta s + M s^2} \tag{2-62}$$

The relationship J_1, J_2, and K_T, η, and M for an optimum system is to be determined. To obtain a solution, Eq. (2-18) gives

$$Y\bar{Y} = 1 - \frac{k^2 \eta^2}{K_T{}^2} s^2 + \frac{k^2 M^2}{K_T{}^2} s^4 \tag{2-63}$$

The function $Y(s)$ can be written as

$$Y(s) = (1 + as)(1 + bs) \qquad (2\text{-}64)$$

where $\pm a$ and $\pm b$ are roots of $1/s$ of the expression on the right-hand side of Eq. (2-63). If $k\eta^2/2MK_T < 1$, the roots are complex:

$$a = \tau e^{j\theta} \qquad (2\text{-}65)$$
$$b = \tau e^{-j\theta} \qquad (2\text{-}66)$$

$$\tau = \sqrt{\frac{kM}{K_T}} \qquad (2\text{-}67)$$

$$\cos 2\theta = \frac{k\eta^2}{2MK_T} \qquad 2\theta < 90° \qquad (2\text{-}68)$$

If $k\eta^2/2MK_T > 1$, the roots are real:

$$a = \tau e^{\theta'} \qquad (2\text{-}65a)$$
$$b = \tau e^{-\theta'} \qquad (2\text{-}66a)$$

The constant τ is given in Eq. (2-67), and the constant θ' is given by

$$\cosh 2\theta' = \frac{k\eta^2}{2MK_T} \qquad (2\text{-}68a)$$

The two forms are identical if imaginary values of θ are allowed. Since $\cos 2\theta$ is always positive, the locations of a and b are within $\pm 45°$ of the real axis. Equation (2-44) gives

$$\frac{C}{R}(s) = \frac{1}{(1 + as)(1 + bs)} \qquad (2\text{-}69)$$

Assuming $R(s) = c_1/s$, we can evaluate the integrals J_1 and J_2 from the table of Appendix D. The results are

$$J_1 = \frac{c_1^2}{2}\left(a + b + \frac{ab}{a + b}\right) \qquad (2\text{-}70)$$

$$J_2 = \frac{c_1^2}{2k^2}\left(a + b - \frac{ab}{a + b}\right) = \frac{c_1^2 M^2}{2K_T^2\tau^4}\left(a + b - \frac{ab}{a + b}\right) \qquad (2\text{-}71)$$

Substituting Eq. (2-69) in Eq. (2-60) gives

$$G_0(s) = \frac{1}{(a + b)s + abs^2}$$

The gain and time constants of the optimally compensated system are

$$K_v = \frac{1}{a + b} \qquad (2\text{-}72)$$

$$T = \frac{ab}{a + b} \qquad (2\text{-}73)$$

Using Eqs. (2-65) to (2-68), Eqs. (2-70) to (2-73) can be expressed in terms of dimensionless functions of θ:

$$J_1 = \frac{c_1{}^2 M}{\eta} C_E \tag{2-74}$$

$$J_2 = \frac{c_1{}^2 \eta^3}{K_T{}^2 M} C_L \tag{2-75}$$

$$K_v = \frac{\eta}{M} C_K \tag{2-76}$$

$$T = \frac{M}{\eta} C_T \tag{2-77}$$

where

$$C_E = \left(\cos\theta + \frac{1}{4\cos\theta}\right)(2\cos 2\theta)^{1/2} \tag{2-78}$$

$$C_L = \left(\cos\theta - \frac{1}{4\cos\theta}\right)(2\cos 2\theta)^{-3/2} \tag{2-79}$$

$$C_K = \frac{(2\cos 2\theta)^{-1/2}}{2\cos\theta} \tag{2-80}$$

$$C_T = \frac{(2\cos 2\theta)^{1/2}}{2\cos\theta} \tag{2-81}$$

Equations (2-78) to (2-81) can be extended in range by substituting $\cosh\theta'$ and $\cosh 2\theta'$ for $\cos\theta$ and $\cos 2\theta$, respectively. The four coefficients are calculated for various values of θ and θ'. In Fig. 2-13, C_L, C_K, and C_T are plotted versus C_E. For a specified integral-square error, the motor dissipation, gain, and time constants of the compensated open-loop transfer function can be read directly from these curves. Alternatively, if the allowable dissipation is known, the minimum integral-square error can be read. The gain and time constants to use are the ones that correspond to C_E.

2-10. Summary. In this chapter we have given a solution of the problem of minimizing the integral-square error with a specified limit on the integral-square value of a certain plant variable. The system configuration is completely free. The method is then extended to the design of systems which meet conventional specifications of response time, system bandwidth, etc., with least likelihood of saturation. Its application is also made easier by deriving a graphical method, the root-square-locus method.

The method is by no means above criticism in its treatment of the saturation problem. No calculation of the nonlinear effect is actually made. Only the integral-square value of the saturable plant variable is minimized under the assumption that the system is linear. Nevertheless, it is an improvement over conventional linear design techniques.

One difficulty in conventional design techniques is that they leave too

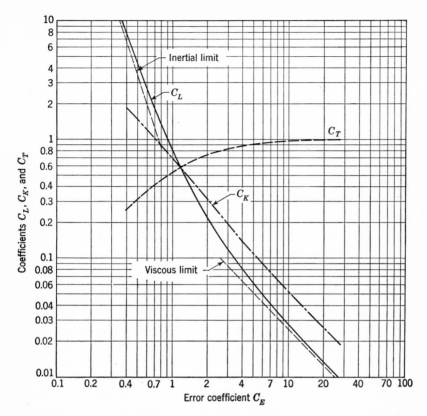

Fig. 2-13. Universal curves showing loss, gain, and time constants of an optimum second-order system versus integral- (or mean-) square error.

much to the designer. To meet the same performance criterion, a wide variety of compensating networks or means can be used, and one of the common ills of an inexperienced design is unnecessary saturation of the plant or controlled system. The root-square-locus method does not require much more effort than Evans's root-locus method; however, it does away with this unwelcome prospect.

Another advantage of the method is that it can be used to investigate general trends or relationships between the performance of a system and its hardware requirements. The problem of integral-square error versus motor heating is used to illustrate the method.

CHAPTER 3

STATISTICAL PROPERTIES OF SIGNAL AND NOISE

3-1. Introduction. This chapter gives the basic material of random-signal analysis. It is assumed that the reader has some previous knowledge of statistics or has read Appendix A.

We begin by discussing the significance of mean-square error when the input signals are Gaussian. The merit of a control system is usually judged on the basis of some cost figure which increases with the absolute value of the error, but the exact form of the cost-versus-error function varies from application to application. It is shown in Sec. 3-2 that, no matter what form the cost function takes, a system with a lower value of mean-square error has a lower expected cost figure. The same cannot be said for systems with non-Gaussian inputs. In Chap. 2, we used the integral-square error as a convenient merit measure of a system's transient response to deterministic inputs. Now we see that it is also an absolute merit measure of a system's response to Gaussian random inputs. Since the inputs to a system are neither completely deterministic nor Gaussian random, the use of mean-square error as a merit measure is more reliable than it is in the purely deterministic case, although it is not so absolutely reliable as in the Gaussian case.

Once we have decided upon the mean-square error as a system merit measure, the problem is then how to calculate the mean-square error with random inputs and how to design a system with least-mean-square error. The calculations are much simpler if the system is stationary. Section 3-3 points to the difference between stationary and nonstationary processes and introduces the ergodic hypothesis which states that, for a stationary process, the ensemble average of any quantitative measure is equal to its time average. This facilitates the analytical work of the remaining sections of the present chapter, which are concerned only with stationary systems. In Secs. 3-4 to 3-7 we show how to calculate the mean-square value of any system variable from some statistical properties of the inputs, known as power spectra and correlation functions, and how these properties are defined in terms of measurements made on the signal itself. The equivalence of power spectra and correlation functions is established by showing that one is the Laplace transform of the other. The problem of zero crossing is also discussed.

Quite frequently, the power spectrum is not measured but estimated from the generating process of the signal. The method of doing this is given in Secs. 3-8 to 3-12.

3-2. Random Signals in a Control System. In contrast to deterministic signals, random signals cannot be described as given functions of time such as a step, a ramp, or a sine wave. The exact function is unknown to the system designer; only some of its average properties are known.

A random signal may be generated by one of nature's processes, for instance, radar noise and wind- or wave-induced forces and moments on a radar antenna or a ship. Alternatively, it may be generated by human intelligence, for instance, the bearing of a zigzagging aircraft, the contour to be followed by a duplicating machine, etc.

One outstanding experimental fact about nature's random processes is that these signals are very closely Gaussian. The word Gaussian is a mathematical concept which describes one or more signals $i_1, i_2, \ldots, i_n$ having the following properties:

1. The amplitude of each signal is normally distributed.

2. The joint distribution function of any number of signals at the same or different times taken from the set is a multivariate normal distribution. This experimental fact is not surprising in view of our derivation of the multivariate distribution function in Secs. A-6 to A-8. A nature's random process is usually the sum total of the effects of a large number of independent contributing factors. These contributing factors can be considered as the variables y in Sec. A-8, while the measurable entities or signals of the random process are the variables x. For instance, thermal noise is due to the thermal motions of billions of electrons and atoms. An ocean-wave height at any particular time and place is the sum of wind-generated waves at previous times over a very large area.

In a problem involving random inputs, there is no definite answer to the question of what is the value of a certain system variable x at a certain time. All we can say is that associated with each possible value of x there is a probability density $p(x)$ of its occurrence, and $p(x)$ contains all the information we need. For instance, in fire-control problems, we talk about the probability of a hit or a miss. The latter probability is simply that of the error exceeding a given value, or, mathematically, it is the integral of the probability density of the system error from a maximum allowable value E_1 to ∞. As another example, consider the seaworthiness of a ship in a rough sea. The roll angle as a function of time cannot be calculated, because of the randomness of the ocean waves. However, for a given ship and a given sea state, there is a definite probability associated with each value of roll angle of the ship, and the probability of capsizing is that of the roll angle exceeding its maximum allowable value.

If the fluctuation of a certain system variable x is caused by noise, turbulence, or other form of Gaussian random inputs, or if it is due to a rapid succession of deterministic inputs such as steps or ramps but the individual steps or ramps are applied so fast that the system has little time to settle, or if it is due to any combination of inputs and disturbances of the above description, $p(x)$ can be closely approximated by a normal distribution function:

$$p(x) = \frac{1}{\sqrt{2\pi}\,\sigma} \exp\left[-\frac{(x - \bar{x})^2}{2\sigma^2}\right] \tag{3-1}$$

In Eq. (3-1), $\bar{x}$ is the mean value of x, and σ^2 is the mean value of $(x - \bar{x})^2$. In most applications we are interested only in the variations of x instead of x itself; furthermore, positive and negative excursions of x from its steady state, or quiescent value, are equally likely. If we use x to denote the deviation of a system variable from its quiescent value, rather than the variable itself, $\bar{x}$ is always zero, and σ^2 is simply $\sigma^2 = \overline{x^2}$. We see that, for a system variable the amplitude of which is normally distributed, once its mean-square value is determined, its complete distribution function is determined.

If the system variable obeys normal distribution, the least-square criterion is the absolute criterion in the following sense: If we are interested in keeping the system error within a certain tolerance limit for most of the time, the system with the least-mean-square error has the largest percentage of time within such a tolerance limit. If we are interested in keeping a certain system variable below a certain assigned maximum for reason of saturation or safety, the system with the least-mean-square value of the variable has the least likelihood of violating this restriction. These points can be established by proving the following theorem:

Theorem. If $p_1(x) = (1/\sigma_1)f(x/\sigma_1)$ and $p_2(x) = (1/\sigma_2)f(x/\sigma_2)$, where $\sigma_1 > \sigma_2$ and $f(x) \geq 0$, and $g(x)$ is a nondecreasing function of the absolute value of x in both positive and negative directions of x, then

$$\int_{-\infty}^{\infty} p_1(x)g(x)\,dx \geq \int_{-\infty}^{\infty} p_2(x)g(x)\,dx \tag{3-2}$$

PROOF. Let Δ denote the difference:

$$\Delta \equiv \int_{-\infty}^{\infty} p_1(x)g(x)\,dx - \int_{-\infty}^{\infty} p_2(x)g(x)\,dx$$

$$\equiv \int_{-\infty}^{\infty} \frac{1}{\sigma_1}f\left(\frac{x}{\sigma_1}\right)g(x)\,dx - \int_{-\infty}^{\infty} \frac{1}{\sigma_2}f\left(\frac{x}{\sigma_2}\right)g(x)\,dx$$

Let ξ denote x/σ_1 in the first integral and η denote x/σ_2 in the second integral; then we have

$$\Delta = \int_{-\infty}^{\infty} f(\xi)g(\sigma_1\xi)\, d\xi - \int_{-\infty}^{\infty} f(\eta)g(\sigma_2\eta)\, d\eta$$

$$= \int_{-\infty}^{\infty} f(\xi)[g(\sigma_1\xi) - g(\sigma_2\xi)]\, d\xi$$

The function $f(\xi)$ cannot be negative and must be positive for some value of ξ. Since $|\sigma_1\xi| > |\sigma_2\xi|$, and $g(x)$ is a nondecreasing function of $|x|$, $g(\sigma_1\xi) - g(\sigma_2\xi)$ is always positive or zero. Therefore $\Delta \geq 0$, QED.

The physical interpretation of the above theorem is as follows: The normal distribution function of Eq. (3-1) obviously fits the requirements of the theorem with $f(\xi) = (1/\sqrt{2\pi})\exp(-\xi^2/2)$. The function $g(x)$ is usually referred to as a cost function. Its functional form depends on the application. For instance, $g(x)$ may represent the cost of a miss and x represent the error. Then

$$g(x) = 0 \qquad |x| < x_1$$
$$g(x) = 1 \qquad |x| > x_2$$
$$\frac{dg}{d|x|} > 0 \qquad x_1 \leq |x| \leq x_2$$

With $|x| < x_1$, it is a definite hit. With $|x| > x_2$, it is a definite miss. With some in-between value of x, the probability of a miss increases with the error. As another example, $g(x)$ may represent motor heating and x represent motor current. Then $g(x)$ is equal to a constant times x^2.

It should be noted that the theorem holds as long as $g(x)$ increases with an increasing magnitude of x in both positive and negative directions of x. It is not necessary for $g(x)$ to be symmetrical. For instance, in metal working, if the positive tolerance limit is exceeded, the work piece is rejected for rework; if the negative tolerance limit is exceeded, the piece is rejected, period. The cost is obviously not equal in the two directions.

The integrals on the two sides of the inequality (3-2) represent expected costs of the two systems. We may summarize the significance of the theorem as follows: *With a normally distributed system error (or some other relevant variable) the system with the least-mean-square error has the least expected cost.*

3-3. Stationary and Nonstationary Processes, Ergodic Hypothesis. The random processes encountered in control work can be classified as stationary and nonstationary processes. To gain some insight into the subject, let us think of the underlying mechanism that generates a random process. It can usually be described in physical or mathematical terms. For instance, the underlying mechanism that generates shot-effect noise is thermionic emission; the underlying mechanism that generates ocean waves is essentially wind force in conjunction with the earth's gravity;

and the outcome of dice throwing is determined by a probability of $\frac{1}{6}$ for each face of each die independent of all others.

If the generating mechanism does not change with time, any measured average property of the random process is independent of the time of measurement aside from some statistical fluctuations, and the random process is called stationary. For instance, ocean-wave height in a given sea state, thermal noise, and a telegraphic signal of a certain language are examples of stationary random processes. If the generating mechanism does change, the random process is called nonstationary, in which case the generating mechanism may change in a predetermined fashion or at random. An example of the former is found in missile launching where the unwanted fluctuations in vertical and lateral thrusts are generated by one or a group of rocket motors of which the operating condition is a predetermined function of time. Alternatively, the generating mechanism may change at random, as in the course of flight of an aircraft, where the wind disturbance depends on the local atmospheric condition which is sometimes calm and sometimes turbulent.

The random processes or events generated by the same underlying mechanism form a statistical ensemble. When we say the averaged value of a certain quantity, we usually mean the ensemble average, which is the averaged value over all possible events weighted according to the probabilities of such events. However, for a stationary process we find little reason to distinguish between the ensemble average at any particular time and the time average of a single event. The life history of a single event can be chopped up into an infinite number of events. Since these events are generated by the same underlying mechanism which does not change with time, they can be thought of as arbitrarily selected from the entire ensemble, and therefore they represent the latter. *The assumption of equivalence between time and ensemble averages is called the ergodic hypothesis.* As we shall see, using the time average instead of the ensemble average, and vice versa, is essential to our analytical work at a number of places.

3-4. Basic Properties of Correlation Functions. The analysis of Sec. 3-2 points to the logic or desirability of the least-square criterion for systems with random inputs. We shall proceed to derive the basic mathematics required in such an optimization procedure. Without loss of generality, we define the random signals as variations from their mean values, and therefore they have zero mean themselves.

The statistical properties of a set of random signals (which may include the random inputs and system variables in response to these inputs) can be described by their *correlation functions*. The correlation function $\phi_{ab}(t_1,t_2)$ is defined as the ensemble average of signal $a(t)$ at time t_1 and $b(t)$ at time t_2.

$$\phi_{ab}(t_1,t_2) \equiv \langle a(t_1)b(t_2)\rangle \tag{3-3}$$

When the two signals $a(t)$ and $b(t)$ are different, $\phi_{ab}(t_1,t_2)$ is called the *cross-correlation function*. When $a(t)$ and $b(t)$ are one and the same, $\phi_{aa}(t_1,t_2)$ is called the *autocorrelation function*.

As discussed in Sec. A-12, correlation functions can be viewed as a generalization of correlation coefficients in the regresssion technique but without normalization by the rms values of the two variables. Because of this exception, mathematicians usually refer to $\phi_{ab}(t_1,t_2)$ as the *covariance function* instead of the correlation function.

In the subsequent sections of this chapter, we are concerned only with stationary systems. It follows from the definition of stationarity that for arbitrary T

$$\phi_{ab}(t_1 + T,\, t_2 + T) = \phi_{ab}(t_1,t_2)$$

Therefore the only significant independent variable is $t_2 - t_1$, which we shall denote as τ. Instead of Eq. (3-3) we may write

$$\phi_{ab}(\tau) = \overline{a(t)b(t + \tau)} \tag{3-4}$$

The time interval τ is called the correlation time. A number of useful properties of the correlation function follow directly from Eq. (3-4):

$$\phi_{aa}(0) = \overline{[a(t)]^2} \tag{3-5}$$
$$\phi_{ab}(-\tau) = \phi_{ba}(\tau) \tag{3-6}$$
$$\phi_{aa}(-\tau) = \phi_{aa}(\tau) \tag{3-6a}$$
$$|\phi_{ab}(\tau)| \leq \sqrt{\phi_{aa}(0)\phi_{bb}(0)} \tag{3-7}$$
$$|\phi_{aa}(\tau)| \leq \phi_{aa}(0) \tag{3-7a}$$

Inequality (3-7) can be proved as follows:

$$\left|\frac{[a(t)]^2}{\phi_{aa}(0)}\right| + \left|\frac{[b(t+\tau)]^2}{\phi_{bb}(0)}\right| - \frac{2|a(t)b(t+\tau)|}{\sqrt{\phi_{aa}(0)\phi_{bb}(0)}}$$
$$= \left[\left|\frac{a(t)}{\sqrt{\phi_{aa}(0)}}\right| - \left|\frac{b(t+\tau)}{\sqrt{\phi_{bb}(0)}}\right|\right]^2 \geq 0 \tag{3-8}$$

Averaging the above inequality gives

$$2 - \frac{2|\phi_{ab}(\tau)|}{\sqrt{\phi_{aa}(0)\phi_{bb}(0)}} \geq 0 \tag{3-8a}$$

It can be rewritten into inequality (3-7).

Equation (3-5) shows that the autocorrelation function at $\tau = 0$ is the mean-square value of the random signal itself. Equation (3-6a) shows that $\phi_{aa}(\tau)$ is an even function of τ. Inequality (3-7) shows that the magnitude of the cross-correlation function cannot exceed the product of the rms values of the two signals.

Example 3-1. Let $v = di/dt$, where $i(t)$ is a stationary random signal. Show that $\phi_{iv}(0) = 0$.

Solution. By definition

$$\phi_{iv}(0) = \left\langle i(t) \frac{di(t)}{dt} \right\rangle$$

since

$$\frac{d}{dt}[i(t)]^2 = 2i(t)\frac{di(t)}{dt}$$

Taking the ensemble average of both sides, we obtain

$$\frac{d}{dt}\phi_{ii}(0) = 2\phi_{iv}(0)$$

The left-hand side of the above equation is obviously zero.

3-5. Spectral Densities and Wiener's Theorem. Quite similarly to the treatment of deterministic signals, we find it mathematically expedient to transform the random variables into the frequency domain. Let the chopped signals $a_T(t)$ and $b_T(t)$ be defined as the same random signals $a(t)$ and $b(t)$, respectively, in the interval $0 \le t \le T$ but zero outside this interval, and $A_T(s)$, $B_T(s)$ represent their Laplace transforms. Then

$$\frac{1}{T}\int_0^{T-\tau} a(t)b(t+\tau)\,dt = \frac{1}{T}\int_0^\infty a_T(t)b_T(t+\tau)\,dt$$
$$= \frac{1}{2\pi jT}\int_0^\infty a_T(t)\int_{-j\infty}^{j\infty} B_T(s)e^{s(t+\tau)}\,ds\,dt$$
$$= \frac{1}{2\pi jT}\int_{-j\infty}^{j\infty} A_T(-s)B_T(s)e^{s\tau}\,ds$$

Performing the ensemble average over the above equation, we have

$$\frac{T-\tau}{T}\phi_{ab}(\tau) = \frac{1}{2\pi j}\int_{-j\infty}^{j\infty}\frac{1}{T}\langle A_T(-s)B_T(s)\rangle e^{s\tau}\,ds \qquad (3\text{-}9)$$

Let a function $\Phi_{ab}(s)$ be defined as

$$\Phi_{ab}(s) \equiv \lim_{T\to\infty}\frac{1}{T}\langle A_T(-s)B_T(s)\rangle \qquad (3\text{-}10)$$

As T approaches infinity, Eq. (3-9) becomes

$$\phi_{ab}(\tau) = \frac{1}{2\pi j}\int_{-j\infty}^{j\infty}\Phi_{ab}(s)e^{s\tau}\,ds \qquad (3\text{-}11)$$

The function $\Phi_{ab}(s)$ is called the spectral-density function when a and b are the same, or the cross-spectral-density function when $a(t)$ and $b(t)$ represent different signals. Its physical significance will be made clear in the next section. Equation (3-11) shows that $\phi_{ab}(\tau)$ is the inverse Laplace transform of $\Phi_{ab}(s)$. It follows that $\Phi_{ab}(s)$ is the Laplace transform of $\phi_{ab}(\tau)$. Since, in general, $\phi_{ab}(-\tau) \neq 0$, the Laplace transform is double-ended:

$$\Phi_{ab}(s) = \int_{-\infty}^{\infty} \phi_{ab}(\tau)e^{-s\tau}\, d\tau \tag{3-12}$$

The transform relationship between correlation functions and spectral densities as represented by the pair of Eqs. (3-11) and (3-12) is called Wiener's theorem.

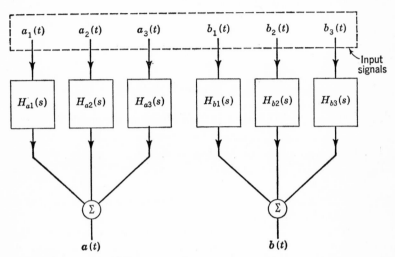

FIG. 3-1. When the spectral densities of inputs are known, Eq. (3-22) gives the spectral densities of the output signals $a(t)$ and $b(t)$.

Presently we shall derive a number of significant properties of the spectral densities.

1. *Symmetry Properties.* Equation (3-10) implies that

$$\Phi_{ab}(j\omega) = \Phi_{ba}(-j\omega) \tag{3-13}$$
$$\Phi_{aa}(j\omega) = \Phi_{aa}(-j\omega) > 0 \tag{3-13a}$$

Equations (3-13) and (3-13a) show that $\Phi_{ab}(j\omega)$ is the complex conjugate of $\Phi_{ba}(j\omega)$ and that $\Phi_{aa}(j\omega)$ is a real positive even function of ω.

2. *Transmission Properties.* In Fig. 3-1, $a(t)$ is the sum of a number of signals $a_1(t)$, $a_2(t)$, $\ldots$, $a_n(t)$ through filters with transfer functions $H_{a1}(s)$, $\ldots$, $H_{an}(s)$, respectively. Similarly, $b(t)$ is the sum of a number of signals $b_1(t)$, $b_2(t)$, $\ldots$, $b_m(t)$ through filters with transfer functions $H_{b1}(s)$, $H_{b2}(s)$, $\ldots$, $H_{bm}(s)$, respectively. The spectral density $\Phi_{ab}(j\omega)$ is to be expressed in terms of the spectral densities $\Phi_{a_i b_k}(j\omega)$,

$i = 1, 2, \ldots, n, k = 1, 2, \ldots, m$. We shall show that

$$\Phi_{ab}(j\omega) = \sum_{i=1}^{n} \sum_{k=1}^{m} H_{a_i}(-j\omega)H_{b_k}(j\omega)\Phi_{a_ib_k}(j\omega) \tag{3-14}$$

Equation (3-14) can be proved as follows: Let the chopped signals be defined as

$$a_{Ti}(t) = a_i(t)$$
$$b_{Ti}(t) = b_i(t) \qquad 0 \le t \le T$$
$$a_{Ti}(t) = b_{Ti}(t) = 0 \qquad t < 0 \qquad t > T$$

Let $a_T(t)$ and $b_T(t)$ represent the sum signals when the inputs are replaced by the respective chopped inputs.   Then

$$A_T(-j\omega) = \sum_{i=1}^{n} H_{ai}(-j\omega)A_{Ti}(-j\omega) \tag{3-15}$$

$$B_T(j\omega) = \sum_{k=1}^{m} H_{bk}(j\omega)B_{Tk}(j\omega) \tag{3-16}$$

Multiplying Eqs. (3-15) and (3-16) and dividing the result by T,

$$\frac{1}{T} A_T(-j\omega)B_T(j\omega) = \sum_{i=1}^{i=n} \sum_{k=1}^{k=m} \frac{1}{T} H_{ai}(-j\omega)H_{bk}(j\omega)A_{Ti}(-j\omega)B_{Tk}(j\omega)$$

If we take the ensemble average over the above equations and let T approach infinity, this becomes Eq. (3-14).

We note that $a_T(t)$ and $b_T(t)$ as defined here are the responses to chopped inputs and are not exactly the same as the chopped response signals which should be used in Eq. (3-10).   However, the differences are appreciable only at the two ends of the 0 to T interval and become insignificant when we let T approach infinity.

Two interesting special cases of Eq. (3-14) are the following:

FILTERING PROPERTY.   If a signal $i(t)$ is passed through a filter with the transfer function $H(s)$, and a signal $e(t)$ is obtained at the output, then

$$\Phi_{ee}(j\omega) = H(j\omega)H(-j\omega)\Phi_{ii}(j\omega) \tag{3-17}$$

Equation (3-17) is obtained by letting $a_1(t) = b_1(t) = i(t), H_{a1}(s) = H_{b1}(s)$, and $n = m = 1$.

ADDITION PROPERTY.   Let all the H's equal unity, $a_i(t) = b_i(t)$, and $m = n$; then Eq. (3-14) becomes

$$\Phi_{ac}(j\omega) = \sum_{i=1}^{n} \sum_{k=1}^{n} \Phi_{a_ia_k}(j\omega)$$

$$= \sum_{i=1}^{n} \Phi_{a_ia_i}(j\omega) + \sum_{i=2}^{n} \sum_{k=1}^{i-1} [\Phi_{a_ia_k}(j\omega) + \Phi_{a_ka_i}(j\omega)] \tag{3-18}$$

The spectral density of the sum signal is equal to the sum of the spectral densities of the individual signals, if these signals are uncorrelated; otherwise, the real components of the cross-spectral densities give rise to an additional term.

Example 3-2. For the problem of Sec. 2-2, $\Phi_{rr}(j\omega)$ is given instead of $r(t)$. Find integral expressions for the mean-square values of $e(t)$ and $i(t)$ in terms of the control ratio $F(s)$.

Solution. Since

$$E(s) = R(s) - C(s) = [1 - F(s)]R(s)$$
$$I(s) = \frac{C(s)}{G(s)} = \frac{F(s)R(s)}{G(s)}$$

Eq. (3-17) gives

$$\Phi_{ee}(j\omega) = [1 - F(j\omega)][1 - F(-j\omega)]\Phi_{rr}(j\omega)$$
$$\Phi_{ii}(j\omega) = \frac{F(j\omega)F(-j\omega)\Phi_{rr}(j\omega)}{G(j\omega)G(-j\omega)}$$

By letting $a(t) = b(t) = e(t)$, and $\tau = 0$ in Eq. (3-11), we obtain

$$\overline{[e(t)]^2} = \phi_{ee}(0) = \frac{1}{2\pi j} \int_{-j\infty}^{j\infty} \Phi_{ee}(s)\, ds$$
$$= \frac{1}{2\pi j} \int_{-j\infty}^{j\infty} [1 - F(s)][1 - \bar{F}(s)]\Phi_{rr}(s)\, ds \qquad (3\text{-}19)$$

Similarly,
$$\overline{[i(t)]^2} = \frac{1}{2\pi j} \int_{-j\infty}^{j\infty} \frac{F(s)F(-s)\Phi_{rr}(s)}{G(s)G(-s)}\, ds \qquad (3\text{-}20)$$

Example 3-3. A signal $i(t)$ consists of a random series of impulses:

$$i(t) = \sum_{n=-\infty}^{n=\infty} I_n\delta(t - t_n)$$

where t_n occurs at random but on an average there are ν impulses per second, and the mean-square value of I_n is I^2. Determine $\Phi_{ii}(j\omega)$.

Solution. Consider a large interval T and chopped signal $i_T(t)$:

$$I_T(j\omega) = \int_0^T i(t)e^{-j\omega t}\, dt = \sum_{0 \le t_n \le T} I_n e^{-j\omega t_n}$$
$$\Phi_{ii}(j\omega) = \frac{1}{T}\left\langle \sum_{0 \le t_n, t_m \le T} \sum I_n I_m e^{j\omega(t_n - t_m)} \right\rangle$$

We note that, as t_n and t_m occur at random, $\langle e^{j\omega(t_n - t_m)}\rangle = 0$ unless $t_n = t_m$. Therefore

$$\Phi_{ii}(j\omega) = \frac{1}{T}\left\langle \sum_{0 \le t_n \le T} I_n^2 \right\rangle = \nu I^2 \qquad (3\text{-}21)$$

Example 3-4. A Gaussian signal $i(t)$ with zero mean has a spectral density

$$\Phi_{ii}(j\omega) = \frac{10}{\omega^4 - 5\omega^2 + 9}$$

Determine the fraction of time in which $|i(t)| \ge 5$.

Solution. The mean-square value of $i(t)$ is determined first:

$$\Phi_{ii}(s) = \frac{10}{s^4 + 5s^2 + 9} = \frac{10}{(s^2 + s + 3)(s^2 - s + 3)}$$

$$\overline{i^2} = \frac{1}{2\pi j} \int_{-j\infty}^{j\infty} \Phi_{ii}(s) \, ds = \frac{10}{2 \times 1 \times 3} = 1\frac{2}{3} = \sigma^2$$

When $\overline{i^2}$ is known, the probability for $|i| \geq 5$ is obtained by integrating the density function:

$$p(|i| \geq 5) = \frac{2}{\sqrt{2\pi}\,\sigma} \int_5^\infty e^{-(i^2/2\sigma^2)} \, di = \frac{2}{\sqrt{\pi}} \int_{5/\sqrt{2}\,\sigma}^\infty e^{-x^2} \, dx$$

$$= 1 - \Phi\left(\frac{5}{\sqrt{2}\,\sigma}\right) = 1 - \Phi(2.74) = 1 - 0.99989 = 1.1 \times 10^{-4}$$

The function $\Phi(x)$ is called the error integral.

3-6. Physical Significance of Spectral Densities. In the preceding section, the spectral density is defined mathematically and used in calculating the mean-square value of the output variable of a system with random inputs. However, it has a physical significance of its own which will be shown presently.

In case a of Fig. 3-2, we have a narrow bandpass filter having a transfer function $H(j\omega)$ such that $|H(j\omega)|^2$ is unity at ω_0 and has an effective bandwidth $\Delta\omega$. The signal $i(t)$ is applied to the input of the filter, and its output $a(t)$ is squared and averaged by a low-pass filter which has unity gain for d-c signals:

$$\overline{[a(t)]^2} = \frac{1}{2\pi j} \int_{-\infty}^{\infty} H(j\omega)H(-j\omega)\Phi_{ii}(j\omega) \, d\omega$$

The phase angles of $H(j\omega)$ and $H(-j\omega)$ cancel out. If $\Delta\omega$ is small enough so that $\Phi_{ii}(j\omega)$ does not change much in the passband,

$$\overline{[a(t)]^2} = \frac{2\,\Delta\omega}{2\pi} \Phi_{ii}(j\omega_0) = 2\,\Delta f \Phi_{ii}(j\omega_0) \tag{3-22}$$

The factor 2 is caused by integrating over both the positive and negative ends of ω.

We may think of $i(t)$ as an electric current passing through a load of 1-ohm resistance. Then $[i(t)]^2$ is the total power, and $\overline{[a(t)]^2}$ is the portion of power within the passband of $H(j\omega)$. While from an engineering point of view we regard the bandwidth of $H(j\omega)$ as Δf, mathematically it is $2\,\Delta f$, because of the presence of a passband in the negative frequency range. Therefore, $\Phi_{ii}(j\omega_0)$ is the power content of $i(t)$ per unit bandwidth at $\omega = \omega_0$. It is also called the power-density spectrum.

In some textbooks Δf is regarded as the bandwidth and the spectral density is twice the value that we use here. However, the present usage is becoming more common in the literature.

Similarly, for case b of Fig. 3-2

$$\overline{a(t)b(t)} = \frac{\Delta\omega}{2\pi}[\Phi_{iv}(j\omega_0) + \Phi_{iv}(-j\omega_0)]$$

$$= 2\,\Delta f \times \text{real component of } \Phi_{iv}(j\omega_0) \qquad (3\text{-}23)$$

The real component of $\Phi_{iv}(j\omega_0)$ is called the cospectrum. It represents the power of $i(t)v(t)$ per unit bandwidth at ω_0. Similarly, for case c of

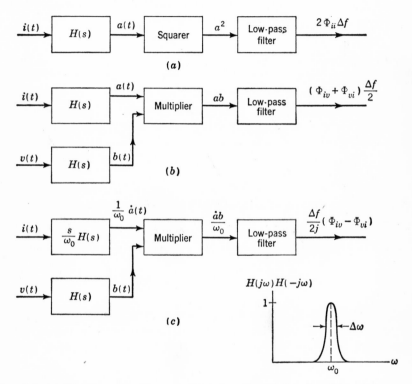

Fig. 3-2, in which $I(j\omega_0)$ undergoes an additional phase shift of $90°$,

$$\frac{\overline{ab}}{\omega_0} = \frac{\Delta f}{j}(\Phi_{iv} - \Phi_{vi}) = 2\,\Delta f \times \text{imaginary component of } \Phi_{iv}(j\omega_0) \quad (3\text{-}24)$$

The imaginary component of $\Phi_{iv}(j\omega_0)$ represents the reactive power of $i(t)v(t)$ per unit bandwidth at ω_0. It is also called the quadrature spectrum.

3-7. The Zero-crossing Problem. In some applications, we are not so much interested in the fraction of time for which $i(t)$ exceeds a threshold level h as in the average number of times $i(t)$ goes over h per second, as illustrated in Fig. 3-3. It can be calculated as follows: Let $v \equiv di/dt$ and $p(i,v)$ represent the joint probability density of i and v. The time that it takes $i(t)$ to change from h to $h + dh$, or vice versa, is

$$\tau = \frac{dh}{|v|}$$

Let dN represent the number of crossings per unit time with di/dt in the range v to $v + dv$. Then $\tau \, dN$ is the fraction of time for di/dt to be in

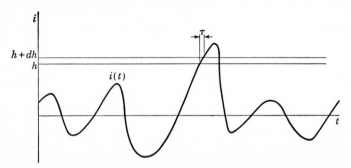

FIG. 3-3. Crossing of level h by a random signal.

the range v to $v + dv$ and i to be in the range h to $h + dh$. But by definition of the joint probability density $p(i,v)$, this is $p(h,v) \, dh \, dv$. Therefore

$$dN = \frac{1}{\tau} p(h,v) \, dh \, dv = p(h,v)|v| \, dv \qquad (3\text{-}25)$$

$$N(h) = \int_{-\infty}^{\infty} |v| p(h,v) \, dv \qquad (3\text{-}26)$$

For Gaussian signals, Eq. (3-26) can be expressed in terms of the correlation functions. Since $\phi_{iv}(0) = 0$ (Example 3-1), $p(i,v)$ can be written as

$$p(i,v) = \frac{\exp\{-\frac{1}{2}[i^2/\phi_{ii}(0) + v^2/\phi_{vv}(0)]\}}{2\pi \sqrt{\phi_{ii}(0)\phi_{vv}(0)}}$$

Substituting the above expression for $p(h,v)$ in Eq. (3-26) and integrating give

$$N(h) = \frac{1}{\pi} \left[\frac{\phi_{vv}(0)}{\phi_{ii}(0)} \right]^{1/2} e^{-h^2/2\phi_{ii}(0)}$$
$$= N(0)e^{-h^2/2\phi_{ii}(0)} \qquad (3\text{-}27)$$

where $N(0)$ is the number of zero crossings per second:

$$N(0) = \frac{1}{\pi} \left[\frac{\phi_{vv}(0)}{\phi_{ii}(0)} \right]^{1/2} \qquad (3\text{-}28)$$

In Eq. (3-27), $N(h)$ is the number of times $i(t)$ crosses the level h in both directions. Therefore, $N(h)/2$ is the number of times $i(t)$ goes over h, and $N(h)$ is the number of times $|i(t)|$ goes over h.

Example 3-5. For the signal $i(t)$ of Example 3-4, calculate:
(a) The number of zero crossings per second.
(b) The number of times per second that $|i(t)|$ exceeds 5.
Solution. Since $V(s) = sI(s)$, Eq. (3-17) gives

$$\Phi_{vv}(s) = \frac{-10s^2}{s^4 + 5s^2 + 9}$$

$$\phi_{vv}(0) = \frac{1}{2\pi j} \int_{-j\infty}^{j\infty} \frac{-10s^2}{s^4 + 5s^2 + 9} \, ds = \frac{10}{2 \times 1 \times 1} = 5$$

As calculated in Example 3-4, $\phi_{ii}(0) = \frac{5}{3}$. Equation (3-28) gives

$$N(0) = \frac{\sqrt{3}}{\pi} = 0.551 \text{ sec}^{-1}$$

Equation (3-27) gives

$$N(5) = N(0) \exp\left(-\frac{5^2}{2 \times \frac{5}{3}}\right) = N(0)e^{-7.5} = 3.1 \times 10^{-4} \text{ sec}^{-1}$$

3-8. Generalized Shot Effect. There are two types of random inputs, the ones that we can only measure and the ones that we define by a set of probabilities or conditional probabilities. An ensemble of the former

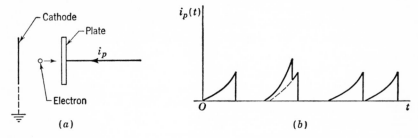

FIG. 3-4. Shot-effect current pulses of (b) are due to individual electrons in transit, as shown in (a).

consists of measured records of a random variable under well-defined physical conditions, as well as the infinite number that are not measured but probably exist under the same set of conditions. One example is the pressure record of atmospheric turbulence. The spectral-density function is found to depend essentially on two parameters, rms gust velocity and mean length of turbulence. These two parameters are then used to define the ensemble. Alternatively, the condition that defines the ensemble of records of internal noise of a radio receiver is simply the receiver itself. The analytical problem here is how accurately we can determine the ensemble-average power spectrum from the limited number of sample records that we measure and analyze. This problem is taken up in Chap. 7.

For random signals defined by a set of probabilities, the infinite collection of sequences of outcomes that obey the set of probabilities constitutes an ensemble, and each sequence is a member of the ensemble. In the subsequent sections, we shall develop methods for calculating the ensemble-average spectral densities directly from the set of probabilities.

One special class of probabilistic ensembles is of utmost interest in control work. It is referred to in the literature as generalized shot effect. We shall use the shot effect to illustrate its significance. In Fig. 3-4a, a plate current i_p is induced by discrete electrons traveling from cathode to the plate. If it is assumed that the space-charge effect, or the interaction between electrons in transit, can be neglected, the induced burst of current of each individual electron in transit is then independent of that of all others, as illustrated in Fig. 3-4b. Let $f(t)$ represent the induced current of an electron emitted at $t = 0$. The total plate current is

$$i_p(t) = \sum_l f(t - \tau_l) \qquad (3\text{-}29)$$

Since the emissions occur at random, the exact time of emission, τ_l, of each individual electron is not known. However, the average number of τ_l's per second, which is the same as the average number of electrons emitted per second, is known as I_p/e, where I_p is the average plate current and e is the electron charge. Thus $i_p(t)$ is defined by the function $f(t)$, the randomness of τ_l, and the average number of τ_l's per second. It should be noted that, in any given period of time T, the number of electrons emitted is very unlikely to be exactly TI_p/e. It usually differs from this expected number by a small margin.

Equation (3-29) can be generalized as follows:

$$i(t) = \sum_{k=1}^{N} \sum_{l=-\infty}^{\infty} a_{kl} f_k(t - \tau_{kl}) \qquad (3\text{-}30)$$

where both a_{kl} and τ_{kl} are random values with known probabilities of amplitude distribution and of occurrence, respectively, and $f_k(t) = 0$ for all $t < 0$. Equation (3-30) represents a composite series of recurring events the nature of which is represented by the functions $f_k(t)$. In some cases, there are fixed instants of occurrence. However, in most cases we know only the average number of occurrences per second but not the exact instant of occurrence. Furthermore, we know beforehand only the probability function for various amplitudes a_k but not the exact amplitude. Sometimes, the amplitude distribution depends on previous amplitudes. For instance, the transverse position of a zigzagging aircraft is usually considered a random series of ramp inputs, while a dial position is usually considered a random series of step inputs. However, there is a fundamental difference in the randomness of the two examples.

In the former, the component of aircraft velocity in the transverse direction is limited. Consequently, each subsequent input depends on the previous ones. If the speed is already at its maximum, the next input can only be in the opposite direction. In the latter example, the dial may turn any number of turns in one direction, and each input can be completely independent.

To calculate its spectral density, $i(t)$ is broken down into a number of component series $i_k(t)$:

$$i_k(t) \equiv \sum_{l=-\infty}^{\infty} a_{kl} f_k(t - \tau_{kl}) \tag{3-31}$$

Then

$$i(t) = \sum_{k=1}^{n} i_k(t) \tag{3-32}$$

In many applications, the $i_k(t)$'s are independent of each other, and Eq. (3-18) gives

$$\Phi_{ii}(j\omega) = \sum_{k=1}^{n} \Phi_{i_k i_k}(j\omega) \tag{3-33}$$

where $\Phi_{ii}(j\omega)$ and $\Phi_{i_k i_k}(j\omega)$ are spectral densities of $i(t)$ and $i_k(t)$, respectively.

To determine $\Phi_{i_k i_k}(j\omega)$, we shall define a unit step series:

$$u_k(t) \equiv \sum_{l=-\infty}^{\infty} a_{kl} u(t - \tau_{kl}) \tag{3-34}$$

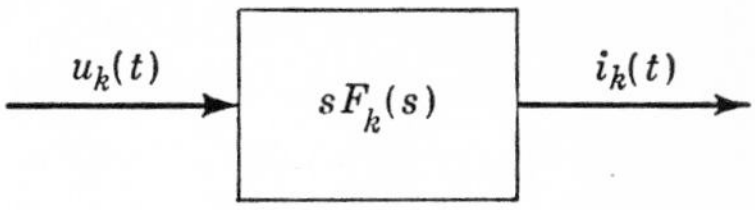

where $u(t)$ is the unit step function. If we apply $u_k(t)$ at the input end of a filter with transfer function $sF_k(s)$, where $F_k(s)$ is the Laplace transform of $f_k(t)$, $i_k(t)$ is obtained as the output (Fig. 3-5). From Eq. (3-17) we have

FIG. 3-5. Relation between a random series of known time functions and corresponding series of step functions.

$$\Phi_{i_k i_k}(j\omega) = \omega^2 F_k(j\omega) F_k(-j\omega) \Phi_{u_k u_k}(j\omega) \tag{3-35}$$

Equations (3-33) and (3-35) can be combined as

$$\Phi_{ii}(j\omega) = \omega^2 \sum_{k=1}^{n} F_k(j\omega) F_k(-j\omega) \Phi_{u_k u_k}(j\omega) \tag{3-36}$$

In the following we shall study the statistical properties of a random series of step inputs. The spectral densities of the more general class of random inputs are then calculated from Eq. (3-36).

3-9. Spectral Density of Recurring Step Function with Fixed Occurrences and Random Amplitudes. Let $y(t)$ be a random function of time as illustrated in Fig. 3-6. The value of $y(t)$ is a constant y_n in the interval $(n - 1)T < t < nT$. We may consider $y(t)$ as a series of step inputs occurring at . . . , T, $2T$, . . . , nT, . . . , with amplitudes . . . , $a_1, a_2, \ldots, a_n, \ldots$, and

$$a_n = y_{n+1} - y_n \tag{3-37}$$

In some applications, where the input function can be represented by a random series of step or ramp inputs, y_n has direct physical significance, since it represents the position or speed. In other applications, where the waveform factor $f_k(t)$ of Eq. (3-30) is, for instance, an exponentially

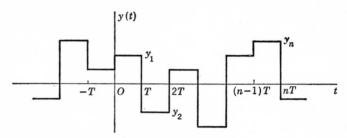

FIG. 3-6. Recurring step inputs with fixed occurrences and random amplitudes.

decaying function, y_n of the corresponding unit step series would lose much of its meaning, since it is no longer a measurable, physical entity. The most significant quantities then are the input amplitudes a_n.

For a stationary time series, $y_n{}^2$ is obviously independent of n. We have

$$\phi_{yy}(0) = \overline{y_n{}^2} \tag{3-38}$$

and $\overline{y_n y_{n+l}}$ depends on l only. Let the correlation coefficient c_l be defined as

$$c_l = \frac{\overline{y_n y_{n+l}}}{\phi_{yy}(0)} \tag{3-39}$$

Once the sequence of c_l's is known, the autocorrelation function and spectral density of $y(t)$ can be calculated as follows: If $\tau = lT$, obviously $\overline{y(t)y(t + \tau)} = \overline{y_n y_{n+l}}$.

In general, $lT < \tau < (l + 1)T$. Let $\tau = lT + \tau'$. With reference to Fig. 3-6, when t is in the range nT to $(n + 1)T - \tau'$, the ensemble average of $\overline{y(t)y(t + \tau)}$ is $\overline{y_n y_{n+l}}$. When t is in the range $(n + 1)T - \tau'$ to $(n + 1)T$, the ensemble average of $\overline{y(t)y(t + \tau)}$ is $\overline{y_n y_{n+l+1}}$. Considering all values of t, we have

$$\phi_{yy}(\tau) = \overline{y(t)y(t + \tau)} = \left(1 - \frac{\tau'}{T}\right)\overline{y_n y_{n+l}} + \frac{\tau'}{T}\overline{y_n y_{n+l+1}}$$

$$= \phi_{yy}(0)\left[\left(1 - \frac{\tau'}{T}\right)c_l + \frac{\tau'}{T}c_{l+1}\right] \tag{3-40}$$

A plot of $\phi_{yy}(\tau)/\phi_{yy}(0)$ is shown in Fig. 3-7.

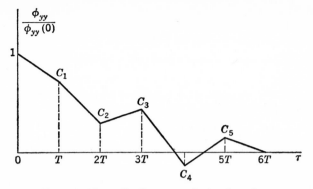

FIG. 3-7. Normalized autocorrelation function.

The spectral density $\Phi_{yy}(j\omega)$ can be calculated from Eq. (3-12). Since $\phi_{yy}(\tau) = \phi_{yy}(-\tau)$,

$$\frac{\Phi_{yy}(j\omega)}{\phi_{yy}(0)} = \int_0^\infty \frac{\phi_{yy}(\tau)}{\phi_{yy}(0)} \left(e^{-j\omega\tau} + e^{j\omega\tau}\right) d\tau$$

$$= \int_0^T \sum_{l=0}^\infty e^{-j\omega lT} \left[\left(1 - \frac{\tau'}{T}\right) c_l + \frac{\tau'}{T} c_{l+1}\right] e^{-j\omega\tau'} d\tau'$$

$$+ \text{ complex conjugate}$$

$$= \sum_{l=0}^\infty \left[\left(-\frac{j}{\omega}\right) e^{-j\omega lT} + \frac{1}{\omega^2 T} e^{-j\omega lT} - \frac{1}{\omega^2 T} e^{-j\omega(l+1)T}\right] c_l$$

$$+ \sum_{l=0}^\infty \left[\frac{j}{\omega} e^{-j\omega(l+1)T} + \frac{1}{\omega^2 T} e^{-j\omega(l+1)T} - \frac{1}{\omega^2 T} e^{-j\omega lT}\right] c_{l+1}$$

$$+ \text{ complex conjugate}$$

$$= \left\{-\frac{j}{\omega} + \frac{1}{\omega^2 T} \left(1 - e^{j\omega T}\right)\right.$$

$$\left. + \sum_{l=1}^\infty \frac{1}{2}\left[2e^{-j\omega lT} - e^{-j\omega(l+1)T} - e^{-j\omega(l-1)T}\right]\right\} c_l$$

$$+ \text{ complex conjugate}$$

$$= \frac{4 \sin^2 (\omega T/2)}{\omega^2 T} \left(1 + 2 \sum_{l=1}^\infty c_l \cos l\omega T\right) \qquad (3\text{-}41)$$

Example 3-6. Let us consider as an example $c_l = b^l$, where b is a real constant with its absolute value less than unity.

$$1 + 2 \sum_{l=1}^{\infty} b^l \cos l\omega T = 1 + \sum_{l=1}^{\infty} b^l(e^{jl\omega T} + e^{-jl\omega T})$$

$$= 1 + \frac{be^{j\omega T}}{1 - be^{j\omega T}} + \frac{be^{-j\omega T}}{1 - be^{-j\omega T}}$$

$$= \frac{1 - b^2}{1 - 2b \cos \omega T + b^2} \tag{3-42}$$

Equations (3-41) and (3-42) give

$$\frac{\Phi_{yy}(j\omega)}{\phi_{yy}(0)} = \frac{4(1 - b^2) \sin^2 (\omega T/2)}{\omega^2 T(1 - 2b \cos \omega T + b^2)} \tag{3-43}$$

Equation (3-43) is illustrated in Fig. 3-8 with values of b equal to 0.5 and -0.5, respectively.

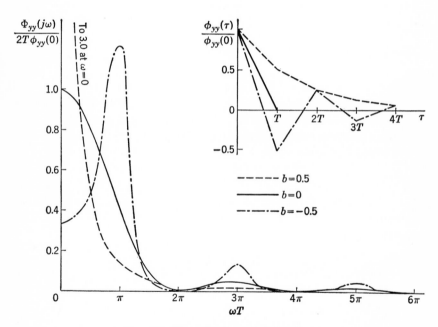

FIG. 3-8. Normalized spectral density.

3-10. Calculation of the Correlation Coefficients from Conditional Probabilities of Input Amplitude.

In general, the correlation coefficients c_l are not known, and the distribution function of a_n is given instead. The distribution of a_n depends on the present state of the system, which is simply y_n. Before the time nT, we do not know what a_n will be. We do know, however, that the probability of its being within the infinitesimal range $a_n \pm \frac{1}{2}\delta a_n$ is $P(a_n, y_n)\delta a_n$. Let us assume further that the probability density function $P(a_n, y_n)$ depends on the absolute value $|a_n + (1 - b)y_n|$ only. If $b = 1$, the input amplitude a_n is completely independent of the past. If $b = 0$, the instantaneous amplitude y_{n+1} is completely independent of the past.

To start with, let us compute the average value of $\overline{y_n y_{n+l}}$. This can be done by mathematical induction. For any given value of y_n, there is a set of average values $\widetilde{y}_{n+1}, \widetilde{y}_{n+2}, \ldots, \widetilde{y}_{n+l}, \ldots$ which depend on y_n. We use the wavy line to indicate that this is a conditional average taken under the condition that y_n is known. If we form the product $y_n \widetilde{y}_{n+l}$ and make a weighted average over all possible values of y_n, $\overline{y_n y_{n+l}}$ would be obtained. When the value of y_{n+l-1} is known, the average value of y_{n+l} is

$$(y_{n+l})_{av} = \int_{-\infty}^{\infty} (a_{n+l-1} + y_{n+l-1})p(a_{n+l-1}, y_{n+l-1})\, da_{n+l-1} \quad (3\text{-}44)$$

Let us introduce a new variable ξ; $\xi \equiv a_{n+l-1} + (1 - b)y_{n+l-1}$. Since y_{n+l-1} is fixed, $da_{n+l-1} = d\xi$, and Eq. (3-44) can be written as

$$\begin{aligned}
(y_{n+l})_{av} &= \int_{-\infty}^{\infty} (\xi + by_{n+l-1})p(\xi)\, d\xi \\
&= \int_{-\infty}^{\infty} p(\xi)\xi\, d\xi + by_{n+l-1} \int_{-\infty}^{\infty} p(\xi)\, d\xi \quad (3\text{-}45)
\end{aligned}$$

Since $p(\xi)$ depends only on the absolute value of ξ, the first integral on the right-hand side of Eq. (3-45) vanishes. The total probability of the input a_{n+l-1} having whatever possible value is unity; consequently, the second integral is unity. Therefore,

$$(y_{n+l})_{av} = by_{n+l-1} \quad (3\text{-}46)$$

$(y_{n+l})_{av}$ has been taken over a fixed value of y_{n+l-1}. If we make a weighted average on the two sides of Eq. (3-46) over all possible y_{n+l-1} under the condition that y_n is known, it becomes

$$\widetilde{y}_{n+l} = b\widetilde{y}_{n+l-1} \quad (3\text{-}47)$$

The wavy line above denotes conditional average. Repeating Eq. (3-47), we get

$$\begin{aligned}
\widetilde{y}_{n+l} &= b^l y_n \\
\overline{y_n y_{n+l}} = \overline{y_n \widetilde{y}_{n+l}} &= b^l \overline{y_n^2} \quad (3\text{-}48)
\end{aligned}$$

To evaluate $\overline{y_n^2}$, we note that, for any given y_n, the average value of y_{n+1}^2 is

$$\begin{aligned}
y_{n+1}^2 &= \int_{-\infty}^{\infty} (a_n + y_n)^2 p[a_n + (1 - b)y_n]\, da_n \\
&= \int_{-\infty}^{\infty} (\xi + by_n)^2 p(\xi)\, d\xi \\
&= \int_{-\infty}^{\infty} (\xi^2 + 2b\xi y_n + b^2 y_n^2)p(\xi)\, d\xi \\
&= \int_{-\infty}^{\infty} \xi^2 p(\xi)\, d\xi + b^2 y_n^2 \quad (3\text{-}49)
\end{aligned}$$

Averaging Eq. (3-49) over y_n, we have

$$\overline{y_{n+1}^2} = \int_{-\infty}^{\infty} \xi^2 p(\xi)\, d\xi + b^2 y_n^2 \tag{3-50}$$

Since the average y_n^2 should be the same for all n in a stationary random process, Eq. (3-50) can be solved for y_n^2. It is

$$\phi_{yy}(0) = \overline{y_n^2} = \frac{\int_{-\infty}^{\infty} \xi^2 p(\xi)\, d\xi}{1 - b^2} \tag{3-51}$$

$\overline{y_n^2}$ is $\phi_{yy}(0)$ by definition. From Eqs. (3-43), (3-48), and (3-51), the spectral density $\Phi_{yy}(j\omega)$ can be calculated. While we have written $\pm \infty$ for all the limits of integration, this does not rule out the case of limited amplitude. For the latter case, we may simply define $p(\zeta) = 0$ for $|\xi| > \xi m$. Once y_n reaches $\xi m/(1 - b)$, a_n can be negative. The upper limit of y_n is therefore $\xi m/(1 - b)$. It does indicate, however, that if y_n is limited, $b \neq 1$, and the input amplitude a_n cannot be independent of y_n.

If $b = 1$, the autocorrelation function $\phi_{yy}(\tau)$ is infinity, but the spectral density of Eq. (3-43) becomes

$$\Phi_{yy}(j\omega) = \frac{1}{\omega^2 T} \int_{-\infty}^{\infty} \xi^2 p(\xi)\, d\xi = \frac{\overline{\xi^2}}{\omega^2 T} \tag{3-52}$$

These results are to be expected. With completely independent input, the expected value of $[y(t)]^2$ is the mean-square deviation times the number of inputs (see Sec. A-4). Its expected stationary value is infinity. However, its a-c power is limited. Each step input contributes an amount $2\overline{\xi^2}/\omega^2$. Since each input is independent of the other, the total power adds to the value given in Eq. (3-52).

The normalized autocorrelation function is unity. This corresponds to the fact that, with an existing amplitude approaching infinity, the new inputs cannot make much difference one way or the other.

3-11. Spectral Density of Recurring Step Function with Random Occurrences and Random Amplitudes. In a majority of applications, the exact moments of the inputs are not known. However, we know that, on the average, there are ν inputs per second. The statistics of the amplitudes are the same as those given in Sec. 3-9. In mathematical language,

$$y(t) = \sum_{k=-\infty}^{\infty} a_k u(t - T_k) \tag{3-53}$$

where $\cdots T_{-1} < T_0 < T_1 < T_2 \cdots$ and $u(t)$ is the unit step function (see Fig. 3-9).

$$\lim_{l \to \infty} \frac{l}{T_{n+l} - T_n} = \nu \qquad \text{for all } n \tag{3-54}$$

We shall follow the same procedure as before, namely, determine the autocorrelation function first and then determine the spectral density in terms of the autocorrelation function.   To begin with, we shall calculate the probability $p_\tau(l)$ that, within a period τ, l inputs have occurred.   Let us divide τ into small intervals $\delta\tau$.   The probability of two occurrences in any single interval is $(\nu\,\delta\tau)^2$.   The total probability of having such double occurrences is of the order of $(\tau/\delta\tau)(\nu\,\delta\tau)^2 = \nu\tau\,\delta\tau$.   Therefore, by making $\delta\tau$ sufficiently small, the probability of multiple occurrences in any single interval can be neglected.

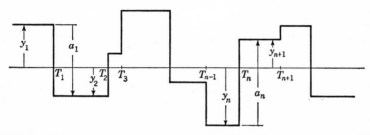

FIG. 3-9. Recurring step inputs with random occurrences and random amplitudes.

Let N denote the total number of intervals, $\tau/\delta\tau$.   The probability of having l single occurrences is

$$p_\tau(l) = \underbrace{\frac{N!}{(N-l)!\,l!}}_{\substack{\text{total number} \\ \text{of ways}}} \underbrace{(1 - \nu\,\delta\tau)^{N-l}}_{\substack{\text{nothing occurred} \\ \text{in } N-l \text{ intervals}}} \underbrace{(\nu\,\delta\tau)^l}_{\substack{\text{single occurrences} \\ \text{in } l \text{ intervals}}}$$

The above expression can be rewritten in the following form:

$$\frac{\nu^l \prod\limits_{k=0}^{l-1} [\delta\tau(N-k)]}{l!} (1 - \nu\,\delta\tau)^{(1/\nu\delta\tau)(\nu N\delta\tau - \nu l\delta\tau)}$$

$$= \frac{\nu^l}{l!}\left[\prod_{k=0}^{l-1}(\tau - k\,\delta\tau)\right]\left[(1 - \nu\,\delta\tau)^{1/\nu\delta\tau}\right]^{\nu\tau - \nu l\delta\tau} \quad (3\text{-}55)$$

In the limit of $\delta\tau$ approaching zero, it becomes

$$p_\tau(l) = \frac{(\nu\tau)^l}{l!}\,e^{-\nu\tau} \quad (3\text{-}56)$$

Equation (3-56) gives the probability of having exactly l occurrences in an interval τ.   It is known as Poisson's distribution.

The autocorrelation function is the weighted average of $\overline{y_n y_{n+l}}$:

$$\phi_{yy}(\tau) = \sum_{l=0}^{\infty} p_\tau(l)\overline{y_n y_{n+l}} \quad (3\text{-}57)$$

Substituting the result of Eq. (3-56) in (3-57), we have

$$\phi_{yy}(\tau) = \sum_{l=0}^{\infty} \frac{(\nu\tau)^l}{l!} e^{-\nu\tau} \overline{y_n y_{n+l}} \qquad (3\text{-}58)$$

The spectral density can be calculated from Eqs. (3-12) and (3-58):

$$\frac{\Phi_{yy}(j\omega)}{\phi_{yy}(0)} = \sum_{l=0}^{\infty} \frac{c_l}{l!} \int_0^{\infty} (\nu\tau)^l e^{-\nu\tau}(e^{j\omega\tau} + e^{-j\omega\tau}) \, d\tau$$

$$= \sum_{l=0}^{\infty} c_l \nu^l \left[\frac{1}{(\nu - j\omega)^{l+1}} + \frac{1}{(\nu + j\omega)^{l+1}} \right]$$

$$= 2 \sum_{l=0}^{\infty} \frac{c_l}{\nu} \left(1 + \frac{\omega^2}{\nu^2} \right)^{-(l+1)/2} \cos \frac{(l+1)\theta}{2} \qquad (3\text{-}59)$$

where $\theta = \tan^{-1}(\omega/\nu)$.

In the special case of $c_l = b^l$, $\phi_{yy}(\tau)$ reduces to a very simple form, and $\Phi_{yy}(j\omega)$ can be easily calculated from $\phi_{yy}(\tau)$. From Eq. (3-58),

$$\frac{\phi_{yy}(\tau)}{\phi_{yy}(0)} = \sum_{l=0}^{\infty} \frac{(\nu\tau)^l}{l!} e^{-\nu\tau} b^l = e^{-(1-b)\nu\tau} \qquad (3\text{-}60)$$

The spectral density $\Phi_{yy}(j\omega)$ is

$$\Phi_{yy}(j\omega) = \phi_{yy}(0) \int_0^{\infty} e^{-(1-b)\nu\tau}(e^{-j\omega\tau} + e^{j\omega\tau}) \, d\tau$$

$$= \phi_{yy}(0) \left[\frac{1}{(1-b)\nu - j\omega} + \frac{1}{(1-b)\nu + j\omega} \right]$$

$$= \frac{2(1-b)\nu\phi_{yy}(0)}{(1-b)^2\nu^2 + \omega^2} \qquad (3\text{-}61)$$

$$\Phi_{yy}(j\omega) = \frac{2\nu \int_{-\infty}^{\infty} \xi^2 p(\xi) \, d\xi}{(1+b)[(1-b)^2\nu^2 + \omega^2]} \qquad (3\text{-}62)$$

In the limiting case of completely independent inputs, $b = 1$,

$$\Phi_{yy}(j\omega) = \frac{\nu\overline{\xi^2}}{\omega^2} \qquad (3\text{-}63)$$

while $\phi_{yy}(\tau)$ becomes infinity. However, the normalized autocorrelation function is

$$\frac{\phi_{yy}(\tau)}{\phi_{yy}(0)} = 1 \qquad (3\text{-}64)$$

These relations are the same as the corresponding ones in Sec. 3-10 and can be explained in the same way.

In the case of completely independent y_n's, $b = 0$,

$$\phi_{yy}(\tau) = \overline{\xi^2} e^{-\nu\tau} \tag{3-65}$$

and $$\Phi_{yy}(j\omega) = \frac{2\nu\overline{\xi^2}}{\omega^2 + \nu^2} \tag{3-66}$$

From the above derivations, we see that, if a certain signal is a random series of step inputs, its spectral density is of the form $1/\omega^2$ only if the amplitude of each input is completely independent of all others. Otherwise, the spectral density becomes of the form $1/(\omega^2 + \omega_1^2)$, where the corner frequency ω_1 is $(1 - b)\nu$. Correspondingly, the spectral density for a random series of inputs of the waveform $f_k(t)$ is

$$\Phi_{i_k i_k}(j\omega) = \frac{A\omega^2 F_k(j\omega) F_k(-j\omega)}{\omega^2 + \omega_1^2} \tag{3-67}$$

where A is a proportionality constant.

3-12. Spectral Densities of Signals Containing Pure Sinusoidal Components. In Fig. 3-2, the spectral density represents the power within a narrow frequency band per unit bandwidth, and the cross-spectral density represents a similar product involving two signals. In case both signals are sinusoidal and of the same frequency ω_0, the measured power is zero if ω_0 is not included in the passband, and a finite power P if ω_0 is included in the passband. For instance, P may be the power dissipated in a 1-ohm resistor or the vector power of an a-c source, depending on whether the spectral density of an alternating current alone or the cross-spectral density of emf and current are being considered. In any case, we may write for positive values of ω_1 and ω_2

$$\frac{1}{\pi} \int_{\omega_1}^{\omega_2} \Phi_{ij}(j\omega) \, d\omega = \begin{cases} P_{ij} & \text{if } \omega_1 < \omega_0 < \omega_2 \\ 0 & \text{if } \omega_1 > \omega_0 \quad \text{or} \quad \omega_2 < \omega_0 \end{cases} \tag{3-68}$$

Obviously, $\Phi_{ij}(j\omega)$ is zero for all values of $\omega \neq \omega_0$. In order that the integral of Eq. (3-68) be finite, $\Phi_{ij}(j\omega)$ must be infinity at $\omega = \omega_0$. A function of this nature is called an impulse function or delta function and is denoted by $\delta(x)$. Its properties are discussed in Appendix B. Considering that $\Phi_{ij}(-j\omega) = [\Phi_{ij}(j\omega)]^*$, the spectral density Φ_{ij} can be written as

$$\Phi_{ij}(j\omega) = \pi[P_{ij}^* \delta(\omega + \omega_0) + P_{ij}\delta(\omega - \omega_0)] \tag{3-69}$$

If a random time function contains a number of purely sinusoidal components,

$$i(t) = f(t) + \sum_k A_k \sin(\omega_k t + \phi_k) \tag{3-70}$$

where $\Phi_{ff}(j\omega)$ is bounded with perhaps an exception at $\omega = 0$, then

$$\Phi_{ii}(j\omega) = \Phi_{ff}(j\omega) + \frac{\pi}{2} \sum_k A_k{}^2[\delta(\omega - \omega_k) + \delta(\omega + \omega_k)] \qquad (3\text{-}71)$$

Equation (3-71) is a direct consequence of Eqs. (3-18) and (3-69). Obviously, the cross-spectral densities of sinusoidal functions of different frequencies vanish. Since $\Phi_{ff}(j\omega)$ is bounded, there cannot be any coherent sinusoidal component in $f(t)$, and the cross-spectral densities between $f(t)$ and the various sinusoidal terms are vanishingly small compared with the δ functions. Equation (3-71) gives $\Phi_{ii}(j\omega)$ as the sum of the spectral densities of all the individual components.

In practice, a purely sinusoidal signal perhaps does not exist. There is always some frequency or phase or amplitude fluctuation, and the only question is how much. Such a signal can be approximated by a random series of damped sinusoidal functions in which each input amplitude a_l is completely independent of all previous a_l's:

$$y(t) = \sum_l a_l u(t - \tau_l) e^{-\epsilon(t-\tau_l)} \sin \omega_0(t - \tau_l) \qquad (3\text{-}72)$$

From Sec. 3-8, the spectral density of $y(t)$ is the same as that of each individual term except for a constant multiplier. Therefore

$$\Phi_{yy}(j\omega) = \frac{A}{(j\omega + a)(j\omega + a^*)(j\omega - a)(j\omega - a^*)} \qquad (3\text{-}73)$$

where $a = \epsilon + j\omega_0$, and A is a constant which depends on the amplitude distribution of a, the number of τ_l's per second, and ϵ. Since

$$\phi_{yy}(0) = \frac{1}{2\pi} \int_{-\infty}^{\infty} \Phi_{yy}(j\omega) \, d\omega = \frac{A}{4\epsilon aa^*} \qquad (3\text{-}74)$$

Eq. (3-73) becomes

$$\Phi_{yy}(j\omega) = \frac{4aa^*\phi_{yy}(0)}{(j\omega + a)(j\omega + a^*)(j\omega - a)(j\omega - a^*)} \qquad (3\text{-}75)$$

Equation (3-75) is useful in studying the optimum filtering of a sinusoidal noise signal from a random input signal.

As ϵ approaches zero, $y(t)$ approaches a purely sinusoidal wave. It is always possible to adjust the distribution of a_l in such a way that $\phi_{yy}(0)$ remains constant as ϵ approaches zero.

3-13. Summary. In this chapter, we have defined spectral densities and correlation functions for random signals, both mathematically and physically; derived their transforms and other properties; and formulated ways of calculating these functions for random signals of the generalized-shot-effect type directly from the probabilities which specify these signals.

The concept of a distribution function for system error or other system variables is introduced.   When the system inputs are either Gaussian or highly random in other predesignated ways, normal distribution can be used to approximate the actual distribution.   Under such conditions, once the mean-square amplitude of fluctuation of a system variable is known, its distribution is completely known.   A corollary of this is that a system with the least-square error gives the least cost no matter how the cost function is defined as long as it is a non-decreasing function of the error.   Similarly, a system with the least-square amplitude of the input to a saturable fixed component has the least tendency to saturate.   The concept of stationary processes is introduced, together with the ergodic hypothesis which states the equivalence between time and ensemble averages.

Having thus established the plausibility of the least-square criterion, we have shown that for stationary systems the only required data for optimum design based on this criterion are the spectral densities of the input signals.   As another facet of spectral densities, the correlation functions are defined and are shown to be the inverse Fourier or Laplace transforms of the former.   The physical and statistical significances of these functions are also illustrated.   Equations relating the spectral densities of the output functions to those of the input signals and transfer functions of the system are derived.

The spectral densities of random signals of the generalized-shot-effect type can be calculated by calculating first the spectral densities of the corresponding unit step series, and the waveform factor is taken into consideration later as a separate step in Eq. (3-36).   The correlation function of a unit step series is calculated from two given factors: (1) the distribution as well as the interdependence of the successive amplitudes and (2) the distribution of the breaking points or times of change in amplitude. When the latter is completely random, Poisson's distribution is derived and used as a basis for such calculations.   Once the correlation functions are determined, the spectral densities are calculated by Laplace or Fourier transform.

Sometimes purely or nearly sinusoidal components are present in a random signal.   The former give rise to δ functions in the spectral density, while the latter introduce a sharp but finite peak which can be described by a rational function of ω^2.

In closing, it may be remarked that the use of spectral densities to represent stationary signals is not only a powerful technique but is a natural one for electrical engineers.   Because of the transform relationship between spectral densities and correlation functions, whatever analytical results are obtainable from the use of one representation are also obtainable from the use of the other.   However, as the relation between input and output spectra of a linear network is exactly the same for random signals as it is for steady-state sinusoidal signals, our analytical work is on familiar ground when spectral densities are used. No such familiarity exists for correlation functions.

On the other hand, correlation functions are readily defined for non-stationary signals, as we shall see in Chap. 5. The spectral-density function is essentially a time-averaged quantity. Its significance is lost when time average becomes meaningless.

We may conclude that spectral densities should be used for analyzing stationary (or approximately stationary) systems, whereas correlation functions should be used for analyzing nonstationary systems.

CHAPTER 4

OPTIMUM SYSTEMS WITH RANDOM INPUTS

The design of systems with random inputs is perhaps the most significant problem that makes least-square optimum-design techniques worthwhile. In practically every high-performance system, the ultimate error is caused by noise or load disturbance or some other undesirable random inputs. There is always the thermal noise or the induced noise in a highly sensitive sensing element or in the inertial or some other reference system. After every removable source is eliminated, the residue is always there and most likely random in nature. Load disturbance is even more fundamental. We can say with some justification that, without consideration of load disturbance, a feedback control system has little to offer over a feedforward system.

In this chapter, we shall formulate the optimum-design problem in general terms, give a general solution, and then proceed to show its various applications. One advantage of this approach is that it shows how various design considerations can be incorporated into the same procedure. However, our purpose is not to present the derived procedure as a cookbook solution of design problems of this type but rather to illustrate the method.

The mathematics is basically the same as that used in Chap. 2. In fact, for simple problems, very little change needs to be made. For instance, if in Example 3-2 $F(s)$ is to be determined so that

$$\overline{[e(t)]^2} = \min$$
$$\overline{[i(t)]^2} \leq K_2$$

the method and solution of Sec. 2-4 can be taken over almost in their entirety, with $\Phi_{rr}(j\omega)$ taking the place of $R(s)R(-s)$. As we have little need for preliminaries, we shall proceed to the general case directly.

GENERAL PROCEDURES AND METHODS

4-1. Optimization Criterion and Constraints. Figure 4-1 illustrates a typical system with a single controlled variable. The given elements are the controlled system or fixed component $G_1(s)$ and the main-loop feedback function $H_m(s)$ [$H_m(s)$ is usually a constant]. The desired output $c_d(t)$ results from a specified linear operation $L(s)$ on the reference input $r(t)$. $L(s)$ is purely hypothetical and may or may not be physically realizable. For instance, the desired output $c_d(t)$ may be the reference input τ sec later:

$$c_d(t) = r(t + \tau)$$

The Laplace transform of the above equation gives

$$C_d(s) = \mathcal{L}\{r(t + \tau)\} = e^{\tau s}R(s) \tag{4-1}$$

The linear operator $L(s)$ is then $e^{\tau s}$, which obviously does not represent any physically realizable network. Other types of linear operation may

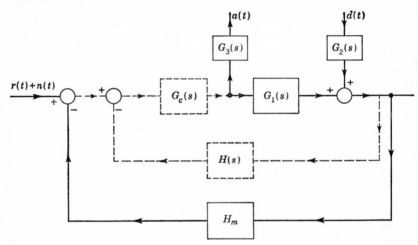

Fɪɢ. 4-1. Block diagram of a system with multiple inputs. Solid line, fixed elements; broken line, possible arrangement and compensating elements to be designed.

be physically realizable; for instance, a follow-up system is represented by $L(s) = 1$. Besides the reference input, there are also undesirable or spurious inputs into the system, such as noise $n(t)$ and load disturbance $d(t)$. The transfer function $G_2(s)$ represents the process through which the controlled variable $c(t)$ is affected by the load disturbance $d(t)$. For instance, $d(t)$ may be a torque and $c(t)$ the shaft position, and $G_2(s)$ is then $1/Ms^2$, where M is the moment of inertia. The system error $e(t)$ is defined as

$$e(t) = c_d(t) - c(t) \tag{4-2}$$

Our design problem is to select the series-compensating function $G_c(s)$ and/or the parallel-compensation function $H(s)$ so that

$$\overline{[e(t)]^2} = \min \tag{4-3}$$

Sometimes there is a multiplicity of inner loops and compensating networks. These apparently complicated systems are, however, reducible to the form shown in Fig. 4-1, but the latter cannot be further reduced without altering one or the other of the closed-loop system functions C/R and C/D. From Fig. 4-1, C/R and C/D can be readily expressed as

$$\frac{1}{(C/R)(s)} = H_m(s) + H(s) + \frac{1}{G_1(s)G_c(s)} \tag{4-4}$$

$$\frac{C}{D}(s) = \frac{G_2(s)}{G_c(s)G_1(s)}\frac{C}{R}(s) \tag{4-5}$$

Equations (4-4) and (4-5) illustrate that C/R and C/D can be independently determined. Given these two functions, $G_c(s)$ can be determined from Eq. (4-5), and $H(s)$ is then determined from Eq. (4-4).

Because of the presence of a fixed component, there are two types of constraints or limiting factors on the system:

1. *Functional Constraints.* In order that the closed-loop system be stable, all the poles of the system functions C/R and C/D are confined to the LHP interior. Additional restrictions exist if the fixed component has one or both of the following properties:

a. TRANSPORTATION LAG OR DEAD TIME. If the fixed component has absolutely no response for a period τ subsequent to the application of a forcing signal, the period τ is referred to as transportation lag or dead time. Mathematically, we may write $G_1(s)$ as having a factor $e^{-\tau s}$.

b. NONMINIMUM PHASE. If $G_1(s)$ has one or more zeros in the RHP, it is referred to as a nonminimum-phase function. The term minimum phase was used by Bode to define the class of functions that obey his famous theorem relating gain and phase. For a transfer function to represent a stable system and to have minimum phase, all its characteristic frequencies must be in the LHP, including the origin. A pole in the RHP causes the component to be unstable without feedback, and a zero in the RHP causes it to have a greater phase lag for the same gain characteristics. The latter point can be illustrated by an example: Let us compare two transfer functions, one with $1 + s$ and the other with $1 - s$ in the numerator but identical otherwise. The gain of the two functions is identical at all frequencies. However, the phase lag of the latter is greater than that of the former by $2 \tan^{-1} \omega$.

Physically, if the initial response of a component to a step input is opposite to its steady-state response, the component must have nonminimum phase. Obviously this initial reversal necessarily causes delay in the closed-loop system response.

From the above discussion, $G_1(s)$ is expressed as

$$G_1(s) = e^{-\tau s}P(s)G_{11}(s) \tag{4-6}$$

where
$$P(s) = \prod_i \left(1 - \frac{s}{\lambda_i}\right) \tag{4-7}$$

The λ_i's are zeros of $G_1(s)$ in the RHP, and $G_{11}(s)$ represents the balance of the transfer function. The question is: What are the restrictions imposed by $e^{-\tau s}P(s)$ on C/R and C/D?

With reference to Fig. 4-1, let $i(t)$ denote the input to the fixed component $G_1(s)$. The closed-loop transfer functions I/R and I/D can be expressed as follows:

$$\frac{I}{R}(s) = \frac{1}{G_1(s)}\frac{C}{R}(s) \tag{4-8}$$

$$\frac{I}{D}(s) = \frac{1}{G_1(s)}\left[\frac{C}{D}(s) - G_2(s)\right] \tag{4-9}$$

It is physically impossible to apply to the fixed component a forcing signal $i(t)$ in anticipation of the system input or load disturbance. Therefore the system functions I/R and I/D cannot possess the factor $e^{\tau s}$. Furthermore, I/R and I/D cannot possess $1/P(s)$, because in that case $i(t)$ would rise exponentially as a result of any thermal agitation or a sudden input. While the system is stable in the sense that the controlled variable $c(t)$ has only exponentially decreasing terms as long as the system is linear, it would not operate within the linear range for long, because of the exponentially rising $i(t)$. Therefore the factor $e^{\tau s}/P(s)$ which is implicit in $1/G(s)$ on the right-hand side of Eqs. (4-8) and (4-9) must be canceled by a factor $e^{-\tau s}P(s)$ in $(C/R)(s)$ and $(C/D)(s) - G_2(s)$, respectively.

The fact that the fixed component is open-loop unstable, as exhibited by poles in the RHP, does not cause any restriction on its closed-loop response. The poles are readily removed by inner-loop feedback, which can be considered as part of $H(s)$.

The functional constraints are taken into consideration in the optimization procedure by assuming appropriate unknown functions which will be denoted as $F_i(s)$, $i = 1, 2, \ldots$. The only restriction on the $F_i(s)$'s is that all their poles be confined to the LHP interior.

Let us consider $(C/R)(s)$ first. If $G_1(s)$ is known to be stable, we can write

$$\frac{C}{R}(s) = F(s)G_1(s)$$

The above expression automatically takes into account the restrictions due to transportation lag and nonminimum phase. It is not adequate if $G_1(s)$ has one or more poles in the RHP. On the other hand, if we write

$$\frac{C}{R}(s) = F(s)$$

poles of $G_1(s)$ in the RHP do not present a problem; however, additional provisions must be made for the zeros. An expression which is good for all situations is

$$\frac{C}{R}(s) = e^{-\tau s}P(s)F_1(s) \tag{4-10}$$

In Eq. (4-10), only the RHP zeros of $G_1(s)$ are explicitly expressed. Similarly,

$$\frac{C}{D}(s) = e^{-\tau s}P(s)F_2(s) + G_2(s) \tag{4-11}$$

$F_1(s)$ and $F_2(s)$ are unknown functions to be determined. The condition that all the poles of $F_1(s)$ and $F_2(s)$ be in the LHP, together with Eqs. (4-10) and (4-11), is sufficient to ensure that the functional constraints on $(C/R)(s)$ and $(C/D)(s)$ are met.

2. *Amplitude Constraints.* The amplitude constraints may be expressed as

$$\overline{[a_i(t)]^2} \le K_i \qquad i = 1, 2, \ldots, N \tag{4-12}$$

In Eqs. (4-12), the $a_i(t)$'s represent N signals which either exist in the controlled system or may be obtained by given linear operations on such signals.

It should be emphasized at this point that there are two aspects of our problem: the analytical aspect and the engineering aspect. From the analytical point of view, we pose Eqs. (4-3) and (4-12) at the start and obtain a system which satisfies these conditions, without questioning why. From the engineering point of view, we can never exhaust the various possible situations under which these criteria are justifiable. While our study is concerned mainly with the analytical aspect, it may be worthwhile to mention a few situations which give rise to Eqs. (4-12).

1. Heat loss. The copper loss in a motor is proportional to the square of the winding current, which can be considered one of the constrained signals.

2. Saturation. The fixed component saturates when the input level is too high. The saturation may take many forms: for instance, magnetic saturation in a motor, maximum effective displacement of a rudder or an elevator, maximum flow of a hydraulic valve, etc. As saturation always gives rise to an undesirable effect, the simplest way to take saturation into account is to avoid it as much as possible by limiting the mean-square value of the variable $a_i(t)$ as expressed by Eqs. (4-12). Let ξ_i represent the saturation limit. For Gaussian random inputs, it can be readily shown from Sec. 3-2 that the probability or fraction of time for $a_i(t)$ to exceed ξ_i is

$$p(|a_i| > \xi_i) = 1 - \Phi\left(\frac{\xi_i}{\sqrt{2K_i}}\right) \tag{4-13}$$

If $\sqrt{K_i}$ is selected as a small fraction of ξ_i, $1 - \Phi(\xi_i/\sqrt{2K_i})$ is very close to zero. Therefore the inequality of (4-12) controls the probabilities of saturation at various points in the system.

3. System bandwidth. The cost of components increases with the system bandwidth. This is partly because of the saturation effect which is accentuated by any attempt to speed up the system response and partly because of the resonant frequencies and phase lags of the various components in the higher frequency range. The transfer functions that we use in ordinary design work are approximations at best, in the sense that small time constants are neglected and distributed lags are treated as simple time constants. Notable examples of the latter are the transmission lag in hydraulic conduits and torsional shafts. It is costly to elevate these effects to a higher frequency range; furthermore, there is a limit on what we can do, considering cost or not.

Newton introduced an artificial measure of the bandwidth and posed as a condition for system design that the bandwidth so measured be below a specified value. One would accomplish the same result by requiring that the mean-square value of the system output in response to a hypothetical random input $w(t)$ be limited or at a minimum. The spectral density of the hypothetical input $\Phi_{ww}(j\omega)$ is a rising function of ω. By assuming different functions for $\Phi_{ww}(j\omega)$, we can reflect the practical undesirability, in cost or otherwise, of a high-frequency system.

4. Other criteria. There are many other ways of establishing constraints. For instance, we may not wish to limit the complete system as much as to limit to lower frequencies the input $i(t)$ of a certain component. A high-pass filtering function operating on $i(t)$ gives the constrained signal $a_i(t)$.

4-2. Solution of the General Problem. Having thus far put our optimization criterion and the various constraints into mathematical expressions, we shall proceed to obtain a solution of the problem. The first step is to express the system error in terms of the inputs and the unknown functions $F_1(s)$ and $F_2(s)$:

$$E(s) = C_d(s) - C(s) = L(s)R(s) - \frac{C}{R}(s)R_1(s) - \frac{C}{D}(s)D(s)$$

$$= L(s)R(s) - e^{-\tau s}P(s)F_1(s)R_1(s) - [e^{-\tau s}P(s)F_2(s) + G_2(s)]D(s)$$
(4-14)

To make the problem more definite, let the constrained signal $a(t)$ be specified by the following equation:

$$A(s) = G_3(s)I(s) = \frac{G_3(s)}{G_1(s)}[C(s) - G_2(s)D(s)]$$
(4-15)

where $G_3(s)$ may be unity or some other network function, as discussed in the preceding section. Making the same substitutions as was done in Eq. (4-14), we obtain

$$A(s) = \frac{e^{-\tau s}P(s)G_3(s)}{G_1(s)} [F_1(s)R_1(s) + F_2(s)D(s)] \tag{4-16}$$

Equation (3-11) gives the mean-square values $\overline{e^2}$ and $\overline{a^2}$ as the following integrals:

$$\overline{e^2} = \frac{1}{2\pi j} \int_{-j\infty}^{j\infty} \Phi_{ee}(s)\, ds \tag{4-17}$$

$$\overline{a^2} = \frac{1}{2\pi j} \int_{-j\infty}^{j\infty} \Phi_{aa}(s)\, ds \tag{4-18}$$

From Eqs. (3-14), (4-14), and (4-16) the spectral densities $\Phi_{ee}(s)$ and $\Phi_{aa}(s)$ can be expressed in terms of the spectral densities of the inputs, $r(t)$, $n(t)$, and $d(t)$. It is assumed that no correlation exists between $r_1(t)$ and $d(t)$: $\Phi_{r_1 d}(s) = \Phi_{rd}(s) = 0$.

$$\Phi_{ee}(s) = \bar{L}L\Phi_{rr} + \Phi_{cc} - \bar{L}\Phi_{rc} - L\Phi_{cr} \tag{4-19}$$

$$\Phi_{cc}(s) = \bar{P}P\bar{F}_1 F_1 \Phi_{r_1 r_1} + (e^{-\tau s}PF_2 + G_2)(e^{\tau s}\bar{P}\bar{F}_2 + \bar{G}_2)\Phi_{dd} \tag{4-20}$$

$$\Phi_{rc}(s) = e^{-\tau s}P\bar{F}_1 \Phi_{rr_1} \tag{4-21}$$

$$\Phi_{cr}(s) = e^{\tau s}\bar{P}\bar{F}_1 \Phi_{r_1 r} \tag{4-22}$$

$$\Phi_{aa}(s) = \frac{\bar{G}_3 G_3 \bar{P}P}{\bar{G}_1 G_1} (\bar{F}_1 F_1 \Phi_{r_1 r_1} + \bar{F}_2 F_2 \Phi_{dd}) \tag{4-23}$$

Equations (4-17) to (4-23) give $\overline{e^2}$ and $\overline{a^2}$ in terms of the unknown functions F_1 and F_2. Our design criterion is that $\overline{e^2}$ should be a minimum, while $\overline{a^2}$ is limited by inequality (4-12). We can follow the same procedure as was used in Sec. 2-4 to derive optimum forms of F_1 and F_2. Alternatively, we may use the optimization theorem which will be derived in the next section. It gives the conditions to be satisfied as

$$\frac{\partial \Phi_{ee}}{\partial \bar{F}_1} + k^2 \frac{\partial \Phi_{aa}}{\partial \bar{F}_1} = X_1(s)$$
$$\frac{\partial \Phi_{ee}}{\partial \bar{F}_2} + k^2 \frac{\partial \Phi_{aa}}{\partial \bar{F}_2} = X_2(s) \tag{4-24}$$

where k^2 is Lagrange's undetermined multiplier and $X_1(s)$ and $X_2(s)$ are unspecified except that they do not possess any poles in the LHP. The reason for using k^2 instead of the conventional λ is explained in Sec. 2-4. This condition, when taken together with the restriction on the pole locations of F_1 and F_2, gives a unique solution of the problem, as will be shown below. In taking the derivatives, F_1, F_2, $\bar{F}_1$, and $\bar{F}_2$ are considered independent.   Equations (4-24) give

$$\bar{Y}YP\bar{P}F_1\Phi_{r_1r_1} - e^{\tau s}\bar{P}L\Phi_{r_1r} = X_1(s) \tag{4-25}$$
$$\bar{Y}YP\bar{P}F_2\Phi_{dd} + e^{\tau s}\bar{P}G_2\Phi_{dd} = X_2(s) \tag{4-26}$$

where Y is a function with all its poles and zeros in the LHP and is defined by

$$Y \equiv \left\{1 + \frac{k^2\bar{G}_3G_3}{\bar{G}_1G_1}\right\}^+ \tag{4-27}$$

The two unknown functions F_1 and F_2 can be solved independently. Let

$$\begin{aligned} Z &\equiv \{\Phi_{r_1r_1}\}^+ \\ \mathbf{D} &\equiv \{\Phi_{dd}\}^+ \end{aligned} \tag{4-27a}$$

All the poles and zeros of Z and $\mathbf{D}$ are in the LHP.   The function $\mathbf{D}$ is boldfaced so that it will not be confused with the Laplace transform of $d(t)$.   Following the steps which led to Eq. (2-29), we arrive at the following solutions:

$$F_1 = \frac{1}{\bar{P}YZ}\left[\frac{e^{\tau s}\bar{P}L\Phi_{r_1r}}{P\bar{Y}\bar{Z}}\right]_+ \tag{4-28}$$

$$F_2 = -\frac{1}{\bar{P}Y\mathbf{D}}\left[\frac{e^{\tau s}\bar{P}G_2\mathbf{D}}{P\bar{Y}}\right]_+ \tag{4-29}$$

Let $Y_1(s)$ be defined as

$$Y_1(s) \equiv \frac{P(-s)Y(s)}{P(s)} \tag{4-30}$$

From Eqs. (4-10), (4-11), (4-28), and (4-29) we obtain

$$\frac{C}{R}(s) = \frac{e^{-\tau s}}{Y_1Z}\left[\frac{e^{\tau s}L\Phi_{r_1r}}{\bar{Y}_1\bar{Z}}\right]_+ \tag{4-31}$$

$$\frac{C}{D}(s) = G_2(s) - \frac{e^{-\tau s}}{Y_1\mathbf{D}}\left[\frac{e^{\tau s}G_2\mathbf{D}}{\bar{Y}_1}\right]_+ \tag{4-32}$$

From Eq. (4-27) we see that $1/Y$ can be obtained by a root-square-locus plot from G_1/G_3.   The zeros of $1/Y$, however, are in the LHP by definition.   They may or may not be the original zeros of G_1/G_3.   The definition of $Y_1(s)$ implies that all the zeros of $1/Y(s)$ which are not zeros of G_1 are replaced by the latter.   Since none of the poles of G_3 can be in the RHP, all the zeros of $1/Y_1(s)$ are the same as zeros of G_1/G_3, while all the poles of $1/Y_1(s)$ are obtained by the root-square-locus plot.   This description allows $Y_1(s)$ to be determined directly, without resorting to Eq. (4-30).

An alternative way of solving the above problem is to consider $d'(t)$ of Fig. 4-1 as the load disturbance. Let the primed functions represent the ones to be used instead of the original functions. Then

$$\Phi_{d'd'}(s) = G_2(s)G_2(-s)\Phi_{dd}(s)$$
$$G_2'(s) = 1 \qquad\qquad (4\text{-}33)$$

If $G_2(s)$ has minimum phase, the two methods are equivalent. If $G_2(s)$ has zeros in the RHP or transportation lag, the two methods represent different physical situations: The former method applies when $d(t)$ is directly measurable, and the system block diagram of Fig. 4-1 is correspondingly modified. The latter applies when $d(t)$ is not measurable, and its effect on $c(t)$ is the only quantity measurable through the error-sensing device, as illustrated by Fig. 4-1.

4-3. An Extension of Variational Calculus. In most applications with least-square criteria, the integrand of the integrals which are being minimized, or limited in value, is of quadratic form in the unknown functions $F_i(s)$ and $F_i(-s)$. However, it may be desirable to state the variational problem in a relatively general form. Let the integrals I_m be defined as

$$I_m \equiv \frac{1}{2\pi j} \int_{-j\infty}^{j\infty} \Phi_m(s;F_1,F_2,\ \ldots\ ,F_n;\bar{F}_1,\bar{F}_2,\ \ldots\ ,\bar{F}_n)\ ds$$

$$m = 0, 1, 2, \ldots, M \quad (4\text{-}34)$$

The functions Φ_m and F_i, $m = 0, 1, 2, \ldots, M$, $i = 1, 2, \ldots, n$, satisfy the following conditions:†

1. $F_i(s)$'s are physically realizable network functions, in the sense that they are real functions of s with all the poles in the LHP, thus excluding the imaginary axis.

2. Φ_m's satisfy the conjugate condition that, for all subscripts i and m and arbitrary ω_1,

$$\left.\frac{\partial\Phi_m}{\partial F_i}\right|_{s=j\omega_1} = \left.\frac{\partial\Phi_m}{\partial\bar{F}_i}\right|_{s=-j\omega_1} \qquad (4\text{-}35)$$

In taking the partial derivatives, F_i and $\bar{F}_i$ are considered independent.

† Condition 1 is obvious. Condition 2 is equivalent to the following: Given that the functions $F_i(s)$, $i = 1, 2, \ldots, n$, are real functions of s, Φ_m is real on the $j\omega$ axis and is even in ω, $\Phi_m(j\omega) = \Phi_m(-j\omega)$. This condition obviously holds for physical systems and is sufficient for condition 2. The proof will not be given here as it is routine and lengthy. Condition 3 can be interpreted as follows: Let us regard s, $e^{\tau s}$, $F_i(s)$, and $\bar{F}_i(s)$ as a set of variables. If Φ_m can be expressed as a polynomial in these variables, condition 3 is easily shown to be true. We shall see that in all the application problems of this chapter Φ_m can be expressed as a polynomial in these variables. However, as condition 3 also holds for some other form of Φ_m, it is the weaker condition of the two. It is always desirable to use a weaker assumption, as the result of the theorem is then more general.

3. For admissible $F_i(s)$'s, that is, the $F_i(s)$'s which give convergent values of all the integrals I_m,

$$\lim_{s \to \infty} s\bar{F}_i \frac{\partial \Phi_m}{\partial \bar{F}_i} = 0 \tag{4-36}$$

In case $\partial \Phi_m / \partial F_i$ has essential singularities at infinity, such as $e^{\tau s}$, Eq. (4-36) is required to hold only for s with a negative real component. An optimization theorem may be stated as follows:

If conditions 1, 2, and 3 hold, a necessary and sufficient condition for

$$I = \sum_{m=0}^{M} \lambda_m I_m$$

to be stationary with respect to infinitesimal variations of $F_1(s)$, $F_2(s)$, . . . , $F_n(s)$ and corresponding variations of $F_1(-s)$, $F_2(-s)$, . . . , $F_n(-s)$ is that the partial derivatives

$$X_i(s) = \sum_{m=0}^{M} \lambda_m \frac{\partial \Phi_m}{\partial \bar{F}_i} \tag{4-37}$$

do not have any pole in the LHP including the imaginary axis, where the λ_m's are arbitrary constants.

From Lagrange's method of undetermined multipliers, we see that $\sum_{m=0}^{M} \lambda_m \Phi_m$ being stationary is a necessary condition for the following:

$$\begin{aligned} I_0 &= \min \\ I_m &\leq K_m \qquad m = 1, 2, \ldots, M \end{aligned} \tag{4-38}$$

The proof of the theorem is as follows:

Let $\epsilon H_i(s)$'s be an arbitrary set of infinitesimal difference functions, where ϵ is an infinitesimal constant and the $H_i(s)$'s are finite. Since the admissible $F_i(s)$'s satisfy conditions 1 and 3, the difference functions $\epsilon H_i(s)$ between two sets of admissible $F_i(s)$'s must meet the same conditions. The first-order variation δI is

$$\epsilon \sum_{m=0}^{M} \frac{\lambda_m}{2\pi j} \int_{-j\infty}^{j\infty} \sum_{i=1}^{n} \left(\frac{\partial \Phi_m}{\partial F_i} H_i + \frac{\partial \Phi_m}{\partial \bar{F}_i} \bar{H}_i \right) ds = 0 \tag{4-39}$$

Since the $H_i(s)$'s are independent of each other, Eq. (4-39) is equivalent to

$$\sum_{m=0}^{M} \frac{\lambda_m}{2\pi j} \int_{-j\infty}^{j\infty} \left(\frac{\partial \Phi_m}{\partial F_i} H_i + \frac{\partial \Phi_m}{\partial \bar{F}_i} \bar{H}_i \right) ds = 0 \qquad i = 1, 2, \ldots, n \tag{4-40}$$

By using Eq. (4-35) and substituting $-s$ for s in the following integral, it becomes

$$\int_{-j\infty}^{j\infty} \frac{\partial \Phi_m}{\partial F_i} H_i \, ds = \int_{-j\infty}^{j\infty} \frac{\partial \Phi_m}{\partial \bar{F}_i} \bar{H}_i \, ds \qquad (4\text{-}41)$$

Substitution of Eq. (4-41) in (4-40) gives

$$\int_{-j\infty}^{j\infty} \sum_{m=0}^{M} \lambda_m \frac{\partial \Phi_m}{\partial F_i} \bar{H}_i \, ds = 0 \qquad (4\text{-}42)$$

As a result of condition 3, the path of integration of Eq. (4-42) may be extended from $+j\infty$ through a large semicircle to $-j\infty$ enclosing the entire LHP, and there results

$$\oint_{\text{LHP}} X_i(s) H_i(-s) \, ds = 0 \qquad i = 1, 2, \ldots, n \qquad (4\text{-}43)$$

Since $H_i(s)$ does not have any poles in the RHP including the imaginary axis, it follows that $H_i(-s)$ does not have any poles in the LHP including the imaginary axis. A sufficient condition for $\delta I = 0$ is that the functions $X_i(s)$ do not have any poles in the LHP including the imaginary axis. This is also the necessary condition, because of the arbitrariness of $H_i(-s)$. If any of the functions $X_i(s)$ has one or more poles in the LHP, a function $H_i(-s)$ can be found such that the sum of residues does not vanish, and the condition embodied in Eq. (4-43) will be violated.

Equation (4-37) with the above specification on $X_i(s)$ can be easily remembered as an extension of variational calculus. If we do not require the poles of $F_i(s)$ to be in the LHP, the result of variational calculus is that the expressions for $i = 1, 2, \ldots, n$ on the right-hand side of Eq. (4-37) vanish. With the additional restriction on the locations of the poles of $F_i(s)$, the result is correspondingly relaxed and the same expression is only required to be analytic in the LHP. This kind of relaxation is essential to finding a solution satisfying simultaneously the restriction on the location of the poles of $F_i(s)$ and Eq. (4-37).

Some of our friends may ask, with Eq. (4-37) and the restriction on $F_i(s)$, can we find a unique solution to the set of unknown functions $F_i(s)$? As mathematicians, we may simply turn up our noses to imply that to answer such questions is beneath our dignity. A mathematical theorem need only establish the equivalence of two sets of conditions or establish that one set of conditions implies another set; whether or not any set leads to any useful result is not the point. However, as engineers, we do have to answer such questions. If Φ_m is bilinear in $F_i(s)$ and $\bar{F}_i(s)$, Eq. (4-37) leads to a set of simultaneous linear equations in $F_i(s)$. These equations, together with the restriction on the locations of the poles of $F_i(s)$, do lead to unique solutions of $F_i(s)$.

APPLICATION PROBLEMS

In the following sections, we shall utilize the previous result to study the effects on system performance due to various limiting conditions and to obtain the optimum forms of filtering and compensation under various special circumstances.   In order to demonstrate the physical significances, only one or two limiting conditions are taken up each time. Admittedly, a larger number of limiting conditions may be present in a system; the difference in arriving at a solution is, however, in the amount of effort required rather than in kind.

4-4. Optimum System in the Presence of Load Disturbance.   As an example, we shall study the optimum structure of a positioning system in the presence of load disturbance.   The block diagram of the system is shown in Fig. 4-1, in which $G_3(s) = H_m = 1$, $G_1(s)$ and $G_2(s)$ are known, and G_c and H are to be determined.   In case the controlled system is of the minimum-phase type, we can usually save computation by defining F_1 and F_2 as the system functions C/R and C/D.   The optimization procedure of Sec. 4-2 gives

$$F_1 = \frac{1}{YZ}\left[\frac{\Phi_{r_1 r}}{\bar{Y}\bar{Z}}\right]_+ \tag{4-44}$$

$$F_2 = \frac{k^2}{Y\mathbf{D}}\left[\frac{G_2\mathbf{D}}{G_1\bar{G}_1\bar{Y}}\right]_+ \tag{4-44a}$$

The functions Y, Z, and $\mathbf{D}$ are given in Eqs. (4-27) and (4-27a), with $G_3 = 1$.   The spectral density of the reference input signal, the transfer functions $G_1(s)$ and $G_2(s)$, and the fixed components are given as

$$\Phi_{r_1 r_1} = \Phi_{rr} = \frac{A^2(\omega^2 + \omega_1{}^2)}{\omega^2(\omega^2 + \omega_0{}^2)} \tag{4-45}$$

$$G_1(s) = K_T G_2(s) = \frac{K_T}{\eta s + M s^2} \tag{4-45a}$$

Equation (4-45) implies that the noise is negligible, and (4-45a) implies a disturbing torque or force.

Two different types of load disturbance are studied:

1. White Gaussian disturbance.

$$\Phi_{dd} = B^2$$

2. A random series of step inputs.

$$\Phi_{dd} = \frac{B^2}{\omega_2{}^2 + \omega^2}$$

The load disturbance is assumed to be uncorrelated to the reference input signal.   The closed-loop transfer function F_1 is, according to Eq.

(4-44),

$$F_1 = \frac{1}{YZ}\left[\frac{Z}{Y}\right]_+ \tag{4-46}$$

where $\quad Y = (1 + as)(1 + bs) = \dfrac{1}{\omega_k{}^2}(s^2 + 2\zeta\omega_k s + \omega_k{}^2) \tag{4-47}$

$$Z = \frac{A(s + \omega_1)}{s(s + \omega_0)} \tag{4-48}$$

The constants a and b are the same as those given in Eqs. (2-65) and (2-66), $\zeta = \cos\theta$, and $\omega_k = 1/\tau$. Substituting Eqs. (4-47) and (4-48) in Eq. (4-46), routine calculation gives

$$F_1 = \frac{(s + \omega_1')\omega_1\omega_k{}^2/\omega_1'}{(s + \omega_1)(s^2 + 2\zeta\omega_k s + \omega_k{}^2)} \tag{4-49}$$

where $\quad \omega_1' = \omega_1 \dfrac{\omega_k{}^2 + 2\zeta\omega_0\omega_k + \omega_0{}^2}{\omega_k{}^2 + 2\zeta\omega_1\omega_k + \omega_1\omega_0} \tag{4-50}$

Next we shall determine $F_2(s)$ for the two different types of load disturbance:

Case 1

$$\Phi_{dd} = B^2 \qquad \mathbf{D}(s) = \bar{\mathbf{D}}(s) = B$$

Equation (4-44a) gives

$$\begin{aligned}
F_2(s) &= \frac{k^2}{K_T{}^2}\frac{1}{Y(s)}\left[\frac{-\eta s + Ms^2}{(1 - as)(1 - bs)}\right]_+ \\
&= \frac{k^2}{K_T{}^2}\frac{1}{Y(s)}\left[\frac{M}{ab} + \frac{C_1}{1 - as} + \frac{C_2}{1 - bs}\right]_+
\end{aligned} \tag{4-51}$$

where C_1 and C_2 are constants. We note that the constant term represents a pole at infinity.† Since $Y(s)$ and $\bar{Y}(s)$ are of the order of s^2 at infinity, it is possible for $F_2(s)Y(s)$ to have a pole at infinity but not for $X_2/\bar{Y}(s)$. Consequently the term M/ab is considered an LHP term, and we have

$$F_2(s) = \frac{k^2 M}{K_T{}^2 ab}\frac{1}{Y(s)} = \frac{k\omega_k{}^2/K_T}{s^2 + 2\zeta\omega_k s + \omega_k{}^2} \tag{4-52}$$

† If a is finite and nonvanishing, a pole at a can be written as either $C/(s - a)$ or $C'/(1 - s/a)$. As a approaches infinity, the former form cannot be used since it becomes identically zero, unless we make the assumption that C is proportional to a, which reduces it to the latter form. The latter form reduces to a constant C' as a approaches infinity.

Another way of obtaining the same result is to determine the limiting form of the function YDF_2 as s approaches infinity. Since the loop gain of the system must approach 0 as ω becomes infinity,

$$F_2 \to G_2 \qquad \text{and} \qquad YDF_2 \to \frac{k}{G_1}BG_2 = \frac{kB}{K_T}$$

From Eqs. (4-4) and (4-5), the compensating network G_c and feedback function H are obtained:

$$G_c = \frac{1}{k} \frac{\omega_1}{\omega_1'} \frac{s + \omega_1'}{s + \omega_1} \tag{4-53}$$

$$H = -\frac{k\eta\omega_1's}{K_T\omega_1} \frac{s + \omega_1}{s + \omega_1'} + \frac{2\zeta\omega_1's}{\omega_1\omega_k} \frac{s + \omega_1 - \omega_k(\omega_1/\omega_1' - 1)/2\zeta}{s + \omega_1'} \tag{4-54}$$

Equations (4-53) and (4-54) are illustrated in Fig. 4-2. If there is additional damping due to armature speed emf, η in the regenerative feedback branch is replaced by $\eta + K_eK_T/R_a$, as shown by the dashed line in Fig. 4-2.

If ω_0 is negligibly small, the term $\omega_1 - \omega_k(\omega_1/\omega_1' - 1)/2\zeta$ vanishes, and the lead network in the degenerative feedback branch is replaced by a differentiating circuit with time constant $\omega_1'^{-1}$. The system becomes a type 2 system. Physically, Φ_{rr} of Eq. (4-45) may represent a composite series of random step and ramp inputs, and ω_0 is due to the correlation between successive ramp inputs. If the slope of the reference input $r(t)$ does not change frequently, ω_0 would be relatively small, and we obtain a type 2 system as the optimum result.

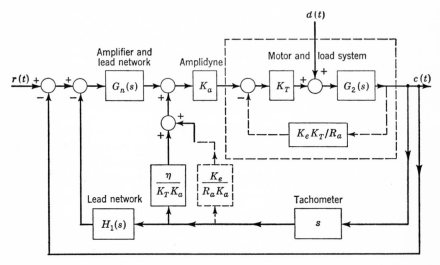

FIG. 4-2. Optimum compensation of a system in the presence of white Gaussian load disturbance.

$$H_1(s) = \frac{2\zeta\omega_1''}{\omega_1\omega_k} \frac{1 + s/\omega_1''}{1 + s/\omega_1'} \quad \text{lead network}$$

$$\omega_1'' = \omega_1 - \frac{\omega_k(\omega_1/\omega_1' - 1)}{2\zeta}$$

$$G_n(s) = \frac{1}{kK_a} \frac{1 + s/\omega_1'}{1 + s/\omega_1}$$

Case 2

$$\Phi_{dd} = \frac{B^2}{\omega_2{}^2 + \omega^2} \qquad D = \frac{B}{s + \omega_2}$$

Equation (4-44a) gives

$$F_2(s) = \frac{k^2}{K_T{}^2} \frac{s + \omega_2}{Y(s)} \left[\frac{-\eta s + M s^2}{(1 - as)(1 - bs)(s + \omega_2)} \right]_+$$

$$= \frac{k^2}{K_T{}^2} \frac{M\omega_2{}^2 + \eta\omega_2}{(1 + a\omega_2)(1 + b\omega_2)} \frac{1}{Y(s)}$$

$$= \frac{k}{K_T} \frac{\alpha(\omega_2)}{Y(s)} = \frac{k\omega_k{}^2 \alpha(\omega_2)/K_T}{s^2 + 2\zeta\omega_k s + \omega_k{}^2} \tag{4-55}$$

where

$$\alpha(\omega_2) = \frac{\omega_2{}^2 + \eta\omega_2/M}{\omega_2{}^2 + 2\zeta\omega_2\omega_k + \omega_k{}^2} \tag{4-56}$$

From Eqs. (4-4) and (4-5), G_c and H are obtained as

$$G_c = \frac{1}{k\alpha(\omega_2)} \frac{\omega_1}{\omega_1'} \frac{s + \omega_1'}{s + \omega_1} \tag{4-57}$$

$$H = \frac{k\alpha\omega_1'}{K_T\omega_1} \frac{s + \omega_1}{s + \omega_1'} \left(-\eta s + \frac{1 - \alpha}{\alpha} M s^2 \right)$$

$$+ \frac{2\zeta\omega_1' s[s + \omega_1 - \omega_k(\omega_1/\omega_1' - 1)/2\zeta]}{\omega_1\omega_k(s + \omega_1')} \tag{4-58}$$

Equations (4-57) and (4-58) are illustrated in Fig. 4-3. Physically, the spectral density Φ_{dd} of case 2 corresponds to persistent load disturb-

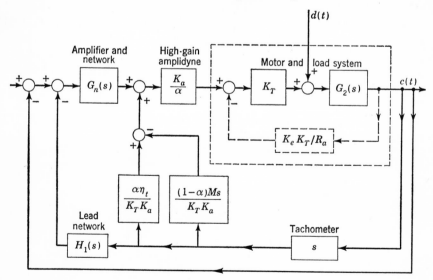

FIG. 4-3. Optimum compensation of a system in the presence of persistent load disturbance. $\eta_t = \eta + K_e K_T/R_a$. $H_1(s)$ and $G_n(s)$ are the same functions of s as in Fig. 4-2.

ance.   The smaller the value of ω_2, the longer the load disturbance is applied before it shifts in value.   From Eq. (4-56), we see that $\alpha(\omega_2)$ is approximately proportional to ω_2, and the amplifier gain varies as $1/\omega_2$.   With increased amplifier gain, the output variable is less and less affected by the presence of load disturbance.   Equation (4-58) shows that the higher amplifier gain is offset by additional degenerative feedback, so that the closed-loop transfer function $F_1 = C/R$ is not altered.

The above two cases are an interesting illustration of the "engineering common sense" of the optimization process.   If the load disturbance is of the impulse type given in case 1, it would pay to save the motor power and let the load system inertia play some part in counteracting the disturbance.   If the load disturbance is a series of persistent step inputs, it must be balanced to a greater extent by motor power, and the amplifier gain is raised to make this possible.

4-5. Noise and Optimum Filtering.   In the literature there are various ways of reducing the undesirable effects of noise: nonlinear devices which operate on the amplitude and linear devices which operate on the frequency.   We may say that, if phase coherence exists between the various Fourier components of the desired signal, a nonlinear device is sometimes effective.   Without such phase coherence, linear filtering appears to be the only method.   At present, we shall take up only optimum linear filtering and omit the nonlinear devices completely.

There is a significant difference between conventional filter theory and the optimum filtering that we are about to discuss.   In conventional filters we usually disregard the phase relationship between the input and output signals; however, in servo work the phase error is at least as important as the amplitude error.   The system error is defined as $r(t) - c(t)$ in the time domain.   When transformed into the frequency domain, the Fourier component of the error is the vector difference between the Fourier components of the input and output signals.

We shall illustrate our method for determining the optimum filter in the presence of noise of the following two types:

1. Sinusoidal noise
2. White Gaussian noise

Case 1.   Sinusoidal Noise

$$\Phi_{nn}(j\omega) = \frac{4aa^*(a + a^*)P_n}{(\omega^2 + a^2)(\omega^2 + a^{*2})} \tag{4-59}$$

where P_n is the noise power, a^* is the conjugate of a,

$$a = \epsilon + j\omega_0$$

and ϵ is a very small constant.   If the noise is a perfect sinusoidal wave,

ϵ approaches 0 as its limit. From Eq. (4-27a) we have

$$Z\bar{Z} = \Phi_{rr}(j\omega) + \frac{4aa^*(a + a^*)P_n}{(\omega^2 + a^2)(\omega^2 + a^{*2})}$$

$$= \Phi_{rr}(j\omega)\left[1 + \frac{4aa^*(a + a^*)}{(\omega^2 + a^2)(\omega^2 + a^{*2})}\frac{P_n}{\Phi_{rr}(j\omega_0)}\right] \quad (4\text{-}60)$$

It is permissible to replace the function $\Phi_{rr}(j\omega)$ in the brackets by its value at ω_0, since $\Phi_{nn}(j\omega)$ vanishes except at the vicinity of ω_0. Equation (4-60) becomes

$$\frac{Z\bar{Z}}{\Phi_{rr}(j\omega)} = \frac{\omega^4 + \omega^2(a^2 + a^{*2}) + a^2a^{*2} + 4aa^*(a + a^*)P_n/\Phi_{rr}(j\omega_0)}{(\omega^2 + a^2)(\omega^2 + a^{*2})} \quad (4\text{-}61)$$

Next, we shall proceed to determine the roots of the numerator polynomial. Since it is a real and even polynomial of ω and s, the roots are symmetrically located in foursomes. We write these roots as $\pm b$ and $\pm b^*$.

$$(\omega^2 + b^2)(\omega^2 + b^{*2}) = \omega^4 + \omega^2(a^2 + a^{*2}) + a^2a^{*2} + \frac{4aa^*(a + a^*)P_n}{\Phi_{rr}(j\omega_0)}$$

$$\quad (4\text{-}62)$$

Comparing coefficients of the ω^2 term and the constant term,

$$b^2 + b^{*2} = a^2 + a^{*2} = 2(\epsilon^2 - \omega_0^2) \quad (4\text{-}63)$$

$$b^2b^{*2} = a^2a^{*2} + \frac{4aa^*(a + a^*)P_n}{\Phi_{rr}(j\omega_0)} \quad (4\text{-}64)$$

Substituting $\epsilon + j\omega_0$ for a, Eq. (4-64) becomes

$$b^2b^{*2} = (\epsilon^2 + \omega_0^2)\left(\epsilon^2 + \omega_0^2 + \frac{8\epsilon P_n}{\Phi_{rr}}\right) \quad (4\text{-}65)$$

Taking the square root on both sides of Eq. (4-65) and expressing the right-hand side in a power series, we obtain

$$bb^* = \omega_0^2 + \frac{4P_n}{\Phi_{rr}}\epsilon + \left(1 + \frac{8P_n^2}{\omega_0^2\Phi_{rr}^2}\right)\epsilon^2 + \cdots \quad (4\text{-}66)$$

If we define ϵ' and ω_0' by $b \equiv \epsilon' + j\omega_0'$, Eqs. (4-63) and (4-66) can be combined as

$$\epsilon'^2 = \frac{1}{4}(b^2 + b^{*2}) + \frac{1}{2}bb^* = \frac{2P_n}{\Phi_{rr}}\epsilon + \left(1 + \frac{4P_n^2}{\omega_0^2\Phi_{rr}^2}\right)\epsilon^2 + \cdots \quad (4\text{-}67)$$

Neglecting ϵ^2 and smaller terms, we have

$$\epsilon' = \sqrt{\frac{2P_n\epsilon}{\Phi_{rr}(j\omega_0)}} \quad (4\text{-}68)$$

$$\omega_0'^2 = \frac{1}{2}bb^* - \frac{1}{4}(b^2 + b^{*2}) = \omega_0^2 + \frac{2P_n}{\Phi_{rr}}\epsilon + \frac{4P_n^2}{\omega_0^2\Phi_{rr}^2}\epsilon^2 + \cdots \quad (4\text{-}69)$$

Neglecting ϵ and smaller terms, Eq. (4-69) gives

$$\omega_0' = \omega_0 \tag{4-70}$$

We note that the accuracy of Eqs. (4-68) and (4-70) improves as ϵ becomes smaller. As ϵ approaches zero, both equations become exact.

From Eq. (4-61) we have

$$\frac{\bar{Z}Z}{\bar{R}R} = \frac{(s^2 + b^2)(s^2 + b^{*2})}{(s^2 - a^2)(s^2 - a^{*2})} \tag{4-71}$$

Consequently

$$\frac{Z}{R} = \frac{(s + b)(s + b^*)}{(s + a)(s + a^*)} = \frac{s^2 + 2\epsilon's + \omega_0^2}{s^2 + 2\epsilon s + \omega_0^2} \tag{4-72}$$

Equation (4-44) becomes

$$F_1 = \frac{R}{Z} \frac{1}{YR} \left[\frac{R}{\bar{Y}} \left(\overline{\frac{R}{Z}} \right) \right]_+ \tag{4-73}$$

Since $(\overline{R/Z})$ is very close to unity except at the vicinities of $s = \pm j\omega_0$, and $j\omega_0$ is not likely to be one of the poles, the factor $(\overline{R/Z})$ has negligible effect on the LHP terms in the partial-fraction expansion. Equation (4-73) can be written as

$$F_1 = \frac{s^2 + 2\epsilon s + \omega_0^2}{s^2 + 2\epsilon's + \omega_0^2} \frac{1}{YR} \left[\frac{R}{\bar{Y}} \right]_+ \tag{4-74}$$

We see that Eq. (4-74) can be realized by inserting a filter at the input end of the system, as shown in Fig. 4-4. For purely sinusoidal noise, the

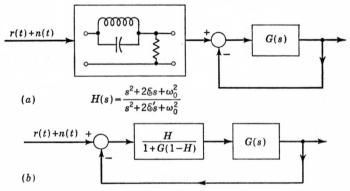

FIG. 4-4. Optimum filtering of sinusoidal noise. (a) Filtering ahead of summing point; (b) filtering after summing point.

constant ϵ is determined by the Q value of the available resonant circuit: $\epsilon = \omega_0/2Q$, and the constant ϵ' is determined by Eq. (4-68).†

Case 2. White Gaussian Noise

$$\Phi_{nn}(j\omega) = A_n{}^2$$

When the noise spectrum distributes over a wide range of frequencies, we would expect the optimum filter to depend on $\Phi_{rr}(j\omega)$ for all frequencies

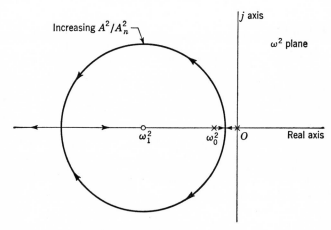

FIG. 4-5. Root-square-locus plot of Φ_{rr}/Φ_{nn}. The roots are zeros of $Z\bar{Z}$.

rather than on $\Phi_{rr}(j\omega_0)$ of one single frequency, as shown in case 1. Let us assume the spectral density $\Phi_{rr}(j\omega)$ of Eq. (4-45). From Eq. (4-27a) we have

$$\bar{Z}Z = \frac{A^2(\omega^2 + \omega_1{}^2)}{\omega^2(\omega^2 + \omega_0{}^2)} + A_n{}^2 \qquad (4\text{-}75)$$

The zeros of $\bar{Z}Z$ can be obtained, in general, by making the root-square-locus plot of $A^2(\omega^2 + \omega_1{}^2)/A_n{}^2\omega^2(\omega^2 + \omega_0{}^2)$, as shown in Fig. 4-5. In a

† In Eq. (4-74), the engineering "common sense" of the optimization process is again illustrated. In most applications, ω_0 is outside the servo bandwidth; nevertheless Eq. (4-74) prescribes a notch filter rather than a low-pass filter. The reason is that a notch filter has much less phase-shift at lower frequencies compared with that of a low-pass filter, and therefore its phase error is much less. Sometimes the sinusoidal noise is generated inside a control element in the servo loop, e.g., the phase-sensitive detector in a carrier system. The same procedure leads to a notch filter for the second-harmonic carrier current with the only difference that the constant ϵ is determined by the bandwidth of $r(t)$ instead of by the available Q because the second-harmonic carrier current has a bandwidth twice that of $r(t)$. A notch filter in the servo loop does not reduce the phase margin nearly as much as does a low-pass filter.

simple case such as the present one the zeros can also be easily calculated:

$$\bar{Z}Z = \frac{A_n^2(\omega^2 + \omega_3^2)(\omega^2 + \omega_4^2)}{\omega^2(\omega^2 + \omega_0^2)} \tag{4-76}$$

where

$$\omega_3^2, \omega_4^2 = -\frac{1}{2}\left(\omega_0^2 + \frac{A^2}{A_n^2}\right) \pm \frac{1}{2}\sqrt{\left(\omega_0^2 + \frac{A^2}{A_n^2}\right)^2 - \frac{4\omega_1^2 A^2}{A_n^2}}$$

From Eq. (4-76),

$$Z = \frac{A_n(s + \omega_3)(s + \omega_4)}{s(s + \omega_0)} \tag{4-77}$$

Let Φ_{rr} be factored into $\bar{R}R$. Since $\Phi_{r_1r} = \Phi_{rr}$, Eq. (4-44) becomes

$$F_1 = \frac{1}{YZ}\left[\frac{\bar{R}R}{\bar{Y}\bar{Z}}\right]_+ = \frac{1}{YZ}\left[\frac{A\omega_1\bar{R}(0)}{\omega_0\bar{Y}(0)\bar{Z}(0)}\frac{1}{s} - \frac{A(\omega_1 - \omega_0)\bar{R}(-\omega_0)}{\omega_0\bar{Y}(-\omega_0)\bar{Z}(-\omega_0)}\frac{1}{s + \omega_0}\right]$$

$$= \frac{A}{YZ}\left[\frac{\omega_1}{\omega_0}\frac{1}{s} - \frac{\omega_1 - \omega_0}{\omega_0}\frac{R(\omega_0)}{Y(\omega_0)Z(\omega_0)}\frac{1}{s + \omega_0}\right] \tag{4-78}$$

$$F_1 = \frac{A}{YZ}\frac{\omega_1(s + \omega_1'')}{\omega_1'' s(s + \omega_0)} \tag{4-79}$$

where $\omega_1'' = \dfrac{\omega_1\omega_0}{\omega_1[1 - R(\omega_0)/Y(\omega_0)Z(\omega_0)] + \omega_0 R(\omega_0)/Y(\omega_0)Z(\omega_0)}$ (4-80)

Equations (4-77) and (4-79) give

$$F_1 = \frac{A}{A_n}\frac{\omega_1}{\omega_1''}\frac{s + \omega_1''}{(s + \omega_3)(s + \omega_4)}\frac{1}{Y(s)}$$

$$= \frac{\omega_3\omega_4}{\omega_1''}\frac{s + \omega_1''}{(s + \omega_3)(s + \omega_4)}\frac{1}{Y(s)} \tag{4-81}$$

Without noise, the optimum system function F_1 is

$$F_{10} = \frac{\omega_1}{\omega_1'}\frac{s + \omega_1'}{s + \omega_1}\frac{1}{Y(s)} \tag{4-82}$$

where $\omega_1' = \dfrac{\omega_1\omega_0}{\omega_1[1 - 1/Y(\omega_0)] + \omega_0/Y(\omega_0)}$ (4-83)

Equation (4-81) can be interpreted as inserting a lag network $1/(s + \omega_4)$ for filtering and as shifting the critical frequencies ω_1' and ω_1 to ω_1'' and ω_3, respectively, so that the low-frequency response is least disturbed.

Obviously, $F_1(s)$ of Eqs. (4-74) and (4-81) can be paired with $F_2(s)$ of Sec. 4-4 to synthesize an optimum system in the presence of both noise and load disturbance. The technique is entirely the same as that given in Sec. 4-4.

4-6. Systems with Multiple Constraints. Systems with multiple constraints can be optimized by a slight extension of the general method.

As will be shown in the following paragraphs, the main effect of additional constraints is to alter the function $Y(s)$.

Let us consider the system of Fig. 4-6. There are two essential constraints in the system: the control field current i_f of the amplidyne and the heat loss in both the servomotor and the amplidyne. As the variable portions of the heat loss in both components are proportional to the armature current $\overline{i_a^2}$, we shall impose the more severe limitation of the two on $\overline{i_a^2}$. In case the servomotor is driven by a shunt generator instead of

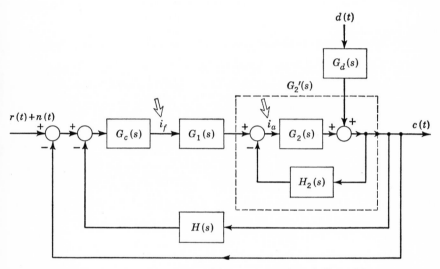

FIG. 4-6. Block diagram of a system with two constraints (indicated by arrows).

the amplidyne, the instantaneous generator field emf e_f should be used instead of i_f.

The Laplace transforms of i_a and i_f are expressed in terms of the input as

$$I_a(s) = \frac{1}{G_2(s)} \{[R(s) + N(s)]F_1(s) + [F_2(s) - G_d(s)]D(s)\} \quad (4\text{-}84)$$

$$I_f(s) = \frac{1}{G_1(s)G_2'(s)} \{[R(s) + N(s)]F_1(s) + [F_2(s) - G_d(s)]D(s)\} \quad (4\text{-}85)$$

where $G_2'(s)$ is the transfer function of the servomotor including the effect of counter emf. The integral to be minimized is

$$J_t = \overline{e^2} + k_1{}^2\overline{i_a{}^2} + k_2{}^2\overline{i_f{}^2} = \frac{1}{2\pi} \int_{-j\infty}^{j\infty} \psi_t(s)\, ds \quad (4\text{-}86)$$

where

$$\psi_t(s) = (\bar{F}_1 - 1)(F_1 - 1)\Phi_{rr} + \bar{F}_1 F_1 \Phi_{nn} + \bar{F}_2 F_2 \Phi_{dd} + \bar{F}_1 F_2 \Phi_{nd} + \bar{F}_2 F_1 \Phi_{dn}$$
$$+ (\bar{F}_1 - 1)F_1 \Phi_{rn} + (F_1 - 1)\bar{F}_1 \Phi_{nr} + (\bar{F}_1 - 1)F_2 \Phi_{rd}$$
$$+ (F_1 - 1)\bar{F}_2 \Phi_{dr} + \left(\frac{k_1^2}{\bar{G}_2 G_2} + \frac{k_2^2}{\bar{G}_1 G_1 \bar{G}_2' G_2'}\right)[\bar{F}_1 F_1 (\Phi_{rr} + \Phi_{nn})$$
$$+ \Phi_{rn} + \Phi_{nr}) + (\bar{F}_2 - \bar{G}_d)(F_2 - G_d)\Phi_{dd}$$
$$+ \bar{F}_1 (F_2 - G_d)(\Phi_{dr} + \Phi_{nd}) + F_1 (\bar{F}_2 - \bar{G}_d)(\Phi_{dr} + \Phi_{dn})] \quad (4\text{-}87)$$

Differentiating Eq. (4-87) with respect to $\bar{F}_1$ and $\bar{F}_2$, respectively, gives

$$X_{R1} = \left(1 + \frac{k_1^2}{\bar{G}_2 G_2} + \frac{k_2^2}{\bar{G}_1 G_1 \bar{G}_2' G_2'}\right)[(\Phi_{rr} + \Phi_{nn} + \Phi_{rn} + \Phi_{nr})F_1$$
$$+ (\Phi_{rd} + \Phi_{nd})F_2] - (\Phi_{rr} + \Phi_{nr}) - G_d\left(\frac{k_1^2}{\bar{G}_2 G_2} + \frac{k_2^2}{\bar{G}_1 G_1 \bar{G}_2' G_2'}\right)(\Phi_{rd} + \Phi_{nd})$$

$$(4\text{-}88)$$

$$X_{R2} = \left(1 + \frac{k_1^2}{\bar{G}_2 G_2} + \frac{k_2^2}{\bar{G}_1 G_1 \bar{G}_2' G_2'}\right)[\Phi_{dd} F_2 + (\Phi_{dn} + \Phi_{dr})F_1]$$
$$- \Phi_{dr} - \left(\frac{k_1^2}{\bar{G}_2 G_2} + \frac{k_2^2}{\bar{G}_1 G_1 \bar{G}_2' G_2'}\right)G_d \Phi_{dd} \quad (4\text{-}89)$$

We shall assume as before that $r(t)$, $n(t)$, and $d(t)$ are not correlated, and consequently all the cross-spectral densities vanish. Equations (4-88) and (4-89) reduce to the same form as Eqs. (4-25) and (4-26) except that the function $Y(s)\bar{Y}(s)$ is replaced by

$$\bar{Y}(s)Y(s) = 1 + \frac{k_1^2}{\bar{G}_2 G_2} + \frac{k_2^2}{\bar{G}_1 G_1 \bar{G}_2' G_2'} \quad (4\text{-}90)$$

In a positioning system employing an amplidyne-driven shunt motor,

$$G_1 = \frac{K_a}{1 + T_q s} \qquad G_2 = \frac{K_T}{\eta s + M s^2}$$

and $G_2' = K_T/(\eta_t s + M s)$, where $\eta_t = \eta + K_T K_e/(R_g + R_a)$. Equation (4-90) becomes

$$\bar{Y}(s)Y(s) = 1 - \frac{k_1^2}{K_T^2} s^2(\eta^2 - M^2 s^2) - \frac{k_2^2}{K_T^2} s^2(\eta_t^2 - M^2 s^2)(1 - T_q^2 s^2)$$

$$(4\text{-}91)$$

The right-hand side of Eq. (4-91) can be factored by solving a third-order algebraic equation in s^2. While this is not difficult to do, a more general method appears desirable. Equation (4-90) gives

$$\bar{Y}(s)Y(s) = 1 + \frac{k_1^2}{\bar{G}_2 G_2}\left(1 + \frac{k_2^2 \bar{G}_2 G_2}{k_1^2 \bar{G}_1 G_1 \bar{G}_2' G_2'}\right) \quad (4\text{-}92)$$

Equation (4-92) can be solved, in general, by two root-square-locus plots in succession. We shall plot first the root-square locus with (k_1^2/k_2^2) $\bar{G}_1 G_1 \bar{G}_2' G_2'/\bar{G}_2 G_2$ as the "open-loop" transfer function. The set of closed-loop poles so obtained are joined by the poles and zeros of $\bar{G}_2 G_2$, and another set of root-square loci is plotted. The procedure is similar to the root-locus plot for multiloop systems.

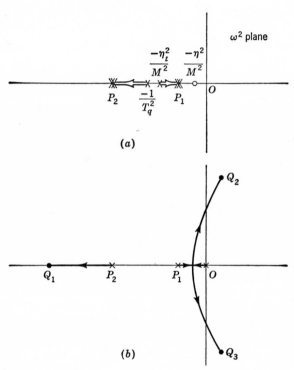

FIG. 4-7. Successive root-square-loci plot for determining the roots Q_1, Q_2, Q_3 of $Y\bar{Y}$.

Figure 4-7 illustrates such a plot for Eq. (4-91). Letting Ω denote $-s^2$, we have

$$\frac{k_1^2}{k_2^2} \frac{\bar{G}_1 G_1 \bar{G}_2' G_2'}{\bar{G}_2 G_2} = \frac{k_1^2 K_a^2 (\eta^2 + M^2 \Omega)}{k_2^2 (1 + T_q^2 \Omega)(\eta_t^2 + M^2 \Omega)} \tag{4-93}$$

There are two "open-loop" poles at $-1/T_q^2$ and $-\eta_t^2/M^2$ and one zero at $-\eta^2/M^2$. The first set of root-square loci is shown in Fig. 4-7a as double lines on the negative real axis. For a given ratio of k_1^2/k_2^2, a pair of poles P_1 and P_2 are obtained. If the saturation value I_{fs} of i_f is much larger than $(R_g + R_a) I_{as}/K_a$, where I_{as} is the limiting value of i_a, the "gain" ratio k_1^2/k_2^2 would be relatively large. P_1 is very close to $-\eta^2/M^2$, and P_2 is approximately $-k_1^2 K_a^2/k_2^2 T_q^2$.

For the second set of root-loci plots, we notice that $\bar{G}_2 G_2$ has a pole at the origin and a pole at $-\eta^2/M^2$. The latter cancels the zero at $-\eta^2/M^2$, and we have altogether three poles at O, P_1, and P_2 to start with. In Fig. 4-7b the root-square loci are shown as the heavy lines. For large gain or small k_1, the three branches approach three asymptotes 120° apart.

Corresponding to a given value of $K_T{}^2/k_1{}^2$, there are three "closed-loop" poles Q_1, Q_2, and Q_3. Let q_1, q_2, and q_3 denote $\sqrt{-Q_1}$, $\sqrt{-Q_2}$, and $\sqrt{-Q_3}$ with their signs so selected that all three are located in the LHP. The function $Y(s)$ is obtained as

$$Y(s) = \left(1 - \frac{s}{q_1}\right)\left(1 - \frac{s}{q_2}\right)\left(1 - \frac{s}{q_3}\right) \tag{4-94}$$

Once $Y(s)$ is determined, the rest of the procedure in synthesizing the system is the same as that of Sec. 4-4.

4-7. Examples of Unstable Systems and Systems with Nonminimum Phase. We may define a nonminimum-phase dynamical system as one which has at least one zero in the RHP. In contrast, an unstable system is one which has at least one pole in the RHP. The latter appears to be more difficult to control while operating alone; however, it is far less a problem in a closed-loop system. A pole in the RHP can easily be removed by closing the feedback loop, but a zero in the RHP remains intact no matter what we do with the servo system, using series or parallel compensation or any combination thereof.

As examples in practice, a two-phase servomotor with a rotor resistance which is not sufficiently high would possess a pole in the RHP. A tail-controlled steering system may have a pole in the RHP, a zero in the RHP, or both. We shall discuss the servomotor first. The torque-versus-speed curve of a servomotor depends very much on the internal impedance of the control phase amplifier. The standard procedure of a manufacturer's test is to connect both phases into sources of zero internal impedance. If the rotor resistance (in stator terms) is larger than the leakage impedance, the motor torque would reduce as it speeds up, as shown by the set of solid lines of Fig. 4-8. However, in actual operation, the internal impedance of the control amplifier is by no means negligible, especially when a capacitor is connected across its output end. If the rotor resistance is approximately equal to or lower than the magnetizing impedance, the motor torque may increase with speed for small speeds in actual operation, as shown by the broken lines of Fig. 4-8. Let α denote the slope of the torque-versus-speed curve at zero speed (Y axis). For small signals,

$$J \frac{d^2\theta}{dt^2} = T = T_0 + \alpha \frac{d\theta}{dt} = K_T e_i + \alpha \frac{d\theta}{dt} \tag{4-95}$$

where e_i is the input voltage to the control amplifier and θ is the shaft position. Equation (4-95) can be written as the following transfer function:

$$\frac{\Theta(s)}{E_i(s)} = \frac{K_T}{Js^2 - \alpha s} \tag{4-96}$$

There is a pole at α/J. If α is positive, the pole is in the RHP, indicating that the motor is liable to run away by itself under open-loop conditions.

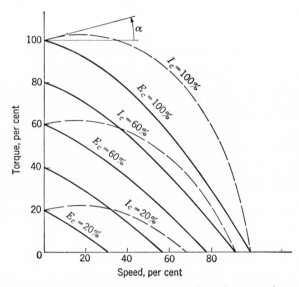

FIG. 4-8. Typical torque-versus-speed characteristics of a two-phase servomotor. Solid lines, operation with zero control phase impedance; dashed lines, operation with large control phase impedance.

The pole is readily removed by introducing a minor feedback loop, as shown in Fig. 4-9a. The feedback element may be either an a-c tachometer or a friction cup, and the equivalent transfer function including minor feedback loop is

$$G_e(s) = \frac{K_T}{Js^2 + (\beta - \alpha)s} \tag{4-97}$$

If β is numerically larger than α, the pole in the RHP is removed. An alternative is that we may leave the motor as it is and stabilize the closed-loop system by means of a lead network, as shown in Fig. 4-9b. The latter method, however, requires precision gears. Gear backlash is outside the stabilizing loop in case a but inside the stabilizing loop in case b, since the main loop is the stabilizing loop. It is not difficult to see why in the latter case any gear backlash would result in chatter noise.

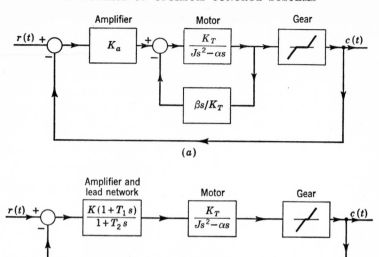

FIG. 4-9. Two methods of removing an RHP pole of the load system. (a) Minor feedback loop; (b) lead-network compensation.

Neither case imposes a restriction on the form that the closed-loop transfer function C/R takes.

The aircraft-pitch control problem furnishes an interesting illustration of the nonminimum-phase effect. With reference to Fig. 4-10, the dynamics of a tail-controlled airframe is described by the following equations:

$$Ma = MV \frac{d\beta}{dt} = C_L\alpha - C_F\delta \tag{4-98}$$

$$J \frac{dq}{dt} = C_T\delta - C_M\alpha - C_q q \tag{4-99}$$

where the variables α, β, γ, and δ are measured from a set of initially balanced values. The angles α, β, and γ are assumed to be small enough so that the gravitational force can be regarded as constant and absorbed into the initial values. The forward velocity V is also assumed constant. Equations (4-98) and (4-99) describe the balance of force and balance of moments, respectively. Their physical meaning can be understood from the following example: Suppose that there is a commanding input for the aircraft to accelerate upward. The acceleration error signal causes the controller to actuate a hydraulic transmission system which in turn raises the elevator of the aircraft. The immediate aerodynamic force tends, however, to push the aircraft downward as a whole, and particularly to push its tail downward. This results in a slanting of the plane with its nose pointing up, and the plane gradually accelerates upward but at an oscillatory rate. Mathematically, the immediate downward force is represented by the term $-C_F\delta$ in Eq. (4-98) and the turning moment is represented by $C_T\delta$ in Eq. (4-99). The term $C_L\alpha$ represents the essential lift force which accelerates the aircraft upward.

Since $\alpha = \gamma - \beta$, the linear acceleration a can be expressed in terms of α and q. It is

$$a = V\frac{d\beta}{dt} = V\left(q - \frac{d\alpha}{dt}\right) \tag{4-100}$$

A differential equation of a in terms of δ is obtained by eliminating α and q in Eqs. (4-98) to (4-100):

$$\frac{d^2a}{dt^2} + \left(\frac{C_q}{J} + \frac{C_L}{MV}\right)\frac{da}{dt} + \left(\frac{C_M}{J} + \frac{C_qC_L}{JMV}\right)a = -\frac{C_F}{M}\frac{d^2\delta}{dt^2}$$
$$- \frac{C_FC_q}{JM}\frac{d\delta}{dt} + \frac{1}{JM}(C_TC_L - C_FC_M)\delta \tag{4-101}$$

From the above equation, the transfer function of the controlled system is obtained:

$$\frac{A(s)}{\Delta(s)} = \frac{-(C_F/M)s^2 - (C_FC_q/JM)s + (C_TC_L - C_FC_M)/JM}{s^2 + (C_q/J + C_L/MV)s + C_M/J + C_qC_L/JMV} \tag{4-102}$$

We see that a zero in the RHP is introduced by the $-C_F\delta$ term which represents an immediate downward force following an elevator movement upward. The locations of the poles depend primarily on the sign of C_M/J, which is numerically larger than C_qC_L/JMV in most cases. If

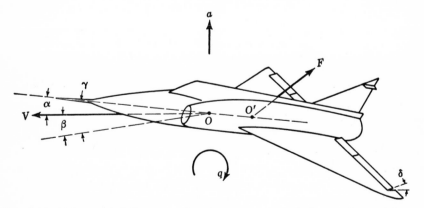

Fig. 4-10. Airframe-pitch linear acceleration system, a typical case of nonminimum phase.

the center of force, O', is behind the center of mass, O, as shown in Fig. 4-10, C_M is positive and the open-loop system is stable.   If the center of force is sufficiently ahead of the center of mass, the constant term $C_M/J + C_qC_L/JMV$ is negative, and a pole in the RHP is introduced.   The system will not be stable without automatic control.

Ship and submarine steering problems are dynamically similar to the aircraft-pitch control problem and can be described by substantially the same equations.   However, because of the appreciable inertia of the surrounding water, the effective mass of a ship or a submarine is larger than its actual mass and is different in different directions.   Let M_t denote the transverse mass and M_l denote the longitudinal mass.   For aircraft control, Eqs. (4-98) and (4-100) can be combined as

$$MVq - MV\frac{d\alpha}{dt} = C_L\alpha - C_F\delta \tag{4-103}$$

For ship and submarine control, the above equation becomes

$$M_lVq - M_tV\frac{d\alpha}{dt} = C_L\alpha - C_F\delta \tag{4-104}$$

Equation (4-104) will replace Eq. (4-98) while Eq. (4-99) and the kinematical relation (4-100) remain unaltered.   The transfer function is of the same form as Eq. (4-102).

Example 4-1.   For the system of Fig. 4-1, the following functions are given:

$$\Phi_{rr}(j\omega) = \frac{A^2}{\omega^2} \qquad \Phi_{dd}(j\omega) = \frac{B^2}{\omega^2} \qquad \Phi_{nn} = 0$$
$$G_2(s) = 1$$
$$G_1(s) = \frac{K_m(z_1 - s)(z_2 + s)}{s(s^2 + 2\zeta\omega_0 s + \omega_0^2)}$$

where z_1, z_2, ζ, and ω_0 are positive constants.   Determine the optimum system, under the assumption that there is no limitation on the mean-square amplitude of the input function to $G_1(s)$.   Determine the transient responses of the optimum system to step inputs in $r(t)$ and $d(t)$.

Solution.   Without power constraint, $k = 0$ in Eq. (4-27), and $Y = \bar{Y} = 1$.

$$P = z_1 - s \qquad \bar{P} = z_1 + s$$
$$Z = R = \frac{A}{s} \qquad \mathbf{D} = \frac{B}{s}$$

Equation (4-28) gives

$$F_1 = \frac{s}{A(z_1 + s)}\left[\frac{(z_1 + s)A}{(z_1 - s)s}\right]_+ = \frac{1}{z_1 + s}$$

Similarly, Eq. (4-29) gives

$$F_2 = \frac{1}{z_1 + s}$$

From Eqs. (4-31) and (4-32) we have

$$\frac{C}{R}(s) = \frac{z_1 - s}{z_1 + s}$$

$$\frac{C}{D}(s) = 1 - \frac{z_1 - s}{z_1 + s} = \frac{2s}{z_1 + s}$$

The compensating network G_c, and feedback function H are determined from $(C/R)(s)$ and $(C/D)(s)$:

$$G_c(s)G_1(s) = \frac{(C/R)(s)}{(C/D)(s)} = \frac{z_1 - s}{2s}$$

Therefore,

$$G_c(s) = \frac{1}{2sG_{11}(s)} = \frac{s^2 + 2\zeta\omega_0 s + \omega_0^2}{2K(z_2 + s)}$$

$$H = \frac{1}{C/R} - 1 - \frac{1}{G_cG_1} = \frac{z_1 + s}{z_1 - s} - 1 - \frac{2s}{z_1 - s} = 0$$

The system response to a step input in $r(t)$ is

$$c(t) = \mathcal{L}^{-1}\left\{\frac{z_1 - s}{z_1 + s}\frac{1}{s}\right\} = \mathcal{L}^{-1}\left\{\frac{1}{s} - \frac{2}{z_1 + s}\right\}$$

$$= 1 - 2e^{-z_1 t} \tag{4-105}$$

The system response to a step input in $d(t)$ is

$$c(t) = \mathcal{L}^{-1}\left\{\frac{2s}{z_1 + s}\frac{1}{s}\right\} = 2e^{-z_1 t} \tag{4-106}$$

Equations (4-105) and (4-106) are plotted in Fig. 4-11.

The mean-square error is

$$\overline{e^2} = \frac{1}{2\pi j}\int_{-j\infty}^{j\infty}\left\{\left(1 - \frac{C}{R}\right)\left[1 - \overline{\left(\frac{C}{R}\right)}\right]\left(-\frac{A^2}{s^2}\right) + \frac{C}{D}\overline{\left(\frac{C}{D}\right)}\left(-\frac{B^2}{s^2}\right)\right\}ds$$

$$= \frac{A^2 + B^2}{2\pi j}\int_{-j\infty}^{j\infty}\frac{2}{z_1 + s}\frac{2}{z_1 - s}\,ds = \frac{2}{z_1}(A^2 + B^2) \tag{4-107}$$

The significance of Eq. (4-107) is that it gives the lowest possible error even if unlimited power is available. This error is completely due to the nonminimum-phase characteristic of the load system.

Example 4-2. In Example 4-1, assume that $\overline{[i(t)]^2}$ is limited, where $i(t)$ is the input to the fixed elements $G_1(s)$, and determine $(C/R)(s)$ and $(C/D)(s)$.

Solution. From Eq. (4-27) the functions Y and $\bar{Y}$ are determined by the root-square-locus plot of Sec. 2-7. Note that $Z_1 = -z_1^2$, $Z_2 = -z_2^2$ as before. Let q_1, q_2, and q_3 be the same closed-loop roots with negative real components as in Sec. 2-7. However, as z_1 and z_2 are now positive, Eq. (2-55) gives

$$Y(s) = \frac{(1 - s/q_1)(1 - s/q_2)(1 - s/q_3)}{(1 + s/z_1)(1 + s/z_2)} \tag{4-108}$$

since the critical frequencies of $Y(s)$ are in the LHP, by definition. Equations (4-28) and (4-31) give

$$F_1(s) = \frac{1}{Y\bar{P}}$$

$$\frac{C}{R}(s) = \frac{P}{Y\bar{P}} = \frac{(1 - s/z_1)(1 + s/z_2)}{(1 - s/q_1)(1 - s/q_2)(1 - s/q_3)} \tag{4-109}$$

Equations (4-29) and (4-32) give

$$\frac{C}{D}(s) = 1 - \frac{P}{Y\bar{P}} = 1 - F_1(s) \tag{4-110}$$

Equation (4-110) would result in a system without minor feedback loop. This is because of our assumption that $\Phi_{dd} = B^2/\omega^2$ and $G_d(s) = 1$. In steering systems and aircraft-pitch control systems, the worst type of load disturbance is a turning moment rather than a force applied to the center of mass. In such a case, $G_d(s)$ is a function of s, and a different form of $F_2(s)$ is obtained.

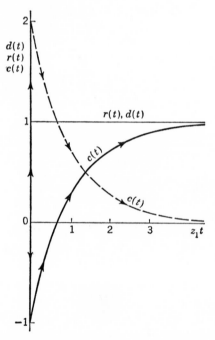

FIG. 4-11. Transient response of an optimum nonminimum-phase system without power constraint. Solid curve, system response to unit step input; dashed curve, system response to unit step load disturbance.

4-8. Wiener's Problem of Optimum Prediction. An obvious situation in fire-control problems is that the desired output variable $c(t)$ is not the input variable $r(t)$ at the present but is $r(t + \alpha)$ at a time α sec later. In Sec. 4-1, it is shown that this requirement can be represented by a predictive operator $L(s) = e^{\alpha s}$. If we assume that there is no constraint due to controlled plant or fixed component, Eq. (4-31) gives the optimum filtering function as

$$F = \frac{1}{Z}\left[\frac{e^{\alpha s}\Phi_{r_1 r}}{\bar{Z}}\right]_+ \tag{4-111}$$

To evaluate the minimum value of mean-square error, we obtain from Eqs. (4-19) to (4-22)

$$\Phi_{ee}(s) = \Phi_{rr} + \bar{F}F\bar{Z}Z - \bar{L}F\Phi_{rr_1} - L\bar{F}\Phi_{r_1r} \qquad (4\text{-}112)$$

Substituting Eq. (4-111) in (4-112), the latter becomes

$$\Phi_{ee}(s) = \frac{1}{\bar{Z}Z}(\Phi_{rr}\Phi_{nn} - \Phi_{rn}\Phi_{nr}) + \left[\frac{e^{\alpha s}\Phi_{r_1r}}{\bar{Z}}\right]_{-}\left[\frac{e^{-\alpha s}\Phi_{rr_1}}{Z}\right]_{+} \qquad (4\text{-}113)$$

Equation (4-113) can be interpreted as follows: The first term represents the error power spectrum with an optimum linear filter having no restriction on its physical realizability or pole locations. The second term represents an additional error power spectrum when the condition of physical realizability is imposed. The proof will be given below. Without consideration of physical realizability, the values of $F(s)$ for different s are independent, or we may say that $F(s)$ is an arbitrary real function of s.

To find the optimum function without any constraint, we differentiate $\Phi_{ee}(s)$ with respect to $\bar{F}(s)$ and set the result to zero:

$$F\bar{Z}Z - L\Phi_{r_1r} = 0 \qquad (4\text{-}114)$$

Therefore
$$F = \frac{e^{\alpha s}\Phi_{r_1r}}{\bar{Z}Z} \qquad (4\text{-}115)$$

Substituting Eq. (4-115) in (4-112),

$$\Phi_{ee}(s) = \Phi_{rr} - \frac{\Phi_{rr_1}\Phi_{r_1r}}{\bar{Z}Z} = \frac{1}{\bar{Z}Z}(\Phi_{rr}\Phi_{nn} - \Phi_{rn}\Phi_{nr}) \qquad (4\text{-}116)$$

Equation (4-116) shows that the first term of Eq. (4-113) is the minimum error resulting from an optimum but unrealizable filter.

Normally $\Phi_{nr} = 0$, $\Phi_{r_1r} = \Phi_{rr}$, and $\bar{Z}Z = \Phi_{rr} + \Phi_{nn}$. This will be assumed in integrating Eq. (4-112) to obtain an explicit expression for the least-mean-square error. Let $R(s)$ be defined by

$$R(s) \equiv \{\Phi_{rr}(s)\}^{+} \qquad (4\text{-}117)$$

$R(s)$ can be written in a partial-fraction expansion:

$$R(s) = \sum_{i} \frac{b_i}{s + p_i} \qquad (4\text{-}118)$$

Let $B(s)$ be defined as
$$B(s) \equiv \frac{e^{-\alpha s}R(s)}{Z(s)} \qquad (4\text{-}119)$$

It follows from the definition of $B(s)$ that all the poles of $B(s)$ are in the

LHP, including that at infinity.   Equation (4-111) gives

$$FZ = [\mathbf{R}(s)B(-s)]_+ = \sum_i \frac{b_i B(p_i)}{s + p_i} \tag{4-120}$$

With the aid of Eqs. (4-118) and (4-119), the four terms of Eq. (4-112) can be readily integrated:

$$\frac{1}{2\pi j} \int_{-\infty}^{j\infty} \Phi_{rr}\, ds = \frac{1}{2\pi j} \int_{-\infty}^{j\infty} \sum_i \sum_j \frac{b_i b_j\, ds}{(s + p_i)(-s + p_j)}$$

$$= \sum_i \sum_j \frac{b_i b_j}{p_i + p_j} \tag{4-121}$$

The above expression is also the mean-square value of the input $r(t)$.
   The second term gives

$$\frac{1}{2\pi j} \int_{-j\infty}^{j\infty} F e^{-\alpha s} \Phi_{rr}\, ds = \frac{1}{2\pi j} \int_{-j\infty}^{j\infty} (FZ) B\bar{R}\, ds$$

$$= \sum_i \sum_j \frac{b_i b_j B(p_i) B(p_j)}{p_i + p_j} \tag{4-122}$$

The above result is obtained by closing the contour of integration with a large semicircle at infinity enclosing the RHP.   It is easy to see that integration of the third and fourth terms gives exactly the same result. Combining all four terms, we obtain finally

$$\overline{e^2} = \sum_i \sum_j \frac{b_i b_j}{p_i + p_j} [1 - B(p_i) B(p_j)] \tag{4-123}$$

Example 4-3.   Given $\Phi_{rr}(j\omega) = A^2/\omega^2(\omega^2 + \omega_1{}^2)$ and $\Phi_{nn}(j\omega) = 1$, determine the optimum system function which predicts $r(t + \alpha)$.
   Solution

$$\Phi_{rr}(s) = \frac{A^2}{s^2(s^2 - \omega_1{}^2)} \tag{4-124}$$

$$\mathbf{R}(s) = \frac{A}{s(s + \omega_1)}$$

$$Z(s) = \frac{(s + a_1)(s + a_2)}{s(s + \omega_1)}$$

where a_1, a_2 are given by

$$a_1, a_2 = \pm \left(\frac{\omega_1{}^2}{2} \pm \sqrt{\frac{\omega_1{}^4}{4} - A^2} \right)^{1/2} \tag{4-125}$$

The signs are so selected that the real components of a_1 and a_2 are positive.   Equation

(4-115) gives

$$F(s) = \frac{1 + Ts}{(1 + s/a)(1 + s/a_2)} \tag{4-126}$$

where $T = [1 - B(\omega_1)]/\omega_1$, and

$$B(\omega_1) = \frac{e^{-\omega_1 \alpha}}{(1 + \omega_1/a_1)(1 + \omega_1/a_2)} \tag{4-127}$$

The mean-square error can be calculated from Eq. (4-123). The two roots of $R(s)$ are 0 and ω_1. Among the four terms of Eq. (4-123), the term with $p_1 = p_2 = 0$ gives the indeterminate form 0/0. In order to determine its value, we assume that $p_1 = p_2 = \epsilon$, a negligibly small but nonvanishing constant:

$$\frac{A^2}{2\epsilon\omega_1{}^2}[1 - B(\epsilon)B(\epsilon)] = \frac{A^2}{\omega_1{}^2}\left(\alpha + \frac{1}{a_1} + \frac{1}{a_2}\right)$$

Equation (4-123) gives

$$\overline{e^2} = \frac{A^2}{\omega_1{}^2}\left(\alpha + \frac{1}{a_1} + \frac{1}{a_2} - T - \frac{\omega_1 T^2}{2}\right) \tag{4-128}$$

4-9. Optimum Filtering of Two Related Signals.

When we have a single signal mixed with noise, any attempt to filter out the noise would also filter out some of the signal. This is no longer true when we have two independent ways of measuring the same signal. Let I_1 and I_2 be the outputs of two independent instruments measuring the same signal R:

$$I_1(s) = H_1(s)R(s) + N_1(s) \tag{4-129}$$
$$I_2(s) = H_2(s)R(s) + N_2(s) \tag{4-130}$$

where $H_1(s)$ and $H_2(s)$ are known operators and N_1, N_2 are independent noise sources with known power spectrum. The problem is to find linear operators $G_1(s)$ and $G_2(s)$ such that

$$C(s) \equiv G_1(s)I_1(s) + G_2(s)I_2(s) = R(s) + N_3(s) \tag{4-131}$$

where N_3 is independent of $R(s)$ and is to have least-mean-square value.

To see how a problem of this sort comes about, let us consider a navigation problem: The latitude of a submarine is to be determined without the benefit of taking a star fix. A gyro pointing north can be fairly accurately maintained since it does not mutate within a 24-hr period. The angle between the vertical axis and the gyro axis gives a direct determination of the latitude. Alternatively, the change in latitude can be determined by integrating the velocity or twice integrating the acceleration in the north-south direction. The integrated signal is more accurate in giving the instantaneous variations in latitude while the gyro signal is more accurate in giving the long-range or averaged latitude. What is the best way of combining these signals to come as close as possible to the instantaneous latitude?

To solve the mathematical problem as outlined above, let us note that $G_1(s)$ and $G_2(s)$ are not independent, owing to the requirement that N_3 is to be independent of $R(s)$.   Let $F(s)$ be defined by

$$G_1(s) = \frac{F(s)}{H_1(s)} \tag{4-132}$$

Substituting Eqs. (4-129), (4-130), and (4-132) in (4-131) and comparing the coefficients of $R(s)$ give

$$G_2(s) = \frac{1 - F(s)}{H_2(s)} \tag{4-133}$$

and $$N_3(s) = \frac{F(s)N_1(s)}{H_1(s)} + \frac{[1 - F(s)]N_2(s)}{H_2(s)} \tag{4-134}$$

Since N_1 and N_2 are independent, Eq. (4-134) gives the following relation between the spectral densities Φ_{11}, Φ_{22}, and Φ_{33} of N_1, N_2, and N_3, respectively:

$$\Phi_{33} = \frac{\bar{F}F\Phi_{11}}{\bar{H}_1 H_1} + \frac{(1 - \bar{F})(1 - F)\Phi_{22}}{\bar{H}_2 H_2} \tag{4-135}$$

For the minimum mean-square value of $n_3(t)$, Eq. (4-37) gives

$$\frac{\Phi_{11}F}{\bar{H}_1 H_1} + \frac{\Phi_{22}(F - 1)}{\bar{H}_2 H_2} = X \tag{4-136}$$

The solution of Eq. (4-136) is

$$F = \frac{1}{Z}\left[\frac{\Phi_{22}}{\bar{H}_2 H_2 \bar{Z}}\right]_+ \tag{4-137}$$

where Z is obtained by factoring

$$\bar{Z}Z = \frac{\Phi_{11}}{\bar{H}_1 H_1} + \frac{\Phi_{22}}{\bar{H}_2 H_2} \tag{4-138}$$

Example 4-4. Given measured position and velocity signals i_1 and i_2 which are mixed with noise of spectral densities Φ_{11} and Φ_{22}, respectively:

$$\Phi_{11} = \frac{A^2}{\omega^2 + a^2} \tag{4-139}$$

$$\Phi_{22} = \frac{B^2}{\omega^2 + a^2} \tag{4-140}$$

(a) Determine G_1 and G_2 to obtain a position signal with least noise.
(b) Determine G_1 and G_2 to obtain a velocity signal with least noise. Calculate the mean-square value of the noise in each case.
Solution. For case a, $H_1 = 1$, $H_2 = s$.

$$\bar{Z}Z = \frac{A^2}{-s^2 + a^2} + \frac{B^2}{-s^2(-s^2 + a^2)} = \frac{A^2(-s^2 + b^2)}{-s^2(-s^2 + a^2)}$$

$$Z = \frac{A(s + b)}{s(s + a)}$$

where $b = B/A$. Equation (4-137) gives

$$F = \frac{s(s + a)}{A(s + b)} \left[\frac{B^2}{As(s + a)(-s + b)} \right]_+$$
$$= \frac{b^2 s(s + a)}{s + b} \left[\frac{1}{abs} - \frac{1}{a(a + b)(s + a)} \right] = \frac{b(s + a + b)}{(a + b)(s + b)}$$

Equations (4-132), (4-133), and (4-135) give

$$G_1(s) = \frac{b(s + a + b)}{(a + b)(s + b)} \tag{4-141}$$

$$G_2(s) = \frac{a}{(a + b)(s + b)} \tag{4-142}$$

$$\Phi_{33} = \frac{b^2[\omega^2 + (a + b)^2 + a^2]}{(a + b)^2(\omega^2 + a^2)(\omega^2 + b^2)} \tag{4-143}$$

Integrating Eqs. (4-139) and (4-143) gives

$$\overline{n_1^2} = \frac{A^2}{4a}$$

$$\overline{n_3^2} = \frac{A^2}{4a} \frac{b(2a + b)}{(a + b)^2}$$

$$\overline{n_1^2} - \overline{n_3^2} = \overline{n_1^2} \left(\frac{a}{a + b} \right)^2 \tag{4-144}$$

Equation (4-144) gives the improvement over using signal i_1 alone.

For case b, $H_1 = 1/s$, $H_2 = 1$.

$$\bar{Z}Z = \frac{A^2(-s^2 + b^2)}{-s^2 + a^2}$$

$$Z = \frac{A(s + b)}{s + a}$$

$$F = \frac{s + a}{A(s + b)} \left[\frac{B^2}{A(s + a)(-s + b)} \right]_+ = \frac{b^2}{(a + b)(s + b)}$$

Equations (4-132), (4-133), and (4-135) give

$$G_1(s) = \frac{b^2 s}{(a + b)(s + b)} \tag{4-145}$$

$$G_2(s) = \frac{s + ab/(a + b)}{s + b} \tag{4-146}$$

$$\Phi_{33} = \frac{B^2[(a^2 + 2ab + 2b^2)\omega^2 + a^2 b^2]}{(a + b)^2(\omega^2 + a^2)(\omega^2 + b^2)} \tag{4-147}$$

Integrating Eqs. (4-140) and (4-147) gives

$$\overline{n_2^2} = \frac{B^2}{4a}$$

$$\overline{n_3^2} = \frac{B^2(a + 2b)}{4(a + b)^2}$$

$$\overline{n_2^2} - \overline{n_3^2} = \overline{n_2^2} \left(\frac{b}{a + b} \right)^2 \tag{4-148}$$

Equations (4-141), (4-142), (4-145), and (4-146) show that the best way of obtaining the velocity signal is not to differentiate the optimum filtered positional signal.   In fact, if the latter method is used, the mean-square value of n_3 turns out to be infinite.   This is to be expected, since an ideal differentiator increases the noise power in proportion to ω^2.

4-10. Summary.   In Chap. 4, we have formulated in general terms the mathematical problem encountered in minimizing mean-square error in the presence of noise, disturbance, and conditions of constraints.   The problem involves simultaneous determination of a number of unknown system functions.

An optimization theorem is stated and proved.   In order that the error integral be a minimum, the functional derivatives of the integrand must not possess any poles in the LHP.   This is an interesting contrast to ordinary variational calculus which states that for an integral to be stationary the functional derivatives of the integrand must be zero.

When load disturbance is present, two optimum closed-loop transfer functions, $F_1 = C/R$ and $F_2 = C/D$, are simultaneously determined. These two functions in turn determine the series- and parallel-compensating elements.   When noise is present, the optimization procedure automatically specifies a noise filter as an integral part of the system.

The presence of additional constraints can be taken into account by successive root-square-locus plots.   It modifies the function $Y(s)$, which represents system compensation.

A nonminimum-phase system is defined as one with a zero in the RHP. An unstable system is defined as one with a pole in the RHP.   The pole can easily be removed and does not constitute a limitation on the system response.   A zero in the RHP is shown to be an essential limitation which cannot be removed by any means whatsoever.   It restricts the forms of C/R and C/D and thereby imposes an intrinsic error on the system response.   As typical illustrations, a two-phase servomotor with insufficiently high rotor resistance is unstable under open-loop conditions.   A tail-controlled airframe or ship represents a nonminimum-phase system. It may also be unstable, depending on the relative positions of center of force and center of mass.

Optimum filtering and prediction of a stationary random signal with and without noise are treated as a special case of the general procedure and are illustrated by typical examples.   Both the optimum system function and an expression for the least-mean-square error are obtained.

While the optimum-design method is based on the assumption of a stationary system, its application is much wider.   Whenever the changes in a nonstationary system are slow enough so that the prevailing condition can be approximated by transfer functions and spectral densities (which vary with time), the method may be used to advantage.   The exact methods of analysis and synthesis of nonstationary systems are handicapped by a number of factors:

1. The exact variations in system dynamics and signal statistics must be known beforehand.

2. The methods are numerically complicated. More often than not, digital computers are needed.

3. The optimum system as calculated is usually difficult to realize as far as hardware is concerned.

4. Whenever the variations in system dynamics and signal statistics are slow in terms of system response time, the advantages to be gained by the exact methods are slight.

For the above reasons, what we may do for slowly varying nonstationary systems is to design a system which would be optimum if the prevailing condition were stationary. A number of constants in the controller depend on the spectral densities and transfer functions, which represent the prevailing condition, and are adjusted with an auxiliary servo to the optimum setting from time to time as the latter varies. A system of this type is known as an adaptive system. Alternatively, we may optimize the system for the heaviest load or worst condition. In other words, the spectral densities corresponding to the worst conditions are used. Another alternative is to optimize on a weighted-average basis, by using the weighted-average spectral densities. Obviously, combinations of such techniques can also be used if the nature of the problem so dictates.

CHAPTER 5

NONSTATIONARY SYSTEMS AND SYSTEMS
WITH LIMITED OBSERVATION TIME

In the present chapter, we shall take up the problem of optimum design of nonstationary systems and systems with limited observation time. While analysis in the s domain is simple and closely related to traditional servo theory, the method is not applicable to nonstationary systems and systems with limited observation time. The time-domain treatment of this chapter will be put in more general terms to include the above-mentioned systems.

We shall start by generalizing the definitions of correlation function and impulse-response function, so that nonstationary signals and time-dependent systems can be described. An integral equation for the impulse-response function of an optimum system is derived for the general case. Reduction to special cases and methods of solution of the integral equation are then given.

5-1. Nonstationary Systems. Nonstationary systems can be classified into the following types:

1. Systems with time-varying fixed component
2. Systems with nonstationary inputs
3. Systems with both time-varying fixed component and nonstationary inputs

As examples of the above types, let us consider first the missile-control problem: The fixed component, which is synonymous with the controlled-system dynamics, varies because of the diminishing weight of the fuel, the changing speed of the missile, and the changing density, temperature, composition, etc., of the surrounding atmosphere. If the disturbing forces and moments due to atmospheric turbulence are negligible or are stationary and if the statistical nature of the instructions to the controlling elements does not change, then the inputs are stationary and the system belongs to type 1. Otherwise, the inputs are also nonstationary and the system belongs to type 3. Fire-control systems are usually of type 2. Another example of type 2 is encountered at the initial seconds of applying an input signal to a system. Since the stochastic inputs do not go back to infinity, the statistics of the system output are not the same as those which exist after the input signals have been applied for some time.

In order to obtain optimum control in the least-square-error sense, the controlling elements also have to be time-dependent. Therefore, the response of the total system must vary with time whenever the above-mentioned situations arise.

5-2. Mathematical Representation of Time-varying Linear Systems. A linear system may be defined as one that obeys the superposition

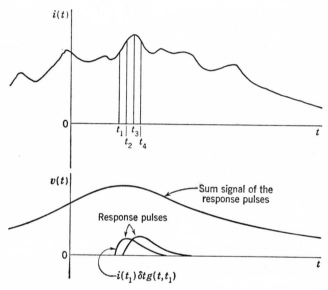

FIG. 5-1. Response of a linear system can be approximated by the sum of impulse responses to input at various times.

theorem. Its characteristics are completely specified by the impulse-response function $g(t,t_1)$ which represents the system output at time t due to a unit impulse input at time t_1.

An arbitrary input function $i(t)$ can be approximated to as close a degree as desired by a sum of impulse functions of magnitude $i(t_1)$ δt, $i(t_2)$ δt, . . . , at time t_1, t_2, . . . , as shown in Fig. 5-1, by making the interval δt arbitrarily small. Owing to the superposition theorem, the system output $v(t)$ is the sum of responses to these impulse functions. Therefore

$$v(t) = \lim_{\delta t \to 0} \sum_n [i(t_n) \ \delta t] g(t,t_n)$$

$$= \int_{-\infty}^{t} g(t,t_1) i(t_1) \ dt_1 \tag{5-1}$$

A physical system is incapable of responding to inputs which are not yet applied, and the upper limit of the integral is t. However, in a hypothetical system representing a desired performance (e.g., prediction), this restriction is not always valid. Equation (5-1) can be written alternatively as

$$v(t) = \int_{-\infty}^{\infty} g(t,t_1)i(t_1) \, dt_1 \tag{5-2}$$

The incapability of a physically realizable system to respond to future inputs can be expressed as

$$g(t,t_1) = 0 \qquad \text{for } t_1 > t \tag{5-3}$$

For a linear system that does not change with time, the system response to an impulse function depends only on the time interval between the application of the input impulse and the time of observation. It may be described as invariant under time translation. Instead of writing $g(t,t_1)$ we may write $g(t - t_1)$. Equation (5-1) becomes

$$v(t) = \int_{-\infty}^{t} g(t - t_1)i(t_1) \, dt_1 = \int_{0}^{\infty} g(\tau)i(t - \tau) \, d\tau \tag{5-4}$$

The second equality sign is obtained by substituting τ for $t - t_1$. Physically, τ is the interval that has elapsed since application of the input. Equation (5-4) is known as a convolution integral in the time domain. We note that Eq. (5-4) holds if the system satisfies two conditions:

1. Linear
2. Invariant under time translation

If condition 2 fails, Eq. (5-4) fails also; however, Eq. (5-1) still holds. The Laplace transform of Eq. (5-4) is

$$V(s) = \int_{0}^{\infty} e^{-st} \int_{0}^{\infty} g(\tau)i(t - \tau) \, d\tau \, dt$$

$$= \int_{0}^{\infty} \int_{0}^{\infty} e^{-s\tau}g(\tau)e^{-s(t-\tau)}i(t - \tau) \, d\tau \, dt = G(s)I(s)$$

The system can be represented by a transfer function in the s domain. Physically, the system is composed of constant elements. However, with an impulse-response function $g(t,t_1)$ which depends independently on t and t_1, the above transformation is not possible. The function $g(t,t_1)$ represents a system with time-dependent elements, or varying parameters.

The correlation function of two random signals is defined, in general, as

$$\phi_{12}(t_1,t_2) \equiv \langle i_1(t_1)i_2(t_2) \rangle \tag{5-5}$$

where the pointed brackets represent the ensemble average. For stationary signals, $\phi_{12}(t_1,t_2)$ depends on the interval $\tau = t_2 - t_1$ only. Equation (5-5) becomes

$$\phi_{12}(\tau) = \langle i_1(t_1)i_2(t_1 + \tau)\rangle \tag{5-6}$$

From Eq. (5-5), it is trivial to verify the following symmetry properties:

$$\begin{aligned}\phi_{11}(t_1,t_2) &= \phi_{11}(t_2,t_1)\\ \phi_{12}(t_1,t_2) &= \phi_{21}(t_2,t_1)\end{aligned} \tag{5-7}$$

Another important relation expresses the correlation functions of the output variables in terms of the inputs. In Fig. 5-2, the correlation function $\phi_{i_1i_2}(t_1,t_2)$ is known and the correlation functions of the output variables $v_1(t)$ and $v_2(t)$ are to be determined. From Eq. (5-2),

$$\begin{aligned}v_1(t)v_2(t') &= \int_{-\infty}^{\infty} g_1(t,t_1)i(t_1)\, dt_1 \int_{-\infty}^{\infty} g_2(t',t_2)i(t_2)\, dt_2\\ &= \int_{-\infty}^{\infty}\int_{-\infty}^{\infty} g_1(t,t_1)g_2(t',t_2)i_1(t_1)i_2(t_2)\, dt_1\, dt_2\end{aligned}$$

Taking the ensemble average of the above equation results in

$$\phi_{v_1v_2}(t,t') = \int_{-\infty}^{\infty}\int_{-\infty}^{\infty} g_1(t,t_1)g_2(t',t_2)\phi_{i_1i_2}(t_1,t_2)\, dt_1\, dt_2 \tag{5-8}$$

Equation (5-8) is good whether $g_1(t,t_1)$ and $g_2(t,t_1)$ are physically realizable or not.

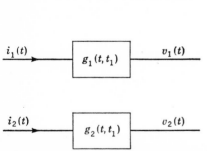
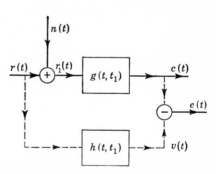

FIG. 5-2. Relation between correlation functions of nonstationary input and output signals to and from a time-varying linear system [Eq. (5-8)].

FIG. 5-3. Desired system response $h(t,t_1)$ and actual system response $g(t,t_1)$.

5-3. Least-square Optimization of a Linear Nonstationary System.

Figure 5-3 illustrates the criteria by which the system function $g(t,t_1)$ is to be determined. The desired output $v(t)$ is obtained by a given linear operation, with impulse response $h(t,t_1)$, on $r(t)$. The system input is masked by additive random noise $n(t)$. The error $e(t)$ is defined as $v(t) - c(t)$, and the ensemble mean-square value $\langle e^2(t)\rangle$ is to be minimized for every instant of time.   By definition of $e(t)$,

$$\phi_{ee}(t,t) = \phi_{vv}(t,t) + \phi_{cc}(t,t) - 2\phi_{cv}(t,t) \tag{5-9}$$

We note that $\phi_{vv}(t,t)$ is independent of $g(t,t_1)$, and the dependence of $\phi_{cc}(t,t)$ and $\phi_{cv}(t,t)$ on $g(t,t_1)$ can be exhibited by making use of Eq. (5-8):

$$\phi_{ee}(t,t) = \phi_{vv}(t,t) + \int_{-\infty}^{\infty} \int_{-\infty}^{\infty} g(t,t_1)g(t,t_2)\phi_{r_1 r_1}(t_1,t_2)\,dt_1\,dt_2$$
$$- 2\int_{-\infty}^{\infty}\int_{-\infty}^{\infty} g(t,t_1)h(t,t_2)\phi_{r_1 r}(t_1,t_2)\,dt_1\,dt_2 \tag{5-10}$$

Let $g_0(t,t_1)$ denote the optimum system function and $\phi_{opt}(t)$ denote the minimum value of $\phi_{ee}(t,t)$ which is obtained by substituting $g_0(t,t_1)$ in Eq. (5-10).   Then an arbitrary system functin $g(t,t_1)$ can be written as

$$g(t,t_1) = g_0(t,t_1) + \epsilon g_1(t,t_1) \tag{5-11}$$

The condition of physical realizability requires Eq. (5-3) to hold for all three functions, $g(t,t_1)$, $g_0(t,t_1)$, and $g_1(t,t_1)$.   We require further that the system have finite memory $T(t)$:

$$g(t,t_1) = g_0(t,t_1) = g_1(t,t_1) = 0 \qquad \text{for all } t_1 < t - T(t) \tag{5-12}$$

Equation (5-12) does not restrict our solution but rather generalizes it, since we can always apply the solution to the case of infinite memory by making $T(t)$ approach infinity for all t.   Substituting Eq. (5-11) in (5-10), rearranging terms, and writing Eqs. (5-3) and (5-12) into the limits of integration give

$$\phi_{ee}(t,t) = \phi_{opt}(t) + \epsilon^2 \int_{t'}^{t}\int_{t'}^{t} g_1(t,t_1)g_1(t,t_2)\phi_{r_1 r_1}(t_1,t_2)\,dt_1\,dt_2$$
$$+ 2\epsilon \int_{t'}^{t}\int_{t'}^{t} g_1(t,t_1)g_0(t,t_2)\phi_{r_1 r_1}(t_1,t_2)\,dt_1\,dt_2$$
$$- 2\epsilon \int_{t_1=t'}^{t_1=t}\int_{t_2=-\infty}^{t_2=\infty} g_1(t,t_1)h(t,t_2)\phi_{r_1 r}(t_1,t_2)\,dt_1\,dt_2 \tag{5-13}$$

where $t' = t - T(t)$.   Equation (5-13) is obtained by making use of Eq. (5-7).   Since the second term on the right-hand side is positive definite, a sufficient condition for making $g_0(t,t_1)$ the optimum system function is that the net value of the last two terms vanish for arbitrary $g_1(t,t_1)$. Therefore

$$\int_{t'}^{t} g_0(t,t_2)\phi_{r_1 r_1}(t_1,t_2)\,dt_2 = \int_{-\infty}^{\infty} h(t,t_2)\phi_{r_1 r}(t_1,t_2)\,dt_2 \qquad t' \le t_1 \le t \tag{5-14}$$

Equation (5-14) is also a necessary condition, since the second term is of the order of ϵ^2 and the last two terms are of the order of ϵ.   If Eq. (5-14) does not hold, it is always possible to make ϵ small enough so that the second term is insignificant and to choose the sign of ϵ such that $\phi_{ee}(t,t) <$

$\phi_{opt}(t)$. This clearly contradicts the proposition that $g_0(t,t_1)$ is the system function that minimizes the ensemble average of $[e(t)]^2$.

Both $h(t,t_2)$ and $\phi_{r_1r}(t_1,t_2)$ are known functions, and the right-hand side of Eq. (5-14) can be integrated. The result is readily seen from Eq. (5-8) to be the correlation function $\phi_{r_1v}(t_1,t)$. Equation (5-14) becomes

$$\int_{t'}^{t} \phi_{r_1r_1}(t_1,t_2)g_0(t,t_2)\, dt_2 = \phi_{r_1v}(t_1,t) \qquad (5\text{-}15)$$

Equation (5-15) was derived by Booton.

For every value of t, $\phi_{r_1r_1}(t_1,t_2)$ and $\phi_{r_1v}(t_1,t)$ are known functions, and t and t' are known constants. The function $g_0(t,t_2)$ is to be determined as a function of t_2. Equation (5-15) is an example of Fredholm's equation of the first kind, for which no general solution is known. However, if $r_1(t)$ can be represented as the output of a linear differential operator with time-dependent coefficients operating on white noise, Eq. (5-15) can be solved by a method devised by Miller and Zadeh. The steps are rather involved even for a single value of t. Their solution is useful for research purposes to gauge the closeness of any approximate solution to their exact solution in extremely simple or extremely important cases. It is too complicated to be used for ordinary work.

The function $\phi_{r_1r_1}(t_1,t_2)$ is called the kernel of the equation. It determines the complexity in arriving at a solution. In the present case, the kernel is symmetrical, since $\phi_{r_1r_1}(t_1,t_2) = \phi_{r_1r_1}(t_2,t_1)$.

5-4. Filtering or Prediction of Deterministic Inputs in Random Noise with Finite Observation Time. In fire-control and inertial-guidance systems, one significant problem is the recovery of a deterministic signal that is masked by random noise. The desired signal can be described as a linear combination of a set of known signals with unknown coefficients. For instance, the bearing of an airplane can be closely approximated by a low-order polynomial in time t, except when it suddenly switches course. We should like to be able to predict its course as closely as possible, not counting the sudden switches, and to do this in as short a time as possible. Obviously, if the observation time is too short, we cannot distinguish signal from noise. If the required observation time is too long, the system becomes impractical; furthermore, it would take into consideration irrelevant data as well as relevant data. Another example is optimum filtering: The error of an inertial reference system has both a random component and a coherent or sinusoidal component of extremely long period. While the former is unavoidable, the latter can be eliminated by accurate adjustment, which depends, of course, on the sensitivity and reliability of detecting such coherent components. The observation time must be considered limited because of the long period of the sinusoidal error.

To attack this problem, we shall start by modifying the results of the previous section.   The input signal to the system is assumed to have three components:

1. Random noise $n(t)$
2. Random signal $r(t)$
3. Signal $\xi(t)$, which is a linear combination of known signals $f_i(t)$ with unknown coefficients A_i, namely,

$$\xi(t) = \sum_i A_i f_i(t) \tag{5-16}$$

As before, $r_1(t)$ denotes the sum of random inputs $r(t) + n(t)$.

We shall require the impulse-response function $g(t,t_1)$ to satisfy the conditions that

$$\int_{t'}^{t} \xi(t_1) g(t,t_1) \, dt_1 = \int_{-\infty}^{\infty} \xi(t_1) h(t,t_1) \, dt_1 \tag{5-17}$$

and that the mean-square error $\phi_{ee}(t,t)$ due to random inputs $r_1(t)$ as given by Eq. (5-10) be a minimum.

Equation (5-17) means that the system gives exactly the desired linear operation on $\xi(t)$.   Owing to the arbitrariness of A_i in Eq. (5-16), Eq. (5-17) is equivalent to

$$\int_{t'}^{t} f_i(t_1) g(t,t_1) \, dt_1 = \int_{-\infty}^{\infty} f_i(t_1) h(t,t_1) \, dt_1 \qquad i = 1, 2, \ldots, N \tag{5-18}$$

For any t, the right-hand side of Eq. (5-18) is a known constant.   There are infinite points on the line segment $t' \leq t_1 \leq t$.   If the second condition is disregarded, corresponding to each point (or each value of t_1) there is an independent value of $g(t,t_1)$.   For the infinite number of values of $g(t,t_1)$, only N linear equations exist.   Consequently there are an infinite number of solutions which satisfy Eq. (5-18).   Among these, the one that yields a minimum value $\phi_{ee}(t,t)$ is the optimum system function.

Assuming Eq. (5-11) as before, we obtain Eq. (5-13) together with N equations arising out of Eq. (5-18):

$$\epsilon \int_{t'}^{t} f_i(t_1) g_1(t,t_1) \, dt_1 = 0 \qquad i = 1, 2, \ldots, N \tag{5-19}$$

Equation (5-19) can be multiplied by a set of Lagrange's multipliers $2\lambda_i(t)$ and added to Eq. (5-13).   As mentioned before, we are determining optimum $g_0(t,t_1)$ for each given value of t.   A different set of values of λ_i is required for each t, and the functional relationship is expressed by $\lambda_i(t)$.

Equation (5-15) becomes

$$\int_{t'}^{t} g_0(t,t_2)\phi_{r_1 r_1}(t_1,t_2)\, dt_2 = \phi_{r_1 v}(t,t_1) + \sum_{i=1}^{i=N} \lambda_i(t)f_i(t_1) \tag{5-20}$$

The solution of Eq. (5-20) can be expressed as

$$g_0(t,t_1) = g_{00}(t,t_1) + \sum_{i=1}^{N} \lambda_i(t)g_{0i}(t,t_1) \tag{5-21}$$

where $g_{00}(t,t_2)$ satisfies Eq. (5-15), and $g_{0i}(t,t_2)$ satisfies the following:

$$\int_{t'}^{t} g_{0i}(t,t_2)\phi_{r_1 r_1}(t_1,t_2)\, dt_2 = f_i(t_1) \qquad i = 1, 2, \ldots, N \qquad t' \le t_1 \le t \tag{5-22}$$

The functions $\lambda(t)$ are determined by substituting Eq. (5-21) in Eq. (5-18).

It is interesting to note that the set of integral equations (5-22) is of exactly the same form as Eq. (5-15). These equations are usually difficult to solve. However, there are special cases which are practically significant and mathematically manageable. These will be taken up in the following sections.

5-5. Time-invariant System with Finite Observation Interval. As shown in the previous section, the general solution $g_0(t,t_1)$ represents an impulse-response function having a waveform depending on the exact time of applying the input. The optimum system is not only difficult to instrument, it is also difficult to use, because the problem of synchronizing the system to the observed object is not always trivial. Under reasonable assumptions of the nature of the input, however, the solution is reduced to time-invariant form, that is, $g_0(t,t_1)$ is a function of $t - t_1$ only. The above mentioned practical difficulties are then alleviated.

The assumptions are as follows:

1. The random inputs $r(t)$ and $n(t)$ are stationary.
2. The desired linear operation does not change with time, $h(t - t_1)$.
3. The allowed interval of observation T is independent of t.
4. The set of known functions $f_i(t)$ satisfy the following equations:

$$f_i(t + \tau) = \sum_{j=1}^{N} a_{ij}(\tau)f_j(t) \qquad i = 1, 2, \ldots, N \tag{5-23}$$

To demonstrate that condition 4 is not too stringent, we note that it is satisfied by the following functions:

1. Exponential function e^{at}
2. The set of sine and cosine functions, $\sin \omega t$ and $\cos \omega t$
3. The set of powers in t, from zeroth to $(N - 1)$st: $1, t, t^2, \ldots, t^{N-1}$

On the other hand, Eq. (5-23) is not satisfied by most other functions, for instance, any set of functions including $1/t$.

If it is assumed that conditions 1 to 4 are satisfied, Eq. (5-18) becomes

$$\int_{t-T}^{t} f_i(t_1)g(t,t_1)\,dt_1 = \int_{-\infty}^{\infty} f_i(t_1)h(t - t_1)\,dt_1 \qquad i = 1, 2, \ldots, N \quad (5\text{-}24)$$

Let $t_1 = t_3 + t - T$. Using Eq. (5-23), Eq. (5-24) becomes

$$\sum_j a_{ij}(t - T) \int_0^T f_j(t_3)g(t, t_3 + t - T)\,dt_3$$

$$= \sum_j a_{ij}(t - T) \int_{-\infty}^{\infty} f_j(t_3)h(T - t_3)\,dt_3 \qquad i = 1, 2, \ldots, N$$

A sufficient condition for satisfying the above equation is

$$\int_0^T f_i(t_3)g(t, t_3 + t - T)\,dt_3 = \int_{-\infty}^{\infty} f_i(t_3)h(T - t_3)\,dt_3$$
$$i = 1, 2, \ldots, N \quad (5\text{-}25)$$

Equation (5-25) is also the necessary condition, provided that the determinant of a_{ij} does not vanish. The latter condition is always satisfied.

Similarly, by the substitution $t_{1,2} = t_{3,4} + t - T$, Eq. (5-10) becomes

$$\phi_{ee}(t,t) = \phi_{vv}(0) + \int_0^T \int_0^T g(t, t_3 + t - T)g(t, t_4 + t - T)$$
$$\phi_{r_1 r_1}(t_4 - t_3)\,dt_3\,dt_4 - 2\int_{t_3=0}^{t_3=T} \int_{t_4=-\infty}^{t_4=\infty} g(t, t_3 + t - T)$$
$$h(T - t_4)\phi_{r_1 r}(t_4 - t_3)\,dt_3\,dt_4 \quad (5\text{-}26)$$

We note that t_3 and t_4 are dummy variables and can be switched to whatever symbols we like. The unknown function $g(t, t_3 + t - T)$ is required to satisfy Eq. (5-25) and to yield a minimum value for the right-hand side of Eq. (5-26). Since none of the other functions and parameters involved depend on t, the solution is obviously independent of t. The only possible solution is then

$$g(t,t_1) = g(t - t_1) \qquad (5\text{-}27)$$

which implies that $g(t, t_3 + t - T) = g(T - t_3)$. This proves our proposition that, if conditions 1 to 4 are assumed, the optimum system is invariant with time. Stated in another way, if a system is shown to be optimum at the end of the first T sec, it continues to be optimum thereafter.

In the equations, $\lambda_i(t)$ are no longer dependent on t. In Eqs. (5-15) and (5-22), we may set $t = T$. Let $\tau_{1,2} \equiv T - t_{1,2}$. Equations (5-15),

(5-22), and (5-21) become

$$\int_0^T g_{00}(\tau_2)\phi_{r_1r_1}(\tau_1 - \tau_2)\, d\tau_2 = \phi_{r_1v}(\tau_1) \qquad 0 \le \tau_1 \le T \quad (5\text{-}28)$$

$$\int_0^T g_{0i}(\tau_2)\phi_{r_1r_1}(\tau_1 - \tau_2)\, d\tau_2 = f_i(T - \tau_1) \qquad 0 \le \tau_1 \le T \quad (5\text{-}29)$$

$$g_0(\tau) = g_{00}(\tau) + \sum_{i=1}^N \lambda_i g_{0i}(\tau) \qquad\qquad (5\text{-}30)$$

The N coefficients λ_i are determined by substituting Eq. (5-30) in the following N equations, which are obtained from Eq. (5-25):

$$\int_0^T g_0(\tau)f_i(T - \tau)\, d\tau = \int_{-\infty}^\infty h(\tau)f_i(T - \tau)\, d\tau \qquad i = 1, 2, \ldots, N$$
$$(5\text{-}31)$$

Example 5-1. A signal $\xi(t) = a_0 + a_1t$ with unknown coefficients a_0 and a_1 is masked by white noise, $\phi_{nn}(\tau) = B\,\delta(\tau)$. Determine $g(\tau)$ of a system which gives unerring prediction for α sec ahead, if the noise power is negligible, and the least-square error in general. The observation time is T sec. Determine also the mean-square error for the system.

Solution. In terms of the previous notation, we have

$$h(\tau) = \delta(\tau + \alpha) \qquad \phi_{r_1r}(\tau) = 0$$
$$f_1(t) = 1 \qquad\qquad f_2(t) = t$$

Equation (5-28) gives

$$g_{00}(\tau) = 0$$

Equation (5-29) gives

$$\int_0^T Bg_{0i}(\tau_2)\delta(\tau_1 - \tau_2)\, d\tau_2 = Bg_{0i}(\tau_1) = f_i(T - \tau_1)$$

Therefore,

$$g_{01} = \frac{1}{B} \qquad g_{02}(\tau) = \frac{1}{B}(T - \tau)$$
$$g_0(\tau) = \frac{\lambda_1}{B} + \frac{\lambda_2}{B}(T - \tau) \qquad\qquad (5\text{-}32)$$

Substituting (5-32) in (5-31), we obtain

$$T\lambda_1 + \frac{T^2}{2}\lambda_2 = B$$
$$\frac{T^2}{2}\lambda_1 + \frac{T^3}{3}\lambda_2 = B(T + \alpha)$$

Solving the above equations for λ_1 and λ_2,

$$\lambda_1 = -\frac{B}{T}\left(2 + 6\frac{\alpha}{T}\right)$$
$$\lambda_2 = \frac{B}{T^2}\left(6 + 12\frac{\alpha}{T}\right)$$
$$g_0(\tau) = \frac{1}{T}\left[\left(6 + 12\frac{\alpha}{T}\right)\left(1 - \frac{\tau}{T}\right) - \left(2 + 6\frac{\alpha}{T}\right)\right]$$
$$= \frac{1}{T}\left[\left(4 + 6\frac{\alpha}{T}\right) - \left(6 + 12\frac{\alpha}{T}\right)\frac{\tau}{T}\right] \qquad (5\text{-}33)$$

Equation (5-26) gives

$$\overline{e^2} = \int_0^T [g_0(\tau)]^2 \, d\tau = \frac{4B}{T} \left(1 + 3\frac{\alpha}{T} + 3\frac{\alpha^2}{T^2} \right) \tag{5-34}$$

Equation (5-33) shows that the optimum impulse-response function is independent of B which represents the noise power per unit bandwidth, and Eq. (5-34) shows that the mean-square error is proportional to B. Figure 5-4 gives a plot of $g(\tau)$ as a function of τ for $\alpha/T = 0$ and $\frac{1}{3}$. We note that, as α is increased, the area representing the response of reversed polarity is also increased.

There is a significant difference in basic concept between the optimum-design method presented here and the one presented in Chap. 4. We recognize here that the input has a coherent component $\xi(t)$ and random components $r(t)$ and $n(t)$. While the least-square criterion is the best for the random components, it may not be so for the coherent component. In fire-control problems, a miss may as well be a mile. It is more desirable to have a tolerable error for the largest fraction of time than a least-mean-square error over all times. This concept was introduced by Zadeh and Ragazzini.

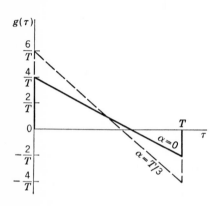

FIG. 5-4. Impulse-response function $g(\tau)$ of an optimum system in the presence of white noise for the prediction of $a_0 + a_1 t$ with finite observation time T.

To see what the result means, let us consider the problem of shooting at a zigzagging airplane in its simplest version. We assume that the plane has a constant-velocity component in the x direction, a changing-velocity component in the y direction with uniform distribution between $\pm V$, and switching at random intervals, the averaged value of which is $\frac{1}{2}$. The prediction time α is the interval required for the projectile to reach the plane, and our problem is to predict the transverse position $y(t + \alpha)$ correctly. It is further assumed that the radar introduces a positional uncertainty with uniform power spectrum but very low-mean-square amplitude. We shall compare the "optimum" systems according to the two different concepts.

For strictly least-square-error criteria, the solution is given in Sec. 4-8. The spectral density $\Phi_{yy}(j\omega)$ is

$$\Phi_{yy}(j\omega) = \frac{A^2}{\omega^2(\omega^2 + \nu^2)} \tag{5-35}$$

which is the same as Eq. (4-124) with $\omega_1 = \nu$. The condition of negligible radar uncertainty is equivalent to letting A approach infinity, and Eq. (4-126) gives the optimum system function as

$$F(s) = 1 + T_1 s$$
$$T_1 = \frac{1}{\nu}(1 - e^{-\nu\alpha}) < \alpha$$

Alternatively, we may use the Zadeh-Ragazzini system. One problem is to select the set of known functions. It is, of course, possible to use a polynomial of high order to approximate not only the straight path

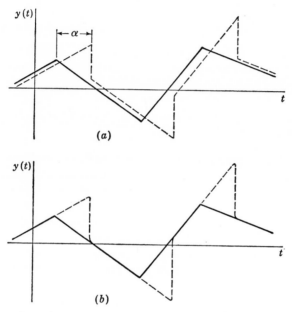

Fig. 5-5. Comparison of a system with least-square prediction (a) and a system with errorless constraint for a number of deterministic signals (b). Solid line, actual variable; broken line, predicted variable.

between two switchings but also a longer path including a few switchings. However, this is undesirable, because as soon as we include a large number of known functions, or powers of t in the predictable set, the mean-square error due to noise or radar uncertainty becomes untolerably large. The best compromise appears to be the least ambitious one. We shall approximate the plane's y position by a linear function of t. If the plane switches course before the arrival of the projectile, it has to be a miss. The solution is given in Example 5-1. As the radar uncertainty is very low, it is permissible to use a short observation interval T.

Figure 5-5 illustrates the situation with somewhat exaggerated error. The actual $y(t)$ as a function of t is shown by a solid line. In Fig. 5-5a, the broken line represents the predicted $y(t)$ of a system with strictly least-mean-square error. The fact that $T_1 < \alpha$ gives insufficient anticipation of the subsequent change. In Fig. 5-5b, the broken line represents the predicted $y(t)$ of the system of Example 5-1. We see that, in the first α sec after switching to a new course, the error is larger in b than in a. However, in the remaining intervals the predicted $y(t)$ of Fig. 5-5b coincides with the actual $y(t)$. While Fig. 5-5a gives the least-mean-square error, b represents a much greater probability of bagging the target plane. Where the effect of noise is considered, the predicted $y(t)$ is distributed about the broken line, with the broken line as mean value in both cases. The above observation still holds.

5-6. General Solution of a Time-invariant System. Example 5-1 represents an extremely simple case with its kernel being a δ function. Normally the solution is much more involved. We shall discuss a general solution under the assumption that $\Phi_{r_i r_i}(s)$ is a rational function of s.

The most difficult hurdle is to solve the integral equations (5-28) and (5-29). Both equations are of the form

$$\int_{T_1}^{T_2} g(\tau)\phi(t - \tau)\, d\tau = f(t) \qquad T_1 \le t \le T_2 \qquad (5\text{-}36)$$

and $g(t) = 0$ for $t < T_1$, and $t > T_2$.

We know also that $\phi(t)$ is an even function and that its Laplace transform $\Phi(s)$ is a rational function of s. Since $\phi(t)$ is even, $\Phi(s)$ is a function of s^2 and can be expressed as $N(s)/D(s)$, where both $N(s)$ and $D(s)$ are real polynomials of s^2. First, we shall consider the simpler case.

Case 1. $N(s) = 1$, $\Phi(s) = 1/D(s)$. Let p denote the operator d/dt. Operating $D(p)$ on Eq. (5-36) results in

$$\int_{T_1}^{T_2} g(\tau)[D(p)\phi(t - \tau)]\, d\tau = D(p)f(t) \qquad (5\text{-}37)$$

What is this function $D(p)\phi(t - \tau)$? Its Laplace transform is

$$D(s)\Phi(s)e^{-s\tau} = e^{-s\tau}$$

Therefore $$D(p)\phi(t - \tau) = \delta(t - \tau) \qquad (5\text{-}38)$$

When Eq. (5-38) is substituted in (5-37), the result is

$$g(t) = D(p)f(t) \qquad T_1 < t < T_2 \qquad (5\text{-}39)$$

At the two ends of the integral, $t = T_1$ and $t = T_2$, the δ function and its derivatives possibly exist. It will be shown that the δ functions are, in general, necessary. Let the roots of the polynomial $D(p)$ be denoted $\pm b_i$, $i = 1, 2, \ldots, m$, where $2m$ is the order of $D(p)$ in p, and *the real components of the b_i's are negative by definition.* We assume that $b_i \ne b_j$, if $i \neq j$. Then, for arbitrary coefficients A_i and B_i we have

$$D(p) \left[f(t) + \sum_i A_i e^{b_i t} + \sum_i B_i e^{-b_i t} \right] = D(p)f(t) \qquad (5\text{-}40)$$

From Eq. (5-40) we see that different $f(t)$ can lead to the same $g(t)$, according to Eq. (5-39). On the other hand, if the values of $g(t)$ are bounded at $t = T_1$ and $t = T_2$, the integral on the left-hand side of Eq. (5-36) gives a uniquely determined $f(t)$. This contradiction can be alleviated by allowing δ functions at both ends:

$$g(t) = D(p)f(t) + \sum_{i=0}^{n} \alpha_i \delta^{(i)}(t - T_1) + \sum_{i=0}^{n'} \beta_i \delta^{(i)}(T_2 - t) \qquad (5\text{-}41)$$

From Eq. (3-11),

$$\phi(t - \tau) = \sum_i C_i e^{b_i |t - \tau|} \qquad (5\text{-}42)$$

where the C_i's are known constants. From Eqs. (5-41) and (5-42),

$$\int_{T_1-}^{T_2+} g(\tau)\phi(t - \tau)\, d\tau = f_0(t) + \sum_{i=1}^{m} C_i \sum_{j=0}^{n} \alpha_j (b_i)^j e^{b_i(t - T_1)}$$

$$+ \sum_{i=1}^{m} C_i \sum_{j=0}^{n'} \beta_j (b_i)^j e^{b_i(T_2 - t)} \qquad (5\text{-}43)$$

where $f_0(t)$ is obtained by integrating $g(\tau)\phi(t - \tau)$ without considering the δ functions. In general,

$$f(t) = f_0(t) + \sum_i A_i' e^{b_i(t - T_1)} + \sum_i B_i' e^{b_i(T_2 - t)} \qquad (5\text{-}44)$$

Comparing Eqs. (5-43) and (5-44),

$$\sum_{j=0}^{n} \alpha_j (b_i)^j C_i = A_i' \qquad i = 1, 2, \ldots, m$$

$$\sum_{j=0}^{n'} \beta_j (b_i)^j C_i = B_i' \qquad i = 1, 2, \ldots, m \qquad (5\text{-}45)$$

Since the m A_i''s are arbitrary, at least m α_j's are required to satisfy Eq. (5-45). The same holds for the β_j's:

$$n \geq m - 1 \qquad n' \geq m - 1 \qquad (5\text{-}46)$$

To summarize the above: The solution of Eq. (5-36) is given by Eq. (5-41). By substituting $D(p)f(t)$ for $g(t)$ in Eq. (5-36) and integrating, $_0(t)$ is obtained. By comparing $f_0(t)$ and $f(t)$, the coefficients A_i and B_i

are determined.   The coefficients α_i and β_i are then determined from Eq. (5-45).

If Eq. (5-36) is the only condition for determining $g(t)$, the equality signs of (5-46) may or may not hold.   In the latter event, α_i's and β_i's are not uniquely determined.   However, this ambiguity can be removed by a physical consideration: In Fig. 5-3, the mean-square value of the output function $c(t)$ is

$$\phi_{cc}(0) = \int_{T_1}^{T_2} \int_{T_1}^{T_2} g(t)g(\tau)\phi_{r_1r_1}(t - \tau) \, dt \, d\tau \qquad (5\text{-}47)$$

It is convenient to discuss the convergence of the above integral in terms of Laplace-transformed functions: $\Phi_{r_1r_1}(s)$ is of the order $1/s^{2m}$ for large value of s. $\Phi_{cc}(s)$ is of the order of

$$\frac{1}{s^{2m}} s^{2N} = \frac{1}{s^{2(m-N)}}$$

where N is the larger one of n,n'.   In order that $\Phi_{cc}(0)$ be bounded, $\Phi_{cc}(s)$ must be of the order of $1/s^2$ or smaller as s approaches infinity.   Therefore

$$n \leq m - 1 \qquad n' \leq m - 1 \qquad (5\text{-}48)$$

Considering inequalities (5-46) and (5-48), we have

$$n = n' = m - 1$$

There is only one solution for $g(t)$ that satisfies the above and is therefore physically feasible.

While $g(t)$ can be obtained by the brute-force method outlined above, the computations are rather tedious.   A much faster method will now be derived: The anomalous situation at $t = T_1$ and $t = T_2$ can be removed by extending the range of integration.   Equation (5-36) holds only for the interval $T_1 < t < T_2$.   Whatever value $f(t)$ may take outside this range has no effect on $g(t)$.   Let us define $f_1(t)$ and $f_2(t)$ as follows:

$$f_1(t) = \sum_{i=1}^{m} C_i e^{-b_i t}$$
$$f_2(t) = \sum_{i=1}^{m} C_i' e^{b_i t} \qquad (5\text{-}49)$$

The constants C_i and C_i' are selected to match the function $f(t)$ and its first $m - 1$ derivatives at the two ends:

$$\begin{aligned} f_1^{(i)}(T_1) &= f^{(i)}(T_1) & i &= 0, 1, 2, \ldots, m - 1 \\ f_2^{(i)}(T_2) &= f^{(i)}(T_2) & i &= 0, 1, 2, \ldots, m - 1 \end{aligned} \qquad (5\text{-}50)$$

It follows from Eq. (5-49) that

$$D(p)f_1(t) = D(p)f_2(t) = 0 \tag{5-51}$$

$$\lim_{t \to -\infty} f_1(t) = 0$$
$$\lim_{t \to \infty} f_2(t) = 0 \tag{5-52}$$

Let $x(t)$ be defined as follows:

$$
\begin{aligned}
x(t) &= f(t) & T_1 \le t \le T_2 \\
x(t) &= f_1(t) & t < T_1 \\
x(t) &= f_2(t) & t > T_2
\end{aligned}
\tag{5-53}
$$

The integral equation

$$\int_{-\infty}^{\infty} g(\tau)\phi(t-\tau)\, d\tau = x(t) \qquad -\infty < t < \infty \tag{5-54}$$

is then equivalent to Eq. (5-36), as will be shown presently. Since the limits are extended to infinity, the ambiguities at the limits no longer exist. We have

$$g(t) = D(p)x(t) \tag{5-55}$$

Equations (5-51), (5-53), and (5-55) give

$$g(t) = 0 \qquad t < T_1 \qquad t > T_2$$

Therefore, Eq. (5-54) is reduced to

$$\int_{T_1}^{T_2} g(\tau)\phi(t-\tau)\, d\tau = x(t) \tag{5-56}$$

We note that, for the range $T_1 \le t \le T_2$, Eq. (5-56) is the same as Eq. (5-36).

In the neighborhood of $t = T_1$, Eq. (5-55) can be written as

$$g(t) = D^+(p)D^-(p)x(t) \tag{5-57}$$

where $\quad D^+(p) = \sqrt{A} \prod_{i=1}^{m} (p - b_i) \qquad D^-(p) = \sqrt{A} \prod_{i=1}^{m} (p + b_i)$

the real components of the b_i's are *negative*, and A is the coefficient of p^{2m} in $D(p)$.

Let us determine the function

$$y(t) = D^-(p)x(t) \tag{5-58}$$

From Eqs. (5-49) and (5-53),

$$
\begin{aligned}
y(t) &= 0 & t < T_1 \\
y(t) &= D^-(p)f(t) & t > T_1
\end{aligned}
\tag{5-59}
$$

From Eq. (5-50), $x(t)$ and its derivatives up to the $(m - 1)$st order are continuous at $t = T_1$. Since $x(t)$ is differentiated, at most, m times, there can be a step function but not a δ function at $t = 0$. Considering Eq. (5-59), we have

$$y(t) = u(t - T_1)D^-(p)f(t) \tag{5-60}$$
$$g(t) = D^+(p)[u(t - T_1)D^-(p)f(t)] \tag{5-61}$$

where $u(t)$ is the unit step function. Similarly, in the neighborhood of $t = T_2$,

$$g(t) = D^-(p)[u(T_2 - t)D^+(p)f(t)] \tag{5-62}$$

Equations (5-61) and (5-62) give the δ functions at $t = T_1$ and $t = T_2$ directly from $D(p)$ and $f(t)$.

Case 2. Both $N(s)$ and $D(s)$ Are Real Polynomials of s^2. Let us denote the roots of $N(s)$ by a_i, $i = 1, 2, \ldots, 2n$, where $2n$ is the order of the polynomial $N(s)$. From the fact that $\phi_{cc}(0)$ must be bounded for any physical system, we obtain the following conditions:

1. The order of the derivatives of the δ function at $t = T_1$ and $t = T_2$ must not be greater than $m - n - 1$.

2. If $m - n = 1$, only δ functions are allowed.

3. If $n = m + r$, then $g^{(i)}(T_1) = g^{(i)}(T_2) = 0, i = 0, 1, \ldots, r - 1$.

These conditions can be realized as follows: Let us consider the integral equation

$$\int_{T_1}^{T_2} g(\tau)\phi_I(t - \tau)\, d\tau = \frac{f(t)}{N(p)} + \sum_{i=1}^{2n} K_i e^{a_i t} = f_I(t) \tag{5-63}$$

where

$$\phi_I(t) = \mathcal{L}^{-1}\left\{\frac{1}{D(s)}\right\} \tag{5-64}$$

is an even function of t. The constants K_i are selected so that if we define

$$y_1(t) = D^-(p)f_I(t)$$
$$y_2(t) = D^+(p)f_I(t)$$

then $\quad y_1^{(i)}(T_1) = y_2^{(i)}(T_2) = 0 \qquad i = 0, 1, 2, \ldots, n - 1 \tag{5-65}$

Equation (5-63) is obviously of the form discussed in the preceding section. Its solution is given as

$$\begin{aligned} g(t) &= D(p)f_I(t) & T_1 < t < T_2 \\ &= D^+(p)u(t - T_1)y_1(t) & t = T_1 \\ &= D^-(p)u(T_2 - t)y_2(t) & t = T_2 \end{aligned} \tag{5-66}$$

Owing to Eq. (5-65), the boundary conditions at the ends are satisfied. Operating on Eq. (5-63) by $N(p)$, we obtain Eq. (5-36). Therefore $g(t)$ of Eq. (5-66) is a solution of Eq. (5-36).

Example 5-2. The problem is the same as Example 5-1 except for one change: $\phi_{nn}(\tau) = Be^{-b|\tau|}$, where b is a positive real constant.

Solution. The Laplace transform of $\phi_{nn}(\tau)$ is

$$\Phi_{nn}(s) = \int_{-\infty}^{\infty} d\tau \, Be^{-b|\tau|}e^{-s\tau} = \frac{2bB}{b^2 - s^2} \tag{5-67}$$

Equation (5-28) gives

$$g_{00}(\tau) = 0$$

Equation (5-29) gives

$$\int_0^T g_{01}(\tau_2)\phi_{nn}(\tau_1 - \tau_2) \, d\tau_2 = 1$$

$$\int_0^T g_{02}(\tau_2)\phi_{nn}(\tau_1 - \tau_2) \, d\tau_2 = T - \tau_1$$

$$D^+(p) = \frac{1}{\sqrt{-2bB}} (p + b)$$

$$D^-(p) = \frac{1}{\sqrt{-2bB}} (p - b)$$

Equations (5-39), (5-61), and (5-62) give

$$g_{01}(\tau) = \frac{1}{2B} [b + \delta(\tau) + \delta(T - \tau)] \tag{5-68}$$

$$g_{02}(\tau) = \frac{1}{2bB} [b^2(T - \tau) + (1 + bT) \delta(\tau) - \delta(T - \tau)] \tag{5-69}$$

$$g(\tau) = \lambda_1 g_{01}(\tau) + \lambda_2 g_{02}(\tau) \tag{5-70}$$

Equation (5-31) gives

$$\int_0^T g(\tau) \, d\tau = \frac{\lambda_1}{2B} (bT + 2) + \frac{\lambda_2 T(bT + 2)}{4B} = 1$$

$$\int_0^T g(\tau)(T - \tau) \, d\tau = \frac{\lambda_1 T}{4B} (bT + 2) + \frac{\lambda_2 T}{6bB} (b^2T^2 + 3bT + 3) = T + \alpha$$

Solving the above equations, we obtain

$$\frac{\lambda_1}{2B} = \frac{12 - 2b^2T^2 - 6bT(2 + bT)\alpha/T}{(2 + bT)(12 + 6bT + b^2T^2)} \tag{5-71}$$

$$\frac{\lambda_2}{2bB} = \frac{6 + 12\alpha/T}{12 + 6bT + b^2T^2} \tag{5-72}$$

Substitution of Eqs. (5-68), (5-69), (5-71), and (5-72) in (5-70) gives the optimum $g(\tau)$.

If the noise bandwidth b is sufficiently wide, bT approaches infinity, and Eq. (5-70) gives the same result as Eq. (5-33). On the other hand, if the noise is of very low frequency, b approaches zero, and we have

$$g(\tau) = \frac{1}{2} [\delta(\tau) + \delta(T - \tau)] + \left(\frac{1}{2} + \frac{\alpha}{T}\right) [\delta(\tau) - \delta(T - \tau)]$$

$$= \delta(\tau) + \frac{\alpha}{T} [\delta(\tau) - \delta(T - \tau)] \tag{5-73}$$

Equation (5-73) can be interpreted as taking the readings at the present and at T sec ago and projecting the result linearly to α sec later. Obviously, we shall not be able to filter out the low-frequency noise by such a procedure. However, as the system is required to duplicate a constant signal faithfully and as a low-frequency noise for a short interval $T \ll 1/b$ cannot be distinguished from a constant signal, filtering is not possible.

As a numerical example, let $bT = 2$, and $\alpha/T = \frac{1}{3}$; Eqs. (5-71) and (5-72) give

$$\frac{\lambda_1}{2B} = -\frac{3}{28} \qquad \frac{\lambda_2}{2bB} = \frac{10}{28}$$

Equation (5-70) gives

$$g(\tau) = \frac{17}{14T} - \frac{20\tau}{14T^2} + \frac{27}{28}\delta(\tau) - \frac{13}{28}\delta(T - \tau) \qquad (5\text{-}74)$$

Equations (5-73) and (5-74) are plotted in Fig. 5-6. Figures 5-4 and 5-6a and b illustrate the step-by-step change in the optimum form of $g(\tau)$ as the noise bandwidth b is decreased.

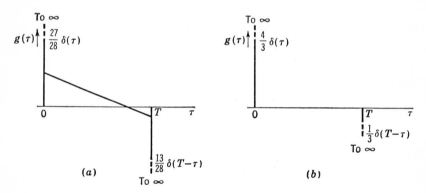

FIG. 5-6. Impulse-response function $g(\tau)$ of an optimum system in the presence of band-limited noise. (a) $bT = 2$, $\alpha/T = \frac{1}{3}$; (b) $bT = 0$, $\alpha/T = \frac{1}{3}$.

5-7. System with Finite Observation Time and Power Constraint Due to Fixed Output Element. Consider the problem of Secs. 5-3 to 5-5 with the following modification: Instead of producing an idealized output $c(t)$, which represents the best estimate of $r(t + \tau)$, and applying this signal to a separately designed servo follow-up system, the over-all system, including the power component, is designed as a whole. We shall limit our study to time-invariant systems. Let $c(t)$ represent the output of the power component, $i(t)$ the input to the power component, and $g(\tau)$ the impulse-response function of the over-all system. In addition to the requirements that $\phi_{ee}(0)$ be a minimum and Eq. (5-17) be satisfied, we require further that $\phi_{ii}(0)$ be limited in amplitude. The function $i(t)$ can be represented as a linear differential operator $H(p)$ operating on $c(t)$. Given the transfer function of the power component as $G_m(s)$, $H(p)$ is simply $1/G_m(p)$.

Let $x(t)$ represent the total input:

$$x(t) \equiv r(t) + n(t) + \xi(t) \tag{5-75}$$

If we assume that $\xi(t)$ is uncorrelated to the random inputs $r(t)$ and $n(t)$, Eq. (5-75) leads to the following:

$$\phi_{xx}(\tau) = \phi_{r_1 r_1}(\tau) + \phi_{\xi\xi}(\tau) \tag{5-76}$$

In determining $\phi_{\xi\xi}(\tau)$, the statistics of the unknown coefficients are taken into consideration. To illustrate what we mean, each segment of $y(t)$ of Example 5-1 can be represented by $y(t) = a_0 + a_1 t$. From the assumption that $y(t)$ is continuous at each switching and from the given statistical data of a_1, $\Phi_{yy}(s)$ is calculated, as shown in Eq. (5-35).

By definition of $g(\tau)$,

$$c(t) = \int_0^T g(\tau)x(t - \tau)\, d\tau \tag{5-77}$$

Operating $H(p)$ on Eq. (5-77),

$$i(t) = H(p)c(t) = \int_0^T g(\tau)H(p)x(t - \tau)\, d\tau \tag{5-78}$$

The operator p in Eq. (5-78) denotes d/dt. Since

$$\frac{d}{dt} x(t - \tau) = -\frac{d}{d\tau} x(t - \tau)$$

Eq. (5-78) can be written as

$$i(t) = \int_0^T g(\tau_1)H(-p_1)x(t - \tau_1)\, d\tau_1 \tag{5-79}$$

where p_1 represents $d/d\tau_1$. From Eq. (5-79) we have

$$[i(t)]^2 = \int_0^T \int_0^T g(\tau_1)g(\tau_2)H(-p_1)H(-p_2)x(t - \tau_1)x(t - \tau_2)\, d\tau_1\, d\tau_2$$

Taking the ensemble average of the above equation results in

$$\phi_{ii}(0) = \int_0^T \int_0^T g(\tau_1)g(\tau_2)H(-p_1)H(-p_2)\phi_{xx}(\tau_1 - \tau_2)\, d\tau_1\, d\tau_2$$

$$= \int_0^T \int_0^T g(\tau_1)g(\tau_2)H(-p_1)H(p_1)\phi_{xx}(\tau_1 - \tau_2)\, d\tau_1\, d\tau_2 \tag{5-80}$$

If Lagrange's undetermined multipliers are used, the problem of minimizing $\phi_{ee}(0)$ while limiting $\phi_{ii}(0)$ is equivalent to minimizing $\phi_{ee}(0) +$

$k^2\phi_{ii}(0)$, where the unknown coefficient k^2 is determined later by the condition that $\phi_{ii}(0)$ is less than or equal to a given limit. From Eqs. (5-10) and (5-80), we see that the solution of Sec. 5-5 still holds except that, in all the integral equations,

$$\phi(\tau) = \phi_{r_1 r_1}(\tau_1 - \tau_2) + k^2 H(-p_1) H(p_1) \phi_{xx}(\tau_1 - \tau_2) \qquad (5\text{-}81)$$

is used as the kernel instead of $\phi_{r_1 r_1}$.

Example 5-3. The problem of Example 5-2 is modified by an additional constraint on the rms input to the power component which has as its transfer function K/s. Determine the optimum form of $g(\tau)$.

Solution

$$\Phi(s) = \Phi_{r_1 r_1}(s) - \frac{k^2}{K^2} s^2 \Phi_{xx}(s)$$

$$= \frac{2bB}{b^2 - s^2} - \frac{k^2 s^2}{K^2} \left[\frac{2bB}{b^2 - s^2} + \frac{A^2}{-s^2(\nu^2 - s^2)} \right]$$

$$= \frac{2bBk^2}{K^2} \frac{K^2/k^2 - s^2}{b^2 - s^2} + \frac{k^2 A^2}{K^2(\nu^2 - s^2)}$$

For the sake of simplicity, let us assume that the limit on the rms input to the power component is set just right for K/k to be exactly equal to b. The above equation becomes

$$\Phi(s) = \frac{2B}{b} \frac{a^2 - s^2}{\nu^2 - s^2} \qquad (5\text{-}82)$$

where $a^2 = \nu^2 + A^2/2bB$. The constant $2B/b$ can be disregarded since it does not influence the solution. We have $D(p) = p^2 - \nu^2$, and $N(p) = p^2 - a^2$.

We can proceed exactly as we did in Sec. 5-6. However, when $N(s)$ is dependent on s, it is usually desirable to make use of the symmetry properties of the problem. We shall make the following modifications.

1. We shall use the new variables u, v defined as $u = \tau_1 - T/2$, $v = \tau_2 - T/2$. The limits of the integrals become $\pm T/2$. Let $\mathbf{g}(u)$ be defined as

$$\mathbf{g}(u) \equiv g(\tau_1) \qquad (5\text{-}83)$$

2. Equation (5-31) is not changed by replacing $f_i(t)$ with a new set $\mathbf{f}_i(t)$, where

$$\mathbf{f}_i(t) = \sum_j a_{ij} f_j(t)$$

as long as the determinant $a_{ij} \neq 0$.

Instead of using 1 and t as the two known functions, we shall have

$$f_1(t) = 1$$
$$f_2(t) = t - \frac{T}{2}$$

Consequently,
$$f_2(T - \tau_1) = T - \frac{T}{2} - \tau_1 = -u$$

$$f_2(T + \alpha) = \frac{T}{2} + \alpha$$

Equation (5-29) becomes

$$\int_{-T/2}^{T/2} \mathbf{g}_{01}(v)\phi(u - v)\, dv = 1 \tag{5-84}$$

$$\int_{-T/2}^{T/2} \mathbf{g}_{02}(v)\phi(u - v)\, dv = -u \tag{5-85}$$

$$\mathbf{g}_0(v) = \lambda_1 \mathbf{g}_{01}(v) + \lambda_2 \mathbf{g}_{02}(v) \tag{5-86}$$

From Eq. (5-84), it is readily seen that $g_{01}(v)$ is an even function while $g_{02}(v)$ is an odd function. Therefore Eq. (5-31) gives

$$\lambda_1 \int_{-T/2}^{T/2} \mathbf{g}_{01}(v)\, dv = 1 \tag{5-87}$$

$$\lambda_2 \int_{-T/2}^{T/2} \mathbf{g}_{02}(v)(-v)\, dv = \frac{T}{2} + \alpha \tag{5-88}$$

The solution of Eqs. (5-84) and (5-85) is given by Eq. (5-66). Since $n = m = 1$, there are no δ functions at the two ends; however, Eq. (5-65) has to be satisfied. For Eq. (5-84) we have

$$f_1(u) = -\frac{1}{a^2} + C_1 \cosh au$$

The constant C_1 is determined by the boundary condition at $u = T/2$ only, since at $u = -T/2$ the boundary condition is automatically satisfied because of symmetry.

$$C_1 a \sinh \frac{aT}{2} + C_1 \nu \cosh \frac{aT}{2} - \frac{\nu}{a^2} = 0$$

Let $\theta = aT/2$; C_1 can be written as

$$C_1 = \frac{\nu/a^2}{a \sinh \theta + \nu \cosh \theta} \tag{5-89}$$

Equation (5-66) gives

$$\mathbf{g}_{01}(u) = \frac{\nu^2}{a^2} + C_1(a^2 - \nu^2) \cosh au \tag{5-90}$$

Similarly,

$$\mathbf{g}_{02}(u) = -\frac{\nu^2}{a^2} u - C_2(a^2 - \nu^2) \sinh au \tag{5-91}$$

$$C_2 = \frac{2 + \nu T}{2a^2(a \cosh \theta + \nu \sinh \theta)} \tag{5-92}$$

From Eqs. (5-87) and (5-88) we obtain

$$\lambda_1 = \frac{a^2}{\nu^2 T + 2aC_1(a^2 - \nu^2) \sinh \theta} \tag{5-93}$$

$$\lambda_2 = \frac{6a^2(T + 2\alpha)}{\nu^2 T^3 + 24C_2(a^2 - \nu^2)(\theta \cosh \theta - \sinh \theta)} \tag{5-94}$$

As a numerical example, let $aT = 2$, and $\nu T = \frac{1}{2}$. Then

$$\mathbf{g}_{01}(u) = 0.0625 + 0.150 \cosh au$$
$$\mathbf{g}_{02}(u) = -0.0625u - 0.319T \sinh au$$
$$\lambda_1 = \frac{4.19}{T} \qquad \lambda_2 = \frac{13.03}{T^2}$$

$$\mathbf{g}_0(u) = \frac{1}{T}\left(0.262 - 0.815\frac{u}{T} + 0.628 \cosh au - 4.15 \sinh au\right) \tag{5-95}$$

Making the substitution $u = \tau - T/2$, Eq. (5-95) becomes

$$g_0(\tau) = \frac{1}{T}\left(0.670 - 0.815\frac{\tau}{T} - 0.648e^{a\tau} + 6.50e^{-a\tau}\right) \tag{5-96}$$

Equation (5-96) gives the optimum impulse-response function for the over-all system and is plotted in Fig. 5-7. Comparing Figs. 5-6a and 5-7, we note that one effect of the power limitation of the fixed component is to round off the impulse-response function.

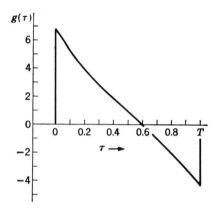

FIG. 5-7. Impulse-response function $g(\tau)$ of an optimum system with constraint on the rms input to the power component.

5-8. Solution of Nonstationary Problems by Eigenfunctions.   Let us consider the general nonstationary problem of Secs. 5-3 and 5-4.   For any given t, $g_0(t,t_1)$ is to be determined as a function of t_1 by solving the integral equations (5-15) and (5-22).   Both equations are of the form

$$\int_a^b x(t')K(t,t')\,dt' = f(t) \tag{5-97}$$

where $f(t)$ and $K(t,t')$ are known functions, and $K(t,t') = K(t',t)$.   Equation (5-97) can be solved if the set of eigenfunctions associated with $K(t,t')$ is known.   The eigenfunctions are defined by considering the following equation:

$$E \int_a^b x(t')K(t,t')\,dt' = x(t) \tag{5-98}$$

where E is a constant.   Equation (5-98) is known as a homogeneous Fredholm equation of the second kind.   There is always the trivial solution $x(t) = 0$.   However, for a discrete set of values of E, there are also nontrivial solutions.   These values of E are called eigenvalues and will be denoted by $E_1, E_2, \ldots, E_n, \ldots$.   Associated with each eigenvalue E_n, there is a nontrivial solution of Eq. (5-98); it is called its eigenfunction. Obviously any solution multiplied by a constant is also a solution. A normalized eigenfunction $u_n(t)$ is defined as one which satisfies

$$E_n \int_a^b u_n(t')K(t,t')\,dt' = u_n(t) \qquad (5\text{-}99)$$

$$\int_a^b [u_n(t)]^2\,dt = 1 \qquad (5\text{-}100)$$

The kernel $K(t,t')$ is called nondegenerate if, for each E_n, there is one and only one $u_n(t)$. When $K(t,t')$ is symmetrical in t and t', the set of eigenfunctions are orthogonal to each other:

$$\int_a^b u_n(t)u_m(t)\,dt = 0 \qquad \text{if } n \neq m \qquad (5\text{-}101)$$

Equation (5-101) is easy to prove. Consider the following integral:

$$J = \int_a^b \int_a^b u_n(t)u_m(t')K(t,t')\,dt\,dt'$$

If it is integrated first with respect to t, the result is

$$J = \frac{1}{E_n} \int_a^b u_n(t')u_m(t')\,dt'$$

If it is integrated first with respect to t', the result is

$$J = \frac{1}{E_m} \int_a^b u_n(t)u_m(t)\,dt$$

Therefore Eq. (5-101) must hold.

The set of orthonormal eigenfunctions $u_n(t)$ is called *complete* if, for any arbitrary function $f(t)$ defined in the interval $a \leq t \leq b$, a set of coefficients a_n can be found such that

$$f(t) = \sum_n a_n u_n(t) \qquad (5\text{-}102)$$

Now we return to Eq. (5-97). If we assume that $K(t,t')$ gives a complete, nondegenerate set of orthonormal eigenfunctions $u_n(t)$, $x(t)$ can be expressed as

$$x(t) = \sum_n b_n u_n(t) \qquad (5\text{-}103)$$

Substituting Eqs. (5-102) and (5-103) in Eq. (5-97) and making use of Eq. (5-99) result in

$$\sum_n \frac{b_n}{E_n} u_n(t) = \sum_n a_n u_n(t) \qquad (5\text{-}104)$$

Multiplying Eq. (5-104) by $u_m(t)$ and integrating, we obtain, for all m,

$b_m = a_m E_m$.   Therefore Eq. (5-103) becomes

$$x(t) = \sum_n a_n E_n u_n(t) \tag{5-105}$$

As a_n, E_n, and $u_n(t)$ are known, Eq. (5-105) is the solution of Eq. (5-97).

For the set of integral equations (5-15) and (5-22), t' and t are the fixed limits of integration, and t_1 and t_2 are the independent variable and variable of integration.   The kernel $\phi_{r_1 r_1}(t_1, t_2)$ and therefore the eigenfunctions depend on the parameter t.   Let the set of eigenfunctions be denoted by $u_n(t, t_1)$.   Let $f_0(t_1)$ denote $\phi_{r_1 v}(t_1, t)$, and coefficients $a_{ij}(t)$ be defined by

$$f_i(t_1) \equiv \sum_{j=1}^{\infty} a_{ij}(t) u_j(t, t_1) \qquad i = 0, 1, 2, \ldots, N \tag{5-106}$$

Owing to the orthonormal relations (5-100) and (5-101),

$$a_{ij}(t) = \int_{t'}^{t} f_i(t_1) u_j(t, t_1) \, dt_1 \tag{5-107}$$

Equations (5-15), (5-22), and (5-105) give

$$g_{0i}(t, t_1) = \sum_{j} a_{ij}(t) E_j(t) u_j(t, t_1) \tag{5-108}$$

$$g_0 = \sum_{i=0}^{N} \lambda_i(t) g_{0i}(t, t_1) \qquad \lambda_0 = 1 \tag{5-109}$$

The coefficients $\lambda_i(t)$ are to be determined.

From Eqs. (5-18), (5-106), and (5-108),

$$\sum_{i=0}^{N} \sum_{j=1}^{\infty} \lambda_i(t) a_{ij}(t) a_{kj}(t) E_j(t) = \sum_{j=1}^{\infty} a_{kj}(t) \int_{-\infty}^{\infty} u_j(t, t_1) h(t, t_1) \, dt_1$$
$$k = 1, 2, \ldots, N \tag{5-110}$$

Equation (5-110) represents N linear equations in $\lambda_i(t)$ from which the N unknowns $\lambda_i(t)$, $i = 1, 2, \ldots, N$, can be solved.

The above represents a formal solution of the general nonstationary problem.   Its applicability is strictly limited because the set of eigenfunctions $u_n(t, t_1)$ is usually difficult to determine.   Only for a very limited number of kernels are these functions known analytically. If the importance of the problem warrants, one may determine the eigenfunctions by the Miller and Zadeh method.   The reader is referred to their original paper for a treatment of this method.

5-9. Summary.   In this chapter the least-square synthesis technique using time-domain variables is formulated in general terms.   The inputs may be nonstationary, the observation time may be limited, there may be power constraint on the input to a fixed component, and, in addition to the least-square-error requirement for random inputs, the system may have to predict without error certain inputs which can be described as a linear combination of known functions with unknown coefficients. For a system with stationary random inputs and possibly limited observation time, a complete solution is given. For nonstationary systems, a solution is given in terms of the eigenfunctions which are obtained with the correlation function of the random inputs as the kernel. However, this solution is only formal, since the eigenfunctions are generally not known.

A correlation function $\phi_{12}(t_1,t_2)$ is defined in terms of the ensemble average, and its reduction to the stationary case is shown. Integral equations which give the impulse-response function $g(t,t_1)$ of the optimum system in terms of the correlation functions of the random inputs and the above-mentioned known functions are derived [Eqs. (5-15), (5-20) to (5-22)].

A running prediction is possible with the time-invariant optimum system function, if the random inputs are stationary and the set of known functions satisfies certain conservation conditions [Eq. (5-23)]. A complete solution including possible δ functions at both ends is given in terms of differential operators [Eq. (5-66)]. The presence of a fixed component together with its power constraint can be taken into consideration by modifying the kernel of the integral equations (5-81). Its practical effect is to reduce the order of discontinuity of the impulse-response function (Examples 5-2 and 5-3).

Eigenfunctions and eigenvalues of a homogeneous Fredholm equation of the second kind are defined, and their properties, including completeness and orthogonality, are briefly discussed. A solution of the integral equations for the general, nonstationary case is given in terms of the eigenfunctions (Sec. 5-8).

Besides the applications discussed in the main body of this chapter, the ideas and mathematical methods developed here can also be applied to a large class of problems in statistical communication. Among these are optimum detection of signal in noise and optimum signal waveform for transmission through a noisy channel. Readers who wish to pursue this subject further will find useful the reference-material section at the end of the book.

CHAPTER 6

OPTIMUM DESIGN OF SAMPLED-DATA SYSTEMS

In the present chapter we shall study a class of control systems that receive intermittently monitored signals at regular intervals to control a continuous plant. The subject matter being treated is limited to optimum-design techniques of such systems, and the reader is assumed to have some familiarity with the usual nomenclature for sampled-data systems and the z-transform method.

As is generally known, the errors between sampling instants are far more tedious to calculate than the error at sampling instants. Fortunately, no such difficulty exists when an integrated criterion is used. In the following sections, we shall discuss the various techniques that enable one to design an optimum system, in a prescribed sense, which gives equal consideration to error at all times, between as well as at the sampling instants.

6-1. Criteria for Optimum Design. The design theory for sampled-data systems is almost an exact parallel to that for continuous systems. The criteria depend on the nature of the inputs: (1) optimization of transient response to deterministic inputs and (2) minimizing of mean-square error in response to random inputs.

In the case of mixed inputs, e.g., step input mixed with random noise, the design procedure is the same as that for random inputs.

As discussed in Sec. 3-2, with random inputs, the distribution function of the system error has a tendency toward approximating the normal distribution, and the mean-square value of the error is most significant in various applications. However, such is not the case if transient response to deterministic input is of primary interest. Two different criteria of optimization will then be discussed: (1) zero transient error in the shortest time and (2) least-integral-square error.

Control systems designed according to criterion (1) are generally known as deadbeat systems. They have the shortest settling time. Criterion (2) is an obvios extension of the least-mean-square-error criterion with random inputs.

As mentioned previously, there is a close parallel between the design theories of continuous systems and sampled-data systems. The similarities are better exhibited by pointing out a few differences at the start:

1. For a sampled-data system, the term "deterministic inputs" has a much stricter implication than for a continuous system. With the obvious exception of step inputs, the starting time must be fixed in relation to the sampling instant. Otherwise, the input can at best be represented as a random combination of deterministic inputs but cannot be treated as a single deterministic input. As it is inconceivable that an external source can be synchronized to the sampling of a control system, the above consideration points to the necessity for certain modifications when unsynchronized deterministic inputs are involved. These modifications will be discussed along with the main theory.

2. For continuous systems without constraint, the system with the shortest settling time as well as the system with the least-square error has

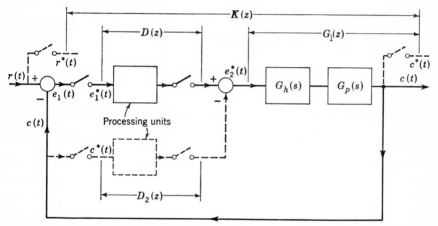

FIG. 6-1. Block diagram showing definitions of transfer functions and system variables in a sampled-data system.

1 as its closed-loop system function. For sampled systems, the solution is by no means trivial. We may reason the difference as follows: The sampling process itself introduces an average delay of half a sampling period, which is, in effect, a functional constraint placed upon the system.

6-2. Restrictions on the Sampled System Function $K(z)$. Before proceeding to optimum-design techniques, we would do well to review the restrictions on $K(z)$, which is the equivalent of C/R in a continuous system.

Figure 6-1 illustrates a typical sampled-data system. The transfer functions $G_p(s)$ and $G_h(s)$ of the controlled plant and hold circuit, respectively, are known. The data-processing unit $D(z)$ which operates on the sampled error signal $e_1^*(t)$ is to be designed. Sometimes it is desirable to introduce an auxiliary processing unit $D_2(z)$ which operates on the sampled output variable $c^*(t)$, as shown by the broken line. $D(z)$ and

$D_2(z)$ take the places of series and shunt compensations, respectively, of a continuous system. In practice, $D(z)$ and $D_2(z)$ can be built into a single digital processing unit. The input functions are either $r^*(t)$ and $c^*(t)$ or $e_1^*(t)$ and $c^*(t)$, and the output is $e_2^*(t)$. Especially in the former case, we may analyze the system as one with z-dependent main-loop

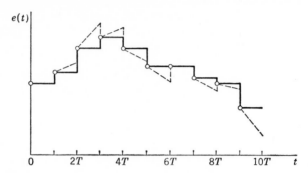

FIG. 6-2. Response of hold systems. Circles, sampled input to hold systems; solid lines, output of zeroth-order hold; broken lines, output of first-order hold.

feedback rather than one with an inner loop. The equivalent feedback function then is $1 + D_2(z)/D(z)$.

The sampled system function $K(z)$ is defined as

$$K(z) \equiv \frac{C(z)}{R(z)} \tag{6-1}$$

In terms of the control elements,

$$K(z) = \frac{D(z)G_1(z)}{1 + D_2(z)G_1(z) + D(z)G_1(z)} \tag{6-2}$$

where $G_1(z)$ is the z transform of $G_1(s) = G_h(s)G_p(s)$. In most applications, $G_p(s)$ is a rational function of s multiplied possibly by a factor e^{-as} representing transportation lag; $G_h(s)$ usually represents a zeroth-order hold system:

$$G_h(s) = \frac{1 - e^{-Ts}}{s} \tag{6-3}$$

Sometimes a first-order hold system is used; then

$$G_h(s) = \frac{(1 - e^{-Ts})^2}{s} + \frac{(1 - e^{-Ts})^2}{Ts^2} \tag{6-4}$$

The input-output relationship of a hold system is illustrated in Fig. 6-2. A zeroth-order hold system holds the sampled value for a single sampling period T. A first-order hold system gives the extrapolation of the two preceding sampled values. It cannot give an interpolation of the two nearest sampled values since no physical system is capable of utilizing future data.

With $G_p(s)$ and $G_h(s)$ of the above description, $G_1(z)$ can be written as

$$G_1(z) = \frac{V(z)}{U(z)} \tag{6-5}$$

where $U(z)$ and $V(z)$ are two polynomials of z^{-1} written in the order of rising powers of z^{-1}. Without losing generality, the first term of $U(z)$ is assumed to be 1. The first term of $V(z)$ is, in general, z^{-m} because of possible transportation lag, and m is the number of sampling periods that have elasped before observing the first nonzero sampled output. Sometimes there are roots of $V(z)$ outside or on the unit circle. Let these roots be denoted by λ_i, $i = 1, 2, \ldots$. $V(z)$ can be expressed as

$$V(z) = V_1(z)V_2(z) \tag{6-6}$$

where
$$V_2(z) = z^{-m} \prod_{i=1}^{l} (1 - \lambda_i z^{-1}) \tag{6-7}$$

and $V_1(z)$ is a polynomial in rising powers of z^{-1} with all its roots inside the unit circle. The first term of $V_1(z)$ is a constant term, by definition of m.

In the literature on sampled-data systems, rational functions of z are usually written as a ratio of two polynomials in z^{-1}. However, when one refers to "roots," "poles," and "zeros," the "roots" of z and "poles" and "zeros" on the z plane are usually meant. The apparent confusion is resolved once we know the above-mentioned rules. On the other hand, these rules are rather convenient for recognizing possible transportation lag in a system. If a certain sampled transfer function implies negative lag or anticipation, it obviously does not represent a physical element.

Similarly to the continuous case, if a sampled network function $F(z)$ is to represent a stable physical system, it must meet either of the following conditions, which are equivalent to each other:

1. $F(z)$ is expressible as a series in z^{-1}, without the presence of any positive powers of z, and the coefficient of z^{-n} approaches zero as n approaches infinity.

2. $F(z)$ is expressible as $A(z)/B(z)$, where $A(z)$ and $B(z)$ are polynomials in z^{-1}. The first term of $B(z)$ is 1, and all the roots of $B(z)$ are inside the unit circle on the z plane.

We note that condition 1 is similar to the requirement on the impulse-response function of a physically realizable continuous system, and condition 2 is similar to requiring that all the poles of $F(s)$ be inside the LHP. These conditions are referred to as conditions of "physical realizability."

For a system to be closed-loop stable, $K(z)$ must meet these conditions. However, they are not sufficient. The factor $V_2(z)$ represents the transportation lag and nonminimum-phase effect of the fixed component which includes both the plant and the hold system.   If $V_2(z)$ is not to appear as a factor in $K(z)$, the manipulated signal $e_2^*(t)$ would have either to anticipate $r^*(t)$ or to rise exponentially following any initial disturbance. The proof is similar to that for the continuous system as given in Sec. 4-1.   The restrictions on $K(z)$ can be summarized into the following equation:

$$K(z) = V_2(z)F(z) \tag{6-8}$$

where $F(z)$ meets the condition of physical realizability.

Equation (6-8) is equivalent to a set of conditions first derived by Bergen and Ragazzini.   They based their deductions on the impossibility of canceling exactly a zero in $G_1(z)$ by a pole in $D(z)$.   While a slight dislocation is not overly harmful when the unintended dipole pair is inside the unit circle, it causes instability if the dipole pair is outside.   Using the same argument, with reversed roles of pole and zero, Bertram derived a condition on $K(z)$ for a system with an unstable plant: For a series-compensated system with unity feedback, any pole of $G_1(z)$ outside the unit circle must appear as a zero of $1 - K(z)$.   As this restriction can be removed by either z-dependent feedback or shunt compensation $[D_2(z) \neq 0]$, it will not be considered in the following sections.   On the other hand, our derivation of Bergen and Ragazzini's condition is independent of system configuration.   Equation (6-8) must be observed no matter how we propose to compensate a system.

6-3. Design of a Deadbeat System.†   If the reference input $r(t)$ can be represented as an nth-order polynomial in t, then

$$R(z) = \frac{Q(z)}{(1 - z^{-1})^{n+1}} \tag{6-9}$$

where $Q(z)$ is a polynomial of z^{-1}.   If $K(z)$ satisfies

$$1 - K(z) = (1 - z^{-1})^{n+1}W(z) \tag{6-10}$$

where $W(z)$ is a polynomial in z^{-1}, the sampled error e_1^* vanishes after a finite number of samples.   This is easy to prove.   Since

$$E_1(z) = R(z) - C(z) = [1 - K(z)]R(z) = Q(z)W(z) \tag{6-11}$$

the number of nonvanishing sampled errors is equal to the order of the polynomial $Q(z)W(z)$.

† Parts of Secs. 6-3 to 6-9, inclusive, are reprinted from the following two papers by the author: Statistical Design Theory for Strictly Digital Sampled-data Systems, *Trans. AIEE*, pt. I, vol. 76, pp. 702–709, 1957, and Statistical Design Theory of Digital Controlled Continuous Systems, *Trans. AIEE*, pt. II, vol. 77, pp. 191–201, 1958.

We note that $K(z)$ must satisfy Eq. (6-8) in addition to (6-10). $W(z)$ being a polynomial implies that, $F(z)$ being also a polynomial, Eq. (6-10) can be satisfied by selecting $F(z)$ in such a way that

$$K(1) = 1$$
$$K^{(i)}(1) = 0 \qquad i = 1, 2, \ldots, n \qquad (6\text{-}12)$$

There are $n + 1$ simultaneous equations in (6-12). In order to satisfy these equations, the polynomial $F(z)$ has a minimum of $n + 1$ terms. Therefore $F(z)$ is of at least nth order. We note that a lower-order $F(z)$ implies a lower-order $W(z)$ and consequently fewer terms of sampled error. The system with an nth order polynomial $F(z)$ in z^{-1} is called a prototype design. It reduces the sampled error to zero within minimum time.

However, reducing the error e^* to zero is not the same as reducing e to zero. For the latter, the requirements are stricter, as expected. Since $r(t)$ is a polynomial in t, and $c(t) = r(t)$ for all $t > t_1$, the input to the plant $e_2(t)$ must be a polynomial in t for all $t > t_1$. It follows that $e_2(t)$ cannot be discontinuous. The order of $e_2^*(t)$ must not exceed the order of the hold system. For instance, with a zeroth-order hold, if $e_2^*(t)$ is a constant, $e_2(t)$ is the same constant. Otherwise $e_2(t)$ is a series of steps. With a first-order hold $e_2^*(t)$ is allowed to be a linear function of time, etc. $E_2(z)$ can be expressed as

$$E_2(z) = \frac{K(z)R(z)}{G_1(z)} = \frac{K(z)U(z)R(z)}{V(z)} \qquad (6\text{-}13)$$

From the above discussion, we see that the following conditions must be satisfied:

1. With a kth-order hold system, $E_2(z)$ is allowed a $(k + 1)$st-order pole at $z = 1$. Since $K(z)$ cannot have a zero at $z = 1$, Eq. (6-13) implies that $U(z)$ has a zero at $z = 1$ of at least $(n - k)$th order. In other words, $G_p(s)$ must have a $(n - k)$th-order pole at $s = 0$.

2. Since $e_2(t)$ is a polynomial in t, $E_2(z)$ cannot have any pole other than 1. But none of the roots of the polynomial $V(z)$ is at 1. Thus $K(z)$ must be divisible by $V(z)$. Instead of Eq. (6-8), we have

$$K(z) = V(z)F(z) \qquad (6\text{-}14)$$

3. Equation (6-10) is required since the sampled error $e_1^*(t)$ must be zero after a finite number of sampling periods.

Condition 1 is a condition on the controlled plant. If it is not satisfied, a deadbeat design is simply not possible. If it is satisfied, we can use Eq. (6-12) to determine $F(z)$ as before. The system with an nth-order polynomial $F(z)$ (in z^{-1}) is called a prototype design. It reduces the error $e(t)$ to zero within minimum time.

Equations (6-10) and (6-14) and condition 1 are the *necessary* conditions. In order to be *sufficient*, another condition on the plant has to be added to the group.   That is the following:

4. None of the roots of $G_p(s)$ are at a distance $j(2\pi/T)$ from each other on the s plane.

To prove this, let us consider the state of affairs after a time interval t_1, which is sufficient for both of the following to have occurred:

1. As a result of Eq. (6-10), the error $e_1^*(t) = 0$ for $t > t_1$.

2. As a result of conditions 1 and 2, $e_2(t)$ can be expressed as a polynomial in t for $t > t_1$.

Let $t' = t - t_1$.   The output function $c(t')$ consists of a polynomial in t together with a number of transient terms $e^{a_i t'}$, where the a_i's are the nonzero poles of $G_1(s)$.   The input $r(t')$ is a polynomial in t'.   Since

$$e_1(t') = r(t') - c(t')$$

$e_1(t')$ can be written as

$$e_1(t') = \sum_{j=0}^{n} B_j t'^j + \sum_i A_i e^{a_i t'} \tag{6-15}$$

The z transform of $e_1(t')$ is

$$E_1(z) = \sum_{j=0}^{n} \frac{C_j}{(1 - z^{-1})^{j+1}} + \sum_i \frac{A_i}{1 - e^{a_i T} z^{-1}} \tag{6-16}$$

Owing to condition 4, none of the poles $e^{a_i T}$ are identical.   As $e_1^*(t) = 0$, $E_1(z) = 0$.   Consequently, $C_j = B_j = A_i = 0$ for all i and j.   Equation (6-15) gives $e_1(t') = 0$ for $t' \geq 0$.   We note that condition 4 is necessary in the proof.   If $e^{a_1 T} = e^{a_2 T}$, we have the possibility that $A_1 = -A_2 \neq 0$. Physically, it represents a transient term which vanishes at every sampling instant.

There are two remaining points to be discussed:

1. The first is the matter of unsynchronized deterministic input. Fortunately, deadbeat systems do not require synchronized inputs. Only the order of the polynomial $r(t)$ enters into the design equation. Since an nth-order polynomial in $t - t_1$ is a different nth-order polynomial in t, the same system results no matter which polynomial is used. However, the coefficients of the polynomial do have some effect on the required number of sampling periods for reducing system error to zero. The order of the polynomial $Q(z)$ of Eq. (6-9) depends on the coefficients of $r(t)$.   The lower the order of $Q(z)$, the faster the system arrives at the errorless state.

2. While a prototype design requires the least time to reduce system error to zero, it is usually not the best design.   For instance, plant saturation is a consideration, and a prototype design tends to force the system

by sending large inputs to the plant. This is especially true in a system with high sampling rates. One way to modify a prototype design is to use the following sampled system function.

$$K(z) = K_0(z) + V(z) \sum_{i=1}^{N} A_i(1 - z^{-1})^{i+n} \qquad (6\text{-}17)$$

We note that, with arbitrary constants A_i, Eq. (6-17) satisfies both Eqs. (6-10) and (6-14). The settling time of the system is increased by N sampling periods. However, by properly choosing the N coefficients A_i, the coefficients of $E_2(z)$ (as a polynomial or series in z^{-1}) can be very substantially reduced. Alternatively, the A_i's may be determined by some other criteria, such as least-square error, least-square error with limited mean-square input to the plant, etc.

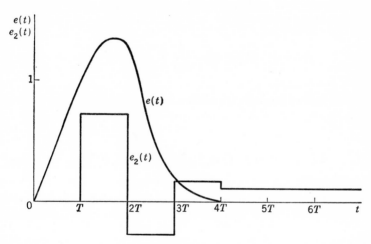

FIG. 6-3. System error and manipulated variable of a deadbeat system subsequent to a ramp input (Example 6-1).

Example 6-1. For the system of Fig. 6-1, let T be the sampling period, and

$$G_p(s) = \frac{10/T}{s(1 + Ts)^2}$$

$$R(s) = \frac{1}{s^2}$$

$D(z)$ is to be designed to give zero error in the least time.

Solution. The transfer function for the plant and hold system is

$$G(s) = \frac{1 - e^{-Ts}}{s} \frac{10}{Ts(1 + Ts)^2}$$

Correspondingly,

$$G(z) = \frac{z^{-1}(1 + 2.34z^{-1})(1 + 0.16z^{-1})}{(1 - z^{-1})(1 - 0.368z^{-1})^2}$$

$$V(z) = z^{-1}(1 + 2.34z^{-1})(1 + 0.16z^{-1})$$

Since $n = 1$, we write

$$K(z) = (c_0 + c_1 z^{-1}) V(z)$$

The coefficients c_0 and c_1 are determined by Eq. (6-12) with the following results:

$$c_0 = 0.732$$
$$c_1 = -0.473$$
$$K_0(z) = 0.732 z^{-1}(1 + 2.34 z^{-1})(1 + 0.16 z^{-1})(1 - 0.647 z^{-1})$$
$$D(z) = \frac{0.732(1 - 0.647 z^{-1})(1 - 0.368 z^{-1})^2}{(1 - z^{-1})(1 + 1.108 z^{-1})(1 + 0.16 z^{-1})}$$

The system error $e(t)$ and manipulated signal $e_2(t)$ are calculated and plotted in Fig. 6-3.

6-4. Systems with Least-integral-square Error.   The integral-square error following an input $r(t)$ is

$$J_e = \int_0^\infty [e(t)]^2 \, dt = \frac{1}{2\pi j} \int_{-j\infty}^{j\infty} E(s) E(-s) \, ds \qquad (6\text{-}18)$$

where $E(s)$ is the Laplace transform of the transient error $e(t)$.   With reference to Fig. 6-1, $E(s)$ can be expressed as

$$E(s) = R(s) - C(s) = R(s) - R^*(s) K^*(s) \frac{G_1(s)}{G_1^*(s)} \qquad (6\text{-}19)$$

To evaluate J, the path of integration is divided into segments of length ω_s, as shown in Fig. 6-4.   Let $\bar{E}(s)$ denote $E(-s)$.   Equation (6-18) can

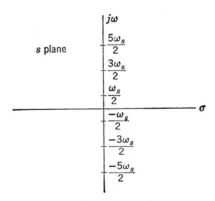

Fig. 6-4. Diagram showing division of $j\omega$ axis into length ω_s ($\omega_s = 2\pi/T$).   (*From S. S. L. Chang, Statistical Design Theory of Digital Controlled Continuous Systems, Trans. AIEE, pt. II, vol. 77, pp. 191–201, 1958.*)

be written as

$$J_e = \frac{1}{2\pi j} \int_{-j\infty}^{j\infty} \bar{E}(s)E(s) \, ds$$

$$= \frac{1}{2\pi j} \sum_{n=-\infty}^{\infty} \int_{-(j\omega_s/2)}^{j\omega_s/2} \bar{E}(s + jn\omega_s)E(s + jn\omega_s) \, ds$$

$$= \frac{T}{2\pi j} \int_{-(j\omega_s/2)}^{j\omega_s/2} (\bar{E}E)^*(s) \, ds \tag{6-20}$$

The last equality sign is obtained by interchanging the order of summation and integration. It is justified on the physical basis that $|E(j\omega)|^2$ must converge rapidly to zero at least as fast as $1/\omega^2$ for large ω, and therefore the series $\sum_{n=-\infty}^{\infty} \bar{E}(s + jn\omega_s)E(s + jn\omega_s)$ converges uniformly.

In terms of the variable z, Eq. (6-20) becomes

$$J_e = \frac{1}{2\pi j} \oint \bar{E}E(z) \frac{dz}{z} \tag{6-21}$$

The contour of integration is the unit circle. From Eq. (6-19), $\bar{E}E(z)$ can be evaluated as follows:

$$E(s)E(-s)$$
$$= \left[R(s) - R^*K^*(s) \frac{G_1(s)}{G_1^*(s)} \right] \left[R^*(-s) - R^*(-s)K^*(-s) \frac{G_1(-s)}{G_1^*(-s)} \right]$$
$$= R(s)R(-s) + \frac{R^*(s)R^*(-s)K^*(s)K^*(-s)}{G_1^*(s)G_1^*(-s)} G_1(s)G_1(-s)$$
$$- \frac{R^*(s)K^*(s)}{G_1^*(s)} G_1(s)R(-s) - \frac{R^*(-s)K^*(-s)}{G_1^*(-s)} G_1(-s)R(s)$$

Applying the z transform to the above equation and noting that $z^{-1} = e^{-sT}$ result in

$$\bar{E}E(z) = \bar{R}R(z) + \frac{R(z)R(z^{-1})K(z)K(z^{-1})}{G_1(z)G_1(z^{-1})} \bar{G}_1G_1(z)$$
$$- \frac{R(z)K(z)}{G_1(z)} \bar{G}_1R(z^{-1}) - \frac{R(z^{-1})K(z^{-1})}{G_1(z^{-1})} \bar{G}_1R(z) \tag{6-22}$$

Similarly, the integral-square value of an arbitrary system variable $a(t)$ in the controlled plant can be expressed as

$$J_a \equiv \int_0^\infty [a(t)]^2 \, dt = \frac{1}{2\pi j} \oint \bar{A}A(z) \, dz \leq M \tag{6-23}$$

where
$$A(s) = E_2^*(s)G_3(s) \tag{6-24}$$
$$\bar{A}A(z) = E_2(z)E_2(z^{-1})\bar{G}_3G_3(z)$$
$$= \frac{R(z)R(z^{-1})K(z)K(z^{-1})}{G_1(z)G_1(z^{-1})} \bar{G}_3G_3(z) \tag{6-25}$$

The transfer function $G_3(s)$ of Eq. (6-24) relates $a(t)$ to the manipulated variable $e_2^*(t)$.

As shown before, minimizing J_e while holding the value of J_a below a given limit M is the same as requiring that

$$J_e + k^2 J_a = \text{min} \qquad (6\text{-}26)$$

The functional constraint on $K(z)$ is given by Eq. (6-8) in conjunction with Eq. (6-7). To facilitate further manipulations, we shall write $V_2(z)$ as $(-1)^l z^{-m'} P(z) \prod_{i=1}^{l} \lambda_i$, where $m' = m + l$ and

$$P(z) = \prod_{i=1}^{l} \left(1 - \frac{z}{\lambda_i} \right) \qquad (6\text{-}27)$$

The functions $G_1(z)$ and $K(z)$ can be written as

$$G_1(z) = z^{-m'} P(z) G_{11}(z) \qquad (6\text{-}28)$$
$$K(z) = z^{-m'} P(z) F(z) \qquad (6\text{-}29)$$

where $F(z)$ is an unknown function to be determined and $G_{11}(z)$ represents the remaining factor of the transfer function $G_1(z)$. In general, both $G_{11}(z)$ and $F(z)$ are ratios of polynomials in z^{-1} with nonvanishing constant terms. It is obvious that, if the constant term of any of the polynomials vanishes, mT would not be the correct value of transportation lag in $G_1(z)$ or in $K(z)$. Another condition is that all the poles of $F(z)$ be confined to the interior of the unit circle, but not necessarily the zeros, while all the zeros of $G_{11}(z)$ must be confined to the interior of the unit circle, but not necessarily the poles.

The derivation of the optimum form of $F(z)$ is similar to the procedure used in Sec. 2-4. Instead of s and $-s$, we now have z and z^{-1}. Instead of the imaginary axis, LHP, and RHP, we now have the unit circle, inside, and outside the unit circle, respectively. Let $F_1(z)$ represent the difference between an arbitrary admissible function $F(z)$ (satisfying the conditions of physical realizability of Sec. 6-2) and the optimum function $F_0(z)$. The same steps from Eqs. (2-11) to (2-15) give

$$\frac{1}{2\pi j} \oint \left[z^{-1} R(z) R(z^{-1}) P(z) P(z^{-1}) \frac{\bar{G}_1 G_1(z) + k^2 \bar{G}_3 G_3(z)}{G_1(z) G_1(z^{-1})} F_0(z) \right.$$
$$\left. - z^{m'-1} P(z^{-1}) R(z^{-1}) \frac{\bar{G}_1 R(z)}{G_1(z^{-1})} \right] F_1(z^{-1}) \, dz = 0 \quad (6\text{-}30)$$

for arbitrary admissible $F_1(z^{-1})$, as the necessary and sufficient condition for $F_0(z)$ to satisfy Eq. (6-26). Since all the poles of admissible $F_1(z)$'s are inside the unit circle, all the poles of $F_1(z^{-1})$ are outside the unit circle.

A necessary as well as sufficient condition for Eq. (6-30) is that the expression in the brackets not have any pole inside the unit circle. Let

$$Y(z)Y(z^{-1}) \equiv \frac{\bar{G}_1G_1(z) + k^2\bar{G}_3G_3(z)}{G_1(z)G_1(z^{-1})} \tag{6-31}$$

$$Z(z)Z(z^{-1}) \equiv R(z)R(z^{-1}) \tag{6-32}$$

$Y(z)$ and $Z(z)$ are further characterized by the condition that all their poles and zeros be inside the unit circle. To illustrate how this is done: The right-hand side of Eq. (6-31) is factored into

$$A^2 \frac{\prod_i (1 - \alpha_i z^{-1})(1 - \alpha_i z)}{\prod_j (1 - \beta_j z^{-1})(1 - \beta_j z)}$$

where $|\alpha_i| < 1$ and $|\beta_j| < 1$ for all i and j.

The function $Y(z)$ is given as

$$Y(z) = \frac{A \prod_i (1 - \alpha_i z^{-1})}{\prod_j (1 - \beta_j z^{-1})} \tag{6-33}$$

The reason that the factors are written as above is to avoid introducing extra poles on the wrong side of the unit circle. For instance, $z - \alpha$ has a zero at α and a pole at ∞, while $1 - \alpha z^{-1}$ has a zero at α and a pole at the origin. The pole and zero of $1 - \alpha z^{-1}$ are located inside the unit circle. It follows that all the poles and zeros of $Y(z)$ are inside the unit circle. Whenever a root is larger than unity in magnitude, we write the factor as $1 - \alpha z$, where α is the reciprocal of the root. The pole and zero of $1 - \alpha z$ are outside the unit circle.

The function $Z(z)$ is obtained by factoring $R(z)R(z^{-1})$ in a similar manner. We note that, no matter how the poles and zeros of $R(z)$ are located, all the poles and zeros of $Z(z)$ are inside the unit circle. However, $Z(z)$ usually has poles on the unit circle. What do we do with these poles? Just as in the continuous case, we consider these poles as approaching the unit circle from inside in a physical sense. For instance, for a step input, we may write

$$R(z) = \frac{1}{1 - e^{-\epsilon T}z^{-1}} \tag{6-34}$$

The small constant ϵ may be the reciprocal of 1 million years. For all practical purposes, $R(z)$ represents a step input. When the location of a pole is significant mathematically, $e^{-\epsilon T}$ is obviously a pole inside the unit circle. For all numerical computations, however, $e^{-\epsilon T}$ is the same as unity. We may write, instead of Eq. (6-34),

$$R(z) = \frac{1}{1 - z^{-1}} \qquad (6\text{-}35)$$

with the understanding that there is a factor $e^{-\epsilon T}$ ahead of z^{-1}.

Another reason for introducing $Z(z)$ is to dispose of any factor z or z^{-1} in $R(z)$. For instance, for a ramp input,

$$R(z) = \frac{z^{-1}}{(1 - z^{-1})^2} \qquad Z(z) = \frac{1}{(1 - z^{-1})^2} \qquad (6\text{-}36)$$

With the functions $Y(z)$ and $Z(z)$ as defined above, the condition for optimum $F_0(z)$ is

$$z^{-1}Z(z)Z(z^{-1})Y(z)Y(z^{-1})P(z)P(z^{-1})F_0(z) - z^{m'-1}P(z^{-1})R(z^{-1})\frac{\bar{G}_1 R(z)}{\bar{G}_1(z^{-1})}$$
$$= X(z) \quad (6\text{-}37)$$

Dividing Eq. (6-37) by $Z(z^{-1})Y(z^{-1})P(z)$,

$$z^{-1}P(z^{-1})Z(z)Y(z)F_0(z) - \frac{z^{m'-1}P(z^{-1})R(z^{-1})\bar{G}_1 R(z)}{P(z)Y(z^{-1})Z(z^{-1})G_1(z^{-1})}$$
$$= \frac{X(z)}{P(z)Z(z^{-1})Y(z^{-1})} \quad (6\text{-}38)$$

We note that all the poles of $z^{-1}P(z^{-1})Z(z)Y(z)F_0(z)$ are inside the unit circle and all the poles of $X(z)/P(z)Z(z^{-1})Y(z^{-1})$ are outside the unit circle. Writing the remaining term into a partial-fraction expansion and collecting the terms in the expansion according to their pole locations, we have

$$\frac{z^{m'-1}P(z^{-1})R(z^{-1})\bar{G}_1 R(z)}{P(z)Y(z^{-1})Z(z^{-1})G_1(z^{-1})} = \sum_i \frac{A_i}{z - a_i} + \sum_i \frac{B_i}{z - b_i} + W(z) \quad (6\text{-}39)$$

where $|a_i| < 1$ and $|b_i| > 1$ and $W(z)$ is a polynomial in z.

$Q_i(z)$ and $Q_0(z)$ are defined as follows:

$$Q_i(z) \equiv \sum_i \frac{A_i}{z - a_i} \qquad (6\text{-}40)$$

$$Q_0(z) \equiv \sum_i \frac{B_i}{z - b_i} + W(z) \qquad (6\text{-}41)$$

Equation (6-38) can be written as

$$z^{-1}P(z^{-1})Z(z)Y(z)F_0(z) - Q_i(z) = \frac{X(z)}{P(z)Z(z^{-1})Y(z^{-1})} + Q_0 \quad (6\text{-}42)$$

The expression on the left-hand side does not have any poles outside the unit circle, while the expression on the right-hand side does not have any poles inside the unit circle.   Therefore both expressions must be equal to a constant ξ, and

$$P(z^{-1})Z(z)Y(z)F_0(z) = zQ_i(z) + \xi z$$

$$= \sum_i \frac{A_i}{1 - a_i z^{-1}} + \xi z \qquad (6\text{-}43)$$

By definition, neither $P(z^{-1})$, $Z(z)$, $Y(z)$, nor $F(z)$ can have a pole at infinity.   Consequently $\xi = 0$, and Eq. (6-43) becomes

$$F_0(z) = \frac{1}{Z(z)P(z^{-1})Y(z)} \sum_i \frac{A_i}{1 - a_i z^{-1}} \qquad (6\text{-}44)$$

We note that the summation on the right-hand side of Eq. (6-44) can be obtained by "partial fractioning" the function

$$U(z) = \frac{z^{m'}P(z^{-1})R(z^{-1})\bar{G}_1 R(z)}{P(z)Y(z^{-1})Z(z^{-1})G_1(z^{-1})}$$

into terms of the form $A_i/(1 - a_i z^{-1})$ directly and collecting terms inside the unit circle.   We shall denote this operation as $[U(z)]_+$.   Equations (6-29) and (6-44) give

$$K_0(z) = \frac{z^{-m'}P(z)}{Z(z)P(z^{-1})Y(z)} \left[\frac{z^{m'}P(z^{-1})R(z^{-1})\bar{G}_1 R(z)}{P(z)Y(z^{-1})Z(z^{-1})G_1(z^{-1})} \right]_+ \qquad (6\text{-}45)$$

Let $Y_1(z)$ be defined as

$$Y_1(z) \equiv \frac{z^{m'}P(z^{-1})}{P(z)} Y(z) \qquad (6\text{-}46)$$

Equation (6-45) can be written as

$$K_0(z) = \frac{1}{Z(z)Y_1(z)} \left[\frac{R(z^{-1})\bar{G}_1 R(z)}{Y_1(z^{-1})Z(z^{-1})G_1(z^{-1})} \right]_+ \qquad (6\text{-}47)$$

There is a simple graphical method for determining $Y(z)$ and $Y_1(z)$. On the right-hand side of Eq. (6-31), the variable z appears in pairs of factors

$$(1 - az^{-1})(1 - az) = 1 + a^2 - a(z + z^{-1}) \qquad (6\text{-}48)$$

Let $\Omega = \frac{1}{2}(z + z^{-1})$.   The right-hand side of Eq. (6-31) can be written as a function of Ω.   If necessary, the function $1/\bar{Y}Y(\Omega)$ can be obtained by a root-locus plot on the Ω plane. $Y(z)$ is then obtained from $\bar{Y}Y(\Omega)$, as shown by Eq. (6-33).   Equation (6-46) gives $Y_1(z)$ by switching a number of poles of $Y(z)$ to their reciprocal values and also attaching the factor $z^{m'}$ which represents transportation lag.

6-5. Statistical Properties of Sampled Signal. For continuous random signals, we have two distinctive though equivalent representations of their statistical properties, namely, spectral density and correlation function. We still have sampled spectral density and sampled correlation function for sampled signals; however, the two representations tend to merge. This is rather characteristic of the z-transform method. For instance, the z transform of a sampled signal $i(nT)$ is

$$I(z) = \sum_{n=0}^{\infty} i(nT)z^{-n}$$

The values of the time function $i(nT)$ are simply the coefficients of the power-series representation of $I(z)$.

The correlation function of sampled signals i_1 and i_2 is $\phi_{12}(nT)$. Their sampled cross-spectral-density function can be defined in two ways:

z transform of $\Phi_{12}(s)$

$$\sum_{n=-\infty}^{n=\infty} \phi_{12}(nT)z^{-n}$$

We note that, in order to use the first definition, the two signals must be continuous to begin with, so that their cross-spectral density $\Phi_{12}(s)$ is defined. To use the second definition, the two signals may be sampled. It is only necessary to know $\phi_{12}(nT)$, which may be calculated as

$$\phi_{12}(nT) = \overline{i_1(mT)i_2(mT + nT)}$$

where the averaging may be taken over m or the ensemble. Thus the signals may be undefined except at sampling instants.

In case the two signals are continuous and stationary, we shall show that the two definitions are equivalent. Readers who are not interested in the mathematical details may skip the remainder of this section.

Let $\Phi(s)$ be a real, rational function of s, with roots in both the RHP and LHP, and converging at least as fast as s^{-2} as $s \to \infty$. Three differently defined $\Phi(z)$'s will be denoted as $\Phi_a(z)$, $\Phi_b(z)$, and $\Phi_c(z)$, respectively. We shall show that they are identical with each other.

Case 1.   Single-ended Series, $\Phi_a(z)$

$$\Phi_a(z) = \sum_{n=0}^{\infty} \phi_a(nT)z^{-n} \tag{6-49}$$

where
$$\phi_a(t) = \frac{1}{2\pi j} \int_{\Gamma_1} \Phi(s)e^{st}\,ds \tag{6-50}$$

and Γ_1 is the contour shown in Fig. 6-5. It consists of a vertical line aa'

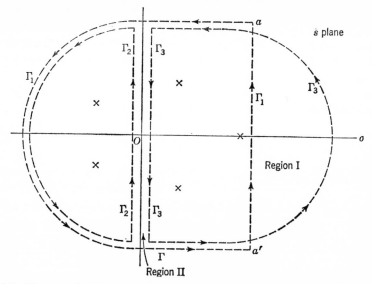

FIG. 6-5. Diagram showing pole locations, contours of integration, and regions of convergence. (*From S. S. L. Chang, Statistical Design Theory of Digital Controlled Continuous Systems, Trans. AIEE, pt. II, vol. 77, pp. 191–201, 1958.*)

to the right of all the poles of $\Phi(s)$ and a large semicircle at infinity enclosing all the region to the left of aa'. Correspondingly, the series of Eq. (6-49) converges for values of z outside a circle on the z plane, with radius larger than unity. However, once expressed in closed form, $\Phi_a(z)$ also exists for values of z inside the circle. The tables for z-transform functions are usually calculated on this basis.

Case 2.   Double-ended Series, $\Phi_b(z)$

$$\Phi_b(z) = \sum_{n=-\infty}^{\infty} \phi_b(nT)z^{-n} \tag{6-51}$$

where

$$\phi_b(t) = \begin{cases} \dfrac{1}{2\pi j} \displaystyle\int_{\Gamma_2} \Phi(s)e^{st}\, ds & \text{for } t \geqq 0 \\[3mm] \dfrac{1}{2\pi j} \displaystyle\int_{-\Gamma_3} \Phi(s)e^{st}\, ds & \text{for } t \leqq 0 \end{cases} \tag{6-52}$$

Case 3. Z Transform of $\Phi(s)$, $\Phi_c(z)$

$$\Phi_c^*(s) = \frac{1}{T} \sum_{n=-\infty}^{\infty} \Phi(s + jn\omega_s) \tag{6-53}$$

and $\Phi_c(z)$ is obtained by substituting z for e^{sT} in $\Phi_c^*(s)$. The series of Eq. (6-51) is convergent on the unit circle of the z plane or in the neighborhood of the imaginary axis on the s plane (shown as region II in Fig. 6-5). Integrals involving $\Phi_b(z)$ and $\Phi_c(z)$ are evaluated along the unit circle.

It will be shown that the three definitions of $\Phi(z)$ are identical. In other words, when $\Phi_a(z)$, $\Phi_b(z)$, and $\Phi_c(z)$ are expressed in closed form, they are one and the same function.

Let $\Phi_a^*(s)$, $\Phi_b^*(s)$, and $\Phi_c^*(s)$ represent the respective sampled Laplace transforms. Let

$$\delta_{T+}(t) = \sum_{n=0}^{\infty} \delta(t - nT) \tag{6-54}$$

and

$$\delta_{T-}(t) = \sum_{n=1}^{\infty} \delta(t + nT) \tag{6-55}$$

The Laplace transform of Eq. (6-54) gives

$$\Delta_{T+}(s) = \sum_{n=0}^{\infty} e^{-nsT} \tag{6-56}$$

The series on the right-hand side of Eq. (6-56) is convergent for positive values of s. In the region of convergence, it can be expressed in closed form as

$$\Delta_{T+}(s) = \frac{1}{1 - e^{-sT}} \tag{6-57}$$

Similarly, for negative values of s the Laplace transform of Eq. (6-55) gives

$$\Delta_{T-}(s) = \sum_{n=1}^{\infty} e^{nsT} = \frac{e^{sT}}{1 - e^{sT}} = -\frac{1}{1 - e^{-sT}} \tag{6-58}$$

From Eqs. (6-49), (6-50), and (6-56), $\Phi_a^*(s)$ can be written as

$$\Phi_a^*(s) = \mathcal{L}\{\phi_a(t)\delta_{T+}(t)\}$$
$$= \frac{1}{2\pi j} \int_{\Gamma_1} \Delta_{T+}(s - s')\Phi(s')\,ds' \tag{6-59}$$

where s' is the dummy variable of integration and the path of integration Γ_1 is traversed by s'. Equation (6-59) is a convolution integral in the s domain. For the value of s to the right of aa', $s - s'$ is positive along the entire path of integration. Therefore writing $\Delta_{T+}(s - s')$ in closed form, according to Eq. (6-57), is allowable.

$$\Phi_a^*(s) = \frac{1}{2\pi j} \int_{\Gamma_1} \frac{\Phi(s')\,ds'}{1 - e^{-(s-s')T}} \qquad \text{for } s \text{ in region I} \tag{6-60}$$

Similarly, from Eqs. (6-51), (6-52), (6-57), and (6-58),

$$\Phi_b^*(s) = \mathcal{L}\{\phi_b(t)\delta_{T+}(t)\} + \mathcal{L}\{\phi_b(t)\delta_{T-}(t)\}$$

$$= \frac{1}{2\pi j} \int_{\Gamma_2} \frac{\Phi(s')\,ds'}{1 - e^{-(s-s')T}} + \frac{1}{2\pi j} \int_{\Gamma_3} \frac{\Phi(s')\,ds'}{1 - e^{-(s-s')T}} \qquad (6\text{-}61)$$

Equation (6-61) holds for s in region II, that is, the space between Γ_2 and Γ_3. With s in region II, the conditions of convergence for both Eqs. (6-57) and (6-58) are satisfied.

In evaluating the contour integrals, considering s as being in region I in Eq. (6-60) means simply disregarding the poles at $(s - s')T = j2\pi n$, where n is an arbitrary integer, and considering s as being in region II in Eq. (6-61) means the same. Since $\Phi(s)$ does not have any pole in region II, Γ_2 and Γ_3 of Eq. (6-61) can be combined to give Γ_1. Therefore,

$$\Phi_a^*(s) = \Phi_b^*(s) \qquad (6\text{-}62)$$

To prove that $\Phi_c^*(s)$ is also the same function, let us consider an integral with a large circle of infinite radius as the contour of integration Γ_∞;

$$\frac{1}{2\pi j} \int_{\Gamma_\infty} \frac{\Phi(s')\,ds'}{1 - e^{-(s-s')T}} = 0 \qquad (6\text{-}63)$$

The integral vanishes since $\Phi(s')$ approaches zero at least as fast as $1/s^2$. The left-hand side of Eq. (6-63) can be considered as the sum of two integrals, J_1 and J_2. In evaluating J_1, the poles at $(s - s')T = j2\pi n$ are disregarded, and in evaluating J_2, the poles of $\Phi(s')$ are disregarded. Therefore,

$$\Phi_a^*(s) = J_1 = -J_2 \qquad (6\text{-}64)$$

Let $\omega_s = 2\pi/T$. The residue at $s' = s + jn\omega_s$ is $-\Phi(s + jn\omega_s)/T$. Therefore

$$J_2 = -\frac{1}{T} \sum_{n=-\infty}^{\infty} \Phi(s + jn\omega_s) = -\Phi_c^*(s) \qquad (6\text{-}65)$$

From Eqs. (6-62), (6-64), and (6-65), the following equality is established:

$$\Phi_a^*(s) = \Phi_b^*(s) = \Phi_c^*(s) \qquad (6\text{-}66)$$

This is the same as

$$\Phi_a(z) = \Phi_b(z) = \Phi_c(z) = \Phi(z) \qquad (6\text{-}67)$$

The above proof justifies the use of standard z-transform tables for the calculation of $\Phi(z)$. While it is proved only for the case of $\Phi(s)$ not having any pole on the $j\omega$ axis, the result is nevertheless applicable to cases in which $\Phi(s)$ has a finite number of poles on the $j\omega$ axis, in the limiting sense that these poles can be approximated to any degree of desired accuracy by poles not exactly on the $j\omega$ axis, as discussed in Sec. 6-4.

6-6. Input-Output Relationships of a System with Sampling. In Sec. 3-6, we have shown that in a continuous, linear system, if the spectral densities of the input signals are known, the spectral densities of the output signals can be readily calculated. We shall derive here similar relations for sampled-data systems. There are necessarily more varieties, because of the possibilities of changing a continuous signal into a digital

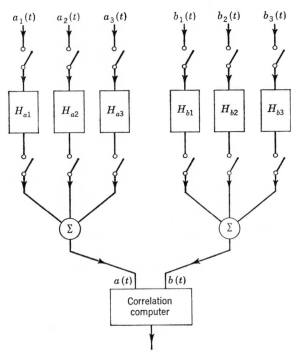

Fig. 6-6. Block diagram illustrating input and output relationship of a sampled system (case 1). (*From S. S. L. Chang, Statistical Design Theory for Strictly Digital Sampled-data Systems, Trans. AIEE, pt. I, vol. 76, pp. 702–709, 1957.*)

signal by means of a sampler, or a digital signal into a continuous signal by applying it to a hold circuit in combination with a continuous controlled system. There are three basic situations:

Case 1. Correlation of Digital Signals after Transmission through a Linear Network. Let signals $a(t)$ and $b(t)$ be the sum signals, as shown in Fig. 6-6, in which $H_{ai}(z)$ and $H_{bj}(z)$ represent the transfer functions of stable systems or prescribed linear operators, and $a_i(t)$ and $b_j(t)$ are stationary random sequences of time, $t = \ldots , -2T, -T, 0, T, 2T,$ $\ldots$. In terms of the z transform, the two signals can be expressed as

$$A(z) = \sum_i H_{ai}(z) A_i(z) \tag{6-68}$$

$$B(z) = \sum_j H_{bj}(z) B_j(z) \tag{6-69}$$

It will be shown that

$$\Phi_{ab}(z) = \sum_i \sum_j H_{ai}(z^{-1}) H_{bj}(z) \Phi_{a_i b_j}(z) \tag{6-70}$$

where $\Phi_{ab}(z)$ is the sampled spectral density of the resultant signals $a(t)$ and $b(t)$, and $\Phi_{a_i b_j}(z)$ is that of the source signals $a_i(t)$ and $b_j(t)$.

Let $A_m(z)$ and $B_m(z)$ represent the z transforms of the sampled signals $a(t)$ and $b(t)$, respectively, where $t = 0, T, 2T, \ldots, (m-1)T, mT$. Then

$$
\begin{aligned}
A_m(z^{-1}) B_m(z) &= \sum_{i=0}^m a(iT) z^i \sum_{j=0}^m b(jT) z^{-j} \\
&= \sum_{i=0}^m \sum_{k=-i}^{k=m-i} a(iT) b(iT + kT) z^{-k} \\
&= \left(\sum_{k=-m}^{-1} \sum_{i=|k|}^m + \sum_{k=0}^m \sum_{i=0}^{m-k} \right) a(iT) b(iT + kT) z^{-k} \tag{6-71}
\end{aligned}
$$

Dividing Eq. (6-71) by m and taking the ensemble average result in

$$\frac{1}{m} \langle A_m(z^{-1}) B_m(z) \rangle = \sum_{k=-m}^m \left(1 - \frac{k}{m} \right) \phi_{ab}(kT) z^{-k} \tag{6-72}$$

Letting m approach infinity, Eq. (6-72) becomes

$$\lim_{m \to \infty} \frac{1}{m} \langle A_m(z^{-1}) B_m(z) \rangle = \sum_{k=-\infty}^{\infty} \phi_{ab}(kT) z^{-k} = \Phi_{ab}(z) \tag{6-73}$$

For the system of Fig. 6-6, let $A_m'(z)$ and $B_m'(z)$ represent the z transforms of the sum signals $a_m'(t)$ and $b_m'(t)$ when the source signals are limited to m sampled sets of values. Obviously, $a(t)$ and $b(t)$ persist somewhat longer, because of the storage properties of $H_{a_i}(z)$ and $H_{b_j}(z)$. However, this end effect has only a limited number of significant digits and is negligible if m is made large enough. From Eqs. (6-68) and (6-69) we obtain

$$A_m'(z^{-1}) B_m'(z) = \sum_i \sum_j H_{a_i}(z^{-1}) H_{b_j}(z) A_{m_i}(z^{-1}) B_{m_j}(z) \tag{6-74}$$

Dividing Eq. (6-74) by m, taking the ensemble average, and letting m approach infinity result in

$$\lim_{m \to \infty} \frac{1}{m} \langle A'_m(z^{-1}) B'_m(z) \rangle = \sum_i \sum_j H_{a_i}(z^{-1}) H_{b_j}(z) \Phi_{a_i b_j}(z) \qquad (6\text{-}75)$$

Since the end effects become negligible as m approaches infinity, we have

$$\lim_{m \to \infty} \frac{1}{m} \langle A'_m(z^{-1}) B'_m(z) \rangle = \lim_{m \to \infty} \frac{1}{m} \langle A_m(z^{-1}) B_m(z) \rangle = \Phi_{ab}(z) \qquad (6\text{-}76)$$

Equation (6-70) follows from Eqs. (6-75) and (6-76).

Case 2.   Correlation between a Continuous Signal and the Response of a Continuous System to Digital Signal.   For the system of Fig. 6-7, if

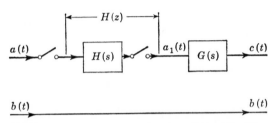

Fig. 6-7. Block diagram illustrating input and output relationship of a sampled system (case 2). (*From S. S. L. Chang, Statistical Design Theory of Digital Controlled Continuous Systems, Trans. AIEE, pt. II, vol. 77, pp. 191–201, 1958.*)

the correlation function $\phi_{ba}(\tau)$ or the spectral density $\Phi_{ba}(s)$ is known, what is $\phi_{bc}(\tau)$ [or $\Phi_{bc}(s)$]? Both source signals $a(t)$ and $b(t)$ are assumed to be ergodic. $H(z)$ and $G(s)$ may represent physical elements or hypothetical linear relations, such as prediction.

Let h_n and $g(t)$ represent the impulse responses of the respective elements. In terms of the z transform, it is

$$H(z) = \sum_{n = -\infty}^{\infty} h_n z^{-n} \qquad (6\text{-}77)$$

It is understood that h_n vanishes for large negative values of n, and $g(t)$ vanishes for large negative values of t. The output variable $c(t)$ can be expressed as

$$c(t) = \sum_n \sum_m a(mT) h_{n-m} g(t - nT) \qquad (6\text{-}78)$$

Equation (6-78) can be interpreted physically as follows: $\sum_m a(mT) h_{n-m}$ is the value of the impulse input to $G(s)$ at time nT. If $H(z)$ represents a physical element, it responds only to past and present inputs; then

h_{n-m} vanishes for all values of $m > n$. If $H(z)$ represents a prediction of k sampling intervals, h_{n-m} vanishes for all $m > n + k$. In either case, the summation can be taken for all values of m, from $-\infty$ to ∞. The output $c(t)$ is the sum total of the impulse response of $G(s)$ to all previous inputs. As before, the summation in n can be taken from $-\infty$ to ∞.

By definition of the correlation function,

$$\phi_{bc}(\tau) = \frac{1}{2T_1} \int_{-T_1}^{T_1} b(t)c(t + \tau) \, dt \tag{6-79}$$

where T_1 is a large interval approaching infinity. Let $b_1(t)$ represent the variable which is equal to $b(t)$ inside the interval $-T_1 < t < T_1$ and zero elsewhere. Substitution of Eq. (6-78) into (6-79) gives

$$\phi_{bc}(\tau) = \frac{1}{2T_1} \int_{-\infty}^{\infty} \sum_{n=-\infty}^{\infty} \sum_{m=-\infty}^{\infty} b_1(t)a(mT)h_n g(t + \tau - nT - mt) \, dt \tag{6-80}$$

Let $t' = t - mT$. Equation (6-80) can be written as

$$\phi_{bc}(\tau) = \frac{1}{2T_1} \int_{-\infty}^{\infty} \sum_{n=-\infty}^{\infty} \sum_{m=-\infty}^{\infty} b_1(t' + mT)a(mT)h_n g(t' + \tau - nT) \, dt' \tag{6-81}$$

In Eq. (6-81), the only factors depending on m are $b_1(t + mT)$ and $a(mT)$. Since b_1 is nonvanishing in an interval $2T_1$, there are, within a tolerance of ± 1, $2T_1/T$ nonvanishing terms in the summation over m. Because of the ergodic (or stationary) property of $a(t)$ and $b(t)$, one has for large T_1

$$\sum_{m=-\infty}^{\infty} b_1(t' + mT)a(mT) = \frac{2T_1}{T} \phi_{ba}(-t') \tag{6-82}$$

Substituting Eq. (6-82) in Eq. (6-81) results in

$$\phi_{bc}(\tau) = \frac{1}{T} \int_{-\infty}^{\infty} \sum_{n=-\infty}^{\infty} \Phi_{ba}(-t')h_n g(t' + \tau - nT) \, dt' \tag{6-83}$$

Equation (6-83) represents composite convolution, summation, and integration in the time domain. In terms of s-domain variables, it is

$$\Phi_{bc}(s) = \frac{1}{T} H^*(s)G(s)\Phi_{ba}(s) \tag{6-84}$$

Case 3.   Correlation between Outputs of Continuous Systems with Digital Inputs.   For the system of Fig. 6-8, if $\phi_{ab}(nT)$ or $\Phi_{ab}(z)$ is known, what is $\phi_{ce}(t)$ or $\Phi_{ce}(s)$?   The same assumptions for $a(t)$, $b(t)$, $G_a(s)$, and $G_b(s)$ are made as in the previous case.

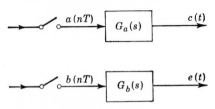

FIG. 6-8. Block diagram illustrating input and output relationship of a sampled system (case 3).   (*From S. S. L. Chang, Statistical Design Theory of Digital Controlled Continuous Systems, Trans. AIEE, pt. II, vol. 77, pp. 191–201, 1958.*)

The output variable $c(t)$ can be considered the sum total of impulse response of $G_a(s)$:

$$c(t) = \sum_{n=-\infty}^{\infty} a(nT)g_a(t - nT) \tag{6-85}$$

A similar expression holds for $e(t)$.   By definition,

$$\phi_{ce}(\tau) = \frac{1}{2T_1} \int_{-T_1}^{T_1} \sum_{n=-\infty}^{\infty} \sum_{m=-\infty}^{\infty} a(nT)b(mT)g_a(t - nT)g_b(t + \tau - mT) \, dt \tag{6-86}$$

As T_1 approaches infinity, the time interval in which $g_b(t)$ has appreciable value becomes negligible compared with T_1.   Equation (6-86) can be written as

$$\phi_{ce}(\tau) = \frac{1}{2T_1} \int_{-\infty}^{\infty} \sum_{n=-\infty}^{\infty} \sum_{m=-\infty}^{\infty} a(nT)b_1(mT)g_a(t - nT)g_b(t + \tau - mT) \, dt \tag{6-87}$$

where $b_1(nT) = b(mT)$ in the interval $-T_1 < mT < T_1$ but zero elsewhere.   Let $t' = t - nT$, and $m = n + m'$.   Equation (6-87) becomes, by changing variables t and m to t' and m', respectively,

$$\phi_{ce}(\tau) = \frac{1}{2T_1} \int_{-\infty}^{\infty} \sum_{n=-\infty}^{\infty} \sum_{m'=-\infty}^{\infty} a(nT)b_1(nT + m'T)$$
$$g_a(t')g_b(t' + \tau - m'T) \, dt' \tag{6-88}$$

Similarly to Eq. (6-88), one derives

$$\sum_{n=-\infty}^{\infty} a(nT)b_1(nT + m'T) = \frac{2T_1}{T} \phi_{ab}(m'T) \tag{6-89}$$

From Eqs. (6-88) and (6-89),

$$\phi_{ce}(\tau) = \frac{1}{T} \int_{-\infty}^{\infty} \sum_{m'=-\infty}^{\infty} \phi_{ab}(m'T)g_a(t')g_b(t' + \tau - m'T) \, dt' \tag{6-90}$$

Equation (6-90) is the convolution sum and integral of three variables $\phi_{ab}(m'T)$, $g_a(-t)$, and $g_b(t)$. In terms of s-domain variables, it is equivalent to

$$\Phi_{ce}(s) = \frac{1}{T} \Phi_{ab}^*(s)G_a(-s)G_b(s) \tag{6-91}$$

6-7. Stationarity of Continuous-system Variables in a Sampled System. We note that the signals $c(t)$ and $e(t)$ are stationary in the long run but nonstationary within each sampling period. For instance, $G_a(s)$ and $G_b(s)$ may have an impulse response of the form e^{-at}, with $1/\alpha$ much less than T. The mean-square values of $c(t)$ and $e(t)$ immediately after the sampling instant are much larger than those values immediately before. The correlation function $\phi_{ce}(nT)$ actually could be written $\phi_{ce}(nT,t_1)$, indicating that the averaging is taken over values of $c(t)$ and $e(t)$ at exactly t_1 after the sampling instants. Correspondingly, the sampled spectral densities $\Phi_{ce}(z,t_1)$ can be defined as

$$\Phi_{ce}(z,t_1) = \sum_{n=-\infty}^{n=\infty} \phi_{ce}(nT,t_1)z^{-n}$$

The mean-square value of $e(t)$ at t_1 after the sampling instants can be obtained by integrating:

$$\frac{1}{2\pi j} \oint z^{-1}\Phi_{ee}(z,t_1) \, dz$$

The correlation function $\phi_{ce}(\tau)$ of Eq. (6-90) is obtained by integrating over all times, and the dependence on t_1 is averaged out. As a result, $\Phi_{ce}(z)$ of Eq. (6-91) is the sampled spectral density corresponding to averaged $\phi_{ce}(\tau)$. The mean-square value of $e(t)$ obtained from $\Phi_{ee}(z)$ is the averaged value over all times.

6-8. Optimum System with Random Inputs. Figure 6-9 represents the block diagram of a system with random inputs. The spectral densities of the various inputs are known. For simplicity's sake, we assume that the inputs are uncorrelated. Since the treatment can be readily extended in case this assumption is not valid, there is little to be gained in treating a general case.   We assume also that the functional constraints and power constraints are the same as those of Sec. 6-3.

In previous sections, we defined a closed-loop digital transfer function $K(z)$ such that, with an input $r(t)$, the z transform of the output variable is $C(z) = K(z)R(z)$.   This function is now denoted as $K_1(z)$.   We note that, with a total input $r_1(t)$, $r_1(t) = r(t) + n(t)$, the digital signal $e_2^*(t)$ applied to the plant and hold system is given by its z transform,

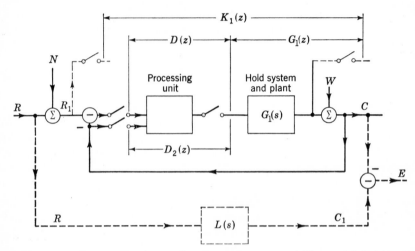

Fig. 6-9. Block diagram showing random inputs, system variables, and definition of a system error in a sampled-data system with inner feedback loop.

$E_2(z) = K_1(z)R_1(z)/G_1(z)$.   To take the effect of load disturbance $w(t)$ into account, a similar transfer function $K_2(z)$ is defined in the following equation:

$$E_2(z) = \frac{1}{G_1(z)} [K_1(z)R_1(z) + K_2(z)W(z)] \qquad (6\text{-}92)$$

where $W(z)$ is the z transform of $w(t)$.   The functional constraint on $K_2(z)$ is the same as that given by Eq. (6-8).

The function $c(t)$ is given by its Laplace transform:

$$C(s) = \frac{G_1(s)}{G_1^*(s)} [K_1^*(s)R_1^*(s) + K_2^*(s)W^*(s)] + W(s) \qquad (6\text{-}93)$$

The system error is given as

$$E(s) = L(s)R(s) - C(s) \qquad (6\text{-}94)$$

The mean-square value of $e(t)$ is

$$\overline{e^2} = \frac{1}{2\pi j} \int_{-j\infty}^{j\infty} \Phi_{ee}(s) \, ds$$

$$= \frac{1}{2\pi j} \oint z^{-1}\Phi_{ee}(z) \, dz \qquad (6\text{-}95)$$

The last equality sign is shown in the same way as Eq. (6-21). Let $c_1(t)$ represent the desired output. Then

$$C_1(s) = L(s)R(s) \qquad (6\text{-}96)$$

From Eq. (6-94),

$$\Phi_{ee}(s) = \Phi_{c_1 c_1}(s) + \Phi_{cc}(s) - \Phi_{c_1 c}(s) - \Phi_{c c_1}(s) \qquad (6\text{-}97)$$

By definition of $c_1(t)$, we have

$$\Phi_{c_1 c_1}(s) = L(s)L(-s)\Phi_{rr}(s) \qquad (6\text{-}98)$$

Equations (6-84) and (6-93) give

$$\Phi_{c_1 c}(s) = \frac{1}{T} \frac{K_1^*(s)G_1(s)}{G_1^*(s)} \Phi_{c_1 r_1}(s) = \frac{1}{T} \frac{K_1^*(s)G_1(s)L(-s)}{G_1^*(s)} \Phi_{rr}(s) \quad (6\text{-}99)$$

From Eqs. (6-91) and (6-93),

$$\Phi_{cc}(s) = \frac{1}{T} \frac{G_1(s)G_1(-s)}{G_1^*(s)G_1^*(-s)} \{K_1^*(s)K_1^*(-s)[\Phi_{rr}^*(s) + \Phi_{nn}^*(s)]$$

$$+ K_2^*(s)K_2^*(-s)\Phi_{ww}^*(s)\} + \frac{K_2^*(s)G_1(s)\Phi_{ww}(s)}{TG_1^*(s)} + \frac{K_2^*(-s)G_1(-s)\Phi_{ww}(s)}{TG_1^*(-s)}$$

$$+ \Phi_{ww}(s) \qquad (6\text{-}100)$$

From Eqs. (6-97) to (6-100) we obtain finally the following z-transform equation:

$$\Phi_{ee}(z) = \bar{L}L\Phi_{rr}(z) - \frac{1}{T} \frac{K_1(z)\bar{G}_1 L\Phi_{rr}(z^{-1})}{G_1(z)} - \frac{K_1(z^{-1})\bar{G}_1 L\Phi_{rr}(z)}{TG_1(z^{-1})}$$

$$+ \frac{1}{T} \frac{\bar{G}_1 G_1(z)}{G_1(z)G_1(z^{-1})} \{K_1(z)K_1(z^{-1})[\Phi_{rr}(z) + \Phi_{nn}(z)] + K_2(z)K_2(z^{-1})\Phi_{ww}(z)\}$$

$$+ \frac{K_2(z)\bar{G}_1 \Phi_{ww}(z^{-1})}{TG_1(z)} + \frac{K_2(z^{-1})\bar{G}_1 \Phi_{ww}(z)}{TG_1(z^{-1})} + \Phi_{ww}(z) \qquad (6\text{-}101)$$

Similarly, the mean-square value of the constrained variable $a(t)$ is shown to be

$$\overline{[a(t)]^2} = \frac{1}{2\pi j} \oint \Phi_{aa}(z) \frac{dz}{z} \qquad (6\text{-}102)$$

where

$$\Phi_{aa}(z) = \frac{1}{T} \frac{G_3 G_3(z)}{G_1(z)G_1(z^{-1})} \{K_1(z)K_1(z^{-1})[\Phi_{rr}(z) + \Phi_{nn}(z)]$$

$$+ K_2(z)K_2(z^{-1})\Phi_{ww}(z)\} \qquad (6\text{-}103)$$

The optimum system functions $K_1(z)$ and $K_2(z)$ can be determined by a method similar to that used in Sec. 6-4. However, as there is more than one unknown function, it is desirable to make use of a variational theorem in the z domain. Let the integrals I_m be defined as

$$I_m = \frac{1}{2\pi j} \oint \Phi_m(z, F_1, F_2, \ldots, R_n; \bar{F}_1, \bar{F}_2, \ldots, \bar{F}_n) \frac{dz}{z}$$

$$m = 0, 1, 2, \ldots, M \quad (6\text{-}104)$$

where $\bar{F}_i(z) = F_i(z^{-1})$. Conditions similar to 1, 2, and 3 of Sec. 4-3 are assumed to be satisfied. The necessary as well as sufficient condition for

$$I = \sum_{m=0}^{M} \lambda_m I_m$$

to be stationary with respect to infinitesimal variations of F_1, F_2, $\ldots$ and corresponding variations of $\bar{F}_1$, $\bar{F}_2$, $\ldots$ is that the functional derivatives

$$X_i = z^{-1} \sum_{m=0}^{M} \lambda_m \frac{\partial \Phi_m}{\partial \bar{F}_i} \quad (6\text{-}105)$$

do not have any pole inside the unit circle.

Making use of the above theorem and following through the steps of Sec. 6-4, we obtain finally

$$K_1(z) = \frac{1}{Z(z) Y_1(z)} \left[\frac{\bar{G}_1 L \Phi_{rr}(z)}{G_1(z^{-1}) Y_1(z^{-1}) Z(z^{-1})} \right]_+ \quad (6\text{-}106)$$

$$K_2(z) = -\frac{1}{W(z) Y_1(z)} \left[\frac{\bar{G}_1 \Phi_{ww}(z)}{G_1(z^{-1}) Y_1(z^{-1}) W(z^{-1})} \right]_+ \quad (6\text{-}107)$$

where

$$Z(z) Z(z^{-1}) = \Phi_{rr}(z) + \Phi_{nn}(z) \quad (6\text{-}108)$$

All the poles and zeros of $Z(z)$ are inside the unit circle. $Y_1(z)$ is defined by Eq. (6-46). From $K_1(z)$ and $K_2(z)$, $D_1(z)$ and $D_2(z)$ can be readily calculated.

The following example illustrates some typical calculations.

Example 6-2. For the system of Fig. 6-9, the known conditions are

$$G_1(s) = \frac{1 - e^{-st}}{s} \frac{10}{1 + 2Ts}$$

$$L(s) = e^{nTs}$$

$$\Phi_{rr}(j\omega) = \frac{2\nu A^2}{\nu^2 + \omega^2}$$

$$\Phi_{rn}(j\omega) = 0$$

$$\phi_{nn}(\tau) = 1 \qquad \tau = 0$$

$$\phi_{nn}(\tau) = 0 \qquad \tau \geq T$$

To design a data-processing unit which gives the lowest mean-square error, without constraint, we calculate

$$G_1(z) = \frac{3.94z^{-1}}{1 - 0.606z^{-1}}$$

$$G_1G_1(z) = \frac{9.7T(1 + 0.264z)(1 + 0.264z^{-1})}{(1 - 0.606z)(1 - 0.606z^{-1})}$$

$$\Phi_{nn}(z) = 1$$

$$\Phi_{rr}(z) = \frac{A^2(1 - q^2)}{(1 - qz)(1 - qz^{-1})} \qquad q = e^{-\nu T}$$

$$Z(z)Z(z^{-1}) = \Phi_{rr}(z) + \Phi_{nn}(z) = \frac{q(1 - az)(1 - az^{-1})}{a(1 - qz)(1 - qz^{-1})}$$

where a is a constant less than unity and satisfies the following equation:

$$\frac{A^2(1 - q^2)}{q} = \frac{(q - a)(1 - aq)}{aq}$$

$$P(z) = 1$$

$$m' = 1$$

$$Y(z) = 2.5 \sqrt{\frac{Tq}{a}} (1 + 0.264z^{-1})(1 - az^{-1})$$

$$G(-s)L(s)\Phi_{r_1r}(s) = \frac{20\nu A^2(1 - e^{Ts})e^{nTs}}{(\nu^2 - s^2)(1 - 2Ts)(-s)}$$

$$= \frac{10A^2(1 - q)q^n}{(\nu + s)(1 + 2T\nu)\nu} + \cdots$$

$$\bar{G}L\Phi_{r_1r}(z) = \frac{10A^2(1 - q)q^n}{\nu(1 + 2T\nu)(1 - qz^{-1})} + \cdots$$

$$\left[\frac{\bar{G}_1L\Phi_{rr}(z)}{G_1(z^{-1})Y_1(z^{-1})Z(z^{-1})} \right]_+ = \frac{10A^2(1 - q)q^n}{\nu(1 + 2T\nu)[Z(z)Y(z)G(z)]_{z^{-1}=q}} \frac{1}{1 - qz^{-1}}$$

$$K_0 = \frac{1.264Cq^n(q - a)z^{-1}}{(1 + 0.264z^{-1})(1 - az^{-1})}$$

where
$$C = \frac{1 - q}{T\nu q(1 + 2T\nu)} \frac{1.264}{1 + 0.264q} \frac{1.606q}{0.394}$$

6-9. Optimization of Transient Response to Unsynchronized Deterministic Inputs.

Unsynchronized deterministic inputs can be treated as random inputs with spectral density

$$\Phi_{rr}(s) = A R(s)R(-s) \tag{6-109}$$

where A is a constant. Equation (6-109) follows directly from Eq. (3-35).

6-10. Optimization of the Presampling Filter and Wave-shaping Filter.[†]

Figure 6-10 illustrates a system for transmitting a continuous signal over a sampled-data link. The sampling switch generally represents the necessity of transmitting the signal as a sequence of numbers, rather than representing an actual switch. For instance, we may wish to transmit a continuous signal accurately by short wave, and the most reliable way of doing this is pulse-code modulation. The sampling opera-

[†] Parts of Sec. 6-10 are reprinted from a paper by the author, Optimum Transmission of Continuous Signal over a Sampled-data Link, *AIEE paper* 60-1243, 1960.

tion, which is part and parcel of pulse-code modulation, is rather undesirable in that it causes frequency aliasing and mixes high-frequency noise into the signal band.   This effect can be substantially reduced by using a low-pass filter $F(s)$ before sampling to filter out most of the high-frequency noise.   At the receiving end, a wave-shaping filter $G(s)$ is used to reconstruct the continuous signal from the sampled signal.

The optimization problem can be formulated with reference to Fig. 6-10.   The input signal is $r_1(t) = r(t) + n(t)$.   The desired output signal $c_1(t)$ is the output of a linear operation $L(s)$ on $r(t)$.   Given the spectral densities $\Phi_{r_1 r_1}(j\omega)$, the network functions $F(s)$ and $G(s)$ to give least

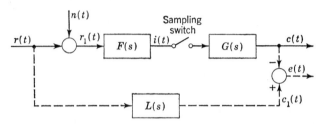

FIG. 6-10. Block diagram of a sampled-data transmission link.   (*From S. S. L. Chang, Optimum Transmission of Continuous Signal over a Sampled-data Link, AIEE paper 60-1243, 1960.*)

$\overline{[e(t)]^2}$ and the minimum value of $\overline{[e(t)]^2}$ are to be determined for the following three cases:

1. $F(s)$ is fixed, and $G(s)$ is to be optimized.
2. $G(s)$ is fixed, and $F(s)$ is to be optimized.
3. $F(s)$ and $G(s)$ are to be optimized simultaneously.

In the present and next sections, our mathematical manipulations are done mostly in the s domain, and we shall use the same shorthand notations explained in Sec. 2-4 following Eq. (2-13).   Whenever sampling is involved, $AB^* \equiv A(s)B^*(s)$, meaning that $B(s)$ alone is sampled, and $(AB)^* \equiv [A(s)B(s)]^*$, meaning that $A(s)B(s)$ are sampled together.   We further define the following mathematical symbols:

$$\{\quad\}^{\pm}: \qquad\qquad \{\quad\}^{+}\{\quad\}^{-} \equiv \{\quad\}$$

The function inside the braces is always symmetrical in s and $-s$ and can be factored so that $\{\quad\}^{+}$ and its reciprocal are analytic in the right half of the s plane and $\{\quad\}^{-}$ and its reciprocal are analytic in the left half of the s plane.

$\{\quad\}^{*\pm}$: The same definition is applied to sampled functions. $\{\quad\}^{*}$ is a rational function of z.   Let λ and $1/\lambda$ be a pair of its poles (or zeros) with $|\lambda| < |$.   Then $\{\quad\}^{*+}$ is written in factors of the form $1 - \lambda z^{-1}$, and $\{\quad\}^{*-}$ is written in factors of the form $1 - \lambda z$.

These rules are the same as the corresponding ones in Secs. 2-4 and 6-4 defining $Y(s)$ and $Y(z)$, respectively.

With reference to Fig. 6-10, the mean-square error is given as

$$\overline{[e(t)]^2} = \frac{1}{2\pi j} \int_{-j\infty}^{j\infty} \Phi_{ee}(s)\, ds \tag{6-110}$$

where $\Phi_{ee} = \Phi_{c_1 c_1} - \Phi_{c_1 c} - \Phi_{c c_1} + \Phi_{cc}$, and the latter spectral densities are given as

$$\Phi_{c_1 c_1} = \bar{L}L\Phi_{rr} \tag{6-111}$$

$$\Phi_{c_1 c} = \frac{1}{T}\, G\Phi_{c_1 i} = \frac{1}{T}\, FG\bar{L}\Phi_{rr_1} \tag{6-112}$$

$$\Phi_{c c_1} = \frac{1}{T}\, \bar{F}\bar{G}L\Phi_{r_1 r} \tag{6-113}$$

$$\Phi_{cc} = \frac{1}{T}\, (\bar{F}F\Phi_{r_1 r_1})^* \bar{G}G \tag{6-114}$$

Equations (6-111), (6-112), and (6-114) are obtained from Eqs. (3-17), (6-84), and (6-91), respectively. Equation (6-113) is obtained by changing s to $-s$ in Eq. (6-112) and noting that $\Phi_{c_1 c}(s) = \Phi_{c c_1}(-s)$.

The only requirement on F and G is that they be analytic in the RHP. With F fixed, Eq. (4-37) gives a condition to be satisfied by the optimum G:

$$\frac{\partial \Phi_{ee}}{\partial \bar{G}} = -\frac{1}{T}\, \bar{F}L\Phi_{r_1 r} + \frac{1}{T}\, (\bar{F}F\Phi_{r_1 r_1})^* G = X_1 \tag{6-115}$$

where $X_1(s)$ is an unspecified function analytic in the LHP. The solution of Eq. (6-115) is readily seen to be

$$G = \frac{Q}{\{\bar{F}F\Phi_{r_1 r_1}\}^{*+}} \tag{6-116}$$

where

$$Q = \left[\frac{\bar{F}L\Phi_{r_1 r}}{\{\bar{F}F\Phi_{r_1 r_1}\}^{*-}} \right]_+ \tag{6-117}$$

To derive an expression for the mean-square error under this condition, we obtain from Eq. (6-115)

$$\frac{1}{2\pi j} \int_{-j\infty}^{j\infty} (\Phi_{c c_1} - \Phi_{cc})\, ds = -\frac{T}{2\pi j} \int_{-j\infty}^{j\infty} X_1 \bar{G}\, ds = 0 \tag{6-118}$$

The last equality sign is due to the fact that both X_1 and $\bar{G}$ are analytic in the LHP. Replacing the dummy variable s by $-s$ on the left-hand side of Eq. (6-118) gives

$$\frac{1}{2\pi j} \int_{-j\infty}^{j\infty} (\Phi_{c_1 c} - \Phi_{cc})\, ds = 0 \tag{6-119}$$

Substituting Eqs. (6-118) and (6-119) in (6-110) gives

$$\overline{[e(t)]^2_{G_{opt}}} = \frac{1}{2\pi j} \int_{-j\infty}^{j\infty} (\Phi_{c_1c_1} - \Phi_{cc}) \, ds = \frac{1}{2\pi j} \int_{-j\infty}^{j\infty} \left(\Phi_{c_1c_1} - \frac{\bar{Q}Q}{T} \right) ds \quad (6\text{-}120)$$

The above completes the equations for optimizing $G(s)$. The problem of optimizing $F(s)$ with $G(s)$ given is reduced immediately to the same as the previous one by proving the following equation:

$$\frac{1}{2\pi j} \int_{-j\infty}^{j\infty} A^*(s)B(s) \, ds = \frac{1}{2\pi j} \int_{-j\infty}^{j\infty} B^*(s)A(s) \, ds \quad (6\text{-}121)$$

The above equality is to hold for all even functions $A(s)$ and $B(s)$ with finite $a(nt)$ and $b(nt)$, respectively.

Equation (6-121) is readily proved as follows:

$$\frac{1}{2\pi j} \int_{-j\infty}^{j\infty} A^*(s)B(s) \, ds = \frac{1}{2\pi j} \int_{-j\infty}^{j\infty} A^*(s)B(-s) \, ds$$

$$= \int_{-\infty}^{\infty} b(t) \sum_{n=-\infty}^{n=\infty} a(t)\delta(t - nT) \, dt$$

$$= \sum_{n=-\infty}^{n=\infty} a(nT)b(nT) \quad (6\text{-}122)$$

The first equality sign is due to the fact that $B(s)$ is even; the second is due to Parseval's theorem. Since the right-hand side of Eq. (6-122) is symmetrical in $a(t)$ and $b(t)$, Eq. (6-121) is proved.

With the help of Eq. (6-121), Eq. (6-110) can be written as

$$\overline{[e(t)]^2} = \frac{1}{2\pi j} \int_{-j\infty}^{j\infty} (\Phi - \Phi_{cc_1} - \Phi_{c_1c} + \Phi_{c_1c_1}) \, ds \quad (6\text{-}123)$$

where

$$\Phi = \frac{1}{T} (\bar{G}G)^* \bar{F}F \Phi_{r_1r_1} \quad (6\text{-}124)$$

In optimizing $F(s)$, Eqs. (6-123) and (6-124) take the place of Eqs. (6-110) and (6-114). The same steps which led to Eqs. (6-115), (6-116), and (6-120) give

$$-\frac{1}{T} \bar{G}L\Phi_{r_1r} + \frac{1}{T} (\bar{G}G)^* \Phi_{r_1r_1}F = X_2 \quad (6\text{-}125)$$

$$F = \frac{U}{\{\bar{G}G\}^{*+}\{\Phi_{r_1r_1}\}^+} \quad (6\text{-}126)$$

$$\overline{[e(t)]^2_{F_{opt}}} = \frac{1}{2\pi j} \int_{-j\infty}^{j\infty} \left(\Phi_{c_1c_1} - \frac{1}{T} \bar{U}U \right) ds \quad (6\text{-}127)$$

where X_2 is an unspecified function analytic in the LHP and U is given as

$$U = \left[\frac{\bar{G}L\Phi_{r_1r}}{\{\bar{G}G\}^* - \{\Phi_{r_1r_1}\}^-} \right]_+ \tag{6-128}$$

To summarize the above results, Eqs. (6-116) and (6-120) give the optimum wave-shaping filter $G(s)$ and the least-mean-square error, respectively, if $F(s)$ is fixed. Equations (6-126) and (6-127) give the optimum presampling filter $F(s)$ and the least-mean-square error, respectively, if $G(s)$ is fixed. For the optimum transmission system, Eqs. (6-115) and (6-125) are to be solved simultaneously. While all four equations (6-116), (6-120), (6-128), and (6-129) are satisfied by the optimized functions $F(s)$ and $G(s)$, they do not represent a solution of the problem since both $F(s)$ and $G(s)$ are unknown.

In order to arrive at a solution of Eqs. (6-115) and (6-125) simultaneously, one more general relation will be derived: Multiplying Eq. (6-115) by $TG(-s)$ and Eq. (6-125) by $TF(-s)$ and taking the difference give

$$\{\bar{F}F\Phi_{r_1r_1}\}^*\bar{G}G - \{\bar{G}G\}^*\Phi_{r_1r_1}\bar{F}F = TX_1\bar{G} - TX_2\bar{F} \tag{6-129}$$

The expression on the right-hand side of Eq. (6-129) is analytic in the LHP. Therefore the expression on the left-hand side is analytic in the LHP. As the latter expression is symmetrical in s and $-s$, it is necessarily analytic in the RHP also. Therefore, it must be a constant. The constant can be determined by integrating the latter expression from $-j\infty$ to $j\infty$. Equation (6-121) gives the integrated result as zero. Therefore, the constant is zero, and it follows that

$$\{\bar{F}F\Phi_{r_1r_1}\}^*\bar{G}G = \{\bar{G}G\}^*\Phi_{r_1r_1}\bar{F}F \tag{6-130}$$

Equation (6-130) is to be satisfied by the simultaneously optimized $F(s)$ and $G(s)$. Substituting Eqs. (6-116) and (6-126) in Eq. (6-130) gives

$$\bar{Q}Q = \bar{U}U \tag{6-131}$$

Because of the requirement that all the poles and zeros of $Q(s)$ and $U(s)$ be in the LHP, Eq. (6-131) gives

$$Q(s) = U(s) \tag{6-132}$$

Equation (6-116) is multiplied by its conjugate to give

$$\bar{G}G = \frac{\bar{Q}Q}{\{\bar{F}F\Phi_{r_1r_1}\}^*}$$

The sampled form of the above equation is

$$\{\bar{G}G\}^*\{\bar{F}F\Phi_{r_1r_1}\}^* = \{\bar{Q}Q\}^* \tag{6-133}$$

On account of Eqs. (6-132) and (6-133), Eq. (6-126) can be written as

$$\frac{\bar{F}}{\{\bar{F}F\Phi_{r_1r_1}\}^{*-}} = \frac{\bar{Q}}{\{\bar{Q}Q\}^{*-}\{\Phi_{r_1r_1}\}^{-}}$$

Equation (6-117) becomes

$$Q = \left[\frac{\bar{Q}L\Phi_{r_1r}}{\{\bar{Q}Q\}^{*-}\{\Phi_{r_1r_1}\}^{-}}\right]_{+} \tag{6-134}$$

Similarly, by using Eqs. (6-132), (6-133), and (6-116), Eq. (6-128) is reduced to exactly Eq. (6-134).

Equation (6-134) can be solved for Q. The only poles of the bracketed expression in the LHP are the ones due to $L\Phi_{r_1r}$. Let these be denoted as λ_i.

$$Q = \sum_i \frac{A_i}{s - \lambda_i} \tag{6-135}$$

The coefficients A_i are determined by substituting Eq. (6-135) back into Eq. (6-134). Equation (6-133) gives

$$\{\bar{G}G\}^{*+}\{\bar{F}F\Phi_{r_1r}\}^{*+} = \{\bar{Q}Q\}^{*+} \tag{6-136}$$

However, there is no way of determining the two factors on the left-hand side of the above equation separately. This is not surprising, since if we write $F = F_1^*F_2$ and $G = G_1^*G_2$ the block diagram of Fig. 6-10 gives

$$C = (RF)^*G = (RF_2)^*F_1^*G_1^*G_2$$

Therefore, $C(s)$ is indifferent to the distribution of $F_1^*(s)G_1^*(s)$ as long as the product remains unchanged, and consequently one is at liberty to choose one of these functions. As the sampled network function is much more costly to realize before sampling than after, one requires that

$$F_1^* = \frac{1}{\{\bar{G}G\}^{*+}} = \frac{1}{B} \tag{6-137}$$

where B is a constant to be selected as one wishes. Equations (6-116) and (6-126) become

$$G = \frac{BQ}{\{\bar{Q}Q\}^{*+}} \tag{6-138}$$

$$F = \frac{Q}{B\{\Phi_{r_1r_1}\}^{+}} \tag{6-139}$$

Equations (6-137) and (6-138) give the simultaneously optimized network functions, while with the optimized $Q(s)$ Eq. (6-120) gives the least value of mean-square error.

Example 6-3. A problem of optimum filtering and prediction in the presence of uncorrelated white noise will be used to illustrate the method.

$$c_1(t) = r(t + \alpha) \qquad L(s) = e^{\alpha s}$$

$$\Phi_{r_1r}(s) = \frac{2a}{a^2 - s^2}$$

$$\Phi_{r_1r_1}(s) = \frac{2a}{a^2 - s^2} + \sigma^2 = \frac{\sigma^2(b^2 - s^2)}{a^2 - s^2}$$

where $b^2 = a^2 + 2a/\sigma^2$. Determine optimum $F(s)$, $G(s)$, and the extra error due to sampling.

Solution. Equation (6-135) gives

$$Q(s) = \frac{A}{s + a}$$

The braced functions in Eqs. (6-137) to (6-139) are calculated to be

$$\{Q(-s)Q(s)\}^* = \frac{A^2(1 - e^{-2aT})/2a}{(1 - e^{-aT}e^{-Ts})(1 - e^{-aT}e^{Ts})}$$

$$\{Q(-s)Q(s)\}^{*-} = \frac{A\sqrt{(1 - e^{-2aT})/2a}}{1 - e^{-aT}e^{Ts}}$$

$$\{\Phi_{r_1r_1}(s)\}^- = \frac{\sigma(b - s)}{a - s}$$

Substituting the above results in Eq. (6-134) gives

$$A = \frac{e^{-\alpha a}\sqrt{2a(1 - e^{-2aT})}}{\sigma(b + a)}$$

For numerical simplicity, let

$$B = e^{-\alpha a}\sqrt{(1 - e^{-2aT})/2a}$$

Equations (6-138) and (6-139) give

$$G(s) = \frac{(1 - e^{-aT}e^{-Ts})e^{-\alpha a}}{s + a} \tag{6-140}$$

$$F(s) = \frac{2a}{\sigma(b + a)(s + a)}\frac{s + a}{\sigma(s + b)} = \frac{2a}{\sigma^2(b + a)}\frac{1}{s + b}$$

Since $\sigma^2 = 2a/(b^2 - a^2)$, the above equation can be written as

$$F(s) = \frac{b - a}{s + b} \tag{6-141}$$

The function $G(s)$ of Eq. (6-140) can be separated into a digital filter and a low-pass filter. Together with $F(s)$ of Eq. (6-141), they are represented by the block diagram of Fig. 6-11.

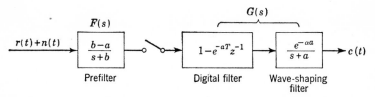

FIG. 6-11. Block diagram for the optimized sampled-data transmission link of Example 6-3.

The mean-square error is given by Eq. (6-120):

$$\overline{[e(t)]^2} = 1 - \frac{A^2}{2aT} = 1 - \frac{e^{-2\alpha a}(1 - e^{-2aT})}{\sigma^2(b + a)^2 T}$$
$$= 1 - \frac{(b - a)(1 - e^{-2aT})e^{-2\alpha a}}{2aT(b + a)} \tag{6-142}$$

At T approaches zero, Eq. (6-142) approaches the known result of a Wiener filter:

$$\overline{[e(t)]^2_{T=0}} = 1 - \frac{b - a}{b + a} e^{-2\alpha a}$$

The excess error due to sampling is found to be

$$\overline{[e(t)]^2} - \overline{[e(t)]^2_{T=0}} = \left(1 - \frac{1 - e^{-2aT}}{2aT}\right)\frac{(b - a)e^{-2\alpha a}}{b + a} \tag{6-143}$$

6-11. Optimum Presampling Filter and Hold Circuit in Control Systems.

The method of the preceding section can be modified slightly to optimize the presampling filter, the digital processing unit, and the hold circuit simultaneously in a sampled-data feedback control system. Sometimes a designer is not at liberty to change the presampling filter or the hold circuit. This presents no problem. As we shall see, the method can be used to optimize the digital processing unit together with either or both of the other two units.

The essential difference between optimum filtering and control problems is that in the latter the constraints due to the controlled plant must be considered. In general, we can find equivalent closed-loop transfer functions $F(s)$ and $G(s)$ such that

$$C(s) = [F(s)R_1(s)]^*G(s) \tag{6-144}$$

where $G(s)$ or $F(s)$ is usually a product of a sampled function and an unsampled function of s. While the method we shall discuss is not based on any particular arrangement of control components or block diagram, it is desirable to use one to illustrate the physical significance of $F(s)$ and $G(s)$. For the system of Fig. 6-12, F_1, G_1, G_p, and H are unsampled functions of s, and D^* is the usual digital processing unit.

$$E_2 = F_1R_1 - E_2^*D^*G_eF_1 \tag{6-145}$$

where
$$G_e = \frac{G_1G_p}{1 + G_pH} \tag{6-146}$$

Applying the sampling operation to Eq. (6-145) and solving for E_2^* give

$$E_2^* = \frac{(F_1R_1)^*}{1 + (G_eF_1)^*D^*}$$
$$C = G_eE_2^* = \frac{G_e(F_1R_1)^*D^*}{1 + (G_eF_1)^*D^*} \tag{6-147}$$

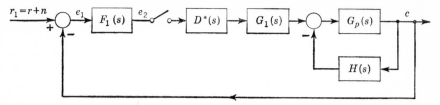

FIG. 6-12. Block diagram of a feedback system with presampling filter $F_1(s)$ and wave-shaping filter $G_1(s)$.

Comparing Eqs. (6-144) and (6-147), we see that

$$F(s) = F_1(s)B^*(s) \tag{6-148a}$$

$$G(s) = \frac{G_e D^*}{[1 + (G_e F_1)^* D^*]B^*} \tag{6-148b}$$

where B^* is arbitrary. If the same reasoning which leads to Eq. (4-10) is applied to Eq. (6-148b), it is obvious that the transportation lag and nonminimum-phase part $[e^{-\tau s}P(s)]$ of $G_p(s)$ must also be a part of $G(s)$. Therefore we write

$$G(s) = e^{-\tau s}P(s)G_2(s) \tag{6-149}$$

where $G_2(s)$ is required to be analytic in the RHP but is otherwise free.

The amplitude constraint can be written as

$$\overline{[a(t)]^2} \le M$$

where $A(s) = G_3(s)C(s)/G_p(s)$. Among the spectral densities given in Eqs. (6-111) to (6-114), the significant modifications and additions are

$$\Phi_{cc_1} = \frac{1}{T} \bar{F} \bar{G}_2 \bar{P} e^{\tau s} L \Phi_{r_1 r} \tag{6-150}$$

$$\Phi_{cc} = \frac{1}{T} (\bar{F} F \Phi_{r_1 r_1})^* \bar{P} P \bar{G}_2 G_2 \tag{6-151}$$

$$\Phi_{aa} = \frac{1}{T} \frac{(\bar{F} F \Phi_{r_1 r_1})^* \bar{P} P \bar{G}_2 G_2 \bar{G}_3 G_3}{\bar{G}_p G_p} \tag{6-152}$$

The integral to be minimized is

$$\overline{[e(t)]^2} + k^2 \overline{[a(t)]^2} = \frac{1}{2\pi j} \int_{-j\infty}^{j\infty} (\Phi_{ee} + k^2 \Phi_{aa}) \, ds \tag{6-153}$$

Following the same steps as in Sec. 6-10, we obtain the optimized functions for the following cases:

1. Prefilter $F_1(s)$ is known; $D(z)$ and $G_e(s)$ are to be optimized. In this case we let $B^*(s) = 1$. $F(s)$ is then completely known. The optimized $G(s)$ is given as

$$G = \frac{e^{-\tau s}}{Y\{\bar{F} F \Phi_{r_1 r_1}\}^{*+}} \left[\frac{\bar{F} e^{\tau s} L \Phi_{r_1 r}}{\bar{Y}\{\bar{F} F \Phi_{r_1 r_1}\}^{*-}} \right]_+ \tag{6-154}$$

where
$$Y = \frac{\bar{P}}{P}\left\{1 + \frac{k^2\bar{G}_3 G_3}{\bar{G}_p G_p}\right\}^+ \tag{6-155}$$

In other words, $1/Y$ is obtained by a root-square-locus plot of the transfer function G_p/kG_3, keeping the original zeros as its zeros. $D(z)$ and $G_e(s)$ are obtained by comparing Eqs. (6-148b) and (6-154). Equation (6-120) is still correct for calculating $\overline{e^2} + k^2\overline{a^2}$ with the new value of Q given as

$$Q = \left[\frac{\bar{F}e^{\tau s}L\Phi_{r_1 r}}{\bar{Y}\{\bar{F}F\Phi_{r_1 r_1}\}^{*-}}\right]_+ \tag{6-156}$$

2. The continuous part $G_e(s)$ is known; $D(z)$ and $F_1(s)$ are to be optimized. Let

$$B^* = \frac{D^*}{1 + (G_e F_1)^* D^*} \tag{6-157}$$

Then $G(s) = G_e(s)$, and the optimized $F(s)$ is given as

$$F = \frac{U}{\{\Phi_{r_1 r_1}\}^+\{\bar{Y}Y\bar{G}G\}^{*+}} \tag{6-158}$$

where
$$U = \left[\frac{\bar{G}e^{\tau s}L\Phi_{r_1 r}}{\{\bar{Y}Y\bar{G}G\}^{*-}\{\Phi_{r_1 r_1}\}^-}\right]_+ \tag{6-159}$$

and Eq. (6-127) is still correct for calculating $\overline{e^2} + k^2\overline{a^2}$ with the new U.

3. All three functions $F_1(s)$, $D(z)$, and $G_e(s)$ are to be optimized simultaneously. The results are

$$Q = U = \left[\frac{\bar{Q}e^{\tau s}L\Phi_{r_1 r}}{\{\bar{Q}Q\}^{*-}\bar{Y}\{\Phi_{r_1 r_1}\}^-}\right]_+ \tag{6-160}$$

$$G = \frac{Be^{-\tau s}Q}{Y\{\bar{Q}Q\}^{*+}} \tag{6-161}$$

$$F = \frac{Q}{B\{\Phi_{r_1 r_1}\}^+} \tag{6-162}$$

where B is an arbitrary constant.

Example 6-4. A follow-up control system has the same signal and noise spectral densities as the one in Example 6-3. The controlled plant has a transfer function K/s, and the mean-square value of the input $i(t)$ to the controlled plant is limited:

$$\overline{[i(t)]^2} \leq M$$

Determine the optimum $F_1(s)$, $D(z)$, and $G_1(s)$.
Solutions. Under the given conditions,

$$L(s) = 1 \qquad e^{\tau s} = 1 \qquad G_3(s) = 1$$
$$Y = 1 + \frac{k}{K}s = 1 + k's$$

Equation (6-160) gives

$$Q = \frac{\sqrt{2a(1 - e^{-2aT})}}{\sigma(b + a)(1 + ak')} \frac{1}{s + a}$$

Let
$$B = \sqrt{(1 - e^{-2aT})/2a} \quad \text{as before; then}$$

$$G(s) = \frac{1 - e^{-aT}e^{-Ts}}{(1 + k's)(s + a)} \tag{6-163}$$

$$F(s) = \frac{b - a}{(1 + ak')(s + b)} \tag{6-164}$$

Equations (6-163) and (6-164) can be readily realized by the block diagram of Fig. 6-13. We note that the optimum data hold has an exponentially decaying characteristic instead of the conventional constant value over a sampling period.

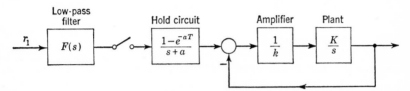

Fig. 6-13. Physical realization of an optimum system (Example 6-4).

6-12. Summary. A few selected topics on the optimum design of sampled-data systems are treated in this chapter:

1. Deadbeat systems
2. Systems with least-integral-square error to deterministic inputs subject to plant saturation
3. Systems with least-mean-square error in the presence of noise and load disturbance and also subject to plant saturation

The emphasis is on the design of a digital computer or sampled-data processing unit which receives and delivers a series of impulses to control a continuous plant. The manipulated impulses are such that they give the best match, in a prescribed sense, of the continuous-plant response to the desired response. In cases where the designer has a free choice of the presampling filter and (or) the hold circuit (postsampling wave-shaping filter), methods are also developed for simultaneous optimization of the sampled-data processing unit together with either or both of the continuous filters.

Various ways of defining the sampled correlation function and sampled spectral densities are given. The equivalence as well as differences of these definitions is shown. The input-output relations of sampled random signals as well as continuous random signals in sampled systems are derived. A variational theorem in the z domain is stated but not proved, as this can be done readily by a method similar to that of Sec. 4-3.

Examples are given to illustrate the various design techniques.

CHAPTER 7

SPECTRAL-DENSITY ESTIMATES

In the previous chapters, we have visualized the significant role played by spectral densities in the design of optimum systems with random inputs. Little has been said about the accuracies of experimentally determined spectral densities. For stationary signals with unlimited data available, the spectral densities can be determined to any degree of accuracy, but this condition does not exist in many situations. Just to name a few:

1. In the experimental study of missiles in flight, every bit of data is obtained at considerable cost.

2. For adaptive systems, admitting random inputs, the input signal is assumed to be undergoing adiabatic change. In order that the system be constantly tuned to give optimum performance, we must be able to determine the most up-to-the-second signal properties with the maximum accuracy. The requirement of up-to-the-second-ness and the requirement of accuracy are not compatible.

3. Even for stationary random signals of unlimited availability, economic considerations of computer and manpower usually limit the amount of data which are actually analyzed.

Considering the above, we see that some basic knowledge of spectral-density estimates is of vital importance in control engineering.

7-1. The Nature of Measured Spectral Densities and Correlation Functions. In Sec. 3-5, the spectral densities and correlation functions are defined in terms of random variables which remain stationary and may be measured for as long a period T_1 as we wish. However, in all practical measurements, the duration T_1 is finite. Because of the random nature of the variables, no two measurements are expected to agree. The spectral densities as computed from one sample record differ from that computed from another, and the results are expected to be scattered somewhat rather than falling exactly on a smooth curve. In Fig. 7-1, the solid curve represents the mean value of measured spectral density from a large number of sample records, while the broken curve represents that from a single sample. The same situation exists with measured correlation functions.

The scattered nature of the measured spectral density does not originate from the measuring technique or the instrumental accuracy. We may think of it as nature's way of baffling us when we try to squeeze too much information out of a single specimen which does not have that much in it. More specifically, there are two main sources of uncertainties:

Uncertainty of Frequency and Time. In order to determine the frequency of a signal to an approximate accuracy of Δf, the length of the sample signal required in the analysis is at least $1/\Delta f$.

Statistical Uncertainty. There is an inherent uncertainty in the process of estimating the properties of the entire ensemble from a limited number of observed samples. For instance, we have to throw a die many more times than the least possible six to know that there are six faces on the die

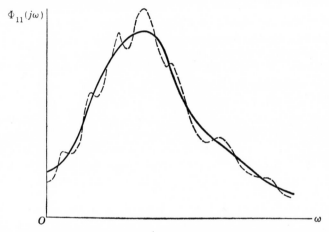

FIG. 7-1. Typical random variation of power spectrum computed from a single sample record of finite duration (broken curve) from the averaged power spectrum computed from a large number of sample records (solid curve).

and that each face has the same probability of appearing, if this knowledge is to be gained entirely by experiment.

In the subsequent sections, we shall determine the inherent limitations on the accuracies of computed spectral densities and correlation functions. These limits depend on the number and length of sample records, required resolution in frequency, and the random nature of the signals being measured. For the latter characterization, we shall assume that the signals are Gaussian. As discussed in Sec. 3-2, a Gaussian signal can be thought of as the sum total of a large number of independent contributing signals, the magnitude of each contributing signal being insignificantly small. In nature, the following signals are among the notably Gaussian ones:

1. Pressure and height of ocean waves
2. Pressure and instantaneous velocity of air turbulence
3. Thermal noise, shot noise, radar noise, etc.

One may think of the Gaussian case as an extreme example in randomness, and reliability estimates based on Gaussian signals are pessimistic for signals that may be random but not Gaussian.

7-2. Error Due to Uncertainty in Spectral-density Measurements.
Let us consider a sample signal $i(t)$, of length T_1, generated by a given stationary random process.   It can be expressed as a Fourier series:

$$i(t) = \frac{A_0}{2} + \sum_{n=1}^{\infty} (A_n \cos \omega_n t + B_n \sin \omega_n t) \tag{7-1}$$

where $\omega_n = 2\pi n/T_1$ and

$$A_n = \frac{2}{T_1} \int_0^{T_1} i(t) \cos \omega_n t \, dt \tag{7-2}$$

$$B_n = \frac{2}{T_1} \int_0^{T_1} i(t) \sin \omega_n t \, dt \tag{7-3}$$

We shall refer to the mean-square value of signal amplitude as power. The power contained in the nth spectral line is

$$P_n = \tfrac{1}{2}(A_n{}^2 + B_n{}^2) \tag{7-4}$$

For a stationary random process, one instant of time is just as good as another, and there is no preferred phase for any sinusoidal component of $i(t)$.   Therefore

$$\langle A_n \rangle = \langle B_n \rangle = 0 \tag{7-5}$$

and
$$\langle A_n{}^2 \rangle = \langle B_n{}^2 \rangle \tag{7-6}$$

The Fourier coefficients A_n and B_n have zero mean, but their standard deviation is, in general, not zero.   These coefficients have the same nature as the net distance traveled in a random-walk problem with equal probability of moving in either direction.   The analogy can be better demonstrated by rewriting Eq. (7-2) as follows:

$$A_n T_1 = 2 \sum_{m=1}^{M} \int_{(m-1)T_2}^{mT_2} i(t) \cos \omega_n t \, dt \tag{7-7}$$

where $M = T_1/T_2$.   In Eq. (7-7) the integral from 0 to T_1 is broken up into little segments of width T_2 each, and T_2 is selected so that the $i(t)$ in different integrals are substantially independent.   Since each integral has equal likelihood of being positive or negative, the expected value of the total sum $A_n T_1$ vanishes, which is in accord with Eq. (7-5).   For the same T_2 the mean-square deviation $\langle (T_1 A_n)^2 \rangle$ increases proportionally with M and therefore with T_1:

$$\langle (T_1 A_n)^2 \rangle = T_1{}^2 \langle A_n{}^2 \rangle \equiv K(\omega_n) T_1$$

where $K(\omega_n)$ is a proportionality constant independent of T_1 but is a function of ω_n.

We may write the above equation in another way:

$$\langle A_n{}^2 \rangle = \frac{K(\omega_n)}{T_1} \tag{7-8}$$

What is the significance of $K(\omega_n)$? With a sample signal of length T_1, the spectral lines or Fourier components are at frequency intervals $1/T_1$ apart. For any given frequency range Δf, the number of spectral lines inside that range is $T_1 \Delta f$, and the total power inside that range is the measured value of $\Phi_{ii}(j\omega_n) \Delta f$, by definition.† Therefore,

$$\Phi_{ii}(j\omega_n)_{meas} \Delta f = \sum_{\Delta f} \tfrac{1}{2}(A_n{}^2 + B_n{}^2) \tag{7-9}$$

where the summation is over all spectral lines inside Δf. The spectral density $\Phi_{ii}(j\omega_n)$ is the expected value of the measured $\Phi_{ii}(j\omega_n)$. Consequently, Eq. (7-9) can be written as

$$\Phi_{ii}(j\omega_n) \Delta f = \sum_{\Delta f} \tfrac{1}{2}(\langle A_n{}^2 \rangle + \langle B_n{}^2 \rangle) \tag{7-10}$$

From Eqs. (7-6), (7-8), and (7-10), we have

$$\Phi_{ii}(j\omega_n) \Delta f = T_1 \Delta f \frac{K(\omega_n)}{T_1}$$

Therefore, $\qquad\qquad K(\omega_n) = \Phi_{ii}(j\omega_n) \tag{7-11}$

In the above we have shown that A_n has zero mean and standard deviation $\sqrt{\Phi_{ii}(j\omega_n)/T_1}$. What is the distribution of A_n? With reference to Sec. A-6, if T_1 is sufficiently long or the number of terms M in Eq. (7-7) is sufficiently large, A_n is expected to have Gaussian distribution:

$$p(A_n) \, dA_n = \frac{1}{\sqrt{2\pi E_n}} e^{-A_n{}^2/2E_n} \, dA_n \tag{7-12}$$

where $E_n = \Phi_{ii}(j\omega_n)/T_1$. From Eqs. (7-4) and (7-12), the power of the nth spectral line P_n has a probability density $p(P_n)$:

$$p(P_n) \, dP_n = \int p(A_n) p(B_n) \, dA_n \, dB_n$$

$$= \frac{1}{2\pi E_n} \int e^{-P_n/E_n} \, dA_n \, dB_n$$

$$= \frac{1}{E_n} e^{-P_n/E_n} \, dP_n \tag{7-13}$$

The integral sign is over a zonal region $P_n < \tfrac{1}{2}(A_n{}^2 + B_n{}^2) < P_n + dP_n$. From Eq. (7-13) we see that the power of each spectral line has an

† To agree with most of the literature on power spectra measurements, $\Phi_{ik}(j\omega)$ is taken to be the power per unit *real* frequency range in Chap. 7. Its value is twice that of the theoretical $\Phi_{ik}(j\omega)$ in other chapters of the book. See Sec. 3-6.

exponential distribution.   Its value could be anywhere from zero to a few times E_n.   The expected value of P_n is E_n, and its mean-square deviation is

$$\langle (P_n - E_n)^2 \rangle = \int_0^\infty (P_n - E_n)^2 p(P_n) \, dP_n = E_n{}^2 \qquad (7\text{-}14)$$

Equation (7-14) shows that, if we measure the spectral density $\Phi_{ii}(j\omega_n)$ by calculating P_n for one frequency alone, the probable error is 100 per cent.   However, if we sum over P_n for all the components in a frequency range Δf, as shown in Eq. (7-9), both the mean value and mean-square deviation are multiplied by the number of components $T_1 \Delta f$.   The percentage of the probable error is reduced:

$$\epsilon \equiv \frac{\sqrt{\langle [\Phi(j\omega)_{meas} - \Phi(j\omega)]^2 \rangle}}{\Phi(j\omega)} = \frac{1}{\sqrt{T_1 \Delta f}} \qquad (7\text{-}15)$$

where ϵ is the expected per-unit error.

The same sort of reduction in probable error can be obtained by averaging the spectral densities analyzed from N independent samples of $i(t)$; Eq. (7-15) is replaced by

$$\epsilon = \frac{1}{\sqrt{N T_1 \Delta f}} \qquad (7\text{-}16)$$

Alternatively, we may write

$$T_1 = \frac{1}{\epsilon^2 N \, \Delta f} \qquad (7\text{-}17)$$

Equation (7-17) gives the required sample length for an expected per-unit error ϵ and resolution Δf.   We note that the same degree of accuracy and resolution can be obtained by either increasing the number of samples or increasing the length of each sample.   However, in the former case, the resolution is always limited by the following relation:

$$T_1 > \frac{1}{\Delta f} \qquad (7\text{-}18)$$

Equation (7-18) states simply the impossibility of distinguishing two frequency components Δf apart in a sample of length less than $1/\Delta f$.†

7-3. Direct Measurement of Spectral Densities by Analog Method. It is generally true in electronic computing devices that, if the desired accuracy is not exacting, analog methods are cheaper or simpler than digital methods.   The dividing line is approximately at an allowed error figure of 0.1 per cent.   In spectral-analysis work, instrument error of the order of 1 or 2 per cent is considered tolerable, since the inherent error due

---

† Inequality (7-18) can be put in a more precise form: If the signal $i(t)$ of length T_1 is repeated indefinitely, the power spectrum becomes bunched into spectral lines

to statistical uncertainties is of the order of 10 per cent or more in most measurements.

The basic arrangements of Fig. 3-2 for measuring spectral densities and cross-spectral densities have been discussed in Sec. 3-5. While there have been various methods published in the literature, they are more or less variations of the basic method in order to overcome one or another of the following difficulties:

1. Servo signals usually have very low frequencies. Some have periods better counted in minutes than in seconds. The filters are costly, and the time it takes to analyze a point on the spectrum is prohibitively long.

2. A tunable filter or a large number of bandpass filters $H(s)$ have to be used in order to obtain sufficient points to plot a spectral-density-versus-frequency curve. It is difficult to keep the area of $|H(j\omega)|^2$ versus frequency curve the same (or even constant) at different frequencies. Scale corrections are neither convenient nor accurate.

3. In measuring cross-spectral densities the bandpass filters have to be closely matched in phase-shift characteristics. This is very difficult to do for filters with narrow passband and sharp cutoff characteristics.

A workable device must overcome all the above difficulties. For the speed-up process, the signal is generally recorded on magnetic tape or sound film and played back at much higher speeds. Magnetic tape

---

separated from each other by $1/T_1$, and the minimum uncertainty in frequency δf is of the order of $1/T_1$. If the signal $i(t)$ is not repeated, we may write

$$i(t) = i_\infty(t)h(t)$$

$$h(t) = \begin{cases} 1 & \text{for } 0 \le t \le T_1 \\ 0 & \text{for other values of } (t) \end{cases}$$

Then
$$I(j\omega) = \frac{1}{2\pi} \int_{-\infty}^{\infty} I_\infty(j\omega - j\omega_1)H(j\omega_1)\,d\omega_1$$

Multiplying the above equation by $2/T_1$ times its conjugate gives

$$\frac{2}{T_1} I(-j\omega)I(j\omega) = \frac{1}{2\pi^2 T_1} \int_{-\infty}^{\infty} \int_{-\infty}^{\infty} I_\infty(j\omega_2 - j\omega)I_\infty(j\omega - j\omega_1)H(j\omega_1)H(-j\omega_2)\,d\omega_1\,d\omega_2$$

Taking the ensemble average gives

$$\langle \Phi_{ii}(j\omega)_{meas} \rangle = \frac{1}{2\pi^2 T_1} \int_{-\infty}^{\infty} \int_{-\infty}^{\infty} \langle I_\infty(j\omega_2 - j\omega)I_\infty(j\omega - j\omega_1) \rangle H(j\omega_1)H(-j\omega_2)\,d\omega_1\,d\omega_2$$

As $\langle I_\infty(j\omega)I_\infty(j\omega') \rangle = \pi\Phi_{ii}(j\omega)\delta(\omega - \omega')$, the above equation becomes

$$\langle \Phi_{ii}(j\omega)_{meas} \rangle = \frac{1}{2\pi T_1} \int_{-\infty}^{\infty} \Phi_{ii}(j\omega - j\omega_1)H(j\omega_1)H(-j\omega_1)\,d\omega_1$$

$$= \frac{1}{2\pi T_1} \int_{-\infty}^{\infty} \Phi_{ii}(j\omega - j\omega_1)\left(\frac{\sin \omega_1 T_1/2}{\omega_1/2}\right)^2 d\omega_1$$

The above equation represents a spreading of the spectral density over a bandwidth of $\delta f = 1/T_1$. In both cases the best resolution obtainable is δf. Therefore $\Delta f > \delta f$, and inequality (7-18) follows.

has proved more convenient to use than sound film. To avoid the necessity of using tunable filters or a large number of filters, heterodyning is the only method that has appeared in the literature. An alternative method for the direct measurement of cross-spectral densities is taking the difference between the power spectra of sum and difference signals. Instead of surveying the literature on this subject, we shall describe in some detail an analyzer initially developed by the author at New York University and later completed under the supervision of J. H. Chadwick of the Marine Division of Sperry Gyroscope Company. It is currently in use for analyzing ocean waves, ship motions, and servo signals in general.

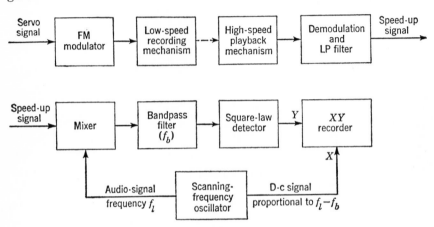

FIG. 7-2. Block diagram of electronic spectrum analyzer.

Figure 7-2 illustrates a block diagram of the device. There are two essential functioning units:

1. *Data Speed-up and Repeating Unit.* The best frequency range for spectral analysis is at the high audio and supersonic region. The speeding-up operation can be done in two ways.

FM TAPE RECORDING. Magnetic tapes are much more reliable in carrying frequency information than straight amplitude information. Frequency-modulated signal is recorded on the tape, and the length of tape for each sample record is made into a loop and played back at a few hundred to a few thousand times the recording speed. For various applications the recording speed and center carrier frequency are proportional to signal frequency range, while the playback speed is fixed and tied to the spectral analyzer.

Frequency modulation is accomplished by varying the positive grid bias of a multivibrator according to the servo signal. With adequate positive bias, a linear range of frequency swing of ±40 per cent of the center carrier frequency is readily obtained.† The carrier frequency can be made as low as desired in so far as the electronics is concerned. However, it must be high enough for the servo signal. The recording-tape speed depends on the carrier frequency. It is normally possible to record 1,000 cycles of carrier on every inch of tape. The playback speed is limited by tape flutter and is much higher. Two typical sets of values are given in Table 7-1.

TABLE 7-1

Servo signal	0–0.5 cps	0–10 cps
Carrier frequency	12.5 cps	250 cps
Recording-tape speed	1⅛ in./min	⅜ in./sec
Frequency swing	7.5–17.5 cps	150–350 cps
Playback speed	45 in./sec	45 in./sec
Speed-up signal	0–1.2 kc	0–1.2 kc

With large-percentage frequency swing, the demodulation is best accomplished by a counter-type demodulator. For each zero crossing of the carrier signal, a voltage pulse of constant magnitude and duration is produced at the output end. A low-pass filter with a cutoff frequency between the highest signal frequency and the lowest carrier frequency is used to recover the signal from the sequence of voltage pulses. The filter is designed to have negligible ripple in its attenuation characteristics in the speed-up signal range. Since the power spectrum of a signal does not depend on phase, the filtering error is also negligible. In measuring the cross-spectral density of two signals, the filtering error is again negligible since there is no change in the relative phase of the two signals.

PARALLEL PCM ON MAGNETIC DRUM.‡ With a magnetic drum, it is possible to record the signal with one set of heads and to take out the speed-up signal simultaneously with another set of heads. The device works as follows: Each sampled signal point is converted into a binary number. The n digits are recorded on n parallel channels, with one channel for each digit. Suppose that there are N digit positions on each

---

† It is easy to see why the frequency-versus-bias-voltage characteristics are extremely linear. When the tube is under conduction, its grid bias is approximately 0. At the commuting instant, a voltage $-E_\Delta$ far beyond cutoff voltage $-E_c$ is impressed on its grid. Subsequently the grid voltage follows an exponentially decaying curve toward the bias voltage E_b: $e_g = E_b - (E_\Delta + E_b)e^{-t/RC}$. At $e_g = -E_c$, the multivibrator commutes again, and the half period is

$$\frac{T}{2} = RC \log \frac{E_\Delta + E_b}{E_c + E_b} = RC \log \left(1 + \frac{1}{x} \right)$$

where $x = (E_b + E_c)/(E_\Delta - E_c)$. The function $1/\log (1 + 1/x)$ is extremely linear for $x > 2$.

‡ Still being developed at the time of writing.

channel. The recording heads skip N digits and record on every $(N + 1)$st digit, while the playback heads read out every digit. By this means the sampled signal is speeded up by a factor $N + 1$. Use of parallel recording of the binary digits allows the maximum number of sampling points for a given drum circumference. It also simplifies the coding and decoding circuits as compared with a time division system.

The system has two advantages: For analyzing the recorded signal it does away with the manual process of forming tapes into loops, which is usually a bottleneck in large-scale data-analysis operation. For adaptive systems, the spectral densities of immediately past data can be analyzed while present data are being recorded simultaneously.

2. *Spectral Analysis Unit.* The repetitive speed-up signal is heterodyned with a local oscillator of slowly varying frequency which scans

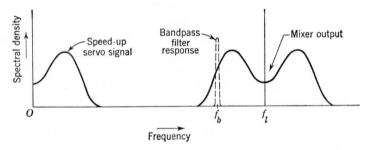

Fig. 7-3. Spectral densities of servo signal and mixer output signal in the electronic spectrum analyzer.

over the required range. To obtain constant conversion gain the local oscillator signal is of square waveform and is applied to the cathode of a balanced linear amplifier (mixer in Fig. 7-2) so that the amplifier is cut off every other half cycle. The signal being analyzed is applied to the grid of the amplifier, and a conversion gain of $1/\pi$ times the amplifier gain is obtained.† The output from the converter is filtered by a bandpass filter with center frequency f_b and detected by a square-law detector to give the spectral density at f_s:

$$f_s = \frac{1}{a} (f_l - f_b) \qquad (7\text{-}19)$$

where a is the speed-up ratio and f_l is the local oscillator frequency. The relation is illustrated in Fig. 7-3.

† Consider an input $A \sin \omega t$. The output is $A \sin \omega t[1 + f(t)]K_a/2$, where $f(t)$ is a square wave of unity amplitude. Expressing $f(t)$ in a Fourier series, we obtain immediately in the output product a term $(K_a A/\pi) \cos (\omega_l - \omega)t$. If $\omega < \omega_b$ and $\omega_l > \omega_b$, the only term that can pass the bandpass filter is the term with $\omega_l - \omega = \omega_b$. All the harmonic terms are filtered out.

The combination of bandpass filter and square-law detector serves an essential averaging function. The repetitive signal has a fundamental period T_1/a, and its power spectrum is a series of lines $\delta f\ (= a/T_1)$ apart. As discussed in Sec. 7-2, the power of any given spectral line of different sample records of the same ensemble is distributed over a wide range, with its standard deviation equal to its mean value. When one or a few sample records are used in the analysis, it is necessary to average the power content over a number of spectral lines to obtain any meaningful result. There are usually a large number of spectral lines in the passband of the filter, and the power content of each spectral line is modified by the attenuation characteristics of the filter. As the square-law detector gives the total power of the filtered signal, its output voltage is proportional to the weighted average of the spectral lines in the passband.

The rate of scanning must be slow enough so that a nearly steady-state condition exists. Another way of looking at this is that, during the time of scanning over each filter bandwidth, the sample signal has to be repeated a sufficient number of times so that different portions of the sample signal are equally emphasized.

The attenuation characteristics of the filter determine the weights used in the averaging process. While it is necessary to average over a number of lines to reduce the statistical variation, the averaging process tends also to smooth out any sharp variation in the power spectrum. The latter effect is called blurring error. It has been shown that the optimum filter characteristics to give a minimum of blurring error for the same statistical error, or vice versa, are the semicircular characteristics† of Fig. 7-4a. The filter emphasizes the spectral lines near the center of the passband and deemphasizes the components near the cutoff. While very sharp cutoff in the attenuation band is desirable, this requirement is not too critical. Figure 7-4b gives the spectrum of the input signal while Fig. 7-4c gives the spectrum of the output of the filter.

The above describes the analyzer function in obtaining the spectral density of a single signal. Figures 7-5a and b illustrate a method for analyzing the cross-spectral density $\Phi_{12}(j\omega)$ of two signals i_1 and i_2. The arrangement for obtaining the real component of $\Phi_{12}(j\omega)$, or cospectrum, is shown in Fig. 7-5a. The sum and difference signals $\frac{1}{2}(i_1 + i_2)$ and $\frac{1}{2}(i_1 - i_2)$ are analyzed, and the difference between the two spectral densities gives the cospectrum. In Fig. 7-5b, the signal i_2 is first inte-

---

† The semicircular filtering characteristics can be approximated by a single-tuned resonant circuit in cascade with a double-tuned critically coupled resonant circuit. The Q value of the latter is 1.414 times that of the former. Let x denote $(f - f_b)/\Delta$, where Δ is a bandwidth equal to the radius. Then $|H(j\omega)|^2 = 1/(1 + x^2 + x^4 + x^6 + \cdots) \cong 1/(1 + x^2)(1 + x^4)$. The frequency response of the single-tuned resonant circuit is $1/(1 + x^2)$, while that of the double-tuned circuit is $1/(1 + x^4)$.

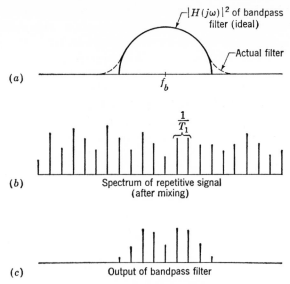

Fig. 7-4. Fine structure of the spectra of input and output signals of the bandpass filter.

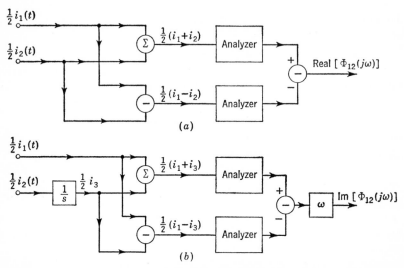

Fig. 7-5. Arrangements for measuring cospectrum and cross spectrum of two signals.

grated to obtain a 90° phase shift at all frequencies, and the subsequent operations are the same as shown in Fig. 7-5a. The difference between the two spectra is multiplied by ω to compensate for the frequency dependence of the gain of the integration process, and the product is the cross spectrum. The methods can be readily proved by applying Eq. (3-14).

An alternative way of determining the cross spectrum is not to integrate or differentiate i_2 but to heterodyne i_1 and i_2 with different square-wave signals which are shifted by one-quarter period. The heterodyned signals are then combined and analyzed. While the latter method requires slightly more electronics, it does away with the necessity of multiplying the results by ω or $1/\omega$.

7-4. Computation of Correlation Functions by Digital and Analog Methods. The correlation function between two signals $i_1(t)$ and $i_2(t)$ (or the same signal) is computed exactly the same way as it is defined, except that the sample signal has finite length T_1:

$$\phi_{12}(\tau) = \overline{i_1(t)i_2(t+\tau)} = \frac{1}{T_1 - \tau} \int_0^{T_1 - \tau} i_1(t)i_2(t+\tau)\, dt \qquad (7\text{-}20)$$

T_1 may be determined by Eq. (7-17) or some other considerations. Equation (7-20) indicates three essential steps, as follows:

1. Time shift: either advancing i_2 or delaying i_1 by an interval τ
2. Multiplication
3. Averaging

The above steps may be accomplished by either analog or digital means. The digital method will be discussed first. Since only a finite number of data points can enter into the computation, we select an interval T, $T = T_1/M$, and take readings of i_1 and i_2 at $t = 0, T, 2T, \ldots, nT,$ $\ldots$. These readings will be denoted as $i_1(n)$ and $i_2(n)$, respectively. Similarly, we shall use $\phi_{12}(h)$ to denote $\phi_{12}(\tau)$ at $\tau = hT$, and $h = 0, 1, 2, 3, \ldots$. Equation (7-20) can be written approximately as

$$\phi_{12}(h) = \frac{1}{M - h + 1} \sum_{n=0}^{n = M - h} i_1(n)i_2(n + h) \qquad (7\text{-}21)$$

The crucial points in this method of computing the correlation function are the following:

1. The choice of T. Too large an interval results in unnecessary work, while too small a T results in mixing of the spectral densities. Let ω_s be defined as $2\pi/T$. It is easy to show that $\sin \omega t$, $\sin (\omega_s + \omega)t$, and $- \sin (\omega_s - \omega)t$ give the same set of readings. The same is true for the cosine functions. Once T is selected, there is no way of distinguishing spectral components of frequencies $\omega_s \pm \omega$ from that of frequency ω. The criterion for determining T is therefore

$$T < \frac{\pi}{\omega_h} \qquad (7\text{-}22)$$

where ω_h is the high-frequency limit of the spectrum in the sense that there is only negligible power content at frequencies beyond ω_h. It may be estimated by inspecting the sample signal.

2. The choice of sample length T_1. The choice of T_1 is determined by the nature of the signal and desired accuracy. Because of the randomness of $i_1(t)$ and $i_2(t)$ and the finite length of the sample, there is a random variation of the computed $\phi_{12}(\tau)$ from its expected value. For instance, no matter how large or how small τ is, the mean-square values of $i_1(t)$ and $i_2(t + \tau)$ are $\phi_{11}(0)$ and $\phi_{22}(0)$, respectively, and the product $i_1(t)i_2(t + \tau)$ may take any value between plus or minus a few times $\sqrt{\phi_{11}(0)\phi_{22}(0)}$. While this scattering of values can be reduced by averaging over a number of data points, as shown in Eq. (7-21), the number of independent data points is limited and is proportional to T_1. If we choose the interval T between data points according to Eq. (7-22), the result is not appreciably different from that obtained by integration, since every bit of independent data is utilized or nearly utilized.

It is shown in Appendix C that the scattering of measured data points varies slightly with the delay time τ. For Gaussian random signals, the mean-square error of the measured correlation function is given as

$$\langle [\phi_{12}(\tau)_{meas} - \phi_{12}(\tau)]^2 \rangle = \frac{1}{T_1 - \tau} \int_{-\infty}^{\infty} [\phi_{11}(\tau_1)\phi_{22}(\tau_1) \\ + \phi_{12}(\tau + \tau_1)\phi_{12}(\tau - \tau_1)] \, d\tau_1 \quad (7\text{-}23)$$

where $\phi_{12}(\tau)_{meas}$ is defined as

$$\phi_{12}(\tau)_{meas} = \frac{1}{T_1 - \tau} \int_0^{T_1-\tau} i_1(t)i_2(t + \tau) \, dt \quad (7\text{-}24)$$

The unlabeled correlation functions are the theoretical or true values for the ensemble. Equation (7-23) is obviously a counterpart of Eq. (7-15). There is a significant contrast, however. Equation (7-15) shows that the standard deviation of the measured spectral density at a given frequency is proportional to the spectral density at that frequency. Equation (7-23) shows that the standard deviation of the measured correlation function depends on the correlation functions at all values of delay time τ.

Equation (7-23) holds approximately if the measured correlation function is computed according to Eq. (7-21).

3. How many values of $\phi_{12}(h)$ need to be computed? At first glance, the answer appears to be trivial. We just calculate $\phi_{12}(h)$ for all values of h starting from 0, 1, 2, 3, . . . until we come to a value m such that $\phi_{12}(h)$ is vanishingly small for all values of h above m. However, this is a false answer. Because of the scattered nature of measured $\phi_{12}(h)$, it is not possible to tell from one sample alone whether the measured $\phi_{12}(h)$ truly reflects the ensemble correlation function or is merely a random

variation. This indistinguishability is especially true at the tail end of the correlation function.

The above discussion points to the flexibility in the selection of m. It is not difficult to see that the choice of m corresponds to the choice of resolution Δf in spectral-density measurements. We recall that spectral density is simply the Fourier transform of the correlation function, and the well-known rules between frequency resolution and duration of a signal apply. If we compute the spectral densities from the measured correlation function which occupies an interval $|\tau| \leq mT$, the best resolution we can obtain is approximately

$$\Delta f \cong \frac{1}{mT} \qquad (7\text{-}25)$$

Equation (7-25) will be substantiated by a more exact analysis. Since Eq. (7-15) holds equally well whether the spectral densities are computed from correlation functions or directly from the sample signals, the expected per-unit error of computed spectral density is

$$\epsilon \cong \frac{1}{\sqrt{T_1 \, \Delta f}} = \sqrt{\frac{m}{M}} \qquad (7\text{-}26)$$

Equation (7-26) shows that, in order to have some degree of statistical reliability in the computed spectral density, m should be no more than a small fraction of M. On the other hand, m has to be large enough to give the desired resolution.

Equations (7-22) to (7-24) are based on the assumption that we are limited by the available signal sample and are doing our best in estimating the statistical properties from the available sample. Another alternative is that the available signal sample is unlimited but we are limited by the number of computing operations, because of cost or other considerations. In that case we would do better by pacing the delay time at intervals T as given in Eq. (7-22) but pacing the time t of data points at much larger intervals, so that each pair of data points is completely independent of any other. The data-sampling process is shown in Fig. 7-6. By averaging N values of $i_1(t)i_2(t + \tau)$, the mean-square deviation of measured $\phi_{12}(\tau)$ is

$$\langle [\phi_{12}(\tau)_{meas} - \phi_{12}(\tau)]^2 \rangle = \frac{1}{N} \{ \phi_{11}(0)\phi_{22}(0) + [\phi_{12}(\tau)]^2 \} \qquad (7\text{-}27)$$

Equation (7-27) is derived in Appendix C. Since the correlation functions usually extend over an interval much larger than T, Eq. (7-23) gives a considerably higher value for the estimated mean-square deviation. A similar situation is found in mining if we draw the analogy between the statistical information contained in a piece of signal sample and iron contained in a mine.   Equations (7-22) and (7-23) represent virtually complete depletion of the mine, whereas Eq. (7-27) represents mining only the choicest ore.   The former gives maximum yield per piece of mine, while the latter gives maximum yield per unit of effort.

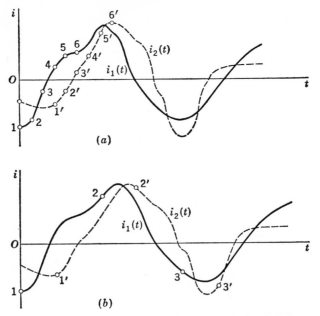

FIG. 7-6. Two ways of signal sampling in computing correlation functions.   (a) When length of sample record is limited; (b) when number of computations is limited.

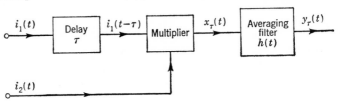

FIG. 7-7. Block diagram of continuous correlator.

While digital computation can be readily programmed on a general-purpose machine, it takes readout devices to convert the sample signal to a sequence of numbers.   The computational process is also time-consuming.   As an alternative, there have been developed various types of electronic correlators which compute the correlation functions by analog techniques.   We shall describe two types:

1. *The Continuous Correlator.*   A block diagram of the continuous correlator is shown in Fig. 7-7.   The output of the multiplier is

$$x_\tau(t) = i_1(t - \tau)i_2(t) \tag{7-28}$$

and the output $y(t)$ of the averaging filter is

$$y(t_1) = \int_0^{t_1} x_\tau(t_1 - t')h(t') \, dt' \tag{7-29}$$

We shall require that the area under the $h(t)$ curve be unity and that the correlator be in operation for a sufficiently long time, so that $h(t)$ has negligible value for $t > t_1$. Then

$$\langle y_\tau(t_1) \rangle = \int_0^\infty \langle x_\tau(t_1 - t') \rangle h(t') \, dt'$$
$$= \int_0^\infty \phi_{12}(\tau)h(t') \, dt' = \phi_{12}(\tau) \tag{7-30}$$

In the above derivation, the expected value of $x(t_1 - t')$ is $\phi_{12}(\tau)$, due to Eq. (7-28). As $\phi_{12}(\tau)$ is independent of t', it is taken out of the integral sign. The balance of the integral is simply the area under the $h(t)$ curve and is required to be unity. Equation (7-30) shows that $y(t)$ is an estimate of $\phi_{12}(\tau)$.

In general, the averaging filter is a low-pass filter and $h(t)$ has the form of curve a of Fig. 7-8. A special case of interest is for $h(t)$ to take the rectangular form of

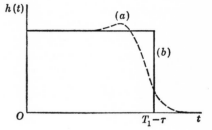

Fig. 7-8. Impulse response of averaging filter.

curve b. It represents integration from 0 to $T_1 - \tau$. At the end of the run, or $t_1 = T_1$, we have

$$y(T_1) = \frac{1}{T_1 - \tau} \int_0^{T_1 - \tau} x(T_1 - t') \, dt'$$

A substitution of the dependent variable $t'' = T_1 - t' - \tau$ gives

$$y(T_1) = \frac{1}{T_1 - \tau} \int_0^{T_1 - \tau} x(t'' + \tau) \, dt''$$
$$= \frac{1}{T_1 - \tau} \int_0^{T_1 - \tau} i_1(t'')i_2(t'' + \tau) \, dt''$$

Equation (7-30) is reduced to Eq. (7-24).

As far as the instruments are concerned, the delay may be accomplished by a delay line or by staggering the playback head if the sample signal is recorded on tape. The multiplication is done by matching two square-law devices, as illustrated in Fig. 7-9. Each square-law device is made up of a large number of diode shapers, and its accuracy can be easily made to approximate 0.2 per cent.

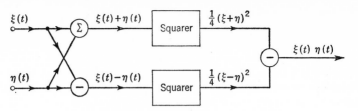

FIG. 7-9. Block diagram of analog multiplier.

2. *The Pulse-type Correlator.* One of the earliest electronic correlators built at MIT utilizes pulse multiplication. A series of pulses of height $i_1(t_1)$, $i_1(t_2)$, . . . are passed through a varying gate of duration $i_2(t_1 + \tau)$, $i_2(t_2 + \tau)$, . . . , respectively. The area of the resulting train of pulses is proportional to $i_1(t_1)i_2(t_1 + \tau)$. By integrating over the area of these pulses and dividing the result by the number of pulses, the average value of $i_1(t)i_2(t + \tau)$ is obtained. Obviously, the spacing of data points is of necessity larger than the delay time τ. As discussed previously, the method works best for direct analysis of live signals or when there is unlimited length of sample record available.

7-5. Computation of Spectral Densities from Correlation Functions.†
Once the correlation functions are determined by either digital or analog computation, the spectral densities can be calculated as follows: The known values are ϕ_h which represent measured $\phi_{12}(\tau)$ at $\tau = hT$, $h = 0$, ± 1, ± 2, . . . , $\pm m$. Suppose that we wish to compute the spectral density at ω_1. From the equation

$$\Phi_{12}(j\omega_1) = 2 \int_{-\infty}^{\infty} \phi_{12}(\tau)e^{-j\omega_1\tau} \, d\tau$$

and by making use of all available data, we arrive at the following approximate form:

$$2T \sum_{h=-m}^{h=m} \phi_h e^{-j\omega_1 hT} \tag{7-31}$$

However, because of the discreteness and finite range of measured $\phi_{12}(\tau)$, the above sum may or may not be the most desirable representation of $\Phi_{12}(j\omega_1)$. We shall denote it by the noncommittal symbol $M(\omega_1)$ and examine its significance. By definition, the expected value of ϕ_h is

$$\langle \phi_h \rangle = \phi_{12}(hT) = \frac{1}{4\pi} \int_{-\infty}^{\infty} \Phi_{12}(j\omega)e^{j\omega hT} \, d\omega \tag{7-32}$$

---

† With minor variations, the analysis of this section follows essentially that of J. W. Tukey, "Measuring Noise Color," lecture notes for distribution at a meeting of the New York Section of the IRE, November, 1951, and The Sampling Theory of Power Spectrum Estimates, *Symposium on Applications of Autocorrelation Analysis to Physical Problems*, Woods Hole, Mass., June 13–14, 1949.

From Eqs. (7-31) and (7-32),

$$\langle M(\omega_1) \rangle = \frac{T}{2\pi} \sum_{h=-m}^{h=m} \int_{-\infty}^{\infty} \Phi_{12}(j\omega) e^{j(\omega-\omega_1)hT} \, d\omega \qquad (7\text{-}33)$$

The integral converges absolutely at infinity, since for all physical cases the spectral densities of the signals are limited within a finite frequency range. In fact, this is the condition upon which T is selected [Eq. (7-22)]. The summation of finite terms in h can be taken up first:

$$\sum_{h=-m}^{h=m} e^{j(\omega-\omega_1)hT} = \frac{e^{-jm(\omega-\omega_1)T} - e^{j(m+1)(\omega-\omega_1)T}}{1 - e^{j(\omega-\omega_1)T}}$$

$$= \frac{\sin (2m+1)(\omega-\omega_1)T/2}{\sin (\omega-\omega_1)T/2} \qquad (7\text{-}34)$$

Note that $(\omega - \omega_1)T/2$ is very small and its sine function is very close to the variable itself. Equation (7-33) can be written as

$$\langle M(\omega_1) \rangle \eqsim \int_{-\infty}^{\infty} \Phi_{12}(j\omega) W(\omega - \omega_1) \, d\omega_1 \qquad (7\text{-}35)$$

where
$$W(\omega - \omega_1) = \frac{\sin (2m+1)(\omega-\omega_1)T/2}{\pi(\omega-\omega_1)} \qquad (7\text{-}36)$$

Equation (7-35) shows that $\langle M(\omega_1) \rangle$ is not $\Phi_{12}(j\omega)$ itself but is the weighted average of the neighboring spectral densities. This is desirable from the standpoint of reducing statistical error, if $W(\omega - \omega_1)$ has the proper waveform.

A plot of $W(\omega - \omega_1)$ versus ω is given in Fig. 7-10. We note that there is a large number of minor lobes, and the nearest minor lobes have a peak

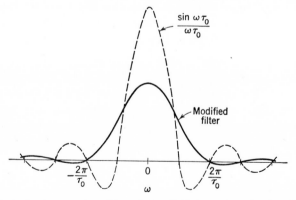

FIG. 7-10. Equivalent averaging filter of the digital computation method. Broken curve corresponds to Eq. (7-35) with $\tau_0 = (2m+1)T/2$; solid curve corresponds to Eq. (7-38) with $\eta = 0.23$. (*Reprinted from H. Press and J. W. Tukey, Bell Telephone System Monograph 2606, 1957.*)

value of approximately -0.22 times that of the major peak. This is embarrassing, especially when the power-density spectrum $\Phi_{11}(j\omega)$ is being computed. In some cases there is a sharp change in $\Phi_{11}(j\omega)$ from a very low value to a very large value, and the computed $\Phi_{11}(j\omega)$ at the low point becomes negative. In computing cross-spectral densities the error is not so obvious but it is still there. One method of remedying this situation is to average over a few values of $M(\omega_1)$:

$$M_a(\omega_1) = (1 - 2\eta)M(\omega_1) + \eta M(\omega_1 + \Delta\omega) + \eta M(\omega_1 - \Delta\omega) \quad (7\text{-}37)$$

where
$$\Delta\omega = \frac{2\pi}{(2m + 1)T} \quad (7\text{-}38)$$

and η is a small fraction which will be determined later. In Eq. (7-35), $W(\omega - \omega_1)$ is replaced by

$$W_a(\omega - \omega_1) = (1 - 2\eta)W(\omega - \omega_1) + \eta W(\omega - \omega_1 + \Delta\omega)$$
$$+ \eta W(\omega - \omega_1 - \Delta\omega) \quad (7\text{-}39)$$

We note that, by selecting $\Delta\omega$ as given in Eq. (7-38), the minor lobes of $W(\omega - \omega_1)$ are matched against the minor lobes of $W(\omega - \omega_1 \pm \Delta\omega)$ of the opposite sign. The fraction η is selected so that as much cancellation is obtained as possible. The centers of the side lobes are at $\omega - \omega_1 = (n/2)\,\Delta\omega$, where $n = 3, 5, 7, 9, \ldots$. At these points, the magnitude of the remaining lobes can be readily evaluated in terms of the major peak:

$$\frac{W_a(n\,\Delta\omega/2)}{W_a(0)} = \frac{2(-)^{(n-1)/2}}{\pi}\left[\frac{1}{n} - \frac{\eta}{1 - 2\eta}\left(\frac{1}{n + 2} + \frac{1}{n - 2}\right)\right] \quad (7\text{-}40)$$

The lobe at $n = 3$ is merged with the major peak, and we would do well to minimize the lobes at $n = 5$ and $n = 7$. Setting the terms inside the brackets to zero at $n = 6$, we obtain

$$\frac{\eta}{1 - 2\eta} = \frac{n^2 - 4}{2n^2} = \frac{4}{9}$$
$$\eta = \frac{4}{17} = 0.235$$

The solid curve of Fig. 7-10 is plotted for $\eta = 0.23$ as recommended by Tukey.

From the above discussion, it is also obvious that the half bandwidth of the averaging filter is $\Delta\omega$. There would be an adequate coverage of the spectral-density curve by selecting ω_1 at $\Delta\omega$ apart.

To summarize the above, the procedure of computing the spectral density from the correlation function is listed below:

1. *Power-density Spectrum* $\Phi_{11}(j\omega)$. The following symbols are defined:

$$M_k \equiv M(k\,\Delta\omega) \qquad k = 0, 1, 2, \ldots, m$$
$$\Phi_k \equiv M_a(k\,\Delta\omega) \qquad k = 0, 1, 2, \ldots, m$$

STEP *a*

$$M_k = 4T\left(\frac{\phi_0}{2} + \sum_{h=1}^{h=m} \phi_h \cos\frac{2\pi hk}{2m+1}\right)$$

STEP *b*

$$\Phi_k = 0.54M_k + 0.23(M_{k+1} + M_{k-1}) \qquad k = 1, 2, \ldots, m$$
$$\Phi_0 = 0.54M_0 + 0.46M_1$$

Φ_k are the measured values of $\Phi_{11}(j\omega)$ at $\omega = k\,\Delta\omega$.

2. *The Cross-spectral Density*

$$A_k + jB_k \equiv M(k\,\Delta\omega)$$
$$P_k + jQ_k \equiv M_a(k\,\Delta\omega)$$

STEP *a*

$$A_k = 2T\left[\phi_0 + \sum_{h=1}^{m}(\phi_h + \phi_{-h})\cos\frac{2\pi hk}{2m+1}\right]$$

$$B_k = 2T\sum_{h=1}^{m}(\phi_{-h} - \phi_h)\sin\frac{2\pi hk}{2m+1}$$

STEP *b*

$$P_k = 0.54A_k + 0.23(A_{k+1} + A_{k-1})$$
$$Q_k = 0.54B_k + 0.23(B_{k+1} + B_{k-1})$$
$$P_0 = 0.54A_0 + 0.46A_1$$
$$Q_0 = 0$$

P_k and Q_k are measured values of the cospectrum and quadrature spectrum, respectively, at $\omega = k\,\Delta\omega$.

Considering Eq. (7-38) and $T_1 = nT$, Eq. (7-16) can be rewritten in terms of n and m:

$$\epsilon = \sqrt{\frac{m + \frac{1}{2}}{Nn}} \cong \sqrt{\frac{m}{Nn}} \qquad (7\text{-}41)$$

where N is the number of sample records used in the analysis, n is the number of data points in each sample record, and m is the number of points in the resulting spectrum. From Eq. (7-41), we see that, in order to arrive at any degree of reliability, the number of points in the resulting spectrum must be many, many times fewer than the number of data points we have to start with. The square root of the ratio of the two gives the probable error.

7-6. Spectral Densities with Independent Variable Other Than Time.

Sometimes the measured variable is a function of space coordinates rather than time. One interesting application relates to the smoothness of a runway. The elevation z of the runway surface is a function of the distance x from the starting point. To estimate the effect of surface roughness on a plane, the spectral density $\Phi_{zz}(jk_x)$ is computed with k_x

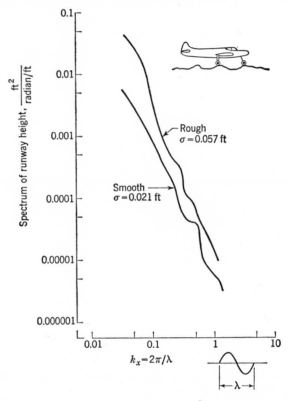

FIG. 7-11. Measured power spectra of runway roughness. σ = mean-square value of surface-height variations. (*Reprinted from H. Press and J. W. Tukey, Bell Telephone System Monograph 2606, 1957.*)

in units of radians per meter instead of the usual radians per second. A typical spectrum is shown in Fig. 7-11.

For a plane running at a speed V, the effect is exactly the same as if it were stationary and a movement $z(t)$ were applied to its landing-gear surface. The frequency ω of $z(t)$ is related to k_x as

$$\omega = Vk_x \tag{7-42}$$

$$\Phi_{zz}(j\omega) = \frac{1}{V} \, \Phi_{zz}\left(j\frac{\omega}{V}\right) \tag{7-43}$$

Therefore, if $\mathbf{\Phi}_{zz}$ is known, $\Phi_{zz}(j\omega)$ can be calculated for various speeds of the plane.

A similar case is a one-dimensional air-turbulence velocity measurement for estimating the forces and moments exerted on a plane's surface, as illustrated in Fig. 7-12. Since the speed of the airplane is considerably higher than the turbulence propagation speed of the surrounding air,

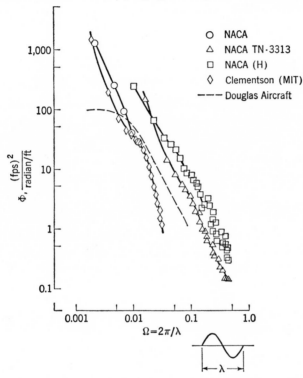

FIG. 7-12. Measured power spectra of atmospheric turbulence. (*Reprinted from H. Press and J. W. Tukey, Bell Telephone System Monograph 2606, 1957.*)

the latter can be considered fixed in position. The forces and moments that it exerts on a wing surface can be obtained by integration of the surface pressure. Because of the motion of the airplane, the forces and moments become functions of time in exactly the same way as shown in Eqs. (7-42) and (7-43).

7-7. Multiple-dimensional Spectrum. Sometimes the random variable in question is a function of more than one independent variable. For instance, ocean-wave height is a function of time and the x,y coordinates, and gust velocity of atmospheric turbulence is a function of time and all three space coordinates. A full representation requires a multiple-dimensional spectral analysis.

One central fact about multiple-dimensional waves is that wave motions of the same frequency but different directions of propagation exist independently.   They do not add up to a single motion toward a single direction with some vectorially summed magnitude.   The waves propagating in various directions are just as independent as waves of different frequencies in the one-dimensional case.   To put it analytically, let v be a random function of the independent variables x_1, x_2, . . . , x_n.   Inside the region $0 \leq x_i \leq X$, $i = 1, 2, . . . , n$, v can be expressed as

$$v = \sum_{N_1 = -\infty}^{\infty} \sum_{N_2} . . . \sum_{N_n} A(N_1, N_2, . . . , N_n) e^{j(2\pi/X)(N_1 x_1 + N_2 x_2 + \cdots + N_n x_n)} \quad (7\text{-}44)$$

The Fourier amplitude $A(N_1, N_2, . . . , N_n)$ is complex and is conjugate to $A(-N_1, -N_2, . . . , -N_n)$.   A set of frequencies f_i are defined as

$$f_i = \frac{\omega_i}{2\pi} = \frac{N_i}{X} \quad (7\text{-}45)$$

Corresponding to the frequency range of the one-dimensional case, we now have a frequency region R, which is defined by the following inequality:

$$\xi_i - \frac{\Delta f}{2} < f_i < \xi_i + \frac{\Delta f}{2} \quad i = 1, 2, . . . , n \quad (7\text{-}46)$$

where Δf is a small frequency range but large enough so that $X \Delta f \gg 1$. The spectral density at $f_i = \xi_i$ is simply the total power inside R divided by the volume of R, in the limit that Δf approaches zero and $X \Delta f$ approaches infinity.

Similarly to the one-dimensional case, the power of each spectral line is independent and has a distribution as given by Eq. (7-13), and the expected value $E(N_1, N_2, . . . , N_n)$ is

$$E(N_1, N_2, . . . , N_n) = \frac{1}{X^n} \Phi_{vv}(j\omega_1, j\omega_2, . . . , j\omega_n) \quad (7\text{-}47)$$

where $\omega_i = 2\pi N_i/X$.   The per-unit error ϵ is given as

$$\epsilon = \frac{1}{(\text{number of spectral lines in } R)^{1/2}} = (X \Delta f)^{-(n/2)} \quad (7\text{-}48)$$

Figure 7-13 illustrates a two-dimensional ocean-wave spectrum obtained by the stereophotographic technique.   The stereophotographs give a complete record of wave height at one single instant over a certain area of ocean surface.   The two-dimensional autocorrelation function of the ocean-wave height is calculated from these photographs, and the two-dimensional spectrum is then calculated from the autocorrelation functions by a method similar to that of Sec. 7-5.   The power spectrum is represented by a contour map with the wave numbers in two mutually perpendicular directions as coordinates, as marked at the edges of the con-

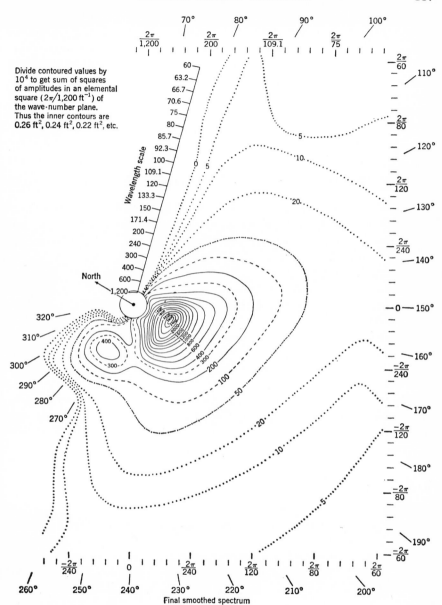

FIG. 7-13. Contour map of measured two-dimensional power spectra of ocean-wave height. (*Reprinted from J. Chase et al., The Directional Spectrum of a Wind Generated Sea, NYU Eng. Research Rept., July, 1957.*)

tour map.   However, in duplication of the cartesian-coordinate representation, polar coordinates are also given by the arrow pointing north, the angular markings from the north direction, and the scale above the origin showing wavelengths in feet.

One complication in applying the ocean-wave spectrum to calculating forces and moments exerted on a ship is that the wave speed and ship speed are of the same order of magnitude.   In contrast to the case of a plane speeding across a runway, we can no longer regard the ocean wave as fixed in space.   Its relative speed to the ship as well as its change of frequency due to ship motion (Doppler effect) must be considered.   A mathematical representation which takes these effects into consideration is given by St. Dennis and Pierson.

7-8. An Appraisal of Various Methods.   In the above sections we have discussed the few basic types or ways of measuring power spectra and correlation functions.   One subject that we have not discussed is the use of correlation techniques in determining transfer functions.   This we shall leave until Chap. 11.   There is a considerable amount of literature on the subject of correlation-function measurements.   However, as this usually is concerned with detailed improvements such as better ways of multiplying, channel multiplexing, etc., and does not represent new basic methods, we shall not go further into the subject.   It may well be said that many of the problems facing earlier workers have already been solved by recent progress in electronic multipliers, integrators, etc., and no longer exist today.

The methods that we have discussed so far are all for stationary signals. For nonstationary signals, ensemble average over a large number of samples by digital computation appears to be the only method.   However, this is too straightforward to warrant any discussion.

For stationary signals, direct analog measurement of power spectra appears to be the best method.   The design techniques of earlier chapters use power spectra directly.   Even with the time-domain synthesis technique, the resulting equations for optimum system functions are expressed in exactly the same form, which of course should be the case since the two methods are equivalent.   While it is necessary to express the power spectrum as a rational function in order to use the methods developed in Chaps. 2 and 4, this has no loss of generality, since within the statistical error limits a measured spectrum can easily be represented as a rational function of $j\omega$.

Bearing in mind that the final data we use in the synthesis procedures are in the form of power spectra, we can make some interesting comparisons between power-spectra measurements and correlation-function measurements:

1. *Frequency Range.*   The frequency range for power-spectra measurements with the heterodyne methods is determined by the central fre-

quency f_b of the bandpass filter. The presence of any Fourier component in the signal with a frequency above f_b will result in frequency aliasing. With correlation-function measurements, it is necessary to change the correlation time in steps. Let T denote the increment in seconds. Then the presence of any Fourier component in the signal with a frequency above $1/2T$ cps will result in frequency aliasing.

2. *Frequency Resolution.* The frequency resolution for direct power-spectra measurements is simply the bandwidth of the filter, while that for correlation-function measurements is approximately $1/2\tau_m$, where τ_m is the longest correlation time (Sec. 7-5).

The frequency-range-to-resolution ratio for direct power-spectra analysis is about 100:1 with ordinary LC for the bandpass filter. To obtain the same ratio by the correlation technique, one would have to divide the range of correlation time into at least 100 steps. This has rarely been done.

Another element is time. As mentioned previously, even with the relatively elementary tape version, the power-spectra analyzer of Sec. 7-3 analyzes and plots on paper a 100-point spectrum well within 5 min. It is very difficult to exceed this by first making correlation computations even with a high-speed digital computer.

7-9. Prewhitening and Duplex Measurements. One difficulty in the practical use of Wiener's prediction technique is the very wide frequency range of power-spectra data required. Owing to the approximate differentiation process (or the use of a lead network) the high-frequency signal and noise are very much exaggerated. Even if the high-frequency power contents of the signal and noise are negligibly low by ordinary servo standards, they are still capable of influencing the error appreciably and make an appreciable difference in the ideal characteristics of a Wiener prediction filter. Of course the requirement of spectra measurements over a wide frequency range with large variations in power level can also arise from other application problems.

One way to accomplish the above with the spectra analyzer described in Sec. 7-3 is to use a prewhitening filter before the signals are recorded and to record the signals with two different tape speeds, usually at a ratio of 10:1. The prewhitening filter has a frequency response

$$|H(j\omega)|^2 \cong \frac{1}{\Phi(j\omega)}$$

in a very rough way and brings the power level throughout the frequency range of interest to the accurate range of the analyzer. The slow-speed tape recording covers a low frequency range in which the power content of the original unwhitened signal is concentrated. The high-speed tape recording extends the frequency range by the speed ratio, and its frequency resolution is worse by the same ratio. The latter is not a serious defect since the asymptotic characteristics of the high-frequency end of the spectrum are generally more important than its detailed structure.

7-10. Confidence Limits. As discussed in Sec. 7-2, the predominant source of error in a measured value of $\Phi(j\omega)$ is the random statistical variations of the samples used. If we assume negligible systematic error due to other sources, Eq. (7-16) gives the rms per-unit error. The frequency range Δf can be replaced by the bandwidth of the bandpass filter $H(j\omega)$:

$$\Delta f = \frac{\left\{ \int_0^\infty [H(j2\pi f)]^2 \, df \right\}^2}{\int_0^\infty [H(j2\pi f)]^4 \, df}$$

In order to obtain any acceptable degree of accuracy, the effective number of independent frequency components $NT_1 \, \Delta f$ is quite high and the measured $\Phi(j\omega)$ has approximately normal distribution. The method of Sec. A-10 can be used to establish its confidence interval. The inequality $|V_{av} - \bar{V}| < a$ in Sec. A-10 becomes

$$\left| \frac{\Phi_{meas} - \Phi}{\Phi} \right| < a$$

It can be rewritten as

$$\frac{1}{1 + a} < \frac{\Phi(j\omega)}{\Phi(j\omega)_{meas}} < \frac{1}{1 - a} \tag{7-49}$$

The ratios $1/(1 - a)$ and $1/(1 + a)$ are called upper and lower confidence limits, respectively.

Example 7-1. The speed-up signal has a length of 0.5 sec, the bandpass filter has a bandwidth of 80 cps, and the power spectra of five independent sample records taken under identical circumstances are averaged to improve the reliability of the measured spectrum. Determine the 90 per cent confidence limits.

Solution. The rms per-unit error of each record is

$$\sigma_1 = \epsilon = \frac{1}{\sqrt{T \, \Delta f}} = \frac{1}{\sqrt{40}}$$

For $p = 0.9$, Table A-1 gives $k_p = 1.163$. Therefore

$$a = 1.163 \times \frac{1}{\sqrt{40}} \times \sqrt{\tfrac{2}{5}} = 0.1163$$

$$\frac{1}{1 - a} = 1.13 \qquad \frac{1}{1 + a} = 0.895$$

There is a probability of 90 per cent that the actual $\Phi(j\omega)$ lies between 0.895 and 1.13 times the measured value.

7-11. Summary. In this chapter, analog and digital methods for measuring spectral densities and correlation functions have been discussed. Their comparative merits and the reliabilities of such measurements are also analyzed.

In making a Fourier analysis of a sample record of a Gaussian random signal, we find that the distributions of Fourier amplitudes are quite similar to the final distances arrived at in a random-walk problem. Mathematical analysis shows that, while the mean value of each Fourier amplitude is zero, its mean-square value is not, but varies at random somewhere between 0 and a few times $\Phi_{ii}(j\omega)/T_1$. This random variation gives rise to the uncertainties in the measured spectrum. The uncertainty, or expected error, is inversely proportional to the square root of the frequency resolution of the measured or estimated spectrum. Its reduction to the irreducible minimum is one of the major considerations in spectrum measuring or estimating techniques.

To make a Fourier analysis of a sample record for every frequency is too time-consuming, and consequently two practical methods are developed:

1. Direct analog computation of the spectrum, in which the speed-up signal is heterodyned, filtered, and detected by a square-law detector
2. Computation from measured or calculated correlation functions

When the second method is used, the frequency resolution of the spectrum is automatically determined by the longest correlation time used in the computations. This also gives some insight into the required resolution in spectrum estimates: If $\Phi_{12}(\tau)$ is expected to be zero for $|\tau| > \tau_1$, there is no point in computing $\Phi_{12}(j\omega)$ for a frequency resolution better than $1/\tau_1$.

Sometimes the independent variable is not time but a space variable x, or there may be more than one independent variable. Spectral densities in terms of wave numbers of these space coordinates are defined. The methods for estimating these "spectral densities" and the associated uncertainties from a given sample record are the same as before.

The frequency range of the measured power spectra is limited either by the center frequency of the bandpass filter or by the increment in correlation time. The frequency resolution is determined by the bandwidth of the bandpass filter or the longest correlation time. All considered, direct analog measurement of power spectra is the simpler and faster method.

Prewhitening can be used to reduce the instrument error at frequencies where the spectral density is low originally. Duplex measurements with recordings at two different speeds can be used to extend the frequency range. When used together, the two methods give accurate measurements over a wide frequency range.

A method for determining the confidence limits of measured spectral densities is also discussed.

CHAPTER 8

EFFECTS OF INACCURACIES OF SYSTEM COMPONENTS

8-1. Scope and Purpose of Error Analysis. One problem facing a system designer is that the actual system and the system he analyzed or specified cannot be expected to be identical. There is always the problem of the stability of a component over periods of operation, because of environmental factors such as temperature, shock, radiation, and atmospherical conditions. There are always the manufacturing tolerances. The dynamics of the controlled system also varies from time to time, because of loading or some other operating situation. Last but not least are the errors due to idealization of transfer functions of system components as well as the controlled system, for instance, the disregard or combination of small time constants or the approximation of distributed parameters by lumped parameters. These approximations are made in order not to complicate the design work unnecessarily.

Therefore what he analyzed is an averaged and idealized system to which we shall refer as the nominal system. At best, it is a close approximation of the actual system. The pertinent question is: Could the actual system with all its possible component variations still be expected to meet given specifications? or, alternatively. What constitutes the least demand on the stability and tolerances of system components to do a given job?

The job requirements usually vary. However, we are in a better position to answer these questions if we know something about error analysis. The subjects treated are as follows:

1. Sensitivity of transient performance to component inaccuracies
2. Sensitivity of closed-loop performance parameters (especially poles and zeros) to component inaccuracies
3. Increase in mean-square error or some other cost function due to component inaccuracies

One assumption of the present analysis is that the inaccuracies are not too high so that first-order variation can be considered adequate as an estimate of the deterioration in performance. Otherwise, direct calculations or one or the other of the self-optimizing schemes discussed in Chap. 10 should be used.

8-2. Calculation of Sensitivity Function of the Transient Response of a Linear System with Constant Coefficients by Transform Method. The sensitivity function is defined as follows: Let $x(t,\alpha)$ represent the response of a certain system with parameter error α to a given input $y(t)$. It is implied that $x(t,0)$ represents the response of the nominal system. For small values of α, $x(t,\alpha)$ can be written in a Taylor series:

$$x(t,\alpha) = x(t,0) + \left[\frac{\partial x(t,\alpha)}{\partial \alpha}\right]_{\alpha=0} \alpha + \left[\frac{\partial^2 x(t,\alpha)}{\partial \alpha^2}\right]_{\alpha=0} \frac{\alpha^2}{2} + \cdots \quad (8\text{-}1)$$

The important term is the linear term, and its coefficient is called the sensitivity function. For a linear system with constant coefficients, the system in question can be represented by a transfer function $F(s,\alpha)$, which links the input $y(t)$ to the variable under consideration $x(t)$. We have

$$x(t,\alpha) = \mathcal{L}^{-1}\{F(s,\alpha)Y(s)\} \quad (8\text{-}2)$$

The differentiability of Eq. (8-2) is assumed at present. Differentiating both sides with respect to α for n times and setting α to zero in the resulting expression,

$$\left[\frac{\partial^n x(t,\alpha)}{\partial \alpha^n}\right]_{\alpha=0} = \mathcal{L}^{-1}\left\{\left[\frac{\partial F^n(s,\alpha)}{\partial \alpha^n}\right]_{\alpha=0} Y(s)\right\} \quad n = 1, 2, \ldots \quad (8\text{-}3)$$

Noting that $F(s,0)Y(s) = X(s,0)$, Eq. (8-3) for $n = 1$ can also be written as

$$\left[\frac{\partial x(t,\alpha)}{\partial \alpha}\right]_{\alpha=0} = \mathcal{L}^{-1}\left\{\left[\frac{\partial \ln F(s,\alpha)}{\partial \alpha}\right]_{\alpha=0} X(s,0)\right\} \quad (8\text{-}4)$$

The sensitivity function can be calculated from either Eq. (8-3) or Eq. (8-4).

Example 8-1. A simple RC network is subjected to a unit step input. Determine the sensitivity function to an error in the time constant. The transfer function of the network is

$$F(s,\alpha) = \frac{1}{1 + (T + \alpha)s} \quad (8\text{-}5)$$

Solution

$$\left[\frac{\partial F(s,\alpha)}{\partial \alpha}\right]_{\alpha=0} = -\frac{s}{(1 + Ts)^2}$$

From Eq. (8-3),

$$\left[\frac{\partial x(t,\alpha)}{\partial \alpha}\right]_{\alpha=0} = \mathcal{L}^{-1}\left\{-\frac{1}{(1 + Ts)^2}\right\} = -\frac{t}{T^2}e^{-t/T} \quad (8\text{-}6)$$

To check our result, direct solution from Eq. (8-5) gives

$$x(t,\alpha) = 1 - e^{-t/(T+\alpha)}$$

Differentiating the above expression with respect to α and setting α to zero give Eq. (8-6).

Example 8-2. Suppose that, in Example 8-1, there is a parasitic inductance L in the RC network. Let λ denote LC. The transfer function of the network can be written as

$$F(s,\alpha) = \frac{1}{\lambda s^2 + Ts + 1} \tag{8-7}$$

Determine the sensitivity of the step-response function to L.

Solution. Equation (8-3) gives

$$\left[\frac{\partial x(t,\lambda)}{\partial \lambda}\right]_{\lambda=0} = \mathcal{L}^{-1}\left\{-\frac{s^2}{(1+Ts)^2}\frac{1}{s}\right\} = \frac{1}{T^2}\left(\frac{t}{T}e^{-t/T} - e^{-t/T}\right) \tag{8-8}$$

Direct calculation from Eq. (8-7) gives

$$x(t,\lambda) = 1 - \frac{1}{2}\left(\frac{1}{a}+1\right)e^{-2t/T(1+a)} + \frac{1}{2}\left(\frac{1}{a}-1\right)e^{-2t/T(1-a)} \tag{8-9}$$

where $a = \sqrt{1 - 4\lambda/T^2}$. For very small values of λ,

$$x(t,\lambda) = 1 - \left(1+\frac{\lambda}{T^2}\right)\left(1-\frac{\lambda t}{T^3}\right)e^{-t/T} + \frac{\lambda}{T^2}e^{-t/T\lambda}$$

$$\cong 1 - e^{-t/T} + \frac{\lambda}{T^2}\left(\frac{t}{T}e^{-t/T} - e^{-t/T} + e^{-Tt/\lambda}\right) \tag{8-10}$$

We note that Eq. (8-10) agrees with Eq. (8-8) for all positive, nonvanishing values of t. However, at $t = 0$, Eq. (8-8) gives the value of the derivative as $-1/T^2$, while Eq. (8-10) gives 0. The discrepancy at $t = 0$ arises out of some improper use of calculus. If we write the inverse transform of Eq. (8-8),

$$\left[\frac{\partial x(t,\lambda)}{\partial \lambda}\right]_{\lambda=0} = \frac{1}{2\pi j}\int_{-j\infty}^{j\infty} -\frac{s}{(1+Ts)^2}e^{st}\,ds$$

we note that the integral is not convergent for $t = 0$. Therefore, the interchange of differentiation and integration in deriving Eq. (8-3) from Eq. (8-2) is not legitimate.

In practice, the problem of interest is the sensitivity function for $t > 0$. At $t = 0$, the solution is no more than the initial conditions, which we already know. However, one may ask if Eq. (8-3) is always correct for $t > 0$. This point will be examined in the next section.

The result may be mentioned here, however. If the parameter errors or inaccuracies in system simulation are of such a nature that they do not change the order of s in the denominator polynomial of $F(s)$, Eq. (8-3) is always justified. If they increase the order of $F(s)$, the following situations would arise:

1. The inaccuracies do not cause high-frequency parasitic oscillations, either permanent or transient; Eq. (8-3) is rigorously correct.

2. The inaccuracies cause high-frequency parasitic oscillations of a transient nature only; Eq. (8-3) neglects such transient oscillations and gives the error in the measurable averaged response. Since the parasitic oscillations are usually very fast and are not detectable by ordinary instruments, we should expect Eq. (8-3) to agree with the measurement. It is justified physically though not mathematically.

3. The inaccuracies cause sustained high-frequency parasitic oscillations. Since these oscillations almost always cause secondary effects by saturating the system components, redesign of the system is called for.

In all, we may say that Eq. (8-3) is good for error analysis of systems without sustained parasitic oscillations. The issue of possible parasitic oscillations has to be examined separately.

8-3. Convergence Problem of the Transform Method, $t > 0$. For a linear system with constant coefficients, the transform function $F(s,\alpha)$ is a rational function in s. Consequently, we may write

$$F(s,\alpha) = \frac{N_0(s) + N_1(s,\alpha)}{D_0(s) + D_1(s,\alpha)} \tag{8-11}$$

where $N_0(s)$, $N_1(s,\alpha)$, $D_0(s)$, and $D_1(s,\alpha)$ are polynomials in s. The polynomials $D_1(s,\alpha)$ and $N_1(s,\alpha)$ are assumed to have the following properties:

1. As α approaches zero, all the coefficients of $N_1(s,\alpha)$ and $D_1(s,\alpha)$ approach zero.

2. All the coefficients of $N_1(s,\alpha)$ and $D_1(s,\alpha)$ are analytic with respect to α in the vicinity of $\alpha = 0$.

Let $N_1^{(1)}(s,\alpha)$ and $D_1^{(1)}(s,\alpha)$ denote the partial derivatives of $N_1(s,\alpha)$ and $D_1(s,\alpha)$ with respect to α. $N_1^{(1)}(s,\alpha)$ and $D_1^{(1)}(s,\alpha)$ are two polynomials in s of the same orders as $N_1(s,\alpha)$ and $D_1(s,\alpha)$, respectively. Condition 2 implies that all the coefficients of $N_1^{(1)}(s,\alpha)$ and $D_1^{(1)}(s,\alpha)$ are continuous at $\alpha = 0$. We assume further that $Y(s)$ is a rational function of s.

For $t > 0$, the inverse transform can be written as

$$x(t,\alpha) = \frac{1}{2\pi j} \int_C F(s,\alpha) Y(s) e^{st} \, ds \tag{8-12}$$

where C is a contour enclosing all the poles of $F(s,\alpha) Y(s)$. The derivative of $F(s,\alpha)$ is

$$\frac{\partial F(s,\alpha)}{\partial \alpha} = \frac{[D_0(s) + D_1(s,\alpha)] N_1^{(1)}(s,\alpha) - [N_0(s) + N_1(s,\alpha)] D_1^{(1)}(s,\alpha)}{[D_0(s) + D_1(s,\alpha)]^2} \tag{8-13}$$

If $D_0(s)$ is a polynomial of equal or higher order than $D_1(s,\alpha)$, obviously the highest-order term of $D_0 + D_1$ cannot be zero in the vicinity of $\alpha = 0$. If the order of $D_0(s)$ is lower, the highest-order term in $D_0 + D_1$ is the highest-order term of $D_1(s,\alpha)$, the coefficient of which is, from our assumption, equal to zero at $\alpha = 0$ and is analytic in the vicinity of $\alpha = 0$. Unless all the derivatives of the coefficient with respect to α vanish (and consequently the coefficient is identically zero in the vicinity of $\alpha = 0$, contradicting the assumption that it is the highest-order term), there is a vicinity around $\alpha = 0$ in which the coefficient is not zero except at $\alpha = 0$. Let us consider α being any point in this vicinity but not at $\alpha = 0$. Since the coefficient of the highest-order term in $D_0 + D_1$ is not zero, it follows that all the roots of $D_0 + D_1$ are finite, and the contour of integration required to enclose all the roots is of finite length. From Eq. (8-13) we see that the value of $(\partial/\partial\alpha)F(s,\alpha)Y(s)$ is bounded everywhere on the contour. Therefore

$$\frac{1}{2\pi j}\int_C \frac{\partial}{\partial\alpha} F(s,\alpha)Y(s)e^{st}\,ds = \frac{1}{2\pi j}\frac{\partial}{\partial\alpha}\int_C F(s,\alpha)Y(s)e^{st}\,ds$$

$$= \frac{\partial}{\partial\alpha}\,x(t,\alpha) \tag{8-14}$$

The above argument can be repeated to obtain

$$\frac{\partial^n}{\partial\alpha^n}\,x(t,\alpha) = \frac{1}{2\pi j}\int_C \frac{\partial^n}{\partial\alpha^n}[F(s,\alpha)Y(s)]e^{st}\,ds \tag{8-15}$$

From Eq. (8-15) we can write

$$\left[\frac{\partial^n}{\partial\alpha^n}\,x(t,\alpha)\right]_{\alpha=0} = \lim_{\alpha\to0}\frac{1}{2\pi j}\int_C \frac{\partial^n}{\partial\alpha^n} F(s,\alpha)Y(s)e^{st}\,ds \tag{8-16}$$

The problem now is whether the limiting process and integration sign can be interchanged. With reference to Eq. (8-13), the contour integral of Eq. (8-15) gives a number of exponential terms with polynomials of t as coefficients. If $D_1(s,\alpha)$ is of the same or lower order than $D_0(s)$, the number of exponential terms is conserved no matter which way we do it. Equation (8-13) gives a number of poles and associated residues as functions of α. If we integrate first, it means that we write the exponential forms and then let α in the time constants and coefficients approach zero. If we take the limit first, it means that we let α in the time constants and coefficients approach zero first and then write the exponential terms. There is no difference.

A problem arises, however, if $D_1(s,\alpha)$ is of higher order in s than $D_0(s)$. By taking the limit first, we are throwing away all the exponential terms not arising out of the roots of $D_0(s)$. The question is: Can these exponential terms be thrown away?

To answer this question, let us examine the roots of $D_0(s) + D_1(s,\alpha)$. Let n and $n + m$ denote the orders of s in $D_0(s)$ and $D_1(s,\alpha)$, respectively.

Proposition 1. As α approaches zero, n roots of $D_0 + D_1$ approach the roots of D_0 and m roots of $D_0 + D_1$ approach infinity.

The first statement is easy to prove, since $D_1(s,\alpha)$ approaches zero as α approaches zero. To prove the second statement, if there is any finite root s_1 other than the roots of $D_0(s)$, then

$$D_0(s_1) + D_1(s_1,\alpha) = 0 \tag{8-17}$$

Since all the coefficients of $D_1(s_1,\alpha)$ approach zero and s_1 is finite, $D_1(s_1,\alpha)$ approaches zero. Therefore $D_0(s_1) = 0$, which contradicts the assumption that s_1 is not a root of D_0. Similarly, by differentiating $D_0 + D_1$ first with respect to s, it is shown that the multiplicity of roots of $D_0(s)$ cannot be increased. Since the m extra roots must go somewhere, this proves our proposition.

The m roots which approach infinity as α approaches zero will be referred to as the m roots.

Proposition 2. *As α approaches zero, the magnitude of the m roots as well as their real and imaginary components approaches powers or fractional powers of $1/\alpha$, and the residues of the m roots cannot approach infinity faster than a finite power of $1/\alpha$.*

Since the coefficients of $D_1(s,\alpha)$ and $N_1(s,\alpha)$ are analytic in the vicinity of $\alpha = 0$, every coefficient can be approximated by the first nonvanishing power in its Taylor's series expansion, and the result mentioned in proposition 2 follows.

Now we are in a position to examine the significance of reversing the order of integration and limiting process:

1. If all the real components of the m roots approach negative infinity as α approaches zero, for any finite $t > 0$

$$\lim_{\alpha \to 0} \left(\frac{1}{\alpha}\right)^a e^{-(1/\alpha)^b t} = 0$$

no matter how large the constant a or how small the constant b as long as $b > 0$. The neglected exponential terms vanish quickly, and the interchange of integration and limiting is justified.

2. If some of the m roots have constant negative real components and none have positive or zero real components, as α approaches zero the terms with constant negative real components introduce transient oscillations of very high frequency. We refer to such a system as having transient parasitic oscillations. The designer may consider such oscillations as objectionable and redesign the system. Alternatively, the designer may tolerate the transient parasitic oscillations as they are too fast to affect any measurable results. Our interchange of integration and limiting neglects the parasitic oscillations and gives the sensitivity function for the measurable part of $x(t,\alpha)$ only. It is exactly the desired result.

3. If some of the m roots have zero or positive real components, sustained parasitic oscillations would result. A redesign of the system would be necessary.

Thus we come to the conclusion at the end of Sec. 8-2.

Example 8-3. The $D_0(s)$ of a system is $1 + 2\zeta s + s^2$, and $D_1(s,\alpha)$ may take any of the following forms:

1. $\alpha(s^2 + s^3)$
2. $\alpha(s^3 + s^4)$
3. $\alpha s^3 + \alpha^2 s^4$
4. αs^5

Determine the nature of parasitic oscillations, if any.

Solution. Since we are interested only in the nature of the roots in the asymptotic limit of very large s and very small α, only the highest-order term in $D_0(s)$ needs to be retained. The other terms in $D_0(s)$ are negligible. In $D_1(s)$, only the terms of higher order than $D_0(s)$ need to be retained. Therefore, as α approaches 0, and s approaches infinity:

Approximate form of $D_0 + D_1$	*Asymptotic roots*
1. $s^2 + \alpha s^3$	$-\dfrac{1}{\alpha}$
2. $s^2 + \alpha s^3 + \alpha s^4$	$-\frac{1}{2} \pm j\sqrt{\dfrac{1}{\alpha}}$
3. $s^2 + \alpha s^3 + \alpha^2 s^4$	$\dfrac{-1 \pm j\sqrt{3}}{2\alpha}$
4. $s^2 + \alpha s^5$	$-\alpha^{-\frac{1}{3}}, \left(\dfrac{1}{2} \pm j\dfrac{\sqrt{3}}{2}\right)\alpha^{-\frac{1}{3}}$

Cases 1 and 3 do not have parasitic oscillations. Case 2 has transient parasitic oscillation. Case 4 has sustained parasitic oscillation.

8-4. Sensitivity Function of Transient Response of Nonlinear Systems and Linear Systems with Time-varying Coefficients.

For linear systems, we may calculate directly and obtain an analytical expression of $x(t,\alpha)$. The sensitivity function $\partial x(t,\alpha)/\partial \alpha$ is calculated from $x(t,\alpha)$ by differentiation. While this procedure would be intractable for all but the simplest systems (for instance, all four cases of Example 8-3 are too complicated for direct calculation), it nevertheless offers an alternative to the transform method.

For nonlinear and time-varying systems, the equations are usually solved by numerical integration or simulation on an analog computer. If we make two runs, one with α equal to zero and one with α equal to some small finite value, and take the difference, it is obvious that the errors in the computations must be much less than the errors introduced by α, if the sensitivity function so obtained is to mean anything at all. To put it another way, the accuracy of the measured sensitivity function is far from as good as that of the computations.

Miller and Murray developed a method which makes possible a direct analog run of the sensitivity functions. Consequently, the sensitivity functions so obtained are as accurate as the computation process. Their work has been intended for analyzing the errors in the output of an analog

computer due to errors in simulation.   The sources of errors are classified
into the following categories:

1. α errors: inaccuracies in system simulation that do not affect the
order of the system
2. β errors: external disturbances
3. λ errors: inaccuracies in system simulation that affect the order of
the system

In terms of Miller and Murray's classification, component inaccuracies
due to manufacturing tolerances and changing environmental factors are
sources for α errors.   Idealization of the transfer function gives rise to
λ errors.   The β errors are what we refer to as noise and load disturbance.
As the latter effects are considered inputs in our analysis and have been
taken up in previous chapters, we are concerned here with only the α and
λ errors.

The differential equations describing the theoretical or specified system
can be written as

$$F_i(\dot{x}_1, \dot{x}_2, \ldots, \dot{x}_n, x_1, x_2, \ldots, x_n, t) = 0 \qquad i = 1, 2, 3, \ldots, n \qquad (8\text{-}18)$$

The n simultaneous equations are perfectly general and may represent
either linear, nonlinear, or time-varying systems, depending on the form
of the function F_i.   In particular, a high-order differential equation can be
represented by letting

$$F_k = \dot{x}_k - x_{k+1} \qquad k = 1, 2, \ldots, m$$

Then in the remaining $n - m$ equations, x_{k+1} simply represents the kth
time derivative of x_1, for all values of k from 1 to m.

Let us consider the α errors first.   The actual system can be represented as

$$G_i(\dot{x}_1, \dot{x}_2, \ldots, \dot{x}_n, x_1, x_2, \ldots, x_n, t, \alpha_1, \alpha_2, \ldots, \alpha_m) = 0$$
$$i = 1, 2, \ldots, n \qquad (8\text{-}19)$$

where

$$G_i(\dot{x}_1, \dot{x}_2, \ldots, \dot{x}_n, x_1, x_2, \ldots, x_n, t, 0, 0, \ldots, 0)$$
$$= F_i(\dot{x}_1, \dot{x}_2, \ldots, \dot{x}_n, x_1, x_2, \ldots, x_n, t) \qquad (8\text{-}20)$$

The solution of Eq. (8-19) gives x_i as a function of t and the α's:
$x_i(t, \alpha_1, \alpha_2, \ldots, \alpha_m)$.   Let $x_i(t, \alpha)$ and $x_i(t, 0)$ be the abbreviated forms of
$x_i(t, \alpha_1, \alpha_2, \ldots, \alpha_m)$ and $x_i(t, 0, 0, 0, \ldots, 0)$, respectively.   Because of
Eq. (8-20), $x_i(t, 0)$ is a solution of Eq. (8-18).   For small values of the
α's, $x_i(t, \alpha_1, \alpha_2, \ldots, \alpha_m)$ can be written as

$$x_i(t, \alpha) = x_i(t, 0) + \sum_{k=1}^{k=m} \left[\frac{\partial x_i(t, \alpha)}{\partial \alpha_k} \right]_{\alpha=0} \alpha_k \qquad (8\text{-}21)$$

The partial derivatives are evaluated by letting all the α's equal zero. Let $w_{ik}(t)$ denote these derivatives. Equation (8-21) can be written as

$$x_i(t,\alpha) = x_i(t,0) + \sum_{k=1}^{k=m} w_{ik}(t)\alpha_k \qquad (8\text{-}22)$$

The functions $w_{ik}(t)$ are generalized forms of transient-response sensitivity functions. From Eq. (8-19),

$$\sum_j \frac{\partial G_i}{\partial \dot{x}_j} \frac{\partial \dot{x}_j(t,\alpha)}{\partial \alpha_k} + \sum_j \frac{\partial G_i}{\partial x_j} \frac{\partial x_j(t,\alpha)}{\partial \alpha_k} + \frac{\partial G_i}{\partial \alpha_k} = 0$$

$$i = 1, 2, \ldots, n; k = 1, 2, \ldots, m \qquad (8\text{-}23)$$

The above equation holds for all values of α's. In particular, for zero values of the α's,

$$\frac{\partial G_i}{\partial \dot{x}_j} = \frac{\partial F_i}{\partial \dot{x}_j} \qquad \frac{\partial G_i}{\partial x_j} = \frac{\partial F_i}{\partial x_j}$$

$$\frac{\partial \dot{x}_j(t,\alpha)}{\partial \alpha_k} = \frac{\partial}{\partial t} \frac{\partial x_j(t,\alpha)}{\partial \alpha_k} = \dot{w}_{jk} \qquad (8\text{-}24)$$

Substituting Eq. (8-24) in Eq. (8-23), we obtain

$$\sum_j \left(\frac{\partial F_i}{\partial \dot{x}_j} \dot{w}_{jk} + \frac{\partial F_i}{\partial x_j} w_{jk} \right) + \left(\frac{\partial G_i}{\partial \alpha_k} \right)_{\alpha=0} = 0 \qquad \begin{array}{l} i = 1, 2, \ldots, n \\ k = 1, 2, \ldots, m \end{array} \qquad (8\text{-}25)$$

The functions $x_i(t,0)$, which are solutions of Eq. (8-18) are assumed to be known. The sensitivity functions w_{jk} can be solved directly from Eq. (8-25) without computing $x_i(t,\alpha)$. Let us now examine the nature of these equations:

Case 1. Equations (8-18) are linear with constant coefficients. The partial derivatives $\partial F_i/\partial \dot{x}_j$ and $\partial F_i/\partial x_j$ are constants. Equations (8-25) are the same linear equations with constant coefficients. The only differences are in the inhomogeneous terms.

Case 2. Equations (8-18) are linear with time-varying coefficients. Equations (8-25) are linear with the same time-varying coefficients but different inhomogeneous terms.

Case 3. Equations (8-18) are nonlinear. Since $\partial F_i/\partial x_j$ and $\partial F_i/\partial x_j$ depend on the $x_i(t,0)$'s, Eqs. (8-25) are linear equations with time-varying coefficients.

The initial values of w_{jk} are known from an inspection of the problem, and Eqs. (8-25) allow the subsequent values of w_{jk} to be determined by calculation or simulation.

In Miller and Murray's work, the λ errors are treated in a much more involved way than the α errors. We shall show how the λ errors can be treated in exactly the same way as the α errors, except for the initial conditions, and then we shall show how the proper initial conditions (at $t = \epsilon > 0$, not $t = 0$) can be obtained. The method is given as follows: Suppose that, because of the λ errors, the actual system equations (8-21) depend on $\ddot{x}_1, \ddot{x}_2, \ldots, \ddot{x}_n$. We may rewrite Eq. (8-19) as

$$F_i(\dot{x}_1, \dot{x}_2, \ldots, \dot{x}_{2n}, x_1, x_2, \ldots, x_{2n}, t) = 0 \qquad e = 1, 2, \ldots, 2n \qquad (8\text{-}26)$$

so that for $1 \leq i \leq n$, and $n + 1 \leq k \leq 2n$, F_i is independent of all x_k and $\dot{x}_k$. For $n + 1 \leq i \leq 2n$, F_i is given as

$$F_i = \dot{x}_{i-n} - x_i \qquad i = n + 1, n + 2, \ldots, 2n \qquad (8\text{-}27)$$

Under these conditions, Eqs. (8-26) are the same as Eqs. (8-18). On the other hand, the functions $G_i(\dot{x}_1, \dot{x}_2, \ldots, \dot{x}_{2n}, x_1, x_2, \ldots, x_{2n}, \alpha_1, \alpha_2, \ldots)$ may depend on $\ddot{x}_{n+1}, \ddot{x}_{n+2}, \ldots, \ddot{x}_{2n}$ when not all the α's are zero. The net result is that the second derivatives $\ddot{x}_1, \ddot{x}_2, \ldots, \ddot{x}_n$ are introduced into Eq. (8-1) while the formalism of α errors is still followed. The above procedure can be extended readily to higher derivatives.

From the above discussion, we see that the λ errors can be written and treated as α errors. A general analysis of the α errors is sufficient for treating both the α and λ errors. However, there is a point of reservation. At $t = 0$, not all the w's are defined. For instance, let us consider the problem of Example 8-2. The differential equation of $x(t,\lambda)$ is

$$\lambda \ddot{x} + T\dot{x} + x = u(t) \tag{8-28}$$

where $u(t)$ is the unit step function. According to the above outlined method, Eq. (8-28) is written as

$$\begin{aligned} F_2 &= G_2 = \dot{x}_1 - x_2 = 0 \\ G_1 &= \lambda \dot{x}_2 + T\dot{x}_1 + x_1 - u(t) = 0 \end{aligned} \tag{8-29}$$

We note that, with $\lambda = 0$, $x_2 = 1/T$ at $t = 0$. With $\lambda \neq 0$, no matter how small, $x_2 = 0$ at $t = 0$. The function

$$w_2(t) = \left(\frac{\partial x_2}{\partial \lambda}\right)_{\lambda=0}$$

cannot exist at $t = 0$. Consequently, Eq. (8-25) is not valid at $t = 0$. This is also true quite frequently in the general case. While Eq. (8-25) is still valid for $t > 0$, its failure to hold at $t = 0$ makes the initial conditions at $t = 0$ useless, and they must be replaced by another set of conditions, initial or otherwise. One readily available set can be obtained by the transform method for $t = \epsilon$, where ϵ is an arbitrarily small positive constant. Since Eq. (8-25) can be extended to as low a value of t as we wish, the initial conditions at $t = \epsilon$ are adequate.

The method is as follows:

1. Approximate the system equations at the vicinity of $t = 0$ by linear equations in the x's. Approximate the inputs by functions that are transformable to rational functions of s.

2. Write out the transform equations and solve for the $X_i(s,\alpha)$'s.

3. Calculate $W_{ik}(s)$ as

$$W_{ik}(s) = \left[\frac{\partial X_i(s,\alpha)}{\partial \alpha_k} \right]_{\alpha=0}$$

These are rational functions in s. $W_{ik}(s)$ may be written as

$$W_{ik}(s) = \frac{N(s)}{D(s)} + Q(s)$$

where $N(s)$, $D(s)$, and $Q(s)$ are polynomials in s, $N(s)$ is of at least one order lower than $D(s)$, and $Q(s)$ may be 0, 1, or any polynomial. The ratio N/D is called the principal part of $W_{ik}(s)$ and is denoted as $P[W_{ik}(s)]$. We note that, as $Q(s)$ does not contribute to $w_{ik}(t)$ for any $t \neq 0$, Eq. (8-3) gives

$$w_{ik}(t) = \mathcal{L}^{-1}\{P[W_{ik}(s)]\}$$

However, it is not necessary to evaluate the inverse transform. The initial-value theorem gives

$$w_{ik}(0^+) = \lim_{s \to \infty} sP[W_{ik}(s)] \tag{8-30}$$

Equation (8-30) is to be used as the initial conditions.

Example 8-4. As an example to illustrate the above, consider the linear equation (8-28). Equations (8-25) and (8-29) give

$$\dot{w}_1 + w_1 + \dot{x}_2 = 0 \tag{8-31}$$

Solving the equation $T\dot{x}_1 + x_1 = u(t)$, we obtain

$$x_1 = 1 - e^{-t/T}$$

$$\dot{x}_2 = \ddot{x}_1 = -\frac{1}{T^2} e^{-t/T}$$

Equation (8-31) gives

$$w_1(t) = \frac{t}{T^3} e^{-t/T} + Ae^{-t/T} \tag{8-32}$$

where A is an arbitrary constant. To determine A, Eq. (8-28) gives

$$W_1(s) = \frac{-s^2}{(1 + Ts)^2} \frac{1}{s} = \frac{-s}{(1 + Ts)^2} \tag{8-33}$$

Equations (8-30) and (8-32) give

$$w_1(0^+) = \frac{-1}{T^2} \tag{8-34}$$

Substituting Eq. (8-34) in (8-32), we obtain $A = -1/T^2$, and

$$w_1(t) = \frac{1}{T^2} \left(\frac{t}{T} e^{-t/T} - e^{-t/T} \right) \tag{8-35}$$

which agrees with Eq. (8-8).   On the other hand, it is obvious that $x(0,\lambda)$ is zero no matter what λ is.

$$w_1(0) = \frac{\partial x(0,\lambda)}{\partial \lambda} = 0 \tag{8-36}$$

If we use Eq. (8-36) as the initial condition, it follows that $A = 0$, and the result is erroneous.

8-5. Sensitivities of Closed-loop Poles of a Linear System.   When we talk about the performance parameters of a closed-loop system, we may be referring to two different types of parameters:

1. Parameters that govern the general characteristic of the response curve, e.g., natural frequency and damping
2. Response to a particular input at a particular time or frequency, e.g., peak overshoot or maximum modulus

The first group will be discussed here while the second group will be discussed in Sec. 8-6.

The natural frequency and damping are well defined for a second-order system but are not so well defined for a system of third order or higher. In general, we may say that the terms refer to the locations of the pair of control poles in a closed-loop system.   By giving an explicit expression for the position shifts of these poles, the problem is solved.

Let p_i denote the poles of $(C/R)(s)$, and let α_j denote the variable parameters of system components, where i and j are running indices. For small variations in the α's, the variations in the p's can be expressed as

$$\delta p_i = \sum_j \frac{\partial p_i}{\partial \alpha_j} \delta \alpha_j \tag{8-37}$$

The partial derivatives $\partial p_i/\partial \alpha_j$ are evaluated for the ideal condition $\delta \alpha_j = 0$ for all j's and are defined as pole sensitivities to the parameter α_j. (The definition of pole sensitivities is not unanimous in the literature. However, as one can be easily obtained from another, the exact definition is not significant.)   The closed-loop function can be written as

$$\frac{C}{R}(s) = \frac{K \prod_k (s - z_k)}{\prod (s - p_i)} \tag{8-38}$$

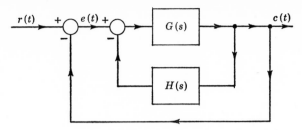

FIG. 8-1. Block diagram illustrating a prototype system with both series and shunt compensation.

Since multiple roots in $(C/R)(s)$ are rather unusual, especially for the control poles, we assume that the poles and zeros are distinct. With reference to Fig. 8-1, $(C/R)(s)$ can be expressed in terms of the transfer functions of the components as

$$\frac{1}{(C/R)(s)} = 1 + H(s) + G^{-1}(s) \qquad (8\text{-}39)$$

Taking the logarithm of the above equations, we obtain

$$\sum_i \log (s - p_i) - \sum_k \log (s - z_k) - \log K$$
$$= \log [1 + H(s) + G^{-1}(s)] \qquad (8\text{-}40)$$

Differentiating Eq. (8-40) with respect to α, multiplying the result by $-(s - p_i)$, and setting s equal to p_i give

$$\frac{\partial p_i}{\partial \alpha_j} = - \left[(s - p_i) \frac{C}{R}(s) \right]_{s=p_i} \left[\frac{\partial H(p_i)}{\partial \alpha_j} + \frac{\partial G^{-1}(p_i)}{\partial \alpha_j} \right] \qquad (8\text{-}41)$$

The expression in the first brackets is the residue of $(C/R)(s)$ at $s = p_i$. Denoting it by R_i, Eq. (8-41) becomes

$$\frac{\partial p_i}{\partial \alpha_j} = - R_i \left[\frac{\partial H(p_i)}{\partial \alpha_j} + \frac{\partial G^{-1}(p_i)}{\partial \alpha_j} \right] \qquad (8\text{-}42)$$

In series-compensated systems, $H(s) = 0$, and Eq. (8-42) can be written in a different form. We note that, since p_i is a pole of $(C/R)(s)$,

$$G^{-1}(p_i) = -1$$

Equation (8-42) becomes

$$\frac{\partial p_i}{\partial \alpha_j} = \frac{R_i}{G^{-1}(p_i)} \frac{\partial G^{-1}(p_i)}{\partial \alpha_j} = R_i \frac{\partial}{\partial \alpha_j} \log G^{-1}(p_i) \qquad (8\text{-}43)$$

For a series-compensated system, $G(s)$ usually represents a product of the form $G_1(s)G_2(s)G_3(s) \cdots$. Equation (8-43) allows the irrelevant G's to drop out of the computation.

Example 8-5. The open-loop transfer function of a lead-lag compensated system can be written as

$$G(s) = \frac{20(1 + 0.5s)(1 + 2s)}{(1 + 0.1s)(1 + 10s)} \frac{K}{(1 + T_1 s)(1 + T_2 s)} \tag{8-44}$$

The nominal values of K, T_1, and T_2 are 5, 0.5, and 2 sec, respectively. Determine the natural frequency and damping of the closed-loop system as well as their sensitivities to variations in K, T_1, and T_2.

Solution. Under the nominal condition,

$$G(s) = \frac{100}{(1 + 0.1s)(1 + 10s)}$$

$$\frac{C}{R}(s) = \frac{100}{s^2 + 10.1s + 101}$$

Therefore,

$$\omega_0 = \sqrt{101} = 10.05$$

$$= \frac{10.1}{10.05 \times 2} = 0.5025 = \cos 59.8°$$

$$p_1 = 10.05 \underline{/120.2°} \qquad p_2 = 10.05 \underline{/-120.2°}$$

Let us consider the pole p_1. Its residue is

$$R_1 = \frac{100}{p_1 - p_2} = -j5.75$$

From Eqs. (8-43) and (8-44),

$$\frac{\partial p_1}{\partial K} = R_1\left(-\frac{1}{K}\right) = \frac{j5.75}{5} = j1.15$$

$$\frac{\partial p_1}{\partial T_1} = R_1 \frac{p_1}{1 + T_1 p_1} = \frac{-j5.75}{0.45 - j0.086} = 12.55\underline{/-79.2°}$$

$$\frac{\partial p_1}{\partial T_2} = \frac{-j5.75}{1.95 - j0.086} = 2.95 \underline{/-87.5°}$$

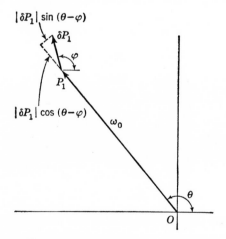

FIG. 8-2. Vector diagram illustrating relationship between the vector δp_1 and the scalors $\delta\omega_0$ and $\delta\zeta$.

From Fig. 8-2,

$$\delta\omega_0 = |\delta p_1| \cos(\theta - \phi)$$

$$\delta\zeta = -\delta \cos\theta \Rightarrow \sin\theta \, \delta\theta = -\frac{|\delta p_1|}{\omega_0} \sin\theta \sin(\theta - \phi)$$

Therefore,

$$\frac{\partial\omega_0}{\partial\alpha} = \left|\frac{\partial p_1}{\partial\alpha}\right| \cos(\theta - \phi) \tag{8-45}$$

$$\frac{\partial\zeta}{\partial\alpha} = \frac{1}{\omega_0}\left|\frac{\partial p_1}{\partial\alpha}\right| \sin\theta \sin(\theta - \phi) \tag{8-46}$$

where α may be any parameter K, T_1, or T_2.
Equations (8-45) and (8-46) give

$$\frac{\partial\omega_0}{\partial K} = 1.15 \cos 30.2° = 0.993 \text{ sec}^{-1}$$

$$\frac{\partial\zeta}{\partial K} = -\frac{1.15}{10.05} \sin 120.2° \sin 30.2° = -0.050$$

$$\frac{\partial\omega_0}{\partial T_1} = -11.8 \text{ sec}^{-2} \qquad \frac{\partial\omega_0}{\partial T_2} = -2.62 \text{ sec}^{-2}$$

$$\frac{\partial\zeta}{\partial T_1} = 0.352 \text{ sec}^{-1} \qquad \frac{\partial\zeta}{\partial T_2} = 0.117 \text{ sec}^{-1}$$

8-6. Sensitivities of Maximum Modulus and Peak Response of a Linear System.

The maximum modulus M is defined as the maximum value of $|(C/R)(j\omega)|$ over varying frequency. Since the peak-response frequency ω_m also varies as the parameters α_i vary, we have

$$\frac{\partial M}{\partial\alpha_i} = \underbrace{\frac{\partial}{\partial\alpha_i}\left|\frac{C}{R}(j\omega_m)\right|}_{\text{constant } \omega_m} + \frac{\partial}{\partial\omega_m}\left|\frac{C}{R}(j\omega_m)\right|\frac{\partial\omega_m}{\partial\alpha_i} \tag{8-47}$$

However, as

$$\frac{\partial}{\partial\omega_m}\left|\frac{C}{R}(j\omega_m)\right| = 0$$

by definition of ω_m, Eq. (8-47) reduces to

$$\frac{\partial M}{\partial\alpha_i} = \frac{\partial}{\partial\alpha_i}\left|\frac{C}{R}(j\omega_m)\right| \tag{8-48}$$

Equation (8-48) is evaluated at the ω_m of the nominal system.

The peak response c_p is defined as the peak value of the unit step response $c(t)$. Similarly to (8-48), we have

$$\frac{\partial c_p}{\partial\alpha_i} = \frac{\partial c(t_p)}{\partial\alpha_i} \tag{8-49}$$

where t_p is the time of peak response of the nominal system. Equation (8-49) reduces the peak-response sensitivity to that of evaluating $c(t)$ at a particular time t_p, which can be done by the transform method of Sec. 8-2.

Let F and $\bar{F}$ represent $(C/R)(j\omega_m)$ and $(C/R)(-j\omega_m)$, respectively. Equation (8-48) can be written as

$$\frac{\partial M}{\partial \alpha_i} = \frac{1}{2M} \frac{\partial}{\partial \alpha_i} (F\bar{F}) = -\frac{M}{2} \frac{\partial}{\partial \alpha_i} \log (F^{-1}\bar{F}^{-1})$$

$$= -M \times \text{real component of} \left[F \left(\frac{\partial H}{\partial \alpha_i} + \frac{\partial G^{-1}}{\partial \alpha_i} \right) \right] \quad (8\text{-}50)$$

For a series-compensated system, Eq. (8-50) becomes

$$\frac{\partial M}{\partial \alpha_i} = -M \times \text{real component of} \left(F \frac{\partial G^{-1}}{\partial \alpha_i} \right)$$

$$= M \times \text{real component of} \left[\frac{(\partial/\partial \alpha_i) \log G(j\omega_m)}{1 + G(j\omega_m)} \right] \quad (8\text{-}51)$$

Example 8-6. For the problem of Example 8-5, determine the maximum modulus and its sensitivity to a change in T_1.

Solution. For the nominal system,

$$\omega_m = \omega_0 \sqrt{1 - 2\zeta^2} = 0.704\omega_0 = 7.08$$

$$M = \frac{1}{2\zeta \sqrt{1 - \zeta^2}} \frac{100}{101} = 1.14$$

To calculate the sensitivity of M to T_1, we evaluate first

$$G(j\omega_m) = \frac{100}{(1 + j0.708)(1 + j70.8)} = 1.153 \underline{/-124.5°}$$

$$\frac{\partial \log G}{\partial T_1} = \frac{-j\omega_m}{1 + T_1 j\omega_m} = 1.92 \underline{/-164.2°}$$

Equation (8-51) gives

$$\frac{\partial M}{\partial T_1} = M \times \text{real component of } 1.90 \underline{/-94.2°} = -0.16 \text{ sec}^{-1}$$

8-7. Physical Significance of a Cost Function. Another phase of error analysis is to take a direct look at the deterioration of system merit due to component inaccuracies. For a system without power constraint (e.g., optimum filtering or prediction) system merit can be taken as synonymous with negative mean-square error. All we need to do is to examine the increase in mean-square error. For a system with power constraint, the criterion is not as simple. The calculated mean-square error $\overline{e^2}$ can obviously be decreased by increasing $\overline{a^2}$. The sum $\overline{e^2} + k^2\overline{a^2}$, however, is always on the rise. Its increased value can be taken as a quantitative indication of the deterioration of system merit. If the constraint in $\overline{a^2}$ is due to heat-loss limitations, we may regard an increased value of $\overline{a^2}$ as an increased cost, since higher temperature reduces the life expectation of the hardware. The sum $\overline{e^2} + k^2\overline{a^2}$ represents total cost in terms of both the expected error and expected life. It will be defined as the "cost function" and denoted by f_c.

Alternatively, the power constraint may be due to saturation. The calculated $\overline{e^2}$ is lower than the actual $\overline{e^2}$. Let the symbols u, v, and w be defined as

$$u = \text{actual } \overline{e^2}$$
$$v = \text{calculated } \overline{e^2} \text{ on linear basis}$$
$$w = \overline{a^2}$$

Obviously we are interested in the increase in u rather than in v. For a system with random inputs and $\overline{a^2}$ considerably below its saturation value, u can be written approximately as

$$u = v + U(w) \tag{8-52}$$

where $U(w)$ is an increasing function of w.

Next, we assume that the level of $\overline{a^2}$ is so selected that u is a minimum. Let k_0 and $F(s,k_0)$ denote the corresponding value of k and optimum system function $F(s,k)$, respectively. For a slightly different $k = k_0 + \delta k$, there is a slightly different $F(s, k_0 + \delta k)$, which gives rise to first-order variations $(\delta v)_1$ and $(\delta w)_1$. Since k_0 is selected to give minimum u, we have

$$\delta u = (\delta v)_1 + \frac{\partial U}{\partial w} (\delta w)_1 = 0 \tag{8-53}$$

However, since $F(s,k_0)$ is an optimum system function, we have

$$(\delta v)_1 + k_0{}^2 (\delta w)_1 = 0 \tag{8-54}$$

Comparing Eqs. (8-53) and (8-54) gives

$$k_0{}^2 = \frac{\partial U}{\partial w} \tag{8-55}$$

Next let us consider an arbitrary but small variation $\epsilon F_1(s)$ from the optimum system function $F(s,k_0)$. Let δu, δv, and δw represent the total variations in u, v, and w, respectively. Then

$$\delta v = C_1 \epsilon + C_2 \epsilon^2$$
$$\delta w = C_3 \epsilon + C_4 \epsilon^2 \tag{8-56}$$

where the coefficients C_1, C_2, C_3, and C_4 are independent of ϵ but dependent on $F_1(s)$. The variation in δu will be evaluated up to the second order in ϵ:

$$\delta u = \delta v + \frac{\partial U}{\partial w} \delta w + \frac{1}{2} \frac{\partial^2 U}{\partial w^2} (\delta w)^2$$
$$= (\delta v + k_0{}^2 \delta w) + \frac{1}{2} \frac{\partial^2 U}{\partial w^2} C_3{}^2 \epsilon^2$$
$$= \delta f_c + \frac{C_3{}^2}{2} \frac{\partial^2 U}{\partial w^2} \epsilon^2 \tag{8-57}$$

Equation (8-57) shows that δf_c is an approximate representation of the increase in actual mean-square error δu.

8-8. Increase of Mean-square Error and the Cost Function.   There are two types of variations which may cause a change in the mean-square error or the cost function:

1. Variations in the spectral densities of the inputs and in the controlled system
2. Variations in the compensating elements

Variations of the first type change the assumed condition of the optimization calculations.   The cost function may be either increased or reduced, depending on what is changed in which way.   The change in cost function is proportional to the parameter change, as long as the latter is small enough.   Variation of the second type does not change the condition of optimization, and consequently the cost function can only be on the rise.   The change of cost function is proportional to the square of the parameter change for small variations.

So far as computation is concerned, the first type is routine.   We simply calculate whatever we wish to calculate in terms of the variable parameters and then take the derivatives.   The second type is more interesting.   We shall derive a method which is faster than direct computation.

As the mean-square error in a system without power constraint can be considered as a special case of the cost function with $k_0 = 0$, we shall consider the cost function only.   In general, it can be represented as

$$f_c = \frac{1}{2\pi j} \int_{-j\infty}^{j\infty} (\Phi_0 + \bar{\Phi}_1 F + \Phi_1 \bar{F} + \Phi_2 \bar{F} F) \, ds \qquad (8\text{-}58)$$

where Φ_0, Φ_1, and Φ_2 are functions of s such that $\Phi_0(s) = \Phi_0(-s)$ and $\Phi_2(s) = \Phi_2(-s)$.   The optimum system function F_0 is determined by the condition

$$\frac{1}{2\pi j} \int_{-j\infty}^{j\infty} (\Phi_1 + \Phi_2 F_0) \bar{F}_1 \, ds = 0 \qquad (8\text{-}59)$$

where F_1 is an arbitrary system function with all its poles in the LHP. As a special case, F_1 may be equal to F_0.   Since

$$\Phi_0 + \bar{\Phi}_1 F_0 + \Phi_1 \bar{F}_0 + \Phi_2 \bar{F}_0 F_0 = \Phi_0 - \Phi_2 \bar{F}_0 F_0 + (\Phi_1 + \Phi_2 F_0) \bar{F}_0$$
$$+ (\bar{\Phi}_1 + \bar{\Phi}_2 \bar{F}_0) F_0 \quad (8\text{-}60)$$

by integrating Eq. (8-60) and making use of Eq. (8-59) we obtain the minimum value of f_c as

$$f_c(0) = \frac{1}{2\pi j} \int_{-j\infty}^{j\infty} (\Phi_0 - \Phi_2 \bar{F}_0 F_0) \, ds \qquad (8\text{-}61)$$

For an arbitrary system function $F = F_0 + \delta F$, Eq. (8-58) gives

$$f_c = f_c(0) + \frac{1}{2\pi j} \int_{-j\infty}^{j\infty} [(\Phi_1 + \Phi_2 F_0) \delta \bar{F} + (\bar{\Phi}_1 + \Phi_2 \bar{F}_0) \delta F] \, ds$$
$$+ \frac{1}{2\pi j} \int_{-j\infty}^{j\infty} \Phi_2 (\delta F)(\delta \bar{F}) \, ds \quad (8\text{-}62)$$

Since the first integral vanishes because of Eq. (8-59),

$$\delta f_c = f_c - f_c(0) = \frac{1}{2\pi j} \int_{-j\infty}^{j\infty} \Phi_2 (\delta F)(\delta \bar{F}) \, ds \quad (8\text{-}63)$$

Equation (8-63) is an exact equation.   It can be evaluated in two ways: either in terms of a variation in the transfer function of the components or in terms of the pole-zero locations of $F(s)$.   Referring to Eq. (8-39), we have $\delta F^{-1} = \delta H + \delta G^{-1}$.   Since

$$F - F_0 = F F_0 \left(\frac{1}{F_0} - \frac{1}{F} \right) = -F F_0 \, \delta F^{-1}$$

Equation (8-63) can be written as

$$\delta f_c = \frac{1}{2\pi j} \int_{-j\infty}^{j\infty} \Phi_2 F_0 \bar{F}_0 F \bar{F} (\delta H + \delta G^{-1})(\delta \bar{H} + \delta \bar{G}^{-1}) \, ds \quad (8\text{-}64)$$

where F_0 is the closed-loop system function of the nominal system.
    Alternatively, Eq. (8-63) may be written as

$$\delta f_c = \frac{1}{2\pi j} \int_{-j\infty}^{j\infty} \Phi_2 F_0 \bar{F}_0 (\delta \log F)(\delta \log \bar{F}) \, ds$$
$$\leq \max_{s=j\omega} |\delta \log F|^2 \frac{1}{2\pi j} \int_{-j\infty}^{j\infty} \Phi_2 F_0 \bar{F}_0 \, ds$$
$$\leq \max_{s=j\omega} |\delta \log F|^2 \frac{1}{2\pi j} \int_{-j\infty}^{j\infty} \Phi_0 \, ds \quad (8\text{-}65)$$

The second inequality sign is justified by Eq. (8-61) since $f_c(0)$ must be positive.   Inequality (8-65) has a certain physical analogy.   If it is assumed that positive and negative unit charges are placed at the poles and zeros in a two-dimensional potential analog, the expression

$$\max_{s=j\omega} |\delta \log F|$$

is the maximum change in potential on the imaginary axis due to displacements of poles and zeros.   The integral

$$\frac{1}{2\pi j} \int_{-j\infty}^{j\infty} \Phi_0 \, ds \quad (8\text{-}66)$$

is the value of the cost function if the control system is turned off.

Inequality (8-65) is meaningless if the integral (8-66) is infinite. This happens when there are poles of Φ_0 on the imaginary axis. However, Eqs. (8-63) and (8-64) can still be used.

8-9. Increase of Cost Function with Steplike Inputs. While the equations derived in the preceding section are general enough, their physical significances are clouded by the generality of the mathematical expressions. By working out the solution for the special case of follow-up systems with steplike inputs, we shall gain some insight into the magnitude of the increase of the cost function. The inaccuracies of the compensating elements may be classified as:

1. Inaccurate gain or time constants
2. Neglected minor time constants

Typical examples of (2) are the time constants of what may be called the driving stage of the system. For instance, in hydraulic systems, a hydraulic booster or a torque motor is commonly used to supply the input to the last stage. Its time constants are of the order of one-tenth those of the final power stage or less. In steering systems, the hydraulic servo for driving the control surfaces can be considered as the driving stage. While it is usually justifiable to neglect these time constants in the initial design, we should like to know, at most how much increase in the cost function is caused by their presence. Since the optimum system designed on the basis of considering these time constants cannot be as good as the idealized system, the disadvantage of neglecting these time constants is not as great as indicated by the present calculations. If the latter values are low, we have reasonable grounds for neglecting these time constants in designing the system.

For the system of Fig. 4-1, with $H_m = 1$, and $n(t) = d(t) = 0$, we have

$$\Phi_{ee} + k^2\Phi_{aa} = \Phi_{rr}(1 - \bar{F})(1 - F) + \frac{k^2\bar{G}_3G_3}{\bar{G}_1G_1}\bar{F}F\Phi_{rr}$$

Therefore,
$$\Phi_2 = \bar{Y}Y\Phi_{rr}$$

where $\bar{Y}Y$ is given in Eq. (4-27). For steplike inputs, $\Phi_{rr}(j\omega) = A^2/\omega^2$, and $F_0 = 1/Y$. Equation (8-64) becomes

$$\delta f_c = \frac{1}{2\pi j}\int_{-j\infty}^{j\infty}\left(-\frac{A^2}{s^2}\right)\bar{F}F(\delta H + \delta G^{-1})(\delta\bar{H} + \delta\bar{G}^{-1})\,ds \quad (8\text{-}67)$$

Now we shall consider variations in G_c only. Equation (8-67) becomes

$$\delta f_c = \frac{1}{2\pi j}\int_{-j\infty}^{j\infty}\left|\frac{A}{s}\frac{F}{G}\delta\log G\right|^2 ds \quad (8\text{-}68)$$

Let G_c be written as

$$G_c = \frac{K(1 + T_a s)(1 + T_b s) \cdots}{(1 + T_1 s)(1 + T_2 s) \cdots}$$

$$\delta \log G = \delta \log G_c = \frac{\delta K}{K} + \sum_{\lambda = a, b, \ldots} \frac{s \, \delta T_\lambda}{1 + T_\lambda s} - \sum_{i = 1, 2, \ldots} \frac{s \, \delta T_i}{1 + T_i s} \qquad (8\text{-}69)$$

We note that, in Eq. (8-68), F/G is simply the closed-loop error to the input transfer function. If the inaccuracy is due to gain K alone, Eq. (8-69) gives

$$\delta f_c = \overline{e^2} \left(\frac{\delta K}{K} \right)^2 \qquad (8\text{-}70)$$

The effect of the time constants can be expressed as

$$\delta f_c = \left(\frac{\delta T}{T} \right)^2 \frac{1}{2\pi j} \int_{-j\infty}^{j\infty} \left| \frac{AF}{sG} \right|^2 \left[\frac{1}{1 + 1/\omega^2 T^2} \right] ds \qquad (8\text{-}71)$$

where T may be one of the T_i's or one of the T_λ's. The function inside the brackets is always less than unity. Therefore

$$\delta f_c < \overline{e^2} \left(\frac{\delta T}{T} \right)^2 \qquad (8\text{-}72)$$

Now we consider the case of the neglected time constants. A function G' is defined as

$$G' = \frac{G}{G_0} = \frac{(1 + T_a' s)(1 + T_b' s) \cdots}{(1 + T_1' s)(1 + T_2' s) \cdots} \qquad (8\text{-}73)$$

where T_a', T_b', $\ldots$ and T_1', T_2', $\ldots$ are the neglected time constants.

$$\delta G^{-1} = \frac{1}{G_0 G'} - \frac{1}{G_0} = \frac{1}{G}(1 - G') \qquad (8\text{-}74)$$

Equation (8-67) becomes

$$\delta f_c = \frac{1}{2\pi j} \int_{-j\infty}^{j\infty} \left| \frac{AF}{sG}(1 - G') \right|^2 ds \qquad (8\text{-}75)$$

Equation (8-75) can be interpreted as shown in Fig. 8-3. AF/sG gives the Laplace transform of the error signal, while $1 - G'$ is another cascaded transfer function before the resulting signal is squared. Figure 8-4 illustrates typical step responses of F/G and $1 - G'$, respectively. Since the time constants in G' are very small, its transient term dies out quickly. The response of $1 - G'$ to the error function a of Fig. 8-4 is not substantially different from its transient response to the step-input function c. Equation (8-75) can be approximated as

$$\delta f_c \cong \frac{1}{2\pi j} \int_{-j\infty}^{j\infty} -\frac{A^2}{s^2}(1 - G')(1 - \bar{G}') \, ds \qquad (8\text{-}76)$$

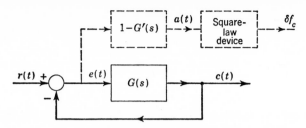

FIG. 8-3. Physical interpretation of the magnitude of δf_c.

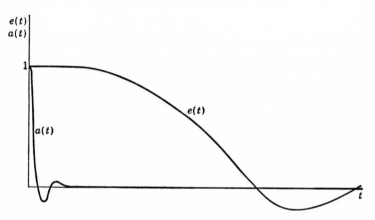

FIG. 8-4. The variables $e(t)$ and $a(t)$ of Fig. 8-3 subsequent to a step input at $t = 0$.

Mathematically, we may say that F/G has a magnitude of nearly unity for large enough values of s. For small values of s, $1 - G'$ is nearly zero, and for the significant range of $1 - G'$, F/G can be considered as unity.

Example 8-7. Determine the increase in cost function to a unit step input, assuming

$$G' = \frac{1}{(1 + as)(1 + bs)}$$

Solution

$$1 - G' = \frac{s(a + b + abs)}{(1 + as)(1 + bs)}$$

$$\delta f_c = \frac{1}{2\pi j} \int_{-j\infty}^{j\infty} \frac{(a + b)^2 - a^2 b^2 s^2}{(1 - a^2 s^2)(1 - b^2 s^2)}\, ds = \frac{1}{2}\left(a + b + \frac{ab}{a + b}\right) \qquad (8\text{-}77)$$

8-10. Error Analysis of Sampled-data Systems. Most of the results for continuous systems can be readily converted to sampled-data systems. The nomenclature of Chap. 6 will be used in the present section.

1. *Transient Response.* Corresponding to Eq. (8-3), we have

$$\left[\frac{\partial c(t,\alpha)}{\partial \alpha}\right]_{\alpha=0} = \mathcal{L}^{-1}\left\{R(s)\,\frac{\partial}{\partial \alpha}\left[\frac{K_0^*(s,\alpha)}{G_1^*(s,\alpha)}\,G_1(s,\alpha)\right]_{\alpha=0}\right\} \qquad (8\text{-}78)$$

If the sensitivity of $c(t,\alpha)$ at sampling instants only is of interest, Eq. (8-78) reduces to

$$\left[\frac{\partial c(nT,\alpha)}{\partial \alpha}\right]_{\alpha=0} = \frac{1}{2\pi j} \oint_{\text{unit circle}} R(z) \left[\frac{\partial K_0(z,\alpha)}{\partial \alpha}\right]_{\alpha=0} z^{n-1}\, dz \quad (8\text{-}79)$$

2. *Pole Sensitivity of* $K_0(z,\alpha)$. Since Eqs. (8-38) and (8-39) still hold with s replaced by z, and $(C/R)(s)$ replaced by $K_0(z,\alpha)$, the results of the analysis also hold in the z plane, namely,

$$\frac{\partial p_i}{\partial \alpha_i} = R_i \left[\frac{\partial H(p_i)}{\partial \alpha_j} + \frac{\partial G^{-1}(p_i)}{\partial \alpha_j}\right] \quad (8\text{-}80)$$

where R_i is the residue of $K_0(z,\alpha)$ at the pole p_i.

In series-compensated systems with $H(z) = 0$, Eq. (8-80) becomes

$$\frac{\partial p_i}{\partial \alpha_j} = R_i \frac{\partial}{\partial \alpha_j} \log G^{-1}(p_i) \quad (8\text{-}81)$$

3. *Increase of the Cost Function.* Corresponding to Eqs. (8-58), (8-63), and (8-65), we have

$$f_c = \frac{1}{2\pi j} \oint [\Phi_0(z) + \Phi_1(z^{-1})K(z) + \Phi_1(z)K(z^{-1})$$

$$+ \Phi_2(z)K(z^{-1})K(z)]\frac{dz}{z} \quad (8\text{-}82)$$

$$\delta f_c = f_c - f_c(0) = \frac{1}{2\pi j} \oint \Phi_2(z)\, \delta K(z)\, \delta K(z^{-1})\frac{dz}{z} \quad (8\text{-}83)$$

$$\delta f_c \leq \max_{|z|=1} |\delta \log K(z)|^2 \frac{1}{2\pi j} \oint \Phi_0(z)\frac{dz}{z} \quad (8\text{-}84)$$

In case there are poles of $\Phi_0(z)$ on the unit circle, these are also poles of $\Phi_2(z)$ and zeros of $\delta K(z)$ if $\overline{e^2} + k^2\overline{a^2}$ of the system is to have finite value. Since $\Phi_0(z) = \Phi_0(z^{-1})$ and $\Phi_2(z) = \Phi_2(z^{-1})$, these poles are in reciprocal pairs a_i and a_i^{-1}. Let $W(z)$ and $\Phi_2'(z)$ be defined as

$$W(z) = \prod_i (1 - a_i z^{-1})$$

$$\Phi_2'(z) = \Phi_2(z)W(z)W(z^{-1})$$

Equation (8-83) can be written as

$$\delta f_c = \frac{1}{2\pi j} \oint \Phi_2'(z)K(z)K(z^{-1}) \left|\frac{1}{W(z)}\,\delta \log K(z)\right|^2 \frac{dz}{z}$$

$$\leq \max_{z=1} \left|\frac{1}{W(z)}\,\delta \log K(z)\right|^2 \frac{1}{2\pi j} \oint \Phi_2'(z)K(z)K(z^{-1})\frac{dz}{z} \quad (8\text{-}85)$$

As the applications of Eqs. (8-78) to (8-85) are similar to the corresponding ones for the continuous systems, they will not be illustrated by examples.

8-11. Summary.   In Chap. 8, we have studied the various effects of component inaccuracies and idealization of transfer functions on the performance of a closed-loop system.   For the transient response as well as the performance parameters (e.g., maximum modulus) of a closed-loop system, the effect of component-parameter change is a first-order effect. Sensitivity functions are defined as the partial derivatives of the system response or response parameters with respect to the component parameter in question.   For the mean-square error or the cost function of an optimum system, the effect of parameter change in the fixed component is a first-order effect, but the effect of parameter change in the compensating elements is a second-order effect.

To give a more detailed account, the effects studied are the following:

1. *Sensitivity of Transient Performance to Component Inaccuracies.* A transform method which gives the sensitivity functions directly is derived for linear systems.   The method is valid in general except at $t = 0$.   For $t = 0$, the method is good if the component inaccuracies do not change the order of the system.   In case the order of the system is changed, the transform method gives the values of the sensitivity functions at $t > 0$ but not at $t = 0$.

For nonlinear and time-varying systems, a set of linear differential equations is derived which makes it possible to compute the sensitivity functions directly on an analog computer.   In case the order of the system is changed by component inaccuracies, the initial values of the sensitivity functions at $t = 0+$ (obtained by the transform method) should be used.   The initial values at $t = 0$ lead to erroneous results because of the discontinuity at $t = 0$.

2. *Sensitivities of Closed-loop Performance Parameters to Inaccuracies.* Simple equations are derived giving the sensitivity functions of maximum modulus, peak response, closed-loop poles, damping factor, etc., to inaccuracies of the gain and time constants of various control elements.

3. *Increase in Mean-square Error or Cost Function Due to Component Inaccuracies.*   The cost function of a system with power constraint is defined as $\overline{e^2} + k_0{}^2\overline{a^2}$, where $\overline{e^2}$ and $\overline{a^2}$ are mean-square values of the system error and constrained variable of the linearized system, and $k_0{}^2$ is the optimum value of the multiplier k^2.   In case the constraint arises out of saturation, it is shown that an increase in cost function is approximately equal to the increase in mean-square error in the actual system.

Simple equations and inequalities are derived which give the increase in cost function in terms of the parameter changes in the compensating elements.   Physical analogs are described for these equations to illustrate the order of magnitude.

CHAPTER 9

MINIMAL-TIME CONTROL OF NONLINEAR SYSTEMS

9-1. Introduction. One hears frequently talk of linear systems and nonlinear systems as if control systems belong to either one or the other of the two big classifications. Logically, this is sound. However, it conveys the impression of equality, and this is not sound. In much the same way, we may classify space into two subspaces, at the origin and not at the origin.

The above analogy can be carried further. If we select points in space at random, the chance of selecting the origin is zero. Similarly, no system is strictly linear in the mathematical sense of the word. All one can say is that a certain system is approximately linear in response to inputs above and below certain magnitudes. In a similar fashion, our space can be classified as away from the origin and in the neighborhood of the origin.

Thus, if we consider the class of all nonlinear systems, it is an infinity of higher order compared with the class of all linear systems. In this chapter, we do not intend to survey all the problems and solutions and studies made on nonlinear systems. Rather, we shall concentrate on a problem of universal importance, namely, the problem of minimal-time control. One well-known special case of minimal-time controls is the predictor control, or "bang-bang" servo.

The problem of minimal-time control arises from the so-called maneuvering problems. Generally speaking, there are two types of applications:

1. *Stabilizing.* The desired dynamical state of the controlled system is fixed or is varying very slowly, and the control force or moments are used primarily to counteract the load disturbance.

2. *Maneuvering.* There is a command to change the dynamical state of the controlled system from one set of values to another, and this change is to be carried out in minimum time with as little overshoot as possible. During this phase of operation, the effects of load disturbances are considered small, and the control force is programmed to carry out the command.

The optimum control for the first application has been treated in Chap. 4. We shall discuss here the optimum control for maneuvering. It will also be shown how, in a single device, the two principles can be reconciled.

9-2. The Maximum Principle. The guiding principle of minimal-time control is the so-called maximum principle. To put it in ordinary language, "*If you wish to get there fastest, give it the mostest.*" While this rudimentary philosophy may not work very well in human affairs, it works in a class of well-defined control problems. In fact, a version of it, the bang-bang servo, has been known for many years and studied by many authors. A very general and precise formulation of the maximum principle has been given fairly recently by a well-known Soviet mathematician, L. S. Pontryagin, and his students V. G. Boltyanskii and R. V. Gamkrelidze. What follows is a heuristic account of this principle.

The controlled dynamical system can be described by a system of first-order differential equations.

$$\dot{x}_i = F_i(\mathbf{x}, \mathbf{f}, t) \qquad i = 1, 2, \ldots, n \qquad (9\text{-}1)$$

where $\mathbf{x}$ and $\mathbf{f}$ stand for the sets of variables $x_1, x_2, \ldots, x_n$, and $f_1, f_2, \ldots, f_m$, respectively, and the functions F are continuous and differentiable in x and f. The set of variables $\mathbf{x}$ is called state variables as it specifies the dynamical state of the controlled system. For instance, in a second-order system, position and velocity constitute a set of state variables. The set of variables $\mathbf{f}$ represents the control forces at our disposal to effectuate the desired changes in the dynamical state of the controlled system. In general, the magnitudes of f_k, $k = 1, 2, \ldots, m$, are limited, but within such limits the f_k's can be varied at will. These limits are referred to as constraints on f. It is seen from Eq. (9-1) that, if at any instant t_1 the values of the x_i's are given and the $f_k(t)$'s for $t \geq t_1$ are given, the state variables x_i as functions of time from the instant t_1 onward are completely determined. In this sense the state variables x_i completely specify the dynamical state of the controlled system. What happened in the past is immaterial.

Equation (9-1) is a very general form of representing dynamical systems. Systems with simple nonlinearities and ordinary transfer functions can readily be rewritten in the form of Eq. (9-1) but not vice versa.

The n-dimensional space with the x_i's as its coordinates is called the phase space. Each point in the phase space specifies a set of values for the x_i's and thereby represents a dynamical state of the system. As t increases, the x_i's vary continuously, and the point x (whose coordinates are the x_i's) traces out a locus in the phase space. The locus is called a trajectory of the system. Obviously, from any given initial point specified by $x_i = \alpha_i$, $i = 1, 2, \ldots, m$, the path of the trajectory depends on the $f(t)_i$'s. Because of the constraints on $\mathbf{f}$, not every curve originating from α (short notation for the point $x_i = \alpha_i$) is a possible trajectory. Let $\Omega(t \leq T)$ denote the collection of all points covered by at least one possible trajectory originating at α at $t = 0$ and ending at $t = T$. Since the $f(t)_i$'s can be varied at will by an infinitesimal amount, the possible trajectories are infinitely close to each other, and $\Omega(t \leq T)$ represents a continuous region in the phase space.

Consider a trajectory Γ originating at a point α and ending at a point β. If no other trajectory can reach β from α in less time, Γ is called an optimum trajectory. The collection of end points at $t = T$ of optimum trajectories originating from α at $t = 0$ is denoted by $\Omega_0(T)$.

Bearing the above definitions in mind, we shall proceed to consider the following propositions:

Proposition 1. *Any part of an optimum trajectory is an optimum trajectory.* Let us select any two points γ and δ on an optimum trajectory Γ from α to β, as shown in Fig. 9-1. Let the parts of Γ between $\alpha\gamma$,

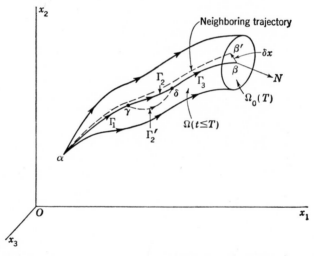

Fig. 9-1. The region Ω generated by optimal trajectories.

$\gamma\delta$, and $\delta\beta$ be labeled Γ_1, Γ_2, and Γ_3, respectively. The proposition states that Γ_2 is an optimum trajectory from γ to δ. This can be readily proved. If there is a possible trajectory Γ'_2 along which δ can be reached in less time from γ, then β can be reached in less time from α by following the trajectory $\Gamma_1\Gamma'_2\Gamma_3$ instead of following Γ. This contradicts Γ being the optimum trajectory.

Proposition 2. $\Omega_0(T)$ *is at the surface of the region* $\Omega(t \leq T)$. Intuitively this is easy to see. In Fig. 9-1, $\Omega(t \leq T)$ is generated by all the points on the trajectories of interval T, and $\Omega_0(T)$ is generated only by the farthest end points which are not covered by other trajectories. Therefore $\Omega_0(T)$ must be on the surface of $\Omega(t \leq T)$.

Now let us consider the optimum trajectory Γ from α to β. To traverse Γ, the functions $f_k(t)$ are completely determined and will be denoted as $\hat{f}_k(t)$. Let Γ' denote an adjacent trajectory (also of duration T) obtained by letting $f_k(t)$ vary by an infinitesimal amount $\delta f_k(t)$ in the allowed direction. For instance, if $f_k(t)$ is at one of the limiting values, $\delta f_k(t)$ can only be in the opposite direction, but otherwise $\delta f_k(t)$ is completely arbitrary. Let $\hat{\mathbf{x}}(t)$ and $\hat{\mathbf{x}}(t) + \delta \mathbf{x}(t)$ denote points on Γ and Γ', respectively, at time t. By definition, the end point β' of Γ' is a point in $\Omega(t \leq T)$, and $\delta \mathbf{x}(T) = \beta' - \beta$.

With reference to Fig. 9-1, let the vector N denote a normal of the surface bounding $\Omega(t \leq T)$ pointing outward from β.† Then

$$\mathbf{N} \cdot \delta \mathbf{x}(T) = \sum_{i=1}^{i=n} N_i \delta x_i(T) \leq 0 \qquad (9\text{-}2)$$

Inequality (9-2) holds to the first order of $\delta \mathbf{x}(T)$. The equality sign holds if β' is also a surface point. Taking an infinitesimal variation of Eq. (9-1) gives

$$\delta \dot{x}_i(t) = \sum_j \left(\frac{\partial F_i}{\partial x_j}\right)_\Gamma \delta x_j(t) + \sum_k \left(\frac{\partial F_i}{\partial f_k}\right)_\Gamma \delta f_k(t) \qquad i = 1, 2, \ldots, n \quad (9\text{-}3)$$

The partial derivatives $\partial F_i/\partial x_j$ and $\partial F_i/\partial f_k$ are evaluated for $\mathbf{x} = \hat{\mathbf{x}}(t)$ and $\mathbf{f} = \hat{\mathbf{f}}(t)$ and are independent of the variations $\delta \mathbf{x}$ and $\delta \mathbf{f}$. Equation (9-3) is correct to the first order and is linear in $\delta \mathbf{x}$ and $\delta \mathbf{f}$. In arriving at a solution of Eq. (9-3) there is no need to treat $\delta \mathbf{x}$ and $\delta \mathbf{f}$ as infinitesimal, since the solution of a set of linear equations is independent of the magnitude of the variables.

Let us consider a time-variant linear system represented by a set of differential equations with $u_i(0) = 0$ and

$$\dot{u}_i(t) = \sum_k g_{ik}(t)u_k(t) + v_i(t) \qquad i = 1, 2, \ldots, n \qquad (9\text{-}4)$$

where $u_i(t)$ and $v_i(t)$ are the output and input variables, respectively. Because of the superposition theorem, $u_i(t)$ can be expressed as

$$u_i(t_1) = \sum_k \int_0^{t_1} h_{ik}(t_1,t)v_k(t) \, dt \qquad (9\text{-}5)$$

where $h_{ik}(t_1,t)$ is the response of output variable u_i at t_1 due to a unit impulse of v_k at t. Equation (9-5) is a multivariable version of Eq. (5-1) and can be derived in the same way.

---

† The normal N may not always exist. For instance, β may be located exactly on an edge of the region $\Omega(t \leq T)$. However, the likelihood of this happening is negligibly small. For linear systems with saturation of the type described in Sec. 9-3, it can readily be shown that the region $\Omega(T)$ (the set or collection of all end points of trajectories of duration T) is convex. Then there is at least one vector N which satisfies inequality (9-2) under all circumstances.

Now let us consider the function $h_{ik}(t_1,t_2)$. By assuming $v_k(t)$ to be impulses at $t = t_2$, it is easy to show that

$$\frac{\partial h_{ik}(t_1,t_2)}{\partial t_1} = \sum_j g_{ij}(t_1)h_{jk}(t_1,t_2)$$

and

$$h_{ik}(t_{2+},t_2) = \delta_{ik}$$

However, of greater interest is the variation of $h_{ik}(t_1,t_2)$ with t_2. Equation (9-5) holds no matter what form the functions v_i take. From this fact and Eq. (9-4) this variation can be readily determined.

1. Let $v_k(t)$ be a unit impulse function at t_{1-}, and all the other $v_i(t) = 0$, $i \neq k$. Equation (9-4) gives

$$u_k(t_1) = 1 \qquad u_i(t_1) = 0 \qquad i \neq k$$

Equation (9-5) gives

$$u_i(t_1) = h_{ik}(t_1,t_{1-})$$

Therefore,

$$h_{ik}(t_1,t_{1-}) = \begin{cases} 1 & \text{if } i = k \\ 0 & \text{if } i \neq k \end{cases} \tag{9-6}$$

Equation (9-6) holds for all i and k and is the boundary condition on $h_{ik}(t_1,t)$.

2. Let $v_k(t)$ be an arbitrary set of impulse functions at $t = 0$. The solution is $u_i(t) = y_i(t)$, where $y_i(t)$ satisfies

$$\dot{y}_i(t) = \sum_k g_{ik}(t)y_k(t) \qquad t > 0 \tag{9-7}$$

Suppose that, instead of the impulses at $t = 0$, we have input impulses at $t = t_{2-}$ ($0 < t_2 < t_1$) with moments $y_i(t_2)$. Then $u_i(t_2) = y_i(t_2)$, and the solution from t_2 onward remains unchanged. Equation (9-5) gives

$$u_i(t_1) = y_i(t_1) = \sum_k h_{ik}(t_1,t_2)y_k(t_2) \tag{9-8}$$

Since Eq. (9-8) is to hold for all values of t_2, we may differentiate it with respect to t_2. The result is

$$0 = \sum_k \frac{\partial h_{ik}(t_1,t_2)}{\partial t_2} y_k(t_2) + \sum_k h_{ik}(t_1,t_2)\dot{y}_k(t_2)$$

$$= \sum_k \frac{\partial h_{ik}(t_1,t_2)}{\partial t_2} y_k(t_2) + \sum_k \sum_L h_{ik}(t_1,t_2)g_{kL}(t_2)y_L(t_2)$$

The second equality sign is due to Eq. (9-7). We may call the dummy indices L and k instead of k and L without changing the double summation, and the above equation becomes

$$\sum_k \left[\frac{\partial h_{ik}(t_1,t_2)}{\partial t_2} + \sum_L h_{iL}(t_1,t_2) g_{Lk}(t_2) \right] y_k(t_2) = 0 \qquad (9\text{-}9)$$

Since the initial-impulse functions are arbitrary, the functions $y_i(t_2)$ are also arbitrary.   Equation (9-9) implies that

$$\frac{\partial h_{ik}(t_1,t_2)}{\partial t_2} = - \sum_L g_{Lk}(t_2) h_{iL}(t_1,t_2) \qquad (9\text{-}10)$$

Equation (9-10) together with Eq. (9-6) determines the set of functions $h_{ik}(t_1,t)$.

Equation (9-3) is of the same form as Eq. (9-4), with

$$g_{ij}(t) = \left(\frac{\partial F_i}{\partial x_j} \right)_\Gamma$$

$$v_i = \sum_k \left(\frac{\partial F_i}{\partial f_k} \right)_\Gamma \delta f_k$$

Therefore, Eq. (9-5) gives the solution as

$$\delta x_i(T) = \sum_j \int_0^T h_{ij}(T,t) \sum_k \left(\frac{\partial F_j}{\partial f_k} \right)_\Gamma \delta f_k(t) \, dt \qquad (9\text{-}11)$$

Inequality (9-2) gives

$$\mathbf{N} \cdot \delta \mathbf{x}(T) = \int_0^T \sum_i \sum_j \sum_k N_i h_{ij}(T,t) \left(\frac{\partial F_j}{\partial f_k} \right)_\Gamma \delta f_k(t) \, dt \le 0 \qquad (9\text{-}12)$$

Let $\lambda_j(t)$ be defined as

$$\lambda_j(t) \equiv \sum_i N_i h_{ij}(T,t) \qquad (9\text{-}13)$$

Equations (9-10) and (9-6) give

$$\dot{\lambda}_j(t) = - \sum_L g_{Lj} \lambda_L(t) = - \sum_L \left(\frac{\partial F_L}{\partial x_j} \right)_\Gamma \lambda_L(t) \qquad (9\text{-}14a)$$

$$\lambda_i(T) = N_i \qquad (9\text{-}14b)$$

Equations (9-14a) and (9-14b) specify $\lambda_i(T)$ completely.   In Eq. (9-12) the $\delta f_k(t)$'s for different k and different t can be independently selected, and the necessary and sufficient condition for satisfying Eq. (9-12) is

$$\sum_j \lambda_j \left(\frac{\partial F_j}{\partial f_k} \right)_\Gamma \delta f_k(t) \le 0 \qquad \text{for } \begin{array}{l} k = 1, 2, \ldots, m \\ 0 \le t \le T \end{array} \qquad (9\text{-}15)$$

Equation (9-15) has a simple interpretation: *Along any given optimum trajectory, with $x_i(t)$, $i = 1, 2, \ldots, n$, considered fixed, the function*

$$H(t,\hat{x},f) \equiv \sum_i \lambda_i(t)F_i(\hat{x},f,t) \tag{9-16}$$

is a maximum if $f_k(t) = \hat{f}_k(t)$, $k = 1, 2, \ldots, m$.

The above has shown only that $H(t,\hat{x},f)$ is a local maximum. A stronger version can be proved as follows: Suppose that $\mathbf{f}(t) = \hat{\mathbf{f}}(t)$ except in the interval $t_2 - \delta t \leq t \leq t_2$. Equation (9-1) gives

$$\delta x_i(t_2) = \{F_i[\hat{\mathbf{x}}(t_2-),\mathbf{f}(t_2-),t_2-] - F_i[\hat{\mathbf{x}}(t_2-),\hat{\mathbf{f}}(t_2-),t_2-]\}\, \delta t$$

and $\delta x_i(t)$ satisfies

$$\delta \dot{x}_i(t) = \sum_j \left(\frac{\partial F_i}{\partial x_j}\right)_\Gamma \delta x_j(t) \qquad t \geq t_2$$

The solution at $t = T$ is

$$\delta x_i(T) = \sum_j h_{ij}(T,t_2)\, \delta x_j(t_2)$$

Therefore

$$\mathbf{N} \cdot \delta \mathbf{x}(T) = \sum_i \lambda_i \{F_i[\hat{\mathbf{x}}(t_2-),\mathbf{f}(t_2-),t_2-] - F_i[\hat{\mathbf{x}}(t_2-),\hat{\mathbf{f}}(t_2-),t_2-]\}\, \delta(t)$$

$$= [H(t_2-,\hat{\mathbf{x}},\mathbf{f}) - H(t_2-,\hat{\mathbf{x}},\hat{\mathbf{f}})]\, \delta t$$

Since $\mathbf{N} \cdot \delta \mathbf{x}(T) \leq 0$, the above equation shows that $H(t_2-,\hat{\mathbf{x}},\hat{\mathbf{f}})$ is an absolute maximum. As t_2 is arbitrarily selected, $\mathbf{f} = \hat{\mathbf{f}}$ gives the absolute maximum H at every t.

Thus by assuming an infinitesimal time interval $\delta(t)$ in which $\mathbf{f}$ may differ from $\hat{\mathbf{f}}$ by a finite amount, we have proved that $\hat{\mathbf{f}}$ gives the absolute maximum H at every t.

This is the essence of Pontryagin's maximum principle. The function $H(t,\hat{x},f)$ is called a Hamiltonian function.

9-3. Minimal-time Control of a Linear System with Saturation. The controlled system can be described by a set of linear differential equations:

$$\dot{x}_i = \sum_{j=1}^{j=n} a_{ij}x_j + \sum_{k=1}^{k=m} b_{ik}f_k \qquad i = 1, 2, \ldots, n \tag{9-17}$$

In Eq. (9-17) f_k are the control forces or the independent variables through which the control function is performed. By properly scaling the constants b_{ik}, the constraints on f_k can be written as

$$|f_k| \leq 1 \qquad k = 1, 2, \ldots, m \tag{9-18}$$

Equations (9-14a) and (9-14b) become

$$\dot{\lambda}_j(t) = -\sum_{i=1}^{i=n} a_{ij}\lambda_i \qquad j = 1, 2, \ldots, n \qquad (9\text{-}19a)$$

$$\lambda_i(T) = N_i \qquad i = 1, 2, \ldots, n \qquad (9\text{-}19b)$$

The Hamiltonian function is

$$H = \sum_{i,j=1}^{i,j=m} a_{ij}\lambda_i(t)x_j(t) + \sum_{i=1}^{i=n}\sum_{k=1}^{k=m} b_{ik}\lambda_i(t)f_k(t)$$

With the constraints (9-18), H cannot be maximum unless

$$f_k(t) = \text{sign of } \left[\sum_{i=1}^{i=n} b_{ik}\lambda_i(t)\right] \qquad (9\text{-}20)$$

Equation (9-20) shows that the solution represents a so-called "bang-bang system." Maximum control effort in one direction or the other is always applied.

For control systems with only one input f_1, the transfer function from f_1 to x_1 can be obtained by substituting s for d/dt in Eq. (9-17), setting $f_2 = f_3 = \cdots = 0$, and solving for the ratio $x_1(s)/F_1(s)$. The denominator polynomial $D(s)$ is

$$D(s) = \det |a_{ij} - \delta_{ij}s|$$

The roots α_i of $D(s)$ are called the characteristic roots of the matrix $||a_{ij}||$. The same roots with reversed sign are obtained in solving a similar expression for Eq. (9-19a).

The solution of Eq. (9-19a) is

$$\lambda(t) = \sum_{i=1}^{i=n} b_{i1}\lambda_i(t) = \sum_{i=1}^{n} A_i e^{-\alpha_i t}$$

If all the α_i's are real, $\lambda(t)$ crosses the zero line or t axis at most $n-1$ times. It follows that f_1 reverses sign at most $n-1$ times. If some of the α_i's are complex, $\lambda(t)$ may cross the t axis considerably more than n times in an interval T large compared with the period of oscillation. The same holds for the number of sign reversals of f_1.

In conclusion, the optimum solution of the control force f_1 is always at plus or minus maximum value until the desired steady-state condition is reached, after which $f_1 = 0$. If all the α_i's are real, or if some of the α_i's are complex but T is less than half the natural period, there are, at most, $n-1$ sign reversals of f_1. If some of the α_i's are complex and T is large, the number of sign reversals of f_1 may be more than $n-1$.

Example 9-1. An inertial system of negligible damping is to be moved from one angular position θ to another in the least time. The inertia of the system is J, and the maximum available torque is K. Determine the optimum form of $f_1(t)$.

Solution. While the problem is a simple one, it can be used to illustrate the method. Let x_1 and x_2 represent θ and $\dot\theta$, respectively. The system equations of motion can be written as

$$\dot{x}_1 = x_2$$
$$\dot{x}_2 = \frac{K}{J} f_1$$

The applied torque is $Kf_1(t)$, and the limits of f_1 are ± 1. Equation (9-19a) gives

$$\dot{\lambda}_1 = 0$$
$$\dot{\lambda}_2 = -\lambda_1 \tag{9-21}$$

From Eq. (9-21), λ_2 can be solved:

$$\lambda_2(t) = A_1 + A_2 t$$
$$\lambda(t) = b_{21}\lambda_2(t) = \frac{K}{J}(A_1 + A_2 t) \tag{9-22}$$

Only one sign reversal of f_1 is possible. To satisfy Eq. (9-11), the sign reversal must occur at $t = T/2$. The change in θ is $KT^2/4J$.

Example 9-2. As a second example, consider the system described by

$$\ddot\theta + 2\zeta\dot\theta + \theta = bf_1(t)$$
$$|f_1(t)| \le 1$$

For any initial value of θ and $\dot\theta$, the system is to be brought to rest in a minimum time.

Solution. Let x_1 and x_2 represent θ and $\dot\theta$, respectively. The equations of motion are

$$\dot{x}_1 = x_2$$
$$\dot{x}_2 = -x_1 - 2\zeta x_2 + bf_1(t)$$

Equation (9-19a) gives

$$\dot{\lambda}_1 = \lambda_2$$
$$\dot{\lambda}_2 = -\lambda_1 + 2\zeta\lambda_2$$

Solving the above equations, we obtain

$$\lambda(t) = b\lambda_2(t) = Ae^{\zeta t} \sin\left(\sqrt{1 - \zeta^2}\, t + \phi\right) \tag{9-23}$$

In Eq. (9-23), A and ϕ are constants of integration. We note that A has no effect on the positions of zero crossing, for the time interval between two zero crossings is always the half period $\pi/\sqrt{1 - \zeta^2}$. Consequently, for large T, f_1 must reverse every half period. Physically, large T means a relatively weak control force bf_1. To bring an oscillatory system to rest with a small force, the applied force must be properly phased.

9-4. Predictor Control of a Second-order System.
If the controlled system is linear, it is quite feasible to use the system error and error derivatives as the state variables instead of the controlled variable and its derivatives. An advantage of this is that the desired final state is always at the origin of phase space, with the resulting simplification in electronics. Section 9-3 shows that this point should be reached by applying maximum control effort all the time, either in one direction or the other. The

way for realizing these ideas is the predictor type of control which operates by phase-plane or phase-space criteria.

In 1950 McDonald published his paper on the optimum control of a second-order system by phase-plane criteria.   Essentially the same idea was contained in a paper submitted by Hopkins to the AIEE at about the same time.   Work on systems of third order and higher was reported in later years by Bogner and Kazda, Silvia, Rose, and others.

Consider the second-order system discussed in Example 9-1, with the the assumption that the reference input θ_1 is a linear function of time (step, ramp).   Once the error and error derivatives are simultaneously zero, we

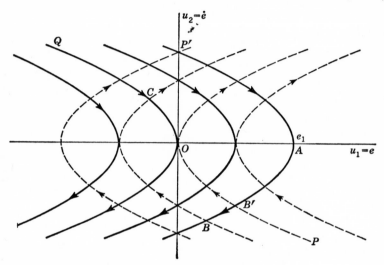

FIG. 9-2. Trajectories in phase plane e-$\dot{e}$.

have the desired steady-state condition, and the applied torque can be removed.

In terms of the error $e = \theta_1 - \theta$, the equation of motion is

$$\frac{d^2e}{dt^2} = -\frac{K}{J} f_1 \qquad (9\text{-}24)$$

For an optimum system, f_1 may take only two values: ± 1.   Within each range of constant f_1, Eq. (9-24) can be integrated:

$$\frac{de}{dt} = -\frac{K}{J} f_1 t + A_1 = -\frac{K}{J} f_1(t - t_0) + \left(\frac{de}{dt}\right)_{t=t_0} \qquad (9\text{-}25)$$

$$e = -\frac{K}{2J} f_1(t - t_0)^2 + \left(\frac{de}{dt}\right)_{t=t_0} (t - t_0) + e(t_0) \qquad (9\text{-}26)$$

The phase-plane diagram of Fig. 9-2 is obtained by plotting error derivative versus error of the controlled system.   For each set of initial conditions, the error and error derivative vary with time, as given by Eqs. (9-25) and (9-26), and trace a curve on the diagram. Each curve is called a trajectory. There are two sets of trajectories in Fig. 9-2, corresponding to the two values of f_1: The solid curves are for $f_1 = +1$, and the broken curves are for $f_1 = -1$.

The life history of a system in operation is traced by a sequence of segments belonging to the two sets. The sequence of curves AB, BC, CO represents a system having an initial error e_1, and $f_1 = +1$, -1, and $+1$. As soon as the representative point of the system reaches 0, both e and ė vanish, and f_1 is made to vanish also.

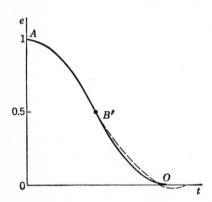

From the discussion of Sec. 9-3, we see that $ABCO$ does not represent an optimum system, since there are two changes of sign of f_1 at B and C, respectively. $AB'O$ is the only trajectory that reaches the origin with one change of sign in f_1, and consequently it represents the optimum system.

There are two trajectories which lead to the origin: $PB'O$ and QCO.

Fig. 9-3. System error subsequent to a step input. Solid curve, idealized predictor-controlled system; dashed curve, actual predictor-controlled system with finite gain. The points A, B', and O correspond to the same points in Fig. 9-2.

The two trajectories join at the origin and can be regarded as a single curve. One way of making an optimum system is to make the curve $PB'OCQ$ a switching boundary in the sense that $f_1 = +1$ if the representative point is above the switching boundary and $f_1 = -1$ otherwise. There is no need to define the value of f_1 on the switching boundary. Consider a system with an initial error e_1. Since the representative point is above the switching boundary, $f_1 = +1$, and the point travels along AB' until it crosses the switching boundary at B'. Theoretically, an infinitesimal amount of crossing is sufficient to reverse the sign of f_1, and the representative point travels along $B'O$ to the origin O. The system error as a function of time is plotted in Fig. 9-3. Similarly, with a ramp input, the representative point starts at P' and traces $P'AB'O$. The system error versus time is plotted in Fig. 9-4.

9-5. Physical Realization of an Approximately Optimum Second-order System. The system described in Sec. 9-4 cannot be realized exactly because of its requirement of infinite gain. Theoretically, the switching boundary is infinitely thin. It takes an infinitesimal change in e or ė at the boundary to change f_1 from maximum positive value to maximum negative value, or vice versa.   While an infinite gain is not possible, it is also not essential in the operation of the system.   With finite gain, a well-designed system is not appreciably slower than the ideal system.

Consider the lead-compensated system of Fig. 9-5.   The torque f_1 is zero if $e + T(de/dt) = 0$.   The switching boundary of the system is shown in Fig. 9-6.   There is a linear region about the neutral boundary $e + T(de/dt) = 0$ in which f_1 is proportional to $e + T(de/dt)$.   Either beyond AA' or below BB' the system is saturated and f_1 equals 1 and -1, respectively.   As the sys-

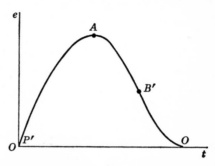

FIG. 9-4. System error subsequent to a ramp input.

tem gain is increased, both AA' and BB' move toward the neutral boundary and merge with the latter in the limit, as the amplifier gain approaches infinity.

Comparing Fig. 9-2 with Fig. 9-6, we see the close parallelism between a lead-controlled system and a predictor-controlled system.   Predictor control can be obtained by bending the switching boundary of the lead-controlled system.   The derivative term is made more effective at large

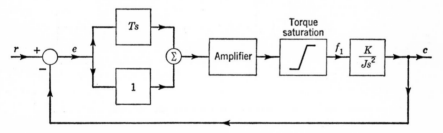

FIG. 9-5. Block diagram of a second-order system with lead compensation.

error, while the straight error term is made more effective at low error. This can be accomplished by introducing nonlinear elements into the controller, as shown in Fig. 9-7.   While two nonlinear elements $N1$ and $N2$ are shown, one is usually sufficient.   For instance, we may have a straight linear element for $N1$ and a nonlinear element for $N2$, with the following input-output relationship:

$$v_{out} = \pm \sqrt{|v_{in}|} \qquad (9\text{-}27)$$

with the same sign as v_{in}.   Alternatively, we may have a straight linear

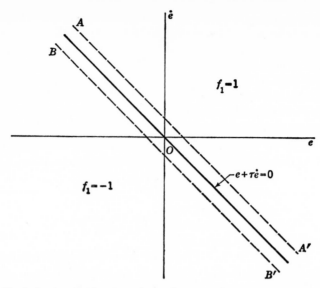

FIG. 9-6. Equivalent switching boundary of a second-order system with lead compensation.

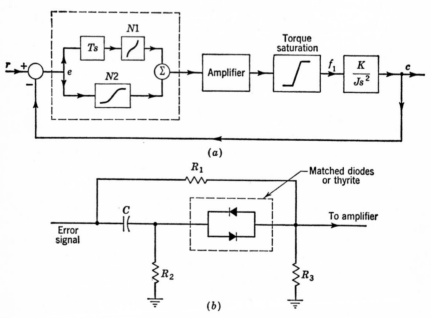

FIG. 9-7. Physical layout of a predictor-controlled system. (a) Block diagram; (b) possible circuitry for nonlinear control (the elements enclosed by broken lines).

element for $N2$ and a nonlinear element for $N1$ with

$$v_{out} = v_{in}|v_{in}| \qquad (9\text{-}28)$$

Of course it is also possible to use two nonlinear elements to give the same over-all effect.

With finite amplifier gain, the ideal switching boundary should not be used as the neutral curve. Rather, the boundaries themselves should be part of the saturation limits, as shown in Fig. 9-8. Part of the ideal switching boundary AB becomes the upper saturation limit, while another

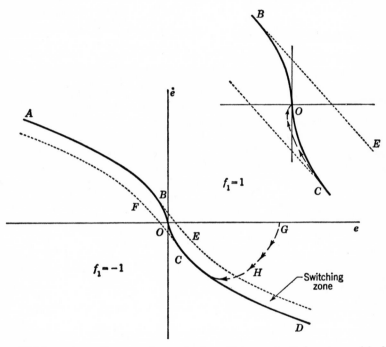

FIG. 9-8. Phase-plane diagram of an actual predictor-controlled system with finite gain. Diagram at upper right corner shows magnified view near origin.

part CD becomes the lower saturation limit. In the region $BECF$ the system is linear and not saturated. Obviously, Eqs. (9-27) and (9-28) are modified to realize the switching zone of Fig. 9-8.

Consider a system with initial error e_1. At first, full $f_1 = +1$ is applied. As soon as the system trajectory enters the switching zone at H, f_1 is reduced in magnitude, and there is less change in $\dot{e}$. Consequently the trajectory moves toward the horizontal direction and bends over gradually until finally it coincides with DC. By now $f_1 = -1$ is applied, and the representative point follows trajectory DC until it passes c. At this point the trajectory for $f_1 = -1$ separates from the lower saturation curve, and the representative point of the system enters into the linear region. It follows a path somewhere between the lower saturation curve and the trajectory for $f_1 = -1$, as illustrated by the broken line. The system-error-versus-time curve is shown as the broken curve in Fig. 9-3.

9-6. Phase-plane Configurations of Second-order Systems with Various Pole Locations.† The trajectories and optimum switching boundaries depend very much on the locations of the poles of the controlled system. We shall study the following cases:

1. Real roots, stable system. Typical example of root locations: 0, -1.

2. Real roots, unstable system. Typical example of root locations: 0, 1.

3. Complex roots, stable system, $\zeta > 0$. Typical example of root locations: $-\zeta \pm j \sqrt{1 - \zeta^2}$.

4. Complex roots, unstable system, $\zeta < 0$. Typical example of root locations: $-\zeta \pm j \sqrt{1 - \zeta^2}$.

In the above, we are referring to the controlled system only, not to the entire servo loop. Because of the existence of nonlinearities in the closed loop, the latter cannot be characterized by root locations.

It is worthwhile to make a detailed study of second-order systems. These systems are simple, and many of the phenomena we observe here can be carried over to higher-order systems.

The differential equation for cases 1 and 2 may be written as

$$\frac{d^2c}{dt^2} + \eta \frac{dc}{dt} = f \tag{9-29}$$

where $\eta = 1$ for case 1 and -1 for case 2, and $f = \pm 1$ for an optimum system. In terms of the error $e = c_1 - c$, where c_1 is a constant, Eq. (9-29) can be written as

$$\frac{d^2e}{dt^2} + \eta \frac{de}{dt} = -f \tag{9-30}$$

Let $x = e$, and $y = de/dt$; Eq. (9-30) becomes

$$\frac{dy}{dt} + \eta y = -f$$

Replacing dt by $(dx)/y$ in the above and rearranging terms,

$$\frac{y \, dy}{f + \eta y} = -dx \tag{9-31}$$

---

† After N. J. Rose, Optimum Switching Criteria for Discontinuous Automatic Controls, *IRE Conv. Record*, pt. IV, vol. 4, 1956, and H. S. Tsien, "Engineering Cybernetics," pp. 154–157, McGraw-Hill Book Company, Inc., New York, 1954.

Integrating Eq. (9-31), we obtain the equations for the trajectories:

$$\eta x + y = \frac{f}{\eta} \log \left(y + \frac{f}{\eta} \right) + \text{constant} \qquad (9\text{-}32)$$

For case 1, $\eta = 1$.   We obtain the two sets of trajectories as shown in Fig. 9-9.   The optimum switching boundary is given by the two trajectories AO and BO.   The case is not substantially different from that of Sec. 9-4.

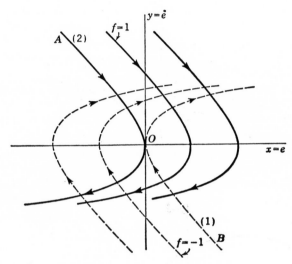

Fig. 9-9. Phase-plane diagram with roots of controlled system at $(0, -1)$.

For case 2, $\eta = -1$.   We obtain the two sets of trajectories as shown in Fig. 9-10.   The optimum switching boundary is given by the two trajectories AO and BO.   However, if $|y| > 1$, all the trajectories are divergent, and there is no way of bringing the system back into the $|y| < 1$ zone.   Physically, the divergence is expected, since with $|dc/dt| > 1$, the negative damping force is larger in magnitude than the control force f.

The differential equation for cases 3 and 4 can be written as

$$\frac{d^2c}{dt^2} + 2\zeta \frac{dc}{dt} + c = f \qquad (9\text{-}33)$$

We shall study the optimum system for reducing c and $\dot{c}$ to zero from some initial values.   Solving Eq. (9-33), we obtain

$$\begin{aligned} x = c &= f + Ae^{-\zeta t} \sin (\sqrt{1 - \zeta^2} + \phi) \\ y = \dot{c} &= Ae^{-\zeta t} \cos (\sqrt{1 - \zeta^2} + \phi + \phi_1) \end{aligned} \qquad (9\text{-}34)$$

where A and ϕ are constants of integration and $\phi_1 = \sin^{-1} \zeta$.

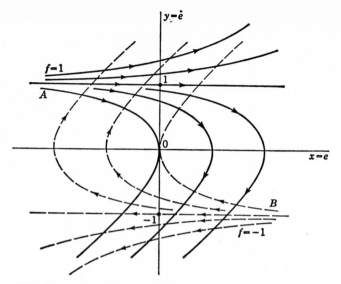

FIG. 9-10. Phase-plane diagram with roots of controlled system at (0,1).

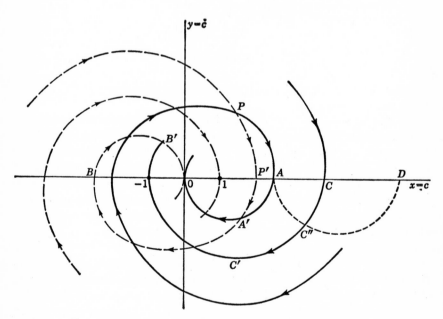

FIG. 9-11. Phase-plane diagram with a pair of complex roots.

For case 3, the trajectories are spiral-like curves converging on $(f,0)$. The set of trajectories with $f = 1$ are shown as solid curves, and the set of trajectories with $f = -1$ are shown as broken curves in Fig. 9-11. The trajectories $AA'O$ and $BB'O$ are two parts of the optimum switching boundary. However, the optimum switching boundary does not extend beyond A and B since it takes more than one-half cycle for points beyond A and B to reach O, and it has been shown in Example 9-2 that f cannot last beyond one-half cycle without changing sign. Consider the point P, for example; it is faster to start with $f = -1$ and to reverse f at A' than to have $f = 1$ all the way. It takes less time to traverse the trajectories $PP'A'O$ than the trajectory $PAA'O$.

To determine the rest of the optimum switching boundary, consider, for instance, the trajectory $CC'B'$ which intersects $BB'O$ at B'. Let C''

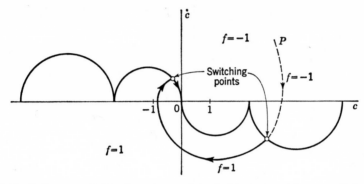

Fig. 9-12. Optimum switching boundary and typical trajectory of a controlled system with a pair of complex roots.

be the point on the trajectory $CC'B'$ from which one-half cycle is required to reach B'. C'' is a point on the optimum switching boundary. If we move the point B' from O to B, the point C'' traces the arc $AC''D$. It can be considered an extension of the optimum switching boundary $OA'A$. If the above process is repeated, the optimum switching boundary of Fig. 9-12 is obtained. Starting with any point P, the trajectory of an optimally controlled system is also shown in Fig. 9-12.

For case 4, most of the above discussion still holds. However, the trajectories of the system are outgoing spirals moving away from the points $(1,0)$ and $(-1,0)$. The optimum switching boundary can be obtained in the same way as in case 3, resulting in two series of nearly half circles of diminishing size, as shown in Fig. 9-13. The circles converge at two points $(\pm a,0)$, where

$$a = \coth \frac{\pi}{2} \frac{|\zeta|}{\sqrt{1 - \zeta^2}}$$

The trajectory starting from $(a,0)$ with $f = 1$ passes the point $(-a,0)$, and the trajectory starting from $(-a,0)$ with $f = -1$ passes the point $(a,0)$. The two critical trajectories mentioned above enclose a region in which the controlled system is convergent. Outside this region, the control force f is too weak to overcome the divergent tendencies of the controlled system.

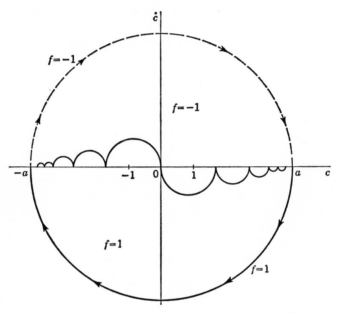

FIG. 9-13. Optimum switching boundary of a system with a pair of divergent complex roots.

9-7. Predictor Control of Higher-order Systems. The general considerations for predictor control of a system of third order or higher are about the same as the ones mentioned in Secs. 9-4 and 9-5. For an nth-order system to be in the desired steady state, we need to have not only zero error but also zero error derivatives up to the $(n - 1)$st order. Therefore, the simultaneous zeroing of n variables is required. The phase-plane technique is carried over into a phase space of n dimensions, as will be described presently.

The controlled system is described by Eq. (9-17). In general, the controlled variable c is a linear combination of the state variables:

$$c = \sum_{i=1}^{i=n} h_i x_i \qquad (9\text{-}35)$$

Let x_{1i} represent the desired final state. To simplify matters, we assume the following:

1. There is only one control force, $m = 1$.
2. The desired final state is a free-running state of the system:

$$\dot{x}_{1i} = \sum_{j=1}^{j=n} a_{ij}x_{1j} \qquad i = 1, 2, \ldots, n$$

Let a set of error variables y_i be defined as

$$y_i \equiv x_{1i} - x_i \qquad i = 1, 2, \ldots, n \tag{9-35a}$$

From Eq. (9-17) and assumptions 1 and 2, we have

$$\dot{y}_i = \sum_{j=1}^{j=n} a_{ij}y_j - b_{i1}f_1 \tag{9-36}$$

$$e = c_1 - c = \sum_{i=1}^{i=n} h_i y_i \tag{9-37}$$

In the following analysis, we shall divide the systems into two groups according to the characteristic roots of the determinant $\|a_{ij}\|$:

1. All the characteristic roots α_i are distinct. Let $\mathbf{y}$ and $\mathbf{b}$ represent the column matrices with $y_1 y_2 \cdots y_n$ and $b_{11} b_{21} \cdots b_{n1}$ as their elements, $\mathbf{h}'$ the row matrix with $h_1 h_2 \cdots h_n$ as its elements, and A the square matrix with a_{ij} as its elements. Equations (9-36) and (9-37) can be written as

$$\dot{\mathbf{y}} = A\mathbf{y} - \mathbf{b}f_1 \tag{9-36a}$$
$$e = c_1 - c = \mathbf{h}'\mathbf{y} \tag{9-37a}$$

Since the characteristic roots α_i of the matrix A are distinct, there is a transformation matrix $\mathbf{T}$ such that

$$\boldsymbol{\alpha} = \mathbf{T}^{-1}A\mathbf{T} \tag{9-38}$$

is diagonal. Let the set of variables $\mathbf{u}$ and the column matrix $\boldsymbol{\beta}$ be defined by

$$\mathbf{u} = \mathbf{T}^{-1}\mathbf{y} \tag{9-39}$$
$$\boldsymbol{\beta} = \mathbf{T}^{-1}\mathbf{b} \tag{9-40}$$

Multiplying the left-hand side of Eq. (9-36a) by $\mathbf{T}^{-1}$, we obtain

$$\dot{\mathbf{u}} = \boldsymbol{\alpha}\mathbf{u} - \boldsymbol{\beta}f_1 \tag{9-41}$$

Since $\boldsymbol{\alpha}$ is a diagonal matrix, Eq. (9-41) can be written in terms of its elements as

$$\dot{u}_i = \alpha_i u_i - \beta_i f_1 \qquad i = 1, 2, \ldots, n \tag{9-42}$$

The solution of Eq. (9-42) can be written as

$$u_i = \frac{\beta_i}{\alpha_i} f_1 + \left(u_{i0} - \frac{\beta_i}{\alpha_i} f_1 \right) e^{\alpha_i(t-t_0)} \tag{9-43}$$

where u_{i0} is the initial value of u_i at $t = t_0$.

The set of variables u_i are called normalized coordinates, since the variables u_i in Eq. (9-42) are separate whereas the variables y_i in Eq. (9-36) are not. Because the transformation matrix T is nonsingular, simultaneous zeroing of the variables u_i is equivalent to simultaneous zeroing of the variables y_i. Therefore the set of variables u_i, $i = 1, 2,$ . . . , n, can be used as coordinates of a phase space, and the origin in the phase space represents the desired steady-state condition. Equation (9-43) represents the parametric equation of a trajectory. Given any set of initial values u_{i0}, $i = 1, 2,$ . . . , n, a trajectory is traced as t increases.

The optimum switching boundaries in phase space u_i can be determined by a reversed time technique as follows: The final or $(n - 1)$st switching boundary is composed of points on either one of two trajectories which will pass the origin in some future time. These points can be obtained by tracing back from the origin. Let us say that the trajectory will pass through u_{i0} at t_0. At some prior time t, $t < t_0$, the representative point is at P, with its coordinates u_i given by Eq. (9-43). Let $\tau = t_0 - t$. That is, τ is the interval of time which the representative point of the system takes to reach the point u_{i0}. Equation (9-43) can be written as

$$u_i(\tau) = \frac{\beta_i}{\alpha_i} f_1 + \left(u_{i0} - \frac{\beta_i}{\alpha_i} f_1 \right) e^{-\alpha_i \tau} \tag{9-44}$$

For the final switching boundary, the destination is the origin, and $u_{i0} = 0$. Let these points be denoted as

$$u_i(\tau,+) = \frac{\beta_i}{\alpha_i} (1 - e^{-\alpha_i \tau}) \tag{9-45}$$

$$u_i(\tau,-) = - \frac{\beta_i}{\alpha_i} (1 - e^{-\alpha_i \tau}) \tag{9-46}$$

The next to final or $(n - 2)$nd switching boundary is a surface generated by trajectories which will intersect the final switching boundary at some future time. Obviously, in order that these trajectories do not coincide with the final switching boundary, f_1 must reverse sign at the point of intersection. The surface generated from trajectories converging on $u_i(\tau,+)$ is

$$u_i(\tau_1,\tau_2;+,-) = - \frac{\beta_i}{\alpha_i} (1 - e^{-\alpha_i \tau_2}) + u_i(\tau_1,+) e^{-\alpha_i \tau_2}$$

$$= \frac{\beta_i}{\alpha_i} [-1 + 2e^{-\alpha_i \tau_2} - e^{-\alpha_i(\tau_1 - \tau_2)}] \tag{9-47}$$

Similarly, the surface generated from trajectories converging on $u_i(\tau, -)$ is

$$u_i(\tau_1, \tau_2; -, +) = \frac{\beta_i}{\alpha_i} [1 - 2e^{-\alpha_i \tau_2} + e^{-\alpha_i(\tau_1 - \tau_2)}] \tag{9-48}$$

Equations (9-47) and (9-48) together give the parametric expression for the $(n - 2)$nd switching boundary.

The process can be continued until we have obtained all the switching boundaries including the first, which is an $(n - 1)$-dimensional continuum in an n-dimensional phase space.   The optimum switching boundaries so obtained are always good for a region near the origin.   If the characteristic roots are real and negative, the optimum switching boundaries are good for the entire phase space.   If the roots are complex with nonpositive real components, at far-away regions the above switching boundaries may not be optimum but the system trajectories still converge.   If the roots have positive real components, the system trajectories at far-away regions diverge.

2. The characteristic roots α_i are not all distinct.   The problem can be treated as a limiting case of a system with all distinct α_i's, but some of the α_i's are approaching each other in the limit.   However, direct solution of the differential equation involved is usually simpler.   This is especially true when the multiple roots occur at $s = 0$.

If the transfer function of the controlled system is expressible as a constant over an nth-order polynomial $D(s)$, the error and error derivatives up to $(n - 1)$st order can be used as coordinates of the phase space. The differential equation of the system is

$$D(p)e = \sum_{j=0}^{n} a_j \frac{d^j e}{dt^j} = bf \tag{9-49}$$

If e and all the time derivatives of e up to the $(n - 1)$st order are simultaneously zero and if f is also made to vanish, the nth derivative is also zero, and there cannot be any changes of the values of e and derivatives of e.   Therefore the origin of phase space represents the desired steady-state condition.   In the solution of Eq. (9-49), the error and error derivatives are expressed as functions of t.   The switching boundaries can be obtained in the same way as in the previous case by the reversed-time technique.

If the transfer function of the controlled system is $N(s)/D(s)$, where both $N(s)$ and $D(s)$ are polynomials of s, not all the error derivatives are continuous when the sign of f is suddenly reversed.   Consequently these derivatives are not suitable coordinates of the phase space, as the representative point in such a space jumps at switching.   A method to remedy this situation will be discussed next.

9-8. Switching Discontinuities in Phase Space. Let the transfer function of the controlled system be

$$G(s) = \frac{\sum\limits_{i=0}^{m} b_i s^i}{\sum\limits_{j=0}^{n} a_j s^j} \qquad (9\text{-}50)$$

For a unit step change in f_1, there is a corresponding step change in the $(n - m)$th derivatives of c. Its magnitude can be evaluated by the limit theorem:

$$\left(\frac{d^{n-m}c}{dt^{n-m}}\right)_{t=0+} = \lim_{s \to \infty}\left[s s^{n-m}\frac{G(s)}{s}\right] = \frac{b_m}{a_n}$$

Since the desired output c_1 is either a constant or a power of t, the same step change will appear in the $(n - m)$th error derivative. It also implies that the higher derivatives are not even finite at the moment of switching. As the operation of predictor control is based on the assumption that the representative point remains at the same position before and after switching, the time derivatives of c of $(n - m)$th order or higher are not suitable as coordinates of the phase space. We shall find a set of variables that are suitable.

Equation (9-50) can be expanded as a power series of $1/s$:

$$G(s) = \sum_{i=n-m}^{\infty} \frac{k_i}{s^i} = \sum_{i=0}^{\infty} \frac{k_i}{s^i} \qquad (9\text{-}51)$$

where the coefficients k_i are zero for $i < n - m$. A set of variables u_i are defined by

$$u_1 = c_1 - c + k_0 f_1 = e + k_0 f_1 \qquad (9\text{-}52)$$

$$u_{i+1} = \frac{du_i}{dt} + k_i f_1 \qquad i = 1, 2, 3, \ldots, n - 1 \qquad (9\text{-}53)$$

The variables u_i are shown to be continuous as follows: From Eq. (9-52)

$$u_1 - c_1 = -c + k_0 f_1 \qquad (9\text{-}54)$$

Taking the Laplace transform of the above equation,

$$\mathcal{L}\{u_1 - c_1\} = \left(-\sum_{i=0}^{\infty} \frac{k_i}{s^i} + k_0\right) F_1(s) = \left(-\sum_{i=1}^{\infty} \frac{k_i}{s^i}\right) F_1(s) \qquad (9\text{-}55)$$

Each sign reversal of f_1 is equivalent to a step change with $F_1(s) = \pm 2/s$.

The immediate change in $u_1 - c_1$ can be calculated by the limit theorem:

$$\delta(u_1 - c_1) = \lim_{s \to \infty} s\left(-\sum_{i=1}^{\infty} \frac{k_i}{s^i}\right) \frac{2}{s} = 0 \qquad (9\text{-}56)$$

The variable u_2 is defined by Eq. (9-53):

$$u_2 = \frac{du_1}{dt} + k_1 f$$

$$u_2 - \frac{dc_1}{dt} = \frac{d(u_1 - c_1)}{dt} + k_1 f_1$$

$$\mathcal{L}\left\{u_2 - \frac{dc_1}{dt}\right\} = \left(-s\sum_{i=1}^{\infty} \frac{k_i}{s^i} + k_1\right) F_1(s)$$

$$= \left(-\sum_{i=1}^{\infty} \frac{k_{i+1}}{s^i}\right) F_1(s)$$

Repeating the above steps, we obtain

$$\mathcal{L}\left\{u_{l+1} - \frac{d^l c_1}{dt^l}\right\} = \left(-\sum_{i=1}^{\infty} \frac{k_{i+l}}{s^i}\right) F_1(s) \qquad l = 1, 2, \ldots, n-1 \qquad (9\text{-}57)$$

From Eq. (9-57) and the limit theorem, it can be readily shown that $u_{l+1} - (d^l c_1/dt^l)$, $l = 1, 2, \ldots, n-1$, is continuous at the moment of switching. Since c_1 is either a constant or a power of t, the time derivatives of c_1 are continuous. Therefore, all the variables u_l, $l = 1, 2, \ldots, n$, are continuous.

In the phase space with coordinates u_k, the representative point remains at the same position while f_1 reverses sign or changes from ± 1 to 0. When the representative point reaches the origin and f_1 is removed, the error and all its derivatives vanish. Thus all the requirements for phase-space criteria are met.

The discontinuity problem arises out of the transfer-function representation of the system. If the system dynamics is put in the form of Eqs. (9-36) and (9-37), the set of variables y_i is always continuous at switching, since the step change in f_1 is absorbed by the $\dot{y}_i$ term. The set of variables y_i or any set of variables which is obtained by a non-singular linear transform of y_i can be used as phase-space coordinates.

Example 9-3. Consider the aircraft-pitch control problem described in Sec. 4-7. The transfer function from elevator angle δ to the linear acceleration a in pitch direction can be written as

$$\frac{A(s)}{\Delta(s)} = \frac{k's^2 + k''s + \omega_n^2 k}{s^2 + 2\zeta\omega_n s + \omega_n^2} \qquad (9\text{-}58)$$

where the constants k, k', k'', and ζ are expressible in terms of the constants in Eq. (4-102). The elevator is rate limited:

$$\left| \frac{d\delta}{dt} \right| \leq \Omega_m \qquad (9\text{-}59)$$

Determine a set of suitable variables for phase-space coordinates and the optimum switching boundaries in the space.

Solution. Let f denote $d\delta/dt$. The transfer function from f to a is

$$\frac{A(s)}{F(s)} = \frac{k's^2 + k''s + \omega_n{}^2 k}{s(s^2 + 2\zeta\omega_n s + \omega_n{}^2)} \qquad (9\text{-}60)$$

Obviously a is continuous at switching, and so is the error $e = a_1 - a$, where a_1 is the ordered value of a. Since this is a third-order system, the desired steady-state condition is represented by simultaneous satisfaction of the following equations:

$$e = 0 \qquad \delta = \text{const} \qquad (9\text{-}61a,b)$$
$$\frac{de}{dt} = 0 \qquad \frac{d^2e}{dt^2} = 0 \qquad (9\text{-}61c,d)$$

Since a_1 is a constant, Eqs. (9-61c,d) are equivalent to

$$\frac{da}{dt} = 0 \qquad \frac{d^2a}{dt^2} = 0$$

From Eqs. (9-52) and (9-53),

$$u_1 = e \qquad (9\text{-}62)$$
$$u_2 = \frac{da}{dt} - k'f = \frac{d}{dt}(a - k'\delta) \qquad (9\text{-}63)$$

A third variable u_3 can be obtained by a straight application of Eq. (9-53). However, it is interesting to use a different method. Equation (9-58) can be written as a differential equation:

$$\frac{d^2a}{dt^2} + 2\zeta\omega_n\frac{da}{dt} + \omega_n{}^2 a = k\frac{d^2\delta}{dt^2} + k''\frac{d\delta}{dt} + \omega_n{}^2 k\delta \qquad (9\text{-}64)$$

At the desired steady-state condition, da/dt vanishes and δ is a constant. If it is also given that $a - k\delta = 0$, Eq. (9-64) ensures $d^2a/dt^2 = 0$. Since both a and δ are continuous at switching, we may use $a - k\delta$ as the third variable:

$$u_3 = a - k\delta \qquad (9\text{-}65)$$

A more direct way of arriving at a set of phase-space variables is by writing the dynamical equations in the form of Eq. (9-17), with α, q, and δ taking the place of x_1, x_2, and x_3:

$$\frac{d\alpha}{dt} = -\frac{c_L}{MV}\alpha + q + \frac{c_F}{MV}\delta \qquad (9\text{-}66)$$
$$\frac{dq}{dt} = -\frac{c_M}{J}\alpha - \frac{c_q}{J}q + \frac{c_T}{J}\delta \qquad (9\text{-}67)$$
$$\frac{d\delta}{dt} = f \qquad (9\text{-}68)$$
$$a = \frac{c_L}{M}\alpha - \frac{c_F}{M}\delta \qquad (9\text{-}69)$$

Equations (9-66) to (9-68) are the same as (9-17), and Eq. (9-69) is the same as (9-35). We note that

$$\det |a_{ij}| = \begin{vmatrix} -\dfrac{c_L}{MV} & 1 & \dfrac{c_F}{MV} \\ -\dfrac{c_M}{J} & -\dfrac{c_q}{J} & \dfrac{c_T}{J} \\ 0 & 0 & 0 \end{vmatrix} = 0 \tag{9-70}$$

Setting the right-hand side of Eqs. (9-66) and (9-67) equal to zero, two equations between α, q, and δ are obtained. From these equations and Eq. (9-69), the steady-state values of α_1, q_1, and δ_1, corresponding to a given a_1, can be calculated:

$$q_1 = \frac{a_1}{V}$$

$$\delta_1 = \frac{a_1}{k}$$

$$\alpha_1 = \frac{M}{c_L}(a_1 - k'\delta_1) = \frac{M}{c_L}\left(1 - \frac{k'}{k}\right)a_1$$

The variables y_1, y_2, and y_3 are defined by Eq. (9-35a):

$$y_1 = \alpha_1 - \alpha = \frac{M}{c_L}\left(1 \frac{k'}{k}\right)a_1 - \alpha$$

$$y_2 = q_1 - q = \frac{a_1}{V} - q$$

$$y_3 = \delta_1 - \delta = \frac{a_1}{k} - \delta$$

Any nonsingular linear transforms of the y's are adequate for phase-space coordinates. It is interesting to show that u_1, u_2, and u_3 are linear combinations of y_1, y_2, and y_3: Eqs. (9-37) and (9-62) show that u_1 is a linear combination of y_1, y_2, and y_3. From Eq. (9-69), u_2 is seen proportional to $\dot{\alpha} = -\dot{y}_1$. Since $b_{11} = 0$, Eq. (9-36) shows that $\dot{y}_1$ is a linear combination of y_1, y_2, and y_3. The variable u_3 is a linear combination of the y's, as it can be written as

$$u_3 = a_1 - k\delta - e = y_3 - u_1$$

We see that the two methods are equivalent.

To determine the switching boundaries, u_1, u_2, and u_3 are solved explicitly in t. Equation (9-64) can be written as

$$\frac{d^2 u_3}{dt^2} + 2\zeta\omega_n \frac{du_3}{dt} + \omega_n^2 u_3 = (-2\zeta\omega_n k + k'')f \tag{9-71}$$

$$u_3 = \frac{f}{\omega_n^2}(-2\zeta\omega_n k + k'') + Ae^{-\zeta\omega_n t}\sin(\psi + \omega_n t\sqrt{1 - \zeta^2}) \tag{9-72}$$

where A and ψ are constants of integration.

$$u_2 = \frac{d}{dt}[u_3 + (k - k')\delta]$$

$$= (k - k')f + \omega_n Ae^{-\zeta\omega_n t}\cos(\psi + \phi + \omega_n t\sqrt{1 - \zeta^2}) \tag{9-73}$$

where $\phi = \sin^{-1} \zeta$.

$$u_1 = a_1 - a = a_1 - u_3 - k\delta$$
$$= B - kft - Ae^{-\zeta\omega_n t} \sin (\psi + \omega_n t \sqrt{1 - \zeta^2}) \qquad (9\text{-}74)$$

The constants A, B, ψ are determined by initial conditions. Equations (9-72) to (9-74) give the system trajectory in parametric form. From these equations, the switching boundaries can be determined by the reversed-time technique.

9-9. Phase-space Technique Versus Programming. There are two ways of realizing optimum controls of high-order systems.

1. *Phase-space Technique.* As described in previous sections, the system operates on error signal and its derivatives or equivalent variables. The system is a feedback system. In practical cases with finite gain, there usually exists a linear region near the origin.

2. *Programming.* For controlled systems with real roots or complex roots of low enough natural frequency, the number of switchings (or sign reversals of f_1) for an optimum system is $n - 1$. Let the time at the various switchings be denoted by t_i, $i = 1, 2, \ldots, n - 1$, with the origin of t coinciding with the entry of an ordered change c_1. Each t_i is a function of c_1. The controller has $n - 1$ nonlinear elements representing the $n - 1$ functions $t_i(c_1)$ and causes f to reverse sign at these predetermined instants. This type of control is a feedforward system. Usually it is used in conjunction with a linear feedback system such that at the end of the operations the controlling function is reverted to the linear system.

Figures 9-14a and b are functional diagrams illustrating the operations of the two types of systems.

Functionally, the phase-space type of control is considerably superior to the programming type. For the latter to operate well, the system must be in a steady-state condition or "in trim" before entering an ordered change c_1. This implies also that, once a change c_1 is ordered, it must be carried out before another change is ordered. There is no such limitation with the phase-space type of control. The system always carries out the best, or fastest, method of reaching the desired steady-state condition, irrespective of the initial conditions. Furthermore, in case there is load disturbance, the phase-space type of control is also superior: Small and constantly present disturbances are counteracted by the linear mode of operation in both systems. Large isolated disturbing forces or moments cause the representative point of the system to be dislodged from the neighborhood of the origin, and the phase-space type of control prescribes the fastest maneuver to restore it. However, as the change caused by disturbance is usually not a simple step change, the programming type of control is totally ineffective.

So far as instrumentation is concerned, the programming type is simpler for systems of third order or higher. It is much easier to assemble $n - 1$ nonlinear functions of a single variable than to assemble $n - 1$ nonlinear surfaces and curves in phase space which are functions of several variables. The noise picked up by measuring instruments affects only the linear mode of a programming type of controller, whereas it affects both the linear and nonlinear operations of the phase-space type of controller. Consequently, noise filtering in the latter is much more of a problem, since the effects of the filters in the phase space are difficult to determine exactly.

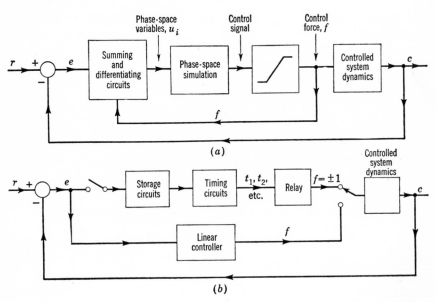

FIG. 9-14. Two ways of optimum maneuvering control. (a) Phase-space controller; (b) programmed controller.

9-10. Preliminary Filtering for Predictor Control. There are two types of noise existing in a measuring instrument: sinusoidal interferences picked up from stray fields of power components and random noises from less artificial sources. The sinusoidal interferences can be removed by carefully shielding the sensing elements or by using sharp antiresonant networks in the earlier amplification stages. The random noise is not so readily removable. It has a much wider bandwidth than the signal bandwidth and usually overlaps the latter. An optimum linear filter carefully designed by the techniques of Chap. 4 is called for, and the same filter is used for both the linear and nonlinear range of operations.

For proper nonlinear operation, time delay in the filters must be compensated for by advancing the switching boundaries. Figure 9-15 illustrates how this can be done for the second-order system described in Sec. 9-5.   Instead of using the two trajectories as the farther boundaries of the switching zone, as shown in Fig. 9-8, the switching zone is moved farther in.   As the error signals are delayed in the noise filter by an interval approximately equal to the phase slope $(d\beta/d\omega)$ of the filter at $\omega = 0$, the trajectory of the system projects slightly beyond the farther boundary of the switching zone, as shown in Fig. 9-15.

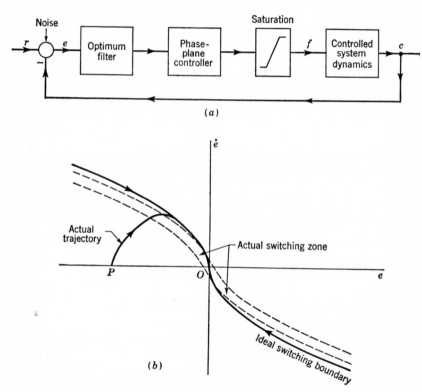

FIG. 9-15. Phase-plane controller with linear filtering.   (a) Block diagram; (b) modification of switching zone.

9-11. Modified Phase-plane Control of a Third-order System.†   As discussed in Sec. 9-9, the phase-space type of controller is more desirable in operation, because it is a feedback system and is inherently more flexible.   However, its cost is high because of the necessity of assimilating surfaces in space which are functions of several variables.   One way of realizing many of the desired features of phase-space control without

† U.S. Patent 2,973,926, Control Apparatus, issued to Sheldon S. L. Chang, March, 1961.

paying the cost is to use a combination system. The arrangement of the system is shown in Fig. 9-16. There are two essential control units.

1. *Stabilizing Unit.* When the contactor is open, the unit admits only derivative signals $\dot{c}$, $\ddot{c}$, or the equivalent, and switches f in such a way that $\dot{c}$ and $\ddot{c}$ are reduced to zero in the least time by the phase-plane method. Once this is accomplished, the contactor closes. This unit is similar to the second-order system described in Sec. 9-5.

2. *Dislodging Unit.* The dislodging unit consists of the nonlinear element 1 and the contactor. It is not effective when the contactor is open. When the contactor is closed, the controlled system is in a steady-state condition with a certain value of c. If c is not equal to c_1, a voltage which is usually a nonlinear function (nonlinear element 1) of the error $c_1 - c$ is introduced into the stabilizing unit and causes f_1 to be at its maximum value in the direction of reducing $c_1 - c$ for an interval depending on $c_1 - c$. At the end of this interval, the contactor opens,

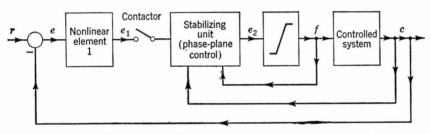

FIG. 9-16. Block diagram of modified *phase-plane* control of a *third-order* system.

and the stabilizing unit takes over the control function. The nonlinear element 1 is designed to hold the first step just long enough so that, after stabilization, $c_1 - c$ is zero or approximately zero.

With the contactor closed, for small inputs and small load disturbances, the system acts like a stable linear system.

An example of such a design is an experimental aircraft-pitch linear acceleration controller for the problem described in Example 9-3. The input signals to the stabilizing unit are u_2 and u_3. Two dimensionless variables are defined as

$$e_\xi = \frac{\omega_n u_3}{(k - k')\Omega_m} \qquad e_\eta = \frac{u_2}{(k - k')\Omega_m} \tag{9-75}$$

Equations (9-72) and (9-73) can be rewritten to give e_ξ and e_η in terms of the dimensionless variable $\omega_n t$. These are the parametric equations of the trajectories in phase space $e_\xi - e_\eta$ and are plotted in Fig. 9-17. The solid and broken curves of Fig. 9-17 correspond to $d\delta/dt = \Omega_m$, $-\Omega_m$, respectively. The two trajectories marked 1 and 2 pass the origin and form the optimum switching boundary.

The operation of the system can be explained with the help of Figs. 9-16 and 9-17.   In Fig. 9-16, the controlled system includes both the aircraft dynamics and the integration from elevator rate to elevator angle. When the contactor is closed and a positive input c_1 is applied to the system, the error voltage e_2 causes δ to increase at the rate Ω_m.   The representative point of the system follows curve 3 into the region of negative f.   However, because of the overriding influence of the error voltage e_1, e_2 remains positive until the representative point reaches a far enough point a to reverse e_2. At this point the contactor opens and e_2 suddenly changes into a large negative voltage.   Consequently f reverses sign and the representative point follows trajectory 6 to point b.   At b, f reverses sign and the representative point follows 1 to the origin, near which point the contactor closes.   There is a net gain in the output variable c.   (In this case c represents the pitch linear acceleration a.)   If the nonlinear element 1 is properly designed, the gain in c is equal to c_1.

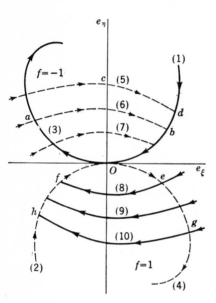

FIG. 9-17. Trajectories in modified phase plane. (*Reprinted from Sheldon S. L. Chang, Proc. Natl. Electronics Conf., vol. 12, pp. 134–151, 1956.*)

Figure 9-18 illustrates the response of a simulated system with the experimental controller on an analog computer.   The elevator angle δ, pitch linear acceleration a, angle of attack α, and pitch angular velocity q are all expressed in per-unit quantities.   In graph b the ordered change in a of two units corresponds approximately to the maximum possible a, because of structural limits.   We note that the elevator angle δ always moves at a maximum rate and reverses twice during the whole process, as required by theory.   There is little overshoot in a.   However, there is a slight dip in a when δ begins to move upward at the start.   This is due to the nonminimum-phase effect described in Sec. 4-7.

Figure 9-19 illustrates the system response to load disturbance of the nature of a pitchwise torque impulse.   With the control on, and an impulse applied at $\omega_n t = 0$, the system disturbance is reduced to zero very quickly.   In contrast, when an equal and opposite impulse is applied at $\omega_n t = 8$, the control is off, and a persistent oscillation is observed.   We note that the controller serves to damp out later oscillations completely

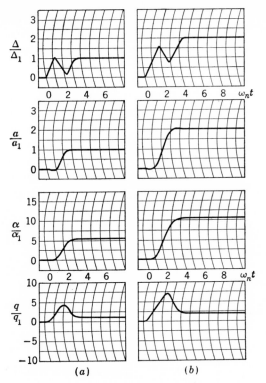

FIG. 9-18. System response to step inputs. (*Reprinted from Sheldon S. L. Chang, Proc. Natl. Electronics Conf., vol. 12, pp. 134–151, 1956.*)

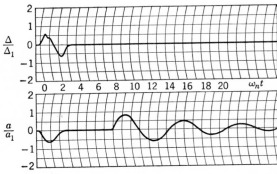

FIG. 9-19. System response to pitchwise torque impulse. (*Reprinted from Sheldon S. L. Chang, Proc. Natl. Electronics Conf., vol. 12, pp. 134–151, 1956.*)

but is not very effective in suppressing the first lobe. This effect is rather characteristic of tail-controlled steering systems in which a relatively small surface is used to control a much larger body. The relatively small control force is adequate to produce desired change as it is magnified by the large number of integrations inherent in the system dynamics. However, as it takes time to integrate, the effect of control on the system is always felt some time later.

This type of control can tolerate a fair amount of component inaccuracies. Figures 9-18 and 9-19 show system responses with a stabilizing

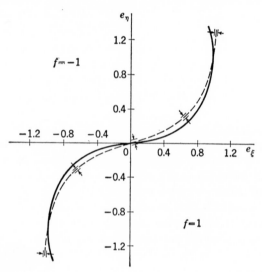

FIG. 9-20. Theoretical and actual switching boundaries in modified phase plane. (*Reprinted from Sheldon S. L. Chang, Proc. Natl. Electronics Conf., vol. 12, pp. 134–151, 1956.*)

unit having a switching zone as indicated by the broken lines of Fig. 9-20. In contrast, the theoretical switching boundary is shown as the solid line. As the performance indicates that a deviation of this order is tolerable, the electronic design does not present a problem.

9-12. Systems with Multiple Limits. It is not unusual for a controlled system to have more than one saturation limit. At times this difficulty can be removed by properly selecting the controlled variable. Take the previous example of aircraft-pitch control; there are at least the following saturation limits:

1. Structural limit, which limits the linear acceleration a
2. Angle of attack limit, which limits α
3. Elevator angle limit
4. Elevator rate limit

The choice of a as a controlled variable removes 1, as we may simply not order too large an a_1. Since the elevator force is small, the angle of attack α is approximately proportional to a in its linear range. At low speed or high altitude or both, 2 is more of a restriction than 1, and we may simply not order an a_1 that requires too large an α. The linear or allowable range of δ is usually large enough to cover the range of a or α in steady state. It does not present a problem if the value of δ during the transient period is not higher than its final value. Figure 9-18 shows that this is the case with predictor control except for very small values of the ordered change a_1, in which case δ is small also. Thus the only limit left is the elevator rate limit.

Another possibility of saturation is in the electronics itself, owing to the presence of the quadrature component of the carrier, harmonics, or some other sources of sinusoidal noise. Such saturation can be removed by a rearrangement of the electronic components and is not essential to the system. For instance, sinusoidal noise, except the quadrature carrier, can be removed by a notch network in the preamplifier stages. The quadrature carrier can be removed to a large extent by careful balancing, and the remainder can be removed by moving ahead the detection stage. To accept a nonessential limit not only complicates the mathematics of the problem; it also makes the solution nonoptimal, since we can make a better system by simply redesigning the electronic circuitry.

The above illustrates the necessity of examining a problem carefully before we come to the conclusion that the system has multiple saturation limits. In such a case, the solution is usually complicated, and we shall limit our study here to a relatively simple case:

A highly idealized ship-steering problem can be formulated as follows:†

$$J \frac{d^2\gamma(t)}{dt^2} = K\delta(t) \qquad (9\text{-}76)$$

where γ is the ship heading and δ is the rudder angle. The rudder-angle and rudder-rate limits can be expressed as

$$|\delta(t)| \leq \delta_m \qquad (9\text{-}77)$$

$$\left| \frac{d\delta(t)}{dt} \right| \leq \Omega_m \qquad (9\text{-}78)$$

The optimum solution is that at any time either one or the other of the following conditions must hold:

$$|\delta| = \delta_m \qquad (9\text{-}79)$$

or $$\left| \frac{d\delta}{dt} \right| = \Omega_m \qquad (9\text{-}80)$$

† This material is condensed from H. G. Doll and T. M. Stout, Design and Analog-computer Analysis of an Optimum Third-order Nonlinear Servomechanism, *Trans. ASME*, pp. 513–525, April, 1957.

First, let us consider the optimum rudder movement for a desired step change in γ, say γ_1. At the desired steady-state condition,

$$\ddot{\gamma} = 0 \tag{9-81}$$
$$\dot{\gamma} = 0 \tag{9-82}$$

Let 0 and t_1 denote the initial time and final time, respectively. Equations (9-81) and (9-82) require that

$$\delta(t) = 0 \qquad \text{for } t > t_1 \tag{9-83}$$
$$\int_0^{t_1} \delta(t)\,dt = 0 \tag{9-84}$$

Equations (9-79), (9-80), (9-83), and (9-84) give the δ versus t, $\dot{\gamma}$ versus t, and $\gamma_1 - \gamma$ versus t curves of Figs. 9-21 and 9-22. Figure 9-21 illus-

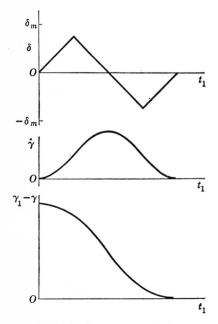

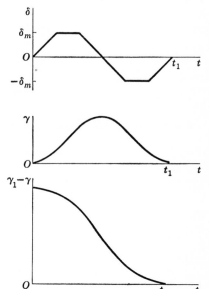

Fig. 9-21. Optimum controlled movements for small step inputs.

Fig. 9-22. Optimum controlled movements for large step inputs (third-order
system with two limits).

trates the situation that the ordered change in γ_1 is small, and consequently the rudder-angle limit has never been reached. Figure 9-22 illustrates the case with large ordered change in γ_1. The dividing line is

$$t_1 = 4\,\frac{\delta_m}{\Omega_m} \tag{9-85}$$

The net change in γ can be obtained by integrating Eq. (9-76). For t_1

equal to $4\delta_m/\Omega_m$ or less,

$$\gamma_1 = \frac{K\Omega_m t_1{}^3}{32J} \tag{9-86}$$

The above simple solution can be readily generalized to include cases with ramp input by modifying Eq. (9-84).

While the above direct solution is quite simple, the switching boundaries in phase space are not so easily determined. First we shall write the system equations in terms of per-unit quantities:

$$\tau = \frac{\Omega_m}{\delta_m} t$$

$$e = \frac{J\Omega_m{}^2}{K\delta_m{}^3} (\gamma_1 - \gamma)$$

With step and ramp inputs, Eq. (9-76) becomes

$$\frac{d^2e}{d\tau^2} = -\frac{\delta}{\delta_m} = -T \tag{9-87}$$

In Eq. (9-87), T represents δ/δ_m. Equations (9-77) and (9-78) become

$$|T| \le 1 \tag{9-88}$$

$$\left| \frac{dT}{d\tau} \right| \le 1 \tag{9-89}$$

Let the phase-space variables x, y, z be chosen as

$$x = e \qquad y = \frac{de}{d\tau} \qquad z = \frac{d^2e}{d\tau^2}$$

From Eqs. (9-87) and (9-88), we see that the phase trajectories are bound between two planes with $z = \pm 1$. On the upper plane, $z = 1$, and the phase trajectories are the set of parabolas

$$x - x_1 = \tfrac{1}{2}y^2$$

Similarly, on the lower plane, the phase trajectories are

$$x - x_1 = -\tfrac{1}{2}y^2$$

In between the two planes, the phase trajectories are obtained by solving the differential equation

$$\frac{d^3e}{d\tau^3} = \pm 1$$

The result is a set of parametric equations:

$$x = e = x_0 + y_0\tau + \frac{z_0}{2}\tau^2 \pm \frac{\tau^3}{6}$$

$$y = \frac{de}{d\tau} = y_0 + z_0\tau \pm \frac{\tau^2}{2} \tag{9-90}$$

$$z = \frac{d^2e}{d\tau^2} = z_0 \pm \tau$$

The switching boundaries can be obtained by the reversed-time technique. Let τ_1 represent the required time to reach the origin. The final switching boundary is for $\tau_1 < 1$:

$$x = \pm \frac{\tau_1^3}{6}$$

$$y = \pm \frac{\tau_1^2}{2} \tag{9-91}$$

$$z = \pm \tau_1$$

The switching surface or first switching boundary is obtained from Eqs. (9-90) and (9-91):

$$x = \pm \left(\frac{\tau_1^3}{6} + \frac{\tau_1^2 \tau_2}{2} + \frac{\tau_1 \tau_2^2}{2} - \frac{\tau_2^3}{6} \right)$$

$$y = \pm \left(\frac{\tau_1^2}{2} + \tau_1 \tau_2 - \frac{\tau_2^2}{2} \right) \tag{9-92}$$

$$z = \pm (\tau_1 - \tau_2)$$

where τ_2 is the time required to reach a point on the final switching boundary of Eq. (9-91). An equation relating x, y, and z can be obtained by eliminating τ_1 and τ_2 from the set of Eqs. (9-92). For the upper signs of Eqs. (9-92),

$$x = -z \left(y + \frac{z^2}{3} \right) - \left(\frac{z^2}{2} + y \right)^{3/2} \tag{9-93}$$

For the lower signs of Eqs. (9-92),

$$x = z \left(y - \frac{z^2}{3} \right) + \left(\frac{z^2}{2} - y \right)^{3/2} \tag{9-94}$$

The switching surface can be represented by a set of constant z lines on the xy plane, as shown in Fig. 9-23. The final switching boundary is the broken curve EOF.

A typical three-dimensional system trajectory is represented by the broken curve $ABDFO$. Let us assume that the system starts at point A with $T = 0$. Since this point lies above the switching surface, a positive movement of the rudder results, with $dT/d\tau = 1$. The representative point P moves in the $-z$ direction while its projection on the xy plane follows the curve AB. At point B, P reaches the lower plane $z = -1$. Thereafter $T = 1$ and P follows the parabolic trajectory to D, where it intersects with the switching surface. After D, $dT/d\tau = -1$ and P follow the trajectory to F, which is a point on the final switching boundary. At F, $dT/d\tau$ becomes 1, and P follows the final switching boundary to the origin. A time representation of δ, $\dot{e}$, and e is shown in Fig. 9-24. It differs from Fig. 9-22 in its lack of symmetry, and the difference can be explained by the presence of a ramp input.

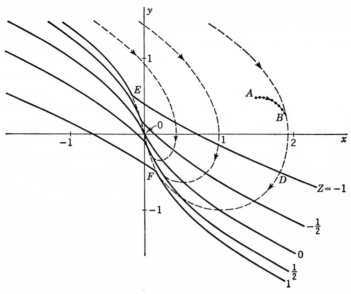

FIG. 9-23. Projection of phase-space trajectories and switching surface on xy plane. (*Reprinted from H. G. Doll and T. M. Stout, Trans. ASME, pp. 513–525, April, 1957.*)

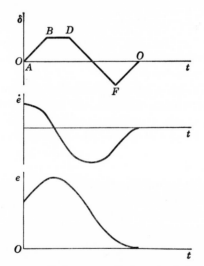

FIG. 9-24. Optimum controlled movements for mixed step and ramp inputs.

9-13. Summary. The maximum principle of Pontryagin for minimal-time control of nonlinear systems is derived. While this broad principle may have other applications, its immediate application is in the minimal-time control of a system with simple saturation and deterministic inputs (step, ramp, etc.). It is shown that the desired final state is reached in the least time by operating the controlled system at its saturated values in either one direction or the other.   If all the poles of a controlled system of nth order lie on the negative real axis including the origin, the desired final state is arrived at by reversing the input to the controlled system $n - 1$ times.   If there are oscillatory poles, the required number of reversals may be greater than $n - 1$.   If the system is unstable uncontrolled, the phase space is divided into convergent and divergent regions, and the above observation applies only to the convergent region.

A controller that realizes the above principle by simulating optimum switching boundaries in phase space is called a predictor type of controller. The switching boundary of a second-order system can be simulated by conventional diode shapers and amplifiers.   While an ideal system with an infinitely thin switching boundary requires an amplifier of infinite gain, the use of finite-gain amplifiers does not slow down the system to any appreciable extent.   In fact, the use of amplifiers with finite gain has an advantage in itself: Once the desired final state is approximately realized, the system automatically becomes a linear feedback control system with lead or proportional plus derivative compensation.

The simulation of switching boundaries of a system of third order or higher is a serious hardware problem.   However, the problem can be alleviated by using a modified version of phase-plane control, which reduces the error derivatives to zero by the predictor technique, and a dislodging unit which operates the system in one extreme value just long enough so that, after subsequent stabilization, the desired change in the controlled variable is realized.

If the transfer function of the controlled system has a numerator polynomial in s other than a constant, the representative point skips to a new position in phase space at each switching.   This effect can be eliminated by using a new set of phase-space coordinates which are signals derived by mixing the error derivatives with the input or actuating signal to the controlled system.

In the presence of noise, prefiltering of the error signal prior to predictor control is necessary.   The switching boundaries should be advanced in position to compensate for the filter time delay.

The problem of multiple saturation limits can usually be avoided by a careful examination of the control problem to separate the essential limits from the nonessential limits.   However, there are systems in which multiple saturation limits are unavoidable.   The problem has not been solved except in the simplest cases, an example of which is given.

CHAPTER 10

SELF-OPTIMIZING SYSTEMS

10-1. What Is a Self-optimizing System? In the previous chapters, our studies have been concerned mainly with the synthesis of systems for which both the plant dynamics and the statistical properties of the inputs are known. The optimum performance as well as the appropriate controller for realizing it can then be determined. However, in many applications, the statistics of the inputs and the plant dynamics are not completely known or are gradually changing. It becomes necessary to

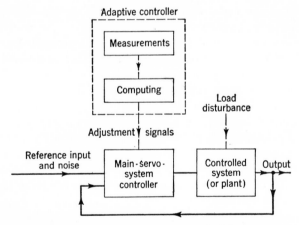

FIG. 10-1. Basic elements of a self-optimizing system.

design a system that learns or estimates the unknown factors during operation and adjusts the controller accordingly to give optimum or approximately optimum performance. A system that is capable of doing the above is called a self-optimizing system, or an adaptive system, in the sense that it is capable of adapting itself to changing environment.

Figure 10-1 illustrates the essential elements of a self-optimizing system. The adaptive controller makes measurements on the main servo loop, computes the changes to be made, and carries out the necessary adjustments on the main servo system. The adaptive control may be either open- or closed-loop, depending on whether the measured quantities are affected by the subsequent adjustments or not.

Functionally speaking, self-optimizing systems can be classified into three different types:

1. Input sensing. The statistical properties of the inputs are uncertain. The adaptive controller measures these properties and automatically makes adjustments on the system controller. In order to make this type of system function, the designer has to know in advance the optimum adjustments for each set of measured data. The adaptive control is usually open-loop. However, it becomes closed-loop if some variable of the system is measured instead of measuring the inputs directly.

2. Plant sensing. Some parameters of the plant dynamics are uncertain. These parameters are measured, and the system controller is adjusted to match the parameters of the plant. There are three ways of estimating the plant parameters:

 a. Measuring the input and output variables of the plant
 b. Measuring the input and the output variables of the closed-loop system
 c. Indirect estimation of the plant parameters by measuring some other physical entity, such as the forward speed of a ship in a steering system

In (*a*) and (*b*) the input variables may be natural inputs to the system or may be a test function, depending on the type of application. In systems where stochastic inputs are constantly present, existing inputs are usually adequate. In other systems where the natural stochastic inputs are negligible and our problem is to hold the system in constant readiness for occasional command, test functions are usually used. The computing device for determining the system parameters from input-output measurements is simpler when a test function is used.

The adaptive control is open-loop for cases *a* and *c* and closed-loop for case *b*.

3. Extremal sensing of certain plant performance criteria. In this type of system the adaptive controller measures directly certain performance merit criteria (e.g., mean-square error or cost function of a servo system) and adjusts the system controller to seek a maximum or minimum of this quantity. The adaptive control is closed-loop. It differs from type 2*b* in that the maximum or minimum value of the given performance criterion is usually unknown, whereas in type 2*b* the desired setting of the controlled parameter is usually known and is not at its extreme value. (An example is the damping coefficient of a closed-loop system, with a desired value somewhere in the range of 0.6 to 0.9.)

In the present chapter we are concerned with the basic principle of adaptive control systems. Examples are given to help explain how the systems work and how to design these systems in situations that are not too critical. The next chapter is devoted to analytical studies of the two essential functions characterizing a self-optimizing system:

1. Learning or measuring
2. Adjusting

It also discusses the best way of accomplishing the above under fast-varying situations.

10-2. Systems with Input Sensing. Input-sensing systems may be designed for two purposes: (1) optimum suppression of noise and (2) optimum allocation of plant power. We shall study the first case first. Given spectral densities $\Phi_{rr}(j\omega)$ and $\Phi_{nn}(j\omega)$, the optimum closed-loop system function is

$$\frac{C}{R}(s) = \frac{1}{Z(s)}\left[\frac{\Phi_{rr}(s)}{Z(-s)}\right]_+. \tag{10-1}$$

where $Z(s)$ is given by Eq. (4-27a). When the signal-to-noise ratio varies gradually with time, C/R also varies. As an example, consider the following case:

Example 10-1

Plant transfer function: $\qquad G(s) = \dfrac{K}{s}$

Signal spectral density: $\qquad \Phi_{rr} = \dfrac{A^2}{\omega^2}$

Noise spectral density: $\qquad \Phi_{nn} = B^2$

$$\Phi_{nr} = \Phi_{rn} = 0$$

The signal-to-noise ratio A^2/B^2 may vary slowly.

Solution. Equation (4-27a) gives

$$Z\bar{Z} = \frac{A^2}{\omega^2} + B^2 = \left(B + \frac{A}{s}\right)\left(B - \frac{A}{s}\right)$$

Therefore $Z = B + A/s$, and Eq. (10-1) gives

$$\frac{C}{R}(s) = \frac{A}{A + Bs} = \frac{1}{1 + (B/A)s} \tag{10-2}$$

The form of Eq. (10-2) suggests that a straight amplifier K_a would do. The closed-loop system function is

$$\frac{C}{R}(s) = \frac{1}{1 + s/KK_a} \tag{10-3}$$

Comparing Eqs. (10-2) and (10-3), we see that

$$K_a = \frac{1}{K}\frac{A}{B} \tag{10-4}$$

Since the signal-to-noise amplitude ratio A/B is known by measurement, K_a is adjusted proportionately. The complete system is shown in Fig. 10-2.

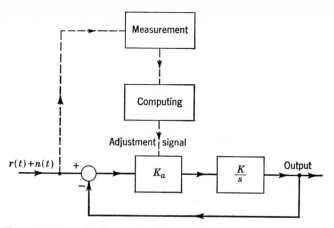

FIG. 10-2. An adaptive system for optimum suppression of noise.

The above example illustrates an extremely simple case for which a single gain control is adequate. However, in general, coordinated changes of a few parameters such as gain, feedback constant, and network time constants are necessary. The design principle is nevertheless the same.

10-3. Systems with Controlled Plant Activity.   As discussed in Chap. 4, when load disturbance is present, plant saturation or heat loss is usually a major consideration in system design.   The problem is usually up to how high a frequency range we wish the controller to counteract the effects of load disturbance.   Beyond this range the disturbances are left to the natural attenuation of plant inertia.   When the magnitude of load disturbance is high, we compensate only for the frequency range where the controlled system is most sensitive in its response.   The compensated range is increased as the magnitude of load disturbance lessens.

The above design concept can be carried out by either open-loop or closed-loop adaptive control.   The latter is usually preferable.   The following examples illustrate how to design and instrument the two types of systems.

Example 10-2.   Known data are:

Plant transfer function:

$$G(s) = \frac{K}{Js^2}$$

Signal spectral density:

$$\Phi_{rr} = \frac{A^2}{\omega^2}$$

Load torque disturbance:

$$\Phi_{TT} = B^2$$

$$\Phi_{rT} = \Phi_{Tr} = 0$$

The value of B is unknown or uncertain. Because of heat loss or saturation, the input to the plant is limited:

$$\overline{i^2} \leq M \tag{10-5}$$

Solution. To determine the optimum system, the load torque disturbance is converted first into a positional disturbance:

$$\Phi_{dd} = \frac{B^2}{J^2 s^4}$$

Equations (4-11), (4-31), and (4-32) give the optimum system functions

$$\frac{C}{R}(s) = F_1(s) = \frac{\omega_1^2}{s^2 + \sqrt{2}\,\omega_1 s + \omega_1^2} \tag{10-6}$$

$$\frac{C}{D}(s) = 1 + F_2(s) = \frac{s^2}{s^2 + \sqrt{2}\,\omega_1 s + \omega_1^2} \tag{10-7}$$

where

$$\omega_1 = \sqrt{\frac{K}{kJ}} \tag{10-8}$$

and k is Lagrange's multiplier.

To determine k or ω_1 in terms of B, we have

$$\overline{i^2} = \frac{1}{2\pi j}\int_{-j\infty}^{j\infty} \frac{1}{G\bar{G}}(F_1\bar{F}_1\Phi_{rr} + F_2\bar{F}_2\Phi_{dd})\,ds$$

$$= \frac{1}{2\pi j}\int_{-j\infty}^{j\infty} \frac{-A^2J^2\omega_1^4 s^2 + B^2(\omega_1^4 - 2\omega_1^2 s^2)}{K^2(s^4 + \omega_1^4)}\,ds \tag{10-9}$$

Equation (10-9) can be readily evaluated by contour integration, as shown in Appendix D. The result is

$$\overline{i^2} = \frac{A^2J^2\omega_1^3 + 3B^2\omega_1}{2\sqrt{2}\,K^2} = M \tag{10-10}$$

Equation (10-10) gives ω_1 as a function of B.

The block diagram of the system is shown in Fig. 10-3. In order to obtain optimum control, simultaneous adjustment of the amplifier gain K_a and feedback constant K_f

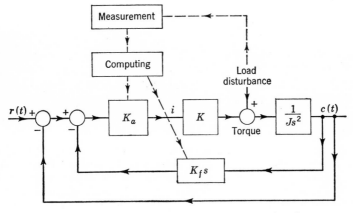

Fig. 10-3. An adaptive system for varying load disturbance.

is necessary:

$$K_a = \frac{\omega_1^2 J}{K} \qquad (10\text{-}11)$$

$$K_f = \frac{\sqrt{2}}{\omega_1} \qquad (10\text{-}12)$$

While it is possible to adjust K_a alone or K_f alone and obtain an optimum setting in the sense of Phillips's procedure (Ref. J1), the result is not as good as that obtained here from Wiener's procedure.

Example 10-3.   Another way of obtaining substantially the same result as Fig. 10-3 is shown in Fig. 10-4.   The function $[i(t)]^2$ is measured directly and compared

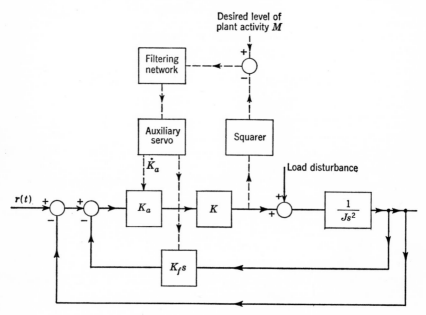

FIG. 10-4. An adaptive system with automatic input-level control.

with the set limit M.   The difference is filtered to average out the random variations of $[i(t)]^2$.   The gain K_a is adjusted upward at a rate proportional to $M - \overline{[i(t)]^2}$, while K_f is varied simultaneously so that at all times

$$K_f = \sqrt{\frac{2J}{KK_a}} \qquad (10\text{-}13)$$

The adaptive control is closed-loop and is illustrated in Fig. 10-5.   The variable x here represents $[i(t)]^2$.   The controlled variable is the expected value $\bar{x}$, and any random fluctuation $x - \bar{x}$ is treated as noise.   Variations in input and load disturbance levels A and B are treated as load disturbance in the adaptive loop.   While only variations in K_a are shown explicitly in Fig. 10-5, the feedback constant K_f is understood to vary according to Eq. (10-13).

From Eqs. (10-10) and (10-11), $\bar{x}$ can be expressed as a function of K_a, A^2, and B^2:

$$\bar{x} = \left(\frac{J}{8K}\right)^{\frac{1}{2}} K_a^{\frac{3}{2}} A^2 + \left(\frac{9}{8JK^3}\right)^{\frac{1}{2}} K_a^{\frac{1}{2}} B^2 \tag{10-14}$$

If variations in A^2 and B^2 are slow, the system is expected to track very well. Change in $\bar{x}$ is expected to be small, and linearization can be used:

$$\delta\bar{x} = \frac{\partial\bar{x}}{\partial K_a}\,\delta K_a + \frac{\partial\bar{x}}{\partial A^2}\,\delta A^2 + \frac{\partial\bar{x}}{\partial B^2}\,\delta B^2 \tag{10-15}$$

The partial derivatives are calculated from Eq. (10-14). Figure 10-5 represents a type 1 system. We note that, under the assumption that variations in A^2 and B^2 are slow, a low gain K_d can be used, and the adaptive loop is stable. If variations in A^2 and B^2 are fast, the filter and K_d determine the effectiveness of the adaptive control loop. The problem requires further study (Sec. 11-10).

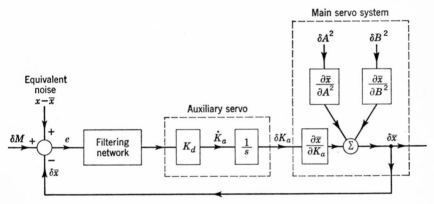

FIG. 10-5. Equivalent block diagram for the adaptive control loop of the system of Fig. 10-4.

10-4. Systems with Plant Sensing by the Use of a Test Signal. If the plant parameters vary with a certain readily measurable quantity in a predetermined manner, the simplest adaptive control is obtained by changing the system controller according to the measurable quantity. In steering systems, practically every constant of the dynamical equations depends on the forward speed, and the system controller is usually adjusted according to the forward speed. An engineering problem arises, however, when the variations in plant parameter are not predetermined. The emphasis of the present section will be on cases a and b mentioned in Sec. 10-1, where the variations in plant parameter have to be measured directly. The measuring techniques for both cases are the same. However, as case b has a closed adaptive loop, an analysis of the adaptive loop is also necessary. We shall discuss the measuring techniques first.

One thing is common among plant-sensing self-optimizing systems that have proved practical or at least seemingly so in the breadboard stage: The form of the transfer function or the pattern of the poles and zeros is assumed known, and only one or two critical parameters are to be measured. This is more or less what one would expect. If we could make an adaptive controller that assumes nothing on the controlled plant, makes all the necessary measurements, adjusts itself accordingly to give satisfactory control performance, and does this sufficiently fast to track any change in the environment or plant dynamics, and with sufficient economy to be practical, we should have no further use for engineering departments.

Presently we shall not try to build a universal adaptive controller but shall limit ourselves to objectives which are much less ambitious. The measured quantities are usually the damping factor and natural frequency of the system, either open- or closed-loop, and the general form of the plant transfer function is assumed to be known. With this limited objective, and using a test signal, the measurements can be quite simple. In general, the test signal does not have to be applied at the input nor the measurements made at the output. These should be done at places most indicative of the response characteristics that we wish to determine while causing least disturbance to the system. Classified according to the nature of the test signal, there are three types of measurements.

1. *Frequency-response Method.* If we know definitely the form of the transfer function and also that the so-called minor time constants are so small that their effects are totally negligible, gain and phase measurement at a single frequency somewhat higher than cutoff is quite adequate to determine the system's response parameters. For instance, consider a second-order system:

$$\frac{C}{R}(s) = \frac{\omega_n{}^2}{s^2 + 2\zeta\omega_n s + \omega_n{}^2} \tag{10-16}$$

The parameters ζ and ω_n can be easily determined from the magnitude and phase of $(C/R)(j\omega)$ for a single ω. The reasons for choosing $\omega > \omega_n$ are that (1) the regular signal level is low for $\omega > \omega_n$ and consequently a weak test signal is all that is necessary and (2), other things remaining equal, the time required for determining gain and phase is inversely proportional to ω.

2. *Impulse-response Method.* One way of determining a system's stability is to examine its response to a test impulse. Of course, the test signal is not an ideal impulse but one with finite pulse width and peak magnitude. As long as the pulse width is considerably narrower than the reciprocal of the system's bandwidth, the system's response approximates impulse response closely.

If the response characteristics of interest are not appreciably masked by other servo signals in the system, adjustments can be made on the basis of each individual impulse response. Otherwise, averaging over the responses to many periodically applied impulses would be necessary.

3. *Correlation Method.* If the input to a system is white noise, the correlation function $\phi_{iv}(\tau)$ between input $i(t)$ and response $v(t)$ is proportional to the impulse-response functon $h(\tau)$. In practice, it is only necessary for $i(t)$ to have nearly constant spectral density in the frequency range in which $H(j\omega)$ is appreciably different from zero.

Since

$$\Phi_{iv}(j\omega) = \Phi_{ii}(j\omega)H(j\omega) \cong \text{const} \times H(j\omega)$$

an inverse transform of the above equation gives the desired conclusion.

The determination of the impulse-response function by correlation was originally proposed by Y. W. Lee (L3). In a recent paper (A1), Anderson, Aseltine, Mancini, and Sarture proposed a method which is fairly easy to instrument. The test signal $i(t)$ has amplitude $\pm I$, where I is a constant, and switches from plus to minus, and vice versa, at random intervals. The average rate of switching is many times higher than the servo bandwidth and consequently the spectral density $\Phi_{ii}(j\omega)$ is approximately constant over a few times the servo bandwidth. The saving in instrumentation is seen from the following equation:

$$\phi_{iv}(\tau)_{\text{meas}} \approx \overline{i(t-\tau)v(t)} = \overline{v(t) \times \text{sign of } i(t-\tau)}I$$

Thus a switching circuit triggered by $i(t-\tau)$ can be used instead of a multiplier in obtaining the product $i(t-\tau)v(t)$. The time averaging is done by either a low-pass filter or integration, as discussed in Sec. 7-4. In the device proposed by Anderson, Aseltine, Mancini, and Sarture, a set of delayed signals $i(t-\tau_n)$, $n = 1, 2, \ldots, 12$, is recorded on a multichannel magnetic tape. By applying these signals to trigger different switching circuits, $\phi_{iv}(\tau)$ with 12 different τ's can be obtained simultaneously.

Once $h(\tau)$ or the equivalent $H(j\omega)$ is determined, there remains the question: How do we make use of this information in adjusting the controller of the main servo system? Usually it is necessary to compute from $h(\tau)$ or $H(j\omega)$ the values of some key parameters that we wish to control. One possible criterion is the area ratio suggested by Anderson et al. It is defined as A_+/A_-, where A_+ and A_- are the total positive and negative areas, respectively, under the $h(\tau)$ curve. Since $h(\tau)$ is the time derivative of unit step response, A_+ measures the total upward movement of the unit step response curve, while A_- measures the total downward movement. The area ratio is a good indication of the overshoot or oscillatory tendency of the system. Once we decide upon a certain area ratio $\xi_0 = A_+/A_-$, we can use as the adjustment signal a "figure of merit" F_a defined by

$$F_a = A_+ - \xi_0 A_-$$

A positive F_a indicates that the system is overdamped, and the reverse is true if F_a is negative. F_a can be easily determined from $h(\tau_n)$ by diodes and summing circuits.

Each of the three methods mentioned above has some comparative merits, depending on where applied. The frequency-response method is simplest to use but is limited by the requirement that one must possess more knowledge about the controlled system. For instance, the existence of a minor time constant T with $1/T$ a few times higher than the servo crossover frequency ω_c can change $(C/R)(j\omega)$ very substantially, since ω of the test signal is larger than ω_c.

The impulse-response method is also simple to use, but one must be certain that the desired response characteristics are not masked by the presence of other servo signals. We shall see this in an example later.

The correlation method is more generally applicable, and both the correlation method and frequency-response method are relatively immune to the presence of other servo signals. However, the correlation method introduces a "noise" of its own into the adaptive control loop because over any finite interval $\Phi_{ii}(j\omega)$ cannot be constant on account of the randomness of $i(t)$. These points will be discussed quantitatively in Sec. 11-4.

Of course we can also determine the system response from measurements made on the servo signals already present in the system without the introduction of a test signal. We gain by not causing any disturbance. However, as the presence of such signals cannot be depended upon all the time, the measurements have to be made over a longer period. A comparison between the two alternatives will be given in Sec. 11-4.

10-5. Stability Analysis of the Adaptive Loop. In some applications, the change in system dynamics is relatively slow, and it is possible to detect such change quickly and accurately. Our problem then is to design a simple and stable adaptive loop.

If there is only one closed-loop performance parameter u to be measured, and correspondingly only one adjustable parameter x, the main servo loop can be represented as giving a value of u for each value of x and y:

$$u = u(x,y)$$

where y stands for one or more variable parameters of the plant transfer function. Let u_0 be the desired value of u. One simple way is to adjust x at a rate proportional to $u_0 - u$:

$$\frac{dx}{dt} = K(u_0 - u) \tag{10-17}$$

To analyze the system's stability, let us assume that, after some initial change, y remains constant thereafter. Then

$$\frac{d}{dt}(u_0 - u)^2 = -2(u_0 - u)\frac{du}{dt} = -2(u_0 - u)\frac{\partial u}{\partial x}\frac{dx}{dt}$$

$$= -2K\frac{\partial u}{\partial x}(u_0 - u)^2$$

We note that $(u_0 - u)^2$ decays exponentially as long as K and $\partial u/\partial x$ are of the same sign. We come to the following conclusion: *An adaptive control loop with a rate of adjustment proportional to the measured error in the performance parameter is always stable if* (1) *the time delay in measurement is negligible and* (2) *the performance parameter is a monotonic function of the adjustable parameter.*

Sometimes it is desirable to control more than one response parameter of a system, and we are likely to find that the adaptive control loops are not independent. While the main servo system has a single controlled variable, the adaptive controller has a number of interdependent variables. It is possible, of course, to separate the various adaptive loops physically at the cost of a computer of varying degrees of complexity, depending on the application. But such a computer is usually unnecessary since most likely the adaptive control loop can be stabilized by some simple means without it.

To analyze the situation, we have in general a set of adjustable parameters $x_1, x_2, \ldots, x_n$; a set of variable system parameters $y_1, y_2, \ldots, y_m$; and a set of response parameters $u_1, u_2, \ldots, u_p$. The main servo system gives u's as functions of x's and y's.

$$u_i = u_i(x_1, \ldots, x_j, \ldots, x_n; y_1, \ldots, y_k, \ldots, y_m)$$

For any given set of values of y's $(y_{1a}, y_{2a}, \ldots, y_{ma})$ which may occur under actual operating conditions, there is a set of values of x's $(x_{1a}, x_{2a}, \ldots, x_{na})$ such that the desired response characteristics can be met:

$$u_i = u_{i0}, \ldots \qquad i = 1, 2, \ldots, p \qquad (10\text{-}18)$$

We note that the existence of a set $x_{1a}, x_{2a}, \ldots, x_{na}$, to satisfy Eq. (10-18) for any possible set $y_{1a}, y_{2a}, \ldots, y_{ma}$ is simply another way of saying that we must provide an adequate range of adjustment so that the desired operating point is not out of range. As an example, consider the second-order system shown in Fig. 10-6. Its closed-loop response is given by Eq. (10-16), and both ζ and ω_n are to be controlled. This is done by introducing tachometer feedback $K_f s$, as shown in Fig. 10-6, and adjusting the loop gain pot K_1 and feedback constant K_f. In terms of the more general terminology, K_1 and K_f are the adjustable parameters

x_1 and x_2. The constants K_a, K_T, J, and η are variable system parameters y_1, y_2, y_3, and y_4; ω_n and ζ are the response parameters u_1 and u_2. Obviously, the adjustable ranges of K_1 and K_f must be large enough to yield desired values of ω_{n0} and ζ_0 for whatever combination of values of K_a, K_T, J, and η may occur in practice; otherwise, the realization of ω_{n0} and ζ_0 is not possible.

As the set of values y_1, y_2, . . . , y_m vary gradually with time, the set x_1, x_2, . . . , x_n which satisfy Eq. (10-18) also vary with time. Let the

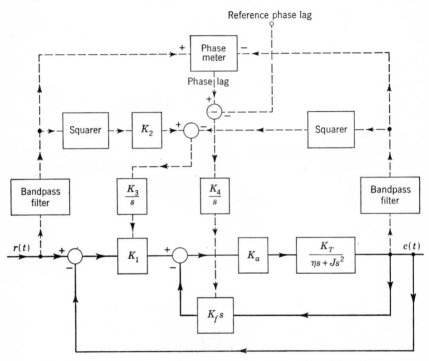

FIG. 10-6. Block diagram of a servo system with controlled ζ and ω_n.

latter set be denoted x_{10}, x_{20}, . . . , x_{n0}. The adaptive controller is designed so that the actual parameters x_1, x_2, . . . , x_n tend to approach x_{10}, x_{20}, . . . , x_{n0}. A block diagram of the adaptive loop is shown in Fig. 10-7, where

$$e_i = x_{i0} - x_i \qquad i = 1, 2, \ldots , n \qquad (10\text{-}19)$$
$$a_i = u_{i0} - u_i \qquad i = 1, 2, \ldots , p \qquad (10\text{-}20)$$

The auxiliary servo is usually linear and can be expressed by the Laplace transform equations:

$$X_i(s) = \sum_j H_{ij}(s) A_j(s) \qquad i = 1, 2, \ldots , n \qquad (10\text{-}21)$$

For small errors, the relation between a_i and e_j can be linearized:

$$a_i = \sum_j B_{ij}e_j \qquad (10\text{-}22)$$

where

$$B_{ij} = \frac{\partial u_i}{\partial x_j}$$

The partial derivatives are evaluated for the present values of y_1, y_2, . . . , y_m and corresponding values of x_{10}, x_{20}, . . . , x_{n0}. We note that as y_1, y_2, . . . , y_m are functions of time, the coefficients B_{ij} are also functions of time, and an exact analysis can be difficult. However, we can always approximate the y's by a series of step changes, and within each step, the y's can be treated as constants. If the adaptive system behaves satisfactorily for all possible values of y, it behaves satisfactorily for the step approximation of y's, which is not substantially different from the

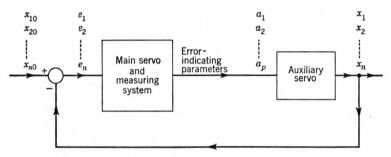

FIG. 10-7. Generalized block diagram of a system with multiple controlled parameters.

actual situation. On the other hand, if the adaptive system is unstable or unsatisfactory in some other way for a possible y set, the adaptive system needs redesigning, because the y's may take on that set of values for some length of time.

The system response can be readily analyzed in matrix notation. Let $\mathbf{X}$, $\mathbf{X}_0$, $\mathbf{A}$, and $\mathbf{E}$ denote column matrices

$$\mathbf{X}(s) = \begin{vmatrix} X_1(s) \\ X_2(s) \\ \cdots \cdot \\ X_n(s) \end{vmatrix}$$

and $\mathbf{H}(s)$ and $\mathbf{B}$ denote rectangular matrices with $H_{ij}(s)$ and B_{ij} as their respective elements. Equations (10-19), (10-21), and (10-22) can be written as

$$\mathbf{E}(s) = \mathbf{X}_0(s) - \mathbf{X}(s) \qquad (10\text{-}23)$$
$$\mathbf{X}(s) = \mathbf{H}(s)\mathbf{A}(s) \qquad (10\text{-}24)$$
$$\mathbf{A}(s) = \mathbf{BE}(s) \qquad (10\text{-}25)$$

From the above equations, $X(s)$ can be solved:

$$X(s) = H(s)BE(s) = H(s)B[X_0(s) - X(s)]$$

Therefore, $$X(s) = [1 + H(s)B]^{-1}H(s)BX_0(s)$$ (10-26)

For arbitrary nonsingular matrices U and V, we have $U^{-1}V = (V^{-1}U)^{-1}$. Using this relation, Eq. (10-26) can be written as

$$X(s) = \{[H(s)B]^{-1} + 1\}^{-1}X_0(s)$$ (10-27)

Let $\Gamma_{ij}(s)$ denote the matrix element of $\Gamma(s) = [H(s)B]^{-1} + 1$, $\bar{\Gamma}_{ij}(s)$ denote the cofactor of $\Gamma_{ij}(s)$, and $\Delta(s)$ denote the determinant. The response $X_i(s)$ due to an input $X_{j0}(s)$ can be written as

$$X_i(s) = \frac{\bar{\Gamma}_{ji}(s)}{\Delta(s)} X_{j0}(s)$$ (10-28)

The poles of $\bar{\Gamma}_{ji}(s)$ are canceled by the poles of $\Delta(s)$. The closed-loop poles are simply roots of $\Delta(s)$. If all the roots of $\Delta(s)$ are in the LHP, the system is stable.

Example 10-4. The above general analysis will be applied to the system illustrated in Fig. 10-6. Instead of measuring ω_n and ζ directly, the gain and phase shift of the system at some $\omega_1 > \omega_{n0}$ are measured. It is assumed that either there is appreciable random noise power at this frequency or, alternatively, a test signal of frequency ω_1 is applied to the input. Two identical filters and amplitude detectors are used at the input and output ends, and K_2 is set at the theoretical gain at ω_1:

$$K_2 = G_0 = \left[\left(\frac{\omega_1^2}{\omega_{n0}^2} - 1\right)^2 + \frac{4\zeta_0^2\omega_1^2}{\omega_{n0}^2}\right]^{-\frac{1}{2}}$$ (10-29)

Let I_1 denote the average power of the filtered signal at the input end; then the gain error signal is

$$a_1(t) = I_1(K_2 - G)$$ (10-30)

where G is the magnitude of the actual $(C/R)(j\omega_1)$ of the main servo system. The error signal $a_1(t)$ is applied to an auxiliary servo which adjusts K_1 of the gain control pot upward at a rate equal to K_3a_1. The phase lag ϕ of $(C/R)(j\omega_1)$ is measured by a phase meter and compared with the theoretical value of $\phi_0 = \pi - \tan^{-1}[2\zeta_0\omega_1\omega_{n0}/(\omega_1^2 - \omega_{n0}^2)]$. The phase error signal is applied to a second auxiliary servo to tune K_f upward at the rate $K_4(\phi_0 - \phi)$.

In terms of the general analysis, G and ϕ take the places of u_1 and u_2; K_1 and K_f take the places of x_1 and x_2. From Fig. 10-6,

$$\frac{C}{R}(s) = \frac{1}{1 + 2\zeta s/\omega_n + s^2/\omega_n^2}$$ (10-31)

where $$\omega_n^2 = \frac{K_1K_TK_a}{J}$$ (10-32)

$$\zeta = \frac{\omega_n}{2}\left(\frac{K_f}{K_1} + \frac{\eta}{K_1K_TK_a}\right)$$ (10-33)

From Eq. (10-31),

$$\log G = -\frac{1}{2} \log \left[\left(1 - \frac{\omega_1^2}{\omega_n^2}\right)^2 + \frac{4\zeta^2 \omega_1^2}{\omega_n^2} \right] \tag{10-34}$$

$$\phi = \pi - \tan^{-1} \frac{2\zeta \omega_1/\omega_n}{\omega_1^2/\omega_n^2 - 1} \tag{10-35}$$

From Eqs. (10-32) to (10-35) B_{ij} can be evaluated:

$$B_{11} = \frac{\partial G}{\partial K_1} = \frac{\partial G}{\partial \zeta} \frac{\partial \zeta}{\partial K_1} + \frac{\partial G}{\partial \omega_n} \frac{\partial \omega_n}{\partial K_1}$$

$$= \frac{G^3 \omega_1^2}{K_1 \omega_n^2} \left[\left(\frac{\omega_1^2}{\omega_n^2} - 1\right) + 4\zeta^2 \right] \tag{10-36}$$

$$B_{12} = \frac{\partial G}{\partial K_f} = -\frac{2G^3 \zeta \omega_1^2}{K_1 \omega_n} \tag{10-37}$$

$$B_{21} = \frac{\partial \phi}{\partial K_1} = -\frac{2G^2 \zeta \omega_1}{K_1 \omega_n} \tag{10-38}$$

$$B_{22} = -\frac{G^2 \omega_1}{K_1} \left(\frac{\omega_1^2}{\omega_n^2} - 1\right) \tag{10-39}$$

The matrix $\mathbf{H}(s)$ is given by

$$H_{11}(s) = \frac{I_1 K_3}{s} \tag{10-40}$$

$$H_{12}(s) = H_{21}(s) = 0 \tag{10-41}$$

$$H_{22}(s) = -\frac{K_4}{s} \tag{10-42}$$

It is assumed that the time constants introduced by the bandpass filter and detection filter are negligible. These time constants are of the order of a few times $1/\omega_1$ and are small compared with the time constants of the adaptive servo. As a numerical example, let $\omega_1 = 2\omega_{n0}$, and $\zeta = 0.707$. The various constants are

$$K_2 = G_0 = \frac{1}{\sqrt{17}} = 0.243$$

$$\phi_0 = 136.7°$$

$$\mathbf{B} = \begin{pmatrix} \dfrac{0.286}{K_1} & -\dfrac{0.0403\omega_1}{K_1} \\ -\dfrac{0.166}{K_1} & -\dfrac{0.176\omega_1}{K_1} \end{pmatrix} \tag{10-43}$$

$$\mathbf{H}(s)\mathbf{B} = \frac{1}{K_1 s} \begin{pmatrix} 0.286 I_1 K_3 & -0.0403\omega_1 I_1 K_3 \\ 0.166 K_4 & 0.176\omega_1 K_4 \end{pmatrix} \tag{10-44}$$

$$\mathbf{H}(s)\mathbf{B}^{-1} = K_1 s \begin{pmatrix} \dfrac{3.08}{I_1 K_3} & \dfrac{0.706}{K_4} \\ -\dfrac{2.91}{\omega_1 I_1 K_3} & \dfrac{5.0}{\omega_1 K_4} \end{pmatrix} \tag{10-45}$$

$$\Delta(s) = 1 + \left(\frac{3.08}{I_1 K_3} + \frac{5.0}{\omega_1 K_4}\right) K_1 s + \frac{17.5 K_1^2 s^2}{I_1 K_3 \omega_1 K_4} \tag{10-46}$$

The adaptive system is obviously stable, no matter what the constraints are. For any step changes in J, η, K_T, and K_a, which result in step changes δ_1 and δ_2 for the theoretical values of K_1 and K_f, respectively, the transient variations of K_1 and K_f

are given by the following equations:

$$(\delta K_1)(s) = \frac{1 + 5K_1s/\omega_1 K_4}{\Delta(s)}\frac{\delta_1}{s} - \frac{0.706K_1\delta_2}{K_4\Delta(s)} \tag{10-47}$$

$$(\delta K_f)(s) = \frac{1 + 3.08K_1s/I_1K_3}{\Delta(s)}\frac{\delta_2}{s} + \frac{2.91K_1\delta_1}{\omega_1 I_1 K_3\Delta(s)} \tag{10-48}$$

The value of K_1 on the right-hand side of the above equations is understood to be the one value that yields ω_{n0} and ζ_0 for the present values of J, η, K_T, and K_a.

If, in Example 10-4, the measurements are made on J, η, K_T, and K_a instead of the closed-loop response at ω_1, the adaptive control is open-loop. While such a system appears simpler on paper, it is much more difficult to instrument than the simple integrations specified by Eqs. (10-40) to (10-42) of Example 10-4.

10-6. Systems Using a Model. Sometimes the dynamics of the controlled system varies too fast for accurate measurement at servo signal frequencies, and we can make the system's response insensitive to such variations by the use of a model in conjunction with adaptive control.

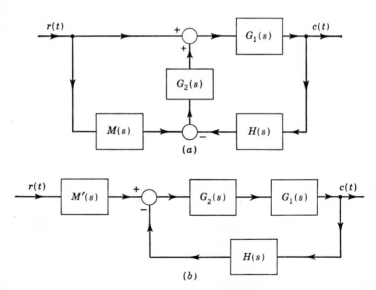

FIG. 10-8. Block diagrams showing conditional feedback (a) and its equivalent (b).

The original idea of using a model was due to Lang and Ham (L1). In Fig. 10-8a, $H(s)$ represents the transfer function of the measuring instruments and is approximately 1 at frequencies for which $M(j\omega)$ is appreciably different from zero, and $G_2(s)$ is a high-gain element. The idea is that any difference between $C(s)$ and $R(s)M(s)$ is negatively fed back through $G_2(s)$, thus forcing the system's response to $R(s)M(s)$. Another interpretation is obtained from the equivalent block diagram of Fig. 10-8b. With very high gain in $G_2(s)$, the system's response is approximately $M'(s) \cong M(s)$, since $1/G_2(s)$ is negligible and $H(s)$ is close to unity.

Theoretically, if there is no noise in the measuring instrument, no load disturbance, and no nonminimum phase or transportation lag in $G_1(s)$, we can introduce a sufficient number of zeros in $H(s)G_2(s)$ to attract all the poles of $G_1(s)$ to these zeros and make the gain of $G_2(s)$ so high that the system's response to $R(s)$ is completely dominated by $M(s)$. However, because of the presence of the aforementioned effects, this approach is not always feasible. Fleischer developed an optimum-linear-design

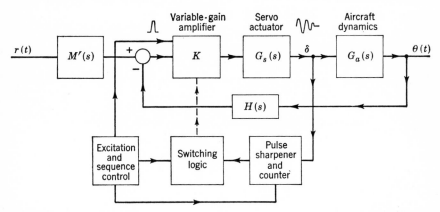

FIG. 10-9. Essential components of an aircraft-pitch control system employing a model and adaptive control of closed-loop stability.

procedure to achieve the best compromise in the least-square-error sense between the system's sensitivity to plant variations on one hand and the aforementioned effects on the other. Because of space limitation, we shall not treat the subject here but refer interested readers to Fleischer's paper.†

Another approach is to adjust the gain of $G_2(s)$ so that the system is just about to oscillate at high frequency. There are a number of ingenious ways of doing this, as published in the *Proceedings of the Self-adaptive Flight Control Systems Symposium*, January, 1959, at Wright Air Development Center. Among these, S. S. Osder (O1) described a method which holds some promise of generality and will be discussed here in its essence.

Figure 10-9 is a block diagram representing the system. The con-

† Paul E. Fleischer, Optimum Design of Passive-Adaptive, Linear Feedback Systems with Varying Plants, *IRE paper* 60 AC-12, 1960; "Synthesis of Linear Control Systems with Low Sensitivity to Plant Variations," D. Eng. Sc. thesis, New York University, June, 1961.

trolled variable is the pitch angle θ, and δ is the elevator or control surface displacement. Without counting the model $M'(s)$, the main servo loop consists of K, $G_s(s)$, $G_a(s)$, and $H(s)$. Its pole-zero pattern is shown in Fig. 10-10. The pitch-control dynamics of a rigid aircraft is represented by poles at P_0, P_1, and P_2 and a zero at z_1. (In Osder's paper, P_0 is replaced by a pair of poles and a zero near the origin. This would happen if we take into consideration the difference in vertical height between the center of weight and center of wing force in the derivation of Sec. 4-7. However, with the loop gain that we are considering, one of the poles goes

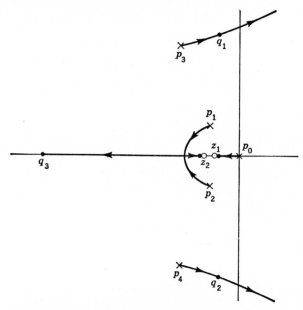

Fig. 10-10. Root loci of aircraft-pitch control system.

very near the zero, and the result is practically the same as a pole P_0 at the origin only.) The poles P_3 and P_4 are due to a second-order servo actuator, and z_2 is due to a lead term in $H(s)$. If we make the gain sufficiently large but not so large as to cause the system to be unstable, the closed-loop system has poles at q_1, q_2, q_3 which are far away from the origin and pole-zero pairs at z_1 and z_2. The system's response from input to θ is approximately $M'(s)/H(s)$. However, such a critical gain value is difficult to maintain without adaptive control since the aircraft's surface effectiveness can vary as much as 10:1 or more, because of wide variations in speed and altitude.

There are also large variations in the positions of P_1 and P_2. One may argue for canceling out the servo poles by a lead network and making the loop gain high enough so that, even with the least surface effectiveness, the aircraft and network poles are either very near a zero or far away from the origin. However, at high speed and low altitude, the loop gain becomes too high, and other minor time constants such as gyro poles and poles due to elastic aircraft structure are liable to show up and cause the system to be unstable. One cannot expect to introduce sufficient lead networks to cancel out all these poles without leaving the system wide open to jamming by instrument noise and load disturbance.

Osder's adaptive control consists of the following:

1. Applying a pulse of narrow width periodically at the input of the variable gain amplifier

2. Counting the output oscillations of the servo actuator with amplitudes exceeding a preset threshold level by a pulse counter

3. Adjusting the gain at a rate according to the count following each pulse

The circuitry gives a slow decrease in gain at a count of three, a relatively fast decrease at a count of four, and a fast decrease at a count of five. The gain is increased if two successive counts of less than two are registered. Thus his logical circuitry tends to keep the count of significant oscillations at two. As shown in Fig. 10-10, the two high-frequency oscillatory poles are kept approximately at q_1 and q_2.

In summary, the use of a model or inner feedback loop in a self-optimizing system has two distinct advantages:

1. The presence of an inner loop or model automatically makes the system's response less sensitive to plant variations.

2. It elevates the critical frequency at which the system's response is measured. The relatively low power content of servo signals at these high frequencies and the fact that measurement is made at high frequency reduce the time required for accurate measurement by at least an order of magnitude. Thus the system is capable of tracking relatively fast variations in controlled system dynamics.

10-7. Optimalizing Control Methods. The "optimalizing" control methods originated by Draper and Li are perhaps the earliest work on extremal sensing systems.† These methods are easy to instrument and are effective in the slow tracking situation. They are:

1. Sensitivity-signal-input optimalizing controllers
2. Continuous-test-signal optimalizing controllers
3. Output-sampling optimalizing controllers
4. Peak-holding optimalizing controllers

† This material is condensed from C. S. Draper and Y. T. Li, "Principles of Optimalizing Control Systems and an Application to the Internal Combustion Engine" (D7). The terminology is modified to be in line with the rest of the book.

In Fig. 10-11a, the sensitivity of merit m to parameter x is defined as dm/dx. If we increase x when dm/dx is positive and decrease x when dm/dx is negative, x would converge to x_0. All the methods 1 to 3 operate on this principle, and their differences are in the way dm/dx is measured.

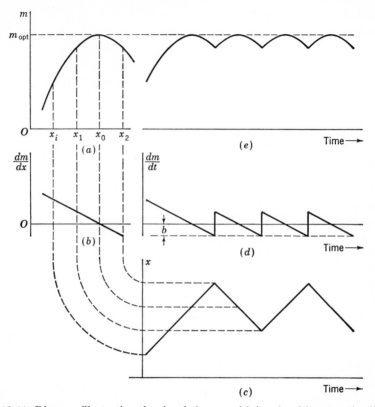

FIG. 10-11. Diagram illustrating the signals in a sensitivity-signal-input optimalizing controller. (*Redrawn from Fig. 11, C. S. Draper and Y. T. Li, "Principles of Optimalizing Control Systems and an Application to the Internal Combustion Engine," American Society of Mechanical Engineers, New York, 1951.*)

Case 1. Optimalizing Systems of Types 1 and 3. In a sensitivity-signal-input optimalizing system, the parameter x is adjusted at a constant rate a, either in one direction or the other:

$$\frac{dx}{dt} = \pm a \tag{10-49}$$

The rate dm/dt is measured. If dm/dt is positive, zero, or not sufficiently negative, x is continually adjusted in the same direction. If dm/dt falls below some preset limit $-b$, where $b > 0$, the direction of adjustment of x

is then reversed, and dm/dt becomes positive again.   The block diagram of the system is illustrated in Fig. 10-12.   The system merit is measured and differentiated to obtain a signal proportional to dm/dt.

When dm/dt is sufficiently negative, it operates a reversing relay to reverse the direction of the adjustor drive.   The operation of the system is illustrated in Fig. 10-11.   If it is assumed that the random variance in measured m is negligible and the initial value of x is x_i, at this point dm/dx is considerably larger than b/a.   If the adjustor drive is in the direction of increasing x initially, dm/dt is positive, and it stays in this position.   If the adjustor drive is in the direction of decreasing x initially, dm/dt is negative and larger in magnitude than b.   The reversing relay immediately operates, and the adjustor drive is again in the direction of increasing x.   As x increases, dm/dx decreases until x_2 is reached, at which point $dm/dx = -b/a$ and the reversing relay operates.   The adjustor drive reverses direction, and x is reduced until x_1 is reached. Afterwards the system hunts between x_1 and x_2.   Figure 10-11a illustrates m versus x; Fig. 10-11b illustrates dm/dx versus x; and Fig. 10-11c, d, and e illustrate x, dm/dt, and m versus time, respectively.

As the value of x hunts between the two limits x_1 and x_2, the averaged value of m is lower than its optimum value.   This difference is called

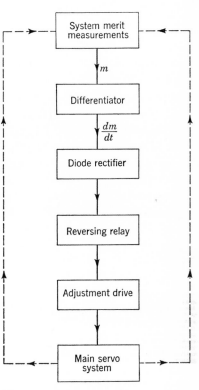

FIG. 10-12. Block diagram of a sensitivity-signal-input optimalizing controller.

hunting loss.   It can be calculated as follows: For small deviations from the optimum value, $m(x)$ can be expanded into a Taylor series.   The first two nonvanishing terms are

$$m = m_{opt} - \frac{m''}{2}(x_0 - x)^2 \qquad (10\text{-}50)$$

Between reversals, dx/dt is constant, and the time-averaged value of $(x_0 - x)^2$ is

$$\overline{(x_0 - x)^2} = \tfrac{1}{3}(x_0 - x_1)^2 \qquad (10\text{-}51)$$

Equation (10-50) gives

$$m_{opt} - \bar{m} = \frac{m''}{6}(x_0 - x_1)^2 = \frac{1}{3}(m_{opt} - m_1) \qquad (10\text{-}52)$$

where m_1 is the value of m at $x = x_1$. Another way of writing the hunting loss is to express it in terms of b. Differentiating m with respect to x and setting $x = x_1$,

$$\frac{b}{a} = m''(x_0 - x_1) \qquad (10\text{-}53)$$

Substituting Eq. (10-53) in (10-52), we obtain

$$m_{opt} - \bar{m} = \frac{b^2}{6m''a^2} \qquad (10\text{-}54)$$

The hunting loss is proportional to b^2. The smaller the margin b we give to dm/dt before reversing, the smaller is the hunting loss. However, if we set b at too low a value, the random variation in measured dm/dt alone is sufficient to cause the reversing relay to operate. Its operation then becomes erratic. The choice of b is therefore a matter of compromise, tolerating either more hunting loss or more erratic operation.

The choice of adjustor speed a is likewise determined by conflicting requirements. The random variations in measured m are of relatively high frequency. If not sufficiently filtered before entering into the differentiating operation, such random variations are greatly exaggerated by differentiation. The filter introduces a time lag which makes the filtered value of m, and consequently dm/dt, represent past data rather than present data. The error so introduced rises sharply with increasing a and is an effect which has not been considered in deriving Eq. (10-54). On the other hand, a system with larger a is better able to cope with the tracking situation.

Output-sampling optimalizing controllers derive dm/dt in a different way. The value of measured m is averaged over one sampling period to give a sampled value of m. The difference between two such successive samples is $T\, dm/dt$, where T is the sampling period. Otherwise the system is entirely the same as the sensitive-signal-input optimalizing controllers. The process of averaging over one sampling period is, in effect, filtering, and taking the difference between two successive samples is equivalent to differentiation. The random variances in sampled m are reduced as T is increased. However, there is a total time lag of one sampling period in the computed value of dm/dt. The considerations in selecting the constants a and b are the same as before.

In both types of systems, the initial settling period is inversely proportional to the adjustor speed a. One way of shortening this period for large initial displacements is to make dx/dt proportional to dm/dx:

$$\frac{dx}{dt} = K_1 \frac{dm}{dx} \tag{10-55}$$

Since

$$\frac{dm}{dt} = \frac{dm}{dx} \frac{dx}{dt} \tag{10-56}$$

dm/dx can be eliminated between Eqs. (10-55) and (10-56):

$$\frac{dx}{dt} = \pm \sqrt{K_1 \frac{dm}{dt}} \tag{10-57}$$

The sign of dx/dt is always so selected as to make dm/dt positive. Equation (10-57) is fairly simple to instrument.

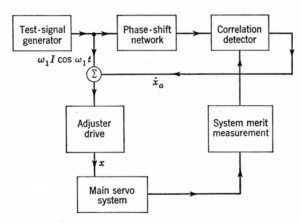

FIG. 10-13. Block diagram of continuous-test-signal optimalizing controller.

Next, we shall study the behavior of the system under the condition of negligible random variance and time delay in measured dm/dt. Differentiating Eq. (10-50),

$$\frac{dm}{dx} = m''(x_0 - x) \tag{10-58}$$

Substituting Eq. (10-58) in (10-55) gives

$$\frac{dx}{dt} = K_1 m''(x_0 - x) \tag{10-59}$$

The solution of Eq. (10-59) is

$$x_0 - x = (x_0 - x_i)e^{-K_1 m''t} \tag{10-60}$$

The parameter error reduces exponentially with the characteristic time constant $1/K_1 m''$.

Case 2. Optimalizing Systems of Type 2. Figure 10-13 illustrates the essential components of a continuous-test-signal optimalizing controller.

A sinusoidal test signal is superimposed on the slowly varying component x_a of x:

$$x = x_a + I \sin \omega_1 t \qquad (10\text{-}61)$$

where ω_1 is the test-signal frequency in radians per second and I is the test-signal amplitude. The amplitude I is small compared with the adjustable range of x. Ideally the test-signal frequency ω_1 satisfies two conditions:

1. ω_1 is very low compared with the operating-frequency range of the main servo system, so that, in determining the merit m of the main servo system, x can be considered as a constant parameter. Consequently m is a function of x only.

2. ω_1 is high compared with the frequency range of x_a, so that the test signal can be considered as a carrier signal in the auxiliary loop.

Expanding $m(x)$ about x_a into a Taylor series,

$$m(x) = m(x_a) + m'(x_a)(x - x_a) + \tfrac{1}{2}m''(x_a)(x - x_a)^2 + \cdots \qquad (10\text{-}62)$$

Substituting $I \sin \omega_1 t$ for $x - x_a$, we see that the only sinusoidal component of frequency ω_1 in the first three terms is from the second term:

$$m'(x_a) I \sin \omega_1 t$$

The higher-order terms can be neglected because of the smallness of I. The signal is applied to the correlation detector, and the output from the latter is $K_d m'(x_a)$, where $m'(x_a)$ is the derivative dm/dx evaluated at $x = x_a$, and K_d is a known constant.

As is usually the case, condition 1 is not strictly followed, and there is a slight time delay in measured m from the instantaneous value of x. Its effect is to introduce a small phase lag ϕ in Eq. (10-62). The phase-shift network in Fig. 10-13 compensates this phase lag as well as any other incidental phase shift of the test signal in the system. For instance, if the adjustor drive of Fig. 10-13 is a rate servo which varies x at a rate proportionate to its input, the resulting integration process introduces a phase lag of 90° in the test signal. The phase-shift network retards the phase of the reference signal by $90° + \phi$ to compensate for the combined effect.

The above discussions show how dm/dx can be measured by introducing a sinusoidal test signal. It is a direct measurement, since the measured quantity is independent of the rate of adjustment dx_a/dt. The signal can be utilized to adjust x, as shown in Fig. 10-13, with K_1/s as the transfer function of the adjustor drive. We have

$$\frac{dx_a}{dt} = K_1 K_d m'(x_a) = K_1 K_d m''(x_0 - x_a) \qquad (10\text{-}63)$$

The second equality sign is obtained from Eq. (10-58). Solving Eq. (10-63), the result is

$$x_0 - x_a = (x_0 - x_i)e^{-K_1 K_d m''t} \tag{10-64}$$

where x_i is the initial value of x_a. Equation (10-64) represents exponential decay with a time constant $1/K_1 K_d m''$.

Under steady-state conditions, $x_a = x_{opt}$, and the hunting loss is

$$m_{opt} - \bar{m} = \frac{m''}{2} \overline{(x_0 - x)^2} = \frac{m''}{4} I^2 \tag{10-65}$$

The hunting loss is proportional to the square of the test-signal amplitude I. However, because of random variations in measured m, I cannot be made too small. The situation is essentially the same as in cases 1 and 3.

Case 3. Optimalizing Systems of Type 4. From the previous discussions, we see that optimalizing systems of types 1 and 3 require differentiating the measured system merit m, a process which accentuates the random variations. The continuous-test-signal optimalizing controllers are relatively advantageous since no differentiation is necessary. The peak-holding system is still better from this standpoint, because it integrates the decline of m from a measured peak value.

The operation of the system is explained with the help of Fig. 10-14. At the beginning of the operation, the value of x is x_i. It is then increased at a constant rate a. The highest measured value of m is recorded in a holding system. If m is going up, the new peaks are recorded. If m is going down, the recorded peak value does not change; however, the deviation from the peak value is integrated with respect to time to obtain a reverse signal. Whenever a new peak value of m is established, the previous reverse signal is erased to minimize the effect of spurious signals. When the reverse signal reaches a preset limit b, the direction of adjustment of x is reversed. The established peak value as well as the reverse signal is simultaneously erased with the reversal of the adjustor drive. Thus everything starts over again.

In Fig. 10-14 the heavy curve shows the expected value of m, but because of random variations the thin curve is measured as the value of x increases linearly with t. The broken curve shows the recorded peak value of m. The area between the broken curve and the thin curve represents the reversing signal. Its value as a function of t is plotted in Fig. 10-14c. At time $t = t_1$, the reversing signal has accumulated to the preset limit b, and thereafter x decreases with t at a constant rate. The value of x hunts back and forth about its optimum value x_0.

In case the random variations in measured m are negligible, Eq. (10-52) expressing the hunting loss as one-third of the hunting zone still

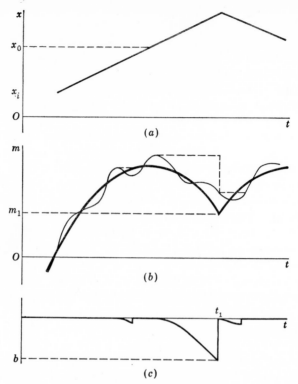

FIG. 10-14. Diagram showing signals in a peak-holding system. (a) Adjustable parameter x versus time; (b) expected and measured m versus time; (c) reversing signal versus time.

holds. In terms of a and b, it is readily shown that

$$b = \frac{m''}{6a} (x_0 - x_1)^3$$

Therefore

$$m_{opt} - \bar{m} = \left(\frac{m''}{6} a^2 b^2 \right)^{\frac{1}{3}} \tag{10-66}$$

As before, the selection of b is determined by considerations of hunting loss and false reversing signal; the selection of a is determined by the time delay in measuring m.

10-8. Summary. The preceding sections give a review of the principle and types of self-optimizing systems in existence or having been proposed. Although it is not all-inclusive, the main species are represented. One way to characterize these systems is as follows:

1. The system operates under a changing situation.
2. The system has a set of adjustable parameters.
3. The ultimate purpose is to keep a set of system-performance parame-

ters at specified or extremal values by automatically adjusting the set of adjustable parameters.

To be more specific, the changing situation may represent a change in the statistical properties of the inputs, either desired or undesired, or a change in the transfer function of the controlled plant. The performance parameters to be kept at specified values may be system bandwidth, damping factor, or mean-square value of control effort. The performance parameters to be kept at extremal values may be engine efficiency, per cent yield in a chemical process, the mean-square value of system error, etc.

There are two types of signal flow in such a control system. The main servo controller receives an input signal and exercises direct control over the plant operation. For any particular setting of the adjustable parameters in the main servo controller, it operates in exactly the same way as an ordinary feedback control system. Simultaneously present is an auxiliary path of signal flow solely for the purpose of making adjustments on the adjustable parameters. This measuring and adjusting operation is a control system in itself and is referred to as adaptive control loop.

The adjustments may be based on two types of data:

1. Measurements on a changing situation
2. Measurements on performance parameters

If data of type 1 are used, the adaptive control is an open-loop system. If data of type 2 are used, the adaptive control is a closed-loop system, as the adjustments change the performance parameters on which the adjustments are based. Consequently, the latter type has all the inherent advantages of a closed-loop system: it is self-correcting and can be instrumented with relatively less hardware.

The successful operation of a self-optimizing system depends on finding a quick and accurate way of detecting any change in the situation or performance parameters. In systems where the main concern is to keep the closed-loop response unchanged while the plant dynamics undergo wide variations, a model or inner feedback loop can be used to advantage in conjunction with adaptive control of the system's stability. The measurement problem is then reduced to a simpler one: that of measuring the closed-loop stability at high frequencies where little servo signal is present instead of direct measurements at servo frequencies.

The methods of analysis and design of self-optimizing systems introduced in the present chapter are limited by one condition: that some means of fast and accurate measurement on the system can be found. When this condition cannot be safely assumed, the design of the adaptive control loop is no longer a simple problem but will be the subject matter of the next chapter.

CHAPTER 11

STOCHASTIC PROCESSES AND OPTIMUM DESIGN
OF ADAPTIVE CONTROL

11-1. Introduction. The preceding chapter on self-optimizing systems is concerned with applications where accurate and fast enough measurements of the situation or performance parameters can be made. The lack of this condition does not necessarily mean that self-optimization will not work but rather that a more careful process of analysis and design is necessary in order to gain most from the self-optimizing operation.

Some of the general problems are as follows:

1. *Measurement.* As a stochastic signal of one form or another is present, the probable error in measurement is large if a very short interval is used. On the other hand, if a long interval is used, the measured result, which is a product of a past situation, would not adequately reflect the present situation. A compromise in the promptness and accuracy has to be made. What represents the best compromise?

2. *Adjustment.* The adjustment is of future operation while it is based on present and past data only. Furthermore, the data are inaccurate because of the compromise mentioned in problem 1. Considering all these factors, the current data are not necessarily the sole criteria for adjustment in an optimum system. What weights should be assigned to previous data in computing the required adjustments?

3. *Evaluation.* Given a statistical description of the changing situation and the probable error in measurement, how close can one hold the performance parameters to specified values or to their respective extremal values?

Preliminary to a solution of these problems is a criterion for the best adaptive control system. For extremal seeking systems, a natural criterion is the difference between the extremal value and the average value of the performance parameter. For systems that regulate a performance parameter to a specified value, the mean-square value of the deviation is used.

In this chapter, the random errors in measuring signal properties and transfer functions are discussed. While these constitute only very limited domains in the entire realm of measurements, they are nevertheless quite representative of the stochastic processes encountered.

A solution of problems 2 and 3 is given for systems which base their adjustment operations on a directly measured performance parameter. The situation parameters are not known or measured. The approach is as follows: Given the values of the interval and probable error of measurement and some statistical description of the changing situation, the optimum weighting factors on present and past data are determined. The deviation from the extremal value or the mean-square deviation from the given value is then calculated. It is the lowest obtainable for a given method of measurement. To solve problem 1, that of the best method of measurement and the optimum T to use, one has to know the dependence of the probable measuring error on T, which is different from one problem to another. However, when this dependence and the solution of 3 are known, the solution of problem 1 becomes a matter of calculus.

11-2. Assumption of Approximate Stationarity in Identification Problems. One common problem in adaptive control systems is to determine quickly and accurately the statistical properties of the signals and transfer functions of the systems in the presence of various disturbances. Strictly speaking, transfer functions and spectral densities are not defined for systems that are not stationary. However, if the time interval in which appreciable change takes place is much larger than the correlation times of the signals or response times of the systems, we may define spectral densities and plant transfer functions in an approximate sense to reflect the immediate situation. Mathematically it is assumed that, in the interval $t - \Delta < t' < t + \Delta$, the correlation function $\phi_{12}(t, t + \tau)$ satisfies

$$\phi_{12}(t, t + \tau) \cong \phi_{12}(t', t' + \tau) \tag{11-1}$$

where Δ is a time interval many times larger than τ_m, the largest τ for which ϕ_{12} is substantially different from zero. Consequently, we may use time average instead of ensemble average to determine $\phi_{12}(\tau)$, and the approximate spectral-density function $\Phi_{12}(s)$ is then the Laplace transform of $\phi_{12}(\tau)$. Of course $\phi_{12}(\tau)$ and $\Phi_{12}(s)$ depend on t in the long run. A similar situation holds for time-varying systems if its impulse-response function satisfies $h(t', t' - \tau) \cong h(t, t - \tau)$.

In the following analysis we assume that the averaging interval is short enough so that the measured quantity has not changed appreciably during the time of measurement, and the error is due only to the finiteness of the measuring interval.

Sometimes a certain amount of prior knowledge about the measured quantity is assumed. This knowledge can always be used to advantage in reducing either the required time of measurement or the probable error.

11-3. Determination of Power Spectrum of Signal $i(t)$. We shall analyze two situations:

1. $\Phi_{ii}(j\omega)$ is completely unknown. In such a case, the rms value of the per-unit error is given by Eq. (7-15):

$$\epsilon = \frac{1}{\sqrt{T\,\Delta f}} \qquad (7\text{-}15)$$

where T is the measuring interval and Δf is the frequency resolution.

2. $\Phi_{ii}(j\omega)$ is known except to a proportionality or magnitude factor. In other words, $\Phi_{ii}(j\omega) = KF(j\omega)$, where $F(j\omega)$ is a known function. Since

$$\phi_{ii}(0) = \frac{1}{\pi}\int_0^\infty \Phi_{ii}(j\omega)\,d\omega = \frac{K}{\pi}\int_0^\infty F(j\omega)\,d\omega \qquad (11\text{-}2)$$

once $\phi_{ii}(0)$ is known, K is determined. If we assume $T \gg \tau_m$, the error in measuring $\phi_{ii}(0)$ in the finite interval T is easily calculated from Eq. (C-15):

$$\langle[\phi_{ii}(0)_{meas} - \phi_{ii}(0)]^2\rangle = \frac{2}{T}\int_{-\infty}^\infty [\phi_{ii}(\tau)]^2\,d\tau \qquad (11\text{-}3)$$

Then
$$\epsilon^2 = \frac{\langle[\phi_{ii}(0)_{meas} - \phi_{ii}(0)]^2\rangle}{[\phi_{ii}(0)]^2}$$

$$= \frac{2\pi\int_0^\infty [\Phi_{ii}(j\omega)]^2\,d\omega}{T\left[\int_0^\infty \Phi_{ii}(j\omega)\,d\omega\right]^2} = \frac{1}{T \times BW} \qquad (11\text{-}4)$$

where BW is the bandwidth of $i(t)$ in cycles per second.

It is interesting to compare Eq. (7-15) with Eq. (11-4). In order to obtain an adequate amount of detail in the measured spectrum, Δf is usually less than one-tenth of the signal bandwidth. The ratio $BW/\Delta f$ represents the advantage of having prior knowledge about the frequency dependence of the power spectrum.

11-4. Determination of the Impulse-response or Transfer Function of a Linear Control Element. Figure 11-1 illustrates a fairly general situation in the experimental determination of the impulse-response function (or transfer function) of a linear control element or system. The input $i(t)$ is either a test signal or a signal that can be measured. The measurable output $v(t)$ is the response to $i(t)$ plus some unknown disturbance $n(t)$, where $n(t)$ represents the equivalent output variation due to

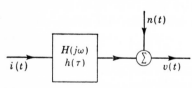

Fig. 11-1. Block diagram for determination of $h(\tau)$ or $H(j\omega)$.

disturbances existing in the measured element and random errors in measuring $i(t)$ and $v(t)$. The signals $i(t)$ and $n(t)$ are uncorrelated. It is obvious that there is no way of separating $n(t)$ from $v(t)$ in a direct determination of $h(\tau)$ with the impulse-response method except by repeating and averaging, which is not an easy thing to do as far as instrumentation is concerned.   The other two methods will now be studied:

1. Correlation measurement with white noise as input, $\phi_{ii}(\tau) = \delta(\tau)$. If the measuring interval is unlimited,

$$\phi_{iv}(\tau) = \int_0^\infty \phi_{ii}(\tau - t')h(t')\,dt' = h(\tau) \tag{11-5}$$

With the measuring interval limited to T, $T \gg \tau_m$, Eq. (C-15) can be used to evaluate the mean-square measuring error:

$$\langle[\phi_{iv}(\tau)_{meas} - \phi_{iv}(\tau)]^2\rangle = \frac{1}{T}\left[\phi_{vv}(0) + \int_{-\infty}^\infty \phi_{iv}(\tau + \tau_1)\phi_{iv}(\tau - \tau_1)\,d\tau_1\right]$$

Owing to Eq. (11-5) and noting that $h(\tau) = 0$ for $\tau < 0$, the above equation can be rewritten as

$$\langle[h(\tau)_{meas} - h(\tau)]^2\rangle = \frac{\phi_{nn}(0)}{T} + \frac{1}{T}\int_0^\infty \{[h(\tau_1)]^2 + h(\tau + \tau_1)h(\tau - \tau_1)\}\,d\tau_1 \tag{11-6}$$

The interesting aspects of Eq. (11-6) are the following:

a. There is a mean-square error of the order τ_m/T even if $\phi_{nn}(0) = 0$. This is due to the randomness of $\phi_{ii}(\tau)$.

b. The mean-square error is proportional to $1/T$.

2. Frequency-response method with a sinusoidal test signal.   Let $I(j\omega)$ and $V(j\omega)$ represent the Fourier transforms of $i(t)$ and $v(t)$ over a finite interval T.   The measured $H(j\omega)$ is obtained as

$$H(j\omega)_{meas} = \frac{V(j\omega)}{I(j\omega)} = H(j\omega) + \frac{N(j\omega)}{I(j\omega)} \tag{11-7}$$

The mean-square error is

$$\langle|H(j\omega)_{meas} - H(j\omega)|^2\rangle = \frac{\langle N(-j\omega)N(j\omega)\rangle}{I(-j\omega)I(j\omega)} \tag{11-8}$$

Let P represent the mean-square amplitude of the input signal.   Then

$$P = \frac{2I(-j\omega)I(j\omega)}{T^2}$$

$$\Phi_{nn}(j\omega) = \frac{2}{T}\langle N(-j\omega)N(j\omega)\rangle$$

Equation (11-8) gives

$$\langle|H(j\omega)_{meas} - H(j\omega)|^2\rangle = \frac{\Phi_{nn}(j\omega)}{TP} \tag{11-9}$$

The measured $H(j\omega)$ is the vector sum of $H(j\omega)$ and a random vector of mean-square amplitude $\Phi_{nn}(j\omega)/TP$ and random phase. Physically, Eq. (11-7) can be carried out in two different ways:

a. A current proportional to $v(t)$ can be applied to an antiresonant circuit of very high Q at frequency ω. If we assume that the circuit is totally discharged at the beginning of T, the voltage across the antiresonant circuit at the end of T has a vector amplitude $V(j\omega)$. Its phase and amplitude are then compared with the known vector $I(j\omega)$.

b. Equation (11-7) can be written as

$$H(j\omega)_{meas} = \frac{I(-j\omega)V(j\omega)}{I(-j\omega)I(j\omega)} \tag{11-10}$$

In Eq. (11-10), $I(-j\omega)I(j\omega)$ is known. The real and imaginary components of $I(-j\omega)V(j\omega)$ can be obtained by integrating the products $i(t)v(t)$ and $\tilde{\imath}(t)v(t)$ for an interval T, where $\tilde{\imath}(t)$ is the same as $i(t)$ with a phase shift of 90° ahead. Since $i(t)$ is a sinusoidal signal, this is not difficult to do.

3. Measurement of $\Phi_{ii}(j\omega)$ and $\Phi_{iv}(j\omega)$ simultaneously for an interval T. The method of measuring $\Phi_{ii}(j\omega)$ and $\Phi_{iv}(j\omega)$ is the same as that discussed in Sec. 7-3. Let us assume that the variation of $H(j\omega)$ in passband $\omega \pm \frac{1}{2} \Delta\omega$ is negligible. Then for all ω' inside the passband

$$V(j\omega') = I(j\omega')H(j\omega) + N(j\omega') \tag{11-11}$$

$$\Phi_{ii}(j\omega)_{meas} = \frac{2}{T \, \Delta f} \sum_{\omega'} I(-j\omega')I(j\omega') \tag{11-12}$$

$$\Phi_{iv}(j\omega)_{meas} = \frac{2}{T \, \Delta f} \sum_{\omega'} I(-j\omega')V(j\omega')$$

$$= \frac{2}{T \, \Delta f} \left[H(j\omega) \sum_{\omega'} I(-j\omega')I(j\omega') + \sum_{\omega'} I(-j\omega')N(j\omega') \right] \tag{11-13}$$

There are $T \, \Delta f$ Fourier components in the frequency range Δf or $\Delta\omega/2\pi$, and the summation signs in Eqs. (11-12) and (11-13) are meant to sum over these components. From these equations we obtain

$$H(j\omega)_{meas} = \frac{\Phi_{iv}(j\omega)_{meas}}{\Phi_{ii}(j\omega)_{meas}}$$

$$= H(j\omega) + \frac{\displaystyle\sum_{\omega'} I(-j\omega')N(j\omega')}{\displaystyle\sum_{\omega''} I(-j\omega'')I(j\omega'')} \tag{11-14}$$

The second term represents an error with random phase. To calculate its mean-square value we write

$$\langle|H(j\omega)_{meas} - H(j\omega)|^2\rangle = \left\langle \frac{\left|\sum\limits_{\omega'} I(-j\omega')N(j\omega')\right|^2}{\left|\sum\limits_{\omega''} I(-j\omega'')I(j\omega'')\right|^2} \right\rangle$$

$$= \sum_{\omega'} \left\langle \frac{|I(j\omega')|^2}{[\sum\limits_{\omega''}|I(j\omega'')|^2]^2} \right\rangle \langle|N(j\omega')|^2\rangle \quad (11\text{-}15)$$

By definition of the spectral density,

$$\langle|N(j\omega')|^2\rangle = \frac{T}{2}\Phi_{nn}(j\omega') = \frac{T}{2}\Phi_{nn}(j\omega) \quad (11\text{-}16)$$

Substituting Eq. (11-16) in (11-15) gives

$$\langle|H(j\omega)_{meas} - H(j\omega)|^2\rangle = \frac{T}{2}\Phi_{nn}(j\omega)\left\langle \frac{1}{\sum\limits_{\omega''}|I(j\omega'')|^2} \right\rangle \quad (11\text{-}17)$$

There are $T\,\Delta f$ terms in the summation over ω''. Let $P_n, n = 1, 2, \ldots$, $T\,\Delta f$, represent $2|I(j\omega'')|^2$ at each ω''. Each term has a density function as given in Eq. (7-13). The assumption

$$\Phi_{ii}(j\omega'') = \Phi_{ii}(j\omega)$$

for all ω'' inside the interval $\omega \pm \Delta\omega/2$ is equivalent to $E_n = E = \Phi_{ii}(j\omega)T$. Then

$$\left\langle \frac{1}{\sum\limits_{\omega''}|I(j\omega'')|^2} \right\rangle = \frac{1}{E^m}\int\!\!\!\int\!\!\!\int\limits_{0}^{\infty}\cdots\int \frac{2}{\sum\limits_{n}P_n} e^{-\sum\limits_{n}P_n/E}\,dP_1\,dP_2\cdots dP_m$$

$$\quad (11\text{-}18)$$

where m is the number of Fourier components in Δf. Since $P_1, P_2, \ldots$, P_m are dummy variables, the integral on the right-hand side of Eq. (11-18) is a function of E only. Let it be denoted as $J(E)$. Then

$$J(0) = 0$$

$$\frac{dJ(E)}{dE} = \frac{2}{E^2}\int\!\!\!\int\!\!\!\int\limits_{0}^{\infty}\cdots\int e^{-\sum\limits_{n}P_n/E}\,dP_1\,dP_2\cdots dP_m$$

$$= \frac{2}{E^2}E^m = 2E^{m-2} \quad (11\text{-}19)$$

Integrating Eq. (11-19) with boundary condition $J(0) = 0$ gives

$$J(E) = \frac{2}{m-1} E^{m-1}$$

Therefore $$\left\langle \frac{1}{\sum_{\omega''} |I(j\omega'')|^2} \right\rangle = \frac{2E^{-1}}{m-1} = \frac{2\Phi_{ii}(j\omega)^{-1}}{T(T\,\Delta f - 1)} \qquad (11\text{-}20)$$

Substituting Eq. (11-20) in (11-17) gives

$$\langle |H(j\omega)_{meas} - H(j\omega)|^2 \rangle = \frac{\Phi_{nn}(j\omega)}{(T\,\Delta f - 1)\Phi_{ii}(j\omega)} \qquad (11\text{-}21)$$

In Eq. (11-21), Δf is the frequency resolution in determining $H(j\omega)$, T is the time of measurement, $\Phi_{ii}(j\omega)$ is the power spectrum of the measurable input signal, and $\Phi_{nn}(j\omega)$ is the power spectrum of the equivalent disturbance at the output end due to unknown inputs (such as load disturbance) and random errors in the measurements.

The signal $i(t)$ may be a test signal already in existence. In the latter case, one must ascertain that $i(t)$ is constantly present and has a fairly consistent power spectrum in the frequency range of measurement.

11-5. The Use of Prior Knowledge in the Determination of $H(j\omega)$. The preceding section gives the basic material in the determination of transfer functions. To see its application to some specific problems, let us consider the following situations:

1. $H(j\omega)$ is completely unknown.
2. $H(j\omega)$ is known except for two parameters.

The problem is to see how much improvement there is in case 2 over case 1 if a test signal is to be used in each case.

For simplicity, let us assume that $H(j\omega)$ is negligible for ω greater than $2\pi f_1$ and that it is required to determine $H(j\omega)$ with frequency resolution Δf and a per-unit mean-square error no more than ϵ^2 within a frequency range 0 to f_1.

For case 1, let T_1 represent the time interval of measurement. Equation (11-21) gives

$$\Phi_{ii}(j\omega) = \frac{\Phi_{nn}(j\omega)}{(T_1\,\Delta f - 1)\epsilon^2 |H(j\omega)|^2}$$

The total disturbance caused by the test signal is

$$\overline{d_1^2} = \int_0^{f_1} \Phi_{ii}(j\omega)|H(j\omega)|^2\,df = \frac{1}{(T_1\,\Delta f - 1)\epsilon^2} \int_0^{f_1} \Phi_{nn}(j\omega)\,df$$

$$= \frac{\Phi_{nn}f_1}{(T_1\,\Delta f - 1)\epsilon^2} \qquad (11\text{-}22)$$

For case 2, it is only necessary to measure $H(j\omega)$ at some ω_2. Then the unknown parameters and $H(j\omega)$ at other ω are determined to approximately the same degree of accuracy. Equation (11-9) gives

$$P_2 = \frac{\Phi_{nn}(j\omega_2)}{T_2\epsilon^2|H(j\omega_2)|^2} \tag{11-23}$$

Since $\overline{d_2^2} = P_2|H(j\omega_2)|^2$, we have from Eqs. (11-22) and (11-23)

$$\frac{\overline{d_1^2}T_1}{\overline{d_2^2}T_2} > \frac{\Phi_{nn}f_1}{\Phi_{nn}(j\omega_2)\,\Delta f} \tag{11-24}$$

The quantity $\overline{d^2}T$ can be called a figure of demerit. For case 2 the figure of demerit is reduced by a factor of $\Delta f/f_1$ times $\Phi_{nn}(j\omega_2)/\overline{\Phi}_{nn}$. The latter ratio represents the advantage of being able to select a frequency at which the noise power is low.

11-6. Stochastic-adjustment Problems. "Stochastic adjustment" means making an adjustment based on data with random error. If some factors about the system are unknown but do not vary with time, the correct settings of the adjustable parameters do not vary with time. Our problem then is to devise a process of adjustment that eventually but unerringly leads to the correct settings. Methods of doing this are called *stochastic-approximation* methods.

Of greater interest to engineers is the *stochastic tracking problem*, in which the system and consequently the correct settings of the adjustable parameters vary with time. Because of the random error in measurement, we can never be completely sure whether an indicated change reflects an actual change of the system or is merely an error in measurement. There is no way of determining the correct settings all the time. Our problem then is to find the best process of adjustment. One way to define "best" is based on the criterion of Sec. 11-1, i.e., least expected difference between the extremal value and actually attained value of the performance parameter for extremal seeking systems and least-mean-square error for systems designed to regulate a performance parameter to a specified value.

In the following analysis the process of measuring and adjusting is assumed discrete. Whenever a performance parameter cannot be computed by continuous analog method, the process has to be discrete. Whenever continuous measurement and adjustment are possible, we may simply carry the analysis over by making the sampling period approach zero.

11-7. Stochastic-approximation Methods. The idea of stochastic approximation was originated in a paper by Robbins and Munro and later generalized to peak-seeking systems by Keifer and Wolfowitz. Before going into the general case, we shall illustrate the underlying idea by a simple example: A certain variable x is to be determined by measurement, and there is a random error δ in the measured value of x (denoted as y):

$$y_i = x + \delta_i \qquad i = 1, 2, \ldots \tag{11-25}$$

The errors δ_i are assumed to be independent for different measurements i, and δ_i has zero mean.

After n measurements, the best estimate of x is

$$x_n = \frac{1}{n} \sum_{i=1}^{i=n} y_i = x + \frac{1}{n} \sum_{i=1}^{i=n} \delta_i \tag{11-26}$$

As n approaches infinity, $\Sigma \delta_i$ approaches $\sqrt{n}\, \delta$ and consequently $x_n - x$ approaches zero.

Another way of looking at Eq. (11-26) is to view it as a successive adjustment process:

$$
\begin{aligned}
x_n &= \frac{1}{n} \sum_{i=1}^{i=n} y_i \\
&= \frac{1}{n} [(n - 1)x_{n-1} + y_n] \\
&= x_{n-1} + \frac{1}{n} (y_n - x_{n-1})
\end{aligned}
\tag{11-27}
$$

After n measurements, our best estimate of x is x_n. However, at the $(n + 1)$st measurement, y_{n+1} is obtained, and some correction has to be made toward y_{n+1}. As the value x_n has the weight of n measurements behind it, we make the coefficient of adjustment smaller as n becomes larger.

The idea can be carried over to the general case. Instead of Eq. (11-25), let m' be the measured value of the performance parameter $m(x)$:

$$m_i' = m(x_i) + \delta_i \qquad i = 1, 2, \ldots \tag{11-28}$$

The variable x is to be adjusted toward a certain unknown setting x_0 which can be defined in two ways:

1. Adjusting for a certain specified m_s:

$$
\begin{aligned}
m(x_0) &= m_s \\
m(x) &> m_s \qquad \text{for } x > x_0 \\
m(x) &< m_s \qquad \text{for } x < x_0
\end{aligned}
\tag{11-29}
$$

2. Adjusting for some unknown peak value of m:

$$m(x_0) > m(x) \qquad \text{for all } x \neq x_0 \tag{11-30}$$

For case 1 we can make successive adjustments on x according to a generalized form of Eq. (11-27):

$$x_{n+1} = x_n + a_n(m_s - m'_n) \qquad n = 1, 2, \ldots \tag{11-31}$$

Let us examine the conditions on the sequence of numbers a_n so that, as $n \to \infty$, x_n converges with probability 1 on x_0.

a. $a_n > 0$. This is to assure that the corrections are to be made in the right direction, on an average.

b. $a_n \to 0$ as $n \to$ infinity. Because of the random variations δ_i in Eq. (11-28), $m_s - m'_n$ is not zero even if $x_n = x_0$. For x_n to converge on any value at all, condition b must be satisfied.

c. $\sum_{n=1}^{n=\infty} a_n^2 \to$ const, or, put in a different way, $\sum_{n=N}^{n=\infty} a_n^2 \to 0$ as N approaches infinity. Condition c is to account for the cumulative effect of δ_i. Equations (11-28) and (11-31) can be combined as

$$x_{n+1} - x_n = -a_n[m(x_n) - m_s] - a_n\delta_n$$

Summing the above equation from $n = N$ upward gives

$$x_\infty - x_N = \sum_{n=N}^{n=\infty} a_n[m_s - m(x_n)] - \sum_{n=N}^{n=\infty} a_n\delta_n \tag{11-32}$$

Equation (11-32) expresses the total variation in x from the Nth step onward. Since

$$\left\langle \left(\sum_{n=N}^{n=\infty} a_n\delta_n \right)^2 \right\rangle = \overline{\delta^2} \sum_{n=N}^{n=\infty} a_n^2 \tag{11-33}$$

condition c assures that the total random variation $\sum_{n=N}^{n=\infty} a_n\delta_n$ approaches zero as N becomes very large.

d. $\sum_{n=1}^{n=\infty} a_n \to \infty$. Conditions a, b, and c assure that x_n converges on some value x_∞. Condition d assures $x_\infty = x_0$. Since condition d also implies $\sum_{n=N}^{n=\infty} a_n \to \infty$, if x_n approaches any value other than x_0, the total corrective effort $\sum_{n=N}^{n=\infty} a_n[m_s - m(x_n)]$ in Eq. (11-32) is infinite. On the other hand, we have no fear of overshoot since each corrective step is very small, because of condition b.

An example of a sequence satisfying conditions a, b, c, and d is $a_n = 1/n$. We note that this is the sequence used in Eq. (11-27).

The above is intended to explain the significances of the conditions

a, b, c, and d on a_n. For a rigorous proof of stochastic approximation, the reader is referred to the paper by Robbins and Munro.

Bertram applied the stochastic-approximation idea to control systems. If the signal part of the input does not change with time, errorless output can be achieved eventually by a process of successively reducing the forward gain of the control system. This can be done with very little knowledge about the controlled system and input-noise statistics.

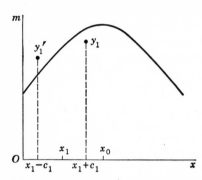

For the peak-seeking case, a satisfactory procedure has been worked out by Keifer and Wolfowitz. The problem is illustrated in Fig. 11-2. The system merit m is a function of a parameter x as given by the solid curve. However, for each measurement, there is a random error δ, and the measured value of system merit, $y = m'$, does not equal m. Let our present estimate of the optimum setting x_0 be denoted by x_1. To improve our estimate, we set x_1 at two different values $x_1 + c_1$ and $x_1 - c_1$ and obtain two readings y_1 and y_1'. Our estimate is shifted in the direction of larger y:

FIG. 11-2. Expected and measured system merit (m and y, respectively) versus adjustable parameter x.

$$x_2 = x_1 + \frac{a_1}{c_1}(y_1 - y_1') \qquad (11\text{-}34)$$

The above processes are repeated with different values of a's and c's:

$$x_{n+1} = x_n + \frac{a_n}{c_n}(y_n - y_n') \qquad n = 1, 2, \ldots \qquad (11\text{-}35)$$

The problem is: Are there two sequences of constants, a_n and c_n, such that in the limit of large n, x_n converges to x_0? The question has been answered in the affirmative under the following rather general assumptions:

1. The function $m(x)$ has no more than a finite number of discontinuities.
2. There is only a single peak of $m(x)$.

The sequences of constants a_n and c_n which give this result are specified by the following:

$$a_n > 0 \qquad c_n > 0 \qquad\qquad (11\text{-}36a)$$
$$a_n \to 0 \qquad c_n \to 0 \qquad \text{as } n \to \infty \qquad (11\text{-}36b)$$
$$\sum \frac{a_n{}^2}{c_n{}^2} < \infty \qquad\qquad (11\text{-}36c)$$
$$\Sigma a_n = \infty \qquad\qquad (11\text{-}36d)$$
$$\Sigma a_n c_n < \infty \qquad\qquad (11\text{-}36e)$$

An example of two such sequences is

$$a_n = \frac{1}{n} \qquad c_n = \frac{1}{\sqrt[3]{n}}$$

An explanation of the above conditions is as follows: The peak seeking is accomplished by finding the point for which $dm/dx = 0$. As $(y_n - y_n')/c_n$ is approximately proportional to dm/dx, it is used in Eq. (11-34) instead of the measured error, $m_s - m(x_n)$. To obtain zero error as $n \to 0$ the excursions c_n for determining dm/dx must approach zero. Conditions (11-36a) to (11-36d) are equivalent to the same conditions in case 1 and are for precisely the same reasons. Condition (11-36e) is to avoid biasing the measurements appreciably when d^2m/dx^2 are not the same as the two sides of the peak.

We note that in the learning situation the method is satisfactory: Not only does x_n approach x_0, but since c_n approaches zero, $x_n \pm c_n$ also approach x_0. After some initial adjustment period, the system operates at the optimum point with vanishing hunting. There is still the problem of the optimum choice of the sequences a_n and c_n such that the speed of convergence to x_0 is fastest. Since there is more than one way of satisfying Eqs. (11-36), which is best?

In the tracking situation, x_0 is a function of time. On the other hand, the sequences specified by Eqs. (11-36) do not allow x_n to change with any finite rate at all, since a_n/c_n approaches zero.

11-8. Basic Assumptions in a Solution of the Stochastic Tracking Problem with Specified m.† In the remainder of the present chapter, we shall study the problem of stochastic adjustment with changing situation parameters. Generally speaking, there are a number of adjustable parameters among which a lesser number are independent. To bring forth the underlying concepts with least mathematics, only one independent adjustable parameter is assumed.

Let α_i, m_i, and x_i denote the situation parameter, performance parameter, and the adjustable parameter, respectively, at the ith measuring interval. The measured performance parameter m_i' can be written as

$$m_i' = m_i(\alpha_1, \alpha_2, \ldots, \alpha_{i-1}, \alpha_i; x_1, x_2, \ldots, x_{i-1}, x_i) + \delta_i \qquad (11\text{-}37)$$

The value of m_i depends on the present as well as previous values of α and x, and δ_i is a random variable representing error in measurement. Let m_s denote the specified value of m_i. A condition representing adequate coverage by x of all possible situations α can be stated as follows: *For every sequence $\alpha_1, \alpha_2, \ldots, \alpha_i$ with nonzero probability, there exists a*

† Sections 11-8 to 11-14, inclusive, are reprinted from a paper by the author, Optimization of the Adaptive Function by Z-transform Method, *Trans. AIEE*, pt. II, July, 1960.

sequence $x_{\alpha 1}$, $x_{\alpha 2}$, . . . , $x_{\alpha i}$ *such that*

$$m_j(\alpha_1, \alpha_2, \ldots, \alpha_{j-1}, \alpha_j; x_{\alpha 1}, x_{\alpha 2}, \ldots, x_{\alpha(j-1)}, x_{\alpha j}) = m_s \quad (11\text{-}38)$$

for all $j = 1, 2, \ldots, i$. This condition is necessary if it is at all possible to hold m_j to the specified value m_s and will be assumed valid.

It will be assumed that the tracking process is fairly good so that $x_{\alpha_i} - x_i$ is small enough for the following approximation to be good:

$$m_i(\alpha_1, \alpha_2, \ldots, \alpha_{i-1}, \alpha_i; x_1, x_2, \ldots, x_i)$$

$$= m_i(\alpha_1, \alpha_2, \ldots, \alpha_i; x_{\alpha 1}, x_{\alpha 2}, \ldots, x_{\alpha i}) + \sum_{j=1}^{i} \left(\frac{\partial m_i}{\partial x_j}\right)_\alpha (x_j - x_{\alpha j}) \quad (11\text{-}39)$$

where the partial derivatives $\partial m_i/\partial x_j$ are evaluated at $x_j = x_{\alpha j}$, $j = 1, 2,$ . . . , i. These derivatives depend on the α's only. Usually the time interval of measurement is larger than the response time of the main servo system, and m_i depends mostly on x_i, slightly on x_{i-1}, and not at all on the previous x's.

As the situation parameter α is unknown, the exact values of the partial derivatives $\partial m_i/\partial x_j$ are not known. The proposed procedure is based on a set of nominal values b_n defined by

$$\left(\frac{\partial m_i}{\partial x_j}\right)_\alpha = b_{i-j} \quad (11\text{-}40)$$

The adjustment procedure is represented by the following equation:

$$x_{i+1} = x_i + \sum_{j=1}^{i} w_{i-j}(m_s - m_j') \quad (11\text{-}41)$$

where w_n, $n = 0, 1, 2, \ldots$, are the weighting factors attached to present and past measurements. The optimum values of w_n are to be determined.

The above assumptions can be summarized as:

1. Condition of adequate coverage: Eq. (11-38).
2. Linearization: Eqs. (11-39) and (11-40) give

$$m_i' = m_s + \sum_{j=1}^{i} b_{i-j}(x_j - x_{\alpha j}) + \delta_i \quad (11\text{-}42)$$

3. Adjustment procedure: Eq. (11-41).

11-9. Z-transform Representation and Optimization. Let the measured difference u_i be defined as

$$u_i = m_s - m_i' \quad (11\text{-}43)$$

Multiplying Eq. (11-42) by z^{-i} and summing over i, it becomes

$$
\begin{aligned}
U(z) + \Delta(z) &= \sum_{i=0}^{\infty} \sum_{j=1}^{i} b_{i-j}(x_{\alpha j} - x_j)z^{-i} \\
&= \sum_{j=0}^{\infty} \sum_{i-j=0}^{\infty} b_{i-j}z^{-(i-j)}(x_{\alpha j} - x_j)z^{-j} \\
&= B(z)[X_\alpha(z) - X(z)] \quad\quad (11\text{-}44)
\end{aligned}
$$

where $U(z)$, $\Delta(z)$, $B(z)$, $X_\alpha(z)$, $X(z)$ are the corresponding z transforms. Multiplying Eq. (11-41) by z^{-i-1} and summing over i, it becomes

$$
X(z) = z^{-1}X(z) + z^{-1}W(z)U(z) \quad\quad (11\text{-}45)
$$

where $W(z)$ is the z transform of the weighting factors. Equation (11-45) can be rewritten as

$$
X(z) = \frac{z^{-1}}{1 - z^{-1}} W(z)U(z) \quad\quad (11\text{-}46)
$$

Equations (11-44) and (11-45) are represented by the block diagram of Fig. 11-3.

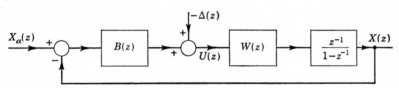

FIG. 11-3. Block diagram of the adaptive control loop. *(From S. S. L. Chang, Optimization of the Adaptive Function by Z-transform Method, Trans. AIEE, pt. II, July, 1960.)*

In Fig. 11-3, the only unknown function is $W(z)$. This function is to be selected such that

$$
D \equiv \overline{(m_s - m_i)^2} = \min \quad\quad (11\text{-}47)
$$

Let $\bar{u}_i$ represent $m_s - m_i$. Equation (11-44) gives

$$
\bar{U}(z) = B(z)[X_\alpha(z) - X(z)] \qu\quad\quad (11\text{-}48)
$$

Equations (11-47) and (11-48) and Fig. 11-3 specify the optimization problems completely. Using the method of Sec. 6-8, we obtain

$$
W(z) = \frac{(z - 1)K(z)}{B(z)[1 - K(z)]} \qu\quad\quad (11\text{-}49)
$$

where $K(z)$ is the closed-loop system function of the adaptive control loop. Its optimum form is

$$
K(z) = \frac{1}{Y(z)} \left[\frac{B(z)B(z^{-1})\Phi_{x_\alpha x_\alpha}(z)}{Y(z^{-1})} \right]_i \qu\quad\quad (11\text{-}50)
$$

In Eq. (11-50), $Y(z)$ is defined by the following two conditions:

1.

$$Y(z)Y(z^{-1}) = B(z)B(z^{-1})\Phi_{x_\alpha x_\alpha}(z) + \Phi_{\delta\delta}(z) \tag{11-51}$$

2. All the poles and zeros of $Y(z)$ are inside the unit circle.

The symbol [ ]$_i$ is defined as follows: Any rational function $Q(z)$ can be expressed as

$$Q(z) = \sum_j \frac{A_j}{z - a_j} + \sum_j \frac{B_j}{z - b_j} + \text{polynomial in } z$$

where $|a_j| \leq 1$ and $|b_j| > 1$.   Then

$$[Q(z)]_i \equiv \sum_j \frac{A_j}{z - a_j} \tag{11-52}$$

From $K(z)$, D can be calculated as

$$D(z) = \frac{1}{2\pi j} \oint \{B(z)B(z^{-1})\Phi_{x_\alpha x_\alpha}(z)[1 - K(z)][1 - K(z^{-1})]$$
$$+ K(z)K(z^{-1})\Phi_{\delta\delta}(z)\} \frac{dz}{z} \tag{11-53}$$

Example 11-1.   Sometimes the operating situation changes in sudden steps.   Correspondingly, x_α is also steplike, and its power spectrum can be approximated as

$$\Phi_{x_\alpha x_\alpha}(s) = \frac{2\nu C_1}{\nu^2 - s^2}$$
$$\Phi_{x_\alpha x_\alpha}(z) = \frac{C(1 - e^{-2\nu T})}{(1 - e^{-\nu T}z^{-1})(1 - e^{-\nu T}z)} \tag{11-54}$$

The random errors in successive measurements are assumed to be independent.

$$\Phi_{\delta\delta}(z) = \Delta \tag{11-55}$$

where Δ is the mean-square value of δ_i.   In case the response time of the main servo system is small compared with T, the constants b_n are approximately

$$b_0 = b \qquad b_i = 0 \qquad \text{for all } i \neq 0 \tag{11-56}$$

The optimum weighting factors w_i and minimum value of D are to be determined.
Solution.   By definition,

$$Y(z)Y(z^{-1}) \equiv \frac{b^2 C_1(1 - e^{-2\nu T})}{(1 - e^{-\nu T}z^{-1})(1 - e^{-\nu T}z)} + \Delta$$
$$= \frac{M^2(1 - az^{-1})(1 - az)}{(1 - e^{-\nu T}z^{-1})(1 - e^{-\nu T}z)} \tag{11-57}$$

where the constant a is given by

$$a + \frac{1}{a} = 2\cosh \nu T + \frac{2b^2 C_1}{\Delta}\sinh \nu T \tag{11-58}$$
$$a < 1$$

and the constant M is given as

$$M^2 = \frac{b^2 C_1 (1 - e^{-2\nu T})}{(1 - ae^{-\nu T})(1 - ae^{\nu T})} \tag{11-59}$$

It follows from Eq. (11-57) and condition (2) that

$$Y(z) = \frac{M(1 - az^{-1})}{1 - e^{-\nu T}z^{-1}} \tag{11-60}$$

From Eqs. (11-52), (11-54), (11-59), and (11-60) we obtain

$$\left[\frac{B(z)B(z^{-1})\Phi_{x_\alpha x_\alpha}(z)}{Y(z^{-1})}\right]_i = \frac{M(e^{-\nu T} - a)}{z - e^{-\nu T}} \tag{11-61}$$

Equations (11-50), (11-60), and (11-61) give

$$K(z) = \frac{(e^{-\nu T} - a)z^{-1}}{1 - az^{-1}} \tag{11-62}$$

Knowing that $K(z)$, $W(z)$, and D are calculated according to Eqs. (11-49) and (11-53), the results are

$$W(z) = \frac{(e^{-\nu T} - a)(1 - z^{-1})}{b(1 - e^{-\nu T}z^{-1})} \tag{11-63}$$

$$D = \left(\frac{1}{a}e^{-\nu T} - 1\right)\Delta \tag{11-64}$$

In case of perfect measurement, $\Delta = 0$. However, as $1/a$ becomes infinity, the value D is indeterminate. To evaluate this limit, let Δ be an arbitrarily small value ϵ, and Eq. (11-58) gives

$$\frac{1}{a} = \frac{2b^2 C_1}{\epsilon} \sinh \nu T \tag{11-65}$$

Substituting Eq. (11-65) into (11-64), we obtain

$$D_0 \equiv \lim_{\Delta \to 0} D = b^2 C_1 (1 - e^{-2\nu T}) \tag{11-66}$$

D_0 represents the probable error involved in predicting the operating situation of the next period.

Next the weighting factors w_i are calculated. Since

$$W(z) = \sum_{i=0}^{\infty} w_i z^{-i}$$

Eq. (11-63) gives

$$w_0 = \frac{e^{-\nu T} - a}{b}$$

$$w_n = -w_0(e^{\nu T} - 1)e^{-n\nu T} \qquad n = 1, 2, 3, \ldots \tag{11-67}$$

To facilitate further discussion, two numerical examples are calculated. The given values and calculated results are listed in Table 11-1.

TABLE 11-1. TWO NUMERICAL CASES

	Case 1	Case 2
Given values:		
νT..............	0.1	0.01
Δ..............	$0.2b^2C_1$	$0.2b^2C_1$
Calculated values:		
a..............	0.380	0.729
D..............	$0.276b^2C_1$	$0.0714b^2C_1$
D_0..............	$0.182b^2C_1$	$0.0198b^2C_1$

The constant b^2C_1 is the mean-square variation in m without adaptive control. It is used here to gauge the mean-square error in measurement as well as the effectiveness of the adaptive control loop. The deviation function D_0 for the ideal situation of perfect measurement is also listed for comparison. In case 1, the variations in operating situation are relatively fast, and one cannot effectively reduce the measuring error by averaging over a number of past samples and still keep up with the changing situation. In case 2, Δ is ten times larger than D_0, and some averaging can be done to reduce the random measuring error.

A surprising fact about Eq. (11-67) is that the weighting factors on past data are negative. However, in close examination of Fig. 11-3 one notices that these weighting factors represent only the immediate contribution. The total contribution of $U(z)$ to the value of $X(z)$ is given as

$$V(z) \equiv \sum_n v_n z^{-n} \equiv \left[\frac{X(z)}{U(z)} \right]_{\text{closed loop}} = \frac{e^{-\nu T} - a}{b} \frac{z^{-1}}{1 - az^{-1}}$$

Therefore, $v_0 = 0$

$$v_n = \frac{e^{-\nu T} - a}{b} a^{n-1} \qquad n = 1, 2, 3, \ldots \qquad (11\text{-}68)$$

The factor V_n gives the total effect of a measured change of one unit at the ith interval on the value of x at the $(i + n)$th interval and will be called the effective weighting factor. In Fig. 11-4, the immediate (solid line) and effective (broken line) weighting factors are plotted for case 1.

Another interesting feature of the system can be illustrated by its transient response to a step input in x_α, if it is assumed that $\Delta(z) = 0$.

$$X_\alpha(z) = \frac{1}{1 - z^{-1}}$$

$$X(z) = K(z)X_\alpha(z) = \frac{(e^{-\nu T} - a)z^{-1}}{(1 - az^{-1})(1 - z^{-1})}$$

$$x_0 = 0$$

$$x_n = (e^{-\nu T} - a)(1 + a + a^2 + \cdots + a^{n-1}) = \frac{(e^{-\nu T} - a)(1 - a^n)}{1 - a}$$

$$(11\text{-}69)$$

The unit step response is plotted in Fig. 11-5. It gradually approaches a final value of 0.847 instead of unity. The reason is that, since the next value of x_α is uncorrelated to its present value, the impending change in x_α is more likely to be in the opposite direction. The adaptive controller does not go all the way in anticipation of this change.

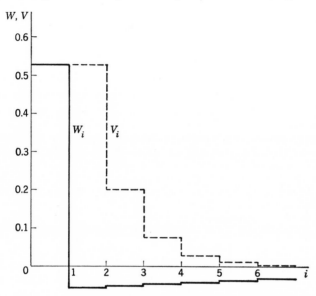

FIG. 11-4. The weighting factors w_i (solid line) and effective weighting factors v_i (broken line) in units of $1/b$. *(From S. S. L. Chang, Optimization of the Adaptive Function by Z-transform Method, Trans. AIEE, pt. II, July, 1960.)*

11-10. Reduction to Continuous Case. Reduction to a continuous case is possible, whenever the variations in situation parameter α are slow enough for the following two effects to be negligible:

1. The adjustment delay of one measuring interval
2. The graininess of a finite number of measured values being weighted or filtered in arriving at an incremental value of x

For instance, case 1 is definitely discrete. A continuous approximation would be too erroneous to be useful. Case 2 is at the borderline region. An indication is that its first four or five effective weighting factors u_i have substantial values.

If we assume the effects 1 and 2 to be small, Eqs. (11-41) and (11-42) become

$$m'(t) = m_s + \int_0^t b(t - \tau)[x(\tau) - x_\alpha(\tau)]\, d\tau + \delta(t) \qquad (11\text{-}70)$$

$$\frac{dx(t)}{dt} = \frac{x_{i+1} - x_i}{T} = \int_0^t w(t - \tau)[m_s - m'(\tau)]\, d\tau \qquad (11\text{-}71)$$

where in the limit of $T \to 0$, $n \to \infty$, and $nT = \tau$

$$b(\tau) = b(nT) = \frac{b_n}{T} \tag{11-72}$$

$$w(\tau) = w(nT) = \frac{w_n}{T^2} \tag{11-73}$$

Let $u(\tau) \equiv m_s - m'(\tau)$. Equations (11-70) and (11-71) can be written as

$$U(s) = B(s)[X_\alpha(s) - X(s)] - \Delta(s) \tag{11-74}$$
$$sX(s) = W(s)U(s) \tag{11-75}$$

Equations (11-74) and (11-75) are represented by the block diagram of Fig. 11-6.

The special density $\Phi_{\delta\delta}(s)$ can be derived as follows: If each measurement is assumed to be independent, the correlation function $\phi_{\delta\delta}(\tau)$ is a tri-

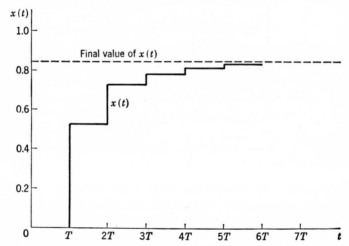

FIG. 11-5. Transient response of the adaptive control loop to unit step at $t = 0$. (*From S. S. L. Chang, Optimization of the Adaptive Function by Z-transform Method, Trans. AIEE, pt. II, July, 1960.*)

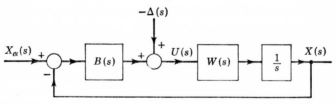

FIG. 11-6. Continuous approximation of a system with slowly varying situation. (*From S. S. L. Chang, Optimization of the Adaptive Function by Z-transform Method, Trans. AIEE, pt. II, July, 1960.*)

angular pulse with height Δ and base $2T$. Therefore

$$\Phi_{\delta\delta}(s) = \int_{-\infty}^{\infty} \phi_{\delta\delta}(\tau)e^{-s\tau}\, d\tau = T\Delta \tag{11-76}$$

The method of Chap. 4 can be used for the subsequent optimization calculations.

11-11. Basic Assumptions of Extremal Seeking Systems. The parameters α_i, m_i, x_i, m_i', δ_i are defined as before. The performance parameter m_i is assumed to depend on α_i and x_i only, and

$$m_i' = m_i(\alpha_i, x_i) + \delta_i \tag{11-77}$$

In contrast to the previous case, m_i is to be held at either an unknown maximum or minimum, depending on the problem. With no loss of generality, it is assumed here that m_i is held at a maximum.

The condition representing adequate coverage is stated as follows: *For every α_i, there exists an x_{α_i} such that*

$$m_i(\alpha_i, x_{\alpha_i}) = \text{max} = m_{opt} \tag{11-78}$$

The optimum value m_{opt} is not known. Equation (11-78) defines x_{α_i}. It is further assumed that the tracking process is fairly good so that $x_{\alpha_i} - x_i$ is small enough for the following approximation to be good:

$$m_i(\alpha_i, x_i) = m_i(\alpha_i, x_{\alpha_i}) + \frac{1}{2}\left(\frac{\partial^2 m_i}{\partial x_i^2}\right)_\alpha (x_{\alpha_i} - x_i)^2 \tag{11-79}$$

A nominal value $-b'$ is selected for the second derivative $(\partial^2 \bar{m}_i/\partial x_i^2)_\alpha$, and Eq. (11-79) becomes

$$m_i(\alpha_i, x_i) = m_{opt} - \frac{b'}{2}(x_{\alpha_i} - x_i)^2 \tag{11-80}$$

The desired result is a procedure for adjusting x_i so that

$$D = \overline{m_{opt} - m_i} = \frac{b'}{2}\overline{(x_{\alpha_i} - x_i)^2} = \text{min} \tag{11-81}$$

One characteristic aspect of extremal sensing systems is the hunting procedure. Even with negligible measuring error δ, one has no way of telling whether m_i is at its peak without introducing some intentional variation in x. The manner in which this variation is made is called the *hunting procedure.*

With reference to Sec. 10-7, Draper and Li have suggested a number of hunting procedures in their work. However, one of their basic assumptions appears to be that the performance parameter can be measured instantaneously and that this measured value depends only on the present value of x. In a relatively fast-varying system, if one makes the measuring interval long enough so that the measured m is sufficiently independent of α and x outside this interval, the measurements can no longer be considered continuous since α is likely to change substantially within a few such intervals.

Two hunting procedures which recognize the discrete nature of the problem will be analyzed:

1. *Derivative Sensing.* The adjustable parameter x of a typical derivative-sensing system is illustrated in Fig. 11-7a. At the end of the

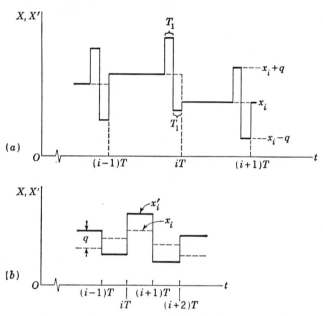

Fig. 11-7. Best estimate of adjustable parameter setting x_i (broken line) and actual adjustable parameter setting x_i' (solid line) of the two types of extremal seeking systems. (a) Derivative sensing; (b) alternative biasing. (*From S. S. L. Chang, Optimization of the Adaptive Function by Z-transform Method, Trans. AIEE, pt. II, July,* 1960.)

ith interval, x is adjusted to $x_i + q$ and $x_i - q$ in succession for smaller intervals T_1, and the subsequent x_{i+1} is determined by $m_{i1}' - m_{i2}'$ measured at the two intervals T_1, as well as all such previous measurements. This method is currently in use in the chemical industry to optimize yield with satisfactory results. However, for systems with relatively fast changing situations, the following proposed method would be preferable.

2. *Alternative Biasing.* The best estimate of the adjustable parameter x_α is illustrated by the broken lines in Fig. 11-7b. However, instead of using this estimated value x_i, the actual x_i' is adjusted to $x_i \pm q$, which

is illustrated by the solid lines. One obvious advantage of this method is that measured data at every interval are utilized on an equal footing.

11-12. Analysis of Derivative Sensing Systems. The changes in x_α and m_{opt} between the two measuring intervals T_1 are assumed negligible. From Eqs. (11-77) and (11-80),

$$m_{i1}' = m_{opt} - \frac{b'}{2}(x_{\alpha_i} - x_i - q)^2 + \delta_{i_1}$$

$$m_{i2}' = m_{opt} - \frac{b'}{2}(x_{\alpha_i} - x_i + q)^2 + \delta_{i_2}$$

The difference of the two equations is

$$m_{i1}' - m_{i2}' = 2b'q(x_{\alpha_i} - x_i) + \delta_{i_1} - \delta_{i_2} \qquad (11\text{-}82)$$

The correction in x_i is given as the weighted sum of all previously measured differences:

$$x_{i+1} = x_i + \sum_{j=0}^{j=i} w_{i-j}(m_{j_1}' - m_{j_2}') \qquad (11\text{-}83)$$

Equations (11-82) and (11-83) are identical with Eqs. (11-41) and (11-42) if we let

$$u_i = m_{i_1}' - m_{i_2}'$$
$$\delta_i = \delta_{i_2} - \delta_{i_1}$$
$$b_0 = 2b'q \qquad b_i = 0 \qquad \text{for all } i \neq 0$$

Consequently, all the analytical results of the preceding section hold.

The average reduction in m is

$$D = \frac{b'}{2T}(T - 2T_1)\overline{(x_{\alpha_i} - x_i)^2} + \frac{b'T_1}{2T}[\overline{(x_{\alpha_i} - x_i - q)^2} + \overline{(x_{\alpha_i} - x_i + q)^2}]$$

$$= \frac{b'}{2}\overline{(x_{\alpha_i} - x_i)^2} + \frac{b'T_1q^2}{T} \qquad (11\text{-}84)$$

From optimum $K(z)$, the value of $\overline{(x_{\alpha_i} - x_i)^2}$ can be calculated. The result is a decreasing function of q. Equation (11-84) implies that D is at a minimum for a certain value of q which can be determined by setting $dD/dq = 0$.

Example 11-2. The power spectra of x_α and δ are given as

$$\Phi_{x_\alpha x_\alpha} = \frac{C_1'}{(1 - z^{-1})(1 - z)} \qquad (11\text{-}85)$$

$$\Phi_{\delta\delta}(z) = 2\Delta \qquad (11\text{-}86)$$

Determine D, q, and $W(z)$.

NOTE: Equation (11-85) represents independent step-like variations in the operating situation, and Eq. (11-86) can be explained as the result of independent measurements with mean-square error Δ for each measurement of period T_1.

Solution. The result of the preceding section gives

$$K(z) = \frac{(1-a)z^{-1}}{1-az^{-1}} \qquad W(z) = \frac{1-a}{2b'q} \tag{11-87}$$

$$a + \frac{1}{a} = 2 + \frac{2b'^2 q^2 C_1'}{\Delta} \tag{11-88}$$

$$\overline{(x_{a_i} - x_i)^2} = \frac{\Delta}{2b'^2 q^2}\left(\frac{1}{a} - 1\right) \tag{11-89}$$

Solving q^2 in terms of a from Eq. (11-88),

$$q^2 = \frac{\Delta}{2b'^2 C_1'} \frac{(1-a)^2}{a} \tag{11-90}$$

From Eqs. (11-89) and (11-90), Eq. (11-84) can be written as

$$D = \frac{b'C_1'}{2(1-a)} + \frac{T_1\Delta}{2b'TC_1'} \frac{(1-a)^2}{a} \tag{11-91}$$

In Eq. (11-91) only a depends on q. For optimum q, dD/da is equated to zero, and the result is

$$\frac{a^2}{(1-a)^2(1-a^2)} = \frac{T_1\Delta}{Tb'^2 C_1'^2} \equiv \eta \tag{11-92}$$

The second equality sign defines the parameter η.

For optimum choice of q, Eq. (11-91) can be written as

$$D = \frac{b'C_1'}{2} f_D \tag{11-93}$$

where

$$f_D = \frac{1 + 2a}{1 - a^2} \tag{11-94}$$

Equation (11-90) can be rewritten as

$$q^2 = \frac{TC_1'}{2T_1} \frac{a}{1 - a^2} \equiv \frac{TC_1'}{2T_1} f_q \tag{11-95}$$

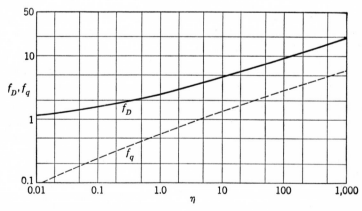

FIG. 11-8. The functions f_D and f_q versus η. (*From S. S. L. Chang, Optimization of the Adaptive Function by Z-transform Method, Trans. AIEE, pt. II, July, 1960.*)

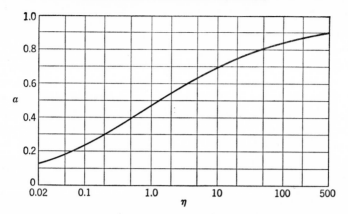

FIG. 11-9. The parameter a versus η. (*From S. S. L. Chang, Optimization of the Adaptive Function by Z-transform Method, Trans. AIEE, pt. II, July, 1960.*)

From Eqs. (11-92), (11-94), and (11-95), η, f_D, and f_q are calculated. The functions f_D and f_q are plotted against η in Fig. 11-8, and a is plotted against η in Fig. 11-9. In a design problem, η is calculated from given data. The minimum value of D, together with the values of q and a to be used, is read from these curves.

11-13. Analysis of Alternative-biasing Systems. For an alternative-biasing system, let the actually applied x'_i be

$$x'_i = x_i + (-1)^i q \tag{11-96}$$

Then
$$m'_i = m_{opt} - \frac{b'}{2}[x_{\alpha_i} - x_i - (-1)^i q]^2 + \delta_i \tag{11-97}$$

The signal $(-1)^i m'_i$ is used for adjustment of x_i and will be denoted by u_i.

$$x_{i+1} = x_i + \sum_{j=0}^{j=1} w_{i-j} u_j \tag{11-98}$$

$$u_i = (-1)^i m'_i = b' q(x_{\alpha_i} - x_i) + (-1)^i \delta_i$$
$$+ (-1)^i \left[m_{opt} - \frac{b'}{2} q^2 - \frac{b'}{2}(x_{\alpha_i} - x_i)^2 \right] \tag{11-99}$$

Except for the terms in brackets, Eqs. (11-98) and (11-99) are identical with Eqs. (11-41) and (11-42) and $b = b'q$. In the brackets, m_{opt} is a slowly varying term, $(b'/2)q^2$ is a constant, $(b'/2)(x_{\alpha_i} - x_i)^2$ is small and always positive. If these terms can be approximated by a constant C_2, the additional disturbance is

$$\delta'_i = (-1)^i C_2$$

and its z transform is

$$\delta'(z) = \frac{C_2}{1 + z^{-1}}$$

Suppose that a filtering factor $1 + z^{-1}$ is introduced in $W(z)$. The disturbance δ' is filtered out except for the initial period $i = 1$. Since the adaptive control loop must be stable, its impulse response is a vanishing function of t. The disturbance due to δ'_i becomes vanishingly small except for the first few sampling periods immediately after turning on the adaptive controller. Allowing a warm-up period, one may assume that, by introducing a filtering factor $1 + z^{-1}$ in $W(z)$, the effect of the terms in brackets on D can be neglected. This point can be verified by a step-by-step calculation.

To summarize the above, Fig. 11-3 gives a fairly good approximation of an alternative-biasing system with the additional requirement that $1 + z^{-1}$ is a factor in the numerator of $W(z)$.

To determine the optimum form of $W(z)$, let

$$K(z) = z^{-1}(1 + z^{-1})F(z) \tag{11-100}$$

where $F(z)$ is an unknown function with all its poles inside the unit circle. The point $z = -1$ is treated as a point outside the unit circle. The method of Sec. 6-8 gives

$$K(z) = \frac{1 + z^{-1}}{Y(z)} \left[\frac{\Phi_{x_\alpha x_\alpha}(z)}{(1 + z^{-1})Y(z^{-1})} \right]_i \tag{11-101}$$

where $Y(z)$ is defined by

$$Y(z)Y(z^{-1}) \equiv \Phi_{x_\alpha x_\alpha}(z) + \frac{\Phi_{\delta\delta}(z)}{b^{-2}q^2} \tag{11-102}$$

and $\bar\Phi_{\delta\delta}(z)$ is the sampled spectrum of $(-1)^i\delta_i$.

$$\overline{(x_{\alpha_i} - x_i)^2} = \frac{1}{2\pi j} \oint \left\{ [1 - K(z)][1 - K(z^{-1})]\Phi_{x_\alpha x_\alpha}(z) \right.$$
$$\left. + \frac{K(z)K(z^{-1})}{b'^2 q^2}\bar\Phi_{\delta\delta}(z) \right\} \frac{dz}{z} \tag{11-103}$$

$$D = \frac{b'}{2}\overline{(x_\alpha - x_i)^2} + \frac{b'}{2}q^2 \tag{11-104}$$

Example 11-3. Assuming the same power spectra as given in Example 11-2, determine optimum $W(z)$, q, and D.

Solution. Since the successive samples of δ_i are uncorrelated,

$$\bar\Phi_{\delta\delta}(z) = \Phi_{\delta\delta}(z) = \Delta$$

Equation (11-101) gives

$$K(z) = \frac{(1 - a)z^{-1}(1 + z^{-1})}{2(1 - az^{-1})} \tag{11-105}$$

$$W(z) = \frac{(1 - a)(1 + z^{-1})}{2b'q\{1 + [(1 - a)/2]z^{-1}\}} \tag{11-106}$$

where

$$a + \frac{1}{a} = 2 + \frac{b'^2 q^2 C'_1}{\Delta} \tag{11-107}$$

Following the same steps as Example 11-2, the results are

$$\overline{(x_{\alpha_i} - x_i)^2} = \frac{5 - a}{4(1 - a)} C_1' \tag{11-108}$$

$$\eta \equiv \frac{\Delta}{C_1'^2 b'^2} = \frac{a^2}{(1 - a^2)(1 - a)^2} \tag{11-109}$$

$$D = \frac{b'C_1'}{2} \frac{5 + 8a - a^2}{4(1 - a^2)} = \frac{b'C_1'}{2} (f_D + \tfrac{1}{4}) \tag{11-110}$$

$$q^2 = C_1' \frac{a}{1 - a^2} = f_q C_1' \tag{11-111}$$

where f_D and f_q are the same functions as defined in Eqs. (11-94) and (11-95). Given η, the values of f_D, f_q, and a can be read from Figs. 11-8 and 11-9.

11-14. Comparison of the Two Types of Extremal Seeking Functions.
The two types of extremal seeking systems can be compared on the basis of equal $\Phi_{x_\alpha x_\alpha}(s)$, measuring interval T_1, and Δ. For a derivative-sensing system, T is much larger than T_1 and will be assumed at least $4T_1$ for the present purpose. For an alternative-biasing system, $T = T_1$. For instance, let the following values be assumed:

$$\nu = \frac{0.025}{T_1}$$
$$\Delta = 0.1b'^2 C_1^2$$

The calculated results are listed in Table 11-2.

TABLE 11-2. COMPARISON OF EXTREMAL SEEKING SYSTEMS

	Derivative $T = 4T_1$	Sensing systems $T = 10T_1$	Alternative biasing $T = T_1$
C_1'	$0.2C_1$	$0.5C_1$	$0.05C_1$
η	0.625	0.04	40
f_D	2.20	1.36	7.05
f_q	0.51	0.17	2.15
a	0.42	0.17	0.79
q^2	$0.204C_1$	$0.42C_1$	$0.107C_1$
D	$0.22b'C_1$	$0.34b'C_1$	$0.182b'C_1$

Table 11-2 shows clearly the advantage of an alternative-biasing system. Not only is its deviation function D lower, the advantage of which is clear, but its lower value of test bias q is also a desirable feature. A lower value of q means less disturbance to the system.

11-15. Summary. The problem of measurement and adjustment in the presence of an appreciable amount of random disturbance is studied.

Two types of measurements are of direct concern to control engineers: measurement of statistical properties of input signals and measurement of transfer functions (or impulse-response functions). For both types the integral-square measuring error is approximately inversely proportional to the time of measurement. Much less time is needed or much less error is obtained if some a priori knowledge of the measured quantity is used.

A study is then made on the optimum utilization of measured data to make adjustments in a self-optimizing system. A basic assumption is that there is a value of the adjustable parameter x_α which gives the desired result in every interval. The desired result is to keep a certain performance parameter either at a prescribed value or at an unknown extremal value.

In the learning situation, x_α is unknown but is a constant. The method of stochastic approximation can be used to arrive at x_α in spite of the random disturbances and the fact that little is known about the adaptive control loop. The method can be described as a process of successively reducing the gain of the adaptive control loop. As the true error signal is coherent but the error introduced by random disturbances is incoherent, it is possible to select a sequence of gain values which decreases slowly enough so that any coherent error is corrected, but fast enough so that the cumulative effect of the disturbances is negligible.

In the tracking situation, the situation parameters vary with time. While the value of x_α is not known to the designer, its power spectrum is assumed to be known. This point is deemed essential. If one does not know how fast the operating situation varies, there is no possible optimization of the adjustment procedure. Assuming a constant situation, the more measurements one averages, the less error one gets. Obviously this is not the answer.

Given the power spectrum of x_α, probable error in each measurement, and the dependence of the performance variable on the adjustable parameter x, the minimum value of D and a set of weighting factors w_i can be obtained. The increment in x is computed as a weighted sum of the present and previous measurements. The set of weighting factors w_i gives optimum adjustment for a nominal situation and near-optimum adjustment in general.

Two types of extremal seeking systems are studied: the derivative-sensing systems and the alternative-biasing systems. In addition to determining the minimum D and the weighting factors, a method for determining the optimum value of test bias is also developed. So far as performance is concerned, the alternative-biasing systems are found to be more satisfactory than the derivative-sensing systems.

CHAPTER 12

COMPUTER OPTIMIZATION OF NONLINEAR SYSTEMS

12-1. Introduction. There are a number of control problems which are far too complex for manual analysis, for instance, the general non-linear problem introduced in Sec. 9-2. Even with $\mathbf{f}(t)$ given, there is no known general method for exact integration of the system of equations (9-1). The maximum principle is no more than an aid to finding $\mathbf{f}(t)$ by doubling the number of unknown dependent variables. A straight analytical solution of the optimal-path problem is not only nonexistent but far from being in sight.

For these and a number of similar problems, it is possible to utilize the high-speed large memory capacity of a modern digital computer for approximate optimal control. There are two stages of operation:

1. The computational stage. The optimum trajectories are computed from the equations describing the system. These trajectories together with the corresponding control forces $\mathbf{f}(t)$ are then stored in the same or a different computer.

2. The control stage. The stored data are utilized in one way or another for actual control of the system.

In this chapter we shall first give a brief description of the various methods of computer control in carrying out the above-mentioned second stage. As the required operations such as data transfer, storage, readout, and interpolation are routine computer operations, we shall not go further into the subject. Our main concern is the first stage: how to compute the optimum trajectories. Two methods can be used, namely:

1. Dynamic programming
2. Digitized maximum principle

These methods as well as their advantages and limitations will be developed in the subsequent sections.

12-2. Types of Computer Control. In utilizing the stored data for actual control of a system, one must provide means for counteracting random disturbances and discrepancies in system parameters. There are at least three ways of accomplishing this.

309

1. *Input Control.* A block diagram of an input control system is shown in Fig. 12-1. The control command is usually a set of data which completely specifies the optimum trajectory, e.g., the terminal point of the trajectory (since the starting point is already known). From these data, the computer selects the optimum trajectory and feeds the instantaneous values of the state variables $\hat{\mathbf{x}}(t)$ to the closed-loop control system. With a high loop gain, the actual $\mathbf{x}(t)$ is kept very close to $\hat{x}(t)$. In computing the optimum trajectory, the assumed limiting values of $\mathbf{f}(t)$ are less than the actual limiting values, and there are some reserved

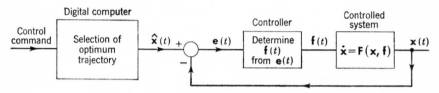

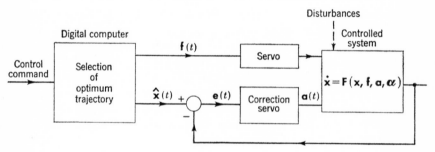

Fig. 12-1. Block diagram of an input control system.

Fig. 12-2. Block diagram of a programming control system with perturbation correction.

capacities in the control forces to overcome load disturbances and any discrepancies between assumed and actual system parameters.

Sometimes the controlled system is a moving vehicle and $\mathbf{x}(t)$ is determined from ground stations. Then $\mathbf{e}(t)$ is sent to the vehicle instead of $\hat{x}(t)$. The principle of operation, however, remains the same.

2. *Programming and Perturbation Correction.* A system of this type is illustrated in Fig. 12-2. From the control command data the computer selects the optimum trajectory and feeds a signal proportional to $\hat{\mathbf{f}}(t)$ to a servo which duplicates the control forces faithfully. Owing to the presence of disturbances and the fact that the system parameters α may not be the same as the ones assumed in the computational stage, $\mathbf{x}(t)$ is not the same as $\hat{x}(t)$. The error is applied to a correction servo which generates a set of correction forces $\mathbf{a}(t)$, which may or may not be modifications on $\mathbf{f}(t)$. If the disturbances and discrepancy in α are small,

the correction loop can be linearized in much the same way as Eq. (9-3). The correction servo loop is essentially a linear system with time-varying coefficients.

3. *Digital Feedback System.* The block diagram of a digital feedback system is shown in Fig. 12-3a. A control command for a terminal point **b** selects not a single optimum trajectory but a whole group of optimum trajectories terminating at **b**. These trajectories form a horn-shaped region in phase space, as shown in Fig. 12-3b. For every measured

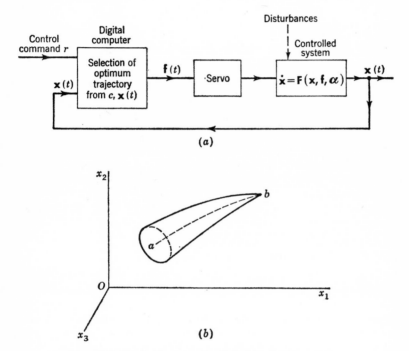

FIG. 12-3. Block diagram of a digital feedback system.

$\mathbf{x}(t)$, the optimum $\hat{\mathbf{f}}(t)$ is interpolated from recorded neighboring trajectories. This information is fed to the servo.

A further improvement can be made by computing the system parameters $\boldsymbol{\alpha}$ from a sufficiently large number of successively measured $\mathbf{x}(t)$'s. If any appreciable change in $\boldsymbol{\alpha}$ is indicated, the horn-shaped region of Fig. 12-3b is modified to suit the new system parameters, thus incorporating the adaptive concept.

The above describes three basic types of computer control. Types 1 and 2 are easier to instrument, while type 3 is closer to being a truly optimum system. In a complex control system consisting of a number of loosely coupled degrees of freedom, the most suitable type for each

degree of freedom may not be the same.   A combination of the three
basic types is then desirable.

12-3. Types of Control Problems.   The controlled system is described
by a system of equations [the same as Eq. (9-1) except that n, m are
replaced by m, m' to save the symbol n for later assignment]:

$$\dot{x}_i = F_i(\mathbf{x},\mathbf{f}) \qquad i = 1, 2, \ldots , m \tag{12-1}$$

where x_1, x_2, $\ldots$, x_m are the state variables and $f_1, f_2, \ldots , f_m$, are the
control forces.   In a general problem, $f_1, f_2, \ldots , f_m$, are also called
choice variables and are restricted by a system of constraints of the following form:

$$|f_k(t)| \leq 1 \qquad k = 1, 2, \ldots , m' \tag{12-2}$$

Equation (12-2) can be generalized by allowing each f_k to have more than
one allowed range.   The optimization problem is to select $\mathbf{f}(t)$ within the
allowed range so that one or the other of the following conditions is
satisfied.

1. *Minimal Time.*   The system is to travel from an initial point $\mathbf{x} = \mathbf{a}$
to a terminal point $\mathbf{x} = \mathbf{b}$ in minimum time.

2. *Maximum Range.*   In a given interval T, $\mathbf{f}(t)$ is selected to maximize
the distance along $\mathbf{c}$:

$$\mathbf{c} \cdot [\mathbf{x}(T) - \mathbf{x}(0)] = \max \tag{12-3}$$

where $\mathbf{c}$ is an arbitrary constant vector.

3. *Minimal Cost between Terminal Points*

$$\int_0^T U(\mathbf{x},\mathbf{f})\, dt = \min \tag{12-4}$$

T is unspecified but the initial and final points are specified:

$$\mathbf{x}(0) = \mathbf{a} \qquad \mathbf{x}(T) = \mathbf{b} \tag{12-5}$$

A given condition on U is

$$U(\mathbf{x},\mathbf{f}) > 0 \tag{12-6}$$

4. *Minimal Cost in Fixed Interval.*   The interval T is given but $\mathbf{x}(T)$
is unknown and Eq. (12-4) is to be satisfied.

We shall show that the above problems are not independent.   Let
$u(t)$ be defined as

$$u(t) \equiv \int_0^t U(\mathbf{x},\mathbf{f})\, dt \tag{12-7}$$

Then
$$\dot{u} = U(\mathbf{x},\mathbf{f}) \tag{12-8}$$

For the problem of minimal cost between terminal points we may use

u as the independent variable and rewrite Eq. (12-1):

$$\frac{dx_i}{du} = \frac{\dot{x}_i}{\dot{u}} = \frac{F_i(\mathbf{x},\mathbf{f})}{U(\mathbf{x},\mathbf{f})} \equiv \Phi_i(\mathbf{x},\mathbf{f}) \tag{12-9}$$

The problem reduces to a minimal-time problem, with Eq. (12-9) as the new system equations. For the problem of minimal cost in the fixed interval T, we may define $x_{m+1}(t)$, $F_{m+1}(\mathbf{x},\mathbf{f})$, and an $(m + 1)$-dimensional vector $\mathbf{c}$ as

$$x_{m+1}(t) \equiv u(t)$$
$$F_{m+1}(\mathbf{x},\mathbf{f}) \equiv U(\mathbf{x},\mathbf{f}) \tag{12-10}$$
$$c_i = 0 \qquad i = 1, 2, \ldots, m \qquad c_{m+1} = -1$$

Thus Eq. (12-8) is combined into Eq. (12-1) with m changed to $m + 1$, and Eq. (12-4) becomes Eq. (12-3).

Using the above reduction, we have only two basic problems left: minimal time and maximum range.

12-4. Digitized System Equations. In order to use a computer, it is necessary to approximate the system equations (12-1) by a set of difference equations. Let the interval from 0 to T be divided into N subintervals T', $T = NT'$. Let $\mathbf{x}(n)$ and $\mathbf{f}(n)$ be defined as follows:

$\mathbf{x}(n)$: value of $\mathbf{x}(t)$ at $t = nT'$
$\mathbf{f}(n)$: average value of $\mathbf{f}(t)$ in the interval $nT' \leq t \leq (n + 1)T'$

With sufficiently large N, Eq. (12-1) can be closely approximated by

$$x_i(n + 1) = x_i(n) + T'F_i[\mathbf{x}(n),\mathbf{f}(n)] \qquad \begin{aligned} i &= 1, 2, \ldots, m \\ n &= 0, 1, 2, \ldots, N - 1 \end{aligned} \tag{12-11}$$

The system of constraints becomes

$$|f_k(n)| \leq 1 \tag{12-12}$$

12-5. Basic Principle of Dynamic Programming.[†] Dynamic programming as developed by Richard Bellman is a very simple and powerful concept. It may be billed as the general technique of optimization using a digital computer. The amount of literature on the subject is quite voluminous despite its relatively short tenure in human knowledge. Because of space limitation, we shall develop here only a very basic version of dynamic programming.

Let us consider a deterministic process in which the state of the system is specified by a set of m state variables $x_1, x_2, \ldots, x_m$. As before, we shall denote these variables by the vector $\mathbf{x}$. Let $T_y (\quad)$ denote a set of transformations which transform one vector $\mathbf{x}$ into another. The

[†] Sections 12-5 and 12-6 are based on R. Bellman, "Dynamic Programming," chap. 3, Princeton University Press, Princeton, N.J., 1957, with some of the present author's own interpretation.

identity of the new vector depends, of course, on both the original vector $\mathbf{x}$ and the transformation selected as specified by the value of y. An example of such a transformation is Eq. (12-11). By selecting $\mathbf{f}(n)$ which specifies the selected transformation, the vector $\mathbf{x}(n)$ is transformed into a new vector $\mathbf{x}(n + 1)$.

An N-stage decision process is defined by the selected sequence of N transformations:

$$\begin{aligned}
\mathbf{x}_1 &= T_{y_0}(\mathbf{x}_0) \\
\mathbf{x}_2 &= T_{y_1}(\mathbf{x}_1) \\
\mathbf{x}_N &= T_{y_{N-1}}(\mathbf{x}_{N-1})
\end{aligned} \qquad (12\text{-}13)$$

These transformations are selected to maximize a given return function of the state variables, $R(\mathbf{x})$, in the final state. In other words, $R(\mathbf{x}_N)$ is to be maximum.

Let $\Omega_N(\mathbf{x}_0)$ be the set of all points that can be reached from $\mathbf{x}_0$ by N transformations. Let $M_N(\mathbf{x}_0)$ denote the maximum value of $R(\mathbf{x})$ for all $\mathbf{x}$ in $\Omega_N(\mathbf{x}_0)$. Then, by definition,

$$M_N(\mathbf{x}_0) = \max_{Y^N} R(\mathbf{x}_N) \qquad (12\text{-}14)$$

where Y^N denotes the sequence of transformations $y_0, y_1, \ldots, y_{N-1}$. The right-hand side of Eq. (12-14) means the maximum value of $R(\mathbf{x}_N)$ by an optimum choice of $y_0, y_1, \ldots, y_{N-1}$ which, of course, is a choice leading to maximum $R(\mathbf{x})$ in $\Omega_N(x_0)$.

We note that the optimum $\mathbf{x}_N$ may not be unique, and for any given $\mathbf{x}_N$ the choice of Y^N may not be unique. But $M_N(\mathbf{x}_0)$ is always unique, since in the closed region $\Omega_N(x_0)$ there must be an upper limit to $R(\mathbf{x})$, and this upper limit is $M_N(\mathbf{x}_0)$.

The selection of a sequence of transformations is called a policy. A policy that leads to maximum return, or $R(\mathbf{x}_N)$, is called an optimal policy. Suppose that Eqs. (12-13) represent an optimal policy. From any point $\mathbf{x}_n$, $n < N$, we assert that it is not possible to arrive at a higher $R(\mathbf{x}_N)$ in $N - n$ steps (or transformations). If this were not true and a higher $R(\mathbf{x}'_N)$ could be obtained by the selection $y'_n, y'_{n+1}, \ldots, y'_{N-1}$, then the policy $y_0, y_1, \ldots, y_{n-1}y'_n, y'_{n+1}, \ldots, y'_{N-1}$ would lead to a higher return from $\mathbf{x}_0$, in contradiction to our assumption that $y_0, y_1, \ldots, y_{N-1}$ is an optimal policy.

The principle of optimality can be stated as follows: *The part of an N-step optimal policy leading from any intermediate state $\mathbf{x}_n$ to the final state $\mathbf{x}_N$ is an $(N - n)$-step optimal policy from $\mathbf{x}_n$.*

In contrast to this principle, any part of an optimal policy which ends before reaching the final state $\mathbf{x}_N$ is not necessarily an optimal policy. To see this, let us consider a simple example as shown in Fig. 12-4. The transformation T consists of T_+, which adds 1 to x, and T_-, which subtracts 1 from x.   Consider a three-stage decision process starting from $x = 0$.   The optimal policy is obviously $+ + +$.   Starting from $x = 1$, $+ +$ is a two-stage optimal policy.   Starting from $x = 0$, $+ +$ is not a two-stage optimal policy.

From the principle of optimality, we can derive a recurrent relation of the maximum return function $M_N(\mathbf{x})$.   In choosing the transform $T_y(\ )$, we know that the sequence of choices following y is also optimum by itself.   For any y we select, the ultimate return function is

$$M_{N-1}[T_y(\mathbf{x})]$$

Therefore, y is selected to maximize the above function.   We have finally

$$M_N(\mathbf{x}) = \max_y M_{N-1}[T_y(\mathbf{x})] \qquad N = 2, 3, 4, \ldots \qquad (12\text{-}15)$$

$$M_1(\mathbf{x}) = \max_y R[T_y(\mathbf{x})] \qquad\qquad\qquad\qquad (12\text{-}16)$$

Equation (12-15) cannot be solved all by itself.   We do not know what $M_{N-1}(\mathbf{x}')$ is for every $\mathbf{x}'$ within reach of one step (or transformation) from $\mathbf{x}$.   However, the class of functions $M_N(\mathbf{x})$ for all x and N can be solved in a rather straightforward manner.

For each $\mathbf{x}$ we can find the maximum value of $R(\mathbf{x}')$ among all $\mathbf{x}'$ in $\Omega_1(\mathbf{x})$ [$\Omega_1(\mathbf{x})$ is the set of all points $\mathbf{x}'$ that can be reached by one step from $\mathbf{x}$].   This is $M_1(\mathbf{x})$.   Then for each $\mathbf{x}$ we can find the maximum value of $M_1(\mathbf{x}')$ among all $\mathbf{x}'$ in $\Omega_1(\mathbf{x})$. This is $M_2(\mathbf{x})$, etc.   Thus, in order to find a solution for $M_N(\mathbf{x}_0)$, we find first a solution for all $M_n(\mathbf{x})$ with $n \leq N$.   As the latter func-

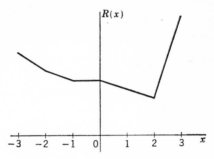

FIG. 12-4. A simple decision process.

tions can be computed as a class, $M_N(\mathbf{x}_0)$ is also determined.   This method of enlarging an unsolvable problem into a solvable class of problems so that a solution can be obtained is called *the technique of invariant imbedding.*

The problem of minimal return can be treated, of course, in exactly the same way, with the symbol max changed to the symbol min.

12-6. Application of Dynamic Programming to the Problem of Minimum Cost in Fixed Interval.   The equations describing the dynamical system are Eqs. (12-11) and (12-12).   The N-stage return function to be minimized is

$$T' \sum_{n=0}^{n=N-1} U[\mathbf{x}(n), \mathbf{f}(n)] \qquad (12\text{-}17)$$

In order to apply dynamic programming, we have to make (12-17) a function of the state variables.   This can be done by introducing a new state variable x_{m+1}:

$$x_{m+1}(n+1) = x_{m+1}(n) + T'U[\mathbf{x}(n),\mathbf{f}(n)] \qquad (12\text{-}18)$$

To minimize (12-17) is the same as to minimize $x_{m+1}(N)$. The return function R is then

$$R(\mathbf{x},x_{m+1}) = x_{m+1} \qquad (12\text{-}19)$$

In Eq. (12-19) and throughout Sec. 12-7, $\mathbf{x}$ is used to denote the m-dimensional vector $x_1, x_2, \ldots, x_m$, not the $(m+1)$-dimensional vector.

The minimum N-stage return $M_N(\mathbf{x},x_{m+1})$ is the initial value of x_{m+1} plus the minimum value of (12-17) which is a function of the initial $\mathbf{x}$ and N only. Therefore

$$M_N(\mathbf{x},x_{m+1}) = x_{m+1} + B_N(\mathbf{x}) \qquad (12\text{-}20)$$

From Eqs. (12-11) and (12-18) we obtain an explicit form for the transform T:

$$T_\mathbf{f}(\mathbf{x},x_{m+1}) = [\mathbf{x} + T'\mathbf{F}(\mathbf{x},\mathbf{f}), \; x_{m+1} + T'U(\mathbf{x},\mathbf{f})] \qquad (12\text{-}21)$$

Substituting Eqs. (12-20) and (12-21) in (12-15) gives

$$x_{m+1} + B_N(\mathbf{x}) = \min_\mathbf{f} \{x_{m+1} + T'U(\mathbf{x},\mathbf{f}) + B_{N-1}[\mathbf{x} + T'F(\mathbf{x},\mathbf{f})]\} \qquad (12\text{-}22)$$

Since x_{m+1} is independent of $\mathbf{f}$, a recurrence relation of $B_N(x)$ is obtained:

$$B_N(\mathbf{x}) = \min_\mathbf{f} \{T'U(\mathbf{x},\mathbf{f}) + B_{N-1}[\mathbf{x} + T'\mathbf{F}(\mathbf{x},\mathbf{f})]\}$$

$$\text{for } N = 2, 3, 4, \ldots \qquad (12\text{-}23)$$

$$B_1(\mathbf{x}) = \min_\mathbf{f} [T'U(\mathbf{x},\mathbf{f})] \qquad (12\text{-}24)$$

Equations (12-23) and (12-24) can be solved by the technique of invariant imbedding in much the same way as Eqs. (12-15) and (12-16). $B_1(\mathbf{x})$ is simply the minimum value of $T'U(\mathbf{x},\mathbf{f})$ for all allowable $\mathbf{f}$. Once $B_{N-1}(\mathbf{x})$ is known for all $\mathbf{x}$, $B_N(\mathbf{x})$ is computed as the minimum sum (for all allowable $\mathbf{f}$) of $T'U(\mathbf{x},\mathbf{f})$ and $B_{N-1}(\mathbf{x}')$, where $\mathbf{x}' = \mathbf{x} + T'\mathbf{F}(\mathbf{x},\mathbf{f})$.

In order to compute $B_N(\mathbf{x})$, we need only the data on $B_{N-1}(\mathbf{x})$. Therefore, once $B_N(\mathbf{x})$ is computed, both $B_{N-1}(\mathbf{x})$ and the optimum $\mathbf{f}$ associated with each $\mathbf{x}$ can be transferred to a magnetic tape. The required fast memory of the computer is not much more than what is necessary for sufficient coverage of $B_N(\mathbf{x})$ for one value of N only. The optimum $\mathbf{f}$ is obviously different for each $\mathbf{x}$ and N, and we shall denote it as $\mathbf{f}(\mathbf{x},N)$.

Suppose that we are interested in finding out the optimum process as well as the minimum return for an N_1-stage process starting from $\mathbf{x}_0$. The minimum return is immediately read from the tape, as it is simply $B_{N_1}(\mathbf{x}_0)$. We also read from the tape $\mathbf{f}(\mathbf{x}_0,N_1)$. This is $\mathbf{f}(0)$ in the notation of Eq. (12-11). For the next point, $\mathbf{x}(1)$ is determined by

$$\mathbf{x}(1) = \mathbf{x}_0 + T'\mathbf{F}[\mathbf{x}_0,\mathbf{f}(0)]$$

Repeated use of

$$\mathbf{f}(n) = \mathbf{f}[\mathbf{x}(n), N_1 - n] \tag{12-25}$$

and Eq. (12-11) gives the complete optimal trajectory. Of course, the past history of $\mathbf{x}$ can also be recorded for each $\mathbf{x}$ and N to save calculation.

One serious drawback of the technique of invariant imbedding is the memory required with a multidimensional vector $\mathbf{x}$. Of course, one cannot record $M_N(\mathbf{x})$ or $B_N(\mathbf{x})$ for every $\mathbf{x}$ even for a one-dimensional problem. However, as most problems have limited range (or region) of $\mathbf{x}$, it is generally possible to place discrete values of $\mathbf{x}$ close enough for one- or two-dimensional problems so that interpolation for the in-between values is accurate enough. For higher dimensions, the required memory quickly rises to astronomical proportions, and a direct application of dynamic programming becomes impractical.

There has been some recent work on how to overcome the difficulty of multidimensionality. However, as the mathematics is quite involved, it will not be treated here.

12-7. Digitized Maximum Principle.† One way to avoid the exponential rise in required memory capacity with the dimensionality of $\mathbf{x}$ is to compute along one single trajectory at a time, rather than one stage in the entire phase space at a time. Pontryagin's maximum principle gives promise of the possibility. However, an arbitrary conversion from continuous to discrete form introduces errors, the cumulative effects of which in hundreds of steps are difficult to determine. In the present section, a maximum principle is derived directly for discrete-time (or sampled-data) systems of the type described by Eqs. (12-11) and (12-12). For computation of continuous systems, the only error introduced is in approximating Eq. (12-1) by Eq. (12-11). Once this is done, the remaining computation process is exact except for the computer round-off error.

In the following development, the assumptions are:

1. The dynamical system is described by Eqs. (12-11) and (12-12) in a region R (R may or may not be bounded in all directions).

2. The function $F_i(\mathbf{x},\mathbf{f})$ is single-valued and has bounded first and second partial derivatives of $\mathbf{x}$ and $\mathbf{f}$ for all $\mathbf{x}$ in R, all $\mathbf{f}$ satisfying the inequality (12-12) and all i, $i = 1, 2, \ldots, m$.

Let Γ be a trajectory defined by

$$\mathbf{f}(n) = \hat{\mathbf{f}}(n) \qquad n = 0, 1, 2, \ldots, N - 1 \tag{12-26}$$

where $\mathbf{f}(n)$ satisfies inequality (12-12). With given $\mathbf{x}(0)$, the solution of Eq. (12-11) is unique and is denoted by $\mathbf{x}(n) = \hat{\mathbf{x}}(n)$, $n = 1, 2, \ldots, N$.

---

† A more complete treatment can be found in a paper by the author, Computer Optimization of Nonlinear Control Systems by Means of Digitized Maximum Principle, presented at IRE International Convention, New York, March, 1961.

Let Γ' be an adjacent trajectory defined by

$$\mathbf{f}'(n) = \hat{\mathbf{f}}(n) + \delta\mathbf{f}(n) \qquad n = 0, 1, 2, \ldots, N - 1 \qquad (12\text{-}27)$$

where
$$|\mathbf{f}'(n)| \leq 1 \qquad |\delta\mathbf{f}(n)| \leq \epsilon \qquad\qquad (12\text{-}28)$$

The solution is denoted as $\hat{\mathbf{x}}(n) + \delta\mathbf{x}(n)$:

$$\hat{x}_i(n + 1) + \delta x_i(n + 1) = \hat{x}_i(n) + \delta x_i(n)$$
$$+ T'F_i[\hat{\mathbf{x}}(n) + \delta x(n), \hat{\mathbf{f}}(n) + \delta\mathbf{f}(n)] \qquad i = 1, 2, \ldots, m$$

Since
$$\hat{x}_i(n + 1) = \hat{x}_i(n) + T'F_i[\hat{\mathbf{x}}(n), \hat{\mathbf{f}}(n)]$$

the difference of the above two equations is

$$\delta x_i(n + 1) = \delta x_i(n) + T' \sum_{j=1}^{j=m} \left(\frac{\partial F_i}{\partial x_j}\right)_n \delta x_j(n)$$

$$+ T' \sum_{k=1}^{k=m'} \left(\frac{\partial F_i}{\partial f_k}\right)_n \delta f_k(n) + O(\epsilon^2) \quad (12\text{-}29)$$

In the above equation, $O(\epsilon^2)$ means a quantity of the order of ϵ^2, and the subscript n denotes that the partial derivatives are evaluated for $\hat{\mathbf{x}}(n)$ and $\hat{\mathbf{f}}(n)$. For any given Γ, these partial derivatives are functions of n only. The boundary condition is $\delta\mathbf{x}(0) = 0$.

It is convenient to express Eq. (12-29) in matrix form: $\delta\mathbf{x}$ and $\delta\mathbf{f}$ can be written as column vectors. Let $\mathbf{P}(n)$ and $\mathbf{B}(n)$ represent $m \times m$ and $m \times m'$ matrices with $\delta_{ij} + T'(\partial F_i/\partial x_j)_n$, and $T''(\partial F_i/\partial f_j)_n$ as their respective elements of the ith row and jth column, where δ_{ij} is the Kronicler symbol $\delta_{ii} = 1$, and $\delta_{ij} = 0$ for $i \neq j$. Equation (12-29) can be written as

$$\delta\mathbf{x}(n + 1) = \mathbf{P}(n)\,\delta\mathbf{x}(n) + \mathbf{B}(n)\,\delta\mathbf{f}(n) + O(\epsilon^2) \qquad (12\text{-}30)$$

Equation (12-30) can be solved step by step:

$$\delta\mathbf{x}(1) = \mathbf{B}(0)\,\delta\mathbf{f}(0) + O(\epsilon^2) \qquad\qquad (12\text{-}31)$$
$$\delta\mathbf{x}(2) = \mathbf{P}(1)\,\delta\mathbf{x}(1) + \mathbf{B}(1)\,\delta\mathbf{f}(1) + O(\epsilon^2)$$
$$= \mathbf{P}(1)\mathbf{B}(0)\,\delta\mathbf{f}(0) + \mathbf{B}(1)\,\delta\mathbf{f}(1) + O(\epsilon^2)$$

There is no need to write $\mathbf{P}(1)O(\epsilon^2) + O(\epsilon^2)$ since it is still a quantity of the order of ϵ^2. Repeated application of the above process gives

$$\delta\mathbf{x}(N) = \sum_{n=0}^{n=N-1} \mathbf{A}(n)\mathbf{B}(n)\,\delta\mathbf{f}(n) + O(\epsilon^2) \qquad (12\text{-}32)$$

where
$$\mathbf{A}(N - 1) = 1 \qquad\qquad (12\text{-}33)$$

$$\mathbf{A}(n) \equiv \mathbf{P}(N - 1)\mathbf{P}(N - 2) \cdots \mathbf{P}(n + 1) \qquad n = 0, 1, \ldots, N - 2$$
$$(12\text{-}34)$$

From Eq. (12-34) we can derive a recurrent relation for $\mathbf{A}(n)$:

$$\mathbf{A}(n - 1) = \mathbf{A}(n)\mathbf{P}(n) \qquad n = 1, 2, \ldots, N \qquad (12\text{-}35)$$

Now let us derive a necessary condition for $\hat{\mathbf{f}}(n)$ to give an optimal Γ.

1. *Maximal-range Problems.*   If Γ is optimal, then from Eq. (12-3) we have

$$\mathbf{c} \cdot [\hat{\mathbf{x}}(N) - \mathbf{x}(0)] \geq \mathbf{c} \cdot [\hat{\mathbf{x}}(N) + \delta\mathbf{x}(N) - \mathbf{x}(0)]$$

The above inequality may be written as

$$\mathbf{c} \cdot \delta\mathbf{x}(N) \leq 0 \tag{12-36}$$

2. *Minimal-time Problems.*   Let $\Omega_N(\mathbf{x}_0)$ represent the set of all possible terminal points of the system at the end of N steps starting from $\mathbf{x}_0$. Since the allowable range of $\mathbf{f}$ is continuous, $\Omega_N(\mathbf{x}_0)$ forms a continuous region in the space $x_1, x_2, \ldots, x_m$. We assume that the number of steps is numerous enough so that $Nm' > m$ and $\Omega_N(\mathbf{x}_0)$ is an m-dimensional region. For any terminal point $\mathbf{b}$, an N can be found such that $\mathbf{b}$ belongs to $\Omega_N(\mathbf{x}_0)$ but does not belong to any $\Omega_{N'}(\mathbf{x}_0)$, $N' < N$. If $\mathbf{b}$ is an interior point of $\Omega_N(\mathbf{x}_0)$, there are, in general, infinitely many optimal trajectories. This point becomes obvious if we recall the geometrical concept of Sec. 9-2 and draw an analogy between the discrete and continuous cases. In the continuous case, terminal points of optimal trajectories of duration T are always on the surface of $\Omega(t \leq T)$. In the discrete approximation, any terminal point $\mathbf{b}$ which has a minimal time from $\mathbf{x}_0$ between $(N-1)T'$ and NT'' will have to be reached at the end of NT'', and generally these points lie inside $\Omega_N(\mathbf{x}_0)$. Since we are using more time than necessary in arriving at $\mathbf{b}$, there are usually infinitely many ways of doing this.

As we are looking for the truly optimal trajectory, what we want is not a trajectory which terminates at $\mathbf{b}$ but passes beyond $\mathbf{b}$ and terminates at a point on the surface of $\Omega_N(\mathbf{x}_0)$. Therefore, the following assumption may be made without loss of generality: *The terminal point of the optimal trajectory is on the surface of $\Omega_N(\mathbf{x}_0)$.*

Let Γ denote an optimal trajectory with its terminating point $\hat{\mathbf{x}}(N)$ lying on the surface of $\Omega_N(\mathbf{x}_0)$. We shall show that there exists a vector ξ such that

$$\xi \cdot \delta\mathbf{x}(N) \leq O(\epsilon^2) \tag{12-37}$$

Inequality (12-37) is easy to prove if we make the assumption that a normal exists to the surface of $\Omega_N(\mathbf{x}_0)$ at $\hat{\mathbf{x}}(N)$. Since $\hat{\mathbf{x}}(N) + \delta\mathbf{x}(N)$ is a point belonging to $\Omega_N(\mathbf{x}_0)$, we may choose ξ as a normal pointing outward from $\hat{\mathbf{x}}(N)$, and inequality (12-37) follows immediately from the definition of a normal. However, for all we know, the surface of $\Omega_N(\mathbf{x}_0)$ may be like sandpaper rather than like that of an apple. Assuming the existence of a normal may be assuming a little too much. We shall give instead a longer proof without this assumption.

To prove (12-37), we shall need the concept of a convex region, which may be defined as follows: *A region Ω is called convex if at every boundary point p_1 there exists a vector ξ_1 such that*

$$\xi_1 \cdot V_{12} < 0$$

for every vector V_{12} joining p_1 to another point p_2 in Ω.

The concept of convexity can be illustrated by the two-dimensional regions of Fig. 12-5: Ω_1 is convex, but Ω_2 and Ω_3 are not since ξ does not exist for p_3 and p_6. A well-known theorem about convex regions is:

A necessary and sufficient condition for a region Ω to be convex is that every point on the straight line joining any two points in Ω is also a point in Ω.

For instance, part of the straight line p_4p_5 lies outside Ω_2, and the straight line p_7p_8 lies outside of Ω_2.

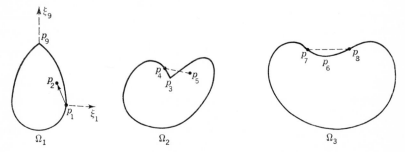

Fig. 12-5. Convex (Ω_1) and nonconvex (Ω_2 and Ω_3) regions.

Let $\Omega_N(\Gamma,\epsilon)$ denote the set of all terminal points $\mathbf{x}(N)$ of all adjacent trajectories defined by Eqs. (12-27) and (12-28). Because $\Omega_N(\Gamma,\epsilon)$ is a subset of $\Omega_N(\mathbf{x}_0)$, and $\hat{\mathbf{x}}(N)$ is on the surface of $\Omega_N(\mathbf{x}_0)$, $\hat{\mathbf{x}}(N)$ is on the surface of $\Omega_N(\Gamma,\epsilon)$ also.

If the small term $O(\epsilon^2)$ is neglected, any point $\delta\mathbf{x}(N)$ on a straight line joining $\delta\mathbf{x}(N)'$ and $\delta\mathbf{x}(N)''$ can be expressed as

$$\delta x(N) = c_1\,\delta\mathbf{x}(N)' + (1 - c_1)\,\delta\mathbf{x}(N)'' = \sum_{n=0}^{n=N-1} \mathbf{A}(n)\mathbf{B}(n)[c_1\,\delta f(n)' \\ + (1 - c_1)\,\delta f(n)'']$$

with $0 < c_1 < 1$. Since both $\delta f(n)'$ and $\delta f(n)''$ satisfy Eqs. (12-27) and (12-28), $c_1\,\delta f(n)' + (1 - c_1)\,\delta\mathbf{f}(n)''$ also satisfies these equations, and $\hat{\mathbf{x}}(N) + \delta\mathbf{x}(N)$ is a point in $\Omega_N(\Gamma,\epsilon)$. Therefore, the region $\Omega_N(\Gamma,\epsilon)$ is convex in this approximation. As $\mathbf{x}(n)$ is a boundary point, there exists a ξ such that

$$\xi \cdot [\hat{\mathbf{x}}(N) + \delta\mathbf{x}(N) - \hat{\mathbf{x}}(N)] = \xi \cdot \delta\mathbf{x}(N) < 0$$

However, as this approximation is good only to the first order of ϵ, we have inequality (12-37) instead.

The weaker condition (12-37) includes (12-36) as a special case. In matrix notation, we can treat ξ as a column vector and denote the transposed ξ (or the corresponding row vector) as ξ'. Inequality (12-37) can be written as

$$\xi' \, \delta\mathbf{x} \leq O(\epsilon^2) \tag{12-38}$$

From Eqs. (12-32) and (12-38) we have

$$\sum_{n=0}^{n=N-1} \xi'\mathbf{A}(n)\mathbf{B}(n) \, \delta\mathbf{f}(n) \leq O(\epsilon^2) \tag{12-39}$$

Let the row vector $\xi'\mathbf{A}(n)$ be denoted as $\lambda'(n)$. It satisfies

$$\lambda'(N - 1) = \xi' \tag{12-40}$$
$$\lambda'(n - 1) = \lambda'(n)\mathbf{P}(n) \qquad n = 1, 2, \ldots, N - 1 \tag{12-41}$$

Inequality (12-39) can be written as

$$\sum_{n=0}^{n=N-1} \lambda'(n)\mathbf{B}(n) \, \delta\mathbf{f}(n) \leq O(\epsilon^2)$$

As $\delta\mathbf{f}(n)$ for each n is independent of all others, we have finally

$$\lambda'(n)\mathbf{B}(n) \, \delta\mathbf{f}(n) \leq O(\epsilon^2) \tag{12-42}$$

for all allowed $\delta\mathbf{f}(n)$ [satisfying (12-27) and (12-28)].

Inequality (12-42) is equivalent to maximizing $\sum_{i=1}^{i=m} \lambda_i(n)F_i[\hat{\mathbf{x}}(n),\mathbf{f}(n)]$ by the choice of $\mathbf{f}(n)$, with $\lambda(n)$ and $\hat{\mathbf{x}}(n)$ considered fixed. It does not rule out the possibility, however, that $\lambda'\mathbf{F}$ is stationary at the optimum value of $\mathbf{f}(n)$. The function $\lambda'\mathbf{F}$ is called the Hamiltonian. The digitized maximum principle can be stated as follows: *Along an optimal trajectory, the Hamiltonian $\lambda'(n)\mathbf{F}[\hat{\mathbf{x}}(n),\mathbf{f}(n)]$ is either maximum or stationary with respect to infinitesimal allowed variations of $\mathbf{f}(n)$.*

Being maximum is not necessarily being stationary in the present case, because of the constraints (12-12) on $\mathbf{f}(n)$.

12-8. Computation Procedure Using the Digitized Maximum Principle. It is convenient to start the computation procedure from the terminal point and work backward. For the minimal-time problem ξ depends on the initial point $\mathbf{x}_0$ but there is no known relationship between ξ and $\mathbf{x}_0$. However, as the problem is usually, with the terminal point $\mathbf{b}$ known, what are the best $f(t)$'s for different initial points $\mathbf{x}_0$, the drawback is not a serious one, and the mapping between ξ and $\mathbf{x}_0$ is automatically carried out in the computing process. For the maximum-range problem $\xi = \mathbf{c}$ but $\mathbf{b}$ is unknown for any given $\mathbf{x}_0$ and the same situation holds.

For each trajectory specified by a terminal point $\mathbf{x}(N) = \mathbf{b}$ and a vector $\xi = \lambda(N - 1)$, a step-by-step computation can be made. The order of computation is as follows:

1. $\mathbf{f}(n)$, $\mathbf{x}(n)$
2. $\mathbf{P}(n)$
3. $\lambda(n - 1)$
4. $\mathbf{f}(n - 1)$, $\mathbf{x}(n - 1)$, etc.

To see how this works, let us assume that $\mathbf{f}$ is a one-dimensional f.   When $\mathbf{x}(N)$ and $\lambda(N - 1)$ are known, the steps are as follows:

1. Determine $f(N - 1)$ and $\mathbf{x}(N - 1)$ simultaneously by the following substeps:

a. Assume an $f(N - 1)$, say 1.

b. Calculate $\mathbf{x}(N - 1)$ from Eq. (12-11) by a looping procedure (successive approximation).   With a small T' the result converges very fast.

c. Calculate $H \equiv \sum_{i=1}^{i=m} \lambda_i(N - 1)F_i[\mathbf{x}(N - 1), \mathbf{f}(N - 1)]$.

d. Assume a slightly different $f(N - 1)$, say 0.99, and recalculate H. We note that, in substep d, $\mathbf{x}(N - 1)$, is *not* recalculated.

If the recalculated H_{N-1} in d is smaller, then the value of $f(N - 1)$ assumed at the beginning is correct, and we go on to the second step.   If not, we repeat the above substeps:

a. Assume $f(N - 1) = -1$.

b. Calculate $\mathbf{x}(N - 1)$.

c. Calculate H from substeps a and b.

d. Assume $f(N - 1) = -0.99$ and calculate H from b and d.

If H as calculated from d is smaller, we proceed to the second step with $f(N - 1) = -1$, and calculate $\mathbf{x}(N - 1)$.   If it is larger, we assume a new value of $f(N - 1)$, say 0, and repeat the above calculations.   The situation is illustrated in Fig. 12-6.   The dot represents the assumed value of f, and the arrow indicates the sense of $\partial H/\partial f$.   In Fig. 12-6a we have $(1,+)$ at the first trial, and it is satisfactory as f maximizes H. In Fig. 12-6b we have $(-1,-)$ at the second trial, and it is satisfactory for the same reason.   In Fig. 12-6c we have $(1,-)$ $(-1,+)$, $(0,+)$ for the first three trials.   Trials 1 and 3 indicate that H has a peak somewhere between 0 and 1, and so we try $\frac{1}{2}$.   Subsequently we get $(\frac{1}{2},-)$, and $(\frac{1}{4},0)$.   At $f = \frac{1}{4}$, H is stationary and we proceed to the next step:

2. Calculate for $i = 1, 2, \ldots, m$ and $j = 1, 2, \ldots, m'$.

$$P_{ii}(N - 1) = 1 + T' \left(\frac{\partial F_i}{\partial x_i}\right)_{N-1}$$

$$P_{ij}(N - 1) = T' \left(\frac{\partial F_i}{\partial x_j}\right)_{N-1} \qquad \text{for } i \neq j$$

The partial derivatives are evaluated for $\mathbf{x}(N - 1)$ and $f(N - 1)$ as calculated from step 1.

3. Calculate for $k = 1, 2, \ldots, m$.

$$\lambda_k(N - 2) = \sum_{j=1}^{j=m} \lambda_j(N - 1)P_{jk}(N - 1)$$

Now we are ready to repeat step 1 again to calculate $f(N - 2)$ and $\mathbf{x}(N - 2)$, etc. In the second and subsequent rounds we can usually save work by assuming at the first trial an $f(n)$ equal to $f(n + 1)$ of the preceding round. The optimal f usually stays at one extreme value for many periods of T' and then at the opposite extreme for more periods of T', etc. Under such situations, step 1 is concluded at the first trial.

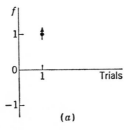

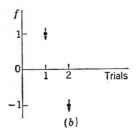

For **f** of two or three dimensions, we can generalize the method of Fig. 12-6 by starting our calculations on the lattice points of a coarse lattice in **f** space, and then refine our calculations on finer and finer lattices until the point for maximum H is found.

It is unusual but not impossible to have two or more values of f which make H locally maximum or locally stationary. In such a case, the computed optimal trajectory branches off into two or more branches.

In computing backward, the significance of $\mathbf{x}(N - n)$ is that it takes n steps to arrive at the terminal point $\mathbf{x}(N)$ from $\mathbf{x}(N - n)$ along an optimal trajectory. The number n is significant but not N or $N - n$. In actual computations, it is desirable to write $\mathbf{x}(N)$ as $\mathbf{x}(0)$, $\mathbf{x}(N - 1)$ as

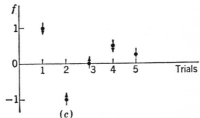

FIG. 12-6. The process of adjusting f.

$\mathbf{x}(1)$, etc. However, the original numbering sequence is kept throughout the present text to avoid confusion.

For the minimal-time problem, the terminal point $\mathbf{x}(N)$ is fixed, and we compute a different trajectory by assuming a different ξ. The collection of trajectories so computed forms a horn-shaped region, as shown in Fig. 12-3b. For the maximal-range problem, $\xi = \mathbf{c}$, and we compute a different trajectory by assuming a different $\mathbf{x}(N)$ satisfying $\mathbf{c} \cdot \mathbf{x}(N) = $ const. The result is a region as shown in Fig. 12-7. The solid lines show the optimal trajectories to be followed, and the broken lines marked $N - n$ mean that, at these points, it takes n periods to arrive at a range of $[\mathbf{x}(N) - \mathbf{x}] \cdot \mathbf{c}$. Sometimes there are two trajectories meeting at the same point such as A. The upper trajectory is the optimal one since it has lower n.

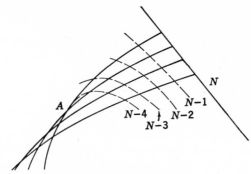

FIG. 12-7. Optimal trajectories for the maximum-range problem.

12-9. Summary. The computation of optimal trajectories for general nonlinear systems has two alternative objectives:

1. It serves as a standard of performance against which the performance of a practical system can be compared.

2. In very important or very expensive systems, it is worthwhile to instrument for the theoretically best by incorporating a digital computer in the control system.

Three ways of realizing the second objective are discussed:

1. Input control
2. Programming with perturbation correction
3. Digital feedback system

Methods 1 and 2 are easier to instrument. However, they are only nearly optimum, since in computing the "optimal trajectories" the full range of control forces cannot be used. This is for the purpose of reserving some corrective capacity to reduce the errors introduced by load disturbance and discrepancies between actual system-parameter values and their design center values. Type 3 is more nearly optimum but is also more expensive in terms of required computer memory and speed.

There are two ways of computing optimal trajectories:

1. Dynamic programming
2. Digitized maximum principle

Dynamic programming in its basic form is absolutely reliable. However, the required computer memory capacity increases exponentially with the number of state variables. Digitized maximum principle is a trajectory-by-trajectory procedure and does not require nearly as much computer memory, but care must be taken that no branches are neglected in the computations. As there is no general method of doing this, the branching problem has to be studied for each individual case.

APPENDIX A

BASIC STATISTICAL THEORY

The following is a brief treatment of the elements of statistical theory which are used throughout this book.

A-1. Distribution, Expected Value, Standard Deviation, Moments. A chance event has a plural number of possible outcomes: a, b, c, ... Let P_a denote the probability of a, P_b the probability of b, P_c the probability of c, . . . ; the set of probabilities P_a, P_b, P_c, . . . is called a distribution.

If we attach a value V to each outcome and denote these values as V_a, V_b, V_c, . . . , the mean value or the expected value of the event is defined as

$$\langle V \rangle = P_a V_a + P_b V_b + P_c V_c + \cdots \tag{A-1}$$

The bracket $\langle \ \rangle$ denotes the expected value of the expression inside. Let $F(V)$ denote an arbitrary function of V; then the expected value of $F(V)$ is

$$\langle F(V) \rangle = P_a F(V_a) + P_b F(V_b) + P_c F(V_c) + \cdots \tag{A-2}$$

Equation (A-1) actually implies Eq. (A-2), since we could have attached $F(V_a)$, $F(V_b)$, $F(V_c)$, . . . , instead of V_a, V_b, V_c, . . . , to outcomes a, b, c, . . . , respectively.

Another point of view is that V is a chance variable, since it may take on any of a number of possible values, and it is called a variate for short. The standard deviation σ is defined as the root-mean-square value of $V - \langle V \rangle$. Mathematically,

$$\sigma^2 = \langle (V - \langle V \rangle)^2 \rangle \tag{A-3}$$

A more complete set of characteristic values of a distribution are the moments, which are defined as the expected values of the powers of its variate. By definition, the nth moment is $\langle V^n \rangle$. The nth moment *about* any point a is $\langle (V - a)^n \rangle$. The expected or mean value of a distribution is simply its first moment. The mean-square deviation, or σ^2, is simply the second moment of a distribution about its mean.

A-2. Continuous Distribution. Sometimes, the possible value of a variate is continuous, for instance, the weight of a human being, the peak voltage of a lightning discharge, or the distance traveled by a thrown ball. The probability of V being within a range of values $V_1 \pm dV/2$ is proportional to dV, if dV is small enough, and can be written $P(V_1)\,dV$. The function $P(V)$ is referred to as the density function of V. Sometimes it is also called the probability density.

The mean value of V and of the function $F(V)$ becomes

$$\langle V \rangle = \int_{-\infty}^{\infty} V P(V)\,dV \tag{A-4}$$

$$\langle F(V) \rangle = \int_{-\infty}^{\infty} F(V)P(V)\,dV \tag{A-5}$$

Obviously,

$$\int_{-\infty}^{\infty} P(V)\,dV = 1 \tag{A-6}$$

The above integration from $-\infty$ to ∞ does not lose any generality. If the range of possible V is limited to $V_1 \leq V \leq V_2$, it is only necessary to require that $P(V) = 0$ for $V < V_1$, and for $V > V_2$.

Sometimes V is discrete in certain ranges and continuous in others. The distribution is then represented by finite probabilities at the discrete points and probability-density functions in the continuous ranges. Equations (A-1) to (A-5) still hold, with the understanding that summation is used in the discrete ranges and integration is used in the continuous ranges.

A more sophisticated approach is to express $P(V)$ in terms of the δ functions (or impulse function, Appendix B) in the discrete ranges. Equations (A-4) to (A-6) would then hold good in general.

A-3. Compound Events. A compound event is one which can be separated into a number of constituent events. Let A, B, C, $\ldots$ denote the constituent events, and a_1, a_2, a_3, $\ldots$; b_1, b_2, b_3, $\ldots$; c_1, c_2, c_3, $\ldots$; $\ldots$ denote the possible outcomes of A, B, C, $\ldots$, respectively. Each combination of a_i, b_j, c_k, $\ldots$ is then a possible outcome of the compound event. The joint probability $P(a_i, b_j, c_k, \ldots)$ is the probability that the combination a_i, b_j, c_k, $\ldots$ occurs.

Two events are said to be independent if the distribution of one is independent of the outcome of the other, and vice versa. Therefore, if all the constituent events are independent of each other, the joint probability $P(a_i, b_j, c_k, \ldots)$ is simply the probability that a_i, b_j, c_k, $\ldots$ have occurred in turn without consideration of what has happened before:

$$P(a_i, b_j, c_k, \ldots) = P(a_i) P(b_j) P(c_k) \ldots \tag{A-7}$$

where $P(a_i)$, $P(b_j)$, $P(c_k)$, $\ldots$ are the individual probabilities of occurrence.

Let V_{ai}, V_{bj}, V_{ck}, $\ldots$ denote the values attached to the outcomes a_i, b_j, c_k, $\ldots$, respectively. From Eqs. (A-7) and (A-2), it can be readily shown that

$$\langle F_1(V_a) F_2(V_b) F_3(V_c) \cdots \rangle = \langle F_1(V_a) \rangle \langle F_2(V_b) \rangle \langle F_3(V_c) \rangle \tag{A-8}$$

where F_1, F_2, F_3 are arbitrary functions of V_a, V_b, V_c, respectively.

A-4. The Law of Large Numbers. Let us consider the sum V_t of the variates of N chance events. For convenience, we shall change our notation somewhat and use the subscript i to denote the ith chance event, and V_i its variate:

$$V_t \equiv \sum_{i=1}^{N} V_i \tag{A-9}$$

The distributions of the events may or may not be the same, and some of the distributions may be continuous while others may be discrete. Since Eqs. (A-1), (A-4), and (A-9) are all linear, it follows that

$$\langle V_t \rangle = \sum_{i=1}^{N} \langle V_i \rangle \tag{A-10}$$

Equation (A-10) states that the mean value of the sum is the sum of the mean. Does the same statement hold for the standard deviation?

$$\sigma_t{}^2 \equiv \langle (V_t - \langle V_t \rangle)^2 \rangle = \left\langle \left[\sum_{i=1}^{N} (V_i - \langle V_i \rangle) \right]^2 \right\rangle = \sum_{i=1}^{N} \langle (V_i - \langle V_i \rangle)^2 \rangle$$
$$+ \sum_{i=1}^{N} \sum_{j=1}^{N}{}' \langle (V_i - \langle V_i \rangle)(V_j - \langle V_j \rangle) \rangle \tag{A-11}$$

The symbol Σ' indicates the sum over all values of j not equal to i. If the constituent events are independent, Eq. (A-8) gives, for $i \neq j$,

$$\langle (V_i - \langle V_i \rangle)(V_j - \langle V_j \rangle) \rangle = \langle (V_i - \langle V_i \rangle) \rangle \langle (V_j - \langle V_j \rangle) \rangle = 0 \qquad \text{(A-12)}$$

Therefore, Eq. (A-11) becomes

$$\sigma_t{}^2 = \sum_{i=1}^{N} \sigma_i{}^2 \qquad \text{(A-13)}$$

Equation (A-13) holds only if all the events are independent of each other.

Next, let us consider the special case of N independent trials of identical chance events:

$$\langle V_i \rangle = \langle V_1 \rangle \qquad \sigma_i = \sigma_1 \qquad \text{with } i = 1, 2, \ldots, N$$

Let V_{av} denote the average value of the N repetitions. By definition,

$$V_{av} = \frac{V_t}{N} \qquad \text{(A-14)}$$

Equations (A-10) and (A-13) become

$$\langle V_{av} \rangle = \langle V_1 \rangle \qquad \text{(A-15)}$$

$$\langle (V_{av} - \langle V_{av} \rangle)^2 \rangle = \frac{\sigma_t{}^2}{N^2} = \frac{1}{N^2} N\sigma_1{}^2 = \frac{\sigma_1{}^2}{N} \qquad \text{(A-16)}$$

Equation (A-15) reaffirms the definition of expected value. Equation (A-16) is very significant. It states that, by averaging the results of N independent trials, the mean-square deviation is reduced by a factor $1/N$. In other words, the averaged outcome of a large number of trials is far more predictable than the outcome of a single trial. This is essentially the law of large numbers.

In the next two sections, two theorems will be discussed which put the above idea into more tangible form.

A-5. Tchebysheff's Inequality. While one would expect a narrow distribution when the standard deviation σ is small, and a widespread distribution when σ is large, the idea is given a more precise formulation by Tchebysheff's inequality.

Let us consider a distribution $P(v)$ with expected value m and standard deviation σ. Our purpose is to determine the probability that v lies outside the range $m \pm a$. For simplicity's sake, the distribution $P(v)$ is assumed to be continuous, although the essence of the arguments applies whether the distribution is continuous or not. By definition of σ and Eq. (A-5),

$$\sigma^2 = \langle (v - m)^2 \rangle = \int_{-\infty}^{m-a} (v - m)^2 P(v)\, dv + \int_{m-a}^{m+a} (v - m)^2 P(v)\, dv$$
$$+ \int_{m+a}^{\infty} (v - m)^2 P(v)\, dv \qquad \text{(A-17)}$$

If we drop out the middle integral on the right-hand side of Eq. (A-17) and replace $(v - m)^2$ by a^2 in the other two integrals, the value of the expression is reduced by both actions. Therefore

$$\sigma^2 > a^2 \left[\int_{-\infty}^{m-a} P(v)\, dv + \int_{m+a}^{\infty} P(v)\, dv \right] \qquad \text{(A-18)}$$

The expression inside the brackets is the probability that v differs from m by a distance of more than a and will be denoted as $P(|v - m| > a)$. Equation (A-18) becomes

$$P(|v - m| > a) < \frac{\sigma^2}{a^2} \tag{A-19}$$

The inequality (A-19) holds, no matter what the nature of the chance event. Suppose that v is the averaged outcome of N independent and identical trials and that the standard deviation of each trial is σ_1; Eq. (A-16) gives $\sigma^2 = \sigma_1^2/N$. Equation (A-19) becomes

$$P(|v - m| > a) < \frac{\sigma_1^2}{Na^2} \tag{A-20}$$

This relation is known as Tchebysheff's inequality. Its significance can be illustrated by the following example:

Example A-1. How many throws of dice do we need to average so that for at least 90 per cent of the time the averaged outcome is between 3 and 4?

Solution

$$m = 3.5$$
$$a = 0.5$$
$$\sigma_1^2 = \tfrac{1}{6} \times (0.5^2 + 1.5^2 + 2.5^2) \times 2 = 2.917$$
$$P(|v - m| > a) = 1 - 0.9 = 0.1$$
$$N < \frac{2.917}{0.5^2 \times 0.1} = 117$$

A-6. Normal Distribution, Central Limit Theorem. The normal distribution for variate v with expected value m and standard deviation σ is defined as

$$P(v) = \frac{1}{\sqrt{2\pi}\,\sigma}\, e^{-(v-m)^2/2\sigma^2} \tag{A-21}$$

It is easily verified that, for the above density function, Eq. (A-6) and the definitions of m and σ are satisfied.

The significance of the normal distribution lies in its universality which is stated in the central limit theorem:

The distribution function of the averaged value of N independent trials of a chance event approaches normal distribution as N approaches infinity.

The most significant part of the above statement is that it says nothing about the distribution of the chance event itself. Thus whether each trial consists of throwing a die or flipping a coin or measured instantaneous velocity in a controlled turbulent flow makes no difference.

The above statement of the theorem may be generalized as follows:

The distribution function of the sum (or averaged value) of N trials approaches the normal distribution as N approaches infinity; whether or not these trials are independent and whether or not these are repetitions of the same or a large number of different chance events make no difference, as long as the contribution of each trial, including its effect on the outcomes of other trials, is of the order of $1/\sqrt{N}$ of the sum (or averaged value).

Let us consider the case of flipping a coin with equally probable outcomes 1 and -1. If each throw is independent, the distribution of the averaged outcome approaches normal distribution with zero mean and $1/N$ as σ^2 for large N [Eqs. (A-15) and (A-16)]. If each throw is partially dependent, for instance, the probability of repeating the previous sign may be $\tfrac{3}{4}$ instead of $\tfrac{1}{2}$, the contribution of each trial is

$$\frac{1}{N}\left(1 + \tfrac{1}{2} + \tfrac{1}{4} + \tfrac{1}{8} + \cdots\right) = \frac{2}{N}$$

The above expression can be explained as follows: A + gives 1 for the value of its own trial, $\frac{1}{2}$ for the expected value of the next trial, and so forth, and the sum is divided by N to give its effect on the averaged outcome. Since the latter is of the magnitude $1/\sqrt{N}$, the generalized version of the theorem states that the distribution of the averaged outcome approaches normal distribution. However its mean-square deviation is larger than $1/N$.

If a variate meets the conditions for normal distribution as stated in the generalized version of the theorem, its distribution function is given by Eq. (A-21), with

$$m = \langle v \rangle$$
$$\sigma^2 = \langle (v - m)^2 \rangle = \langle v^2 \rangle - \langle v \rangle^2$$

Its distribution and higher moments are completely determined by the first and second moments.

The fact that the central limit theorem is pertinent to our study of systems with random inputs can be explained in the following light: The value of a system variable at any given time is determined as the net effect of inputs of all sources at all previous times. If, at any fixed instant, many of these previous inputs are significant and the contribution of none predominates, the amplitude distribution of the system variable is expected to approach normal distribution. Once its mean-square value is known, the entire distribution is determined.

A-7. Characteristic Function and Moment-generating Function. In the preceding section, the central limit theorem is stated without a proof. To prove the theorem, we shall need some powerful mathematical tools, which will be introduced presently. Consider a joint-probability-density function $p(x_1,x_2, \ldots ,x_m)$. Its moment-generating function is defined as

$$M(s_1,s_2, \ldots ,s_m) = \underset{-\infty}{\overset{\infty}{\iiint}} \cdots \int p(x_1,x_2, \ldots ,x_m) \exp \left(\sum_{i=1}^{i=m} s_i x_i \right) dx \quad \text{(A-22)}$$

where dx denotes the product $dx_1\, dx_2 \cdots dx_m$. If we change s_i to $-s_i$ and x_i to t_i we recognize immediately the right-hand side of Eq. (A-22) as the multidimensional, double-ended Laplace transform of $p(x_1,x_2, \ldots ,x_m)$. Another way of interpreting Eq. (A-22) is that the moment-generating function is the average value of the exponential function $\exp \left(\sum_{i=1}^{i=m} s_i x_i \right)$.

If we differentiate the moment-generating function with respect to s_a, s_b, s_c, $\ldots$ in succession, where the subscripts a, b, c, etc., may or may not repeat themselves, and then set $s_i = 0$ for all i, we find

$$\frac{\partial \partial \cdots \partial M(0,0,0)}{\partial s_a\, \partial s_b\, \partial s_c \cdots} = \underset{-\infty}{\overset{\infty}{\iiint}} \cdots \int (x_a x_b x_c \cdots) p(x_1,x_2, \ldots ,x_m)\, dx$$
$$= \langle x_a x_b x_c \cdots \rangle \quad \text{(A-23)}$$

The above equation shows that the statistical moments are the corresponding derivatives of the moment-generating function at the origin.

Next let us consider the convergence range of the integral on the right-hand side of

Eq. (A-23). For purely imaginary values of s_i, $i = 1, 2, \ldots , m$,

$$M(s_1,s_2, \ldots ,s_m) \leq \iiint_{-\infty}^{\infty} \cdots \int p(x_1,x_2, \ldots ,x_m) \left| \exp \left(\sum_{i=1}^{i=m} s_i x_i \right) \right| dx$$

$$= \iiint_{-\infty}^{\infty} \cdots \int p(x_1,x_2, \ldots ,x_m)\, dx = 1$$

Therefore the function $M(s_1,s_2, \ldots ,s_m)$ is convergent in a region adjacent to the imaginary axes of s_i. This is the same as the region of convergence for double-ended Laplace transforms. Similarly to the Fourier transform, we define a characteristic function as

$$C(\omega_1,\omega_2, \ldots ,\omega_m) \equiv M(j\omega_1,j\omega_2, \ldots ,j\omega_m) \equiv \left\langle \exp \left(\sum_{i=1}^{i=m} j\omega_i x_i \right) \right\rangle \quad \text{(A-24)}$$

Sometimes $C(\omega_1,\omega_2, \ldots ,\omega_m)$ is obtained first, and the density function is calculated from it by the inverse transform:

$$p(x_1,x_2, \ldots ,x_m) = \frac{1}{(2\pi)^m} \iint_{-\infty}^{\infty} \cdots \int C(\omega_1,\omega_2, \ldots ,\omega_m) \exp \left(-\sum_i j\omega_i x_i \right) d\omega$$

$$\text{(A-25)}$$

A-8. Mathematical Derivation of the Multivariate Normal Distribution. Presently we shall give a heuristic proof of the central limit theorem for a number of correlated random variables $x_1, x_2, x_3, \ldots , x_m$. The result is more general than that stated in Sec. A-6 as the latter is simply a special case with $m = 1$. Each of the m variables is obtained as a sum of N independent trials:

$$x_i = \sum_{k=1}^{k=N} y_{ik} \qquad i = 1, 2, \ldots , m \qquad \text{(A-26)}$$

The joint distribution of $y_{1k}, y_{2k}, \ldots , y_{mk}$ may be different for different values of k. For a given k, the distribution of some y_{ik} may be independent of others and some y_{ik} may be zero. Without losing generality, we assume that the mean value of each y_{ik} is zero. We assume further that there exist limits $a > 0$ and $b > 0$ such that

$$\underbrace{|y_{ik} y_{jk} \cdots y_{lk}|}_{n \text{ factors}} < a^n \qquad \text{(A-27)}$$

$$\sum_{k=1}^{k=N} \overline{y_{ik}^2} > Nb^2 \qquad \text{(A-28)}$$

The above assumptions are broad enough to suit many situations. For instance, if the joint distributions of the y_{ik}'s of each trial are identical, or if there are a few different distributions of y_{ik}'s which are repeated proportionately in the N trials as N varies, the assumptions are met. We shall derive a joint distribution function for the x_i's as N becomes very large.

As the mean-square values of the x_i's increase proportionately with N, we define a new set of variables $u_i = x_i/\sqrt{N}$. The moment-generating function of u_i is given by

Eq. (A-22):

$$
\left\langle \exp\left(\sum_{i=1}^{i=m} s_i u_i \right) \right\rangle = \left\langle \exp\left(\sum_{i=1}^{i=m} \sum_{k=1}^{k=N} \frac{s_i y_{ik}}{\sqrt{N}} \right) \right\rangle
$$

$$
= \prod_{k=1}^{k=N} \left\langle \exp\left(\sum_{i=1}^{i=m} \frac{s_i y_{ik}}{\sqrt{N}} \right) \right\rangle
$$

$$
= \prod_{k=1}^{k=N} \left\langle 1 + \sum_{i=1}^{i=m} \frac{s_i y_{ik}}{\sqrt{N}} + \sum_{i,l=1}^{i,l=m} \frac{s_i s_l}{2N} y_{ik} y_{lk} + O\left(\frac{1}{N\sqrt{N}} \right) \right\rangle
$$

$$
= \prod_{k=1}^{k=N} \left[1 + \frac{1}{2N} \sum_{i,l=1}^{i,l=m} s_i s_l \langle y_{ik} y_{lk} \rangle + O\left(\frac{1}{N\sqrt{N}} \right) \right]
$$

In the above equation, the second equality sign is due to the independence of the N trials, the fourth equality sign is due to the assumption that $\langle y_{ik} \rangle = 0$, and $O(1/N\sqrt{N})$ stands for terms of the order of magnitude of $1/N\sqrt{N}$ and smaller. Taking the logarithm of the above equation and using the expansion $\log (1 + x) = 1 + x + (x^2/2) + \cdots$ give

$$
\log M(s_1, s_2, \ldots, s_m) = \log \left\langle \exp\left(\sum_{i=1}^{i=m} s_i u_i \right) \right\rangle
$$

$$
= \sum_{k=1}^{k=N} \left[\frac{1}{2N} \sum_{i,l=1}^{i,l=m} s_i s_l \langle y_{ik} y_{lk} \rangle + O\left(\frac{1}{N\sqrt{N}} \right) \right] \tag{A-29}
$$

We note that

$$
\sum_{k=1}^{k=N} O\left(\frac{1}{N\sqrt{N}} \right) = O\left(\frac{1}{\sqrt{N}} \right) \rightarrow 0
$$

It approaches zero as N approaches infinity. Let the coefficients C_{il} be defined as $\langle u_i u_l \rangle$. From Eq. (A-26),

$$
C_{il} = \left\langle \frac{1}{N} \left(\sum_{k=1}^{k=N} y_{ik} \right) \left(\sum_{k'=1}^{k'=N} y_{lk'} \right) \right\rangle
$$

$$
= \frac{1}{N} \sum_{k,k'=1}^{k,k'=N} \langle y_{ik} y_{lk'} \rangle
$$

Since the different trials are independent, $\langle y_{ik} y_{lk'} \rangle = 0$ for $k \neq k'$. The above equation becomes

$$
C_{il} = \langle u_i u_l \rangle = \frac{1}{N} \sum_{k=1}^{k=N} \langle y_{ik} y_{lk} \rangle \tag{A-30}
$$

Substituting Eq. (A-30) in (A-29), we obtain in the limit of very large N

$$\log M(s_1, s_2, \ldots, s_n) = \sum_{i,l=1}^{i,l=m} \tfrac{1}{2} C_{il} s_i s_l$$

The above equation will hold to any desired degree of accuracy by increasing N. Alternatively, it can be written as

$$M(s_1, s_2, \ldots, s_n) = \exp\left(\sum_{i,l=1}^{i,l=m} \tfrac{1}{2} C_{il} s_i s_l\right) \tag{A-31}$$

Correspondingly the characteristic function can be obtained from (A-31) by substituting $j\omega_i$ for s_i, and the joint-probability-density function is given by Eq. (A-25):

$$p(u_1, u_2, \ldots, u_m) = \frac{1}{(2\pi)^m} \int\!\!\!\int\!\!\!\int_{-\infty}^{\infty} \cdots \int \exp\left(-\sum_{i,l=1}^{i,l=m} \tfrac{1}{2} C_{il}\omega_i\omega_l - \sum_i j\omega_i u_i\right) d\omega \tag{A-32}$$

To evaluate Eq. (A-32), it is convenient to use the matrix notation. Let $\mathbf{C}$ denote the $m \times m$ matrix, with C_{il} as its element in the ith row and lth column. $\mathbf{C}$ is a symmetrical positive definite matrix, by definition of C_{il}. Let $\omega'(\omega)$ and $\mathbf{u}'(\mathbf{u})$ denote the row (column) vectors with elements ω_i and u_i, respectively. Since $\mathbf{C}$ is symmetrical, there exists an orthogonal transformation $\mathbf{T}$ such that

$$\mathbf{T}^{-1}\mathbf{C}\mathbf{T} = \mathbf{B}$$

where $\mathbf{B}$ is a diagonal matrix. Let B_i, $i = 1, 2, \ldots, m$, denote the diagonal elements of B. Let vectors $\mathbf{\mu}$ and $\mathbf{v}$ with elements μ_i and v_i be defined as

$$\mathbf{\mu} \equiv \mathbf{T}^{-1}\omega$$
$$\mathbf{v} \equiv \mathbf{T}^{-1}\mathbf{u}$$

Then
$$\mathbf{\mu}' = \omega'(\mathbf{T}^{-1})' = \omega'\mathbf{T}$$
$$\mathbf{v}' = \mathbf{u}'\mathbf{T}$$

$$\sum_{i,l=1}^{i,l=m} C_{il}\omega_i\omega_l = \omega'\mathbf{C}\omega = \omega'\mathbf{T}\mathbf{T}^{-1}\mathbf{C}\mathbf{T}\mathbf{T}^{-1}\omega$$

$$= \mathbf{\mu}'\mathbf{B}\mathbf{\mu} = \sum_i B_i\mu_i^2$$

$$\sum_{i=1}^{i=m} \omega_i u_i = \omega'\mathbf{u} = \omega'\mathbf{T}\mathbf{T}^{-1}\mathbf{u} = \mathbf{\mu}'\mathbf{v} = \sum_{i=1}^{i=m} \mu_i v_i$$

$$d\omega = \det|\mathbf{T}|\, d\mu = d\mu$$

Substituting the above relations in Eq. (A-32) gives

$$p(u_1, u_2, \ldots, u_m) = \prod_{i=1}^{i=m} \frac{1}{2\pi} \int_{-\infty}^{\infty} \exp\left(-\tfrac{1}{2}B_i\mu_i^2 - j\mu_i v_i\right) d\mu_i \tag{A-33}$$

By a change of variable $z_i = \mu_i + jv_i/B_i$, we obtain

$$\frac{1}{2\pi} \int_{-\infty}^{\infty} \exp\left(\tfrac{1}{2}B_i\mu_i^2 - j\mu_i v_i\right) d\mu_i = \frac{e^{-v_i^2/2B_i}}{2\pi} \int_{-\infty+jv_i/B_i}^{\infty+jv_i/B_i} e^{-B_i z_i^2/2}\, dz_i$$

$$= \frac{1}{\sqrt{2\pi B_i}}\, e^{-v_i^2/2B_i}$$

Substituting the above expression in Eq. (A-33) gives

$$p(u_1, u_2, \ldots, u_m) = \frac{e^{-\sum_{i=1}^{i=m} v_i{}^2/2B_i}}{(2\pi)^{m/2}\left(\prod_i B_i\right)^{1/2}} \tag{A-34}$$

The expression on the right-hand side is in terms of the new variables v_i. To change it back to u_i we note that

$$\prod_{i=1}^{i=m} B_i = \det |\mathbf{B}| = \det |\mathbf{T}^{-1}| \det |\mathbf{C}| \det |\mathbf{T}|$$

$$= \det |\mathbf{C}|$$

$$\sum_{i=1}^{i=m} \frac{v_i{}^2}{B_i} = \mathbf{v}'\mathbf{B}^{-1}\mathbf{v} = \mathbf{u}'\mathbf{C}^{-1}\mathbf{u}$$

$$= \frac{1}{\Delta} \sum_{i,j=1}^{i,j=m} \Delta_{ij} u_i u_j$$

where Δ is the determinant of $\mathbf{C}$ and Δ_{ij} is the cofactor of C_{ij}. (There is no need to distinguish Δ_{ij} and Δ_{ji} since $\mathbf{C}$ is symmetrical.) Substituting these relations in (A-34) gives

$$p(u_1, u_2, \ldots, u_m) = \frac{1}{(2\pi)^{m/2}\Delta^{1/2}} \exp\left(-\frac{1}{2\Delta} \sum_{i,j=1}^{i,j=m} \Delta_{ij} u_i u_j\right) \tag{A-35}$$

Equation (A-35) gives the density function of what is known as the multivariate normal distribution. In case there is only one variable, it reduces to Eq. (A-21). In practical work, the density function of Eq. (A-35) and the moment-generating function of Eq. (A-31) are just about equally important.

A-9. Population, Sample, Statistical Inference, Estimate, Maximum-likelihood Criterion. In the previous sections, we have been concerned mainly with a deductive process: Knowing the physical nature of the chance event or events, what can we say about the outcome? However, in many applications, the reverse process is called for: Knowing the results of a large number of trials, what can we say about the physical nature?

While the deductive process is safe, the inductive process is highly tricky and unsafe. Usually, physical insight plays the main part and statistical techniques play only an auxiliary role. Whether the result is worthwhile or not depends on whether the physical insight is right, and there is no textbook which teaches us how to gain physical insights. We shall confine ourselves to an introductory treatment of the statistical techniques.

Population means the results of a large number of trials of the same experiment. Here the word "same" is the most significant. It may mean one of the following:

Case 1. We isolate all the factors we know which may influence the experiment, control these factors so that they are identical in all the trials, and leave only the unknown factors to chance.

Case 2.   We know certain factors that would influence the results of the experiment. However, we do not isolate these factors, as we are interested in the statistics of the population as a whole.

Sample means the small percentage of the population that we analyze.

Inductive inference can be defined as the process of discovering laws or other facts about the population with an analysis of the sample as a starting point.   In case the above-mentioned facts are numerical figures, the process is called *estimation*.

There are two points worth mentioning:

1. The reliability of inductive inference or estimation depends on the selection of the sample.   If the population is defined according to case 1, the samples are selected so that in each sample, all the controlled conditions are met.   If the population is defined according to case 2, the sample must have as nearly as possible proportional representation of all factors appearing in the population.

As an example of the former, in studying the safety of an airplane in a storm or the seaworthiness of a ship, we are interested only in the statistical properties of atmosphere turbulence or ocean waves under stormy conditions.   All the samples representing calm conditions or insufficiently stormy conditions are discarded.   As an example of case 2, in forecasting election returns, the samples must be selected in such a way that they represent every possible classification of the populace.

2. In many cases, the word "population" represents a concept rather than results of actual measurement.   For instance, in determining the spectral density of missile acceleration in rough air, every sample record is obtained at tremendous cost.   In analyzing the samples, our purpose, in the most restrictive sense, is to find out something about the spectral densities of the acceleration of missiles of the same design in atmosphere of the same description of roughness.   It is a conceptual population rather than an actual population which consists of no more than the sample records that we analyzed.   If it were for the latter, we might as well put the sample records on a standard signal analyzer and get the exact height of each spectral line.   No statistics would then be necessary.

The following example illustrates the process of inductive inference: Knowing the exact weight x_i, $i = 1, 2, 3, \ldots, N$, of N individuals of a certain sex and age group, we wish to determine the following for the entire population of the same sex and age description:

1. Mean weight
2. Standard deviation
3. Distribution of weight

The first two items are point estimates.   Let brackets preceded by "est" denote estimated value:

$$\text{est } [\bar{x}] = \frac{1}{N} \sum_{i=1}^{N} x_i \tag{A-36}$$

$$\text{est } [(x - \bar{x})^2] = \frac{1}{N} \sum_{i=1}^{N} (x_i - \text{est } [\bar{x}])^2 = \frac{1}{N} \sum_{i=1}^{N} x_i^2 - \left(\frac{1}{N} \sum_{i=1}^{N} x_i \right)^2 \tag{A-37}$$

The distribution function can be determined on the basis of *maximum likelihood*, that is, finding the distribution function among all possible distribution functions which gives the highest probability or probability density of what already occurred. Physical insight comes into the picture in restricting or specifying possible distribution functions.   To illustrate what we mean, we shall study the following three cases:

Case 1.   Since the weight of an individual can be considered as independent of the weight of another individual selected at random, Eq. (A-7) gives the probability density of all the x_i's occurring as

$$\prod_i P(x_i) = \text{max} \tag{A-38}$$

The only restriction on $P(x)$ is

$$\int_{-\infty}^{\infty} P(x) \, dx = 1 \tag{A-39}$$

The solution of the above variational problem is readily shown to be

$$P(x) = \frac{1}{N} \sum_i \delta(x - x_i) \tag{A-40}$$

Equation (A-40) states that the distribution function is a sum of impulse functions at the measured weights. This is obvious nonsense physically, but it is the correct mathematical solution. It leads to the following observation:

Case 2. Since the weight of an individual fluctuates easily within 5 lb, we arrange the weight scale in 5-lb divisions. Conceivably, a man may weigh anywhere from 50 to 400 lb, and there are 70 such divisions. Let $P(x_\alpha)$ represent the unknown probability of a randomly selected individual's weight being in the range $x_\alpha \pm 2.5$, and n_α represent the number of samples x_i in the range $x_\alpha \pm 2.5$. The probabilities $P(x_\alpha)$ can be determined by the maximum-likelihood criterion:

$$\prod_\alpha [P(x_\alpha)]^{n_\alpha} = \text{max} \tag{A-41}$$

$$\sum_\alpha P(x_\alpha) = 1 \tag{A-42}$$

The solution is

$$P(x_\alpha) = \frac{n_\alpha}{N} \tag{A-43}$$

which is, of course, a well-known result.

Case 3. A more sophisticated form of physical reasoning could be as follows: A man's weight can be considered as the net result of a large variety of factors none of which has a deciding influence. It is expected to approximate the normal distribution,

$$P(x) = \frac{1}{\sqrt{2\pi}\,\sigma} e^{-(x-m)^2/2\sigma^2} \tag{A-44}$$

Therefore, the joint probability density is

$$\prod_{i=1}^{N} P(x_i) = \left(\frac{1}{\sqrt{2\pi}\,\sigma}\right)^N e^{-\sum_i (x_i-m)^2/2\sigma^2} \tag{A-45}$$

Differentiating the above expression with respect to m and σ and setting the results equal to zero, the following results are obtained:

$$m = \frac{1}{N} \sum_{i=1}^{N} x_i$$

$$\sigma^2 = \frac{1}{N} \sum_{i=1}^{N} (x_i - m)^2$$

These are exactly the same as Eqs. (A-36) and (A-37).

What are the comparative advantages of the three cases? The first case has no merit. The second case is the most widely used. It does not require much physical insight and is more or less safe. However, a large number of samples are required. The third case requires far fewer samples; however, if we extend the result to extremes, we get absurd answers. For instance, there is always a nonvanishing probability for negative weight.

The above example has its parallel in spectral-density measurements. For laboratory tests, we collect a large amount of data and impose no more restriction than in the second case. However, for on-the-spot tests, such as in self-adaptive systems, the shape of the spectral density is usually assumed fixed except for the magnitude and maybe one or two other frequency parameters.

A-10. Confidence Interval. When a certain parameter of the population is estimated by averaging over N samples, the sample mean does not necessarily coincide with the population mean. The estimation has little value if we do not know how reliable it is. A confidence interval is defined as a tolerance range about the sample mean which is so selected that the probability for the tolerance range to contain the population mean is a predetermined value. As discussed in Sec. A-6, the sample mean V_{av} is distributed normally about the population mean $\bar{v}$ (same as $\langle v \rangle$):

$$P(V_{av}) = \sqrt{\frac{N}{2\pi}}\frac{1}{\sigma_1} e^{-N(V_{av}-\bar{v})^2/2\sigma_1^2} \tag{A-46}$$

where σ_1 is the standard deviation of each sample. It is either known or can be estimated by Eq. (A-37). The probability that $|V_{av} - \bar{v}|$ is less than a is

$$P(|V_{av} - \bar{v}| < a) = \int_{\bar{v}-a}^{\bar{v}+a} P(V_{av})\, dV_{av} = \frac{1}{\sqrt{\pi}}\int_{-(\sqrt{N/2})(a/\sigma_1)}^{(\sqrt{N/2})(a/\sigma_1)} e^{-x^2}\, dx$$

$$= \Phi\left(\sqrt{\frac{N}{2}}\frac{a}{\sigma_1}\right) \tag{A-47}$$

In Eq. (A-47), $\Phi(x)$ is the error function. An alternative form of writing (A-47) is

$$a = k_p\sigma_1\sqrt{\frac{2}{N}} \tag{A-48}$$

where k_p is a constant depending on the specified probability. It is tabulated as follows:

TABLE A-1

P	k_p
0.5	0.477
0.8	0.906
0.9	1.163
0.95	1.386
0.99	1.82
0.999	2.32

Equation (A-48) can be applied to the problem of Example A-1. Since a large number of throws are required, V_{av} is assumed to be normally distributed. From Table A-1, k_p is found to be 1.163:

$$N = 2\left(\frac{k_p\sigma_1}{a}\right)^2 = 2 \times \frac{1.163^2 \times 2.917}{0.5^2} = 30$$

The result is considerably more optimistic than that obtained from Tchebysheff's inequality. The discrepancy is there because, while Tchebysheff's inequality represents an absolute bound for even the worst possible distribution, Table A-1 holds only if V_{av} is normally distributed.

A-11. Error Analysis. One problem which arises frequently in system design is that of fixing the tolerance limits of components employed in the system. Let b_i represent performance parameters of the system, let α_μ represent parameters specifying properties of the components, and let the prefix δ represent a small change; then

$$\delta b_i = \sum_\mu \frac{\partial b_i}{\partial \alpha_\mu} \delta \alpha_\mu \tag{A-49}$$

If only a few α_μ's are in question, the standard procedure is to consider the worst case:

$$|\delta b_i| \leq \sum_\mu \left| \frac{\partial b_i}{\partial \alpha_\mu} \right| |\delta \alpha_\mu| \tag{A-50}$$

However, if the effect of a large number of independent $\delta \alpha$'s is being considered, it would be desirable to take into account the randomness of the variations. Let σ_i and σ_μ represent the standard deviations of b_i and α_μ, respectively, and $\sigma_{i\mu}$ the standard deviation of b_i due to changes in α_μ alone. From Eq. (A-13), we have

$$\sigma_i{}^2 = \sum_\mu \sigma_{i\mu}{}^2 = \sum_\mu \left| \frac{\partial b_i}{\partial \alpha_\mu} \right|^2 \sigma_\mu{}^2 \tag{A-51}$$

Generally the component parameters are specified by tolerance limits K_μ: $\bar{\alpha}_\mu - K_\mu < \alpha_\mu < \bar{\alpha}_\mu + K_\mu$. If $P(\alpha_\mu)$ is assumed to be uniform within the allowable range $\bar{\alpha}_\mu \pm K_\mu$ and zero outside, σ_μ can be calculated:

$$\sigma_\mu{}^2 = \frac{1}{2K_\mu} \int_{\bar{\alpha}_\mu - K_\mu}^{\bar{\alpha}_\mu + K_\mu} (\alpha_\mu - \bar{\alpha}_\mu)^2 \, d\alpha_\mu = \frac{K_\mu{}^2}{3} \tag{A-52}$$

Combining Eqs. (A-51) and (A-52) results in

$$\sigma_i{}^2 = \frac{1}{3} \sum_\mu \left| \frac{\partial b_i}{\partial \alpha_\mu} \right|^2 K_\mu{}^2 \tag{A-53}$$

A-12. Correlation and Regression. Sometimes two chance events are not independent. If the underlying physical processes are known, this dependence can be expressed in terms of the joint distribution function of the two variates. However, the reverse is true in most instances, and the dependence of the two variates is established by analysis of the samples. Two related techniques, correlation and regression, will now be discussed.

Let u and v denote the two related variates, for instance, weight and height of an individual, temperature and life of a vacuum tube under rated operating conditions, noise amplitudes at one instant of time and at a slightly later time. Each sample is expressed as a pair of values of the two variates (u_i, v_i). A regression line of v on u is defined as a straight line on the u,v plane with least-mean-square vertical distance from the sample points (see Fig. A-1):

$$v = c_v + b_v u \tag{A-54}$$

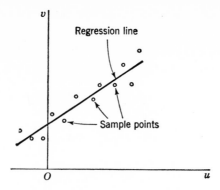

FIG. A-1. Regression line of v on u.

The constants c_v and b_v are determined by minimizing

$$\sum_{i=1}^{N} [v_i - (c_v + b_v u_i)]^2$$

where N represents the total number of samples.   Differentiating the above expression with respect to c_v and b_v and setting the results equal to zero,

$$\sum_{i=1}^{N} [v_i - (c_v + b_v u_i)] = 0 \tag{A-55}$$

$$\sum_{i=1}^{N} u_i[v_i - (c_v + b_v u_i)] = 0 \tag{A-56}$$

Equation (A-55) can be expressed as

$$c_v = v_{av} + b_v u_{av} \tag{A-57}$$

where v_{av} and u_{av} are sample average values.   Substituting Eq. (A-57) in (A-56) and solving for b_v,

$$b_v = \frac{\sum_i u_i(v_i - v_{av})}{\sum_i u_i(u_i - u_{av})} \tag{A-58}$$

Let Du_i and Dv_i represent $u_i - u_{av}$ and $v_i - v_{av}$, respectively.   Since

$$\sum_i (u_i - u_{av}) = \sum_i (v_i - v_{av}) = 0$$

Eq. (A-58) can be written as

$$b_v = \frac{\sum_i (Du_i)(Dv_i)}{\sum_i (Du_i)^2} = \frac{(1/N)\sum_i (Du_i)(Dv_i)}{\sigma_u{}^2} = \frac{(1/N)\sum_i u_i(Dv_i)}{\sigma_u{}^2} = \frac{(1/N)\sum_i v_i(Du_i)}{\sigma_u{}^2}$$

$$\tag{A-59}$$

Equation (A-59) gives three alternative forms for calculating the slope b_v of the regression line of v on u. With reference to Eq. (A-57), (A-54) can be rewritten as

$$v - v_{av} = b_v(u - u_{av}) \tag{A-60}$$

Equation (A-60) shows that the regression line always passes through the center of weight (u_{av}, v_{av}).

The physical significance of the regression line of v on u is that, with u considered as the independent variable, it represents the best estimate of v as a linear function of u in the least-mean-square-error sense. We can also interchange the roles of u and v in the above derivation to obtain the regression line of u on v:

$$u - u_{av} = b_u(v - v_{av}) \tag{A-61}$$

where

$$b_u = \frac{(1/N) \sum_i (Du_i)(Dv_i)}{\sigma_v{}^2} \tag{A-62}$$

Equation (A-61) represents a straight line on the uv plane with least-mean-square horizontal distance from the sample points.

Equations (A-59) and (A-62) give two different values for the two slopes. However, neither value is really significant, since both depend on the selection of units of measurement for the two variates. To remedy this defect, u/σ_u and v/σ_v are used as the variates instead of u and v. Equations for the two regression lines become

$$\frac{v - v_{av}}{\sigma_v} = \phi_{uv} \frac{u - u_{av}}{\sigma_u} \tag{A-63}$$

$$\frac{u - u_{av}}{\sigma_u} = \phi_{uv} \frac{v - v_{av}}{\sigma_v} \tag{A-64}$$

where

$$\phi_{uv} = \frac{(1/N) \sum_i (Du_i)(Dv_i)}{\sigma_u \sigma_v} \tag{A-65}$$

The significant point about the two new regression lines is that they now have identical slope which is also dimensionless. The slope ϕ_{uv} is referred to in the literature as the correlation coefficient, as it is a unique measure of the linear dependence of the two variates.

PROPERTIES OF THE δ FUNCTION

The term "δ function" is synonymous with "impulse function." It is defined by the following equations:

$$\delta(x) = 0 \qquad \text{for all } x \neq 0 \tag{B-1}$$

$$\int_{x_1}^{x_2} \delta(x)\, dx = \begin{cases} 1 & \text{if } x_1 < 0 < x_2 \\ 0 & \text{if } x_1 x_2 > 0 \end{cases} \tag{B-2}$$

The above equations imply that $\delta(x)$ has an infinite peak at $x = 0$. Physically we may think of $y = \delta(x)$ as a finite pulse with unit area under its curve, and the y dimension is stretched to infinity while the x dimension is shrunk to zero in such a way that the area measure xy is conserved. Derivatives of $\delta(x)$ can be considered as derivatives of the pulse function under the same dimensional transform. The situation is illustrated in Fig. B-1.

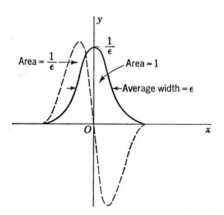

FIG. B-1. Impulse function and its derivative, as ϵ approaches zero.

Equations (B-1) and (B-2) constitute one of the strictest definitions of $\delta(x)$ and allow derivative operations on $\delta(x)$. Sometimes we are not concerned with the derivatives, and Eq. (B-1) can be relaxed somewhat to allow $\delta(x)$ to be represented by a wider class of analytical functions in their limiting forms. This point will be illustrated at the end of this Appendix.

From Eqs. (B-1) and (B-2), the following properties of the δ function can be readily shown:

1.

$$\int_{-a}^{t} \delta(x)\, dx = u(t) \tag{B-3}$$

where a is an arbitrary positive constant and $u(t)$ is the step function.

2.

$$\int_{x_1}^{x_2} f(x)\delta(x)\, dx = \begin{cases} f(0) & x_1 < 0 < x_2 \\ 0 & x_1 x_2 > 0 \end{cases} \tag{B-4}$$

where $f(x)$ is an arbitrary function of x and is continuous at $x = 0$.

3. Let $\delta^{(n)}(x)$ denote $(d^n/dx^n)\delta(x)$, and assume that $f(x)$ has continuous derivatives up to and including the nth. Then

$$\int_{x_1}^{x_2} f(x)\delta^{(n)}(x)\, dx = \begin{cases} (-1)^n f^{(n)}(0) & x_1 < 0 < x_2 \\ 0 & x_1 x_2 > 0 \end{cases} \tag{B-5}$$

Equation (B-5) can be proved as follows: By partial integration,

$$\int_{x_1}^{x_2} f(x)\delta^{(n)}(x)\, dx = \delta^{(n-1)}(x)f(x)\Big|_{x=x_1}^{x=x_2} - \int_{x_1}^{x_2} f^1(x)\delta^{(n-1)}(x)\, dx$$

Owing to Eq. (B-1), $\delta^{(n-1)}(x) = 0$ for all $x \neq 0$. The first term on the right-hand side vanishes. Repeating the above operation, Eq. (B-5) is obtained.

4.

$$\delta(x) = \delta(-x) \tag{B-6}$$

More precisely, what we mean by the above is that

$$\int_{x_1}^{x_2} f(x)\delta(-x)\, dx = \begin{cases} f(0) & x_1 < 0 < x_2 \\ 0 & x_1 x_2 > 0 \end{cases}$$

It is readily shown by a change of variable $y = -x$ and then by making use of Eq. (B-4).

Sometimes it is desirable to replace $\delta(x)$ by one of its analytical forms to facilitate calculation. If such a representation meets both conditions (B-1) and (B-2), with well-defined derivatives all the equations (B-3) to (B-6) hold. An example is

$$\delta(x) = \lim_{c \to \infty} \frac{c}{\sqrt{\pi}} e^{-c^2 x^2} \tag{B-7}$$

$$\delta^{(1)}(x) = \frac{d\delta(x)}{dx} = \lim_{c \to \infty} -\frac{2c^3 x}{\sqrt{\pi}} e^{-c^2 x^2} \tag{B-8}$$

However, if the application does not involve derivatives of the δ function, the requirement of Eq. (B-1) can be relaxed. One frequently used form is

$$\delta(x) = \lim_{T \to \infty} \frac{1}{2\pi} \int_{-T}^{T} e^{ixt}\, dt \tag{B-9}$$

It is easy to verify that the above expression satisfies Eqs. (B-2), (B-3), and (B-4).

STATISTICAL ERROR IN MEASURED
CORRELATION FUNCTIONS

C-1. Continuous Measurement. With reference to the block diagram of Fig. 7-7, $y_\tau(t)$ is the measured correlation function by filtering $x_\tau(t)$:

$$x_\tau(t) = i_1(t - \tau)i_2(t) \tag{C-1}$$

$$y_\tau(t) = \int_0^\infty h(t')x_\tau(t - t') \, dt' \tag{C-2}$$

$$\int_0^\infty h(t') \, dt' = 1 \tag{C-3}$$

$$\langle y_\tau(t) \rangle = \langle x_\tau(t) \rangle = \phi_{12}(\tau) \tag{C-4}$$

The mean-square error in the measured correlation function is

$$\overline{e_\phi{}^2} = \langle [y_\tau(t) - \phi_{12}(\tau)]^2 \rangle = \langle [y_\tau(t)]^2 \rangle - [\phi_{12}(\tau)]^2 \tag{C-5}$$

Equation (C-5) follows directly from (C-4). Presently we shall evaluate $\langle [y_\tau(t)]^2 \rangle$. From Eq. (C-2),

$$\langle [y_\tau(t)]^2 \rangle = \int_0^\infty \int_0^\infty h(t')h(t'')\langle x_\tau(t - t')x_\tau(t - t'') \rangle \, dt' \, dt'' \tag{C-6}$$

Since $i(t)$ is stationary, let $t' - t'' = \lambda$.

$$\langle x_\tau(t - t')x_\tau(t - t'') \rangle = \langle x_\tau(\tau)x_\tau(\tau + \lambda) \rangle$$
$$= \langle i_1(0)i_2(\tau)i_1(\lambda)i_2(\tau + \lambda) \rangle \equiv R(\tau, \lambda) \tag{C-7}$$

Equation (C-7) defines the fourth-order moment $R(\tau, \lambda)$.

Equation (C-6) can be put into a more convenient form. With the understanding that $h(t) = 0$ for all $t < 0$, Eq. (C-6) can be written as

$$\langle [y_\tau(t)]^2 \rangle = \int_{-\infty}^\infty \int_{-\infty}^\infty h(t')h(t'')R(\tau, t' - t'') \, dt' \, dt''$$
$$= \int_{-\infty}^\infty \int_{-\infty}^\infty h(t')h(t' - \lambda)R(\tau, \lambda) \, dt' \, d\lambda$$
$$= \int_{-\infty}^\infty \int_0^\infty h(t')[h(t' - \lambda)R(\tau, \lambda) + h(t' + \lambda)R(\tau, -\lambda)] \, d\lambda \, dt' \tag{C-8}$$

Because of the stationarity of $i(t)$, a time translation gives

$$\langle i_1(0)i_2(\tau)i_1(\lambda)i_2(\tau + \lambda) \rangle = \langle i_1(-\lambda)i_2(\tau - \lambda)i_1(0)i_2(\tau) \rangle$$

Therefore $R(\tau,\lambda) = R(\tau,-\lambda)$, and Eq. (C-8) becomes

$$\langle [y_\tau(t)]^2 \rangle = \int_0^\infty f_h(\lambda) R(\tau,\lambda) \, d\lambda \tag{C-9}$$

where

$$f_h(\lambda) = \int_{-\infty}^\infty h(t)h(t-\lambda) \, dt + \int_{-\infty}^\infty h(t)h(t+\lambda) \, dt$$

$$= 2 \int_{-\infty}^\infty h(t)h(t+\lambda) \, dt = 2 \int_0^\infty h(t)h(t+\lambda) \, dt \tag{C-10}$$

Combining Eqs. (C-5), (C-7), and (C-9) gives

$$\overline{e_\phi^2} = \int_0^\infty f_h(\lambda) R(\tau,\lambda) \, d\lambda - [\phi_{12}(\tau)]^2 \tag{C-11}$$

Equation (C-8) gives a general expression for the mean-square error in the measured correlation function.

If $i(t)$ is Gaussian, $R(\tau,\lambda)$ can be evaluated in terms of the correlation functions. Let x_1, x_2, x_3, and x_4 represent $i_1(0)$, $i_2(\tau)$, $i_1(\lambda)$, and $i_2(\lambda + \tau)$, respectively. Applying Eqs. (A-23) to (A-31) gives

$$R(\tau,\lambda) = C_{12}C_{34} + C_{13}C_{24} + C_{14}C_{23}$$

$$= [\phi_{12}(\tau)]^2 + \phi_{11}(\lambda)\phi_{22}(\lambda) + \phi_{12}(\tau + \lambda)\phi_{12}(\tau - \lambda) \tag{C-12}$$

Substituting Eq. (C-12) in Eq. (C-11) gives

$$\overline{e_\phi^2} = \int_0^\infty f_h(\lambda)[\phi_{11}(\lambda)\phi_{22}(\lambda) + \phi_{12}(\tau + \lambda)\phi_{12}(\tau - \lambda)] \, d\lambda \tag{C-13}$$

In the special case, integration from 0 to T is used instead of filtering:

$$h(t) = \begin{cases} \dfrac{1}{T} & 0 \le t < T \\ 0 & t < 0 \quad \text{and} \quad t \ge T \end{cases}$$

From Eq. (C-10), $f_h(\lambda) = 2(T-\lambda)/T^2$, and Eq. (C-13) becomes

$$\overline{e_\phi^2} = \frac{2}{T^2} \int_0^T (T-\lambda)[\phi_{11}(\lambda)\phi_{22}(\lambda) + \phi_{12}(\tau + \lambda)\phi_{12}(\tau - \lambda)] \, d\lambda \tag{C-14}$$

Let λ_1 be a sufficiently large interval such that, for all $\lambda > \lambda_1$, the correlation functions are negligibly small. If $T \gg \lambda_1$, Eq. (C-14) can be approximated as

$$\overline{e_\phi^2} \approx \frac{2}{T} \int_0^\infty [\phi_{11}(\lambda)\phi_{22}(\lambda) + \phi_{12}(\tau + \lambda)\phi_{12}(\tau - \lambda)] \, d\lambda \tag{C-15}$$

The mean-square error is inversely proportional to T.

C-2. Sampled Measurement. Suppose that instead of Eqs. (C-2) and (C-3) we have

$$y_\tau(t) = \sum_{n=0}^{n=\infty} h(nT)x_\tau(t - nT) \tag{C-16}$$

$$\sum_{n=0}^{n=\infty} h(nT) = 1 \tag{C-17}$$

Equations (C-1), (C-4), and (C-5) still hold.   Equations (C-9) and (C-10) are replaced by

$$\langle [y_\tau(t)]^2 \rangle = \sum_{n=0}^{n=\infty} f_h(nT) R(\tau, nT) \tag{C-18}$$

$$f_h(nT) = 2\epsilon_n \sum_{m=0}^{m=\infty} h(mT)h[(n+m)T] \tag{C-19}$$

where $\epsilon_0 = \frac{1}{2}$, and $\epsilon_n = 1$ for $n \neq 0$.   Substituting Eq. (C-18) in (C-5) gives

$$\overline{e_\phi{}^2} = \sum_{n=0}^{n=\infty} f_h(nT) R(\tau, nT) - [\phi_{12}(\tau)]^2 \tag{C-20}$$

For the Gaussian case, Eq. (C-12) still holds with $\lambda = nT$, and Eq. (C-13) is replaced by

$$\overline{e_\phi{}^2} = \sum_{n=0}^{n=\infty} f_h(nT)[\phi_{11}(nT)\phi_{22}(nT) + \phi_{12}(\tau + nT)\phi_{12}(\tau - nT)] \tag{C-21}$$

In the special case with

$$h(nT) = \begin{cases} \dfrac{1}{N} & 0 \leq n < N \\ 0 & t < 0 \qquad t \geq N \end{cases}$$

Equation (C-19) gives

$$f_h(nT) = 2\epsilon_n \frac{N-n}{N^2}$$

and

$$\overline{e_\phi{}^2} = \frac{2}{N^2} \sum_{n=0}^{n=N-1} (N-n)\epsilon_n[\phi_{11}(nT)\phi_{22}(nT) + \phi_{12}(\tau + nT)\phi_{12}(\tau - nT)] \tag{C-22}$$

There are two special cases:
1. For large N,

$$\overline{e_\phi{}^2} = \frac{1}{N} \sum_{n=-\infty}^{n=\infty} [\phi_{11}(nT)\phi_{22}(nT) + \phi_{12}(\tau + nT)\phi_{12}(\tau - nT)] \tag{C-23}$$

2. For large T such that $\phi_{11}(t)$ and $\phi_{22}(t)$ are negligible for all $t \geq T$, the only significant term in Eq. (C-22) is the $n = 0$ term:

$$\overline{e_\phi{}^2} = \frac{1}{N} \{\phi_{11}(0)\phi_{22}(0) + [\phi_{12}(\tau)]^2\} \tag{C-24}$$

TABLE OF INTEGRALS

This Appendix gives a table of integrals of the type

$$I_n = \frac{1}{2\pi j} \int_{-j\infty}^{j\infty} \frac{g_n(s)}{h_n(s)h_n(-s)} \, ds$$

where
$$h_n(s) = a_0 s^n + a_1 s^{n-1} + \cdots + a_n$$
$$g_n(s) = b_0 s^{2n-2} + b_1 s^{2n-4} + \cdots + b_{n-1}$$

and the roots of $h_n(s)$ all lie in the LHP. The table was computed by G. R. MacLane, following the method developed in Sec. 7.9 of James, Nichols, and Phillips's book "Theory of Servomechanisms." In their original derivation, the path of integration was along the real axis and the condition on $h_n(s)$ was that all its roots lie in the upper half plane. However, their derivation holds equally well if the path of integration is along the imaginary axis and the condition on $h_n(s)$ is that all its roots lie in the LHP. With the present specification, all the coefficients a and b are real.

The table lists the integrals I_n for values of n from 1 to 7 inclusive:

$$I_1 = \frac{b_0}{2a_0 a_1}$$

$$I_2 = \frac{-b_0 + \dfrac{a_0 b_1}{a_2}}{2a_0 a_1}$$

$$I_3 = \frac{-a_2 b_0 + a_0 b_1 - \dfrac{a_0 a_1 b_2}{a_3}}{2a_0(a_0 a_3 - a_1 a_2)}$$

$$I_4 = \frac{b_0(-a_1 a_4 + a_2 a_3) - a_0 a_3 b_1 + a_0 a_1 b_2 + \dfrac{a_0 b_3}{a_4}(a_0 a_3 - a_1 a_2)}{2a_0(a_0 a_3{}^2 + a_1{}^2 a_4 - a_1 a_2 a_3)}$$

$$I_5 = \frac{M_5}{2a_0 \Delta_5}$$

$$M_5 = b_0(-a_0 a_4 a_5 + a_1 a_4{}^2 + a_2{}^2 a_5 - a_2 a_3 a_4) + a_0 b_1(-a_2 a_5 + a_3 a_4)$$
$$+ a_0 b_2(a_0 a_5 - a_1 a_4) + a_0 b_3(-a_0 a_3 + a_1 a_2)$$
$$+ \frac{a_0 b_4}{a_5}(-a_0 a_1 a_5 + a_0 a_3{}^2 + a_1{}^2 a_4 - a_1 a_2 a_3)$$

$$\Delta_5 = a_0{}^2 a_5{}^2 - 2a_0 a_1 a_4 a_5 - a_0 a_2 a_3 a_5 + a_0 a_3{}^2 a_4 + a_1{}^2 a_4{}^2 + a_1 a_2{}^2 a_5 - a_1 a_2 a_3 a_4$$

$$I_6 = \frac{M_6}{2a_0 \Delta_6}$$

$$M_6 = b_0(-a_0 a_3 a_5 a_6 + a_0 a_4 a_5{}^2 - a_1{}^2 a_6{}^2 + 2a_1 a_2 a_5 a_6 + a_1 a_3 a_4 a_6 - a_1 a_4{}^2 a_5 - a_2{}^2 a_5{}^2$$
$$- a_2 a_3{}^2 a_6 + a_2 a_3 a_4 a_5) + a_0 b_1(-a_1 a_5 a_6 + a_2 a_5{}^2 + a_3{}^2 a_6 - a_3 a_4 a_5)$$
$$+ a_0 b_2(-a_0 a_5{}^2 - a_1 a_3 a_6 + a_1 a_4 a_5) + a_0 b_3(a_0 a_3 a_5 + a_1{}^2 a_6 - a_1 a_2 a_5)$$
$$+ a_0 b_4(a_0 a_1 a_5 - a_0 a_3{}^2 - a_1{}^2 a_4 + a_1 a_2 a_3) + \frac{a_0 b_5}{a_6}(a_0{}^2 a_5{}^2 + a_0 a_1 a_3 a_6$$
$$- 2a_0 a_1 a_4 a_5 - a_0 a_2 a_3 a_5 + a_0 a_3{}^2 a_4 - a_1{}^2 a_2 a_6 + a_1{}^2 a_4{}^2 + a_1 a_2{}^2 a_5 - a_1 a_2 a_3 a_4)$$

$$\Delta_6 = a_0{}^2 a_5{}^3 + 3 a_0 a_1 a_3 a_5 a_6 - 2 a_0 a_1 a_4 a_5{}^2 - a_0 a_2 a_3 a_5{}^2 - a_0 a_3{}^3 a_6 + a_0 a_3{}^2 a_4 a_5 + a_1{}^3 a_6{}^2$$
$$- 2 a_1{}^2 a_2 a_5 a_6 - a_1{}^2 a_3 a_4 a_6 + a_1{}^2 a_4{}^2 a_5 + a_1 a_2{}^2 a_5{}^2 + a_1 a_2 a_3{}^2 a_6 - a_1 a_2 a_3 a_4 a_5$$

$$I_7 = \frac{M_7}{2 a_0 \Delta_7}$$

$$M_7 = b_0 m_0 + a_0 b_1 m_1 + a_0 b_2 m_2 + \cdots + a_0 b_6 m_6$$

$$m_0 = a_0{}^2 a_6 a_7{}^2 - 2 a_0 a_1 a_6{}^2 a_7 - 2 a_0 a_2 a_4 a_7{}^2 + a_0 a_2 a_5 a_6 a_7 + a_0 a_3 a_5 a_6{}^2 + a_0 a_4{}^2 a_5 a_7$$
$$- a_0 a_4 a_5{}^2 a_6 + a_1{}^2 a_6{}^3 + 3 a_1 a_2 a_4 a_6 a_7 - 2 a_1 a_2 a_5 a_6{}^2 - a_1 a_3 a_4 a_6{}^2 - a_1 a_4{}^3 a_7$$
$$+ a_1 a_4{}^2 a_5 a_6 + a_2{}^3 a_7{}^2 - 2 a_2{}^2 a_3 a_6 a_7 - a_2{}^2 a_4 a_5 a_7 + a_2{}^2 a_5{}^2 a_6 + a_2 a_3 a_4{}^2 a_7$$
$$- a_2 a_3 a_4 a_5 a_6 + a_2 a_3{}^2 a_6{}^2$$

$$m_1 = a_0 a_4 a_7{}^2 - a_0 a_5 a_6 a_7 - a_1 a_4 a_6 a_7 + a_1 a_5 a_6{}^2 - a_2{}^2 a_7{}^2 + 2 a_2 a_3 a_6 a_7 + a_2 a_4 a_5 a_7$$
$$- a_2 a_5{}^2 a_6 - a_3{}^2 a_6{}^2 - a_3 a_4{}^2 a_7 + a_3 a_4 a_5 a_6$$

$$m_2 = a_0 a_2 a_7{}^2 - a_0 a_3 a_6 a_7 - a_0 a_4 a_5 a_7 + a_0 a_5{}^2 a_6 - a_1 a_2 a_6 a_7 + a_1 a_3 a_6{}^2 + a_1 a_4{}^2 a_7$$
$$- a_1 a_4 a_5 a_6$$

$$m_3 = - a_0{}^2 a_7{}^2 + 2 a_0 a_1 a_6 a_7 + a_0 a_3 a_4 a_7 - a_0 a_3 a_5 a_6 - a_1{}^2 a_6{}^2 - a_1 a_2 a_4 a_7 + a_1 a_2 a_5 a_6$$

$$m_4 = a_0{}^2 a_5 a_7 - a_0 a_1 a_4 a_7 - a_0 a_1 a_5 a_6 - a_0 a_2 a_3 a_7 + a_0 a_3{}^2 a_6 + a_1{}^2 a_4 a_6 + a_1 a_2{}^2 a_7$$
$$- a_1 a_2 a_3 a_6$$

$$m_5 = a_0{}^2 a_3 a_7 - a_0{}^2 a_5{}^2 - a_0 a_1 a_2 a_7 - a_0 a_1 a_3 a_6 + 2 a_0 a_1 a_4 a_5 + a_0 a_2 a_3 a_5 - a_0 a_3{}^2 a_4$$
$$+ a_1{}^2 a_2 a_6 - a_1{}^2 a_4{}^2 - a_1 a_2{}^2 a_5 + a_1 a_2 a_3 a_4$$

$$m_6 = \frac{1}{a_7} \left(a_0{}^2 a_1 a_7{}^2 - 2 a_0{}^2 a_3 a_5 a_7 + a_0{}^2 a_5{}^3 - 2 a_0 a_1{}^2 a_6 a_7 + a_0 a_1 a_2 a_5 a_7 + 3 a_0 a_1 a_3 a_5 a_6 \right.$$
$$- 2 a_0 a_1 a_4 a_5{}^2 + a_0 a_2 a_3{}^2 a_7 - a_0 a_2 a_3 a_5{}^2 - a_0 a_3{}^3 a_6 + a_0 a_3{}^2 a_4 a_5 + a_1{}^3 a_6{}^2$$
$$+ a_1{}^2 a_2 a_4 a_7 - 2 a_1{}^2 a_2 a_5 a_6 - a_1{}^2 a_3 a_4 a_6 + a_1{}^2 a_4{}^2 a_5 - a_1 a_2{}^2 a_3 a_7 + a_1 a_2{}^2 a_5{}^2$$
$$\left. + a_1 a_2 a_3{}^2 a_6 - a_1 a_2 a_3 a_4 a_5 \right)$$

$$\Delta_7 = - a_0{}^3 a_7{}^3 + 3 a_0{}^2 a_1 a_6 a_7{}^2 + a_0{}^2 a_2 a_5 a_7{}^2 + 2 a_0{}^2 a_3 a_4 a_7{}^2 - 3 a_0{}^2 a_3 a_5 a_6 a_7 - a_0{}^2 a_4 a_5{}^2 a_7$$
$$+ a_0{}^2 a_5{}^3 a_6 - 3 a_0 a_1{}^2 a_6{}^2 a_7 - 3 a_0 a_1 a_2 a_4 a_7{}^2 + a_0 a_1 a_2 a_5 a_6 a_7 + 3 a_0 a_1 a_3 a_5 a_6{}^2$$
$$- a_0 a_1 a_3 a_4 a_6 a_7 + 2 a_0 a_1 a_4{}^2 a_5 a_7 - 2 a_0 a_1 a_4 a_5{}^2 a_6 - a_0 a_2{}^2 a_3 a_7{}^2 + 2 a_0 a_2 a_3{}^2 a_6 a_7$$
$$+ a_0 a_2 a_3 a_4 a_5 a_7 - a_0 a_2 a_3 a_5{}^2 a_6 - a_0 a_3{}^3 a_6{}^2 - a_0 a_3{}^2 a_4{}^2 a_7 - a_0 a_3{}^2 a_4 a_5 a_6 + a_1{}^3 a_6{}^3$$
$$+ 3 a_1{}^2 a_2 a_4 a_6 a_7 - 2 a_1{}^2 a_2 a_5 a_6{}^2 - a_1{}^2 a_3 a_4 a_6{}^2 - a_1{}^2 a_4{}^3 a_7 + a_1{}^2 a_4{}^2 a_5 a_6 + a_1 a_2{}^3 a_7{}^2$$
$$- 2 a_1 a_2{}^2 a_3 a_6 a_7 - a_1 a_2{}^2 a_4 a_5 a_7 + a_1 a_2{}^2 a_5{}^2 a_6 + a_1 a_2 a_3{}^2 a_6{}^2 + a_1 a_2 a_3 a_4{}^2 a_7$$
$$- a_1 a_2 a_3 a_4 a_5 a_6$$

APPENDIX E

BIBLIOGRAPHY

In the following chapter-by-chapter description of reference material, the letter and number in the parentheses refer to the Bibliography list at the end of the Appendix.

Chapter 1 is a general introduction. There are some references for the material of Sec. 1-4 on the basic relations of linearly compensated systems, namely, Horowitz's work (H3) and G. C. Newton's discussion of a paper by Lang and Ham (L1).

References for Chap. 2 are Wiener's original work (W2), G. C. Newton's introduction of the quadratic constraint to control saturation tendency (N1,N2), Westcott's work using contour integration in the s domain for optimization (W1), and Chang's root-square-locus method (C7). Truxal's book (T2, chaps. 7 and 8) has both the time-domain and s-domain methods.

References for Chap. 3 are books by Wiener (W2), James, Nichols, and Phillips (J1), Truxal (T2), Newton, Gould, and Kaiser (N2), and Smith (S3).

In Chap. 4 the analysis follows Chang's generalized version of the s-domain optimization method (C5). Most of the subjects are also treated in the book by Newton, Gould, and Kaiser (N2) with time-domain analysis. Bendat's book (B6) has a section on the simultaneous filtering of two related signals which treats the same problem as Sec. 4-9 with a different method.

The original work on time-varying systems (Chap. 5) includes Booton's optimization theory for time-varying linear systems (B14), Zadeh's work on variable networks (Z1), Zadeh and Ragazzini's extension of Wiener's theory to systems with mixed inputs and finite observation time (Z2), and Davis's work (D3) using orthogonal functions. Books by Laning and Battin (L2), Davenport and Root (D2), Bendat (B6), and Seifert and Steeg (S1) also have chapters on the subject. References for further studies on the subject are papers by Bendat (B5), Miller and Zadeh (M2), and the book by Seifert and Steeg (S1).

The essential background material for Chap. 6 is the z-transform method which can be found in any of the following textbooks: Ragazzini and Franklin (R1), Jury (J2), and Tou (T1). The optimization technique follows essentially Chang's three papers (C8, C9, and Optimum Transmission of Continuous Signal over a Sampled Data Link, *Trans. AIEE*). For further reference, Franklin (F3) had worked out earlier a time-domain method, and Kalman gives an interesting extension of the optimization technique (K6).

The original work on the subject matter of Chap. 7, power spectra and correlation-function measurements, is from papers by Rice (R5), Y. W. Lee (L3), Tukey (T6), Press and Tukey (P2), Davenport (D1), and Chang (C3). The book by Blackman and Tukey (B10) is perhaps a classic on the analytical aspect of the subject.

The references for Chap. 8, error analysis, are papers by Huang (H4), Miller and Murray (M3), Papoulis (P1), and Truxal and Horowitz (T3).

In Chap. 9, references for Pontryagin's maximum principle are papers by Boltyanskii, Gamkrelidze, and Pontryagin (B13), Gamkrelidze (G1), and Zadeh (Z4).

References for "bang-bang" servo are books by Flugge-Lotz (F2), Truxal (T2), and Smith (S3) and papers by McDonald (M1), Hopkin (H2), Bogner and Kazda (B12), Rose (R7), Doll and Stout (D5), Chang (C6), and Hung and Chang (H5). General references are books by Ku (K10), Cunningham (C17), Cosgriff (C15), and Gille, Pélegrin, and Decaulne (G5).

References for Chap. 10, self-optimizing systems, are papers by Anderson et al. (A1), Draper and Li (D7), Lang and Ham (L1), Osder (O1), Kalman (K2), Burt (B20), Cosgriff and Emerling (C14), Drenick and Shahbender (D8), Genthe (G3), and Reswick (R4).

References for Chap. 11, random processes and optimization of adaptive control, are papers by Robbins and Munro (R6), Keifer and Wolfowitz (K7), Bertram (B9), Chang (C10), Goodman and Hillsley (G6), and others.

Sources for Chap. 12 are the book and papers by Bellman (B2, B3, B4) and various research reports which are unpublished or are in the process of being published.

General references on mathematics are Cramer (C16), Copson (C13), and Gardner and Barnes (G2).

A1. Anderson, G. W., et al.: A Self-adjusting System for Optimum Dynamic Performance, *IRE Conv. Record*, pt. 4, vol. 7, pp. 182–190, 1958.

B1. Barker, R. H.: The Pulse Transfer Function and Its Application to Sampling Servo Systems, *Proc. IEE (London)*, pt. IV, vol. 99, pp. 302–317, December, 1952.

B2. Bellman, R.: "Dynamic Programming," Princeton University Press, Princeton, N.J., 1957.

B3. Bellman, R.: Some New Techniques in the Dynamic Programming Solution of Variational Problems, *Quart. Appl. Math.* vol. 16, no. 3, October, 1958.

B4. Bellman, R., and R. Kalaba: Dynamic Programming and Adaptive Processes: Mathematical Foundation, *IRE Trans. on Automatic Control*, vol. AC-5, no. 1, pp. 5–10, January, 1960.

B5. Bendat, J. S.: Exact Integral Equation Solutions and Synthesis for a Large Class of Optimum Time Variable Linear Filters, *IRE Trans. on Inform. Theory*, vol. 3, no. 1, March, 1957.

B6. Bendat, J. S.: "Principles and Applications of Random Noise Theory," John Wiley & Sons, Inc., New York, 1958.

B7. Bergen, A. R., and J. R. Ragazzini: Sampled-data Processing Techniques for Feedback Control Systems, *Trans. AIEE*, pt. II, vol. 73, pp. 236–247, November, 1954.

B8. Bertram, J. E.: Factors in the Design of Digital Controllers for Sampled-data Feedback Systems, *Trans. AIEE*, pt. II, vol. 75, pp. 151–159, July, 1956.

B9. Bertram, J. E.: Control by Stochastic Adjustment, *Trans. AIEE*, pt. II, vol. 78, pp. 485–491, 1959.

B10. Blackman, R. B., and J. W. Tukey: The Measurement of Power Spectra, *Bell System Tech. J.*, vol. 37, January and March, 1958; also Dover Publications, New York, 1959.

B11. Bode, H. W., and C. E. Shannon: A Simplified Derivation of Linear Least Square Smoothing and Prediction Theory, *Proc. IEE*, vol. 38, pp. 417–425, April, 1950.

B12. Bogner, I., and L. F. Kazda: An Investigation of Switching Criteria for Higher Order Contactor Servomechanisms, *Trans. AIEE* pt. II, vol. 73, pp. 118–127, July, 1954.

B13. Boltyanskii, V. G., R. V. Gamkrelidze, and L. S. Pontryagin: On the Theory of Optimal Process, *Compt. rend. acad. sci. U.R.S.S.*, vol. 110, p. 7, 1956.

B14. Booton, R. C., Jr.: An Optimization Theory for Time-varying Linear Systems with Non-stationary Statistical Inputs, *Proc. IRE*, vol. 40, pp. 977–981, August, 1952.

B15. Booton, R. C., Jr.: Optimum Design of Final Value Control Systems, *Proc. 1956 Symposium on Nonlinear Circuit Analysis*, pp. 233–241, Polytechnic Institute of Brooklyn, New York.

B16. Bower, J. L., and P. M. Schultheiss: "Introduction to the Design of Servomechanisms," John Wiley & Sons, Inc., New York, 1958.

B17. Brainerd, H. B., in C. S. Draper, Walter McKay, and Sidney Lees: "Instrument Engineering," vol. I, pp. 144–176, McGraw-Hill Book Company, Inc., New York, 1952.

B18. Brown, G. S., and D. P. Campbell: "Principles of Servomechanisms," John Wiley & Sons, Inc., New York, 1958.

B19. Bruns, R. A., and R. M. Saunders: "Analysis of Feedback Control Systems," McGraw-Hill Book Company, Inc., New York, 1955.

B20. Burt, E. G. C.: Self-optimizing Servo Systems with Random Inputs, *Rept. of Seminar on Non-linear Control Problems*, Cambridge University, September, 1954.

C1. Chadwick, J. H.: On the Stabilization of Roll, *Trans. Soc. Naval Architects Marine Eng.*, vol. 63, 1955.

C2. Chadwick, J. H., and S. S. L. Chang: A Recording-Analyzing System for Wave Induced Forces and Motions, *Proc. Symposium on the Behavior of Ships in a Seaway* (1957), Netherlands Ship Model Basin, Wageninger, Netherlands.

C3. Chang, S. S. L.: An Ocean Wave Power Spectrum Analyzer, *Proc. Natl. Electronics Conf.*, vol. 10, pp. 349–357, 1954.

C4. Chang, S. S. L.: On the Filter Problem of the Power-spectrum Analyser, *Proc. IRE*, vol. 42, no. 8, pp. 1278–1282, 1954.

C5. Chang, S. S. L.: Two Network Theorems for Analytical Determination of Optimum-response Physically Realizable Network Characteristics, *Proc. IRE*, vol. 43, pp. 1128–1135, September, 1955.

C6. Chang, S. S. L.: An Airframe Pitch Linear Accelerator Controller, *Proc. Natl. Electronics Conf.*, vol. 12, February, 1957.

C7. Chang, S. S. L.: Root Square Locus Plot—A Geometrical Method for Synthesizing Optimum Servo Systems, *IRE Conv. Record*, 1958.

C8 Chang, S. S. L.: Statistical Design Theory for Strictly Digital Sampled-data Systems, *Trans. AIEE*, pt. I, vol. 76, pp. 702–709, 1957 (January, 1958, section).

C9. Chang, S. S. L.: Statistical Design Theory for Digital Controlled Continuous Systems, *Trans. AIEE*, pt. II, vol. 77, pp. 191–201, 1958.

C10. Chang, S. S. L.: Optimization of the Adaptive Function by Z-transform Method, *Trans. AIEE*, pt. II, vol. 79, 1960.

C11. Chase, J., et al.: The Directional Spectrum of a Wind Generated Sea, *NYU Eng. Research Rept.*, July, 1957.

C12. Chestnut, H., and R. W. Mayer: "Servomechanisms and Regulating System Design," vols. I and II, John Wiley & Sons, Inc., New York, 1951, 1955.

C13. Copson, E. T.: "Theory of Functions of a Complex Variable," Oxford University Press, London, 1935.

C14. Cosgriff, R. L., and R. A. Emerling: Optimizing Control Systems, *AIEE paper* CP-57-778, June, 1957.

C15. Cosgriff, R. L.: "Nonlinear Control Systems," McGraw-Hill Book Company, Inc., New York, 1958.

C16. Cramer, H.: "Mathematical Methods of Statistics," Princeton University Press, Princeton, N.J., 1946.

C17. Cunningham, W. J.: "Introduction to Nonlinear Analysis," McGraw-Hill Book Company, Inc., New York, 1958.

D1. Davenport, W. B., Jr.: Correlator Errors Due to Finite Observation Intervals, *MIT Research Lab. Electronics Tech. Rept.* 191, March, 1951.

D2. Davenport, W. B., Jr., and W. L. Root: "Introduction to Random Signals and Noise," pp. 239–250, 371–382, McGraw-Hill Book Company, Inc., New York, 1958.

D3. Davis, R. C.: On the Theory of Prediction of Non-stationary Stochastic Processes, *J. Appl. Phys.*, vol. 23, pp. 1047–1053, September, 1952.

D4. Derman, C.: Stochastic Approximation, *Ann. Math. Statist.*, vol. 27, p. 879, December, 1956.

D5. Doll, H. G., and T. M. Stout: Design and Analog-computer Analysis of an Optimum Third-order Nonlinear Servomechanism, *Trans. ASME*, pp. 513–525, April, 1957.

D6. Draper, C. S., W. McKay, and S. Lees: "Instrument Engineering," vols. I, II, and III, McGraw-Hill Book Company, Inc., New York, 1952.

D7. Draper C. S., and Y. T. Li: "Principles of Optimalizing Control Systems and an Application to the Internal Combustion Engine," American Society of Mechanical Engineers, New York, 1951.

D8. Drenick, R. F., and R. A. Shahbender: Adaptive Servomechanisms, *Trans. AIEE*, pt. II, vol. 76, p. 286, November, 1957.

E1. Evans, W. R.: "Control-system Dynamics," pp. 96–122, McGraw-Hill Book Company, Inc., New York, 1954.

F1. Fett, G. H.: "Feedback Control Systems," Prentice-Hall, Inc., Englewood Cliffs, N.J., 1954.

F2. Flugge-Lotz, I.: "Discontinuous Automatic Control," Princeton University Press, Princeton, N.J., 1953.

F3. Franklin, G.: The Optimum Synthesis of Sampled-data Systems, D.Eng. Thesis, Columbia University, New York, May, 1955.

G1. Gamkrelidze, R. V.: On the General Theory of Optimal Processes, *Compt. rend. acad. sci. U.R.S.S.*, vol. 123, p. 223, 1958.

G2. Gardner, M. F., and J. L. Barnes: "Transients in Linear Systems," vol. 1, John Wiley & Sons, Inc., New York, 1942.

G3. Genthe, W. K.: Optimalizing Control Design of a Fully Automatic Cruise Control System for Turbo-jet Aircraft, *IRE Wescon Conv. Record*, pt. 4, 1957.

G4. Gibson, J. E., and F. B. Tuteur: "Control System Components," McGraw-Hill Book Company, Inc., New York, 1958.

G5. Gille, J. C., M. J. Pélegrin, and P. Decaulne: "Feedback Control Systems," McGraw-Hill Book Company, Inc., New York, 1959.

G6. Goodman, T. P., and R. H. Hillsley: Continuous Measurement of Characteristics of Systems with Random Inputs: A Step Toward Self-optimizing Control, *ASME paper* 58-IRD-5, 1958.

H1. Hazen, H. L.: Theory of Servomechanisms, *J. Franklin Inst.*, vol. 218, pp. 279–331, 1934.

H2. Hopkin, A. M.: A Phase-plane Approach to the Compensation of Saturating Servomechanisms, *Trans. AIEE*, pt. I, vol. 70, pp. 631–639, 1951.

H3. Horowitz, I. M.: Fundamental Theory of Automatic Linear Feedback Control Systems, *Trans. IRE on Automatic Control*, vol. AC-4, no. 3, pp. 5–19, December, 1959.

H4. Huang, R. Y.: The Sensitivity of the Poles of Linear Closed-loop Systems, *Trans. AIEE*, pt. II, vol. 77, pp. 182–186, 1958.

H5. Hung, J. C., and S. S. L. Chang: Switching Discontinuities in Phase Space, *IRE Conv. Record*, pt. IV, vol. 5, 1957.

J1. James, H. M., N. B. Nichols, and R. S. Phillips: "Theory of Servomechanisms," MIT Radiation Laboratory Series, vol. 25, pp. 308–368, McGraw-Hill Book Company, Inc., New York, 1947.

J2. Jury, E. I.: "Sampled Data Control Systems," John Wiley & Sons, Inc., New York, 1958.

K1. Kalman, R. E.: Analysis and Design Principles of Second and Higher Order Saturating Servomechanisms, *Trans. AIEE*, pt. II, vol. 74, pp. 294–310, 1955.

K2. Kalman, R. E.: Design of a Self-optimizing Control System, *ASME paper* 57-IRD-2, April, 1957.

K3. Kalman, R. E., and J. E. Bertram: General Synthesis Procedures for Computer Control of Single and Multiloop Linear Systems, *Trans. AIEE*, pt. II, vol. 77, pp. 602–609, 1958.

K4. Kalman, R. E., and J. E. Bertram: Control System Analysis and Design via the "Second Method" of Lyapunov. I. Continuous-time Systems, *ASME paper* 59-NAC-2, 1959.

K5. Kalman, R. E., and J. E. Bertram: Control System Analysis and Design via the "Second Method" of Lyapunov. II. Discrete-time Systems, *ASME paper* 59-NAC-3, 1959.

K6. Kalman, R. E.: A New Approach to Linear Filtering and Prediction Problems, *Trans. ASME*, ser. D, pp. 35–45, March, 1960.

K7. Keifer, J., and J. Wolfowitz: Stochastic Estimation of the Maximum of a Regression Function, *Ann. Math. Statist.*, vol. 23, p. 462, September, 1952.

K8. Koschmann, A. H., and J. G. Truxal: Optimum Linear Filtering of Non-stationary Time Series, *Proc. Natl. Electronics Conf.*, vol. 10, pp. 119–127, 1954.

K9. Ku, Y. H.: The Phase Space Method for Analysis of Nonlinear Control Systems, *ASME paper* 56-A-103, 1956.

K10. Ku, Y. H.: "Analysis and Control of Nonlinear Systems," The Ronald Press Company, New York, 1958.

L1. Lang, G., and J. M. Ham: Conditional Feedback Systems—A New Approach to Feedback Control, *Trans. AIEE*, pt. II, vol. 74, pp. 152–161, 1955.

L2. Laning, J. H., Jr., and R. H. Battin: "Random Processes in Automatic Control," McGraw-Hill Book Company Inc., New York, 1956.

L3. Lee, Y. W.: Application of Statistical Methods to Communication Problems, *MIT Research Lab. Electronics Tech. Rept. 181*, September, 1950.

M1. McDonald, D. C.: Nonlinear Techniques for Improving Servo Performance, *Proc. Natl. Electronics Conf.*, vol. 6, pp. 400–421, 1950.

M2. Miller, K. S., and L. A. Zadeh: Solution of an Integral Equation Occurring in the Theories of Prediction and Detection, *IRE Trans. on Inform. Theory*, vol. IT-2, pp. 72–75, June, 1956.

M3. Miller, K. S., and F. J. Murray: A Mathematical Basis for an Error Analysis of Differential Analyzers, *J. Math. Phys.*, vol. 32, nos. 2–3, July-October, 1958.

M4. Minorsky, N.: Directional Stability of Automatically Steered Bodies, *J. Am. Soc. Naval Engs.*, vol. 34, 1922.

M5. Minorsky, N.: "Introduction to Nonlinear Mechanics," J. W. Edwards, Publisher, Inc., Ann Arbor, Mich., 1947.

N1. Newton, G. C., Jr.: Compensation of Feedback Control Systems Subject to Saturation, *J. Franklin Inst.*, vol. 254, pp. 391–413, November, 1952.

N2. Newton, G. C., Jr., L. A. Gould, and J. F. Kaiser: "Analytical Design of Linear Feedback Controls," John Wiley & Sons, Inc., New York, 1957.

N3. Nyquist, H.: Regeneration Theory, *Bell System Tech. J.*, vol. 11, pp. 126–147, 1932.

O1. Osder, S. S.: Sperry Adaptive Flight Control System, *Proc. Self-adaptive Flight Control Systems Symposium*, Wright Air Development Center, January, 1959.

P1. Papoulis, A.: Displacement of the Zeros of the Impedance $Z(p)$ Due to Incremental Variations in the Network Elements, *Proc. IRE*, p. 79, January, 1955.

P2. Press, H., and J. W. Tukey: Power Spectral Methods of Analysis and Application in Airplane Dynamics, *Bell Telephone System Monograph* 2606, 1957.

R1. Ragazzini, J. R., and G. F. Franklin: "Sampled-data Control Systems," McGraw-Hill Book Company, Inc., New York, 1958.

R2. Ragazzini, J. R., and L. A. Zadeh: The Analysis of Sampled-data Systems, *Trans. AIEE*, pt. II, vol. 71, pp. 225–234, November, 1952.

R3. Reintjes, J. F.: An Analogue Electronic Correlator, *Proc. Natl. Electronics Conf.*, vol. 7, pp. 390–400, 1951.

R4. Reswick, J. B.: Disturbance-Response Feedback—A New Control Concept, *Trans. ASME*, vol. 78, p. 153, January, 1956.

R5. Rice, S. O.: Mathematical Analysis of Random Noise, *Bell System Tech. J.*, vol. 23, 1944; vol. 24, 1945.

R6. Robbins, H., and S. Munro: A Stochastic Approximation Method, *Ann. Math. Statist.*, vol. 22, p. 400, September, 1951.

R7. Rose, N. J.: Optimum Switching Criteria for Discontinuous Automatic Controls, *IRE Conv. Record*, pt. IV, vol. 4, 1956.

S1. Seifert, W. W., and C. W. Steeg: "Control Systems Engineering," McGraw-Hill Book Company, Inc., New York, 1960.

S2. Singleton, H. E.: A Digital Electronic Correlator, *MIT Research Lab. Electronics Tech. Rept.* 1952, February, 1950.

S3. Smith, O. J. M.: "Feedback Control Systems," McGraw-Hill Book Company, Inc., New York, 1958.

S4. St. Dennis, M., and W. J. Pierson, Jr.: On the Motions of Ships in Confused Seas, *Trans. Soc. Naval Architects Marine Engs.*, vol. 61, 1953.

T1. Tou, J. T.: "Digital and Sampled-data Control Systems," McGraw-Hill Book Company, Inc., New York, 1959.

T2. Truxal, J. G.: "Automatic Feedback Control System Synthesis," McGraw-Hill Book Company, Inc., New York, 1955.

T3. Truxal, J. G., and I. Horowitz: Sensitivity Considerations in Active Network Synthesis, *IRE Trans. on Circuit Theory*, vol. CT-3, no. 4, December, 1956.

T4. Truxal, J. G. (ed.): "Control Engineer's Handbook," McGraw-Hill Book Company, Inc., New York, 1958.

T5. Tsien, H. S.: "Engineering Cybernetics," McGraw-Hill Book Company, Inc., New York, 1954.

T6. Tukey, J. W.: The Sampling Theory of Power Spectral Estimates, *Symposium on Application of Autocorrelation Analyses to Physical Problems*, Woods Hole, Mass., 1949, Office of Naval Research, Washington, D.C.

W1. Westcott, J. H.: Synthesis of Optimum Feedback Systems Satisfying a Power Limitation, *Frequency Response Symposium*, Dec. 1–2, 1953, *ASME paper 53-A-17.*

W2. Wiener, N.: "The Extrapolation, Interpolation, and Smoothing of Stationary Time Series," John Wiley & Sons, Inc., New York, 1949.

Z1. Zadeh, L. A.: Frequency Analysis of Variable Networks, *Proc. IRE*, vol. 38, no. 3, March, 1950.

Z2. Zadeh, L. A., and J. R. Ragazzini: An Extension of Wiener's Theory of Prediction, *J. Appl. Phys.*, vol. 21, pp. 645–655, July, 1950.

Z3. Zadeh, L. A.: Optimum Filters for the Detection of Signals in Noise, *Proc. IRE*, vol. 40, pp. 1223–1231, October, 1952.

Z4. Zadeh, L. A.: Minimal Time Problems and Maximum Principle, Conference Paper, AIEE, Winter General Meeting, New York, February, 1960.

PROBLEMS

Chapter 1

1-1. Show that, for a linear system with arbitrary configuration, the following relations always hold:

$$\frac{C}{R}(s) = \left(\frac{C}{R}\right)_0 (s) \left[-\frac{C}{N_2}(s) \right] = \left(\frac{C}{R}\right)_0 (s) \left[1 - \frac{C}{D_1}(s) \right]$$

where
- C = controlled variable, output of plant
- D_1 = load disturbance at output end if control loop is open
- N_2 = instrument noise in measured value of C
- R = reference input

C/R, C/N_2, C/D_1 = closed-loop transfer functions as designated

$(C/R)_0(s)$ = required ratio of $C(s)/R(s)$ such that input to plant is zero

1-2. In the literature, at least three different system configurations have been suggested for adaptive control of an aircraft: (1) conditional feedback, (2) prefiltering,

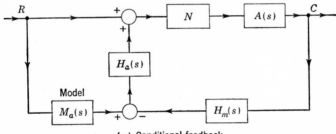

(a) Conditional feedback

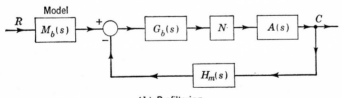

(b) Prefiltering

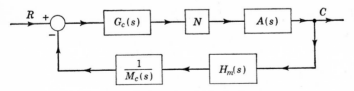

(c) Reciprocal model feedback

FIG. P 1-2

355

and (3) reciprocal model feedback. In the block diagrams of Fig. P 1-2, N represents a nonlinear or variable-gain element, $A(s)$ represents aircraft dynamics, and $H_m(s)$ represents the transfer function of the measuring instrument.

Prove the following:

(a) The three systems are equivalent to each other if

$$1 + M_a(s)H_a(s) = M_b(s)G_b(s) = G_c(s)$$

$$H_a(s) = G_b(s) = \frac{G_c(s)}{M_c(s)}$$

and the same N, $A(s)$, and $H_m(s)$ are used in all three cases.

(b) In case the elements $H_a(s)$, $G_b(s)$, and $G_c(s)$ have very high gain, $H_m(s) = 1$, and the closed loops are stable; then

$$\frac{C}{R}(s) \cong M_a(s) \qquad \text{for (1)}$$

$$\frac{C}{R}(s) \cong M_b(s) \qquad \text{for (2)}$$

$$\frac{C}{R}(s) \cong M_c(s) \qquad \text{for (3)}$$

(c) Is it necessary for the aircraft response to be linear in order to derive the above results?

Chapter 2

2-1. Show that, for any arbitrary $r(t)$, if the only design criterion is

$$\int_0^\infty [r(t) - c(t)]^2 \, dt = \min$$

the optimum system function is

$$\frac{C}{R}(s) = 1$$

2-2. Design an optimum controller that meets the following specifications:

(a) The integral-square error following a step input of one unit is 0.01 sec or less.

(b) The integral-square value of the input to the plant is minimum.

The transfer function of the controlled plant is $G(s) = 10/s$.

2-3. Repeat Prob. 2-2 for a controlled plant with $G(s) = 10/s^3$.

2-4. Repeat Prob. 2-2 if, instead of condition a, the integral-square error following a ramp input of one unit is 0.01 sec or less and $G(s) = 10/s^3$.

2-5. Certain types of control systems are acceleration-limited. For convenience we write

$$\int_0^\infty \left(\frac{d^2c}{dt^2}\right)^2 dt \leq K \tag{1}$$

Determine the optimum control ratios which give least-integral-square errors for the following cases:

(a) The input is a step function of 0.1 unit.

(b) The input is a ramp function of 1 unit.

(c) The input is a mixture of (a) and (b) with equal probability of occurrence, and condition (1) is to be satisfied, on an average.

2-6. Assume unity feedback in Prob. 2-5, and determine the open-loop transfer functions for all three cases. Make Bode plots of the open-loop transfer functions and note the positions of the corner frequencies.

2-7. Plot the root-square locus for a system with plant transfer function

$$G(s) = \frac{5(s + 0.2)}{s^2(s^2 + 0.1s + 0.09)}$$

The desired response time of the closed-loop system is 3 sec, and the integral-square value of the input to $G(s)$ following a step input is to be minimized. Determine the optimum control ratio and discuss the possible ways of realizing this ratio.

2-8. A positional control system is represented by the block diagram of Fig. P 2-8,

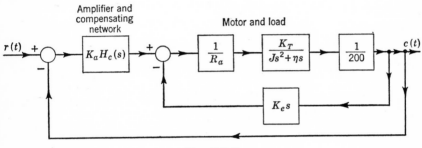

FIG. P 2-8

where $K_T = 2.1$ lb-ft/amp
$\quad K_e = 0.3$ volt/rpm
$\quad R_a = 2.7$ ohms
$\quad \eta = 3.5$ lb-ft/100 rpm   motor + load
$\quad J = 0.11$ slug-ft^2 motor + load

All the above constants refer to the motor shaft. On an average, the load is to be moved one-quarter turn at the rate of approximately five times every minute, and the gear ratio is 200:1.

(a) Determine K_a and $H_c(s)$ to give an integral-square error of no more than $\frac{1}{2}$ sec subsequent to a unit step input with minimum heat loss to the motor (use Fig. 2-13).

(b) What is the armature copper loss under the above-mentioned operating condition?

(c) Plot the transient response of the optimum system.

2-9. If, in Prob. 2-8, no compensating network is to be used, $H_c(s) = 1$. What is the value of K_a to give the least-integral-square error with step input?

2-10. One way of controlling the roll motion of a missile is to use auxiliary jets situated at the tips of the fins to supply the necessary roll moment $m(t)$. The valves controlling the jets are actuated by gyro signals in any desired manner. In designing such a system, it is desirable to achieve the specified speed of response with the least expenditure in ejected gas, the rate of flow of which increases with $|m(t)|$. As a preliminary step, we may assume that the optimum system is one which meets the condition

$$\int_0^\infty \{[r(t) - c(t)]^2 + k^2[m(t)]^2\}\, dt = \min$$

where k is any given constant, $r(t)$ is the ordered roll angle, and $c(t)$ is the actual roll angle.   Given

$$R(s) = \frac{1}{s}$$

$$\frac{C(s)}{M(s)} = \frac{1}{Js^2}$$

Determine:

(a) The optimum $(C/R)(s)$.

(b) The integral-square value of $m(t)$ versus the rise time t_p of the closed-loop system.

(c) The integrated absolute value of $m(t)$ with respect to time versus the rise time t_p.

2-11. In Prob. 2-10, if the reference input consists of ramps and steps instead of steps alone, the equivalent reference input function $R_e(s)$ can be calculated from

$$R_e(-s)R_e(s) = -\frac{a^2}{s^2} + \frac{b^2}{s^4}$$

What is the optimum form of $(C/R)(s)$?

Determine the compensating-network function if series compensation is used.

2-12. The transfer function of an idealized ship-steering system can be written as

$$\frac{C(s)}{A(s)} = \frac{K}{Ms^2}$$

where $c(t)$ is the ship's heading and $a(t)$ is the rudder angle.

(a) With unit step input, find the optimum $(C/R)(s)$ such that

$$J_0 = \int_0^\infty [r(t) - c(t)]^2\, dt = \min$$

$$J_1 = \int_0^\infty \left[\frac{da(t)}{dt}\right]^2 \le L_m$$

(b) Determine J_0, L_m, rise time t_p, and peak values of $a(t)$ and $da(t)/dt$ as functions of the Lagrange multiplier k.

(c) Express peak values of $a(t)$ and $da(t)/dt$ as functions of t_p and parameter K/M.

2-13. The roll motion of an ocean-going ship is stabilized by a pair of activated fins located at the two sides of the ship as shown in Fig. P 2-13a.   The fins are tilted by a hydraulic servo to produce a roll moment in proportion to an actuating signal $v(t)$. The hydraulic servo is usually fast enough so that, as an approximation, its time constants can be neglected.   The equation representing the roll motion is given as

$$J\ddot{\theta}(t) + \eta\dot{\theta}(t) + lW\theta(t) = K_f v(t)$$

where $\theta(t)$ is the roll angle and $K_f v(t)$ is the roll moment generated by the fins.   A block diagram of the system is shown in Fig. P 2-13b.   The values of the constants are given as

$$\omega_n = \sqrt{\frac{lW}{J}} = 0.5 \text{ radian/sec}$$

$$\zeta = \frac{\eta}{2\sqrt{lWJ}} = 0.1$$

$$\frac{K_f}{lW} = 0.04 \text{ radian/volt}$$

Design a control system which has a rise time of 2 sec and is optimum to step inputs in the sense of Sec. 2-6.   Determine the values of the constants K, K_1, and K_2.

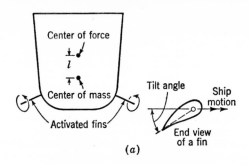

(a)

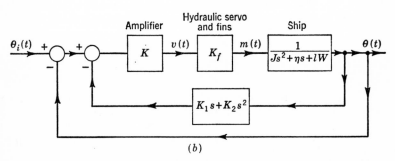

(b)

Fig. P 2-13

2-14. Suppose that in Prob. 2-13, instead of roll-rate and roll-acceleration signals being used to stabilize the system, a series-compensating network $G_c(s)$ is to be used. Determine the function $KG_c(s)$.

In practice, the values of the "constants" change with the loading condition of the ship. A certain combination of changes gives a variation in ω_n of ± 20 per cent from its nominal value but no change in $\zeta\omega_n$ and K_f/J. As the compensating means $\zeta\omega_n$ and K_f/J remain fixed, and ω_n varies from 0.4 to 0.6 radian/sec. What are the closed-loop root loci for the series-compensated system? For the shunt-compensated system of Prob. 2-13? Which system is more desirable?

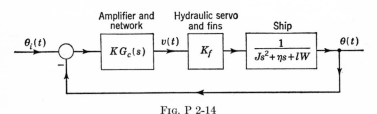

Fig. P 2-14

2-15. Quite frequently, the plant transfer function $G_p(s)$ can be written as

$$G_p(s) = G_1(s)G_2(s)$$

where $G_1(s)$ represents the low-frequency response of the plant and $G_2(s)$ represents some resonant modes at higher frequencies. The exact form of $G_2(s)$ is unknown except that $G_2(j\omega) = 1$ for lower frequencies.   One way of designing such a system is to use the approximation

$$G_p(s) = G_1(s)$$

and require that

$$\frac{1}{2\pi j} \int_{-j\infty}^{j\infty} \left[k^2 \frac{\bar{C}C(-s^2)^n}{\bar{G}_1 G_1} + (\bar{R} - \bar{C})(R - C) \right] ds = \min$$

The above condition has the effect of limiting the bandwidth of the plant input signal $i(t)$ so that the high-frequency resonant modes are not excited.

(a) Show that, with $R(s) = 1/s$, the gain of the closed-loop transfer function I/R decreases at the rate of $6n$ db/octave for large values of ω.

(b) Show that, with arbitrary $R(s)$, the input power to the plant, $|I(j\omega)|^2$, decreases at least at $6(n + 1)$ db/octave at large values of ω.

(c) Given $G_1(s) = K/s(1 + s)$, use the above criterion to determine $(C/R)(s)$ such that the closed-loop system bandwidth is 10 radians/sec and the rate of decrease of $|I(j\omega)|^2$ is 18 db/octave at high frequencies.

(d) Make a Bode plot of the closed-loop transfer functions C/R and I/R for the system you have just derived.

2-16. Show that, in a type 0 system with unit step input, the steady-state value. of $e^2 + k^2 i^2$ is a minimum with the d-c loop gain given by Eq. (2-51).

Chapter 3

3-1. The block diagram of a certain positioning system is shown in Fig. P 3-1.

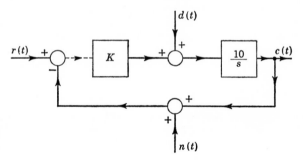

FIG. P 3-1

With control loop open, $c(t)$ responds freely to the load disturbance, and its spectral density is measured to be

$$\Phi_{cc}(j\omega) = \frac{12}{(\omega^2 + 9)\omega^2}$$

What is $\Phi_{dd}(j\omega)$?   With control loop closed, a random noise of spectral density $\Phi_{nn}(j\omega) = 0.1$ is introduced into the system.   Assuming that $r(t) = 0$, determine the new value of $\Phi_{cc}(j\omega)$.   The noise and load disturbance are uncorrelated.

3-2. If, in Prob. 3-1, the random noise and load disturbance are Gaussian, what is the distribution function of $c(t)$?   Does the distribution function vary with time?   Following a step input $r(t) = 10u(t)$, what is the new distribution function of $c(t)$ at various t?

3-3. An ensemble of random signals $r(t)$ is symmetrical about zero:

$$P[r(t)] = P[-r(t)]$$

Signals $x(t)$ and $y(t)$ are obtained by rectifying and squaring $r(t)$, respectively:

$$x(t) = |r(t)|$$
$$y(t) = [r(t)]^2$$

Show that

$$\phi_{rx}(\tau) = \phi_{ry}(\tau) = 0$$

3-4. A random positional variable $\theta(t)$ has a spectral-density function $\Phi_{\theta\theta}(j\omega) = A^2/\omega^2$. What is the mean-square value of $\theta(t)$? Is this possible physically? Is it physically possible to have a spectral-density function

$$\Phi_{\theta\theta}(j\omega) = \frac{A^2}{\omega^4}$$

3-5. The amplifier gain K in Prob. 3-1 is to be adjusted for the least-mean-square value of $c(t)$. Determine K and the least-square value of $c(t)$.

3-6. The transit time of an electron in a vacuum tube is of the order of 10^{-9} sec. Show that, in starved cathode operation (with negligible space-charge effect), the spectral density of the fluctuating component of plate current is eI for the lower frequencies, where e is the electronic charge and $I = \nu e$ is the average or d-c plate current. At what frequency do you expect the spectral density to taper off? Why?

3-7. A function $r(t) = 10 + f(t)$, where $f(t)$ is a Gaussian random fluctuation with

$$\Phi_{ff}(j\omega) = \frac{10}{\omega^4 + 5\omega^2 + 4}$$

Determine the fraction of time that $|r(t)| < 5$ and the number of times per second the value of $r(t)$ goes under 5.

3-8. Determine the autocorrelation functions and spectral densities of the following signals.

(a) A steplike input of mean-square amplitude 1 with probability P of y_n repeating the sign of y_{n-1}.

(b) A series of randomly occurring correlated step inputs as shown in Fig. 3-9 with

$$\overline{y_i y_{i+n}} = q^n \sin n\theta_1$$

(c) A series of randomly occurring pulses of the form of Eq. (3-31), where the a_k's are uncorrelated and $f_k(t) = e^{-bt}$ for $t > 0$, and $f_k(t) = 0$ for $t < 0$.

Assume, on an average, that there are ν inputs or pulses per second in all three cases.

3-9. Repeat Prob. 3-8 with the inputs occurring regularly at $t = n/\nu$, where n is an integer.

3-10. With reference to the block diagram, the spectral densities of i_1 and i_2 are

$$\Phi_{11} = -\frac{1}{s^2}$$
$$\Phi_{22} = 2$$
$$\Phi_{12} = \Phi_{21} = 0$$

What are the spectral densities Φ_{33}, Φ_{44}, and Φ_{34} of the output signals? On the other hand, given Φ_{33}, Φ_{44}, and Φ_{34}, can Φ_{11}, Φ_{22}, and Φ_{12} be determined?

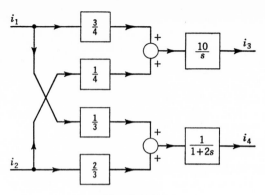

Fig. P 3-10

3-11. Determine the cross-correlation functions and cross-spectral densities of the following pairs of signals:

(a) $\sin \omega_1 t$ and $A \sin (\omega_1 t + \phi) + n(t)$, where ϕ is a constant and $n(t)$ is uncorrelated noise.

(b) $\sin \omega_1 t$ and $|\sin \omega_1 t|$.

(c) $\sin \omega_1 t$ and periodic function $f(t) = f(t + 2\pi/\omega_1)$.

(d) $\Sigma a_n f(t - t_n)$ and $\Sigma a_n g(t - t_n + t_0)$, where $f(t)$ and $g(t)$ are known functions of time, a_n is evenly distributed with mean-square value a^2, and t_n occurs at random with average frequency ν.

(e) $\Sigma a_n f(t - t_n)$ and $\Sigma |a_n| g(t - t_n + t_0)$.

(f) $r(t)$ and $r(t)a(t)$, where $r(t)$ and $a(t)$ are uncorrelated random signals and $a(t)$ has zero mean.

3-12. A missile in horizontal flight can be represented approximately by the block diagram, where $\theta(t)$ is the heading angle and $\delta(t)$ is the angle of deflection of the control surface. Suppose that the disturbing torque due to atmospheric turbulence can be represented by randomly applied torque impulses of root-mean-square magnitude 1 and zero mean and that there are, on an average, ν independent impulses per second. The control loop is open at $t = 0$ (omit the broken lines) [$\delta(t) = 0$ for $t > 0$], with correct heading.

(a) Determine the expected rms heading error at $t = t_1$ sec.

(b) Under what condition would the heading error approach normal distribution?

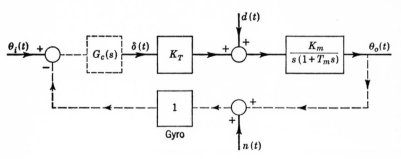

Fig. P 3-12

3-13. From Prob. 3-12, it is obvious that the heading error of an unguided missile operating within the earth's atmosphere increases indefinitely with the time of flight. Suppose that a gyro is used to sense the heading error and to operate the control surface proportionately, as illustrated by the broken lines of the block diagram of Fig. P 3-12, with $G_c(s)$ equal to a constant K. The gyro error can be represented as noise with $\Phi_{nn}(j\omega)$. As a simple approximation, we assume that $\Phi_{nn}(j\omega)$ is a constant within the servo bandwidth and that the desired heading $\theta_i(t)$ does not change with time. Let $e(t) = \theta_i(t) - \theta_0(t)$. Determine for large t (stationary situation):

(a) Spectral density of the heading error.

(b) Mean-square value of the heading error.

(c) The optimum value of K to give the least-square value of the heading error. Assume for computation purposes the following numerical values:

$$T_m = 0.2$$
$$K_m{}^2\Phi_{dd} = 5.76\Phi_{nn}$$

Chapter 4

4-1. With reference to the block diagram, $r(t)$ and $n(t)$ are uncorrelated, and

$$\Phi_{rr}(j\omega) = \frac{3{,}600}{\omega^2(\omega^2 + 169)}$$
$$\Phi_{nn}(j\omega) = 1$$

Determine $H(s)$ such that $\overline{[r(t) - c(t)]^2}$ is minimum. What does it represent physically?

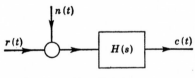

FIG. P 4-1

4-2. An optimum position-control system in the presence of load disturbance is to be designed. With reference to the block diagram, the mean-square value of $a(t)$ is limited. The spectral density $\Phi_{rr}(j\omega)$ of $r(t)$ is $1/\omega^4$, and the spectral density $\Phi_{dd}(j\omega)$ of wind-induced load torque is $A^2/(\omega^2 + \nu^2)$. Determine $G_c(s)$ and $H(s)$. What physical elements do they represent? Neglect $n(t)$ in the present problem.

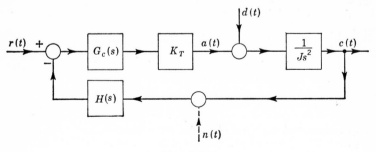

FIG. P 4-2

4-3. A platform-stabilization system has essentially the block diagram of Fig. P 4-2. However, the torque motor usually has sufficient torque $a(t)$ and is not a serious limiting factor on the system's performance. In its place the noise $n(t)$ in the error-sensing element is an important factor to be considered.

Assume

$$\Phi_{dd} = \frac{0.002J^2}{\omega^2 + 0.01}$$

$$\Phi_{nn} = \text{const} = 10^{-10}$$

Determine:

(a) Optimum form of $G_c(s)$.

(b) Mean-square error.

4-4. For the idealized missile-control problem of Prob. 3-13 determine the optimum form of $G_c(s)$, assuming no constraint on the control surface movement. Calculate the least-square values of the heading error and the control surface displacement $\overline{[\delta(t)]^2}$.

4-5. Repeat Prob. 4-4, assuming that the mean-square value of the control surface displacement is limited. Obtain expressions of the optimum form of $G_c(s)$ in terms of the Lagrange multiplier k^2.

4-6. The roll motion of a ship can be stabilized by a pair of activated fins as shown in Fig. P 2-13a. The motions of the fins are opposite to each other so that a net torque is exerted on the ship to neutralize the roll moment exerted by the ocean waves. The stabilizing moment due to the fins is given as

$$m_s(t) = \tfrac{1}{2}wK_L[(\alpha_1 + \beta_1) - (\alpha_2 + \beta_2)]$$

where w is the distance between the centers of force on the fins, K_L is the lift coefficient, α_1 and α_2 are tilt angles of the fins, and β_1 and β_2 represent the instantaneous directions of flow at the two fins. Besides the stabilizing moment, there is a disturbing roll moment $m_d(t)$ exerted on the ship by the ocean waves, and our problem is to use $m_s(t)$ to neutralize the effect of $m_d(t)$ as much as possible. There are two ways of doing this:

1. Tilt-angle control. The tilt angles α_1 and α_2 of the two fins are varied according to the error signal $e(t)$ and its derivatives, as shown in Fig. P 4-6a. The hydraulic servos are assumed to be perfect, and

$$\alpha_1 = -\alpha_2 = \alpha$$

2. Lift control. The lift forces on the two fins are measured by measuring the deflections of their shafts. Two hydraulic servos move the fins in such a way that their lift forces are varied according to $e(t)$ and its derivatives. The part of the control system of Fig. P 4-6a enclosed by broken lines is replaced by two identical branches, one of which is illustrated in Fig. P 4-6b. The hydraulic servos are assumed to be perfect, and

$$L_1 = -L_2 = L$$

(Note: The variations in β_1 and β_2 are slow in terms of the response time of a hydraulic servo. Consequently the fins move with the flow to give the "ordered lift" $\pm L$.)

Assume that the following spectral densities are known:

$\Phi_{dd}(j\omega) = $ spectral density of disturbing roll moment
$\Phi_{\beta_1\beta_1}(j\omega) = \Phi_{\beta_2\beta_2}(j\omega) = \Phi_{\beta\beta}(j\omega) = $ spectral density of variations in flow direction
$\Phi_{\beta_1\beta_2}(j\omega) = \Phi_{d\beta_1}(j\omega) = \Phi_{d\beta_2}(j\omega) = 0$

Derive expressions for $\Phi_{\theta_0\theta_0}(j\omega)$ and $\Phi_{LL}(j\omega)$ in terms of the above spectral densities and transfer functions $G(s)$ of the ship and $(C/M_d)(s)$ which gives minimum $\overline{[\theta_0(t)]^2}$ while $\overline{[L(t)]^2}$ is limited. Do the above problems for both systems.

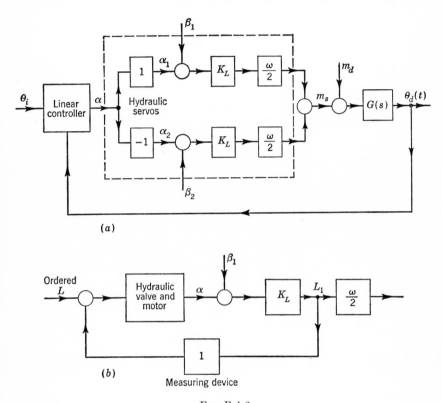

FIG. P 4-6

4-7. For the $(C/M_d)(s)$, $\Phi_{\beta\beta}(s)$, and $\Phi_{dd}(s)$ of Prob. 4-6, compare the relative merits of "tilt-angle control" and "lift control," as described in Prob. 4-6, in the following aspects:

(a) How well is the roll motion "stabilized" as represented by $\Phi_{\theta_0\theta_0}(j\omega)$?

(b) Stress on the fin shafts, as represented by $\Phi_{LL}(j\omega)$.

(c) System's sensitivity to change in ship speed.

Note that $G(s)$ does not change much with speed (see Prob. 2-13) but K_L is approximately proportional to the square of the ship speed.

4-8. Quite frequently, by using physical intuition, a good approximation to the optimal system can be obtained without exact knowledge of the spectral densities. To illustrate this point, we shall indicate an approximate solution of Prob. 4-6, using fin lift control. With reference to the block diagram, it is physically obvious that most of the roll motion is induced by disturbing moments near ω_n, and the essential function of the stabilizing fins is to damp out the resonance. Since the spectral components in $m_d(t)$ at other frequencies are not as significant, we make the approximation $\Phi_{dd}(j\omega) =$

$\Phi_{dd}(j\omega_0)$ in calculating the optimum form of $(C/M_d)(s)$. Show that

$$\frac{C}{M_d}(s)_{opt} = \frac{1}{J(s^2 + 2\zeta_1\omega_1 s + \omega_1{}^2)}$$

where ω_1 is determined by the allowed value of $\overline{[L(t)]^2}$, and ζ_1 is given as

$$\zeta_1 = \sqrt{\left(\zeta^2 - \frac{1}{2}\right)\frac{\omega_n{}^2}{\omega_1{}^2} + \frac{1}{2}}$$

The controller can be realized by the block diagram of Fig. P 4-8b. Determine K and K_v.

Find expressions for the mean-square values of $\theta_0(t)$ and $L(t)$.

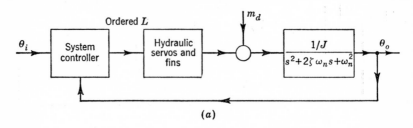

(a)

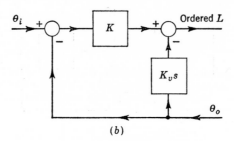

(b)

Fig. P 4-8

4-9. An input signal consists of a desired signal $r(t)$ with $\Phi_{rr}(j\omega) = A^2/(\omega^2 + a^2)$, and uncorrelated noise $n(t)$ with $\Phi_{nn}(j\omega) = B^2$. Determine the optimum filter to give $r(t + \alpha)$ with least-mean-square error.

4-10. Design an optimum predicting differentiator which gives a signal closest to $(d/dt)r(t + 1)$ in the least-square sense. The input-signal and noise spectral densities are given as

$$\Phi_{rr}(j\omega) = \frac{10}{\omega^4} \qquad \Phi_{nn}(j\omega) = 1$$

4-11. For the problem of Sec. 4-9, determine the optimum filtering functions $G_1(s)$ and $G_2(s)$ to give $r(t)$ and $\dot{r}(t)$, respectively, if the known functions are

(a) $r_1(t) = r(t) + n_1(t)$
    $r_2(t) = \dot{r}(t) + n_2(t)$

$$\Phi_{n_1 n_1}(j\omega) = \frac{A^2}{\omega^2 + a^2}$$

$$\Phi_{n_2 n_2}(j\omega) = 1$$

(b) $r_1(t) = r(t) + n_1(t)$
    $r_2(t) = \ddot{r}(t) + n_2(t)$

$$\Phi_{n_1 n_1}(j\omega) = \frac{A^2}{\omega^2 + a^2}$$

$$\Phi_{n_2 n_2}(j\omega) = 1$$

4-12. The method of Sec. 4-9 does not require any prior knowledge of the statistical properties of $r(t)$. Sometimes $r(t)$ is random with a known spectral density $\Phi_{rr}(j\omega)$, and independent filters $G_1(s)$ and $G_2(s)$ are used to give the minimum value of

$$\overline{[r(t) - c(t)]^2}$$

Show that $G_1(s)$ and $G_2(s)$ satisfy the following equations:

$$G_1\Phi_{i_1i_1} + G_2\Phi_{i_1i_2} - \Phi_{i_1r} = X_1$$
$$G_1\Phi_{i_2i_1} + G_2\Phi_{i_2i_2} - \Phi_{i_2r} = X_2$$

where X_1 and X_2 are analytic in the LHP including the imaginary axis.

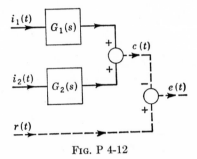

FIG. P 4-12

Chapter 5

5-1. With reference to the block diagram, $\Phi_{nn}(j\omega)$ is a constant ν, and $c(t) = 0$ for all $t < 0$. At $t = 0$, the switch is closed. Find an expression for $\phi_{cc}(t,t')$, where both t and t' are positive. Compare the result with that of Prob. 3-12.

$$n(t) \quad \diagup\!\!\!\!\diagdown \longrightarrow \boxed{\dfrac{K}{s(1+Ts)}} \longrightarrow c(t)$$

FIG. P 5-1

5-2. The switch in Prob. 5-1 is opened after it has been closed for t_1 sec. Show that for $t > t_1$

$$c(t) = C_1 + C_2 e^{-t/T}$$

Determine the distribution functions of C_1 and C_2, assuming that $n(t)$ is Gaussian.

5-3. With reference to the block diagram, the switch is open for $t < 0$ and $c(t)$

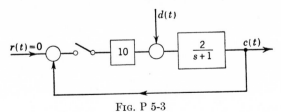

FIG. P 5-3

respond to $d(t)$ freely.   At $t = 0$ the switch is closed.   Given $\Phi_{dd}(j\omega) = 1$, determine $\Phi_{cc}(t,t')$.

5-4. The capacitor C in the circuit diagram is a constant C_0 for $t < 0$ but increases linearly afterwards:

$$C = C_0 + C_1 t$$

Show that the impulse-response function is

$$h(t,t_1) = \begin{cases} \dfrac{1}{R}\,(C_0 + C_1 t_1)^{1/RC_1}(C_0 + C_1 t)^{-(1+1/RC_1)} & t > t_1 > 0 \\ 0 & \text{if } t < t_1 \end{cases}$$

Find also the expression of $h(t,t_1)$ for $t > 0 > t_1$.

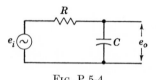

FIG. P 5-4

5-5. For Prob. 5-4, determine the correlation functions between (a) e_0 and e_0 and (b) e_0 and e_i if e_i is a white Gaussian noise with $\Phi_{e_i e_i}(t,t') = \delta(t - t')$.

5-6. Repeat Prob. 5-5 with white Gaussian noise of increasing intensity.

$$\phi_{e_i e_i}(t,t') = \begin{cases} 0 & \text{for } t < 0 \\ (C_0' + C_1' t)\delta(t - t') & \text{for } t \geq 0 \end{cases}$$

5-7. A signal $r(t) = A \sin(\omega_0 t + \phi)$ with unknown A and ϕ is masked by Gaussian noise with spectral density $\Phi_{nn}(j\omega)$. The desired optimum filter should give $r(t)$ unerringly if the noise power is negligible, and least-square error in general. The observation time is T sec. Determine $g(\tau)$ of the optimum filter for the following cases:

(a) $\Phi_{nn}(j\omega) = B$ (b) $\Phi_{nn}(j\omega) = \dfrac{B}{\omega^2 + b^2}$

Determine also the mean-square error for case a.

5-8. Repeat Prob. 5-7 with

$$r(t) = A_0 + A_1 t$$
$$\Phi_{nn}(j\omega) = \omega^2$$

The desired output is $r(t + \alpha)$.   Both A_0 and A_1 are unknown.

5-9. Show that the necessary and sufficient condition for a set of normalized eigenfunctions $U_n(t)$ to be complete is

$$\sum_n U_n(t)U_n(\tau) = \delta(t - \tau) \tag{1}$$

for all values of t and τ in the interval ab.

From Eq. (5-99) and (1) above show that

$$K(t,t') = \sum_n \frac{1}{E_n}\,U_n(t)U_n(t') \tag{2}$$

Given $K(t,t')$, is the set of eigenfunctions $U_n(t)$ uniquely defined? Given the set of eigenfunctions $U_n(t)$, is the kernel $K(t,t')$ uniquely defined?

5-10. A random signal $r(t)$ can be expanded into a set of orthogonal functions $U_n(t)$ in the interval $a \leq t \leq b$:

$$r(t) = \sum_n C_n U_n(t)$$

where the coefficients C_n are random. By some general argument, using the vector-space concept, it can be shown that there exists a set of $U_n(t)$ such that the coefficients C_n are uncorrelated with each other (Karhunen-Loeve theorem):

$$\overline{C_n C_m} = 0$$

for all pairs n, m with $n \neq m$. Our problem is to find this particular set of $U_n(t)$. Show that

$$\phi_{rr}(t,t') = \sum_n \overline{C_n{}^2} U_n(t) U_n(t')$$

and $U_n(t)$ is an eigenfunction of the integral equation with $\phi_{rr}(t,t')$ as kernel.

Chapter 6

6-1. With reference to Fig. 6-1, the known transfer functions are

$$G_p(s) = \frac{5}{s^2(1+s)}$$
$$G_h(s) = \frac{1 - e^{-Ts}}{s}$$

and $T = 1$. Determine $K(z)$ and $D(z)$ so that the following conditions are satisfied after a minimum number of sampling instants:

(a) Errorless at sampling instants only for a unit step input.
(b) Errorless at all times for a unit step input.
(c) Errorless at sampling instants only for a unit ramp input.
(d) Errorless at all times for a unit ramp input.
Calculate also $e_1(t)$ and $e_2^*(t)$ for all four cases.

6-2. In Prob. 6-1, the $D(z)$ of the system is designed for condition d. Determine $e_1(t)$ and $e_2^*(t)$ when a unit step input is applied. Also calculate $e_1(t)$ and $e_2^*(t)$ of a system designed for condition b but with a unit ramp input applied.

6-3. Repeat Prob. 6-1b but allow two additional sampling intervals so that the magnitude of $e_2^*(t)$ can be reduced.

6-4. Repeat Prob. 6-1b for a sampling interval $T = 2$.

6-5. Repeat Prob. 6-1b and d for a plant with transportation lag:

$$G_p(s) = \frac{5e^{-1.5s}}{s^2(1+s)}$$

6-6. Show that

$$\mathcal{Z}\left[\frac{1}{(s^2 - a^2)^{n+1}}\right] = \frac{1}{2na} \frac{d}{da} \mathcal{Z}\left[\frac{1}{(s^2 - a^2)^n}\right]$$

6-7. Given the functions

$$G(s) = \frac{1}{s(1 + Ts)} \qquad R(s) = \frac{1}{s}$$
$$\Phi(j\omega) = \frac{1}{4 + \omega^2 T^2}$$

calculate

(a) $G(z)G(z^{-1})$

(c) $\bar{G}G(z)$

(e) $\bar{G}R(z)$

(g) $\Phi(z)$

(b) $R(z)R(z^{-1})$

(d) $\bar{R}R(z)$

(f) $\bar{G}\bar{R}(z)$

(h) $\bar{G}\Phi(z)$

6-8. With reference to Fig. 6-1, the transfer functions $G_h(s)$, $G_p(s)$ are known and $D(z)$ is to be designed to give the least-integral-square value of $e_1(t)$ following a unit step input in $r(t)$. There is a constraint on $e_2^*(t)$ of the form

$$\sum_{n=0}^{\infty} [e_2(nT)]^2 \leq a^2$$

Determine $D(z)$ for the following cases:

(a) $G_h(s) = \dfrac{1 - e^{-Ts}}{s}$

$G_p(s) = \dfrac{K}{s}$

(b) $G_h(s) = \dfrac{1 - e^{-Ts}}{s}$

$G_p(s) = \dfrac{K}{s^2}$

6-9. The following are expressions for sampled spectral density $\Phi_{12}(z)$:

(a) $\dfrac{1}{(1 + 0.5z^{-1})(1 + 0.5z)}$

(b) $\dfrac{z + 1}{(z + 0.5)(z - 2)}$

Determine $\phi_{12}(nT)$ for each case.

6-10. With reference to Fig. 6-10, the known functions are

$$\Phi_{rr}(j\omega) = \frac{2a}{\omega^2 + a^2}$$
$$F(s) = 1 \qquad n(t) = 0$$

and $G(s)$ is to be selected such that $[r(t + \alpha) - c(t)]^2$ is a minimum. Determine $G(s)$.

Chapter 7

7-1. The power spectrum of a Gaussian random signal of 10-cps bandwidth is to be determined from N independent sample records of 5 min each. The desired frequency resolution is 0.2 cps, and the rms error is to be no more than 5 per cent. What is the minimum number of N?

7-2. Consider two signals

$$u(t) = i_1(t) + i_2(t)$$
$$v(t) = i_1(t)$$

where $i_1(t)$ and $i_2(t)$ are independent and Gaussian. The cospectrum of $u(t)$ and $v(t)$ is measured as shown in Fig. 7-5a. Find an expression for the rms error of the cospectrum.

7-3. Suppose that the bandpass filter of Fig. 7-4 is not the ideal one shown but has the following characteristic:

$$|H(j\omega_n)|^2 = \frac{1}{1 + (0.1n)^4}$$

where $\omega_n = \omega_b + n\Delta$. The constants ω_b and Δ are the center frequency and spacing of the spectral components, respectively. Determine the rms error of the measured spectrum.

7-4. In Prob. 7-1, what is the required N if there is to be 90 per cent confidence that $\Phi(j\omega)$ is within ± 5 per cent of the measured value?

7-5. In Prob. 7-1, what is the required N if there is to be 90 per cent confidence that every point of the 50-point spectrum is within 5 per cent of its measured value?

Chapter 8

8-1. Determine the transient-response sensitivity function with respect to α, where α is a negligibly small constant. Step inputs are assumed.

(a) $F(s) = \dfrac{1 + 2s}{(1 + \alpha + 2s)(1 + s)}$

(b) $F(s) = \dfrac{10}{1 + (2 + \alpha)s + 2\alpha s^2}$

(c) $F(s) = \dfrac{s^2(1 + \alpha^2 s)}{(1 + 2s)(1 + s)(s + \alpha)}$

(d) $F(s) = \dfrac{G(s)}{1 + G(s)}$

$G(s) = \dfrac{1 + 2s}{s^2 + \alpha s}$

8-2. From the following system equations, determine for each system whether it has no parasitic oscillation, transient parasitic oscillation, or sustained parasitic oscillation, where α is a small positive constant approaching zero.

(a) $D(s) = \alpha s^2 + 3s + (2 - \alpha^2)$

(b) $D(s) = \alpha^2 s^4 + 2\alpha^2 s^3 + (1 + \alpha)s^2 + 5s + 4$

(c) $D(s) = -\alpha s^3 + s^2 + 0.2s + 1$

8-3. Find the approximate solutions of the following differential equations to the first order of α. That is,

$$x(t,\alpha) \doteq x(t,0) + \frac{\partial x(t,\alpha)}{\partial \alpha}\bigg|_{\alpha=0} \alpha$$

(a) $\ddot{x} + (1 - \alpha x^2)\dot{x} + x = u(t)$

(b) $\alpha\ddot{x} + \dot{x} + x^3 = \delta(t)$

where $u(t)$ and $\delta(t)$ are the unit step and unit impulse, respectively.

8-4. With reference to Fig. 8-1, the transfer functions are given as

$$H(s) = K_1 s$$
$$G(s) = \frac{K_2}{s^2(1 + Ts)}$$

The nominal values of K_1, K_2, and T are $K_1 = 1$, $K_2 = 2$, and $T = 0.25$. Determine the locations of the closed-loop poles and the sensitivities of these poles with respect to variations of K_1, K_2, and T.

8-5. Determine the nominal value of the damping factor ζ of the control poles (the pair of complex conjugate poles nearest the origin). Assume equal tolerances for K_1, K_2, and T:

$$1 - \eta \leq K_1 \leq 1 + \eta$$
$$1 - \eta \leq \frac{K_2}{2} \leq 1 + \eta$$
$$1 - \eta \leq \frac{T}{0.25} \leq 1 + \eta$$

What is the largest value of η which still satisfies that $\zeta \geq 0.3$ for *any* combination of errors in K_1, K_2, and T? What is the worst combination in K_1, K_2, and T (giving lowest ζ)? Check your result by either root-locus plot or direct factoring.

8-6. Repeat Prob. 8-4 with the following nominal values of K_1, K_2, and T:

$$K_1 = 0.4$$
$$K_2 = 20$$
$$T = 0.04$$

8-7. Show that, at a multiple pole of the control ratio $(C/R)(s)$, the pole sensitivity is infinity. Does that mean that the system is unstable to small component variations?

8-8. Investigate the pole sensitivities of a system with a block diagram as shown in Fig. 8-1, $H(s) = 0$, and

$$G(s) = \frac{K(s + a)}{s^2(s^2 + 2\zeta\omega_0 s + \omega_0^2)}$$

The nominal values of the constants are

$$K = 15 \qquad a = 0.6$$
$$\omega_0 = 4 \qquad \zeta = 0.875$$

Plot the root locus of the system with nominal values of ω_0, a, ζ, and changing value of K.

8-9. With reference to Fig. 8-1, the transfer function of a lead-compensated system is given as

$$G(s) = \frac{1 + 0.5s}{1 + 0.05s} \frac{K}{s(1 + Ts)}$$
$$H(s) = 0$$

The nominal values of K and T are $K = 14$ and $T = 0.5$ sec. Determine the locations of closed-loop poles, peak response, and maximum modulus (for nominal values of K and T) and their sensitivities with respect to small variations in K and T.

If K and T are to have the same percentage tolerances and the maximum modulus is not to exceed 1.4 for the worst combination of errors in K and T, what percentage tolerance can be allowed? Check the last result by making a complex-plane plot, and determine the maximum modulus from the plot or by direct calculation.

8-10. In Example 2-2, the time constants of the actuating solenoids were not taken into consideration. These can be represented as

$$G_1(s) = \frac{1}{1 + 0.1(s/\omega_1) + 0.005(s/\omega_1)^2}$$

Consider $G_1(s)$ as part of $G_c(s)$ and calculate the increase as well as percentage increase in the cost function.

8-11. In an idealized steering system, the transfer function from rudder rate y to ship heading γ is

$$\frac{\Gamma(s)}{Y(s)} = G(s) = \frac{K}{s^3}$$

In a problem with the rms value of the rudder rate $y(t)$ limited, the cost function is assumed to be of the form

$$f_c = \overline{e^2} + k^2\overline{y^2}$$

The spectral density of the desired heading is

$$\Phi_{rr}(j\omega) = \frac{A}{\omega^2}$$

Show that the optimum control ratio is

$$\frac{C}{R}(s) = \frac{\omega_0{}^3}{(s + \omega_0)(s^2 + 2\zeta\omega_0 s + \omega_0{}^2)}$$

and $\zeta = 0.5$.

If the specified limit on peak overshoot is 3 per cent, what value of ζ should be used? What is the percentage increase in the cost function with the new ζ?

If the specified limit on peak overshoot is 20 per cent, what value of ζ should be used?

8-12. For the deadbeat system of Example 6-1 calculate the sensitivity of the system's response to ramp inputs with respect to the gain of $G(s)$.

Chapter 9

9-1. A nonlinear system is represented by

$$\dot{x}_1 = 2x_2$$
$$\dot{x}_2 = -3x_2(x_1{}^2 + x_2{}^2) + y \qquad |y| \leq t$$

For a minimal-time problem, determine the equations to be satisfied by $\lambda_1(t)$ and $\lambda_2(t)$ of Eq. (9-15).

9-2. For Prob. 9-1, if, instead of the minimal-time requirement, the following integral is to be minimized,

$$J = \int_a^b (y^2 + x_1{}^2 + x_2{}^2)\, dt$$

where a, b are fixed terminal points in the phase plane x_1, x_2, rewrite the system equations with a new independent variable τ so that the problem is to arrive at b with minimum τ. Determine the equations to be satisfied by $\lambda_1(\tau)$ and $\lambda_2(\tau)$.

9-3. A control system is represented by

$$J \frac{d^2c}{dt^2} + \eta' \frac{dc}{dt} = f(t) \qquad |f| \leq T_m$$

Determine the optimum switching boundary in the phase plane of the system error $e(t)$, subsequent to a step input. Assume that $J/T_m = 2$ sec^2/radian and $\eta'/T_m = 0.5$ sec/radian. Is it possible to normalize the equation into the form of Eq. (9-29) with $\eta = 1$?

9-4. In Prob. 9-3, the constraint on $f(t)$ is changed to

$$-0.5T_m \leq f(t) \leq 2T_m$$

Does the optimum form of $f(t)$ still take only the limit values? If so, why? Determine the optimum switching boundary in the phase plane of the system error $e(t)$.

9-5. Convert the following transfer functions to state variable representations:

(a) $G(s) = \dfrac{10}{s(s^2 + 2s + 2)}$

(b) $G(s) = \dfrac{25(s + 2)}{s^3 + 4s^2 + 10s + 2}$

(c) $G(s) = \dfrac{-s^2 + 20s + 10}{s^2(1 + s)^2}$

9-6. To reduce noise in measurement, the error $e(t)$ is prefiltered before its application to the phase-plane controller, as shown in Fig. 9-15a. The filter function is

$$H(s) = \frac{10,000}{s^2 + 141.4s + 10,000}$$

The controlled system is the same as given in Prob. 9-3.   Plot on the phase plane the required displacement of the optimum switching boundary to compensate filter delay.

Chapter 10

10-1. Show that the result of Example 10-1 can be generalized as follows: If, instead of the original functions,

$$G(s) = \frac{K}{s + a}$$

$$\Phi_{rr} = \frac{A^2}{\omega^2 + a^2}$$

the optimum system can still be represented by Fig. 10-2 with K/s changed to $K/(s + a)$ and

$$K_a = \frac{1}{K} \left(\sqrt{\frac{A^2}{B^2} + a^2} - a \right)$$

10-2. Show that the actuating error of Prob. 10-1 (input to K_a) has white spectral density.   How does the spectral density change with an increase in K_a?   Find a method of adjustment that converts the system into a closed-loop adaptive system.

10-3. Discuss the possible ways of implementing adaptive control for the roll-stabilization system of Prob. 4-8, assuming that only $\Phi_{dd}(j\omega_n)$ varies from time to time. Investigate the stability of the adaptive loop in case a closed adaptive loop is used.

10-4. In the problem of Example 10-4 find two linear combinations of the phase error and gain error signals that can be used to correct ζ and ω_n independently, at least for small deviations from the nominal operating point.

10-5. A certain controlled plant has a transfer function $G_a(s)$ which drifts slowly but erratically with time:

$$G_a(s) = \frac{K_a}{s(1 + T_1 s)(1 + T_2 s)^2}$$

The ranges of value of T_1, T_2, and K_a are

$$0.5 \leq T_1 \leq 3$$
$$0.01 \leq T_2 \leq 0.05$$
$$2 \leq K_a \leq 4$$

The units are in seconds and second^{-1}, respectively.   The desired control ratio is

$$\left(\frac{C}{R} \right)_d (s) = \frac{1}{1 + s}$$

In order to accomplish the above, an arrangement similar to Fig. 10-9 is used:

$$\theta(t) = c(t)$$
$$M'(s) = G_s(s) = 1$$
$$H(s) = 1 + s$$

and K of the variable-gain amplifier is automatically adjusted.   As an approximation, we may assume that the phase margin of the closed-loop system is 25°.   Make Bode plots of the ratio $\dfrac{(C/R)(j\omega)}{(C/R)_d(j\omega)}$ in the range $0.1 \leq \omega \leq 2$ for two extreme combinations of T_1, T_2, and K_a which give a ratio closest to 1 and a ratio farthest from 1, respectively.

10-6. With reference to Fig. 10-2, the transfer function of the plant is (instead of K/s)

$$G(s) = \frac{1}{Js^2 + \eta s}$$

The signal $r(t)$ is a ramp input Bt and the noise $n(t)$ has a power spectrum $\Phi_{nn}(j\omega) = \sigma^2$. The adaptive controller adjusts K_a so that the total mean-square error under steady-state operation is a minimum. Determine K_a as a function of B and σ^2. Work out three ways of adjusting K_a:

    (a) Open adaptive loop.
    (b) Closed adaptive loop.
    (c) Draper and Li's optimalizing control.
Discuss their relative merits.

Chapter 11

11-1. The power spectrum of a random signal is known except for a constant:

$$\Phi(j\omega) = \frac{K}{\omega^2 + 4}$$

Calculate the required interval of measurement T so that the expected rms error in measured value of K is 1 per cent. Suppose that the functional form of T is unknown and that the frequency resolution is $\Delta\omega = 0.2$ radian/sec. What is the required T for a 1 per cent rms error?

11-2. With reference to Fig. 11-1, $h(\tau)$ and $H(j\omega)$ are to be determined by methods 1 and 3, correlation measurement and cross-spectrum measurement, respectively, described in Sec. 11-4. Suppose that $\Phi_{ii} = 10$, $\Phi_{nn} = 1$, $H(s) = 1/(1 + s)$, $\Delta\omega = 0.1$ radian/sec, and the measuring interval τ is 1 min. Determine the expected mean-square errors for $h(\tau)$ and $H(j\omega)$. Compare the two methods.

11-3. In Example 11-1, the variation of the situation variable is assumed to be steplike. For ramplike variations of the situation variable,

$$\Phi_{x_\alpha x_\alpha}(j\omega) = \frac{2\nu C}{(\nu^2 + \omega^2)\omega^2}$$

and

$$\Phi_{\delta\delta}(z) = \Delta$$

determine the optimum weighting factors w_i and minimum value of D.

11-4. Obtain a solution for the derivative-sensing systems similar to that of Example 11-2 but with the more general form of $\Phi_{x_\alpha x_\alpha}(z)$ as given by Eq. (11-54).

11-5. Repeat Prob. 11-4 for an alternative-biasing system.

INDEX